15th Annual Edition
KNIVES '95

Edited by
Ken Warner

DBI BOOKS. INC.

STAFF

EDITOR
Ken Warner

ASSOCIATE EDITORS
Robert S.L. Anderson
Harold A. Murtz
Ray Ordorica

ASSISTANT TO THE EDITOR
Lilo Anderson

PRODUCTION MANAGER
John L. Duoba

EDITORIAL/PRODUCTION ASSOCIATE
Jamie L. Puffpaff

EDITORIAL/PRODUCTION ASSISTANT
Holly J. Porter

ELECTRONIC PUBLISHING MANAGER
Nancy J. Mellem

ELECTRONIC PUBLISHING ASSOCIATE
Robert M. Fuentes

ELECTRONIC PUBLISHING ASSISTANT
Edward B. Hartigan

COVER PHOTOGRAPHY
John Hanusin

MANAGING EDITOR
Pamela J. Johnson

PUBLISHER
Sheldon L. Factor

DBI BOOKS, INC.

PRESIDENT
Charles T. Hartigan

VICE PRESIDENT & PUBLISHER
Sheldon L. Factor

VICE PRESIDENT—SALES
John G. Strauss

VICE PRESIDENT/MANAGING EDITOR
Pamela J. Johnson

TREASURER
Frank R. Serpone

THE COVER KNIVES

From upper right: Hank Knickmeyer's short hunter in mosaic Damascus and fossil ivory; then an asymetrical dagger in ivory and mokume by Charles Pratt; the all-out large integral hunter by Edmund Davidson, engraved by Jere Davidson; then Jack Davenport's slim liner lock with scrimshaw by Linda Karst; the grand San Francisco folding dirk is by Robert Sidelinger and lies across the fossil ivory grips of a splendid short Bowie in Damascus by Tim Potier; above these in blue titanium is Kit Carson's rendition of Buck's new cross-lock folder design.

Photo by John Hanusin, as ever.

KW

Copyright © MCMXCIV by DBI Books, Inc., 4092 Commercial Ave., Northbrook, IL 60062. Printed in the United States of America. All rights reserved. No part of this book may be reproduced, stored in a retrieval system, or transmitted in any form or by any means, electronic, mechanical, photocopying, recording or otherwise, without prior written permission of the publisher.

The views and opinions of the authors expressed herein are not necessarily those of the publisher, and no responsibility for such views will be assumed.

Arms and Armour Press, London, G.B., exclusive licensees and distributors in Britain and Europe, India and Pakistan; Media House Publications, Sandton, Transvaal, exclusive distributor in South Africa and Zimbabwe. Lothian Books, Auckland, exclusive distributor in New Zealand.

ISBN 0-87349-161-0   Library of Congress Catalog Card #80-67744

CONTENTS

INTRODUCTION 5

FEATURES

TELLING THE TRUTH ABOUT FORGING
      by William W. Wood 6

THE KNIFE BAYONET IN U.S. SERVICE
      by Konrad F. Schreier, Jr. 16

EARLY AMERICAN FRONTIER DAGGERS
      by Gordon Minnis 23

KNIVES ON STAMPS
      by Raymond Schuessler 29

ORIGAMI I HAVE SEEN
      by Allan H. Pressley 34

THE PERFECT KNIVES OF GEORGE LEONARD HERTER
      by Steven Dick 40

THE LOOKOUT'S BOWIE
      by Steven Dick 47

LEVINE'S LATEST
      by Ken Warner 50

THE WOODCRAFT: MARBLE'S BEST SELLER
      by Konrad F. Schreier, Jr. 54

THOUGHTS ON SWORDS
      by Tom Maringer 58

TRENDS

- THE BURGEONING SWORD 64
- INVESTMENT-GRADE KNIVES 70
- FIELD-GRADE KNIVES 79
- THE WORLD OF REALLY SMALL 84
- BIG KNIVES 88
- THE ELEGANT KNIFE 100
- SMALL KNIVES 106
- THE PRIMITIVE EDGE 111
- THAT FOREIGN LOOK 114
- THE MEDIUM KNIFE 118
- THE FOLDING KNIFE 124
- THE AUTOMATIC KNIFE 133
- THE UPGRADED KNIFE 136

STATE OF THE ART

- INTERESTING KNIVES 142
- COMPOSITE BLADES FOR EVERYMAN
  by Hal Davidson 148
- THE ETHNIC KNIFE 150
- STUDY OF STEEL AND SHAPE AND STUFF 152
- EMBELLISHMENT 158
- LEATHERWORK 168

FACTORY TRENDS

- TOUGH LITTLE GUYS 172
- WORKERS OF THE WORLD 173
- NEW KNIVES IN PRODUCTION 174

DIRECTORY

- CUSTOM KNIFEMAKERS 180
  - Centerfold Knives '95 216
- KNIFEMAKERS STATE-BY-STATE 274
- KNIFEMAKERS MEMBERSHIP LISTS 280
- KNIFE PHOTO INDEX
  - Knives '95 283
  - Knives '90-'94 285
- SPECIALTY CUTLERS 292
- GENERAL CUTLERS 293
- IMPORTERS & FOREIGN CUTLERS 293
- KNIFEMAKING SUPPLIES 295
- MAIL-ORDER SALES 297
- KNIFE SERVICES 299
- ORGANIZATIONS & PUBLICATIONS 304

INTRODUCTION

AMONG THE MOST important tools in a savvy pitcher's bag of tricks is a good change-up delivery. In baseball, that's usually a slow ball thrown with the fast-ball motion. A lot of the time it works.

Here, you're going to be looking at a bit of a change-up. However, we're not trying to slip one by or confuse your timing. No, an editor changes things to keep his readers interested.

What we've done is fiddle with the Trends section. For quite a few years now—this is the 15th KNIVES annual, believe it or not—we have presented the year's new knives in arbitrary categories like *hunters, folders, fighters* or *Bowies*. Then, as the available knife illustrations far outgrew the available space, those categories got compressed and we wound up with additional arbitrary categories like *Straight Standards* and *Overseas Knives*.

By now, you have guessed it: This year we have *new* arbitrary categories in Trends. This time *you* get to sort out the types. We have simply judged the knives small, medium or large; plain, fancy or ornate, and so forth.

This is going to provide fewer but larger groups of knives. It is our hope we will all learn something new from the inevitably different juxtapositions in this presentation.

We may also learn this is not a fulfilling way to examine groups of knives. In that case, your Editor is prepared to fall back on the words of a good friend now gone to seek whatever in that place to which we are all bound. When the project of the moment didn't jell, he said, "Oh, well, nothing beats a trial but a failure."

No, I never figured it out, either, but he was a hell of a man. There must be something to it. Please enjoy our trial.

Ken Warner

TELLING THE TRUTH ABOUT FORGING

The dynamics of metallurgy in knifemaking from a professional

by WILLIAM W. WOOD

Wood is not one of your flat-grind, riveted handle slabs, sand-blast economy-model specialists.

THERE HAS BEEN too much debate over the merits of forging versus stock removal in knife making. This controversy is specious because solid-state metallurgy technology clearly defines the properties and limitations of those two methods of fabrication. The facts are known.

There are essentially three methods of producing part shapes in metal alloys: machining, casting and forging. There are other primary methods of metal fabrication, such as rolling and extruding, but those are beyond the scope of this work.

Casting and forging—that is, the forging process often called "drop" forging—enable the reuse of casting moulds or forging dies. Machining has to be repeated for each part produced. Thus, in the case of multiple like parts, casting and forging are less expensive. Hand forging, with fire and hammer and anvil, also requires full repetition for each part.

Industrial casting and forging are generally limited to parts that do not require high strength for a given size or where the size and weight of the part is not critical to its ultimate use. Most automobile parts fall into this category, but some aircraft parts do not because of the weight or strength factor and, as a result, require machining.

Casting produces parts that do not have directional properties; that is, the parts have equal strength in all directions. Cold forging produces parts with directional properties—having greater strength in one direction rather than another.

Forging, and the resulting grain refinement, produces parts that give desirable properties such as fatigue resistance, creep resistance and impact resistance, and forging also works for unilateral parts not requiring high strength or hardness. Examples include such parts as crankshafts or driveshafts for fatigue resistance and connecting rods which are of unilateral dimension. The casting process is used for parts that are generally more intricate and require little strength properties, such as carburetors and distributor caps.

No material is forged just to obtain maximum properties such as hardness and strength. The forge cannot compete with heat-treating for producing parts with these qualities. For example, maximum forging hardness can approach a Rockwell C (Rc) hardness of only 45, whereas the same material can be heat-treated to a Rc of 65. Even that forging hardness can be accomplished only by a final cold forging that imparts higher properties.

Accordingly, smiths of quality knives follow the same steps after forging that the stock removal makers do. These are the final shaping of the blade with a belt sander and heat-treating.

Sometimes, smiths can actually ruin a good piece of steel on the anvil if they let the part cool down too much toward the end of the process. This leaves the blade heavily stressed with fine grains and will considerably reduce hardenability upon subsequent heat-treatment. The reduced hardenability will result in good high strength martensite, but also provides undesirable layered iron carbide called pearlite.

Grinding to shape and heat-treating work much better because the large grains in the annealed condition yield the best hardenability possible and parts with the greatest percentage of uniform martensite, and thus better quality.

Cold forging is defined as working metal below the critical temperature for alloys so that recrystallization is not affected. Hot forging above the critical temperature will result in recrystallization, thereby negating any strength gains.

In order to decisively prove these concepts as they apply to knifemaking, we must define the basic solid-state metallurgy of the metal alloys that are used. As the first step in that process, look at the unit cells of carbon steel alloys in Figure 1.

All iron-carbon alloy systems are composed of unit cells defined as body-centered cubic (BCC) or face-centered cubic (FCC). BCC is a unit cell of eight iron (FE) atoms on the corners of the cell and one carbon (C) atom in the center of the cube. FCC is a unit where there are the same eight atoms of iron, one at each corner of the cube, but there are six carbon atoms, one in the center of each of the six faces of the cube. Those atoms are usually visualized as ping pong balls touching each other at tangent points.

Crystals are aggregates of these unit cells bonded to one another in regular geometric patterns as depicted in Figure 2. These crystals are composed of millions of unit cells, but are in straight geometric alignment as shown. The edges of these straight alignments are called slip lines, which are defined as the atomic planes that glide past one another as the alloy is being worked, such as in forging.

These straight geometric crystal lattices retain their pattern only to the grain boundary edge. Steel alloy grains are the relatively larger unit that contains a single lattice system with a perfect geometric arrangement. Other grains adjoining have their own perfect lattice system, but in a different direction as shown by the three grains in Figure 2.

Steel alloys are made primarily of iron (Fe) and carbon (C). Other alloying elements are often used, but only to control the manner in which Fe and C form martensite for hardenability and strength. It does not take much carbon—less than 1 percent—to effect a great hardening influence on iron, but the carbon is essentially what allows the martensitic transformation to take place.

Because the spheres of atoms touch each other only at tangent points, voids occur between the atoms as shown in Figure 3. These voids are the points where alloying element atoms are deposited. The best alloying elements are the ones whose atoms will fit in the void spaces without too much lattice stretching, which would result in a high energy or unstable situation. These alloying elements do not harden and strengthen the steel like carbon does, but they do help control the manner in which carbon does its job. For example, manganese is added to steel to alleviate brittleness (hot shortness) caused by segregation of iron sulfides at the grain boundaries.

Now that we have defined crystal structure and grains, it will be necessary to establish the effect of temperature, as this factor controls the solid-state metallurgy necessary for hardening and strengthening. Metallurgists use equilibrium diagrams to do this, which is a plot of temperature versus carbon content for a given alloy. All steel alloys have their own equilibrium diagrams, one of which is shown in Figure 4.

Figure 4 delineates a plot of temperature in degrees of Fahrenheit versus carbon content. The carbon content is shown on a logarithmic scale in order to clarify the steel portion of the plot. Such plots are made empirically by selecting steels of varying carbon content and noting their characteristics as they are heated to their melting point.

It is important to note that common steels are formed with up to 2 percent carbon, and cast irons use more than that. Heat-treated steels are formed in the range of .8 to 2 percent carbon. Ferrite, which is a pure form of Fe, develops at low concentrations of carbon, whereas cementite forms as the carbon content is increased to 2 percent. Cementite is an iron carbide (Fe_3C) that precipitates increasingly as the carbon content is raised. The low temperature structure of steel is body-centered cubic (BCC), but at critical temperature—1350 degrees F in this case—austentite begins to form and the alloy becomes face-centered cubic (FCC). This higher energy form of steel occurs because of the heat that is applied to raise the temperature. FCC structures are higher energy—that is, less stable—because the carbon atoms on the cube faces stretch the unit cell into a less dense packing arrangement than the BCC. That is, the cube diagonal in BCC is the same size square as the cube face in FCC. This change in structure while cooling austenite to room temperature and the change in structure from FCC to BCC are the basis for steel heat-treatment of martensite.

The familiar high carbon steels used in knifemaking are superimposed in Figure 4 to illustrate their relationship to these forms of steel as they are heated and cooled; however, it should be realized this is an equilibrium diagram for a typical steel and not for knife steels. Each knife alloy has its own diagram which usually moves the critical temperature and austenite range either up or down slightly. For example, the critical temperature for D2 is 1490 degrees F, and the forging temperature is 2000-2100 degrees F. The solutionizing temperature to transform to austenite for D2, 440C, and 154CM are respectively 1850 F, 1900 F and 1950 F.

The austenite region shown at the higher range is a homogeneous FCC mixture of Fe and C; that is, photomi-

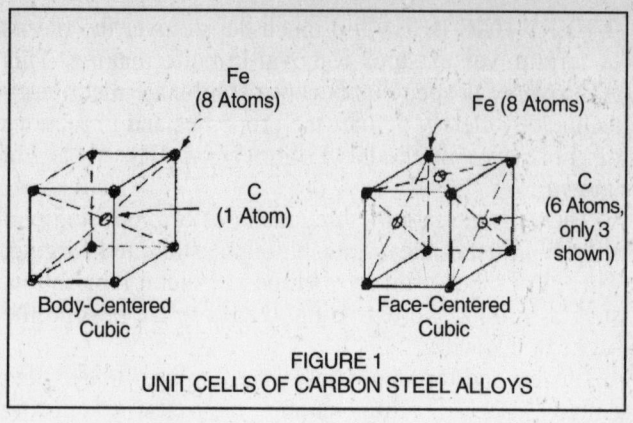

FIGURE 1
UNIT CELLS OF CARBON STEEL ALLOYS

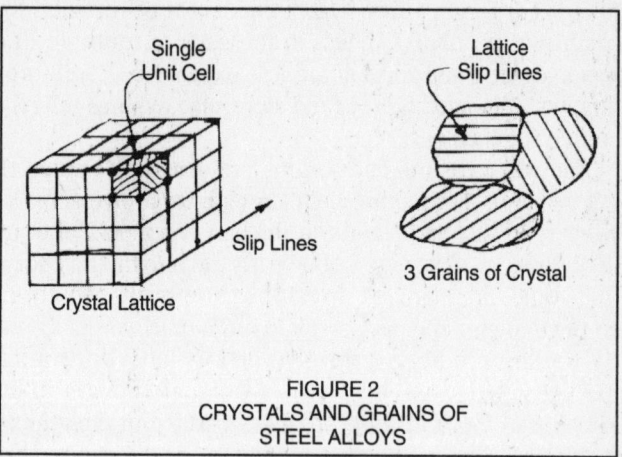

FIGURE 2
CRYSTALS AND GRAINS OF STEEL ALLOYS

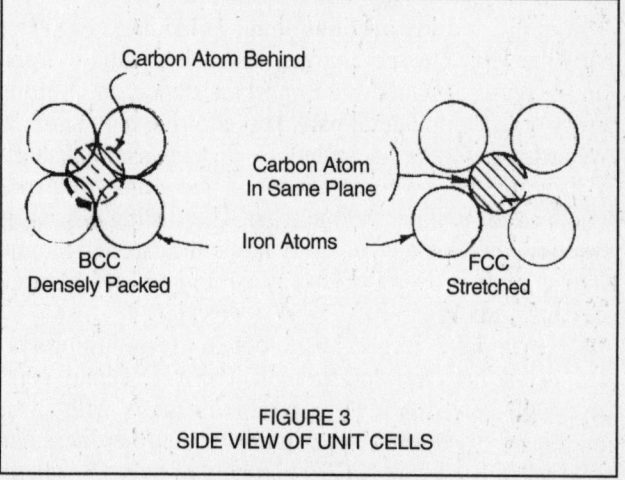

FIGURE 3
SIDE VIEW OF UNIT CELLS

crographs taken of sections of austenite are uniform and show no form of precipitate. However, as the austenite is cooled below the critical temperature, cementite (Fe_3C), an iron carbide, precipitates out at the austenite grain boundaries in distinct layers as shown in Figure 5.

As the cementite precipitates out, it leaves the surrounding austenite depleted of carbon, and ferrite (Fe) is formed. In low carbon steels, this is not much of a problem because the carbide is of such small quantity; however, in the high carbon steel range from .8 to 2 percent carbon, it becomes a considerable problem because alternating layers of carbide reduce strength and hardness, and

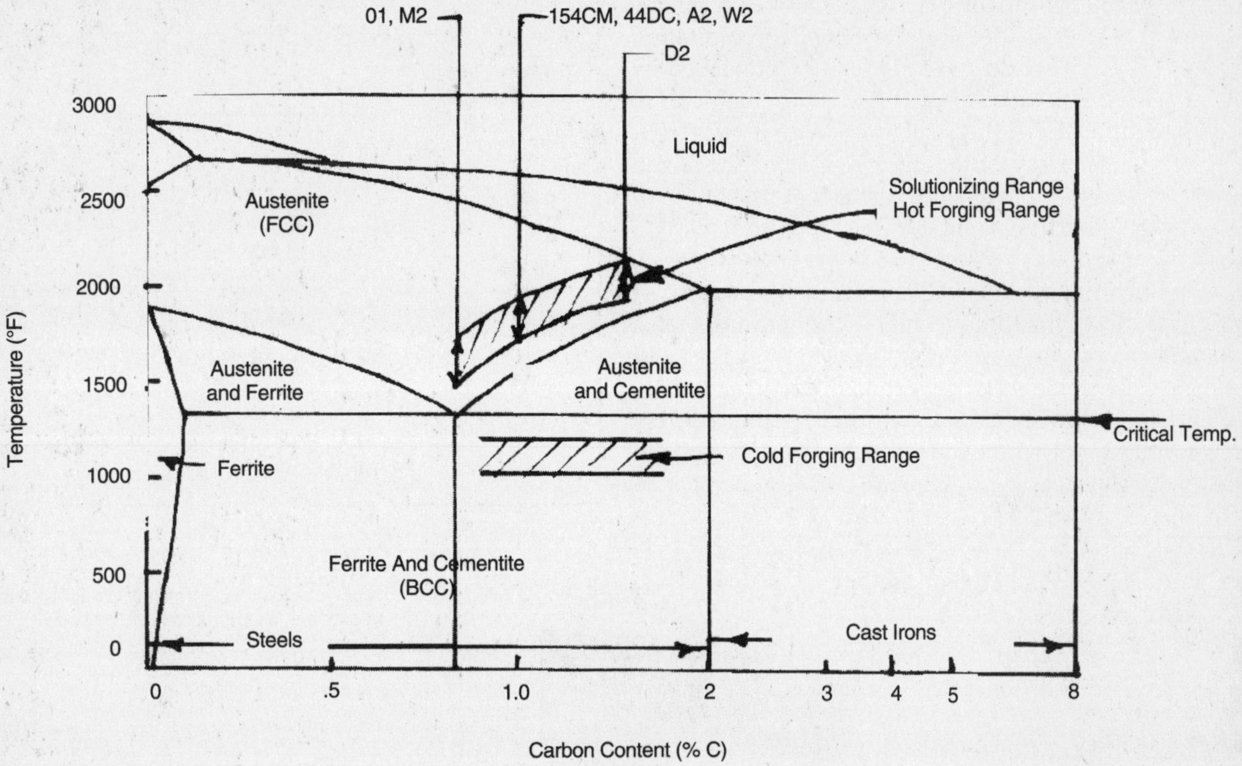

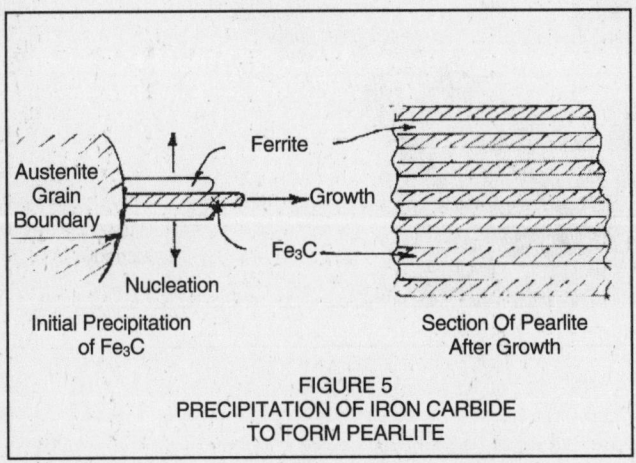

FIGURE 4
TYPICAL EQUILIBRIUM DIAGRAM FOR STEEL

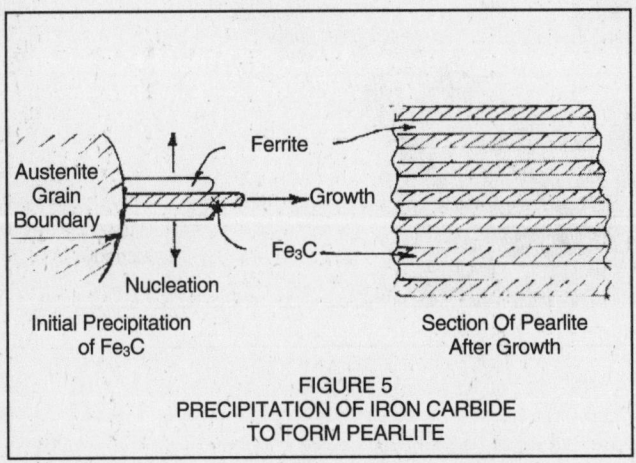

FIGURE 5
PRECIPITATION OF IRON CARBIDE
TO FORM PEARLITE

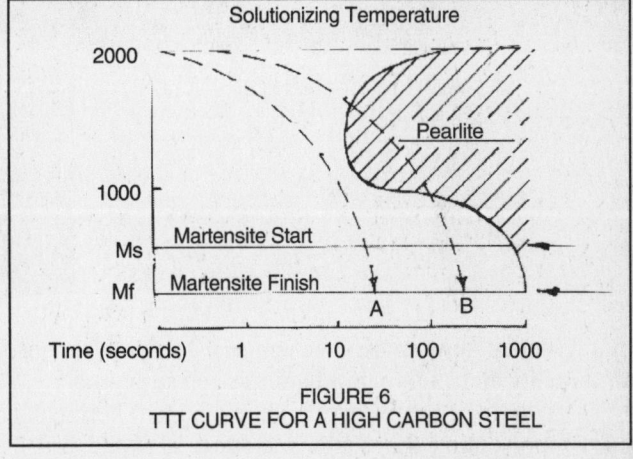

FIGURE 6
TTT CURVE FOR A HIGH CARBON STEEL

make further working almost impossible. This is represented in Figure 5, labeled ferrite and cementite. This happens under slow cooling equilibrium conditions; that is, letting nature take its course. It can be prevented however by rapid cooling (quenching), which allows the steel alloy to form martensite, a stable structure that traps the carbon atoms within the unit cell, preventing it from precipitating.

In order to show this schematically, metallurgical engineers use another diagram called TTT curves, which stands for Time Temperature Transformation, as detailed in Figure 6. This figure represents the basis for heat-treatment of high carbon steel alloys to form martensite. The pearlite section, called a nose, is represented as an S-curve. If the cooling rate is sufficiently slow, then it crosses into the pearlite range, as in cooling rate B, where both martensite and pearlite are formed, making the alloy much less desirable because of the carbide in the pearlite. However, at faster cooling rates such as with water or oil, and even air for some alloys, the pearlite nose can be avoided as in cooling rate A. Thus, a 100-percent martensitic structure can be formed without any precipitated carbide present.

The change to martensite is a fascinating transformation as shown in Figure 7. If allowed to cool slowly, the austenite transforms to alternating layers of BCC ferrite and Fe_3C. However, because the carbon precipitation phenomenon is time-dependent, it can be prevented by rapid cooling. The face-center cubic or FCC unit cell of austenite is transformed instantaneously to a body-centered tetragonal array of iron atoms. The face-centered cubic carbon atoms are retained on the top and bottom of the unit cell, but the rapid cooling traps four carbon atoms between each of the eight corner iron atoms, thereby distorting the unit cell considerably. Because of this distortion, the body-centered Fe atom is also trapped.

This considerable distortion is a high energy-situation, but is stable below the critical temperature. It has a very high hardness of Rc 65 and relatively low ductility and impact resistance. Some of this distortion can be relaxed

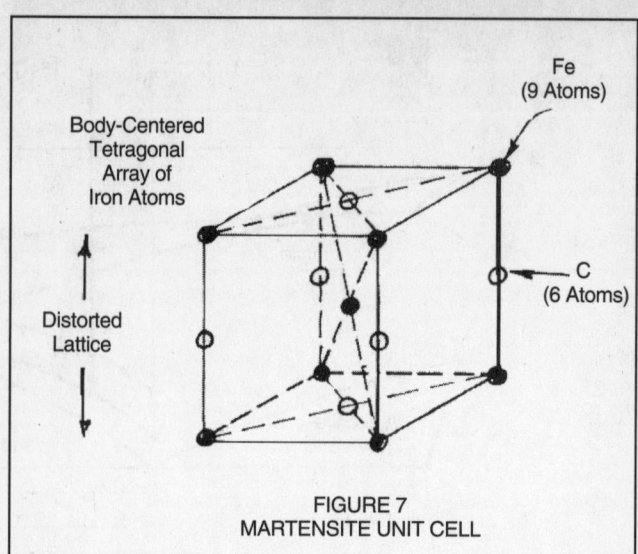

FIGURE 7
MARTENSITE UNIT CELL

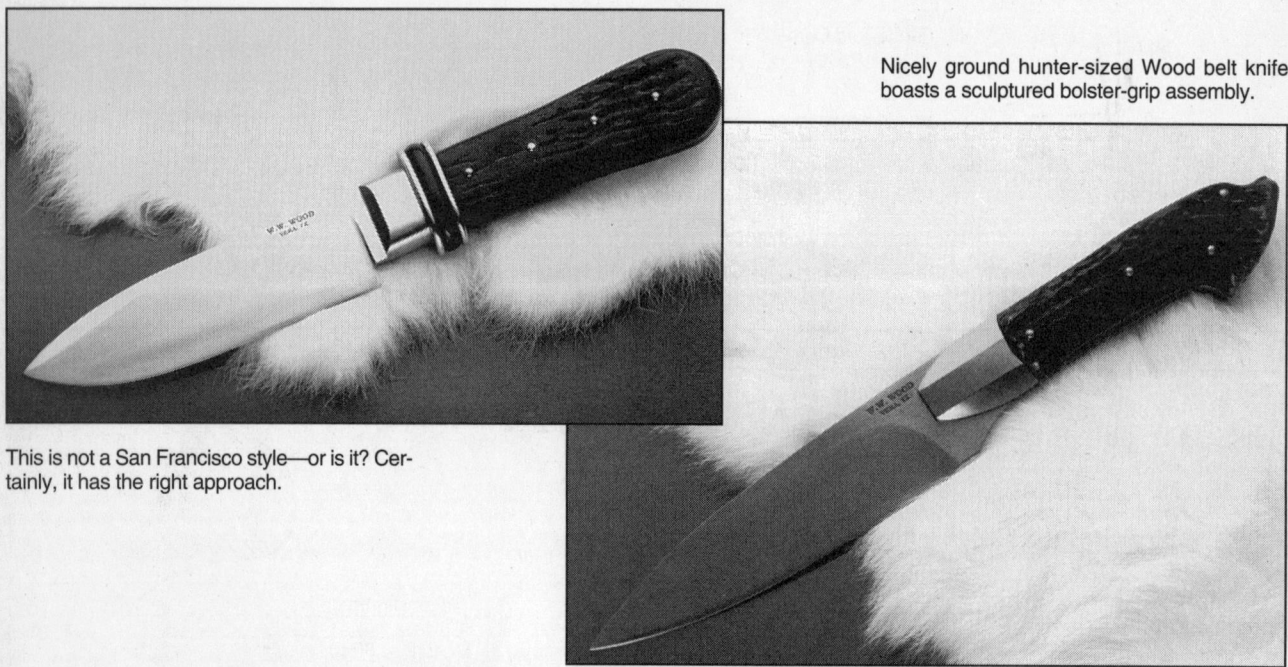

Nicely ground hunter-sized Wood belt knife boasts a sculptured bolster-grip assembly.

This is not a San Francisco style—or is it? Certainly, it has the right approach.

by subsequent low temperature tempering resulting in better ductility and slightly less hardness and strength.

The bottom of the S-curve is shown by two horizontal lines representing the martensite start (Ms) and finish (Mf.) These lines are generally above room temperature on most alloys; however, in some knife steels, the Ms is above room temperature and the Mf is below, resulting in a critical situation for the heat-treater. When cooled to room temperature, some of the austenite will transform to martensite for those alloys, but not all. If allowed to stand, this retained austenite may transform later in a finished knife and cause cracking. For this reason, it is sometimes necessary to sub-zero quench immediately to get full martensitic transformation. Most good heat-treaters know of this phenomenon and will sub-zero quench, but not all have the facility to accomplish this.

The transformation of martensite is also affected by

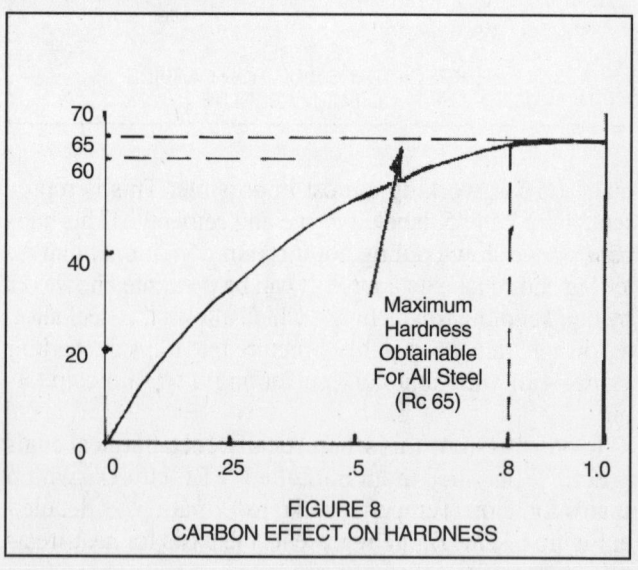

FIGURE 8
CARBON EFFECT ON HARDNESS

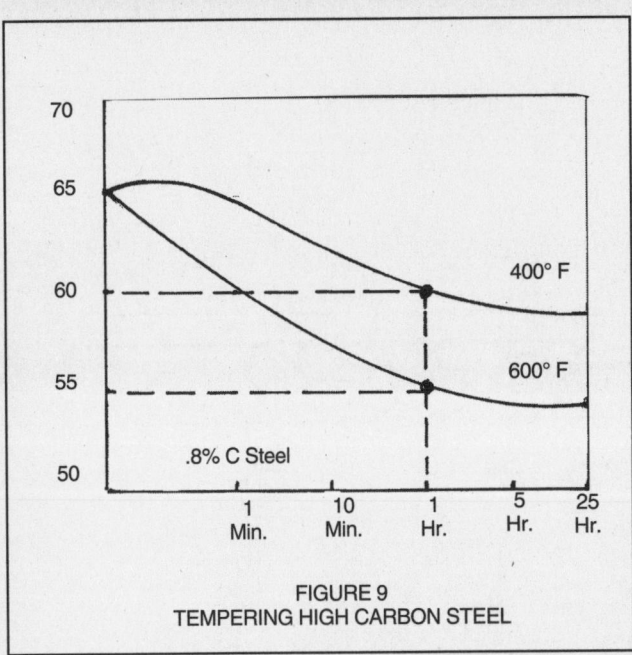

FIGURE 9
TEMPERING HIGH CARBON STEEL

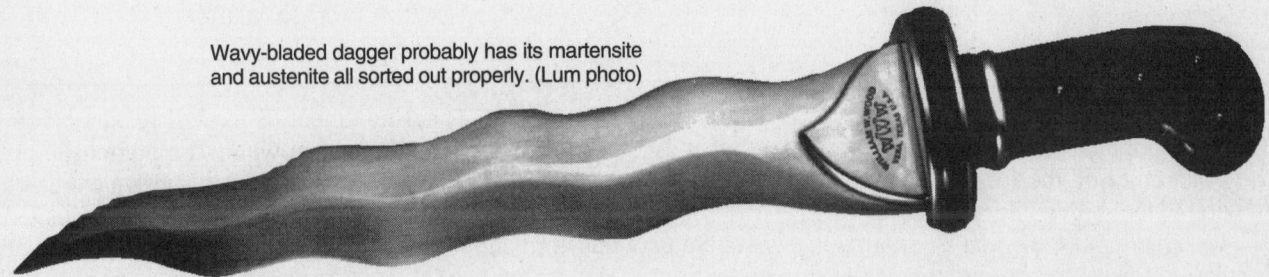

Wavy-bladed dagger probably has its martensite and austenite all sorted out properly. (Lum photo)

against finishing their operation below the critical temperature, as these severely refined grains can inhibit martensitic transformation.

In order to make hardened knife steels useful, it is necessary to reduce the Rc hardness of 65+ to a more manageable range of 55-60, so that ductility and toughness can be improved. Extremely hard and strong martensite can be tempered with temperature and time to improve ductility and toughness. Toughness is that property in steel that makes it less brittle and able to take impact shock, such as you get when a knife is dropped on concrete or when cutting hard objects such as bone.

Tempering steel consists of reheating the hard martensite to below the lower critical temperature for a sufficient time to allow excessive carbon in the martensite to precipitate as iron carbide. The carbon content of the martensite is rapidly reduced and assumes a spherical shape of carbide in ferrite matrix. The optimum combinations of strength, ductility, toughness, etc., of a given steel are controlled by the resulting size of the carbide particles, their distribution and chemistry. These factors, in turn, are controlled by the composition of the steel and the time/temperature combination of tempering.

In order to visualize this, refer to Figure 9. As you can see, it takes between one and twenty-five hours to affect an appreciable hardness drop with the attendant increase in toughness. At one hour, the hardness for this .8 percent C steel has dropped from Rc 66 to Rc 60 for a tempering temperature of 400 degrees F, which is about right for good knife steels. At 600 degrees F tempering temperature, the hardness has dropped to Rc 55 at one hour, which is generally too low for most knife makers.

With knowledge of basic metallurgy and heat-treatment of steel alloys in hand, we can proceed to compare the forging process as it relates to knifemaking. The stock removal process consists of grinding away metal; the forged blade is made by pounding the metal into shape with hammers at a temperature above the critical for that alloy. Cold forging can be done at room temperature, but this is rarely used for knifemaking because of the various problems associated with new knife steels.

Figure 10 is a schematic of forging knife steel above the upper critical temperature. This kind of metal shaping is always performed in the austenite range, generally

the basic steel alloy. The two most important conditions in controlling martensite are (1) the carbon content and (2) the grain size of the austenite as it is about to be quenched.

First, the carbon content must be sufficiently high (.8 percent) to promote martensitic transformation as shown in Figure 8. Beyond this .8 percent C, carbon does not affect the hardenability, shown by a leveling of the curve. This is the reason that all high carbon steels in the range of .8 to 2 percent C are essentially limited to a hardness of Rc 65. It is also the reason low carbon steels, below .8 percent, are not heat-treatable. D2 with its larger carbon content is more hardenable than 154CM, 440C, A2, W2, etc., but the maximum hardness is limited to approximately 65 Rc. All other alloying elements have a negligible effect.

The second factor affecting martensitic transformation is grain size. Large austenite grains retard transformation, as do most secondary alloying elements, and increase hardenability by moving the S curve to the right. However, these secondary elements have less effect than grain size. It is therefore recommended that heat-treaters do not quench from severely refined grains. Solutionizing for a time will let these grains grow to a sufficient size to allow good hardenability. Bladesmiths should be cautioned

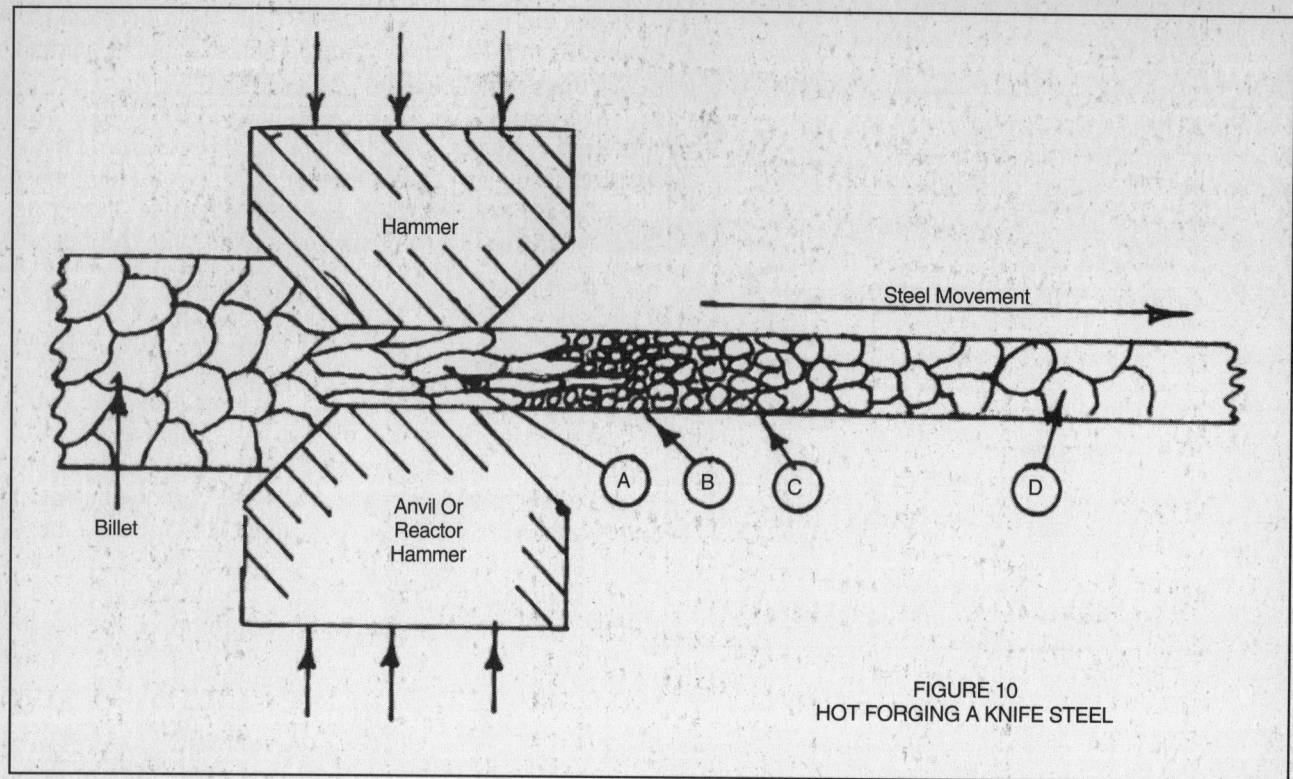

FIGURE 10
HOT FORGING A KNIFE STEEL

above 2000 degrees F, where grain growth is quite rapid. The part continually changes during forging as shown by the billet entering the forging hammers on the left and moving to the right while at temperature.

The large equiaxed—that is, approximately square or round—grains of the hot billet have been pounded into elongated narrow—unidimensional—grains by the forging hammer (A). Then, because the temperature is way above the recrystallization temperature, incipient recrystallization begins (B) shortly after this section leaves the hammer, resulting in small equiaxed grains. Because the part is still hot, grain growth starts immediately (C), resulting in still larger equiaxed grains. Finally, the grains have grown to their original size (D).

Refined grains (C) could be left in the steel by reducing the temperature for the final forging sequence. This should be done for parts that will not be heat-treated, resulting in parts with a range of hardness from Rc 45 to Rc 50, much below heat-treated parts in the range of Rc 60 to Rc 65. For this reason, forging can only help produce a shape in knifemaking and has little if anything to do with the final properties of the knife.

We should note that some knife shapes, especially curved blades, can be most quickly and economically produced by forging. For many, the forge is the easiest place to quickly make small knives, create various tapers, or use perfectly good steel that happens to be in rod form, or even spherical. None of these relate to the technical quality of the finished blade.

If the bladesmith is not careful, he can even make the heat-treating task more difficult, because fine grains actually decrease hardenability, as discussed previously, if taken to final heat-treatment. This will result in some pearlite (iron carbide) present within the martensite giving low hardness and susceptibility to subsequent cracking. Larger grains are desirable for complete martensitic transformation. Most laymen associate refined grains with high strength and hardness, which is true compared with casting, but these small grain structures cannot compare with heat-treated parts obtained by martensitic transformation.

Now let us look at a cold forged steel alloy below the critical temperature and see what happens when it is heated above the recrystallization temperature (Figure 11). The cold forged part (A) shows highly elongated grains that have been hammered into a highly unstable state by the forging hammer. These grains are directionally elongated transverse to the direction of the forging hammer. Slip lines are shown in each grain to denote these have their own lattice direction, although some overall rotation has taken place leaving more alignment than when started. It should be noticed that hardness is relatively high, in the range of Rc 40 to Rc 50, and ductility is low.

As the temperature is increased to above the critical, incipient recrystallization begins (B). These new grains result at the boundaries of the high energy elongated grains (A). Hardness is starting to increase. At higher temperatures, complete recrystallization is affected (C) where all the small grains have consumed the larger elongated grains. At still higher temperature, complete grain growth has been affected (D), with low hardness and high ductility.

In order to put all this knowledge to work in knifemak-

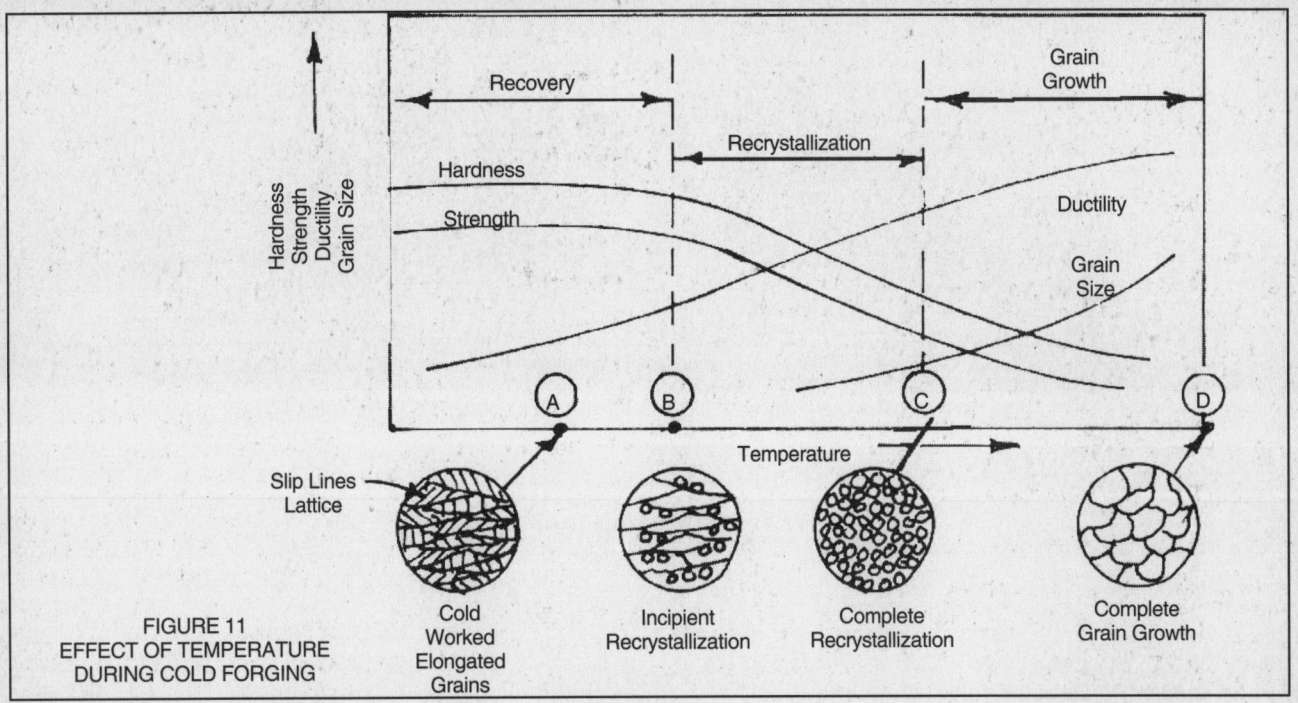

FIGURE 11
EFFECT OF TEMPERATURE
DURING COLD FORGING

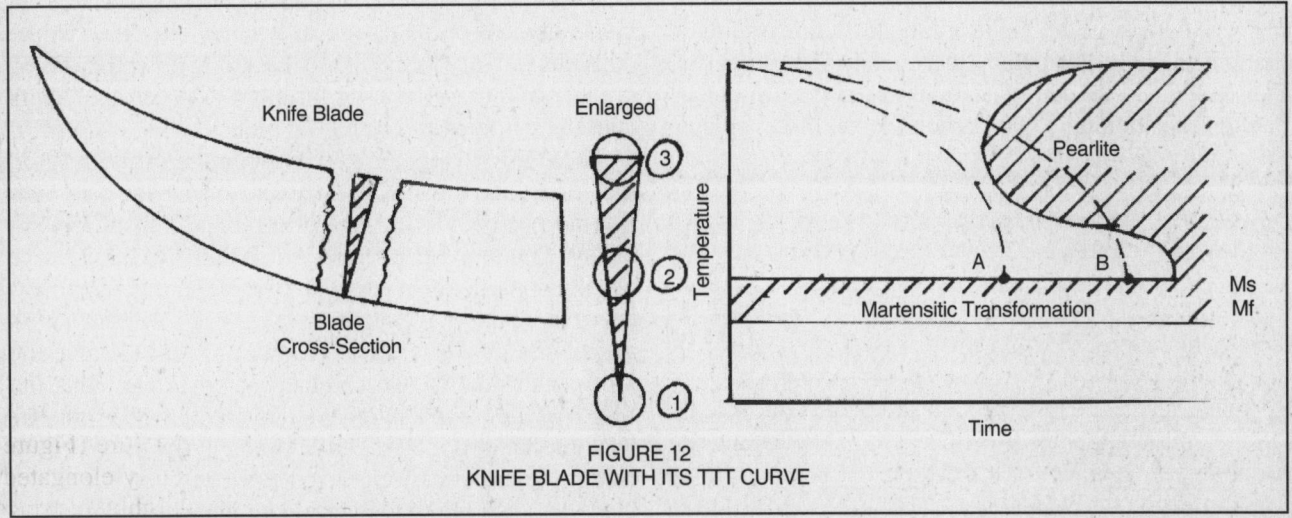

FIGURE 12
KNIFE BLADE WITH ITS TTT CURVE

ing, it will be best to draw a knife blade and relate the various parts of it to the TTT diagram (S-curve) for the appropriate alloy as shown in Figure 12. A cross-section of the blade is shown enlarged with its cutting edge (1), the mid-section (2) and spine (3). The cutting edge will always get more transformed martensite than the rest of the blade because thin sections cool faster during the quenching cycle, as shown by cooling curve A on the S-curve. This is good because the maker wants the cutting edge to be the hardest part of the blade to resist abrading and dulling. Also, retained austenite would possibly result in subsequent cracking at the thin edge.

The spine (3), being the thickest part of the blade, could possibly have a cooling curve such as B, going through the pearlite nose and ending up with alternating layers of iron carbide between a ferrite (pure iron) matrix. Most heat-treaters design their quenching medium to get around this problem; otherwise, we would end up with a lot of delayed cracks in the spine.

Bladesmiths have to be particularly careful at the cutting edge because rapid cooling during forging retards grain growth, making the S-curve move to the left and thereby decreasing hardenability. It is advisable for all knifemakers, those who forge and those who grind, to leave a cutting edge before heat-treatment of approximately .030- to .050-inch thick to ensure maximum hardenability and minimum distortion during heat-treatment. In order to miss the pearlite nose, thick sections such as the spine may require an initial oil quenching to a preselected temperature below the pearlite nose and then air quenching to room temperature.

Damascus steel is a metallurgical problem completely different from what has been discussed heretofore, because it is generally fabricated from alternating layers

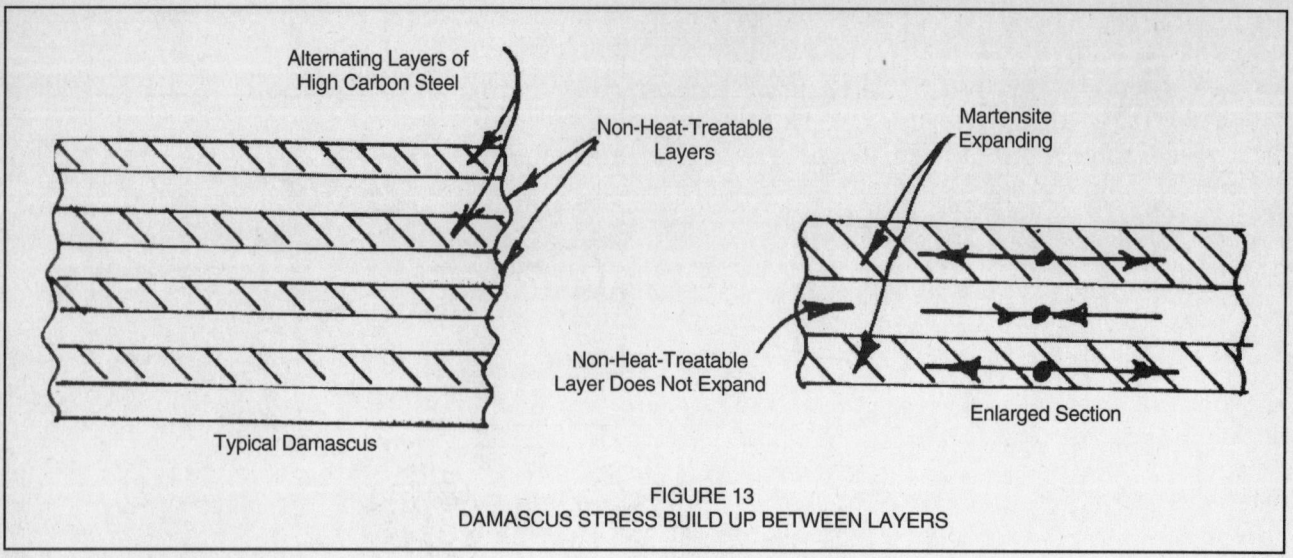

FIGURE 13
DAMASCUS STRESS BUILD UP BETWEEN LAYERS

of a heat-treatable high carbon steel and some other alloy that is not heat-treatable. This results in alternating layers of hard and soft materials as shown in Figure 13.

Stress usually builds up at the juncture of the alternating layers because the high carbon steel transforming to martensite slightly increases in volume. This is because the tetragonal unit cell of martensite has been stretched due to repositioning of the carbon atoms. If the welding process at these junctures has not been performed correctly because of improper heat, pressure and surface cleaning by the smith, these small internal stresses can cause cracking along the layer and sometimes transverse to it. Generally, these stresses are sufficiently alleviated by the adjacent soft layer adhering to the strong layer. However, cracks can occur from a poor bond between the layers caused by improper forging techniques.

These thin layers are generally on the order of .001-inch thick, and it would be desirable to have the hard ones line up perfectly with the cutting edge, but this is not always the case. Because they are so thin, the cutting edge usually consists of an equal number of hard and soft layers running not only with the cutting edge but also across the edge. For these reasons, Damascus cannot give the knifemaker that continuous hard cutting edge along the length of the blade that other knifemaking steels possess.

Some Damascus makers eliminate this problem by using a thick hardenable layer in the very center of the blade and placing the other thinner alternating layers on each side. When this arrangement is correctly forged, the hard layer will remain in the center and will heat-treat with a cutting edge on the order of Rc 60-65. In this way, the maker can have it both ways—the beauty and toughness of Damascus and a cutting edge that will stand abrasion like heat-treated knives.

Damascus is used for its beauty of contrast showing etched surfaces of different patterns that sometimes makes you feel they have been painted by an artist. The

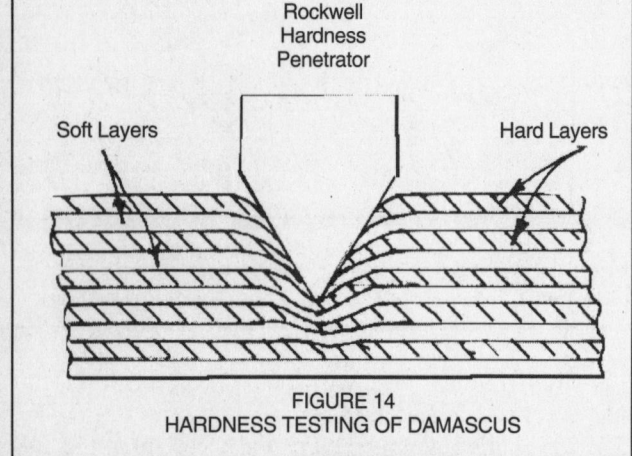

FIGURE 14
HARDNESS TESTING OF DAMASCUS

Wood accepts the idea that stock removal can get tedious in a job as complex as this axe.

material can be hardened, but not like a uniform knife steel. One of the difficulties can be depicted by the Rc hardness schematic shown in Figure 14. As the Rockwell hardness tester generally penetrates to approximately .050-inch, it will encounter around 40-50 layers of hard/soft steel. As the penetrator is only feeling an average hardness of these layers, it is no wonder that it hardly ever picks up a hardness beyond Rc 50, and most of the time around Rc 45.

The toughness of Damascus is good. As the saying goes, it will bend but not break. One story I've heard is that a Damascus sword was bent around on itself to a full circle and returned to the original blade shape upon release. Whether this is true is doubtful, but it does illustrate what people believe about the tough character of Damascus.

Edge holding is another matter. Because of its low average hardness, Damascus steel is not expected to have good edge-holding character. It is generally easy to sharpen and can be sharpened to shave, but it has to be resharpened quite often.

Damascus forging is in a class by itself because there is no other way to produce those beautiful layered art works. However, the knifemaker should realize that the resulting product is not comparable in hardness and edge-holding ability to knives produced from other steel by the stock removal and heat-treating methods. Accordingly, most reputable Damascus knife producers do not make unwarranted claims about those qualities of their knives.

In summary, good knives can be produced by metal removing or forging. However, the metal removal process can produce a knife with fewer problems and less chance of error than the forging process. Unless the mechanic has good knowledge of the metallurgy of his steel, he may forge a blade of inferior quality. If the forger final-shapes his blade by stock removal and then heat-treats, he may equal the blade made by stock removal alone. That, of course, raises the fundamental question: What is gained by the forging process?

Beware of knifemakers claiming of high-quality knives by illustrating grain structure and precipitates in photomicrographs. These fine grains and dispersion of precipitates have nothing to do with the quality of the knife. The quality is determined by the relative amounts of martensite, pearlite and retained austenite. It takes a qualified metallurgist to qualify and quantify those complex interrelated factors.

The metallurgy of knifemaking is complex and intricate. Accordingly, both knifemakers and collectors should be guided by the proven professional reputations of those with whom they deal or buy. Artistic work is one facet of that process. The technical quality of the resultant knife is another. A good artistic knife producer can provide both using proper metallurgical procedures. •

EDITOR'S NOTE

This article is excerpted from a work in progress. William W. Wood is preparing a full book-length treatment of metallurgy in knifemaking to be published soon.

He is perhaps uniquely qualified to write that book and this article. He has made knives professionally for twenty years. The twenty years before that, he was a metallurgist for Ling-Temco-Vought, retiring as chief of manufacturing engineering. He qualified for that work with a Master's Degree, *Magna Cum Laude*, from MIT.

His view here permits of few objections, it seems to us, but there will be some. He says there is no mystery, that the science cited here is the science in use everyday all around the world as thousands of tons of steel are fabricated to serve all the many purposes of industry and commerce.

The book to come promises to answer, in terms of metallurgical knowledge, a wide range of questions on knife steels and their treatment, their uses, their qualities. It is to be a comprehensive presentation of the technical factors involved in the knifemaking process, and we look forward to it.

Ken Warner

Writer, metallurgist, knifemaker Wood.

THE KNIFE BAYONET

GI training in 1942 with a Garand rifle and M1905 bayonet. The bayonet charge was not the way we fought World War II. (U.S. Army Signal Corps photo)

Since the U.S. Army was founded in 1775, there has been the command: "Fix—Bayonets." Dramatic photographs of World War II often show U.S. soldiers and Marines brandishing rifles with bayonets fixed.

There is no question that a rifle with a fixed bayonet in the hand of a determined GI or Marine was a very intimidating weapon. However, during World War II, both the bayonet and the U.S. Armed Forces' attitude toward it and its use changed.

The bayonet was invented to supplement the muzzle-loading musket or rifle to make it a "pike" suitable for hand-to-hand combat. Every U.S. soldier or Marine issued a rifle or musket has always been issued a bayonet for his weapon.

When the U.S. Army adopted its first modern rifle, the bolt-action 30-caliber Krag magazine loader of the 1890s, it adopted its first "knife bayonet" to go with it. It established much of the basic design for the knife bayonet used by the Army and Marine Corps ever since, and also the way it fixed to their rifles.

When the U.S. Army adopted the 30-caliber M1903 Springfield bolt-action rifle, it incorporated many major design changes from the Krag rifle. The '03 Springfield

IN U.S. SERVICE
by KONRAD F. SCHREIER, JR.

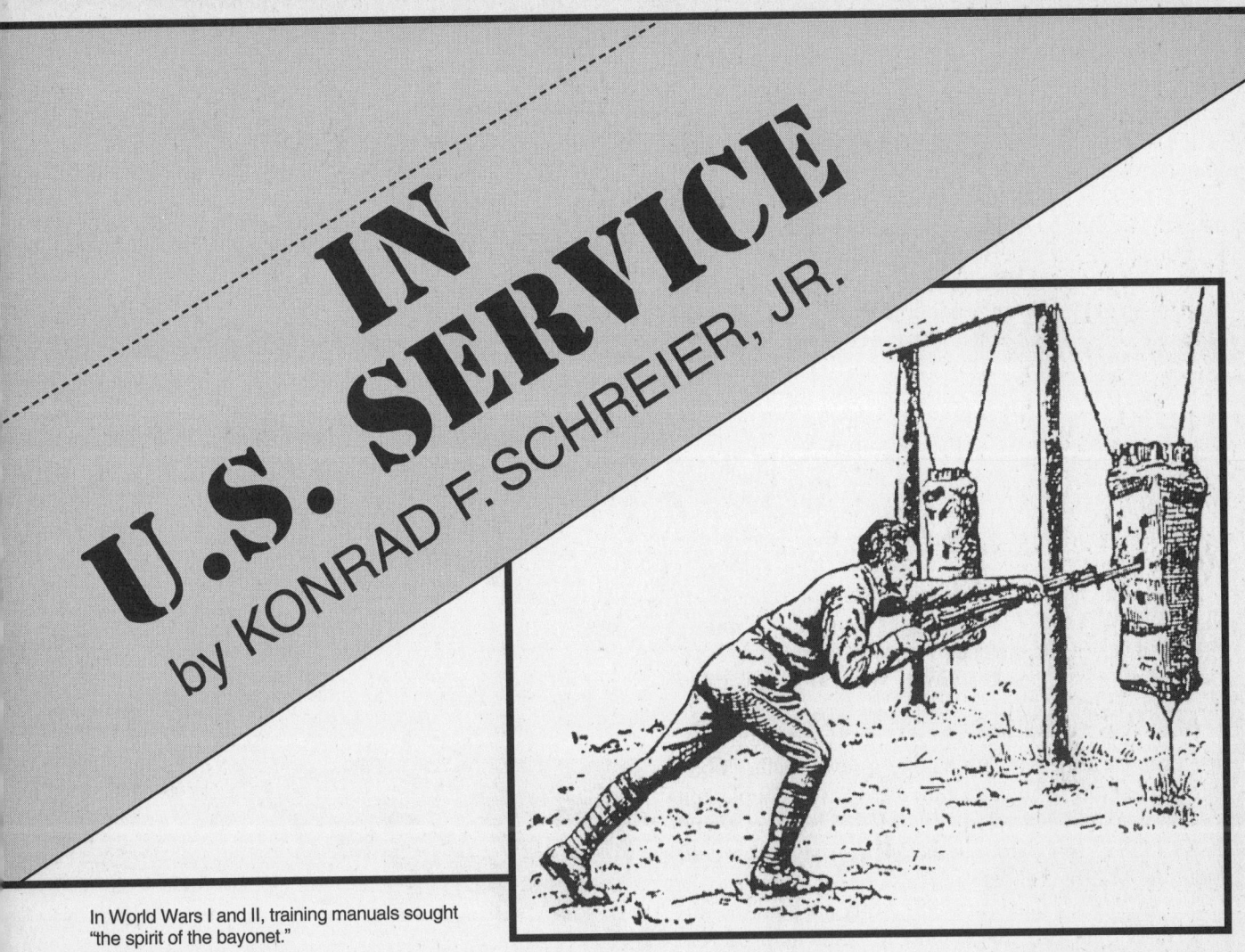

In World Wars I and II, training manuals sought "the spirit of the bayonet."

was 6 inches shorter than the Krag, so it could be used by both foot and mounted troops eliminating the need for separate infantry rifles and cavalry carbines.

Another change in the '03 Springfield was its rod bayonet which telescoped into its stock. This rod bayonet was so unsatisfactory that President Theodore Roosevelt, a soldier himself, ordered it replaced with a knife bayonet almost as soon as he saw it.

The result was a redesign of the '03 Springfield including a new bayonet, Model of 1905 with a 16.2-inch blade, for it. All future '03 Springfields were built to use this bayonet, and all rod bayonet '03 Springfields were ordered rebuilt for it.

The 16.2-inch-long M1905 bayonet brought the length of the '03 Springfield to 59.7 inches overall, about 1.4 inches shorter than the Krag with its 11.7-inch blade bayonet. This ensured the '03 Springfield's bayonet would not be outreached by foreign soldiers' bayonets.

The reorganization of the U.S. Army about 1905 required year model designations for all arms and equipment. Bayonets and their scabbards were considered separate items, so both the new '03 Springfield bayonet and its scabbard were designated Model of 1905. The M1905 scabbard was of the same metal construction as the Krag bayonets, and it was fitted with a metal loop for attachment to a rifleman's leather or web garrison belt.

At the same time, the long-standing bayonet drill specified by the U.S. Army Infantry Drill Regulations received new importance, as did bayonet training. Every rifleman in the Army was taught the carefully choreographed bayonet drill and the aggressive "spirit of the bayonet" which was part of it. The idea was to condition riflemen to subdue their enemies when they could not do it by rifle fire alone. The "spirit of the bayonet" was a part of U.S. Army bayonet training through World Wars I and II.

In 1910, the U.S. Army adopted the Mills web equipment it used through World War II and long after. This system included the rifleman's belt with pockets for clipped rifle ammunition which could not carry a bayonet. It also included a new backpack with provisions to carry the bayonet in a position where it could be easily reached.

To suit the changes of the Mills equipment, a new bayonet scabbard, Model of 1910, was adopted for the M1905 bayonet. Unlike the M1905 scabbard, the M1910 scabbard was a wooden body with a canvas duck cover and the familiar U.S. Army double belt hook system to fasten it to the backpack. The M1910 bayonet scabbard remained standard for the Army into early World War II.

When the United States entered World War I in April of 1917, it required an immense number of modern rifles to equip its troops. The British 303-caliber Enfield Pattern 1914 rifle being manufactured in the United States was brought up to U.S. Army requirements and adopted as the "cal. .30 Rifle, Model of 1917," to be co-standard with the "cal. .30 Rifle Model 1903." The M1917 Enfield had its own bayonet and scabbard also adopted by the U.S. Army as the Models of 1917.

The 17.3-inch-blade M1917 bayonet was of similar construction to the M1905, but they were not interchangeable. Two grooves were cut across the M1917 bayonet's wooden grip to prevent confusion with the M1905.

The overall length of the M1917 rifle and bayonet was 63.4 inches, some 3.7 inches longer than the '03 Springfield with its M1905 bayonet. This was considered something of an advantage for World War I trench warfare bayonet combat.

The M1917 scabbard was of entirely different construction from the M1910, having a sewn leather body with a metal throat including the U.S. Army double belt hook system and a metal tip. The M1905 bayonet would fit the M1917 scabbard, but the M1917 bayonet would not fit the M1910 scabbard.

During World War I, the U.S. Army adopted the 20-inch-barrel riot-type "trench shotgun" and equipped it to use the M1917 bayonet, probably because it was the most available model. This use kept the M1917 bayonet standard in the U.S. Army long after the M1917 rifle became obsolete at the end of World War II.

During World War I, bayonet training was stressed even more in the U.S. Army. Elements were adopted from the British army bayonet training system, and the "spirit of the bayonet" became even more aggressive. This despite the fact that far less costly U.S. Army "extended order" infantry tactics decreased the importance of the time-honored bayonet line charge and the mentality that went with it.

After the end of World War I, the '03 Springfield rifle with its M1905 bayonet and M1910 bayonet scabbard were standard for the Army and Marine Corps. The M1917 Enfield rifle, bayonet and scabbard became "substitute standard" to be issued in the event of war. In addition, the riot-type trench shotgun equipped with the M1917 bayonet and scabbard remained standard issue at the rate of two per company upon request.

By the end of World War I, the U.S. Army had set out to develop a general-issue semi-automatic infantry rifle, the program which led to the adoption of the "cal. .30 Rifle M-1 Garand" of World War II. One of the require-

ments was that the semi-automatic rifle would use the M1905 bayonet, and this determined the design of the M-1 Garand's gas cylinder assembly.

When the controversy over the M-1 Garand rifle versus the Johnson rifle erupted, the U.S. Army strongly objected to the Johnson's inability to use the M1905 bayonet. In actual fact, the recoil-operated Johnson would not function reliably with any bayonet ever designed for it, and this was one of the many reasons the U.S. Armed Forces never adopted it.

As World War II broke out in Europe in 1939, the U.S. Army began preparing, and the production of the M-1 Garand rifle was expanded. This led to a requirement for a new scabbard for the M1905 bayonet which would be easier to manufacture and not use the canvas, rawhide and wood of the M1910 scabbard.

In September of 1940, the Beckwith Manufacturing Co. of Dover, New Hampshire, submitted an experimental prototype that had a metal throat with the Army double belt hook and a body made of plastic. At the time, the use of plastic for such an item of military equipment was a new and novel approach; however, the new experimental scabbard not only passed its tests, but it cost less and was easier to manufacture than the M1910.

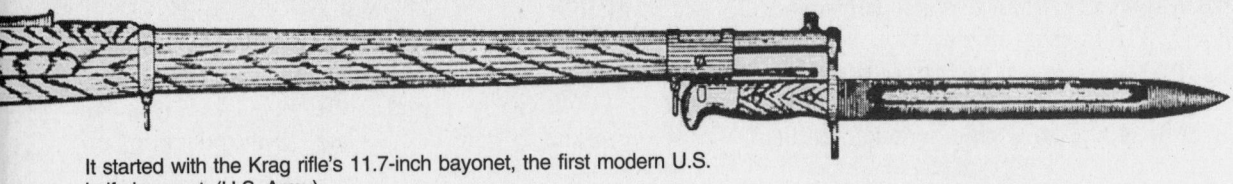

It started with the Krag rifle's 11.7-inch bayonet, the first modern U.S. knife bayonet. (U.S. Army)

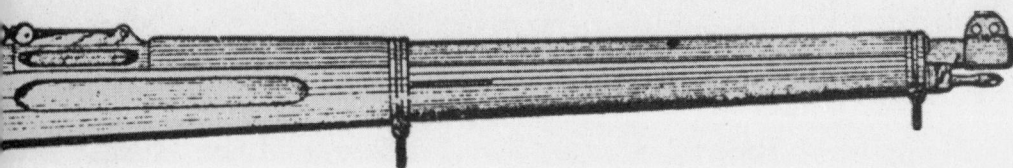

The original 1903 Springfield's rod bayonet—seen under muzzle—was dropped by 1905. (U.S. Army)

The M1903A2 Springfield rifle looked like this with the 16.2-inch blade 1905 bayonet. (U.S. Army)

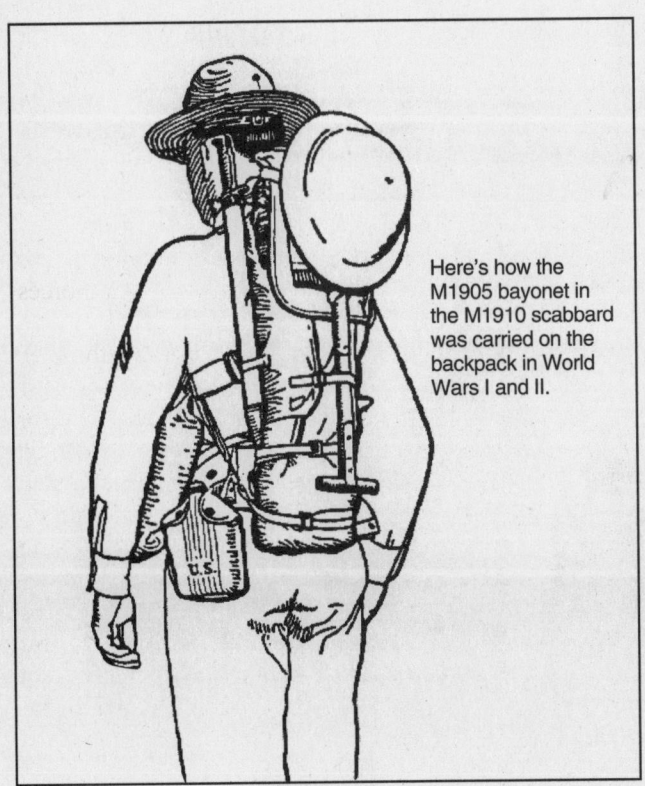

Here's how the M1905 bayonet in the M1910 scabbard was carried on the backpack in World Wars I and II.

After additional development, the new plastic scabbard for the M1905 bayonet was adopted as the Bayonet Scabbard M3. It was already in production, and by 1943, the old M1910 scabbard was made substitute standard. No M1910 scabbards were manufactured during World War II, and the U.S. Army declared it obsolete at the end of World War II.

A plastic scabbard for the M1917 bayonet was developed in 1942, but its production was not pushed since there were large numbers of M1917 scabbards on hand. The new plastic scabbard was designated the M1917, and since the M1917 rifle was not issued to U.S. troops after 1942, the only Army bayonets for which it was issued went on 12-gauge riot shotguns.

Since bayonets and scabbards were relatively easy to manufacture, they were pouring out of a number of factories by the end of 1941. There were a huge number of minor variations from the basic model design, but so long as these did not affect their appearance or ability to fit the rifle, these were allowed and no attempt to keep a record of them was made. Among these variations are the shape of the blade tip and the grips.

When the U.S. Army entered World War II on December 7, 1941, the bayonet was still recognized as an essential rifleman's weapon, but it was also considered a weapon of last resort. Army infantry tactics stressed extended order with a maximum use of cover and concealment based on the firepower of the M-1 Garand rifle and the Browning Automatic Rifle in each infantry squad.

In combat, GIs quickly learned to use these tactics to reduce their casualties, and the use of the bayonet as a weapon occurred only when nothing else would do in either offensive or defensive combat. The spirit of the bayonet was still part of it, but as the war progressed, less and less importance was placed on bayonet training. More effective employment of infantry support weapons such as the machinegun and mortar, and the introductions of new ones like the bazooka hand-held rocket launcher, further reduced the use of the bayonet.

In late 1942, the U.S. Army Cavalry Board requested that the blade of the M1905 bayonet be shortened from

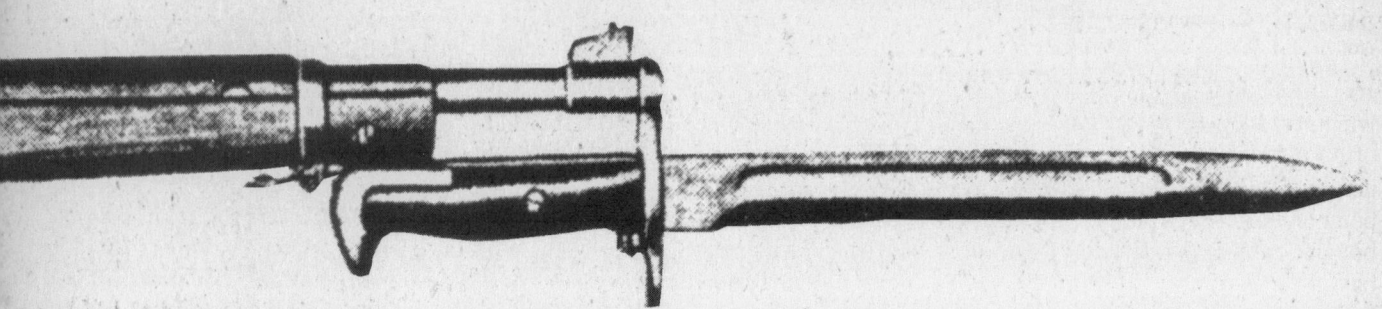

The World War II M1903A3 Springfield rifle with the 10-inch blade M1 bayonet was a different package for a different war. (U.S. Army)

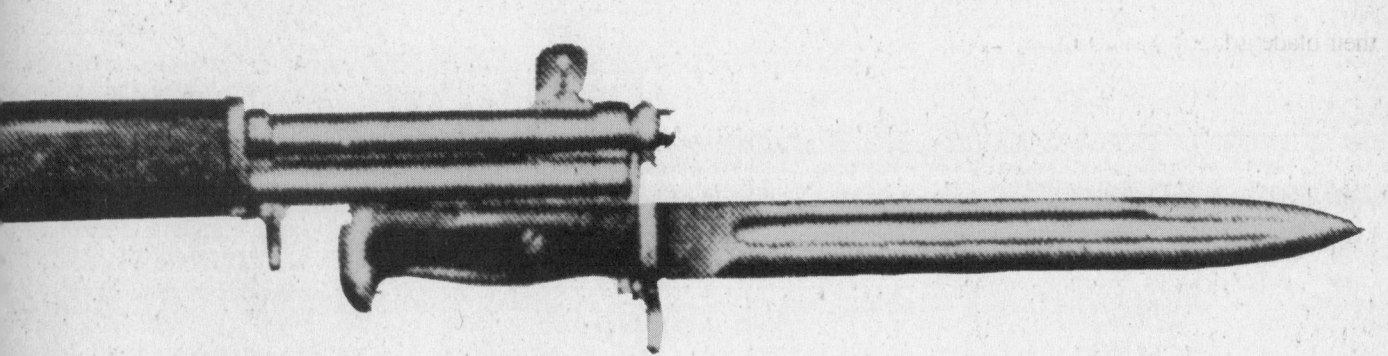

Here's the M1 bayonet on the M1 Garand Rifle. (U.S. Army)

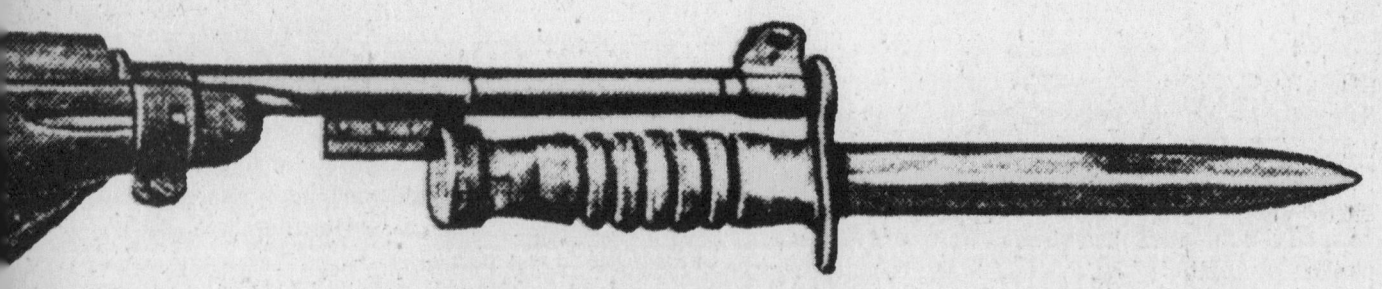

M1 carbine's bayonet lug front band mounts the M4 knife-bayonet. (U.S. Army)

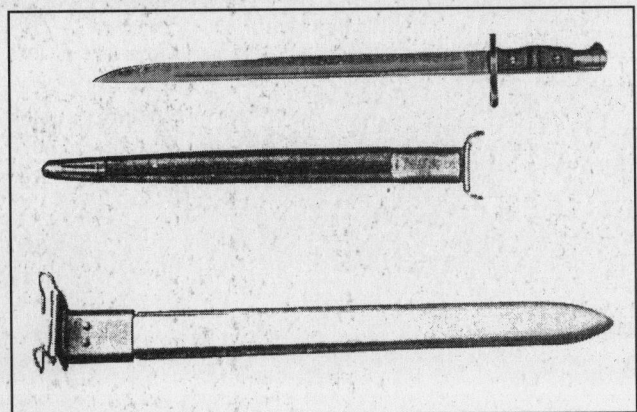

The M1917 bayonet for the M1917 Enfield rifle and its original and World I and II scabbards. (U.S. Army)

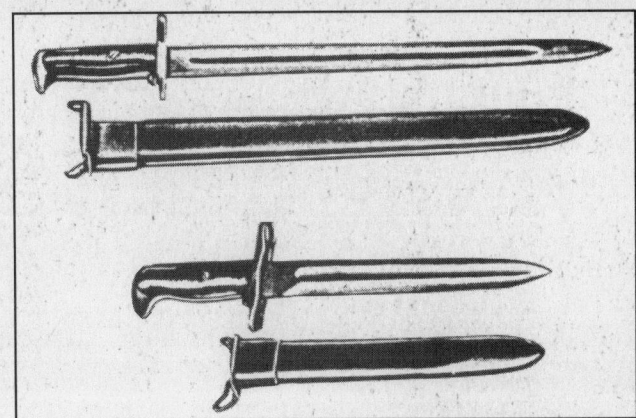

The M1905 and M1 bayonets with World War II plastic scabbards. (U.S. Army)

16.2 to 10 inches so it would be a better utility knife which could be easily carried on a rifleman's belt instead of on his backpack. Tests using cut-down M1905 bayonets carried in cut-down M1910 scabbards were run by both the U.S. Army Cavalry and Infantry boards, and they both recommended the immediate adoption of the shorter bayonet.

The new 10-inch bayonet was adopted as the Bayonet M1 in March, 1943. By this time, large numbers of M1905 bayonets were already being cut down into M1s. When new 10-inch bayonets were manufactured, they were also called M1s, and no distinction was ever made between the cut-down M1905s and new manufacture M1s. During World War II, the cut-down M1905s with their blade gutter running into their tips were more com-

M1905-M1 bayonet was subjected to "production and product improvement" experimenting. In October, 1942, Oneida Limited was given a contract to simplify the basic design so modern manufacturing methods could be used. They produced a series of experimental 10-inch T2 bayonets, some of these produced in substantial numbers for testing. With the available huge quantities of cut-down M1905 and new manufacture M1 bayonets, the new model never required production, and the project was terminated in March, 1945.

In October of 1943, in response to a deluge of requests from both units in combat and in training, the U.S. Army Service Forces issued a requirement for a bayonet for the 30-caliber Carbine M1. At the time, those personnel carrying carbines were issued the Trench Knife M3, and they

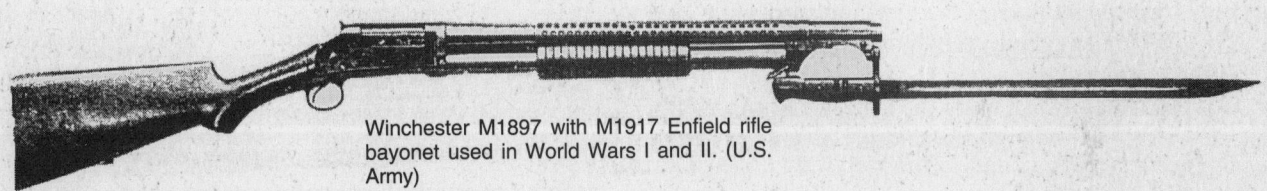

Winchester M1897 with M1917 Enfield rifle bayonet used in World Wars I and II. (U.S. Army)

monly issued than the new manufacture M1s with a tip like the old M1905.

Along with the 10-inch M1 bayonet came the Bayonet Scabbard M3A1 to carry it, and it was nothing but a shortened M3 scabbard. This scabbard was slightly modified late in World War II and redesignated the Bayonet Scabbard M7.

Although the M1905 bayonet quickly became a "limited standard" item, it remained in service long after it was declared obsolete at end of World War II. It was no longer issued for combat troops after 1944, but they were, and still are, issued for special ceremonial color guards and the like, and for use by drill teams. The old 16-inch-long M1905 bayonet is still impressive on parade, especially when its long blade is polished or chrome plated.

During the course of World War II, the design of the

all wanted to be able to use it as a bayonet. The project to design a bayonet for the carbine began with two quite different approaches.

One approach, a blind alley, was to make a variation of the "tent peg" bayonet used with the 303-caliber British No. 4 Lee-Enfield rifle. The U.S. version fastened to the carbine's front sight with a thumb screw, and both blade and "tent peg" types were tested. This approach was quickly dropped for many reasons, among them the fact that the "tent peg" was useless as a utility knife.

The other approach was to modify the Trench Knife M3 and the carbine. The trench knife was very simply modified by using a new guard with a hole that fit the carbine's barrel and supplying a new grip cap with a bayonet retainer spring latch. To accept this bayonet, the carbine's simple front band was replaced with a new

The Bayonet-Knife M4 with M8 and M8A1 scabbards as used in late World War II. (U.S. Army)

front band bayonet lug assembly to which the bayonet latched.

The new carbine bayonet was adopted as the Bayonet-Knife M4 in May of 1944, and its scabbard was either the Scabbard M8 or M8A1 originally designed for the Trench Knife M3. By this time, the Bayonet-Knife M4 had already replaced the Trench Knife M3 in production, and carbines were being built and rebuilt with the front band bayonet lug assembly.

Combat troops began using the carbine bayonet M4 in late 1944, and their comments said it was satisfactory. It was a useful utility knife, but admittedly a 35.6-inch-long carbine tipped by its 6.7-inch blade was only 42.25 inches long and was not a very impressive or effective weapon. However, not unlike many rifles with bayonets fixed, it was frequently seen guarding prisoners of war and in the hand of guards and sentries. By the time World War II ended, the bayonet fitting was standard for all carbines in issue, and many carbines were retrofitted.

There is quite a bit of evidence concerning the U.S. Army's use of bayonets, or lack thereof, in World War II. The massive collections of U.S. Army Signal Corps combat photos don't show many men with bayonets on their rifles.

Another factor was the effect of a bayonet on a rifle's accuracy. Many Army publications and its rifle training instructor cautioned that a rifle with its bayonet fixed would be less accurate than the rifle without it, particularly at ranges over a couple of hundred yards.

The records of the U.S. Army Medical Department show that enemy casualties caused by Army bayonets

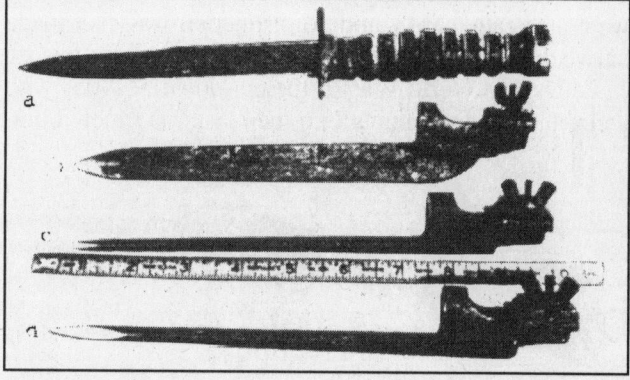

(Below) Experimental carbine bayonets: A is the T4 prototype of the M4 bayonet actually adopted, the others are T5, T6 and T8 "tent peg" prototypes. (U.S. Army)

were rather rare. Unfortunately, they also show there were more Army bayonet casualties caused in bayonet training and by "horse play" not in the line of duty.

The U.S. Army retained the bayonet after the end of World War II and still issues them. However, they have changed a great deal. Before the M-1 Garand rifle went out of service, its World War II 10-inch blade bayonet was replaced by a 6 3/4-inch blade Bayonet-Knife M5 and M5A1. When the 7.62mm rifle M-14 became standard, it used the 6 3/4-inch Bayonet-Knife M5, and the 5.56mm Rifle M-16 series uses the 5-inch Bayonet-Knife M7. All of these are designs based on the World War II carbine Bayonet-Knife M4.

Today, half a century after World War II, the U.S. Army and Marine Corps still have the command, "Fix—Bayonets," and there is no way to expect it to be dropped. Even if there's another design change, the command—and some of the spirit—will still be with us.

EARLY AMERICAN FRONTIER DAGGERS

In a world of single-shot rifles and plentiful bears, a close encounter with a bear was something that could and did happen.

by GORDON MINNIS

THE DAGGER DOES not hold a position of very high visibility in the panoply of American edged weapons. Think of the traditional, historical American knives—the Long Knife of the early riflemen, the Bowie, the Green River, even the Ka-Bar—and there's not a dagger in the lot. In the unlikely event your average American were to have an opinion about daggers, he would doubtless consider them relics of medieval times or the preferred weapon of Mediterranean assassins. The dagger just does not seem to have registered on the American national historical consciousness.

That's all true enough, but a little difficult to explain, because the dagger occupied a significant niche in the armament and culture of early America. From the first colonial years right through the Revolution to the Bowie era and the Civil War, daggers could be seen carried by all manner of frontiersmen, hunters, soldiers, gamblers, politicians, ladies of the evening and anyone else who could imagine needing a defensive weapon.

During much of this period, there was no cutlery industry as such on the North American continent. When commercial cutlery manufacture did develop, it was a long way from the frontier, and the dagger was not a major part of the product line. This is why, I believe, the great majority of surviving early American daggers are of private, as opposed to commercial, make. In this context, that same combination of circumstances can be seen as the beginning of the very long American tradition of "custom" knifemaking.

As might be expected in the case of any object used over such a wide area for so long a time, great variations in the design, construction and materials are found in American daggers. A comprehensive treatment of the subject is far beyond the scope of this article, and it should be understood that the specimens illustrated here are only a sampling of known varieties.

It should also be noted that no attempt was made at very precise dating. American knives of private manufacture made before the Civil War are notoriously difficult to

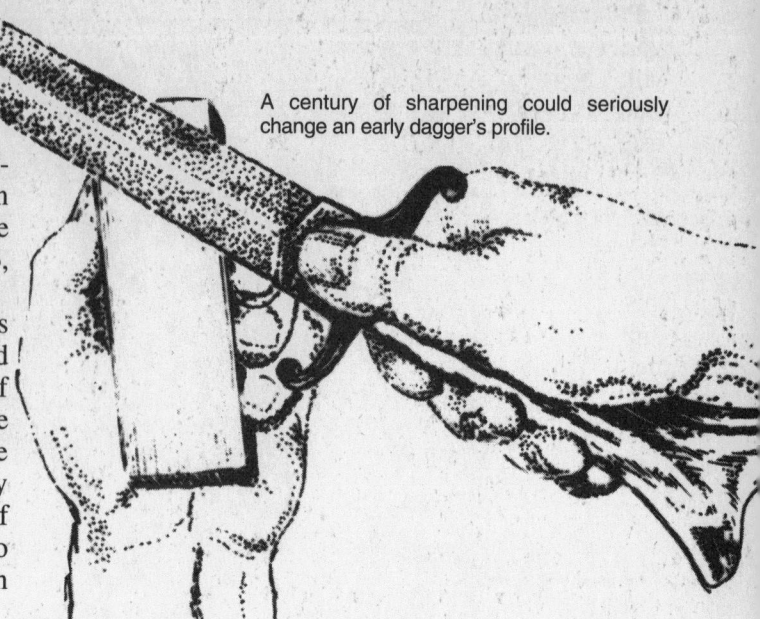

A century of sharpening could seriously change an early dagger's profile.

date with any appreciable accuracy. It is sometimes possible to say, for example, that a piece is of a type used in the Revolutionary War, but this does not mean that the given example absolutely dates between 1775 and 1783, or even 1760 and 1800.

There are, in a general way, some design progressions that provide clues to dating. Daggers early in the period *tend* to be small with narrow, tapered blades and guards of relatively complex form, sometimes integral with the blade stock. Later daggers, as in the Bowie era, *tend* to be larger and heavier with parallel-edged blades less acutely pointed, and with simple guards, often just an oval of sheet metal. However, there are enough exceptions to both these trends that one needs to be very cautious in specifying a period for a particular piece.

DAGGER 1

We begin with an excellent case in point, the first American dagger I ever acquired—now some thirty-five years ago—and a clearer case of plain, dumb beginner's luck you will never see. It would be nice to have those years back again to find a better example, but I wouldn't count on being able to do it.

It's a little tricky to make even a generalized date assignment for this knife, because while it has nice work on the guard and the rich patination of a truly early piece, it is large enough ($9^3/_4$-inch blade, $15^1/_8$ inches overall) to fit right in with the Bowie-period daggers. It is very tempting to consider it an exceptionally large early dagger, and the relatively slim tapered blade tends to confirm this attribution.

The construction system is very unusual for the period; the $^3/_4$-length tang is inletted into the inner faces of the antler slabs which constitute the grip. This produces what some modern makers have called a rabbet tang design and demonstrates once again there's really nothing new under the sun. The handle once had a thin sheet-iron pommel plate held by four small screws; this assembly is now missing. Three iron pins hold the grips to the tang. There is a metal washer between the guard and the antler. The blade is forged from a file, a very common source of steel for all sorts of early American knives and tools.

DAGGER 2

Pointing out errors in the late Harold Peterson's 1958 work *American Knives* has become a popular pastime with some of today's knife writers. Not enough time is spent appreciating some of the valuable and original insights Peterson propounded.

For example, one of Peterson's more significant—and least noticed—observations concerned the use of relatively small daggers as auxiliary weapons by American officers in the Revolutionary War. A few documented specimens are known, and there are a number of very similar surviving examples whose age and style make them rather difficult to explain in any other context.

We show two examples of this class of American dagger, alike in both size and general concept. One has a compound handle of cattle horn with a black walnut pommel and a brass ferrule, while the other has a one-piece grip of deer antler. Both blades are just 7 inches long—slender and tapering as is the case with most early daggers—and both guards show substantial stylistic shaping.

The antler-handled piece is very unusual because the maker's initials—WA—are struck in the base of the blade, perhaps a one-in-a-hundred occurrence in this period. The other dagger's sheath survives—another extremely uncommon feature.

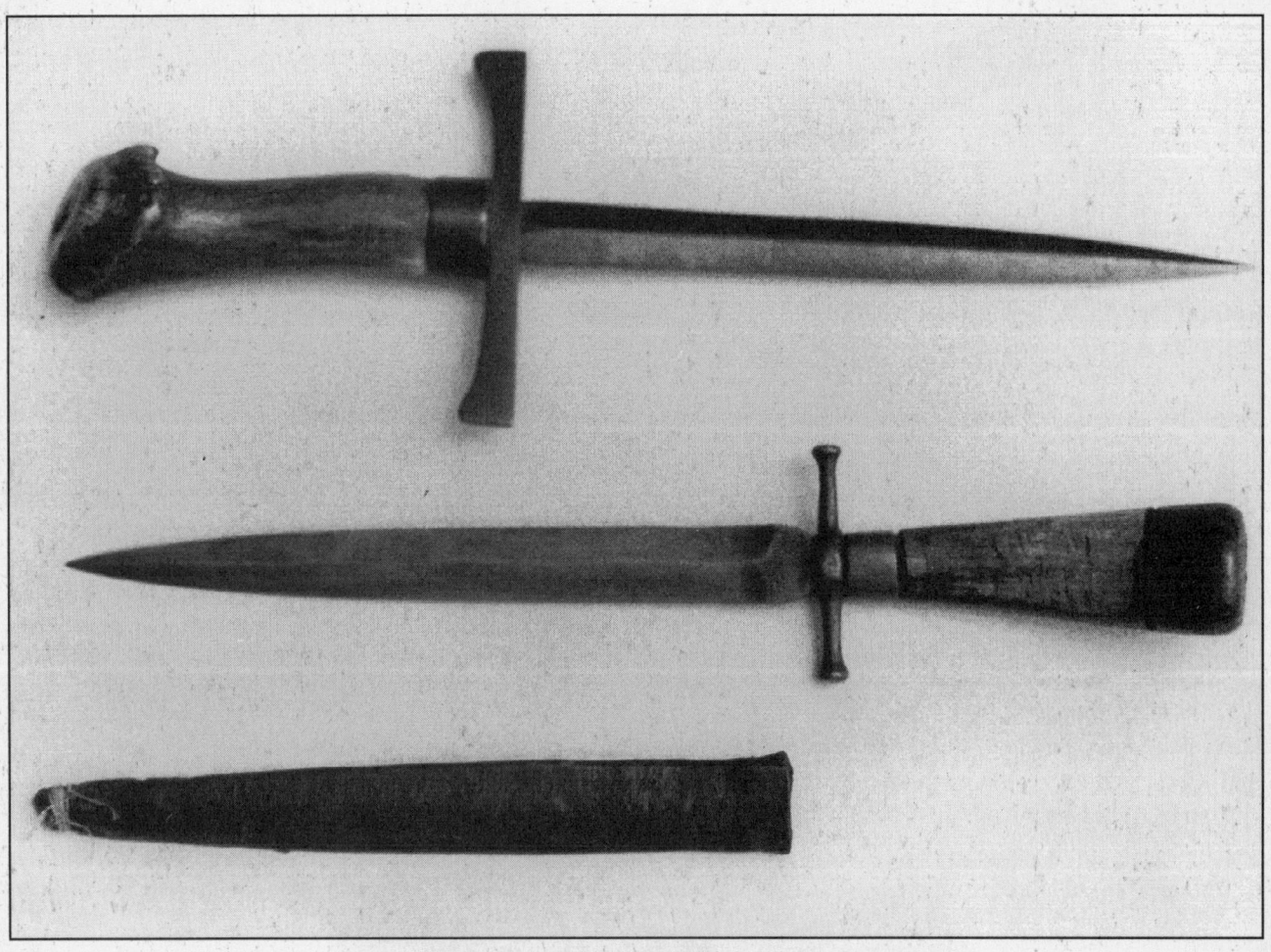

Author's Note

"Dagger," as used herein, refers to fully double-edged, symmetrically spearpointed knives. "Early American" designates, very roughly, what is now the eastern portion of the United States during the last quarter of the 18th century and the first half of the 19th.

DAGGER 3

Two extremely unusual features set this piece apart from the general type of early 19th-century daggers. These are the use of a 2½-inch section of bone for the guard and the date 1804 crudely cut into the rib-bone handle.

Of course, not all names, dates and other inscriptions found on early American artifacts are genuine, as any collector of powder horns, for example, will confirm. This one, however, has been studied with great care by experts, and not only does it give every evidence of real age, it corresponds nicely with the period as estimated on stylistic and structural grounds. I'm going to believe it until somebody proves it's wrong.

In many years of collecting American primitive knives, I have seen one or two with guards of heavy leather and one or two of cattle horn. These are the only instances I can recall of an organic material employed for this purpose, other than the occasional antler tine so used.

The construction of this dagger is a bit of a mystery. A poured-lead ferrule covers the junction of blade, guard and grip. There is probably a pin under this feature, but it's impossible to be sure. The slim, bevelled-edge blade is 7 inches long, and the handle adds another 6 inches.

DAGGER 4

Of all the American primitive knives known to me, I believe this one may best capture the atmosphere of its time. From the battered end of its worn and beautifully patinated antler handle to the tip of its twisted, age-darkened blade, it somehow seems the quintessential early American dagger.

At least part of this effect derives from the intriguing and, as far as I know, unique integral guard and double ricasso feature. This is a powerful design element, and the minor imperfections of its execution only add to its visual strength. Exceptional forge work like this is perhaps the single most desirable element sought after when collecting arms of this class and period.

For all its eye appeal, this is not an especially large weapon, being only 13¾ inches overall with an 8¼-inch blade. The handle is simply driven onto the tang, with no mechanical fastening at all, although there is a metal washer between the grip and the guard.

There would be no reason to hesitate at dating this piece well back in the early 1800s, and it just might precede the turn of the 18th century. But whatever its exact date of manufacture, it's a marvelous piece of Americana.

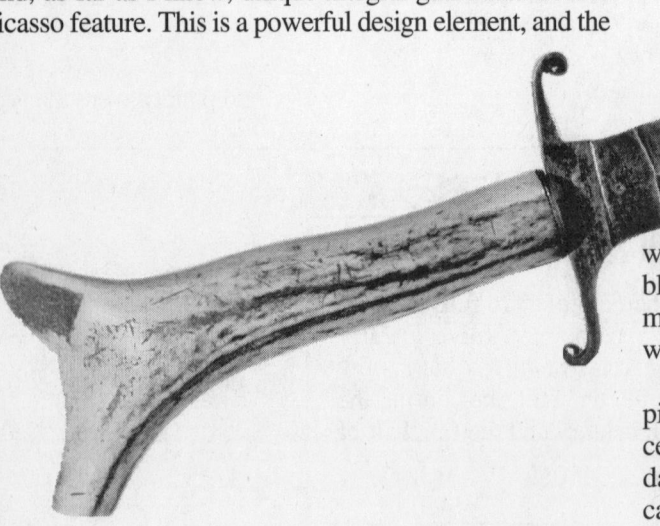

DAGGER 5

This dagger is an oddity which is included here primarily to convey some idea of the strange and curious things one sometimes comes across while pursuing early American knives.

I was told the piece was originally collected in New England, and there seems little reason to doubt this attribution. Stylistically, it varies from the ordinary run of American daggers in much the same way that a New England rifle will differ from a Pennsylvania rifle or a Virginia rifle. Its blade design is reminiscent of some types of early American pole arms of the spontoon pattern, although it is not nearly heavy enough to have been one. The grip is formed from a bit of palmate antler of indeterminate species, with a little pewter finial cast on one point.

This is a knife of fairly substantial proportions (14 1/4 inches overall with an 8 7/8-inch blade) and exceptional workmanship in the forging of the blade and integral guard. Three iron pins hold the handle to the slightly tapered half-tang.

It is rather difficult to assign even an approximate date to this piece, but considering the good forge work and the slender, tapering blade, perhaps somewhere in the first third of the 19th century would be about right.

DAGGER 6

A family tradition of Civil War use is associated with this dagger. I ordinarily pay very little attention to this sort of thing—no attention at all if it seems to be inflating the price—but the piece is easily old enough to have seen that conflict. In fact, it may have been made twenty to thirty years or more before the Civil War, because its blade is of blister steel, a rather primitive cementation-type product which was pretty much obsolete well before the 1860s.

The iron guard is held in place with a pin, a very unusual method, and two more heavy iron pins pass through the half-length flat tang and the slotted antler grip. A poured lead ferrule completes the assembly.

Relatively large (a 9 1/4-inch blade, 14 3/4 inches overall), heavy, strong and sharp, this is a weapon to be taken seriously. It is also ideally balanced and has a wonderful "feel" in the hand, so one can only conclude that its maker knew exactly what he was doing, even if he was not the most artistic of craftsmen.

Daggers of this general size and pattern were the typical variety of the American mid-19th century. Their materials, construction systems and workmanship are virtually identical with those of American Bowies of the period.

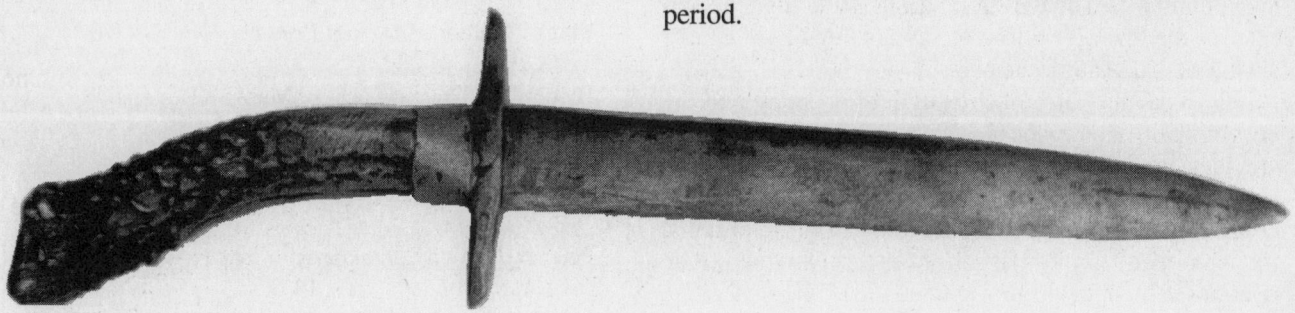

DAGGER 7

Many students and collectors more or less automatically classify knives with tinned-iron scabbards as Confederate. It is true, of course, that a certain percentage of Confederate specimens have sheaths of, or lined with, this material, but I have never seen any reason to believe that knives so equipped were *necessarily* of the Civil War daggers. Unfortunately, the expression is now so entrenched that it is probably ineradicable. At the least, it is useful for designating these long, narrow-bladed daggers as from the Bowie era.

This one is long indeed—a 10¾-inch blade, 15¾ inches overall—and the iron guard is 4 inches across. The

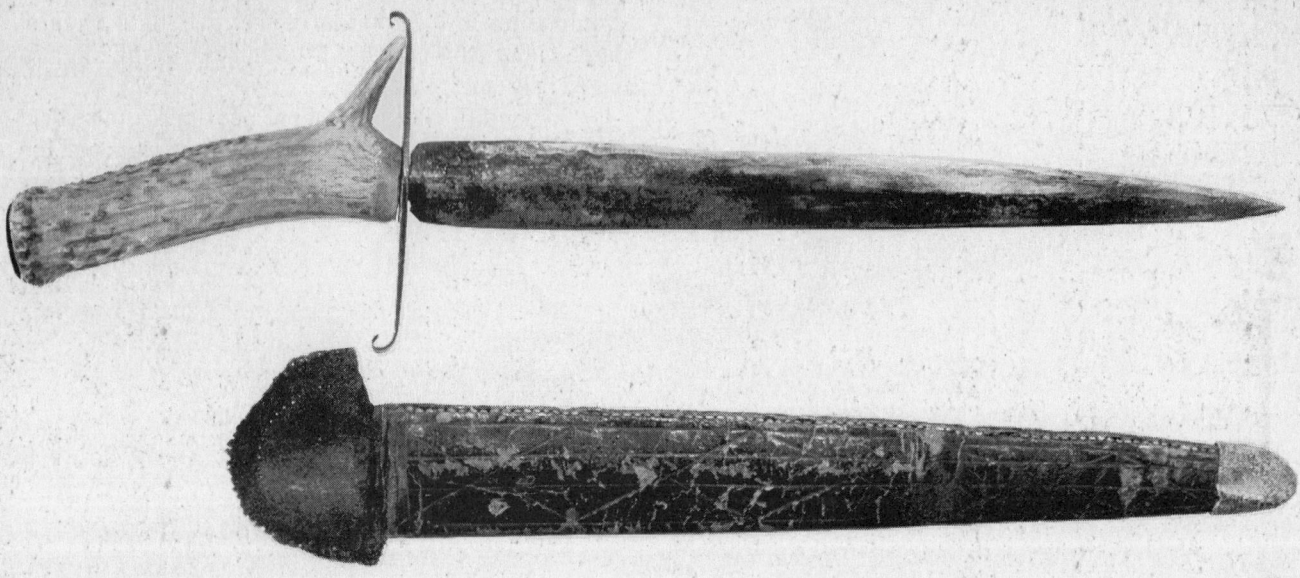

years. This specimen is a case in point; it is almost certainly from the South, but it very possibly predates the 1860s by twenty or thirty years.

This is the sort of dagger that some collectors, perhaps incorrectly, call a "toothpick" or "Arkansas toothpick." This term was originally an ironic reference to the size of the Bowie knife and had nothing whatsoever to do with sheath, as noted, is of tinned sheet iron with a tooled leather cover stitched over it. A remnant of a loop-type suspension is still attached.

Whatever its correct nomenclature may be, this is an exceptional specimen of its class, which is made doubly interesting by the use of the antler tine as an extra guard projection.

CONCLUSION

We have seen here a small selection of one category of the early American dagger. The other category—city-made and/or imported commercial cutlery—is undeniably more artistic in concept and more sophisticated in materials and execution. For many of us, however, these virtues are entirely offset by the strong designs and rugged character of the frontier variety, to say nothing of the latter's appeal as real, using weaponry.

These daggers are much sought after today and are becoming difficult to locate. Prices, as one would expect, are rising, although they remain modest enough by Bowie collector's standards. No doubt we who admire and gather up these old weapons should be sincerely grateful that the American frontier dagger never received the public relations campaign the Bowie knife did.

Bibliography

Grant, Madison. *The Knife in Homespun America*. Privately published, 1984.

Minnis, Gordon. *American Primitive Knives, 1770-1870*. Bloomfield, Ontario, Canada: Museum Restoration Service, 1983.

Neumann, George C. *Swords and Blades of the American Revolution*. Harrisburg, PA: Stackpole Books, 1973.

Peterson, Harold L. *American Knives*. New York: Charles Scribner's Sons, 1958.

Algeria's Yataghan saber and the Finnish puukkos are graceful; the Chinese knife looks tough; Mauretania's "Poignard Damasquine" shows artistic license. Three of the four are handsome stamp designs.

KNIVES on STAMPS

by RAYMOND SCHUESSLER

FOR ALMOST A century and a half, since Great Britain issued the first postage stamp back in 1840, postmasters general from around the globe have commemorated the individuals, events, sports and art that shaped their societies and cultures. Those accorded such a stamp of approval have a permanent niche in the annals of world history. Knives, in all their various forms, have achieved such distinction.

As attendance at knife shows grows, the enthusiasm may be spilling over into stamps. And as the price of rare knives rise in the catalogs, you can expect, eventually, knife stamps to rise, too.

Stamp collecting is the most popular hobby in the world with over 200,000,000 collectors. Since it is difficult and expensive to collect all the stamps of one nation, (often over 2000-plus stamps; Russia has issued over 5000 stamps) the most popular branch of the hobby is topical collecting in which one subject, such as medicine, trains, baseball, ships, etc., is collected.

If archaeologists from some future civilization ever dig up a 20th-century stamp collection, they could learn a great deal about the importance of knives in the history of human development. On stamps you can become a Sultan of Cutlery owning the finest Hassame, Bowie, Wostenholm, a French rondel dagger of 1450, or a sword hilt of Captain Bluebeard—all encased in one desktop notebook, and all for 25¢ to $1 apiece.

The United States, home of the famous Bowie, has not yet stamped a knife aside from a few vague bayonets, but with urging from knife enthusiasts may do so. Wouldn't the magnificent sword of our Marines look great on a commemorative stamp? •

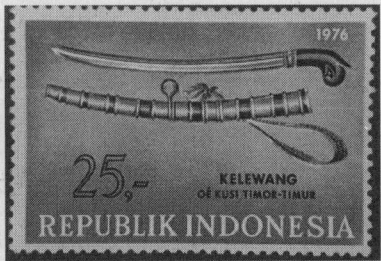  

Indonesia's different regions produce distinctive patterns in knives. Here the *kelewang*, the *mandau*, and the *rencong*.

From a museum in Libreville, the Gabon government chose a whole series of historical arms. The broad-pointed knife has the profile of one pattern of Roman short sword; the others are more local, although the crossbow's pattern is basic, worldwide.

The Turks and Caicos Islands are in the British West Indies—thirty islands on four of which live 12,000 people who own a stamp factory and a lot of pirate legends. Here are four of them, courtesy of Disney—literally.

 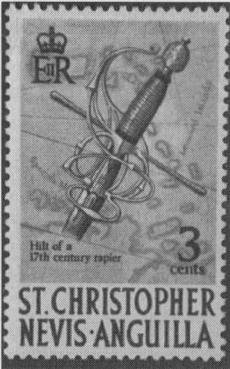  

History of the sword in Peru, the British Indies and Liechtenstein—yes, Pizarro took Peru with a sword and a flair for deception, and sword-bearing Englishmen acquired the West Indies, but when were Viking pattern swords made in Liechtenstein?

Syria and France and Bophuthatswana hail their cutlery factories, while Monaco, Switzerland and Belguim pay tribute to the touring knife sharpeners of, regrettably, another time now gone.

Hewey or Dewey or Louie give point to Disney production; Luxembourg's formal trophy makes a handsome fencer's stamp; and Poland gives fencing real historical weight in a series of four good-looking stamps.

India, Aden and Zambia look at their histories with knives—and a ceremonial axe. All are perfectly OK stamps; one is an outstanding graphic design as well.

And then there are political statements on stamps with knives: The USSR's hero beats a sword into a plowshare; Italy's sword looks Fascistic; a very grim Pole sternly announces his presence; a handsome Frenchman salutes from a Canadian stamp. India shows its tulwars; Hungary goes for the symbolism of swords and a globe; a short sword breaks chains in Liban's 19th year; and the UN's disarmament statement shows, of all possible designs, a Welsh cleaidd.

GETTING STARTED IN KNIFE STAMP COLLECTING

To start your own collection, visit the local library and study the *Scott Catalog of Stamps*, which illustrates or lists most of the stamps ever issued with their official number and current value. The catalog is revised annually.

Subscribe to a good stamp newspaper (*Linn's*), also available at the library. Search their ads for dealers who have the stamps you need.

You can subscribe to a "new issue" service through which you will be sent new issues of knife stamps as they are released.

Also, try your local stamp shop and see if they have the stamps you need.

Stamps should be stored in three-ring plastic sheets with windows to protect the stamps from creasing, humidity and dust. These can be kept in a looseleaf notebook.

The hobby is twice as much fun when you can talk and swap stamps with other collectors. The best way is to join a stamp club. Or why not start your own specialized club with other knife collectors. Bring up the subject at the next knife show. ●

THERE ARE TWO large sword societies in Japan and at least one smaller society that I know about. One of the two large ones is called the *Nihon Token Hozon Kai*, or NTHK for short. It's the Japanese Sword Preservation Society, the oldest sword collecting society in Japan. The man who runs this society, Yoshikawa Kentaro, is a sword polisher and also the curator of the Emperor's sword collection. Traditionally, sword polishers are the people considered to know the most about swords. It takes an enormous amount of knowledge to be able to polish one correctly, which is why an untrained person should never try to polish a Japanese sword.

The second large society is called the *Nihon Bijutsu Token Hozon Kyokai,* or NBTHK for short. This Japanese Art Sword Preservation Society was formed by the Japanese government after World War II to administer the system of designating swords as art objects. They maintain a sword museum in Tokyo and still have a connection with the Japanese government. The NBTHK seems to have a more art-historical orientation with expertise from academics rather than from sword polishers or traditional sword appraisers.

Both these groups conduct *shinsa*. The word means "examine-evaluate" in Japanese. They will evaluate your sword—for a fee—to see if it meets their standards for quality, artistic merit and condition, and if signed, whether the signature is authentic in their judgment. There is a fee for looking at the sword whether it passes or not, and an extra fee for the paper if issued. The fees have recently been $45 and $55 for a U.S. shinsa. If a blade meets their conditions, they will issue a paper called an *origami*, which attests to the quality level of the sword and that it has a correct signature if signed.

Origami means "folded paper" in Japanese. Most origami are in Japanese, so you have to be able to translate them yourself or have somebody do it for you. They are the best assurance in the world that the sword in question is a good one. If the blade is unsigned, they will attribute it to a school or an individual smith when issuing an origami. Complete mountings or individual fittings can be judged, but always separate from the blade.

Working papers in both Japanese and English are used in the actual shinsa. Copies of these are issued to the submitter at a shinsa. About three months later, the actual origami arrives. An origami describes the sword and has a rubbing of the tang of the sword attached. A typical Japanese red stamp overlaps the rubbing, so the rubbing cannot be changed and a good origami used for a bad sword. If it is an origami for a fitting, there is a photograph of the fitting stamped the same way.

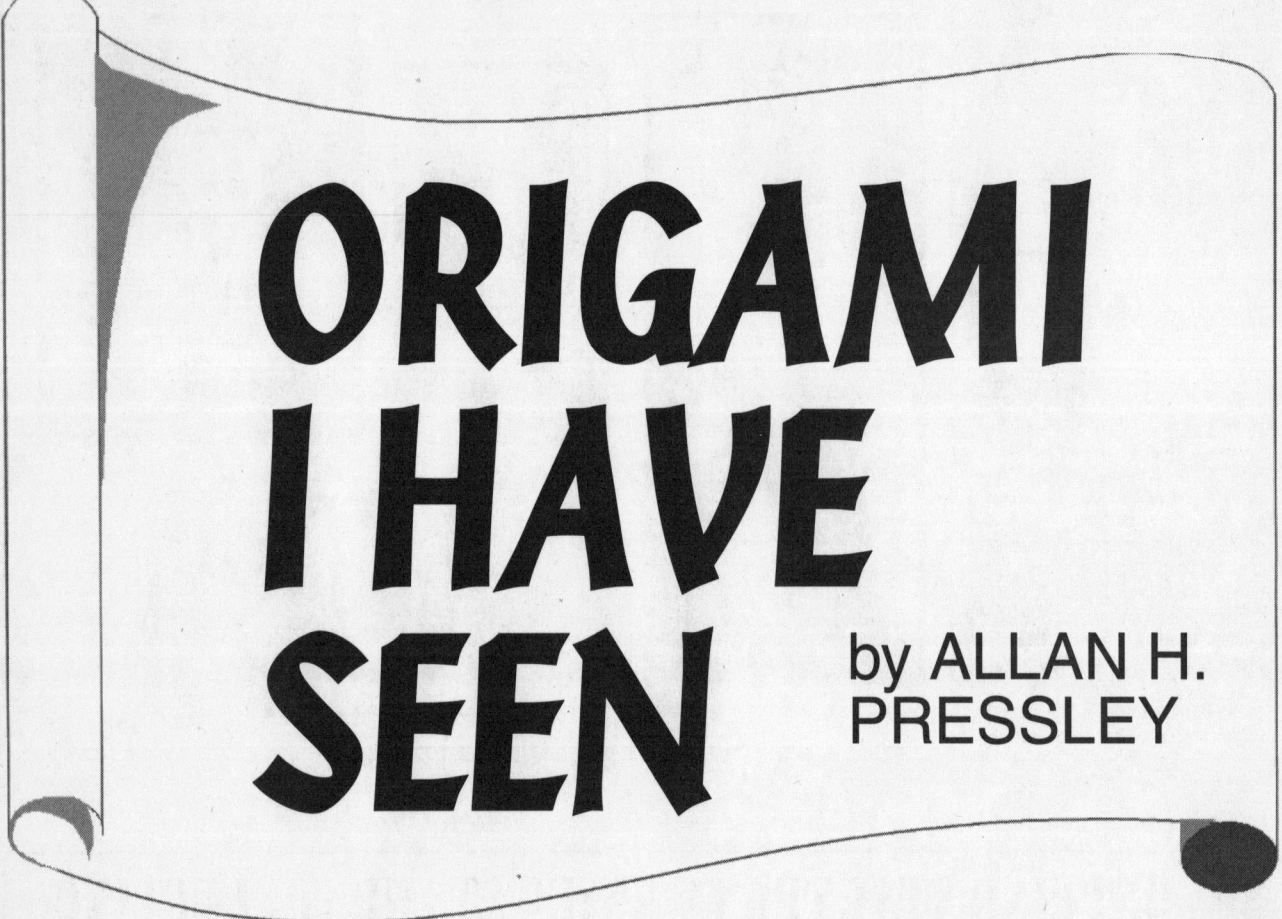

ORIGAMI I HAVE SEEN
by ALLAN H. PRESSLEY

Both societies have several levels of papers. Since I am familiar with the NTHK papers, and because it is more common to see one of their origami than others, I will describe their system. They evaluate swords on a 100-point basis. A 100-point sword would be the highest quality sword made by that school or that man in perfect and unaltered condition; points are taken off for lower quality and condition. Because of these criteria, old swords—Koto swords made between 900 A.D. and 1596 A.D.—are not likely to receive high-scoring papers. Older swords were frequently shortened and are not therefore in unaltered condition. Also, they have been polished a great deal and may have flaws showing.

uted sword. The three small round seals on the second page of the origami are the personal seals of the three senior shinsa team members and have the same legal standing in Japan that signatures do in the West. The large square seal is the seal of the NTHK. The origami does not, as you can see, state the number of points that the sword received on the working paper.

Shinsa were held in 1979, 1984, and 1989 in Chicago by the NTHK and the Chicago Token Study Group. I worked in the shinsa room in 1989. More than half of all swords submitted were rejected as substandard quality. Well over half of the signed swords that were not rejected as substandard were rejected as fake signatures.

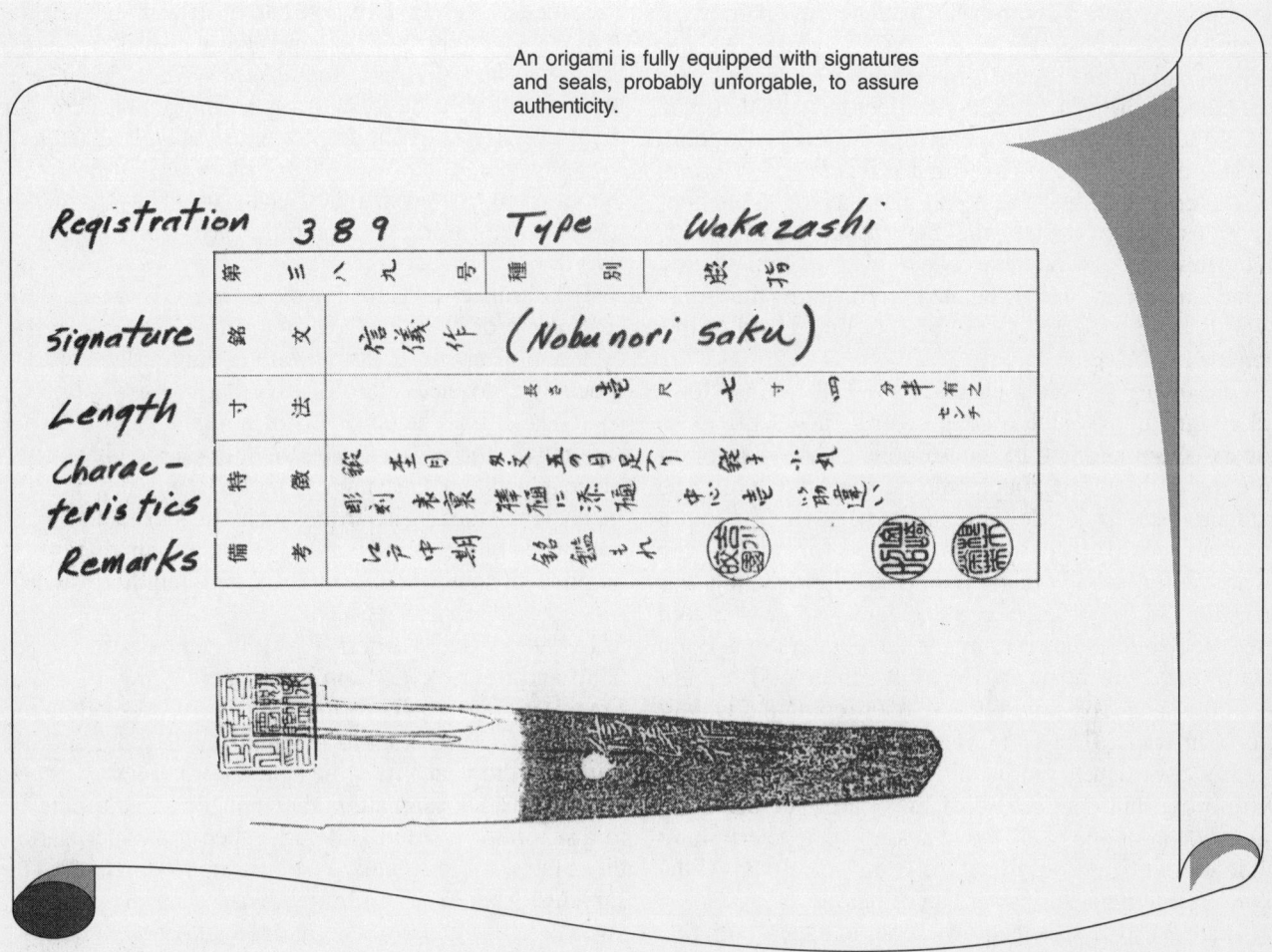

An origami is fully equipped with signatures and seals, probably unforgable, to assure authenticity.

There is no absolute standard. A 70-point sword by one man is not necessarily equal to a 70-point sword by another man. This is an important issue; the sword itself has to be evaluated by the potential buyer.

The levels of NTHK origami scoring:
Shinteisho   60 to 69 points   good quality
Kanteisho   70 to 84 points   fine quality
Yushu-Saku   85 to 94 points   superior quality
Sai-Yusu-Saku   95 to 100 points   highest quality

The point award only appears on the working paper and is not on the origami. Shown nearby are a Shinteisho for a signed sword and a Kanteisho for an unsigned attrib-

These swords were submitted by experienced collectors, or collectors who may have had the advice of experienced collectors. It is very difficult to determine if a signature is valid or not, or if the quality is high enough, even for experienced collectors. I submitted eight unsigned swords in 1989, and they all received origami. I submitted three signed blades and received one origami. This says I have finally learned how to judge a good sword, but still have a long way to go on signatures.

The best way to learn about the next shinsa is to join the Japanese Sword Society of the United States. It will be announced in their newsletter. The NTHK only issue

Shinteisho or Kanteisho on swords judged in this country. If the sword receives a high enough rating here, it can go to Japan for Yushu shinsa and receive a higher rating, but that is an expensive and time-consuming process. The sword has to be registered by a person licensed to handle swords and then submitted to shinsa. Normally, the licensee has to go to the airport to pick up the sword from Japanese customs. The same comments apply to sending swords to Japan for NBTHK shinsa.

It is interesting to stand in the shinsa room and observe. The owners usually stay and watch their blades being judged. When a blade is rejected, it's on a pink sheet instead of the white working paper. When Mr. Yoshikawa picks up a pink sheet, a great groan might be heard from a watching owner, who probably paid serious money for the blade.

It is also interesting to speculate what happens to the rejected sword. Most purist collectors say that you should immediately get rid of a rejected sword. An honest owner will tell the buyer that it is a rejected sword. However, as the sword descends in ownership from honest to less honest owners, that fact probably will be lost, and a new unknowledgable collector will eventually buy it and start the cycle over again. I would guess that some swords have been rejected in all the shinsa held in this country.

One of my swords rejected in the 1989 shinsa for a fake signature is such a good sword—and I like it so much—I am keeping it. Shinsa boils down to an opinion, the opinion of someone more expert than you. The collector has to decide on his own what to do about a rejected sword. If a sword is rejected for quality, the owner will generally learn in time that the rejection was justified. A Japanese collector of Japanese swords told me if the shinsa team is only 99 percent certain about a sword they will reject it. They have to be 100 percent sure to issue an origami because their reputation is their stock in trade. The state of polish affects the shinsa team's confidence in awarding an origami, especially with a big name signature. If they can't see the crystalline detail in the blade—that is as much a determining characteristic as the signature—they don't have the assurance they need to award an origami.

The NBTHK issues their own series of papers with five levels that cover the same criteria as the four levels of NTHK papers. Some U.S. collectors send their swords to Japan to the NBTHK shinsa. This is perhaps because the NBTHK is more lenient than the NTHK. I have heard of several swords that were rejected at the NTHK shinsa and were sent to NBTHK shinsa in Japan where they received origamis.

There were, I believe, two NBTHK shinsa held in this country in the 1970s; occasionally a sword with those papers will be seen. In 1980, there was a scandal involving the NBTHK. In shinsa held outside Tokyo by lower ranking members of the group, pressure was applied by the *Yakusa* (the Japanese Mafia) to issue origami to substandard swords. Because of this, they changed the names and the style of their origami to differentiate them from previous origami. Also, a group split off because of the scandal and called themselves the Tokyo Kantei Club. *Kantei* means to determine the maker of a sword without looking at the signature.

I do not believe there was any problem with NBTHK origami issued in this country, and I would buy a sword with those papers. I would, however, be a little bit wary about swords that had NBTHK origami issued in Japan around 1980.

The NBTHK publishes an English journal called *Token Bijutsu*. In the Number 52 issue, they discussed the load on their shinsa in Japan. They say, "It is evident that significance of the new system has been well established among sword collectors in general as well as those in the trading business." Later, they say, "We are also aware, however, that the Juyo shinsa is an important factor for the prosperity of the trading business as well as the artisans engaged in the maintenance of swords." These sentences strongly suggest to me that the usual buyer in Japan wants to see an origami before he pays a big price for a sword.

The ultimate status for Japanese swords is to be awarded *Kokuho* or National Treasure status. This is awarded by the ministry for Cultural Affairs with judgment by a specially convened board of experts from several of the societies. I have never heard of a non-Japanese owner receiving National Treasure status for one of his swords. Since a National Treasure cannot be legally taken out of Japan, it may be that awarding such status to a non-Japanese owned blade would create a legal problem that is best avoided. There are fewer than two hundred swords classed as National Treasures.

In 1987, the Northern California Japanese Sword Club and the Tokyo Kantei Club held a shinsa in San Francisco. The papers for this shinsa were issued by the Northern California Club in English. They did another thing different at this shinsa: If they judged a signed sword had a fake signature, they nonetheless attributed it to a school or a smith and still issued it a paper stating those facts—if the quality level was up to standards. The Japanese societies would never issue an origami to a sword with a signature they judged fake, no matter how good the quality level. In San Francisco, the swords were rated fair, good, very good and excellent. I believe these four ratings relate to the four levels of the NTHK. A friend of mine worked in the shinsa room there and told me they did not rate any sword excellent, and only two as very good. The rest of the passed swords were evenly divided between fair and good. This is from a very large group of blades submitted, and the usual 50 percent or so of the submitted blades were rejected for low quality. This was, therefore, a very stringent shinsa, and one should not have any qualms about buying a blade with their paper.

I personally like the idea that this shinsa did not reject

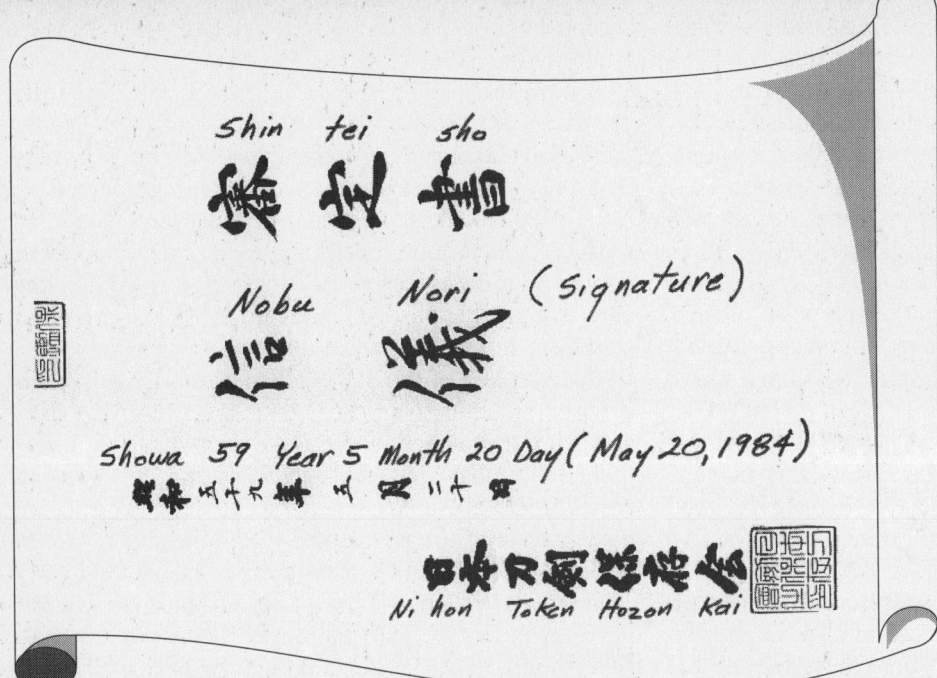

This sword, signed, received a "good quality" rank in this origami, which fully describes the sword.

good swords with fake signatures. I wish the main societies did that, but their belief is that a fake is a fake, no matter how good it is. Signatures can be removed; a Japanese swordsmith can pein out the signature. The owner can then resubmit it. For a blatant fake, that is probably the best solution, but if the signature is very close and the work in the blade seems right, it may be better to leave it alone. Who knows, better scholarship in the future might discover the signature correct. One owner had a signed sword rejected at the 1984 shinsa, but they told him it was a very good sword that would get very good papers if the signature was peined out and the blade resubmitted. Luckily, a Japanese swordsmith from Japan was at the shinsa, and the owner got him to remove the signature. It was resubmitted and did receive a very good attribution and papers.

Swords are rejected for flaws that compromise their status as working weapons. Since their purpose was to be a weapon and not a modern collectible, it is generally thought they are not acceptable if badly flawed. When swords are rejected for low quality, the same reasoning applies. Recently, there has been some speculation whether swords with *showa* or arsenal stamps would pass shinsa. These low-quality blades were made for Japanese military officers between 1926 and 1945. They were marked with either a showa stamp, supposedly from 1926 to 1942, or with a stamp from various arsenals, until 1945. I wrote to the NTHK, and they replied an origami would not be issued on a blade with such a stamp and reminded me that such swords would not be allowed into Japan as Japanese art swords. Personally, I have never seen a blade with such a stamp that I thought had enough artistic merit to pass shinsa. Out of the nearly one thousand smiths making swords in that time, fewer than fifty were considered good, and their swords were not stamped.

There have been and still are some other societies and individuals who are considered authoritative and have issued origami, but they are extremely rare in this country. If such papers accompany a sword, there should be a *lot* of consultation before purchase.

Those who do not collect and understand Japanese swords, but who possess one, often have extremely inflated ideas of value, ideas which do not agree with the practical realities. Generally, this type of person is afraid he will sell a National Treasure for a pittance, but he is not willing to pay dues to learn about Japanese swords. Perhaps this will help:

First, a sword must be in good polish to command a reasonable price and in perfect polish to command the highest price in its category. If it is not in good polish, the cost of polish must be deleted from the market value in perfect polish to arrive at current value. There is also a risk value to be subtracted because some swords have flaws that appear when they are polished.

Suppose I saw a katana out of polish that I thought was worth $5000 in perfect polish because of a signature and papers. The polishing cost for a katana is going to be at least $3000, so that, plus $1000 for risk, has to be deducted from the $5000 to arrive at a logical buying price.

This is why many dealers carry swords around from year to year and wonder why they can't sell them. Some swords will not be worth the cost of polish. And remember, a sword can only be appreciated when it is in, at least, good polish. If the detail in the sword cannot be seen, there is no sense in owning it, unless it is properly repolished in Japan.

Next, to command the highest price, a sword will usually have an origami. Most, but not all, of the swords you see at gun shows and antique shops are either very poor quality or outright junk. To give an example in gun terms, they range from the equivalent of a rusty single barrel shotgun with a broken stock to perhaps the quality of a V-grade Parker, and damn few of those. The problem is that people ask V-grade Parker prices for the rusty single barrel. Be extremely careful and learn what you are doing before you buy.

One could buy a rusty short sword for $1600, have it polished for $1600, and end up with a sword worth less than $1600. If you asked $1600 for a rusty single-barrel shotgun with a broken stock, gun collectors and dealers would have nothing but scorn for you, but they are doing the same thing with Japanese swords at gun shows. I have seen collections of up to thirty swords, and all but one or two were junk. The best advice was given to me when I started: "Save your money for five years and then buy one good sword." I didn't follow this suggestion, but it is good advice if you can stand to be without a sword for five years.

The value of swords on the knowledgeable collector circuit is set by dealers, both Japanese and American, who buy swords to export to Japan where they will sell for more. An American collector has to compete in this market when buying swords. Collectors sell to each other, and if friendly and with a buying-selling history, they may discount some.

Ken Warner asked me, "What is the lowest current price a fellow might expect to pay to a fellow collector for a serious sword, a sword that might have been carried by a real swordsman 300 to 500 years ago, in nice display condition, more or less ready to be worn or to fight?"

The answer: An unsigned katana recently sold with a "fair" paper from the 1987 shinsa. This blade was in very good polish, was fully and correctly mounted, and had a fresh, correctly done hilt wrap. It was dated to the Muromachi period (1394 to 1466 A.D.) and attributed to the Naminohira school, a respectable school but not a great one. It was probably from very early in the Muromachi period because of certain characteristics. It was sold to a dealer for $2400. It had a lot of flaws, even though it was awarded a paper, and this depressed its price. This, I believe, is about the cheapest you could buy a katana with papers on the national market.

You almost always have to pay the national market price for a papered blade, because an owner aware enough to obtain origami will be aware of national market prices. But it is always difficult to tell exactly the fair market value of a Japanese sword. They're all handmade and each is different. It's not like a gun with a specific model and a large body of literature, advertisements and catalogs to suggest the market price. A friend of mine has a katana which has just been polished in Japan and is in *shirasaya* (white scabbard), the plain unfinished wooden scabbard and hilt used to store a blade. This blade has an origami by the NTHK attributing it to a respectable but not great late Koto school. This sword is not ready for fighting because it is not mounted, but it is a good example. A group of us concluded that $8000 is a fair market value for such a sword.

A newly polished blade has to be put in a new scabbard, so rust from the old one does not contaminate the newly polished blade. Wood used for the shirasaya must display certain characteristics: It swells in high humidity to protect the blade from moisture, while in periods of low humidity, it evaporates whatever humidity has been trapped. For these reasons, it is best to store a blade this way, and newly polished blades are almost always put in shirasaya. If it comes with a nice set of old mountings, a wooden replica of the blade called a *tsunagi* is made to hold the mountings together. A lot of dealers sell blades and fittings separately because they think they can make more money that way. I consider this a sin. A phenomenal amount of work is needed to mount a sword from the blade and the fittings, and this ensemble should not be broken up when a new scabbard is needed.

In order to understand the values of signed swords, you have to understand the ranking structure of Japanese swordsmiths. There are 33,000 known Japanese swordsmiths. They are all listed in Hawley's *Japanese Swordsmiths Revised*. There also is a standard reference book in Japanese, Fujishiro's *Nihon Koto/Shinto Jiten*, which lists the top 1700 swordsmiths in five rankings. This is only 5 percent of the 33,000, and these smiths command the highest prices, which vary with the maker's position in the five rankings. The rankings are, from top to bottom:

Saijo saku	Best
Jojo saku	Upper upper
Jo saku	Upper
Chujo saku	Upper middle
Chu saku	Middle

Don't be confused by the "middle" ranking. This means that the Fujishiro brothers considered such a smith

In addition to its "fine" rank, the shinsa judges awarded the unsigned sword an attribution.

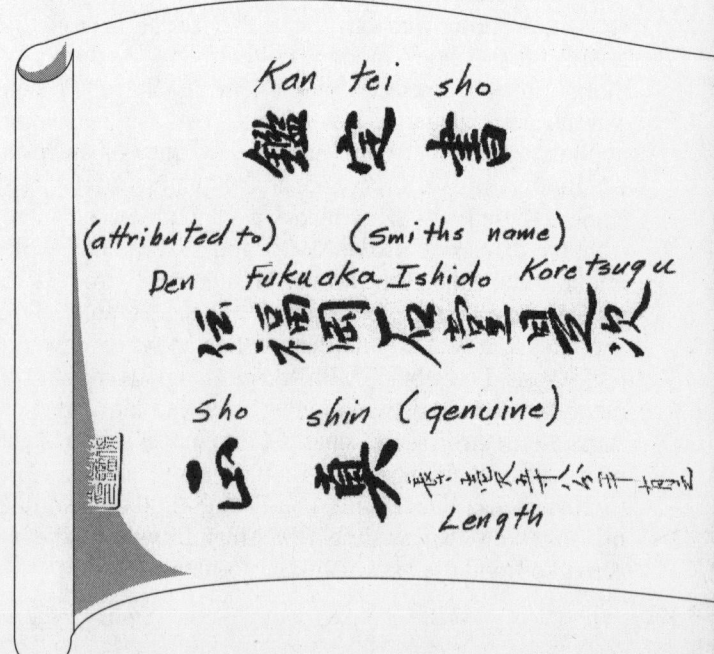

This unsigned sword reached "fine quality" rank.

better than 95 percent of all smiths. There are many other reference books that list many more smiths, but the Fujishiro-listed smiths are always in those books and seem to have the highest status. When a blade is attributed to an individual smith, it will be one of these 1700 smiths. Only their outstanding caliber of work is allowed individual attribution. Generally, work of lesser caliber is ascribed to a school.

I have never heard of a sword attributed to a smith who was not Fujishiro-rated. Some schools had smiths who all worked at the same standard, with the same characteristics, and it is not possible to detect which individual from that school. I have never seen a ranking of the more than 156 known schools of sword making. I think that depends too much on personal taste for any expert to do. Some schools are generally recognized to be consistently very good, and some are outspokenly rated by one Japanese expert to be very poor, but there are a lot in the middle that no expert has ever commented on in English, perhaps because there is too much variation in the quality between various members of such schools.

Recently, a *wakazashi* by a *jo saku* smith in good polish sold between collectors for $4000. (A *wakazashi* is a short sword carried by a samurai along with a katana.) A *wakazashi* by a *jojo saku* smith in perfect polish sold for $5500. Both were probably fair market prices. One blade was in military officer's mounts and the other in shirasaya, so there was no intrinsic mounting value. Both were early *shinto* blades made in the early 1600s. The shinto period lasted from 1596 to 1780 AD. Naturally, both blades had origami. These were both outstanding swords of a quality that you would see in a gun show only once in *many thousand* swords, so you are looking at the very top level of what is available.

Generally, a wakazashi is considered to be worth 30 percent of the value of a katana by the same smith, and a tanto is worth 50 percent. Tanto are very scarce, and that may be why they are worth more, even though they are shorter. Some collectors scorn wakazashi because they are not katana. Still, every samurai carried a wakazashi. Some collectors don't like unsigned blades, either. I have seen many thousands of Japanese swords and perhaps several hundred good ones. The best sword I have ever seen was an unsigned wakazashi.

A moderate quality, signed katana in good mounts, with an interesting provenance, but without an origami, sold recently for about $10,000. It was not one of the top 1700 smiths, so the probability of it being a fake was small. The buyer, an extremely knowledgeable collector, believed the signature to be correct, so he has taken a $10,000 gamble. An early Koto katana in perfect polish and shirasaya, with an origami attributing it to a school, a truly magnificent sword, was sold between collectors for $6000 not long ago.

Recently, the Compton collection of Japanese swords, the largest and best collection of Japanese swords outside Japan, was sold by Christie's in New York in three sales during the course of 1992. This sale contained swords from mediocre to magnificent, according to people who were at the sale. The selling prices of katana in the three sales ranged from about $1000 to $418,000, the highest price ever paid for a sword in an auction, I believe. As you can see, there is a very large value range for Japanese swords.

I would again caution the prospective Japanese sword buyer: It is a tricky business and you had better learn what you are doing before you buy, or get help. That goes for those who already own swords, as well, if they have not begun to study.

ALLAN PRESSLEY

Tragically, Allan Pressley ended his life in November, 1993, while in deep depression.

His friends in sword collecting will miss his presence; his readers in both our *Knives* annuals and *Gun Digest* have lost one more voice of sound experience. He would have produced much more worth reading; there are a few things remaining and we will publish them.

Ken Warner

THE PERFECT

OF GEORGE

KNIVES

by STEVEN DICK

To OUTDOORSMEN OF the 1950s, '60s and early '70s, the name "Herter's" was synonymous with the Sears and Roebuck of sporting equipment. Each year, this mail-order company published a huge (my 1971 catalog is 629 pages) wish book filled with every conceivable outdoor need. Some have compared the company owner, George L. Herter, to P.T. Barnum and say they both shared the belief that a sucker was born every minute. Even the simplest item in the Herter's catalog was often allocated a full page of fine print to describe its many virtues.

Reading these old catalogs, you quickly learn there were two ways of doing anything: the George L. Herter method and the "tenderfoot drugstore outdoorsman" way. A large percentage of the items in the catalog were said to be either "approved by the Official North Star Guide Association" or bore the label "Hudson Bay." As far as I can tell, the "North Star Guide Association" was strictly a marketing ploy on the part of Herter's, and there never was any connection between the mail-order company and the legendary Canadian fur-trading group. Herter's had their own private brand for practically every item of possible use to the sportsman. Some items, like the Herter's 401 Magnum revolver, said to have as much power as a 44 Magnum with less recoil than a 357, were unique but not totally successful. Other products, like the company's knives, gained a wide following among serious outdoorsmen.

The most basic Herter's knife was the "Improved Bowie." My 1953 catalog shows a straight wood-handled knife with no handguard and a 4$\frac{1}{2}$-inch clip-point blade. The catalog states a real outdoor knife must be made of carbon steel rather than stainless and the Improved Bowie was "Belgian formula knife steel." It goes on to state the knife was hand-forged and 200 years of experience had proven 4$\frac{1}{2}$ inches to be the perfect size for outdoor use. Blades shorter than this specific length were said to be only for Boy Scouts. The knife alone was priced at $1.08 or with a "embossed horsehide sheath" at $1.40. I have long wondered what Jim Bowie would have thought of this "improvement" of his original design. Basically, these first Herter's Improved Bowies were short kitchen utility knives combined with lightweight sheaths.

The Improved Bowie must have been popular with customers because by 1956 the catalog had added two more Herter designs, the "Canadian Fish Fillet and Camp Knife" and the "Bull Cook Knife." The Bowie now had a slightly contoured "African Tiger Wood" handle and a 5-inch carbon steel blade. In a reversal of the earlier catalog, it now stated 5 inches had "been established for a woodsman's knife by 200 years of experience." While the price was up to $1.45, you received a "Professional Guide Condensed Information Manual" free with each knife.

The Canadian Fish Fillet and Camp Knife was a narrow, straight-back, stiff 5-inch blade pretty much like any boning knife. Herter's makes a point of telling the reader their filet knife was not 4$\frac{1}{2}$ inches long like its imitators. I assume this is a dig at the trout knife L.L. Bean sold for many years in its own catalog. The Fillet and Camp Knife was priced at $1.15 and came with a copy of "The Only Way To Professionally Fillet and Clean Fish and True French Fry Fish," by George Herter (naturally).

Herter's Bull Cook Knife was basically a 4-inch version of the Improved Bowie. The text explains that the design had been created by log camp cooks making knives from old saw blades. In logging lingo, the word "bull" is still attached to the foreman or boss as in "bullbuck" (a cutting foreman) or "camp bull" (a log camp superintendent). A logger on the prod will often boast he's a real "bull of the woods." While the log camps I've worked in no longer had mess halls, I assume "Bull Cook" was the nickname of the head of the kitchen crew back in Minnesota. The Bull Cook Knife was said to be the perfect tool if you needed to "clean 100 pounds of trout, 50 snowshoe rabbits or 50 partridges in jig time." Like the first two knives, the Bull Cook came with a sheath and booklet titled "Bull Cook Recipes and Practices" by George L. for $1.30.

By 1960, the Improved Bowie had changed to a blade

LEONARD HERTER

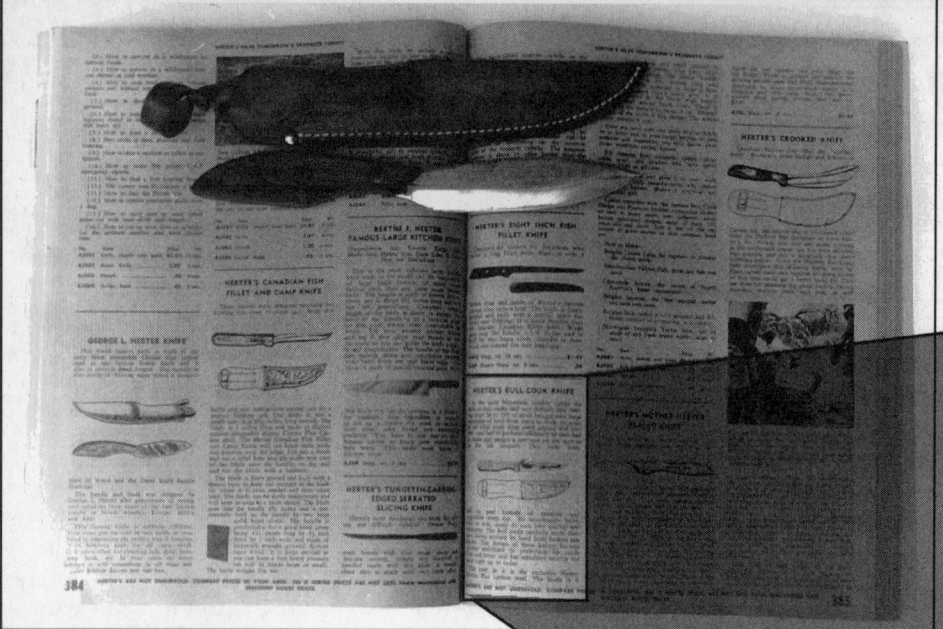

(Left) Each knife listed in Herter's catalog rated a long, detailed and wildly optimistic description and "history."

(Below) Herter's Bull Cook Knife seems to be the hardest to find today, maybe because it was one of the most practical items in the catalog.

of stainless "chrome steel" said to combine the best properties of 1095 carbon and 440B stainless. Of course, this is the only knife steel a real North Star Guide would use. The knife's handle had a more pronounced self-guard notch at the base of the blade, and the price had risen to $1.95. Both the Fillet and Camp Knife and the Bull Cook Knife followed this lead with stainless blades and self-guarded handles. Several new knives were added to the line, the first modestly named the "George L. Herter Knife." One glance will tell anyone familiar with outdoor cutlery that this is actually a close copy of the Grohmann "D.H. Russell Belt Knife." Grohmann, Canada's only commercial knifemaker, introduced the Russell model in 1957 as the perfect cutting tool for woodsmen in the Far North. My own observation in the wilds of British Columbia tells me the Russell Belt Knife remains very popular with Canadian backwoodsmen.

In the Herter version of the knife's history, the "handle and blade were designed by George after generations of testing and opinions from the best known guides in North America, Europe, Africa and Asia." Herter's "Professional Guide's Manual" shows drawings of what are obviously Marble's sheath knives and states only a tenderfoot would carry them. It goes on to state a woodsman's knife blade must be 5 inches long, then shows a "George L. Herter Knife" which has a blade $4^1/2$ inches long! Once, while attending the SHOT show, I asked the Grohmann folks if they had ever made the Herter knives on contract? The reply was, "Who the heck is this George Herter everyone keeps saying our knives look like!!?" Prices for the G.L. Herter Knife were a bit steeper than the Improved Bowie; a knife, sheath and Professional Guide Manual would set you back $3.77.

Another of the new knives was the Herter's "Crooked Knife." Now a real crooked knife is a wood carving tool with J-shaped blade sharpened only around the hook. Traditionally, this was the preferred tool of the North for carving canoe paddles, wood bowls, axe handles and such. The Herter's Crooked Knife was a 6-inch commercial beef skinner combined with a leather sheath. Quoting the catalog, "practically every Indian and Eskimo in Canada has one exactly like it, purchased either from the Hudson's Bay Company or from Herter's." Curved skinners like this find a lot of use anywhere people process large animals for food. I was recently told by an Australian cutlery distributor that the Russell Green River skinner of the same pattern is the favorite knife of their Aborigines. In 1960, the Herter's Crooked Knife, sheath and Pro Guide Book ran $3.10.

At about this same time, Herter's introduced their "Toothpick" folding knives, a $5^1/4$-inch two-blade folding hunter, two-blade muskrat, and a two-blade trapper pattern. George stated these were not "5 and 10¢ store knives nor drug store specials which are good for nothing in the field." Despite that statement, the folders were simply standard Schrades, a brand I've often found in drugstores, with the Herter's trademark etched on the blade!

Herter's also cataloged another folder during this period that, for some reason, didn't last long, the "Jesse Chisholm Wilderness Knife." Chisholm was a half-Cherokee Indian trader in the Kansas area shortly after the Civil War. He is best known for pioneering the "Chisholm Cattle Trail" north from Texas. Supposedly (Herter's version of history), Jesse explained to a traveling knife salesman from Sheffield that he needed a folder with a 3-inch blade for opening deer, antelope, bear, birds and fish. It also had to skin mink and beaver, shave firewood, and turn over meat on the fire. What Herter's was offering was a slightly larger than average seven-bladed Swiss Army-style pocketknife, but you had better make sure you didn't call it that in front of George. To quote, "The wide dull points on so-called Swiss Army Officer's Knives are also worthless and the this type of knife never saw the Swiss Army. It's strictly a phoney." He goes on to say he added the screwdriver, bottle opener, combination beer can opener, sharp punch and Phillips-head screwdriver to bring the knife up to date. So what Chisholm actually asked for was a two-blade pocketknife with a 3-inch spear-point master and short-clip secondary blade?

Right around 1960, Herter's added what became the distinguishing feature of their sheath knives—a serrated hump on the spine directly in front of the handle. I assume this was intended to serve as a thumbrest, but many users I've met felt it only got in the way. Though the catalog never explained why the hump was suddenly an essential part of the perfect outdoor knife, you can bet only a drugstore outdoorsman would have it any other way! The Fillet and Camp Knife was also given a strange up-swept point during this period that was soon dropped for the original straight back.

The early '70s saw Herter's peak popularity as a sporting goods outfitter. An 8-inch fillet was added to the line as well as the "Berthe E. Herter Famous Large Kitchen Knife," a 12½-inch clip-pointed French chef-style knife. "Outperforms any electric knife ever made and makes you look like a cook, not an electrician." I'm sure only a drugstore tenderfoot cook would have used anything else. Prices had risen to $2.65 for the Improved Bowie, $3.97 for the George Herter, $2.97 for the Canadian Fillet and Camp, $2.37 for the Bull Cook and $3.30 for the Crooked Knife. All still came with either the Pro Guide or Bull Cook manual.

During the late '70s, Herter's ran into a number of business setbacks including labor problems, the loss of a large warehouse in Minnesota to a fire, and a bust by Customs for importing endangered bird feathers for fly tying. My last catalog is dated 1978. The long-winded descriptions of each product are gone, and the quality of the knives seems to have slipped. An Improved Bowie was up to $5.27. Berthe Herter's chef knife had lost it clip-point, and the catalog was actually offering Schrade, Camillus and Buck knives under their real trademarks. It was a sad day in this part of the country when the Olympia, Washington, store closed down along with the rest of the Herter's operation. Many still mourn it.

For all the hot air that went with a Herter's product, the buyer still got a good solid tool for a very reasonable price. Any time I bring the company name up, I'm surprised at the number of old Herter's rifles, decoys and reloading tools people admit to owning. An acquaintance of mine grew up on a Montana cattle ranch and has backpacked practically every wilderness area in Oregon,

(Text continues on page 46)

The evolution of the Herter's Improved Bowie. The earliest knife is on the left. The two knives on the right came from the Olympia store's close-out sale in the late 1970s. Though I kind of wonder what Jim Bowie would have to say about the "Improved" part, these knives are better than average outdoor tools.

(Above) A pair of Canadian Fish Fillet and Camp Knives with their "tooled horsehide" scabbards—excellent camp kitchen knives even if they don't follow the modern mini-machete formula.

(Right) These Herter's Crooked Knives were said to see universal use across Canada by the Eskimos and Indians. This was probably true and they are crooked, but were not the *real* crooked knife.

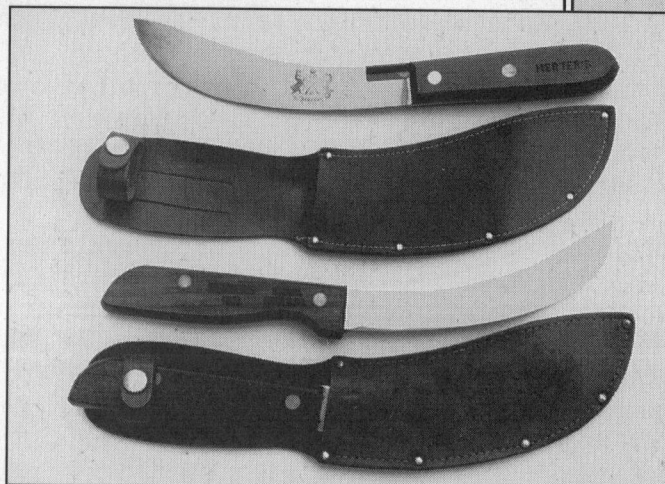

(Above) A pair of fairly straightforward Herter fillet knives—the patterns of these changed often.

(Below) The bottom knife is the George L. Herter Knife; at top is a genuine Grohmann Russell. Grohmann states they never had any dealings with Herter.

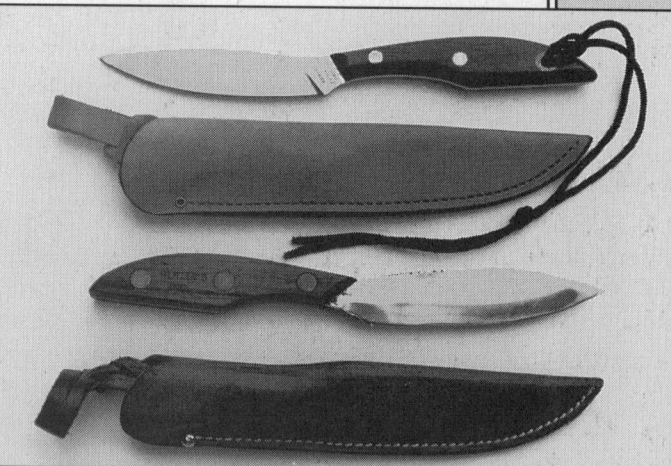

Are Herter's knives collectable? Well, this group of five belong to Rhett Stidham, knife dealer big-time, who deals mostly in high-dollar Randalls and such, and he isn't selling his Herter's yet. It's worth noting whoever owned these particular knives kept them keenly sharp. (Warner photos)

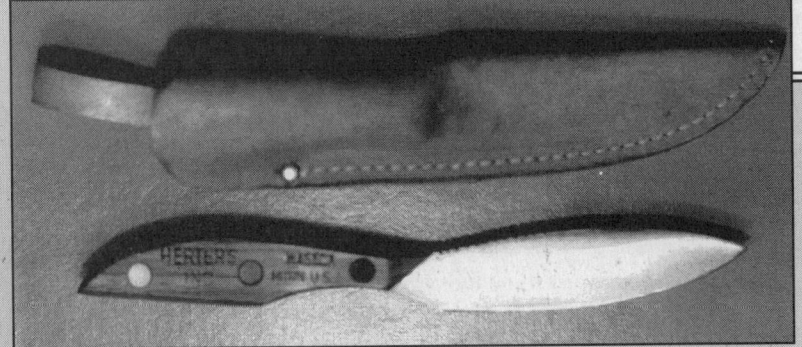

(Text continued from page 43)

Washington, Idaho and Montana. He knows "the Bob" (Bob Marshall Wilderness Area), some of the wildest country in the lower 48, like the back of his hand. His knife for all these outdoor adventures is a humpback Herter's Improved Bowie his brother gave him twenty years ago.

I think most experienced outdoorspersons simply ignored the catalog text and bought what they needed. Even when a less sophisticated outdoorsperson bought the George L. Herter explanation hook, line and sinker, I don't think many would ever say they were actually cheated. For $2 or $3, you could have an Improved Bowie, a knife not much different than those carried by the mountain men that explored the American wilderness. Many of those plain knives are still earning a living in the outdoors all over the country.

Recently, Herter's was reopened as a "Waterfowling Specialist" mail-order company. Much to my personal dismay, the Improved Bowies and Bull Cook knives are totally missing. Hopefully this will change in the future unless the drugstore cowboys and tenderfeet are in charge.

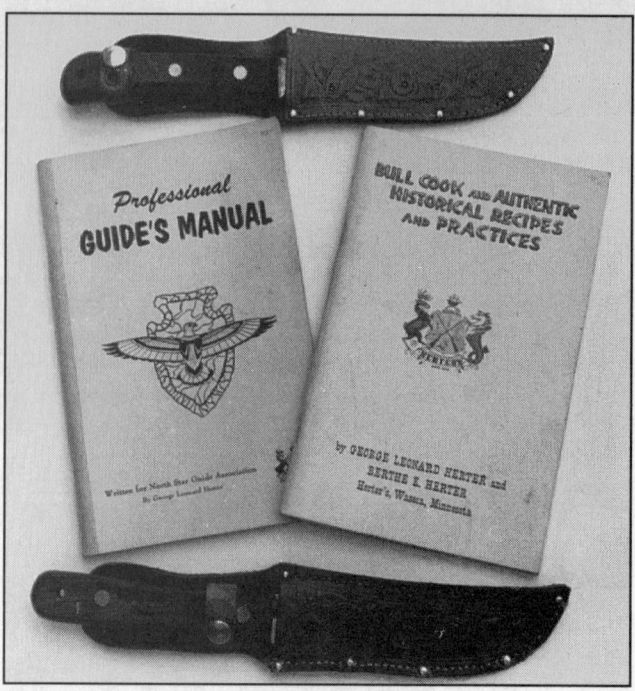

Most knives came with a choice of the "Professional Guide's Manual" or the "Bull Cook and Authentic Historical Recipes and Practices" manual.

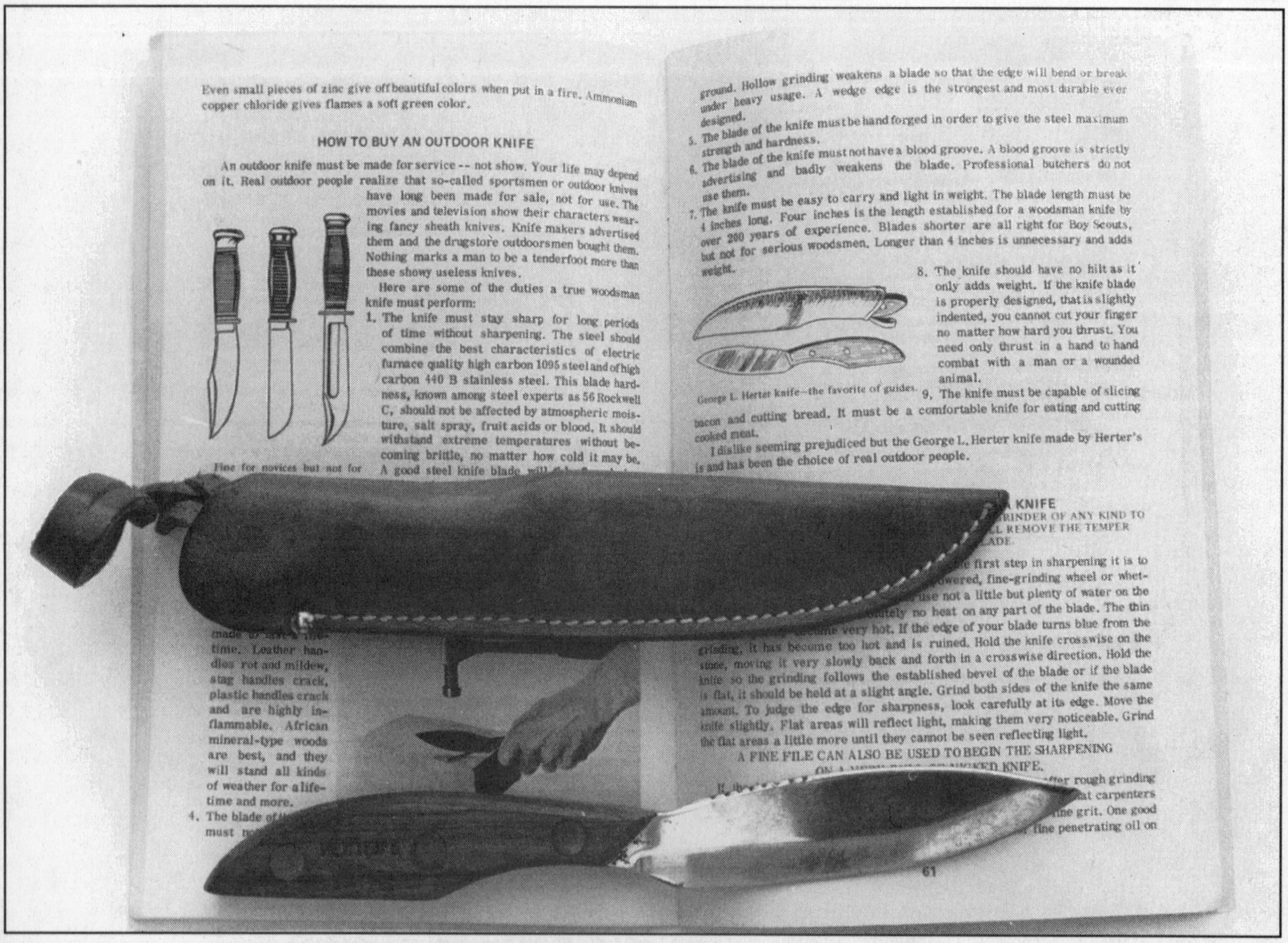

According to George, only a drugstore outdoorsman would have ever carried one of the Marble pattern sheath knives. Real backwoodsmen picked the George L. Herter knife every time.

THE LOOKOUT'S BOWIE

by STEVEN DICK

AFTER SPENDING MOST of the Seventies tearing down fire lookouts and replacing them with aerial patrols, the U.S. Forest Service has now decided the old system was actually less expensive. Once more, lonely individuals are stationed on strategic peaks to scan the surrounding wilderness for the slightest whiff of smoke. Recently, my wife and I hiked a high ridge a few miles south of the Mt. Rainier National Park boundary, and there at the summit was a classic example of a USFS fire lookout, complete with wide windows on all four sides, heavy-duty storm shutters and lightning rods, a topographical map mounted on a table in the center of the room, and a rangefinder for pin-pointing fires. With the exception of the radio that has replaced hand-strung phone lines, little has changed since Gifford Pinchot's days.

After enjoying the view and talking to the two fireguards for a few minutes, we started back down. Just inside the tree line, a few hundred feet below the lookout, I noticed a three-sided lean-to where the guards kept their

The U.S. Forest Service High Rock Lookout in the central Cascade Mountains.

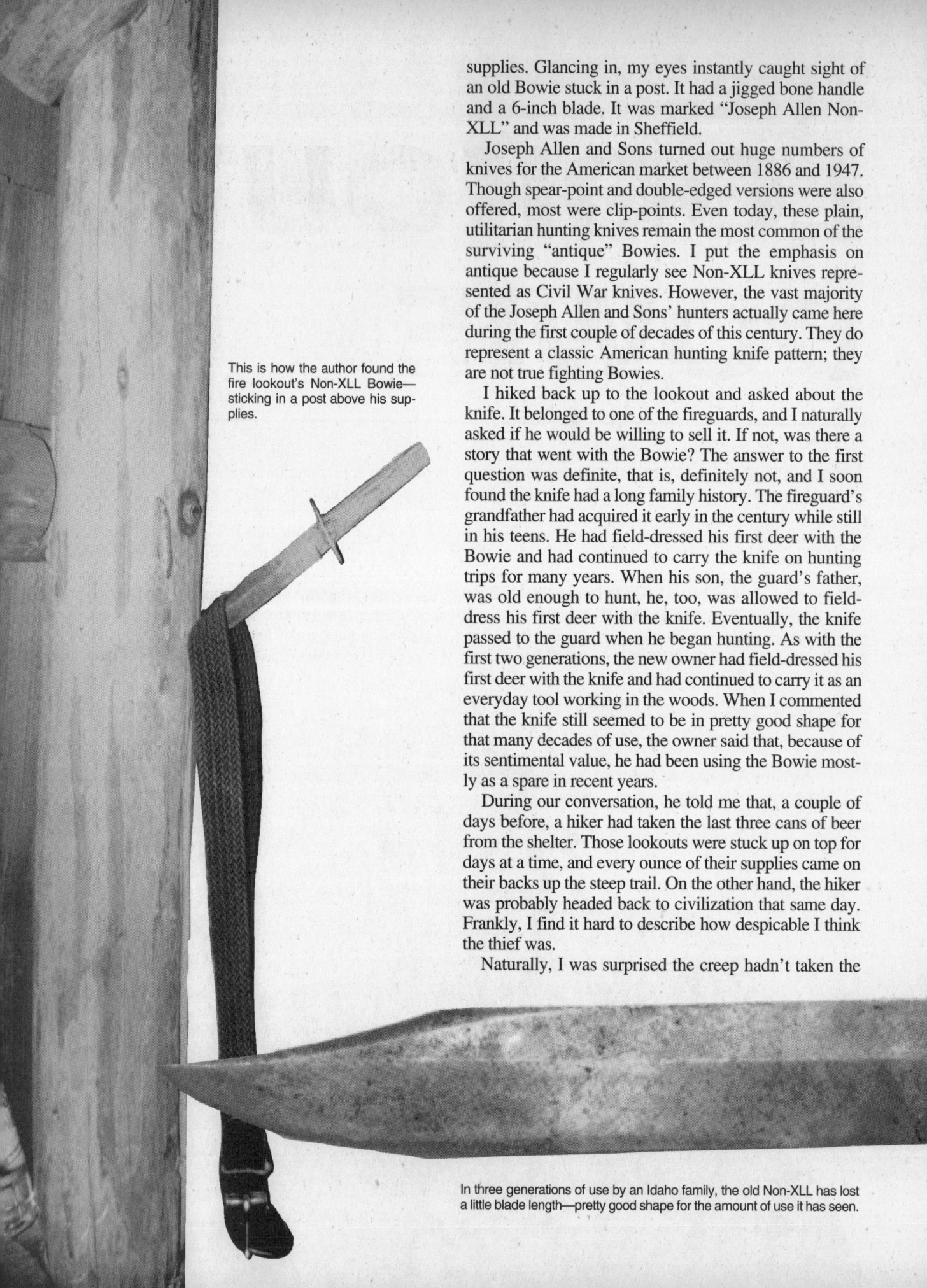

This is how the author found the fire lookout's Non-XLL Bowie—sticking in a post above his supplies.

In three generations of use by an Idaho family, the old Non-XLL has lost a little blade length—pretty good shape for the amount of use it has seen.

supplies. Glancing in, my eyes instantly caught sight of an old Bowie stuck in a post. It had a jigged bone handle and a 6-inch blade. It was marked "Joseph Allen Non-XLL" and was made in Sheffield.

Joseph Allen and Sons turned out huge numbers of knives for the American market between 1886 and 1947. Though spear-point and double-edged versions were also offered, most were clip-points. Even today, these plain, utilitarian hunting knives remain the most common of the surviving "antique" Bowies. I put the emphasis on antique because I regularly see Non-XLL knives represented as Civil War knives. However, the vast majority of the Joseph Allen and Sons' hunters actually came here during the first couple of decades of this century. They do represent a classic American hunting knife pattern; they are not true fighting Bowies.

I hiked back up to the lookout and asked about the knife. It belonged to one of the fireguards, and I naturally asked if he would be willing to sell it. If not, was there a story that went with the Bowie? The answer to the first question was definite, that is, definitely not, and I soon found the knife had a long family history. The fireguard's grandfather had acquired it early in the century while still in his teens. He had field-dressed his first deer with the Bowie and had continued to carry the knife on hunting trips for many years. When his son, the guard's father, was old enough to hunt, he, too, was allowed to field-dress his first deer with the knife. Eventually, the knife passed to the guard when he began hunting. As with the first two generations, the new owner had field-dressed his first deer with the knife and had continued to carry it as an everyday tool working in the woods. When I commented that the knife still seemed to be in pretty good shape for that many decades of use, the owner said that, because of its sentimental value, he had been using the Bowie mostly as a spare in recent years.

During our conversation, he told me that, a couple of days before, a hiker had taken the last three cans of beer from the shelter. Those lookouts were stuck up on top for days at a time, and every ounce of their supplies came on their backs up the steep trail. On the other hand, the hiker was probably headed back to civilization that same day. Frankly, I find it hard to describe how despicable I think the thief was.

Naturally, I was surprised the creep hadn't taken the

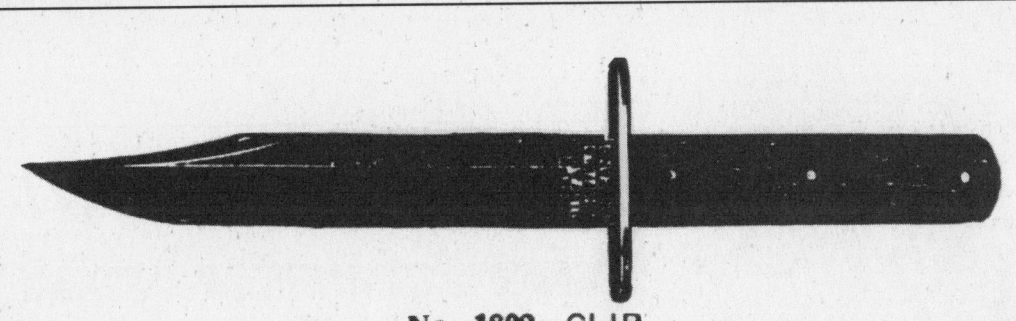

A 20th-century Norvell-Shapleigh Hardware catalog shows this Non-XLL hunter came in several blade lengths. From my own observations, the 6-inch is by far the commonest.

Non-XLL Bowie along with the beer. Up 'til that moment, the lookout hadn't thought the knife might have any particular value to anyone other than his family. At my suggestion, he then decided to store the knife in a safer place back at the tower.

From the 1830s up to fairly recent times, the basic clip-point hunter was a standard part of practically every cutlery company's line. Sheffield firms like Joseph Allen and Sons, Wade & Butcher and Joseph Rogers exported many thousands of these knives to the New World. For years, the majority of sporting goods dealers offered little else in the way of sheath knives. Popular or not, professional outdoor journalists from "Nessmuk" (the pen name of George Washington Sears in the 1880s) on down have discounted the Bowie hunter's utility in the woods. As this family tradition proves, not all those Bowies were in the hands of inexperienced greenhorns. Few of us like to admit it, but the fact remains the person behind the knife is more important than the design of the blade being used. At least one Non-XLL Sheffield Bowie has served three generations of woodsmen just fine.

It's interesting—the history and the knife itself. And there is the rest of the story: Later, after some consideration of various factors, including what seemed to be a very high value for the knife, the Non-XLL left the family and is now owned by—you guessed it—your reporter. •

Despite all the experts' opinions, this fireguard's family found the Bowie-hunter OK for three generations of use.

Book Excerpt

LEVINE'S LATEST

Levine's Guide to Knives and Their Values, Expanded 3rd Edition, has 512 pages, is widely praised in the field. Published at $24.95 by DBI Books.

Pocketknives by Bernard Levine. Available from the author at $15.00 postpaid. (Box 2404, Eugene, OR 97402)

As THIS EDITION was in preparation, Bernard Levine called, and defined himself: He was figuring out some new stuff for the fourth edition of *Levine's Guide to Knives and Their Values,* and number three was just published. Obviously, Bernard R. Levine is a writer of books who thinks about his trade. Certainly, his *Pocket-Knives* from Courage Books, an imprint of Running Press Publishers, Philadelphia, is a thinking man's book. In eighty elegant pages, it provides almost all the key things people who wish to know about pocketknives should know.

By kind permission of Courage Books, we publish here a three-page chapter on Counterfeits from Levine's latest. As a Spencer Tracy character once said in a movie of the Katharine Hepburn character in the same movie: "There ain't much there, but what there is, is 'cherce.'" On this subject—the subject of faked knives—many have written much, much more and said less.

The other seventy-seven pages include chapters on knife history and knife patterns and knife manufacture. There are special chapters on brand names, fancy handles and hand-crafted folders. And there's a very sound chapter of advice to the knife-lorn, advice that will keep any beginning collector (who takes it) out of real trouble.

It's a good book. Right here you can read some of it yourself and confirm our judgment.

Ken Warner

CHAPTER VII

COUNTERFEITS

Knife counterfeiting for the purpose of cheating collectors got its start as a shady cottage industry in the 1950s, with the fabrication of fantasy bowie knives. I do not know exactly when fake pocketknives first appeared, but they were around in 1971 when I first got into the knife business. Like most beginners, I learned my first lessons about counterfeits the hard way, laying out good money for bad knives. I have never made the *same* mistake twice, but there are always new mistakes just waiting to be made.

As pocketknives have grown more popular and more valuable, fakes have grown more common. Most are still relatively easy for the experienced collector to spot, but beginners can be fooled by slick shiny fakes. Today at most knife shows there are entire tables offering nothing but fakes. Show sponsors have not yet come up with a satisfactory solution.

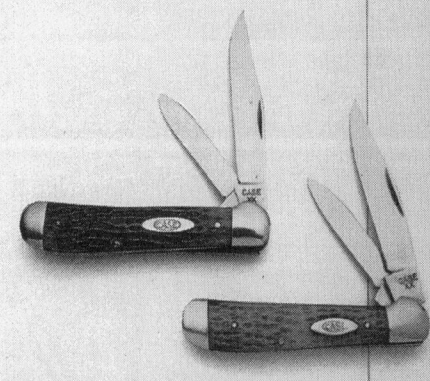

ABOVE
Top: genuine Case XX 6249 "Copperhead" or "Viet Nam" pattern jack knife with red jigged bone handles. Bottom: counterfeit Case XX 6249.

WHERE IT WAS MADE
CAN TELL YOU A LOT

Most fake knives were not made in the same country as the originals which they attempt to copy, so their materials and construction are noticeably different than those of the genuine article. For example, most mass-produced fakes of older American knives are made in Germany and Japan, so once you

COUNTERFEITS

NAZI POCKETKNIVES?

In the 1930s and 1940s the German Nazi party ordered millions upon millions of fancy dress daggers, decorated with party regalia, and in many patterns and variations. These daggers are now popular collector items (and widely faked).

One thing the Nazis did not order was fancy pocketknives. Yet at many knife shows, gun shows, or swap meets, one is sure to see what *look* like Nazi pocketknives. They have all the right regalia, sometimes even a portrait of Hitler or his "autograph." When one ex-Nazi official was shown one of these knives, he said, "We probably would have bought things like this back then, if someone had thought of them, but no one did."

These "Nazi" pocketknives are pure fantasies, dreamed up in the 1970s and sold to the swap-meet trade, mainly by Parker Cutlery Co. of Tennessee. They have now been around long enough to start turning up at antiques stores and estate sales, but they are not genuine, and they have no value.

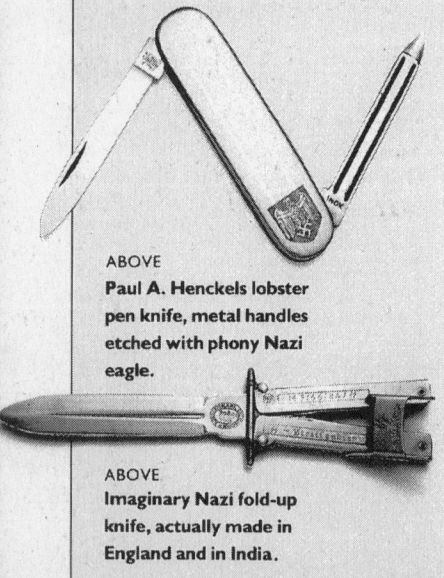

ABOVE
Paul A. Henckels lobster pen knife, metal handles etched with phony Nazi eagle.

ABOVE
Imaginary Nazi fold-up knife, actually made in England and in India.

learn to recognize German and Japanese craftsmanship – both usually good, but quite different from American style – these fakes will become obvious to you.

Long before there were knife collectors, there were already fakes – lots of them – littering the channels of cutlery commerce. In the 17th and 18th centuries Sheffield makers faked London brands. In the 19th century German cutlery firms made up English sounding names to put on knives they sold in America, while in this century cutlers in India did the same thing.

Today Germans make fake American knives for American companies, Italians make fake German knives for German *and* American companies, and North Africans make fake Italian knives for their own consumption because they are cheaper than the real thing. Spaniards make fake French knives for local sale, and so, for that matter, do some French firms. The Japanese fake everyone's knives – and not on their own initiative, but because knife distributors in other countries ask them to (the Japanese are happy to oblige). Meanwhile Pakistani cutlers knock off the Japanese copies, the Chinese copy everyone, and everyone copies Swiss army knives.

So what is a poor collector or other knife buyer to do? Look at knives, especially genuine knives, and study how they are made. Materials and workmanship are surer guides to where and when a knife was manufactured than the markings. Markings only matter when they are consistent with the rest of the knife.

TYPES OF FAKERY

There are three basic types of fake knives. These are counterfeits, re-works, and fantasies.

• **COUNTERFEITS.** A counterfeit is a fake knife which was made in conscious imitation of an authentic knife. Most counterfeits are of decidedly inferior quality, compared to their originals, but beginners who have never seen an original first-hand are likely to be fooled by them. Experience is the best insurance against this type of fake. The overwhelming majority of knife collectors and dealers will be happy to loan you their experience and examine a knife that you are considering acquiring.

The threat of really high-quality counterfeits lurks just over the horizon, but so far it has not arrived (as far as I can tell!). Anyone capable of making a counterfeit of, say, a Remington R1306

COUNTERFEITS

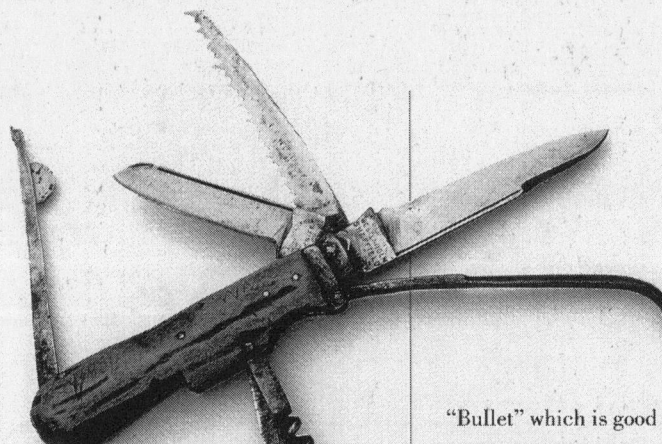

LEFT
George Wostenholm, Sheffield, horseman's knife, genuine stag, repaired with an old Pennsylvania Knife Co. blade; probably an old repair.

"Bullet" which is good enough to fool an advanced collector, could probably make more money by making a folding knife of that quality marked with his own name.

- **RE-WORKS.** Re-works are a much more difficult category than counterfeits. A re-work is a genuine old knife that has been "improved" in some way. The improvement may be relatively minor, such as a patched handle crack or a tightened rivet.

The improvement may instead be major, such as an insignificant marking being ground away, to be replaced by a more popular brand. Most re-stamping is done with modern stamps and is easy for the experienced collector to spot since lettering styles have changed over the years. Some fakers have original old stamping dies, however, and then the collector must be familiar with a particular brand in order to avoid being fooled. Lazy fakers engrave or etch fake marks, which should not fool anyone – but they do.

A common form of re-working is the replacement of broken blades, springs, handle covers, or other components. There is a fine line between legitimate restoration, on one side, and fraud, on the other. A legitimate restoration usually incorporates correct original parts and is always revealed by the seller. Fraud is anything less.

- **FANTASY KNIVES.** Fantasy knives would be a glorious joke, if it were not that so many beginning collectors get burned by them. A fantasy knife is one that a faker dreamed up and then marked with famous names in an effort to tie it to history. Fantasy knives are never based on real prototypes, so strictly speaking they are not counterfeits. Most are glaringly anachronistic in shape, materials, construction, or decoration, but the beginner may not realize this. Many fantasy knives would not function as knives, a sure clue that a "knife" is not genuine.

IT'S IN PRINT, SO IT MUST BE TRUE

I once met a collector, an educated professional, who did not believe in counterfeits. For example, if a knife said WINCHESTER on it, as far as he was concerned it was a Winchester knife. He knew perfectly well that some of the knives that he owned marked WINCHESTER had been made by the Winchester Repeating Arms Company in Connecticut in the 1920s and 1930s, while others were made in Germany in the 1970s, in Japan in the 1980s, in Pennsylvania in the 1990s, or in somebody's basement last week.

None of this bothered him. The knives all said WINCHESTER, so to him they were all WINCHESTER knives, and to him they were all equally valuable.

There, of course, lay the problem. No doubt a few other people share this gentleman's innocent outlook, but most do not. If he ever wants to sell his knives, the ones really made by Winchester will sell right away, while most of the rest will not sell at all.

THE WOODCRAFT
Marble's Best Seller

THE MARBLE'S WOODCRAFT was one of the best and most popular hunting knives of its time, created by that great outdoorsman's equipment designer Webster L. Marble. It was made by his Marble Arms and Manufacturing Co., Gladstone, Michigan, from 1915 until about 1970. According to the available information, it was Marble's all-time best selling knife.

The Woodcraft was an improvement on the De Weese Knife Marble's had introduced about 1902. The De Weese was a lightweight 4-inch-blade knife designed by then-famous outdoorsman Dall De Weese of Cannon City, Colorado. Its features in the Woodcraft included the curved cutting edge, the bone breaker back edge, and a thumbrest on the back of the blade. Although the

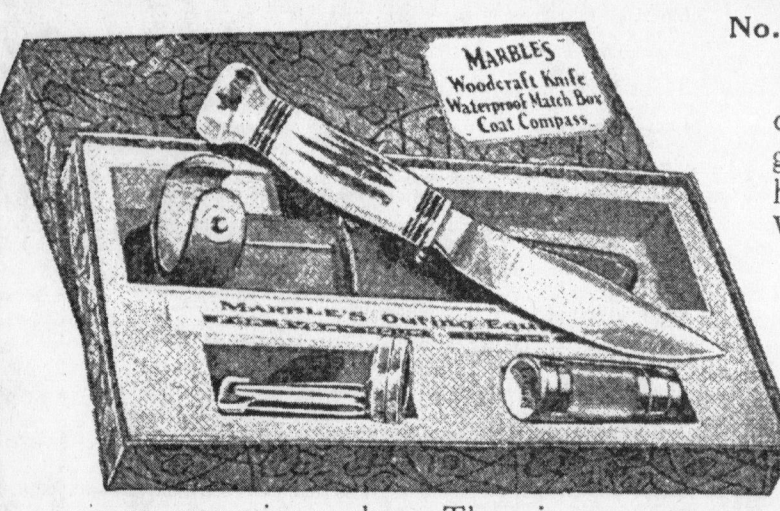

No. 305—Set....$5.00

Consists of one each No. 50 genuine Staghorn Handle Woodcraft Knife in leather sheath, No. 181 Waterproof Match Box, and No. 182 Coat Compass, put up in an attractive package. These items are a necessary part of the equipment of every sportsman and scout. Each insures the safety and convenience of the owner and may save his life.

All are good year 'round sellers, although especially active at Christmas time. When attractively displayed they offer dealers increased volume and profit through their sale.

This boxed set with a Marble's Woodcraft Knife offered other best sellers as well—Marble's pin-on compass and pocket match safe.

by KONRAD F. SCHREIER, JR.

This first ad for Marble's Woodcraft knife appeared in May 1915.

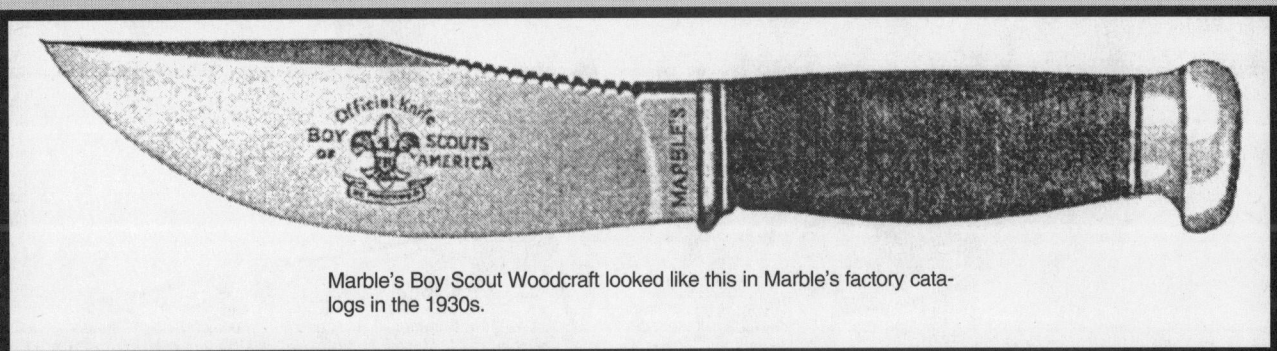

Marble's Boy Scout Woodcraft looked like this in Marble's factory catalogs in the 1930s.

This is the knife—the "most typical"—we think of as the Marble's Woodcraft.

Eagerly sought now by collectors, the full stag version was not nearly so popular then.

FIFTEENTH EDITION 55

DeWeese was still sold by Marble's as late as 1930, it was always too light, had too short a blade, and lacked a guard—a real drawback.

When Webster Marble designed his Woodcraft, he made it a superior utility hunting knife. Introduced in 1915, the basic model cost $1.50. That $1.50 Woodcraft had a leather washer grip with a staghorn cap and a leather sheath. There was a $2.00 model with a full stag-horn grip. The new design received immediate acceptance.

The Woodcraft was made in only one size with a 4 1/2-inch blade, weighing about 5 ounces. Its thick-backed tapered blade was very strong despite its light weight. Its standard leather washer handle with half-guard was very comfortable to use for many tasks. Also, the knurled thumbrest on the blade back made it easy to apply pressure for cutting, and the dull back of the front of the blade was very handy for breaking things like light bones.

When World War I made German stag horn hard to get, Marble began making the leather washer grip model with an aluminum grip cap. Large numbers of Woodcraft knives were used by members of the U.S. Armed Forces in World War I. They were considered an excellent utility sheath knife, but they never earned a reputation as a fighting knife.

After World War I, the Woodcraft knife was as popular with outdoorsmen as any hunting knife then on the market. A number of variations came along, some of which are very rare collectibles. One was the Woodcraft made with fiber washer instead of leather washer grips. Another is the staghorn grip model with an aluminum grip cap.

Despite the rising inflation of the Depression Era, the Woodcraft continued to remain affordable. The standard leather grip model with an aluminum grip cap and leather sheath was $2.25, and a different version with a staghorn grip and grip cap was $3.00 complete with a leather sheath. The Sears Roebuck mail-order catalogs of the late 1920s offered the standard model Woodcraft for $1.79.

In the late 1920s, the Woodcraft was selected as an official knife of the Boy Scouts of America, and it remained one until World War II. A Boy Scout model Woodcraft knife is the regular leather washer hilt type with the Scout emblem etched on its blade and stamped on the leather sheath. In the 1930s, the Scout Woodcraft catalog price was $1.75, while the regular model without the Boy Scout markings was cataloged at $2.00.

At the end of the '30s, the Woodcraft model was at the height of its popularity. Marble's often featured it in their advertising, which appeared in many national magazines, and it could be found in every outdoorsman's store or mail-order catalog. It was considered an excellent hunting knife, and certainly the best available at its price.

Production of the Woodcraft, like many things, was limited during World War II. Most of the production went to U.S. Army Post Exchanges, U.S. Navy Ship's Stores and similar outlets of the Armed Forces, and many American servicemen carried Woodcrafts to war as their personal utility sheath knife. The Woodcraft knife was on many U.S. Armed Forces Unit's lists of non-government issue equipment recommended for purchase by servicemen before they were sent overseas.

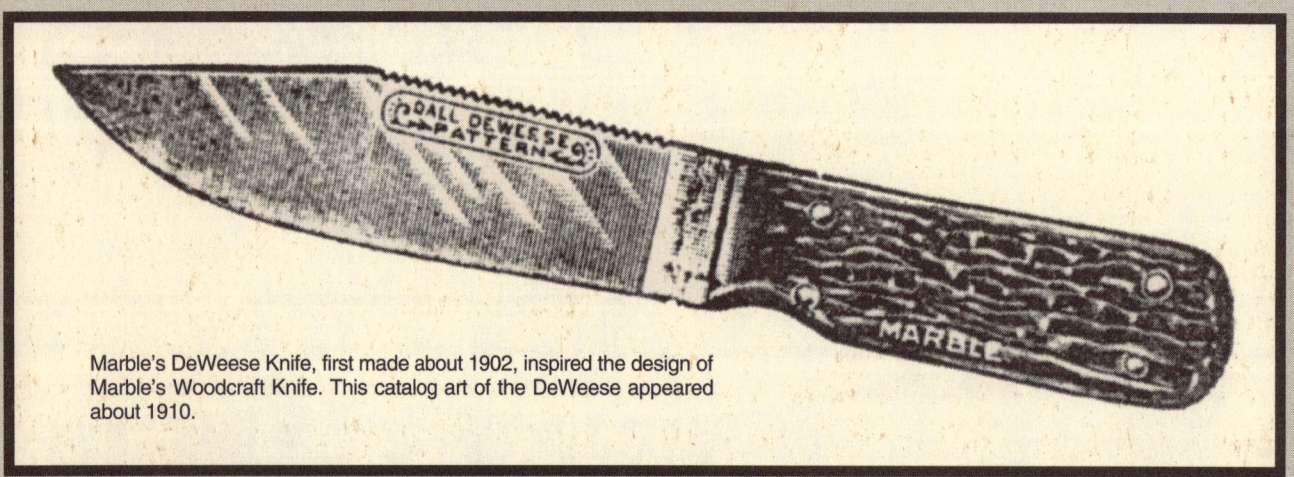

Marble's DeWeese Knife, first made about 1902, inspired the design of Marble's Woodcraft Knife. This catalog art of the DeWeese appeared about 1910.

However, the Woodcraft was never considered a fighting knife.

At the end of World War II, the Marble's Woodcraft was still a very popular outdoorsman's knife, but its price was soon caught in the post-war inflationary spiral. As soon as the U.S. government regulations would allow, its price was raised to $2.50 for the basic leather washer hilt model, and by 1948 it was $3. In the early 1950s, the price was $3.25, and by the late '50s it had risen to $6.25.

At the same time its price rose, the Woodcraft's quality began to deteriorate. Marble's knives were always the product of skilled craftsmen's work, and their workmanship accounts for the variations found in all Marble's knives. As the old-time craftsmen retired after World War II, their replacements were never as good as they had been. By the 1970s, Marble's Woodcraft catalog photographs showed a much more crudely made blade than is

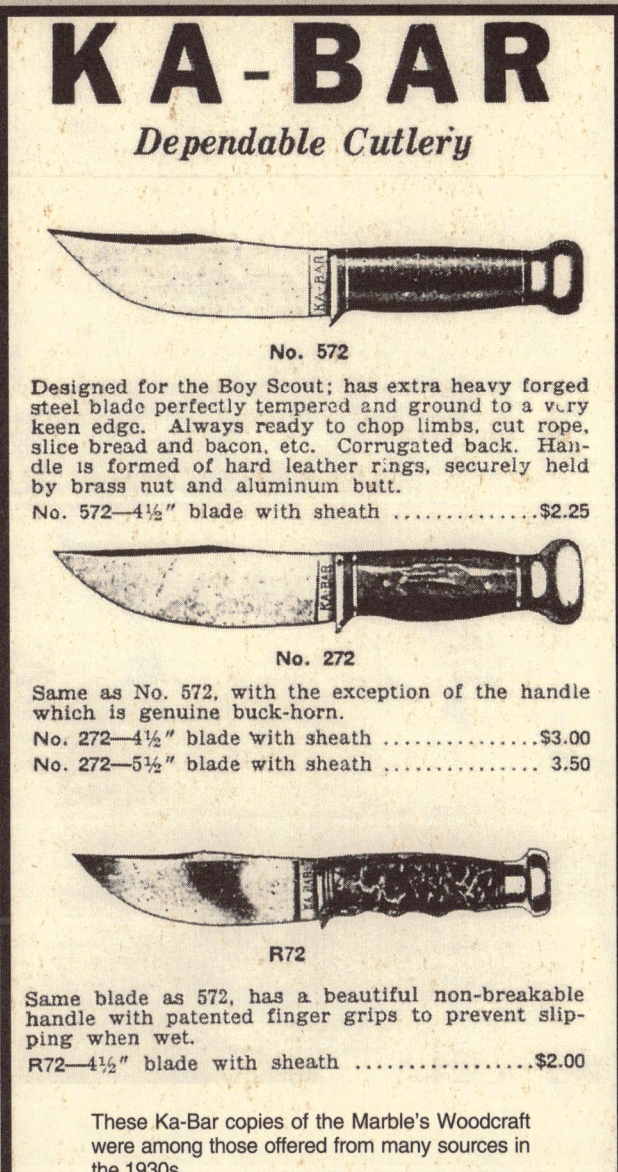

These Ka-Bar copies of the Marble's Woodcraft were among those offered from many sources in the 1930s.

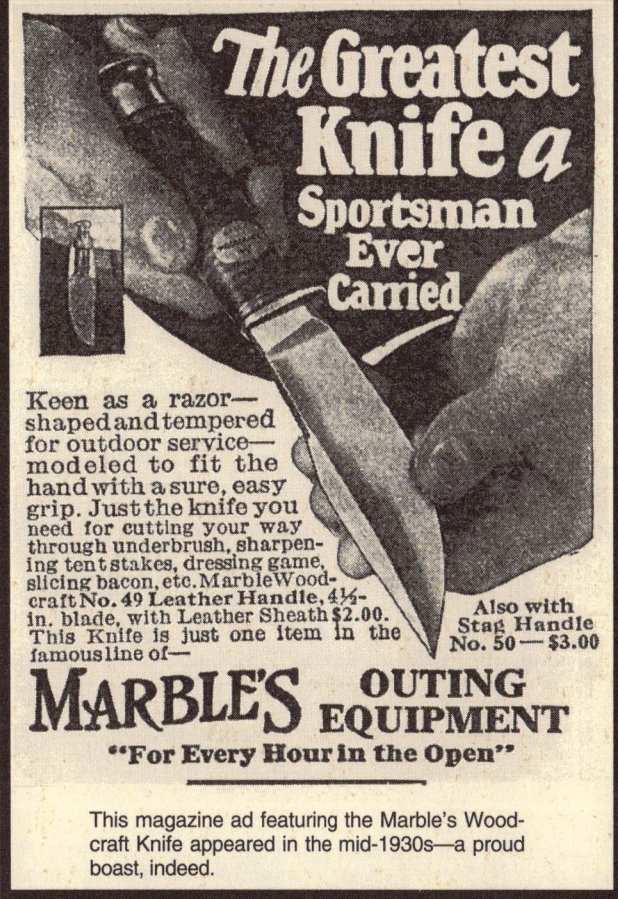

This magazine ad featuring the Marble's Woodcraft Knife appeared in the mid-1930s—a proud boast, indeed.

found on pre-World War II examples.

By the 1970s, the price of a standard leather washer hilt Woodcraft knife had risen to $9.50, and the stag model had been replaced with a "tiger wood" grip model at $10.50. The popularity of the Woodcraft had also fallen off, and its days as America's most popular hunting knife were long over.

From the 1920s on, many copies of it were made. Maher & Grosh's "The Shark" was a $2 copy with a 5-inch blade, and Wade & Butcher made a 4¾-inch-blade copy with a stainless steel blade for $5. In the 1920s, Stillto cutlery made copies with 5- and 6-inch blades they called their "Woodcraft Pattern," and Marble's apparently never contested their use of the name.

Remington made a 5¼-inch-blade copy of the Woodcraft in the 1930s, and Western States Cutlery made a cheap 4¾-inch-blade model selling for $1. In the 1930s, the famous German cutlery firm of J.A. Henckel of Solingen made a 5-inch-blade copy selling for $2.75.

After World War II, Case, Ka-Bar, Western and other knifemakers offered more copies of the Marble's Woodcraft knife, but these drifted away from the original Woodcraft design before long. At the same time, there were some very cheaply made imported copies mostly offered at "war surplus" stores. When handcrafting of knives became popular in the 1960s, imported rough blade forgings in the Woodcraft design began to be offered.

There do not appear to be any copies of the Woodcraft on the market today, and the original model is no longer made. However, when all is said and done, the genuine Marble's Woodcraft knife made by the company's skilled craftsmen in the "good old days" is still an excellent knife. It is also one prized by many blade collectors as a superb example of one of the best American-made knives ever.

●

EDITOR'S NOTE
A well-known fellow named Jim Parker has registered the Marble's trademarks and has knives made in some of the old patterns. They are not generally of typical original Marble's quality. *KW*

I HAVE BEEN a full-time custom swordmaker for more than fifteen years. In that time, over and over again, I have witnessed a peculiar phenomenon: I am at a knife show, a potential customer is looking with polite interest at a sword displayed—perhaps he has never seen a real custom-built sword up-close. He leans over and looks closely and appreciatively, but when his hands touch the handle and he actually picks it up, a strange transformation takes place. His body tenses, the knees flex, the shoulders scrunch, an expression of wild abandon comes over his face as he looks around to see if the area is clear. I usually take a step backward out of range behind the table as it becomes obvious he is smitten with the desire to cut something. Then, reason asserts itself and the sword is closed over the silk-wrapped handle, I felt power surge through my body, circulate, and then concentrate again in the blade. I cannot adequately describe the intensity of the experience, but over the years I would recall it, and I believe it helped lead me into my chosen profession. It has been my goal in swordmaking to craft blades that will allow others to experience that feeling.

Somewhere in our collective unconscious "The Sword" seems to strike a universal chord. Across the centuries and across cultural and religious lines, "The Sword" returns again and again. In Christianity, it is symbolized by the "Sword of the Spirit"—that which divides truth from untruth. The Japanese creation myth holds that the Islands of Japan were formed by the drops of blood falling from

THOUGHTS

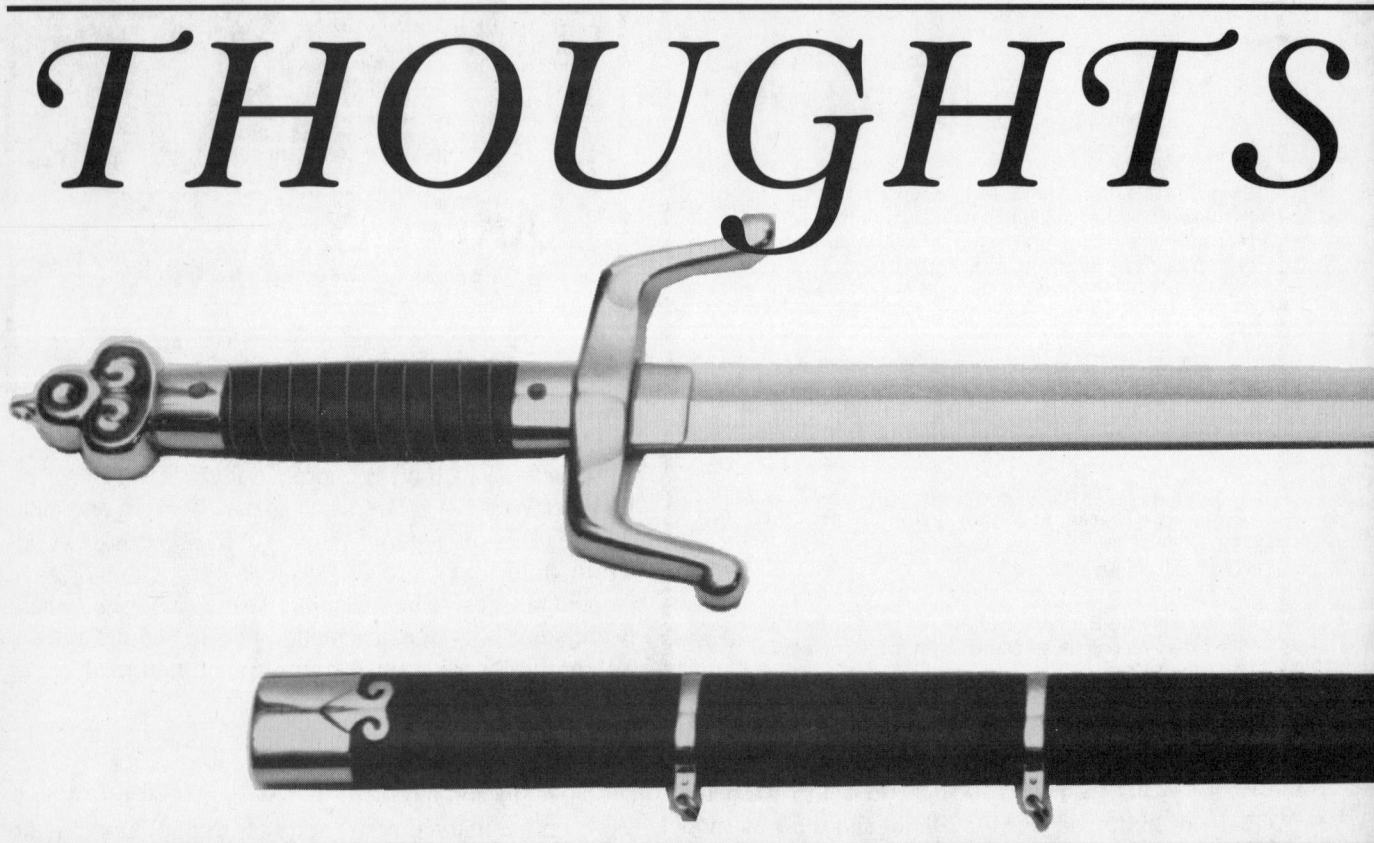

replaced on the table with murmured apologies. He sometimes says, "I had no idea!"

I am often asked some form of the question: "In this day of smart bombs and nuclear weapons, why make swords? Aren't they just totally obsolete?"

It is a completely valid question, and yet it is difficult to give an adequate reply. Some people just know the answer; to them, it is as obvious as the sun rising in the east. To others, understanding the lure of swords may never come, and explanation seems like children's babble.

When I was young, my father showed me a sword he had brought home from World War II. It was a Japanese katana, and when he handed the hilt to me and my hands the edge of the Creator's sword. "The Sword" is not just a weapon of war, nor is it merely a badge of rank or status; it has relevance on deeply philosophic and spiritual levels as well.

As a weapon, the sword is intensely personal. Real battle with swords would have been a horribly grisly affair. The evolution of weapons has always tended to distance one from the opponent, but the sword is just about as close as it gets. The sword is symbolic of the very nature of conflict.

There is an old Irish saying: "Never give a sword to a man who cannot dance." To me, this means that to comprehend swords with a balanced perspective, you must bring with you a playful lightheartedness rather than a brooding seriousness. It does one no good to dwell too much on the gruesome aspects of sword fighting. An appreciation of beauty and balance is absolutely necessary, as is a sense of symmetry.

The Japanese say, "Pen And Sword, In Accord." In *Book of Five Rings,* written in 1645 by the great swordsman Miyamoto Musashi, it says the true path of the warrior is "the twofold way of pen and sword," and that a delicate balance must be maintained between them. The volume is still in print in several languages, remaining popular to this day, assiduously studied by Japanese businessmen for tips on strategy.

To understand why dedicated craftsmen in the modern age would lavish the time and effort to create a finely ries, the sword is almost universally the weapon of choice for the archetypical hero who battles evil to save the world. Why?

I think that the *concept* of the sword is symbolic. It may be, as some say, symbolic of male energy by its phallic shape, which could explain why over 95 percent of sword buyers are male. It could also be symbolic of something deeper and more significant lurking in the human psyche. I don't know which or what, but I know the symbol touches us.

Still, why make new custom swords? Aren't there enough old ones lying around to satisfy the demand? Actually, there are not.

The first knife show I ever attended was the annual

ON SWORDS

———— by TOM MARINGER

Full-sized mild fantasy, but a working sword, all in stainless steel. (VerHoeven photo)

made sword; to comprehend the sword connoisseurs, hobbyists and martial artists who will spend their hard-earned money to purchase such works of art; we first need to define just what a sword is. What is it that makes it different from a long knife? What is it about swords that speaks so eloquently to that inner barbarian lurking in our hearts?

Consider the images of swords that come to your mind. If you're like me, you might see a scene from any one of hundreds of films—Errol Flynn swinging on a rope with sword in hand to save his lady, Conan the Barbarian fighting with his back to the wall against insuperable odds, the Highlander fighting for the very survival of the planet against supernatural foes! In films and sto-
Knifemaker's Guild show in July of 1977 at the Crown Center Hotel in Kansas City, Missouri. I had been making knives only two years and had yet to attempt my first sword. I walked the aisles and gazed upon the finest examples of cutlery the world had yet seen. Swords were few, but present—Jimmy Lile had a Japanese-style katana; Buster Warenski had a beautiful Scottish broadsword; W.W. Cronk showed some huge, elaborate almost-swords; Al Wachowiak showed his collection of "Bodacious Blades," featuring some custom swords and other outlandishly large knives by makers such as Dan Dennehy, Gil Hibben and Rod Chappel.

I toured the room and talked to makers about their swords and was surprised to get the almost-universal

Built to be a boarding cutlass/jungle knife kind of sword, this became the Vorpal sword, and the design is in production in the United States. (VerHoeven photo)

response: "Never again." The problems of scale connected with making swords had so discouraged these makers that they determined not to attempt such pieces in the future.

I found this rather curious and decided then to try my hand at swordmaking, yet for some time I couldn't get started on the project, due to its daunting size, of course. Finally, I mentioned the idea to the teacher of the Tae-Kwon-Do academy I was attending, and he placed an order on the spot. The motivation was now supplied, and I finished my first sword in late 1977 after a gestation period of about three months.

I showed that first sword around a bit, took some photos of it, and suddenly, out of nowhere it seemed, there were people approaching me saying they'd always wanted a custom sword, but could never find a maker willing to put forth the effort necessary. I started accepting orders for custom swords in 1978 and have pursued it as a specialty ever since.

As we said, there are quite a few old swords still in existence. Most are, regrettably, in poor condition, unsuitable for actual use. There are some good older Japanese swords in circulation, of course, but there are very few older European blades in private hands.

Even to get a traditionally styled weapon, a top-quality sword from a living maker is the best possible assurance of satisfaction. If you want a fantasy-style blade, there simply are no old ones, and custom is the only way to go.

Stock-manufactured swords from mail-order catalogs may be the least expensive alternative, if you are not too concerned about exclusivity or the quality of workmanship. And some catalog items are better than others. But if you desire one of the finest swords ever made, you will be best advised to seek a custom maker, work with him on the details of your project, and be willing to pay the necessary price, which in the old days could be a year's income.

The basic techniques involved in swordmaking are almost identical to those used in the making of knives, differing mainly in scale. A custom sword project simply takes more time, more planning, more materials, more knowledge, more space and more patience than the making of a knife.

There are several ways to "define" a sword. I have settled on a standard *physical* definition, as follows:

A sword is an edged weapon with a usable blade length of at least 18 inches and with a handle shorter than the blade.

This definition is useful, allowing a very specific distinction to be drawn between a sword and a big knife, and it very clearly distinguishes the sword from the various forms of the spear by limiting handle length. However, this explanation lacks the flexibility to distinguish between different *kinds* of blades and does not take into account the differences of personal fighting styles or physical stature.

One way to avoid this dilemma is to define a sword *in terms of the person* using it:

A sword is an edged weapon with a usable blade length at least equal to the measurement from the user's elbow to the outstretched fingertips and with a handle shorter than the blade.

Complete outfit in knightly profile, wire wrapped, showing Japanese influence in construction detail—all stainless. (VerHoeven photo)

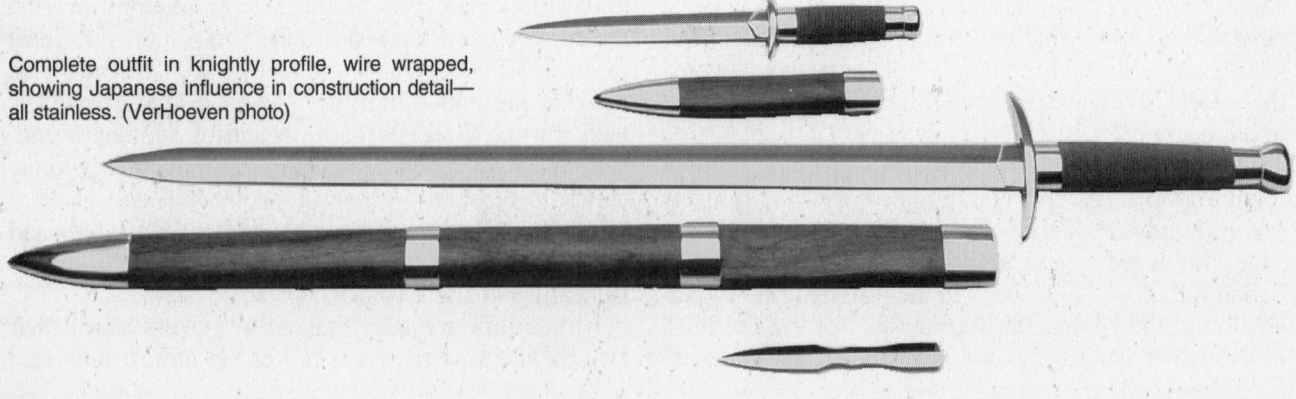

This definition takes personal size into account and is useful when tailoring a sword to an individual who is either much larger or much smaller than average. We are still disregarding any differences in style, however. What about a 17-inch double-edged blade 3½ inches wide? Surely that must qualify as a sword! What about a poniard with a 19-inch blade of quarter-inch round cross-section? Is that an edged weapon? Can it truly be called a sword?

In practice, most of us use the first definition most frequently: an 18-inch blade. Shorter blades which are wide swords generally come in two classes—bashers and wall-hangers.

A basher is a cheaply made sword-like object that is intended for theatrical use or reenactments. Such pieces universally have no edge, and most cannot be sharpened because of the thickness of the blade at the edge. Many are not even made of steel at all. They are intended for bashing, for sword-like play, and are purposefully dull to prevent injuries. They are often well constructed, but some incorporate poor materials and are useless as real weapons except as bludgeons.

Making swords is tough and dirty work, entailing daily health hazards and some danger, and requiring both know-how and facilities. (Berquist photo)

enough to be used as swords we may call short swords. Weapons designed strictly for thrusting, with no edges for cutting, may be referred to as poniards up to a blade length of 22 inches.

Finally, there's the *functional* definition of what a sword is, as follows:

> A sword is an edged weapon with an 18-inch blade that can be depended upon to perform its design function when in the hands of a skilled user.

It follows that items that look like swords, but which cannot be depended upon to perform their design function, are not swords. These visual representations of

A wall-hanger is just what its name implies. It is a sword-like object which is pretty—at least from a distance—but lacks one or more of the characteristics a using sword must have. There is often embellishment on the blade and a complicated looking guard, but the tang might be merely a piece of all-thread welded to a stubby tang. Many such will break on the first blow if an attempt is ever made to actually use them; good ones might go three blows.

Sadly, most commercial swords made today, and some handmade ones, are bashers and wall-hangers.

The functional definition says "...when in the hands of a skilled user." I am often asked by a potential customer,

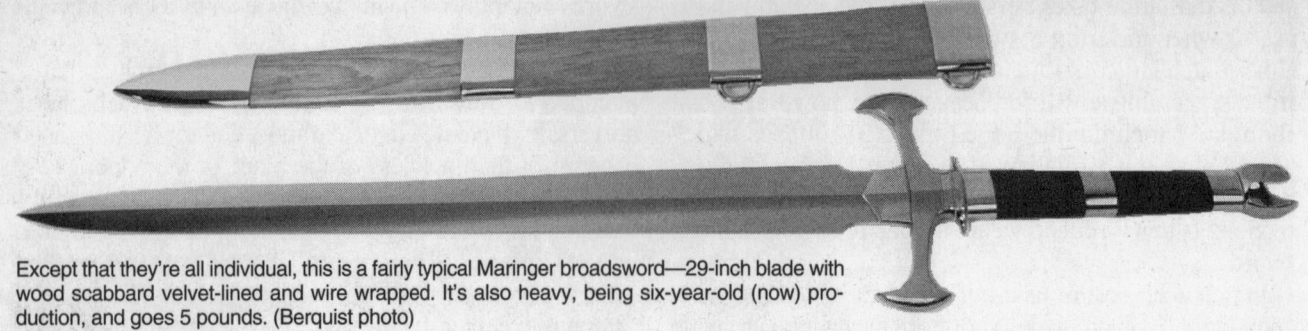

Except that they're all individual, this is a fairly typical Maringer broadsword—29-inch blade with wood scabbard velvet-lined and wire wrapped. It's also heavy, being six-year-old (now) production, and goes 5 pounds. (Berquist photo)

It helps to be a bit whimsical, at swordplay and as a swordmaker—this art adorns letterhead and T-shirts.

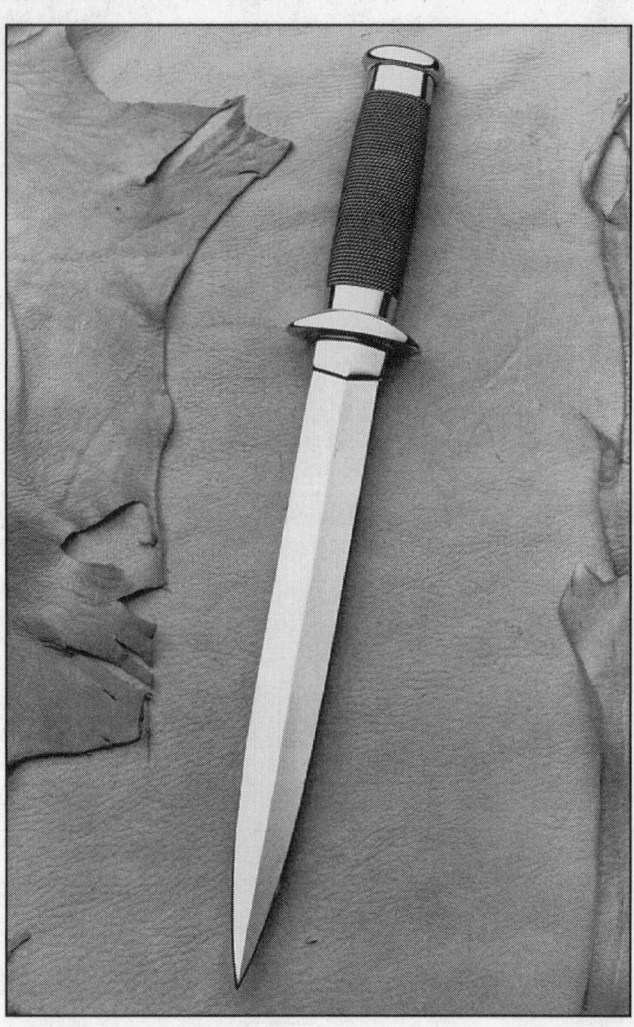

The big dagger is part of the sword business, made either *en suite* with a sword or for fellows who want the style and the class, but don't have the really deep pockets. (Weyer photo)

"What can this sword do?" I sometimes answer that the sword can do nothing; it is merely an inanimate object. The real question is, "What can you do with it?"

In a sword fight, a novice with an excellent sword will almost certainly lose to a master with a poor sword. The value of training and practice must never be underestimated. An excellent sword, for example, may have useful features an excellent swordsman would notice and use, and a novice never. Only swordsmen, perhaps, can fully experience a good sword.

Finally, there is no way to get around this: The design function of a sword is to cleave human flesh and bone. It may be repugnant to contemplate, but all swords of whatever ethnic background or method of manufacture have this feature in common. They are long slivers of steel specifically designed to kill or dismember human beings in the quickest, most efficient manner possible. Any sword-like item which cannot perform this function is not a sword, but merely a visual representation of a sword.

TRENDS

It got to be time for a change, so we changed this section of the book a little. The knives are still the same, but rather than subdivide them by function—hunters, fighters and so forth—we did it by size and by other criteria unrelated to function.

There are rare exceptions, but those aside, the knives you see here, the hundreds of knives you see here, are all handmade or benchmade, the difference being mostly whether or not the knives are produced one at a time or in series or batches.

There are, as with all human activities, extremes in knifemaking. At one end, we have guys who produce knives without power tools; at the other, knifemakers who get as much of the job done as possible without getting their hands on it. The philosophical difference is immense, especially when the knifemakers are talking to their customers. The knives, however, are pretty much the same.

We're only showing you a selection of the photos we get. There are a lot of fine knives that are produced and delivered each year, but never photographed. We're missing some, but not many.

Enjoy them. That's what they are for. That's what this book is for.

Ken Warner

The Burgeoning Sword 64	The Primitive Edge 111
Investment-Grade Knives 70	That Foreign Look 114
Field-Grade Knives 79	The Medium Knife 118
The World of Really Small 84	The Folding Knife 124
Big Knives 88	The Automatic Knife 133
The Elegant Knife 100	The Upgraded Knife 136
Small Knives 106	

TRENDS

THE BURGEONING SWORD

IN FIVE YEARS, this century will be gone, passed into history. It then will be eighty-seven years since the U.S. Army designed, but never used, its last sword—one patterned close to the ninety-two-year-old British 1908 saber—and right at fourteen decades since Japan's samurai were forbade their katanas.

Tactically, on either the personal or military level, the sword died before or during our own Civil War, shot out of its saddle by the rifled musket and the revolving pistol. It remained very useful ceremonially; some men still fought with swords; but the sword's effectively been gone for a good long time.

If, however, the trends continue, the new 21st century will see more swords than now on view. They won't be military, even if some space-opera writers claim the sword is ideal for spaceship boarding actions since, like the neutron bomb, the sword hurts only people. And at least in the early decades, 21st century swords won't be worn and used in public by civilians. They will, however, be there. Consider:

● Americans are buying ten or twenty, perhaps forty, times as many swords—or sword-like objects—as they did when this august journal opened its pages in 1981. (Not an objective study, but this is the educated guess of a careful observer and good guesser.)

● Companies which did not exist even ten years ago now sell (three of them, at least) literally millions of dollars worth of swords every year—some mere decorations, a lot quite serviceable.

● Independent craftsmen, the sort who once made one sword and quit, now specialize in swords. They are getting $1,500, $5,000, even $10,000 for finely made working swords, neither crusted with jewels nor laden with precious metals. Inevitably, some are getting pretty big bucks for inadequate swords, but it was always so.

● There are several partnerships or coalitions of craftsmen doing swords in the U.S. to the same high craft standards as the handmade knife.

● To the world centers of swordmaking, like Japan and Iran and Italy and, now, the United States, we can add India and the Philippines and China and doubtless more to come.

All this means there's money in it. Generally, such trends, having gotten going, continue. We're not looking at hula-hoops or pet rocks, but a genuine effort to meet a public demand—or at least a request.

Of course, we're getting the swords without the fencing masters, without the study, without the training serious sword use absolutely requires. That is probably a good thing—what would a large number of trained swordsmen do in or to this society?

The swords are coming, the swords are coming—and a lot of them are here.

Ken Warner

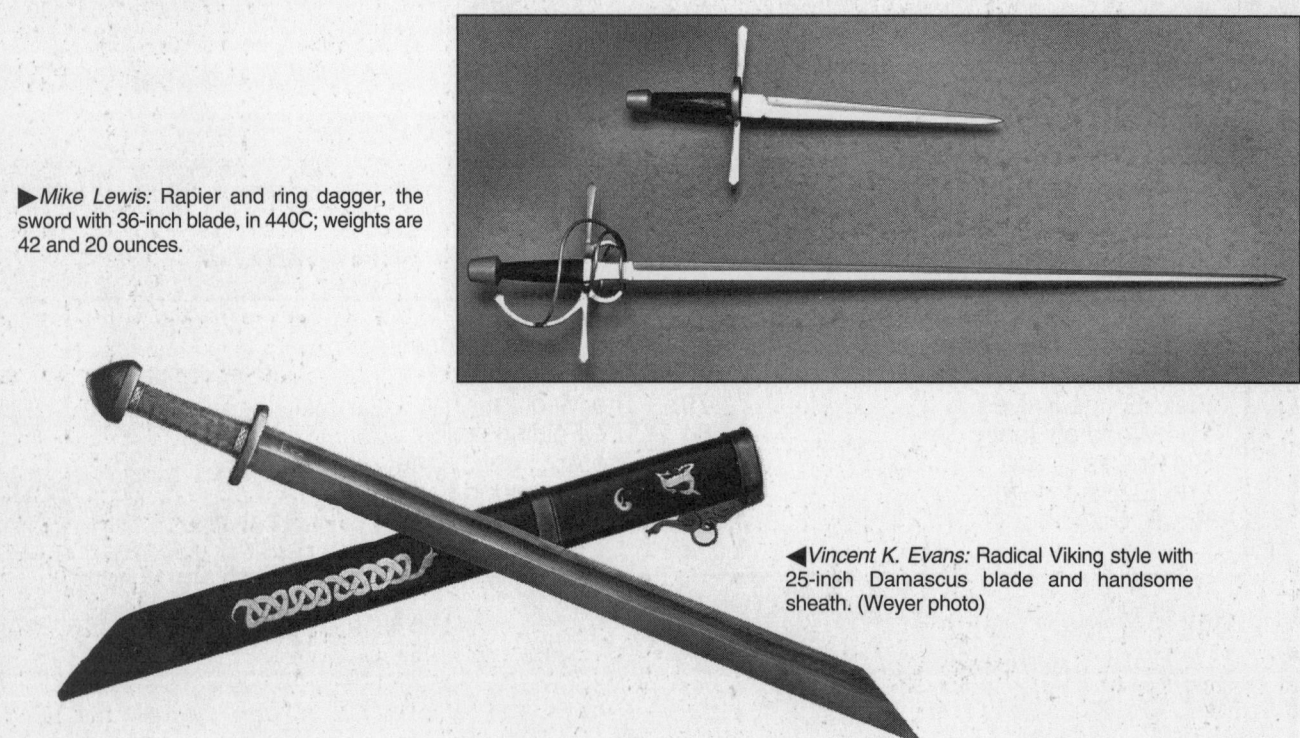

▶*Mike Lewis:* Rapier and ring dagger, the sword with 36-inch blade, in 440C; weights are 42 and 20 ounces.

◀*Vincent K. Evans:* Radical Viking style with 25-inch Damascus blade and handsome sheath. (Weyer photo)

THE BURGEONING SWORD

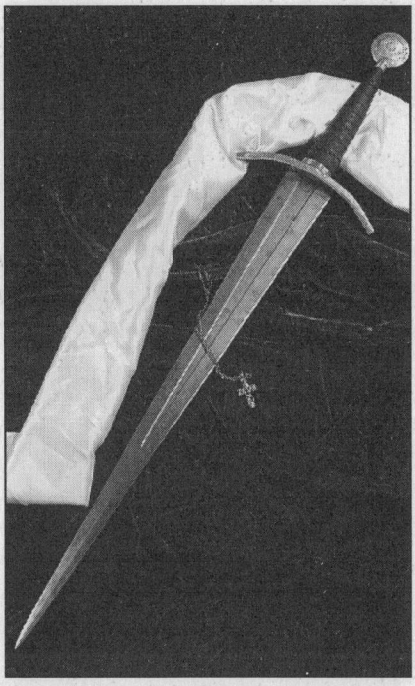

▲*Robert L. Howell:* Mid-15th century styling in 1095 with brass and lots of silver. Sword is artificially aged.

Wm. Dean Mitchell: All-out tulwar is a "whisperer"—internal channels hold gold balls which roll about as the sword moves. The smith demonstrates the complex blade's flexibility; the grip is correctly shaped, but not finished traditionally. (Sword photo by Weyer)

▼*Douglas D. Brack:* A 20th-century design—diamond cross-section 440C blade, Micarta grip, cast nickel-silver guard and pommel, and red spacers. (Fitzgerald photo)

▲*Damascus-USA:* Opulence in bird's-eye Damascus on a 35-inch katana fitted by Don Polzien. (Weyer photo)

FIFTEENTH EDITION **65**

TRENDS

▲ *Joel Mason:* Does not make swords, but creates and styles sword fights.

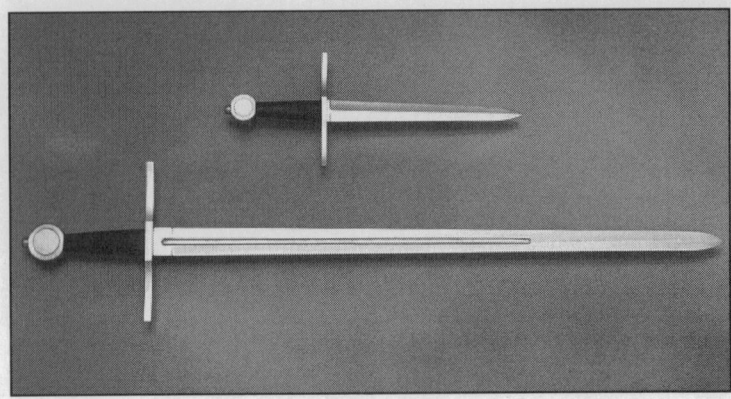

▲ *Mike Lewis:* Sword and dagger pair in 14th-century shape—440C, brass and walnut. The 32-inch sword weighs 52 ounces.

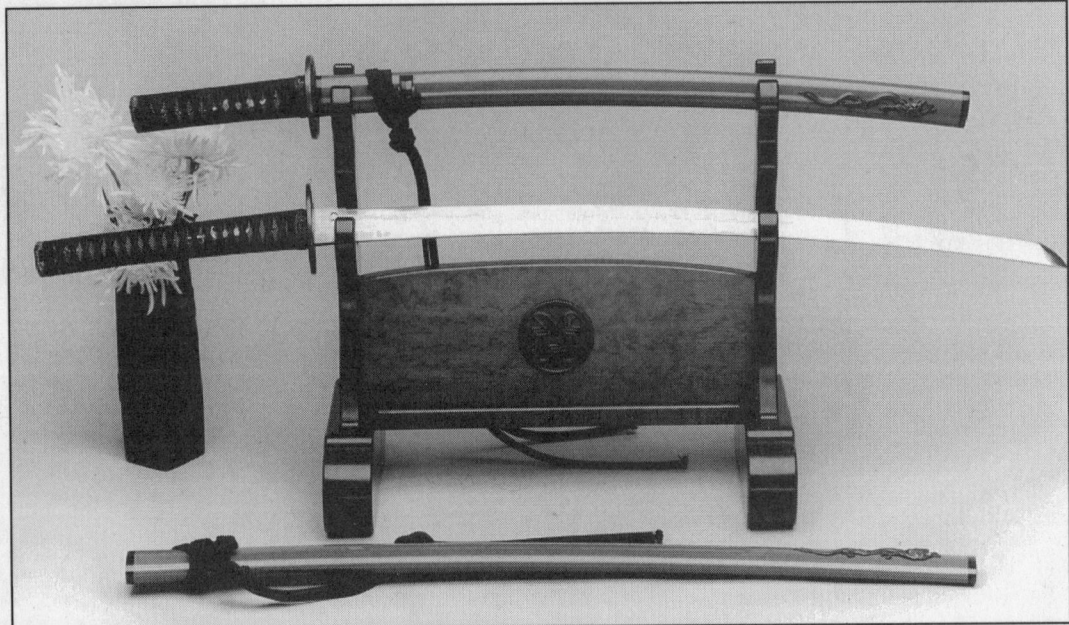

▲ *Scott Slobodian:* A pair of Japanese-style swords in 1045, styled in sterling, copper, iron, rayskin, buffalo horn and exotic wood. (Slobodian photo)

▲ *Fred Lohman:* Does not make swords, but purveys stuff and services to those who do.

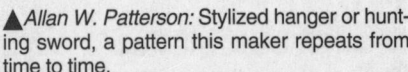

▲ *Allan W. Patterson:* Stylized hanger or hunting sword, a pattern this maker repeats from time to time.

THE BURGEONING SWORD

▶ *Frank J. Dilluvio:* Heavy short broadsword has 19-inch Damascus blade, wire-wrapped grip—28 inches overall. (Weyer photo)

◀ *J. Reese Weiland, Jr.:* Athletic lady demonstrates a mildly fantastic broadsword built for civilized barbarians. (Silhouettes photo)

▼ *Joseph E. Knuth:* Big barbarian sword—47 1/2 inches overall—in 440C, 304 stainless, brass and ebony, also has opals set in gold. (Weyer photo)

▶ *Jimmy L. Fikes:* Short sword in dha-style has 15-inch blade and 15 1/2-inch wrapped handle, and is forged in chisel-edged 5160. chisel-edged. (Weyer photo)

▼ *Philip L. Hagen:* Called "Scarab," this straight sword, nearly 40 inches overall, is a 20th-century design. (Weyer photo)

▶ *Jim Ferguson (Downey, CA):* Battle pair in nickel Damascus—big tools at 24 and 28 inches overall—sterling mounted and handled in ebony. (Slobodian photo)

FIFTEENTH EDITION

TRENDS

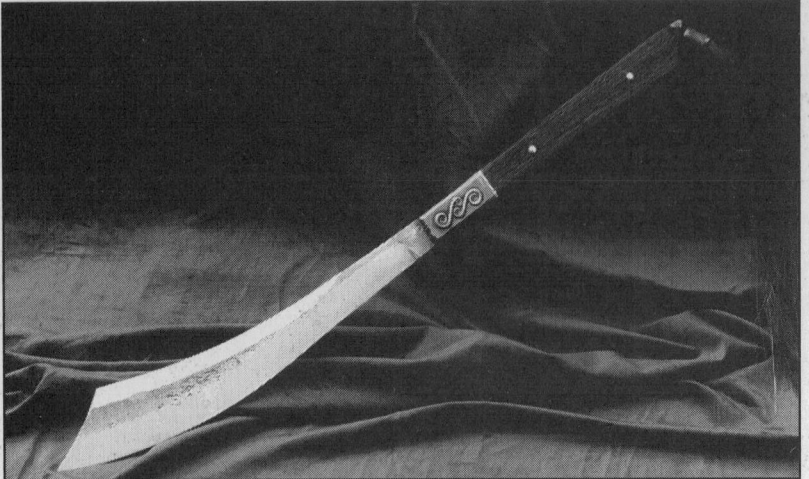

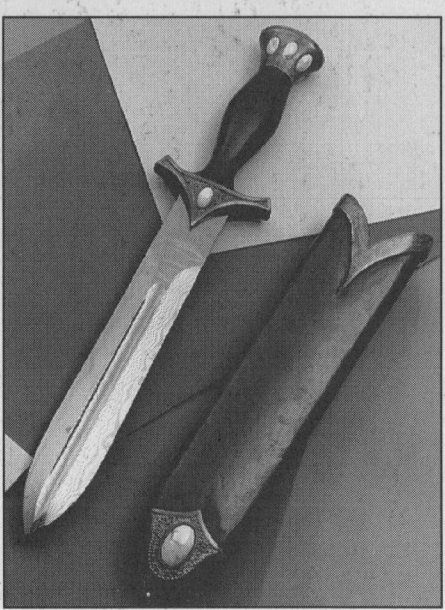

▲ *Don Fogg:* Forge-textured high carbon blade has 25-inch cutting edge. Sword is a Moro style; bolster scroll is forged.

▶ *Wm. R. "Bill" Herndon:* Fantasy short sword at 13 inches in Damascus, bronze and ebony with turquoise. (Weyer photo)

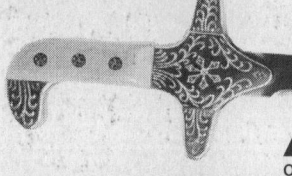

▲▼ *Phill Hartsfield:* A Saudi sword in A2—28-inch blade of $1/8$-inch stock, handled in ivory Micarta and brass.

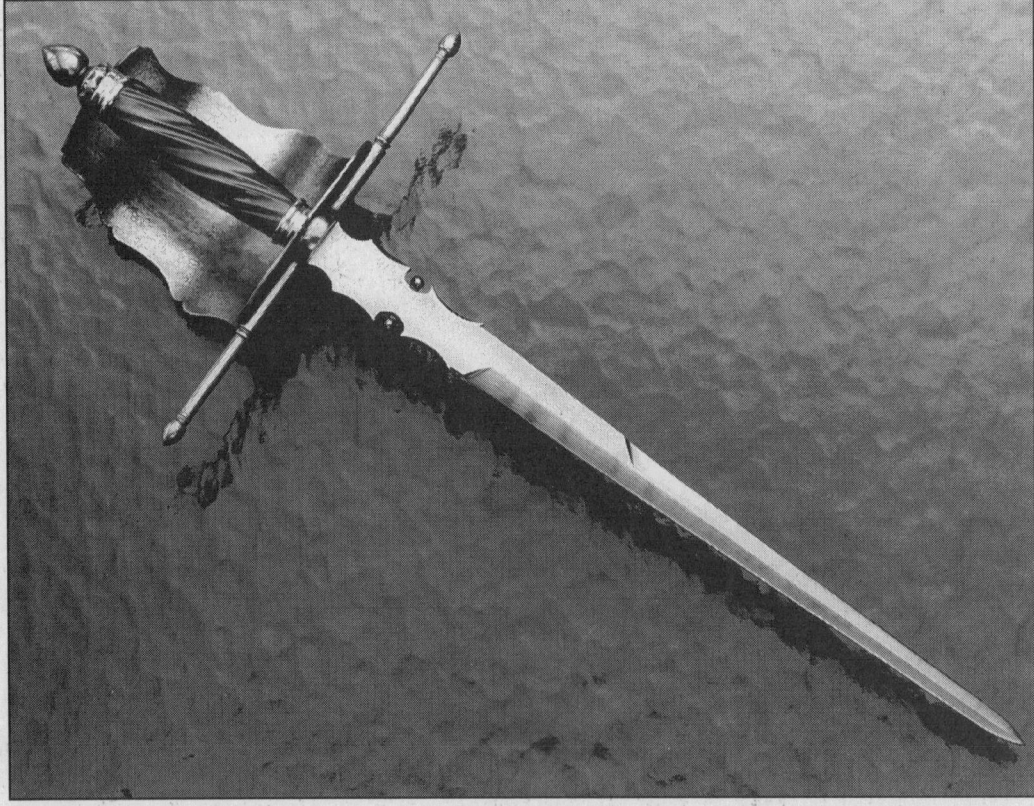

◀ *James E. Porter:* Short sword or lefthand fencing dagger—15-inch blade, delicately styled in Damascus. Handle is amber and stainless. (Weyer photo)

THE BURGEONING SWORD

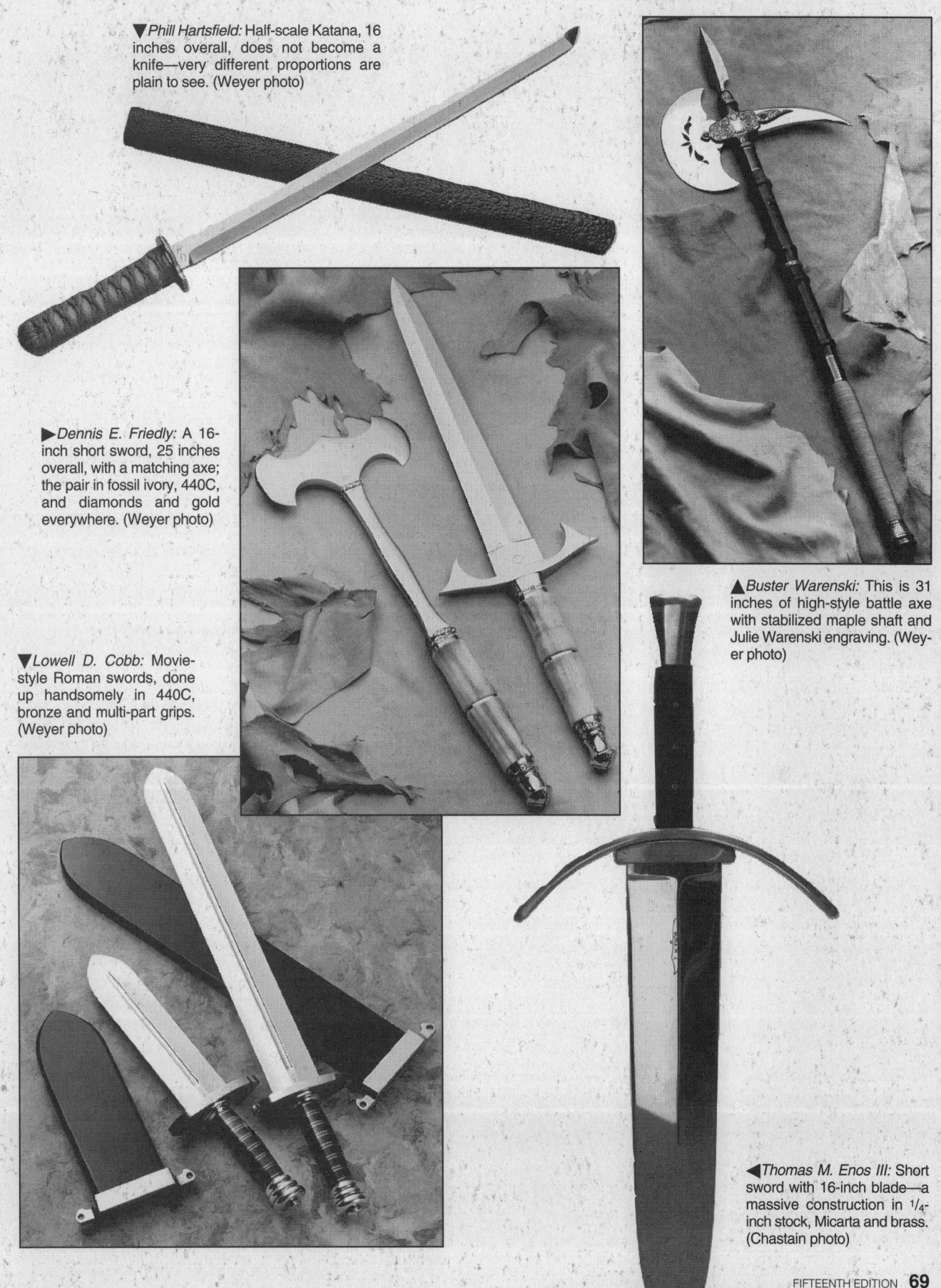

▼*Phill Hartsfield:* Half-scale Katana, 16 inches overall, does not become a knife—very different proportions are plain to see. (Weyer photo)

▶*Dennis E. Friedly:* A 16-inch short sword, 25 inches overall, with a matching axe; the pair in fossil ivory, 440C, and diamonds and gold everywhere. (Weyer photo)

▼*Lowell D. Cobb:* Movie-style Roman swords, done up handsomely in 440C, bronze and multi-part grips. (Weyer photo)

▲*Buster Warenski:* This is 31 inches of high-style battle axe with stabilized maple shaft and Julie Warenski engraving. (Weyer photo)

◀*Thomas M. Enos III:* Short sword with 16-inch blade—a massive construction in 1/4-inch stock, Micarta and brass. (Chastain photo)

FIFTEENTH EDITION 69

TRENDS

INVESTMENT-GRADE KNIVES

WE HAVE TO BE accurate here, so I hope you read this carefully: *Some* of the knives shown here may *not* be investment grade—that's a decision made in the market, not on an editor's yellow pad. *All* of the knives shown here are the investment-grade *type*.

That's why you're not going to see prices here, although we know some of them. A discussion of gent's folders ranging in price at retail from $3,000 to $12,000 could be fascinating, particularly to those of us who think that price range is more for pickup trucks and family cars than pocketknives, but not today.

There are lots—well, some, anyway—of knife buyers who lay down that kind of money with relative alacrity. And what they're buying is charm and style and complete attention to quality detail in distinctively individual creations. That's a mouthful, I agree, but a look close at hand will show you it's an accurate statement.

There are also high-quality knives benchmade in series that are investment-class collectibles. These are the names. The names on the "A list" vary from year to year. Loveless and Lake, for instance, have been on that list for years. Randall was always on the collectible list; now the knives have become investment class.

Why is that? Well, there are people who would tell you dealers helped make a market. There are those—most of them writers or editors—who point to key books and publications. There are a half-dozen factors clearly in play.

But which names make the "A list" is pure chance, a crapshoot, blind luck. Your humble reporter is said by others to have been influential in these matters for thirty years. *Active* for thirty years I'll agree to. *Interesting* for three decades is OK. A fair critic for that time? Probably so. Neither this reporter, however, nor anyone else can claim credit for putting any one name on the "A list."

How about Sylvester Stallone? Neat guy, by all accounts, but was it him or David Morrell, who wrote the original novel, or Jimmy Lile, who made the knife, or Carolco, the movie folks, who designed the posters, that put the Rambo knife up there? Whatever or whichever, none of them had the swat to keep it there.

Although the investment knife scene proceeds by fits and starts, it is growing, in the sense that each year more knifemakers make the step—that is, their knives do—into the big show. The number of patrons—at this level, they are patrons, not customers—varies somewhat in tune with the world financial picture. The number of makers varies by their skill, their talent, their persistence. It's an interesting phenomenon.

What's the difference between an upgraded knife, a fancy knife and an investment-grade knife? Well, an investor looks beyond top quality to an impressive concept carried out to its best expression. If that means gold and diamonds, so be it—an investor will pay. That much you can see in the knives.

The other factor is belief in value and the market. Any market pays what it has to pay to get the goods it wants. If a buyer wants a knife with a $5,000 price tag and is fairly sure someone else will pay $5,000 if he doesn't, he knows the value is there. There are many fine knives very impressively mounted for sale under $1,000 because big-league buyers won't pay more for those knives. And *that* has to do with the first factor—concept and execution.

We said we'd stay away from prices here. That's been our practice in these pages for years. However, it is worth noting that the several dozen knives shown in this presentation aggregate something like $500,000. Most of them have been sold. Fascinating phenomena, these investment-grade knives.

So you have to look at the market. If you have the funds, investment in knives as art and as neat things to own is about as good as thoroughbred horses or Renaissance art, and a whole lot cheaper per piece. Only those engaged daily in the business of buying and selling actually know the prices and the values well enough to bet on them. That may be, besides their splendid good looks, one of the most important things there is about investment knives.

Ken Warner

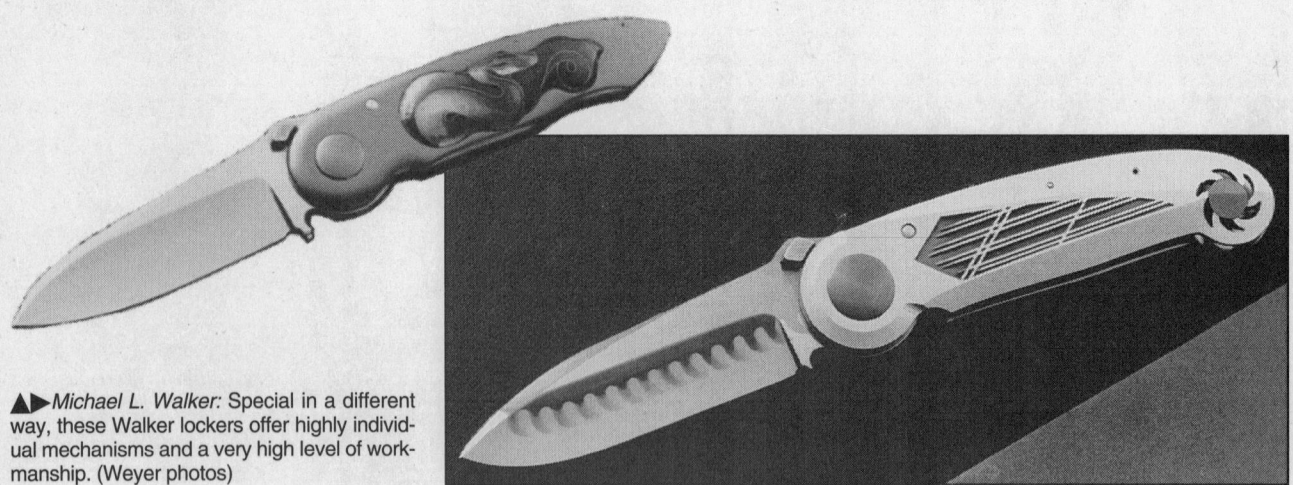

▲▶*Michael L. Walker:* Special in a different way, these Walker lockers offer highly individual mechanisms and a very high level of workmanship. (Weyer photos)

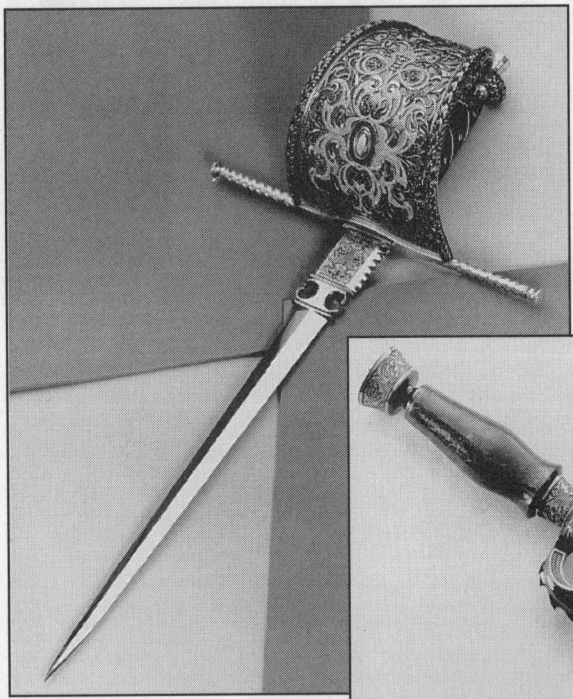

INVESTMENT-GRADE KNIVES

Buster Warenski: Pounds of gold, a lot of diamonds and rubies, and a lot of talent put these three daggers in the big leagues. (Weyer photos)

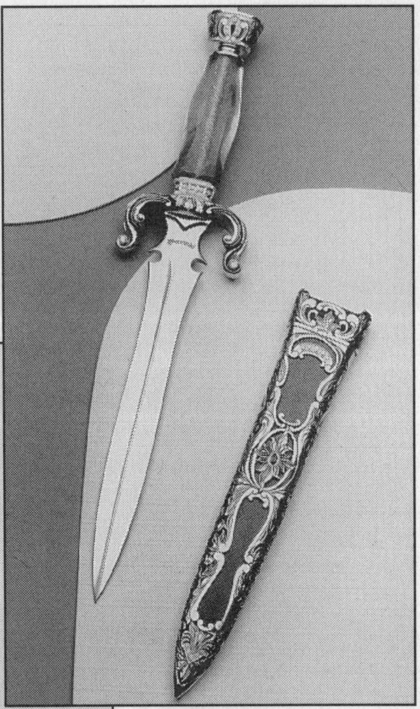

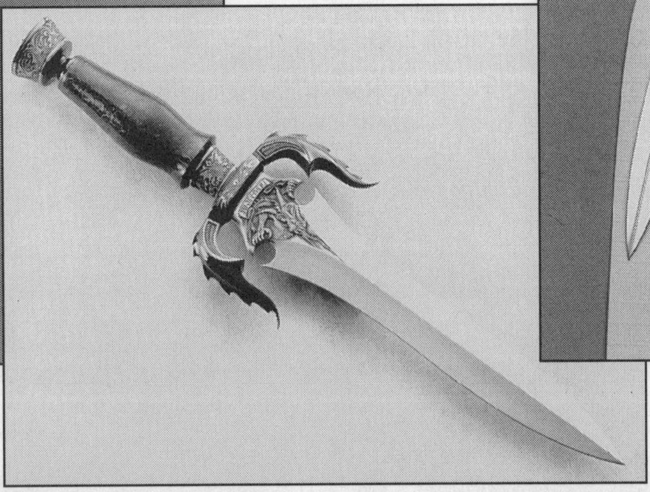

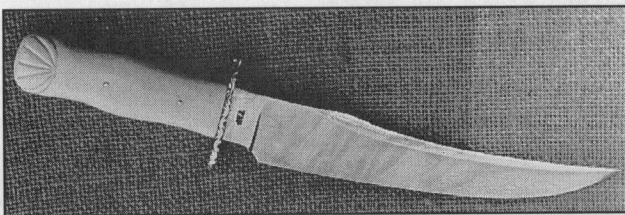

Wm. F. Moran, Jr.: Here is how a special vision works out. These combat knives reflect the quality of their maker, an American knifemaking original himself. (Holter photos)

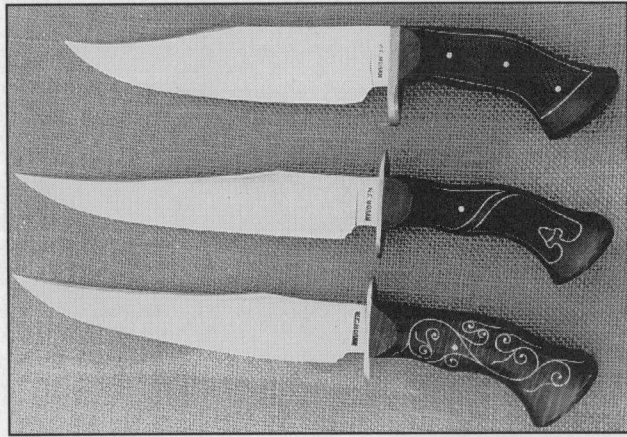

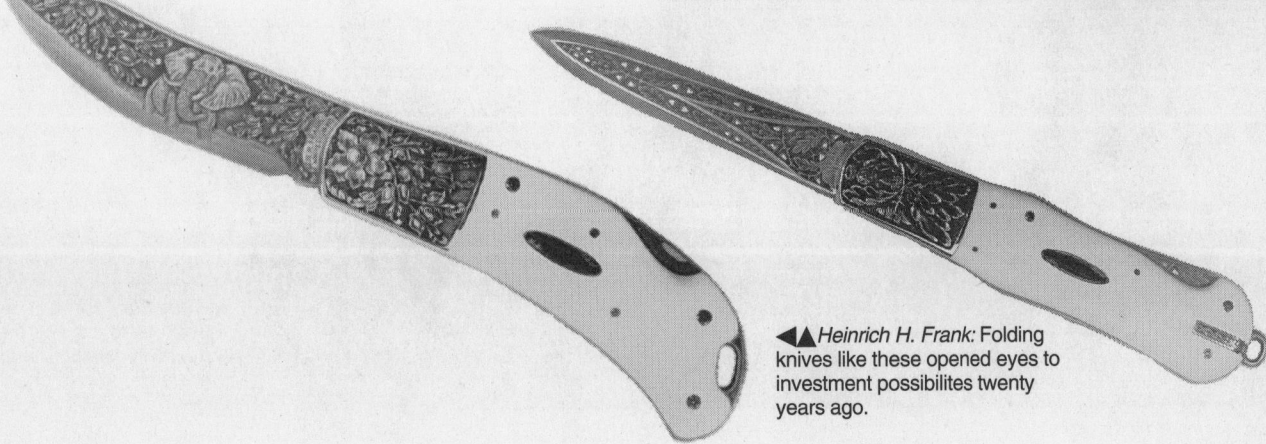

Heinrich H. Frank: Folding knives like these opened eyes to investment possibilites twenty years ago.

FIFTEENTH EDITION 71

TRENDS

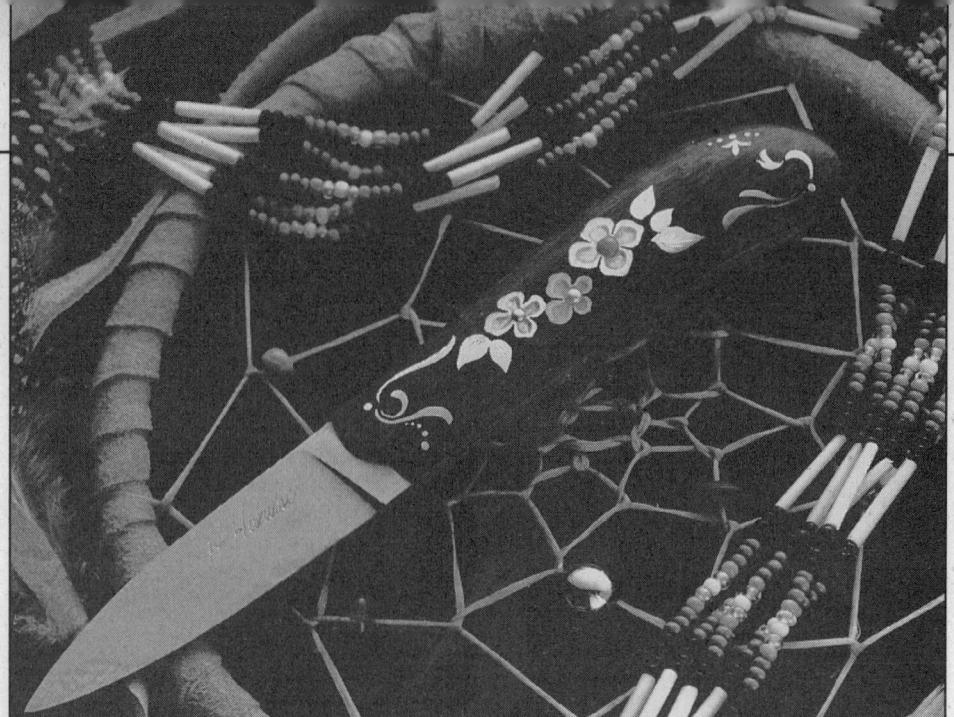

▶ *Harumi Hirayama:* Knives from this maker raised the expectations of taste for makers and buyers. Charm sells. (Tsutsumi photo)

▲▼ *Jim D. Kelso:* Restrained opulence—carved ebony, gold and silver and imagination—surrounds steel by Fogg and by Schwarze.

▼ *Aad V. Rijswijk:* Turquoise-inlaid and gorgeously engraved in a Western frontier motif, this is an outstanding example of the type.

▲ *Frans Van Eldik:* Integral hunter from a wide billet, heavily shaped and engraved by Lovenberg of Liege.

INVESTMENT-GRADE KNIVES

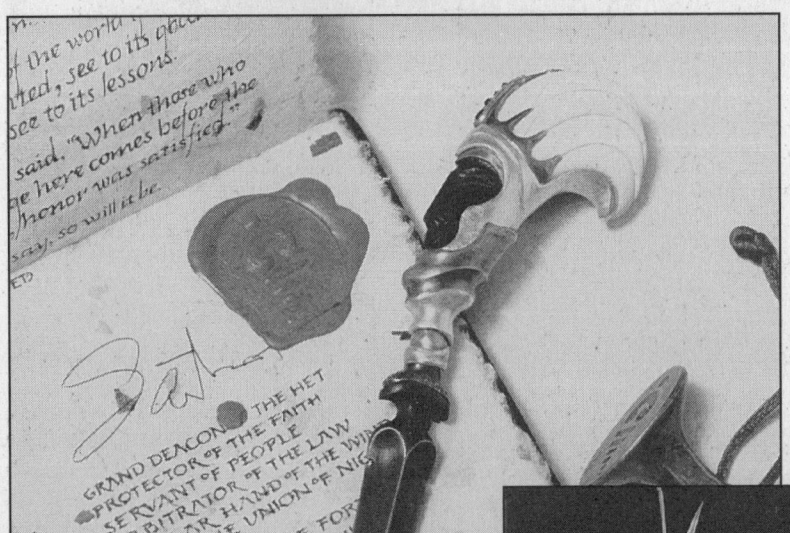

Virgil England: Heard once to say "I'd haul trash before I'd make another 4-inch drop-point hunter," England makes knives for (not from) another world. You see here a Het Temple assassination dagger, a ceremonial hand axe, a stag-handled Hershot fighter, and full samples of the arms of a Hershot Captain of pursuit horse, including shield, mask, scourge, forearm knife. England favors Daryl Meier Damascus and Ron Skaggs gold work.

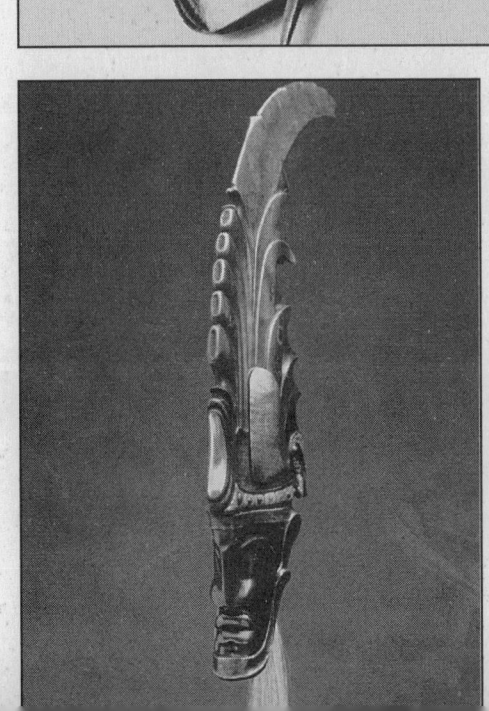

FIFTEENTH EDITION **73**

TRENDS

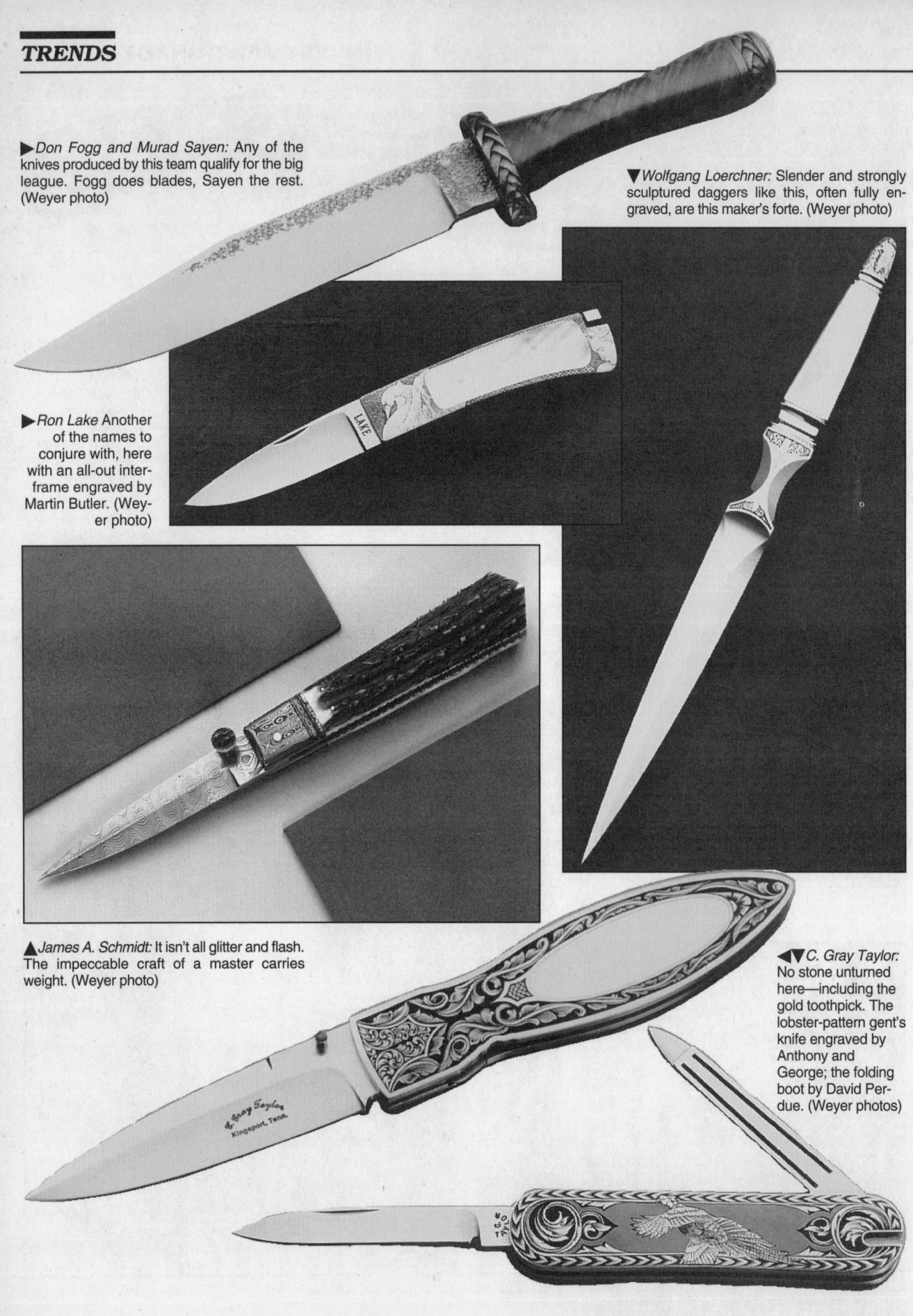

▶ *Don Fogg and Murad Sayen:* Any of the knives produced by this team qualify for the big league. Fogg does blades, Sayen the rest. (Weyer photo)

▼ *Wolfgang Loerchner:* Slender and strongly sculptured daggers like this, often fully engraved, are this maker's forte. (Weyer photo)

▶ *Ron Lake* Another of the names to conjure with, here with an all-out interframe engraved by Martin Butler. (Weyer photo)

▲ *James A. Schmidt:* It isn't all glitter and flash. The impeccable craft of a master carries weight. (Weyer photo)

◀▼ *C. Gray Taylor:* No stone unturned here—including the gold toothpick. The lobster-pattern gent's knife engraved by Anthony and George; the folding boot by David Perdue. (Weyer photos)

74 KNIVES '95

INVESTMENT-GRADE KNIVES

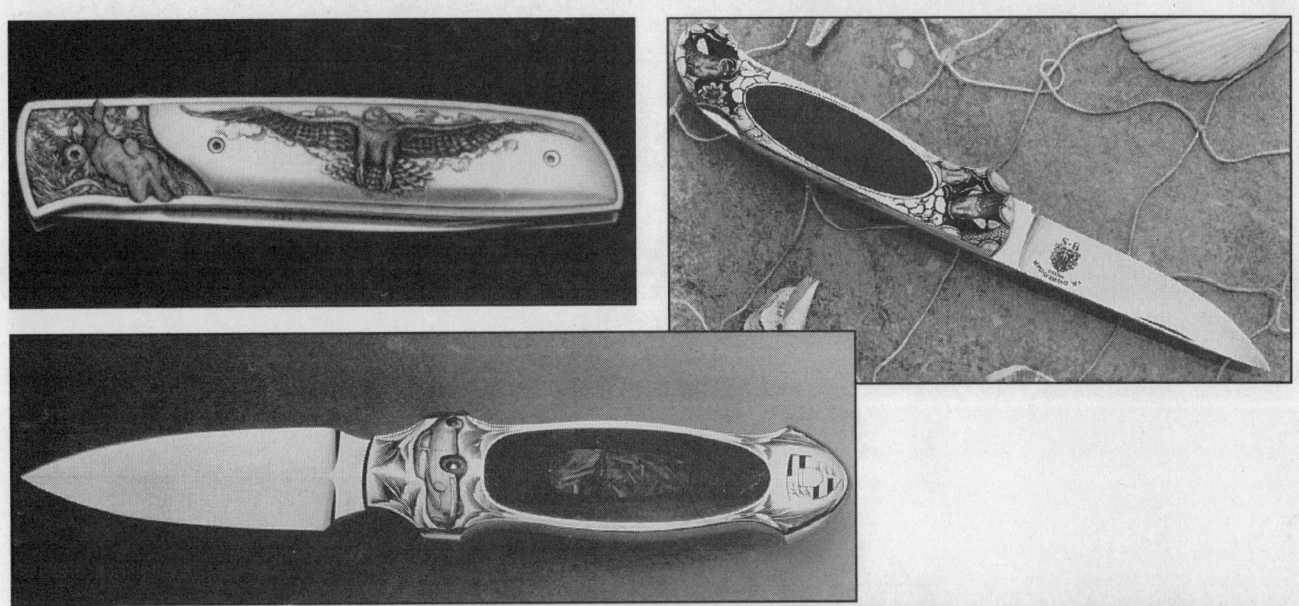

Barrett-Smythe, Ltd.: This company commissions fine knives from a number of makers and sells them like jewelry in a Manhattan store. Shown here: T.R. Overeynder golden carp knife, Wilkerson engraved; Robert Terzuola falcon and rabbit in solid gold, inlaid in gold and silver by Ron Skaggs; a horse's rampant knife by Terzuola and Skaggs; Warren Osborne's dog-and-quail pearl knife engraved by Ron Smith; the Osborne wine maker knife carries Swartley engraving; and the folding dagger with the Porsche/Mercedes theme was made by Scott Sawby and engraved by Ron Skaggs. This is *very* high-end stuff.

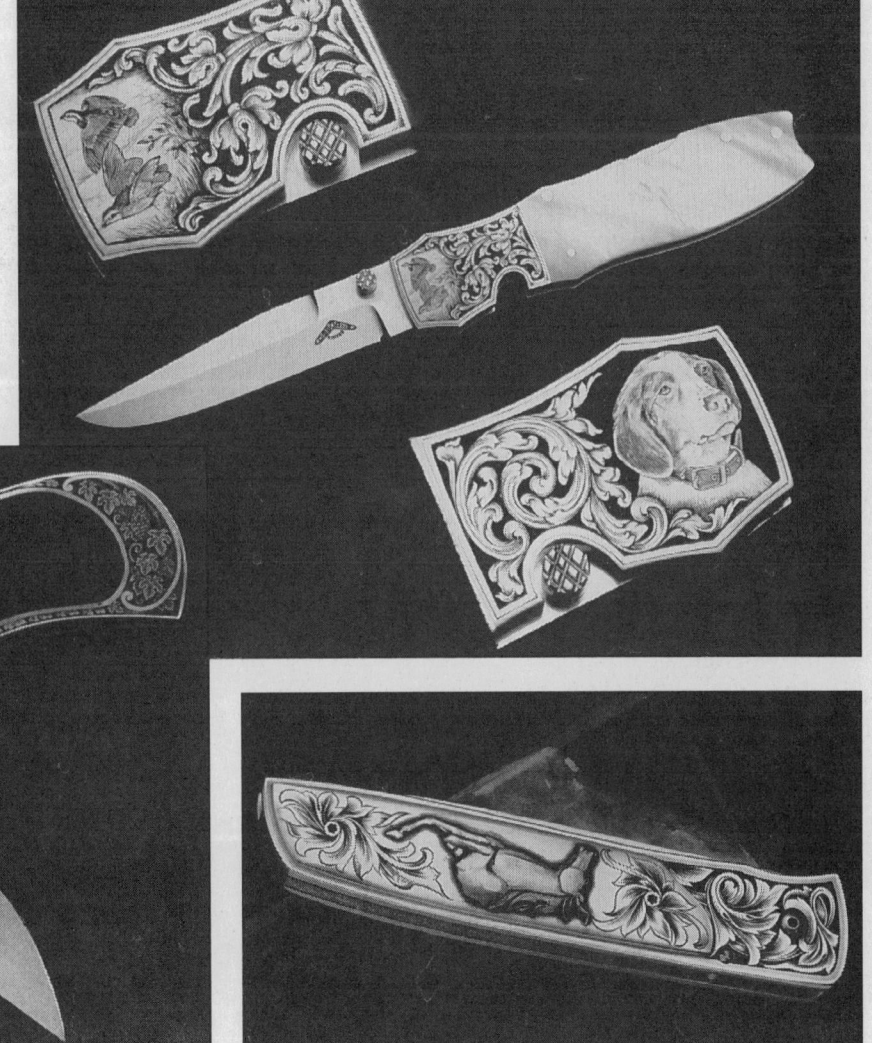

FIFTEENTH EDITION **75**

TRENDS

▲ *Gil Hibben:* For an Art Knife International Show, Hibben did a series of interframes in animal themes, this one the moose. Scrim by Williams; engraved by Shostle. (Weyer photo)

▶ *Richard Spinale:* A full house in pearl, all work by the maker, toothpick included. (Weyer photo)

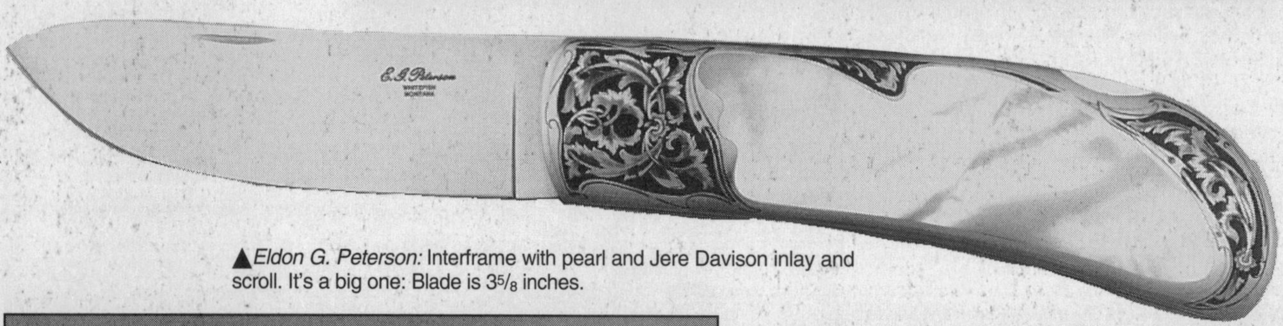

▲ *Eldon G. Peterson:* Interframe with pearl and Jere Davison inlay and scroll. It's a big one: Blade is $3^{5}/_{8}$ inches.

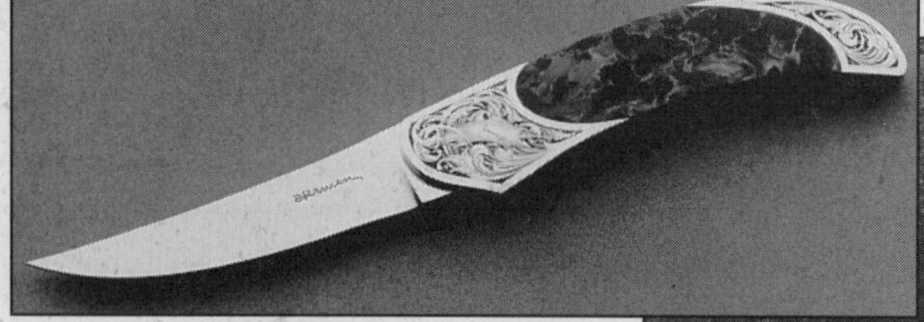

▲▶ *Tim Herman:* The pair of lockers show a frog and a turtle, engraved by Herman himself; in the scroll of the crescent folder Winston Churchill has hidden a billfish. (Weyer photos)

76 KNIVES '95

INVESTMENT-GRADE KNIVES

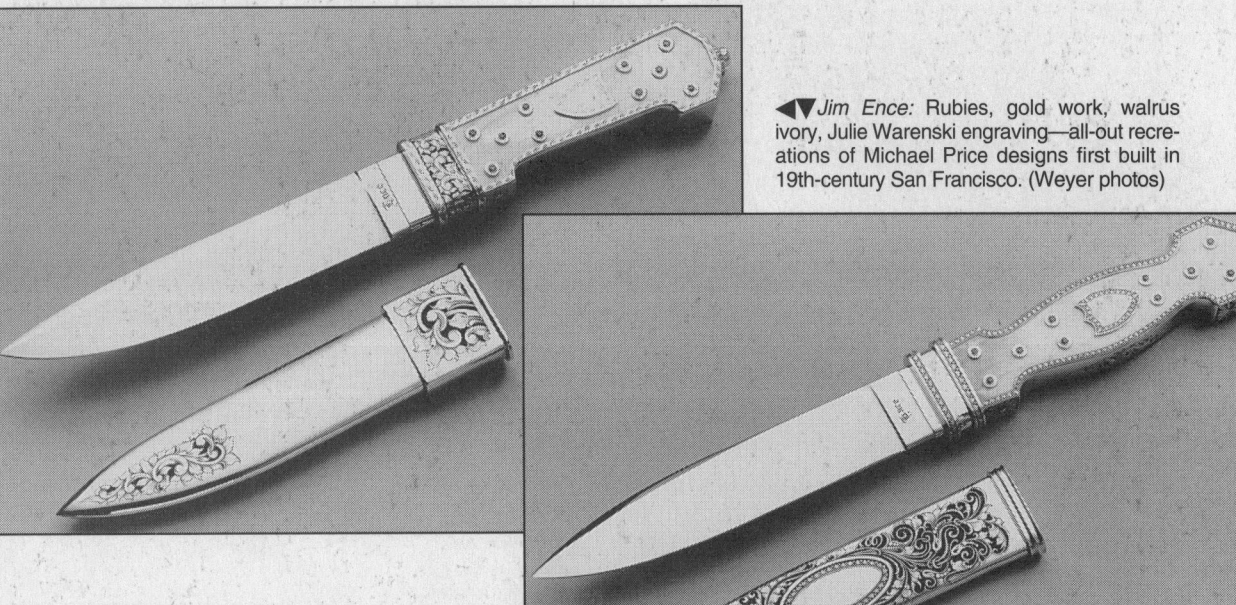

Jim Ence: Rubies, gold work, walrus ivory, Julie Warenski engraving—all-out recreations of Michael Price designs first built in 19th-century San Francisco. (Weyer photos)

Harvey McBurnette: Big folding fighter in 440C and black pearl, all work by the maker. (Weyer photo)

Rick Genovese: Slick folding dagger with stainless frame offers stippled renditions of classical paintings by Steve Lindsay.

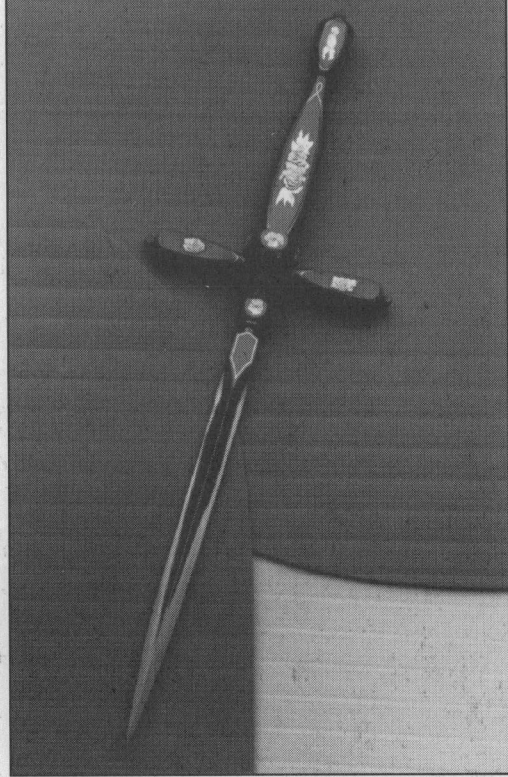

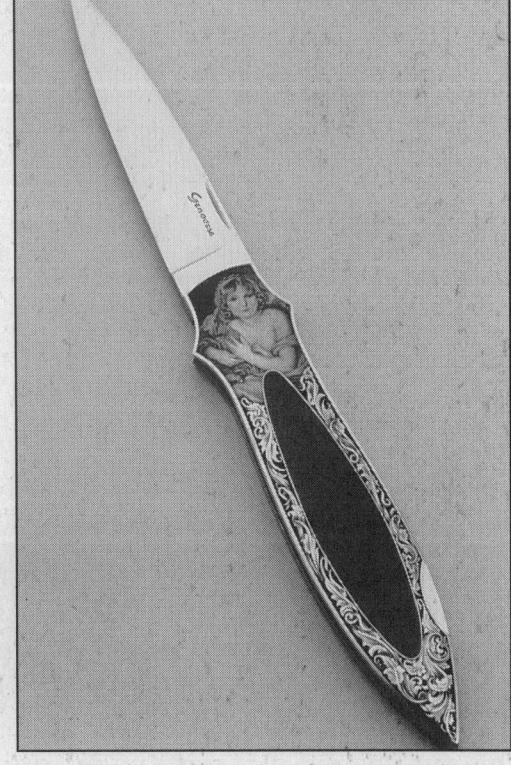

Billy Mace Imel: Slim stylet in black A2 at 10½ inches; gold borders and roses by Ron Skaggs. (Weyer photo)

FIFTEENTH EDITION 77

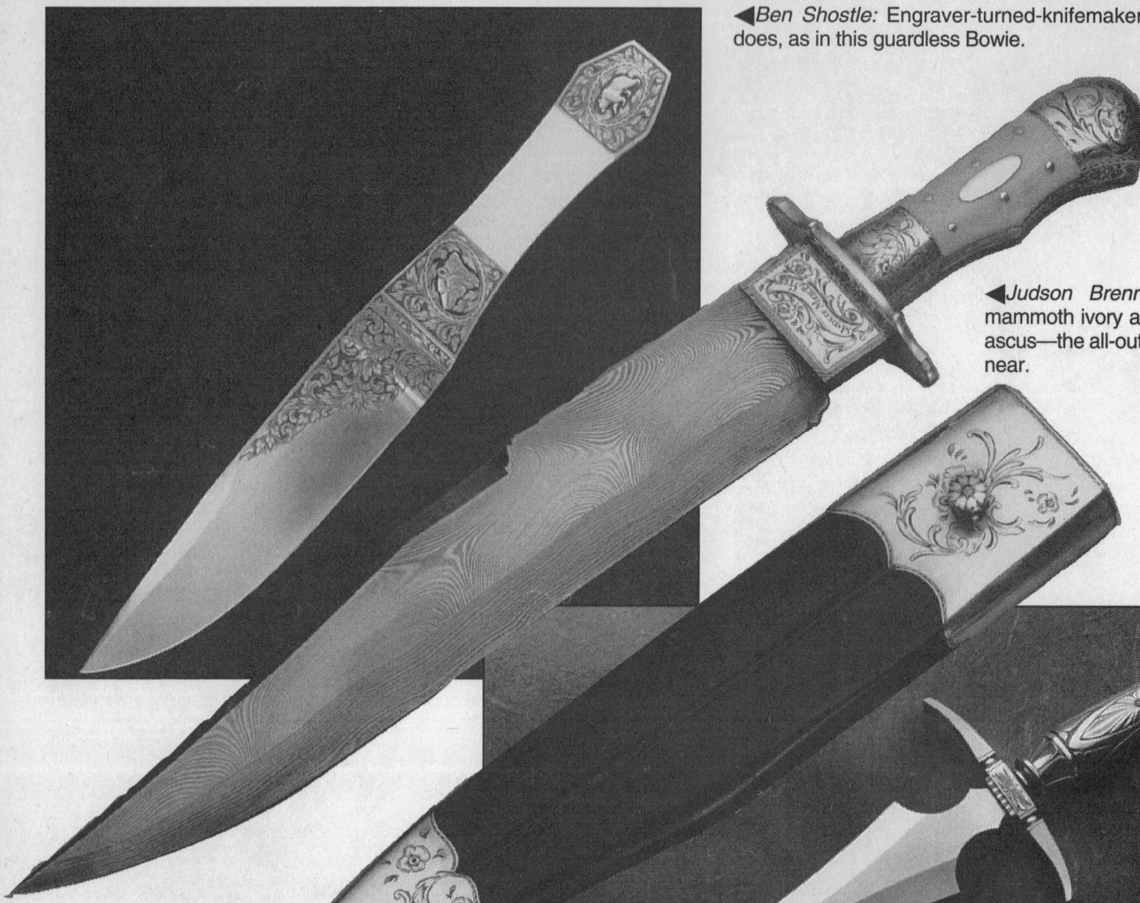

TRENDS

◀ *Ben Shostle:* Engraver-turned-knifemaker can load it up and does, as in this guardless Bowie.

◀ *Judson Brennan:* Sterling silver, mammoth ivory and Daryl Meier Damascus—the all-out Bowie's time may be near.

▲ *Douglas Casteel:* Big dagger in stainless and bronze, all carved by the maker. (Weyer photo)

◀ *James Batson:* If the American Bladesmith Society's dreams can come true, knives with this spirit and feel will do it—all Damascus set off with ivory and sterling silver. (Weyer photo)

TRENDS

FIELD-GRADE KNIVES

AREN'T THEY ALL field grade? Well, we certainly hope they all can cut, but *field grade* as we use it here means something else.

We're talking about presentation, about finish, about the selection of surfaces for tone and color—mostly dull, mostly rough. We're talking a *look*.

How it goes is the maker—or the factory, because there are a *lot* of factory knives in field grades—picks a pattern for one serious use or other, then finishes the blade in sandblasted stainless, or black Teflon, with rough-surfaced grip and a tough demeanor. Often the sheath set-up will be what is called "tactical."

It's not necessary to root through many catalogs to find there are standard finishes and field finishes—same knife, different surface, probably a different sheath. And to find what we could call "ruggedized" standard patterns is pretty easy, too.

There's a bit more than style here—not a lot more, mind you. For generations and centuries, we have taken bright and shiny knives to the woods and on the trail and they worked. So why unshine them?

Because it's *military*, sort of. As the Long Hunters of the 18th century did, crossing their Dark and Bloody Grounds, modern scouts and infiltrators, in real life as in the movies, run as little risk as they can of being spotted because they're carrying something shiny. The field-grade knife—there are, by the way, a myriad of other field-grade things out there, like guns, for one—doesn't draw attention to itself.

Obviously, most field-graded patterns fall into the tactical or defense or all-purpose slots. What to do for hunters is now under examination. The factories are moving toward injection moulding in hunter patterns as well as tactical patterns. Individual knifemakers get that look with Micarta. And then there are the perfectly plain—full or stick tang, brush finish, wood handle, no guard or bolster—designs knifemakers have always made and which factories are copying.

You could say, in fact, that Corbet Sigman was a recent pathfinder for those seeking a style for hunters' field-grade knives. Years ago, he introduced his $60 knives. They were handsome, simple, full-tang shapes—ten of them at the beginning—with wood slabs and impeccable grinds handsome in any company. In Sigman's case, there was a truly unlooked-for result: As soon as they heard about them, his best customers all ordered one each of every new pattern. That meant that hundreds of field-grade knives will never see the field.

Is that true for the bulk of field-grade cutlery, do you suppose? Very likely so, but not more so than with other kinds of knives. Knife customers buy more kitchen knives than they cook with and a lot of pocketknives go from the hardware store straight into the bureau drawer. So the field-grade knife is legitimately part of our scene, as you can see here.

Ken Warner

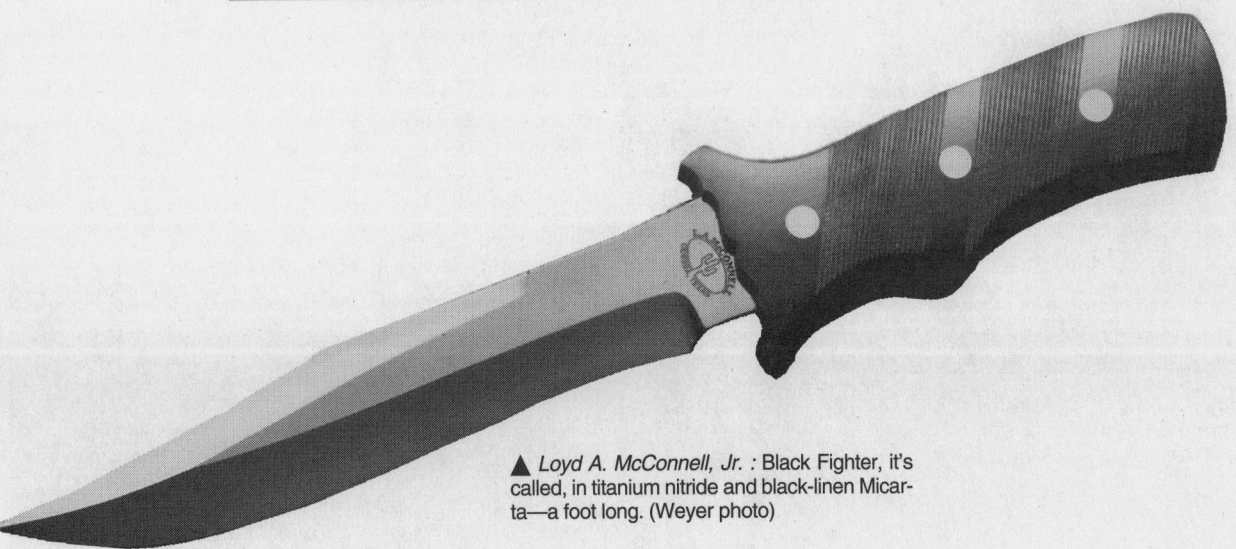

▲ *Loyd A. McConnell, Jr.:* Black Fighter, it's called, in titanium nitride and black-linen Micarta—a foot long. (Weyer photo)

TRENDS

▶ *Ken Largin:* Choice of blade profiles in utility fighters—4-inch blades and wood slabs. (Weyer photo)

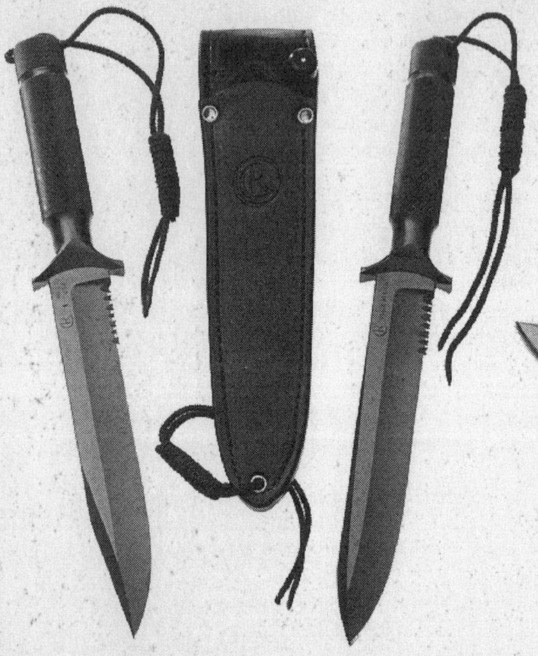

▲▼ *Allen Elishewitz:* Nicely dulled, this pair of single-edge fighters demonstrates field grades can vary.

▲ *Chris Reeve:* All Parkerized steel—can't get much more field grade than that and the look is there. (Weyer photo)

▼ *Robert Rippy:* This is the Tactical Backup—grip and blade back grooved against slippage and sold with hide-out holster. (Box photo)

▲ *Jerry L. Snell:* Bead-blasted fighter blade at 5½ inches offers an edge and a half. (Weyer photo)

FIELD-GRADE KNIVES

◄ *Ken Davis:* Burly chute knife in 440C and black Micarta.

◄ *Chuck Stapel:* A shiny smatchet is a contradiction in terms; this is one of ten in sandblasted Micarta and stainless.

▲ *Jim Hammond:* A folding fighter micro bead-blasted in ATS-34 and Micarta. (Weyer photo)

▲ *Melvin T. Dunn:* Linen Micarta grip, D2 blade—a working sidelock folder. (Weyer photo)

▲ *Phil Boguszewski:* Townsend design takes a titanium-handled folding dagger to field grade. (Weyer photo)

► *Ed Halligan:* Tanto in field grade—cord-wrapped grip on a 6-inch blade. (Weyer photo)

TRENDS

▲ *Barry M. and Phillip G. Jones:* Canvas Micarta and multi-position sheath—a flat-ground D2 field-grade dagger. (Armontrout photo)

▲ *Derek Fraley:* Built for the field, four same-sized hunters handled in Micarta. (Weyer photo)

▲ *Ed Stokes:* Trailing-point hollow-ground hunter in 440C and Micarta laminte. (Box photo)

▲ *Don Maxwell:* Ebony slabs on a short and slick utility blade. (Weyer photo)

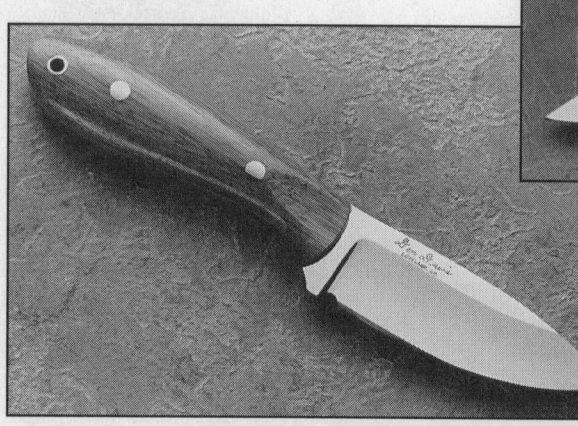

◀ *Don Davis:* Field grade need not mean unfinished, as this padouk-gripped graceful hunter shows. (Weyer photo)

▲ *John Greco:* Two-tone handle wrap on a field-pattern tanto. (Weyer photo)

FIELD-GRADE KNIVES

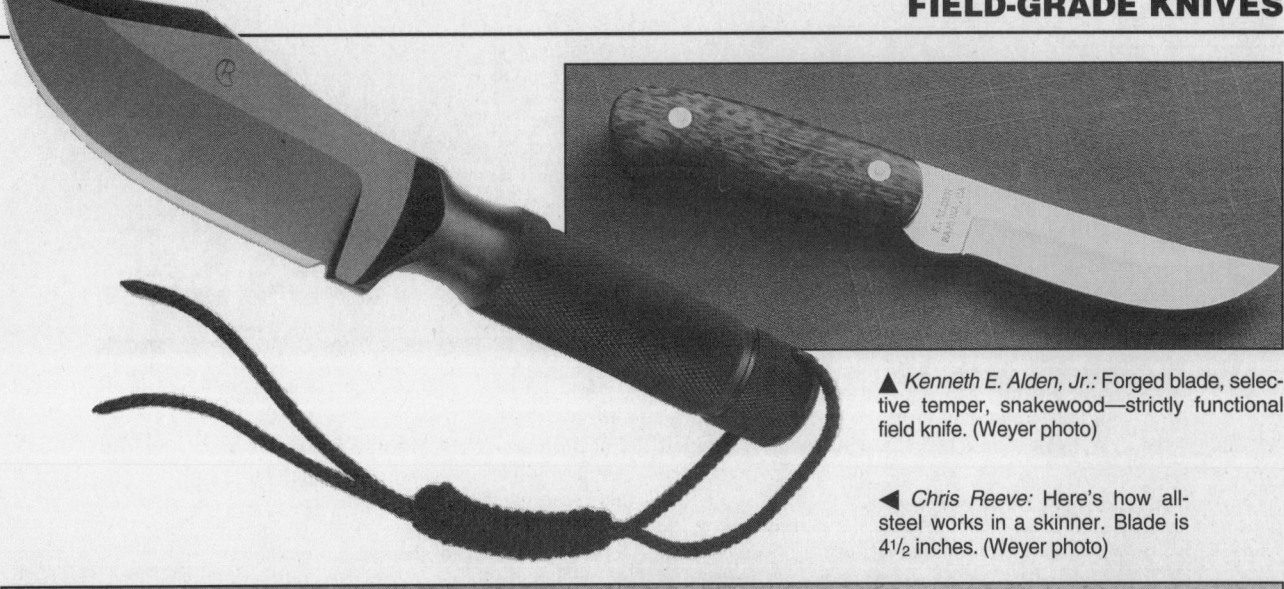

▲ *Kenneth E. Alden, Jr.:* Forged blade, selective temper, snakewood—strictly functional field knife. (Weyer photo)

◀ *Chris Reeve:* Here's how all-steel works in a skinner. Blade is 4½ inches. (Weyer photo)

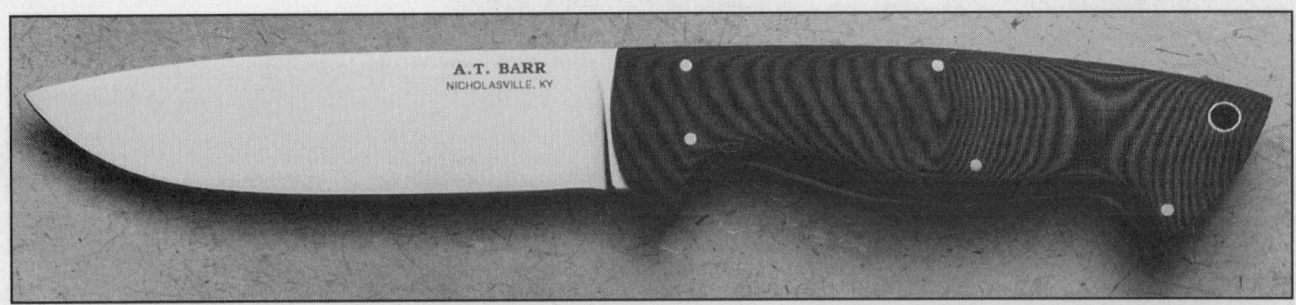

▲ *A.T. Barr:* Sand-blasted grip and 5-inch blade—a utility hunter. (Weyer photo)

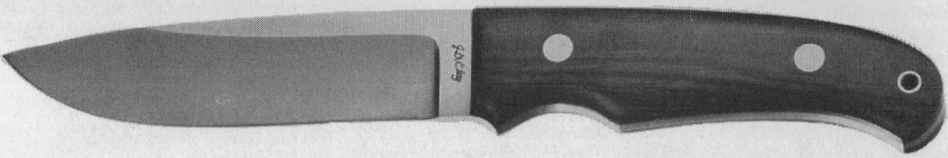

▲▼ *J.D. Clay:* Heavy-duty hunters with plain wood, nicely shaped. (Long photo)

▼ *Robert Rippy:* Styled 5-inch—Micarta is grooved—utility knife, called the Eagle Scout. (Box photo)

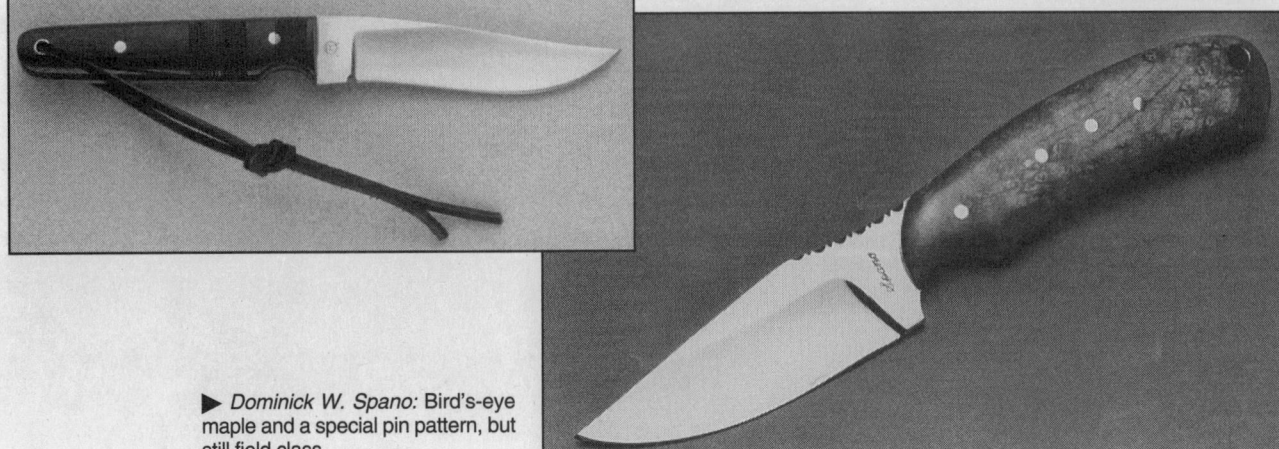

▶ *Dominick W. Spano:* Bird's-eye maple and a special pin pattern, but still field class.

FIFTEENTH EDITION 83

TRENDS

THE WORLD OF REALLY SMALL

THEY DON'T GO away, these miniatures. More examples than ever pass that ultimate test of miniatureness, where without an object of known size also in view you can't tell they're miniature.

To some degree, miniatures follow the example of the trends of other knives. That being the case, we're getting into tiny folders pretty heavily nowadays. And on the straight side, we're getting stuff like *main gauche* daggers and recognizable historical Bowies.

In another area, miniatures are catching up, too. It is not unusual at all to see to-scale embellishment. How an engraver cuts a good scroll at 1/8th his usual scale this reporter does not know, but the work is out there.

For those who want to carry and display a lot of knives in an attache case, the world was never better. Once again we see otherwise normal knifemakers bitten by the miniature bug. There may be more. Stay tuned.

Ken Warner

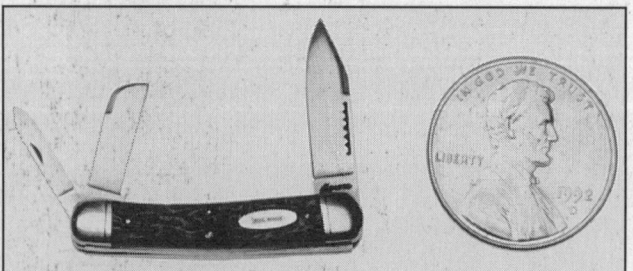

▲*Mike Mercer:* Three-blade Stockman pattern cuts like a real one.

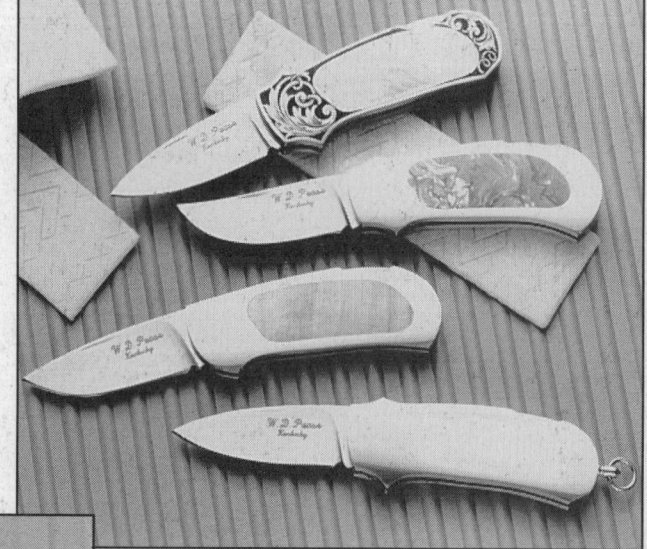

▲*W.D. Pease:* Stellite blades at 1 1/8 inches with various pearls, real interframes, even Tomlin engraving—a good show.

▼*Mike Mercer:* This six-blade Congress is—what?—about 2 inches long as you see it. It's O1 and tortoiseshell with stainless bolsters. (Weyer photo)

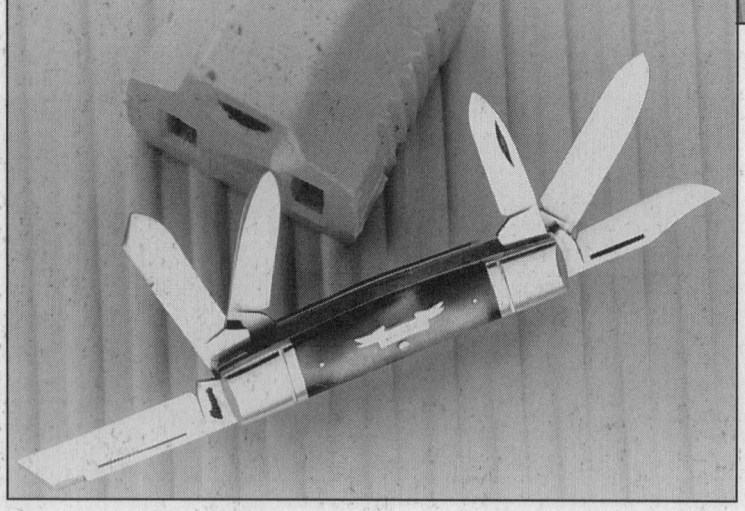

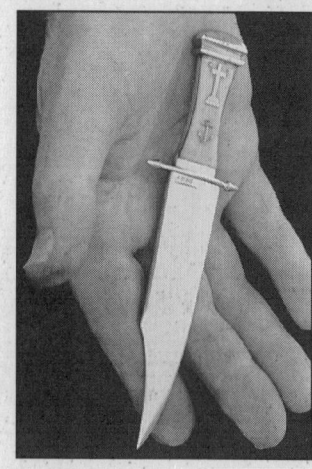

▶*Daniel E. Osterman:* Splendid Bowie—without the hand, you'd think it full-sized.

THE WORLD OF REALLY SMALL

▲*Rick Nowland:* It's just 2½ inches long. Scales are dressed stag. (Long photo)

◀*Mike Mercer:* Scaled-down engraving for a bunch of tiny gent's knives.

▲*Terry L. Kranning:* Oosic grip, brass fittings and 440C blade make a serious Bowie.

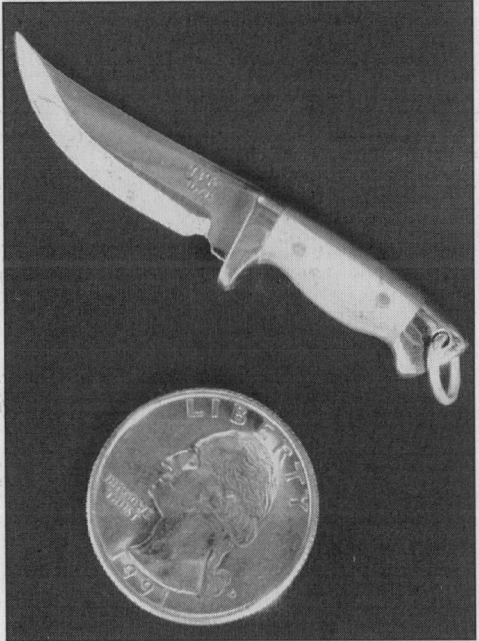
▲*Jeff V. Nielson:* A hunting pattern furnished with a ring for carry as a pendant.

▼*Daniel E. Osterman:* San Francisco dirks in two sizes, one very small.

▲*Dusty Moulton:* Buckeye and O1 steel at 2¾ inches overall—a good-looking hunter. (Long photo)

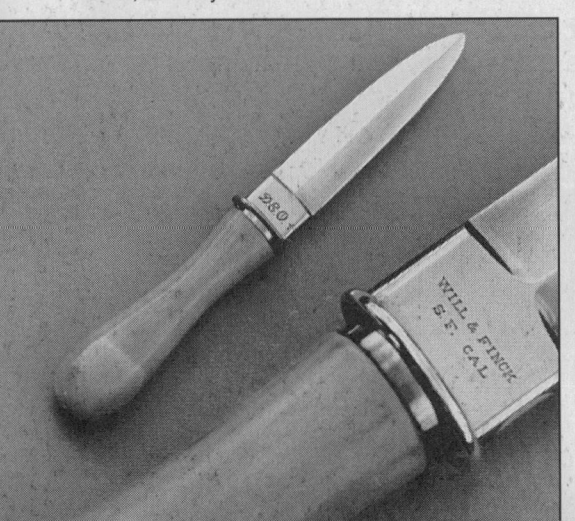

◀*Daniel E. Osterman:* This miniature of an original with a 17-inch (or so) blade is big enough to cut seriously.

TRENDS

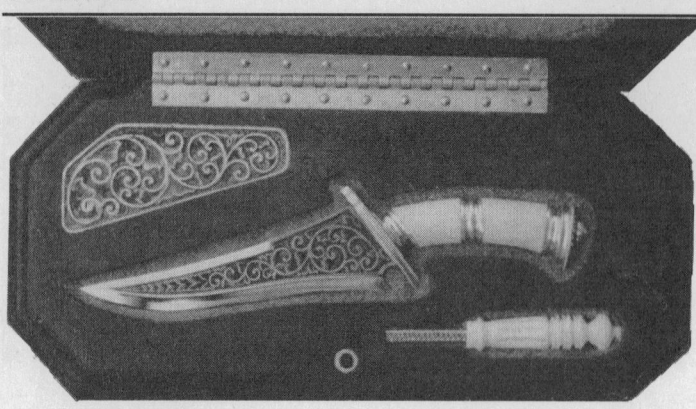

James D. Whitehead: Cased fighter is 2 3/8 inches long in O1 steel, mastodon ivory and sterling silver.

▶ *Phill Hartsfield:* This miniature-sized tanto is smaller than it looks. (Weyer photo)

▲ *Al Eaton:* Blades from 1 3/4 inches to 3 1/6 inches—a nice set of crown-handled Bowies.

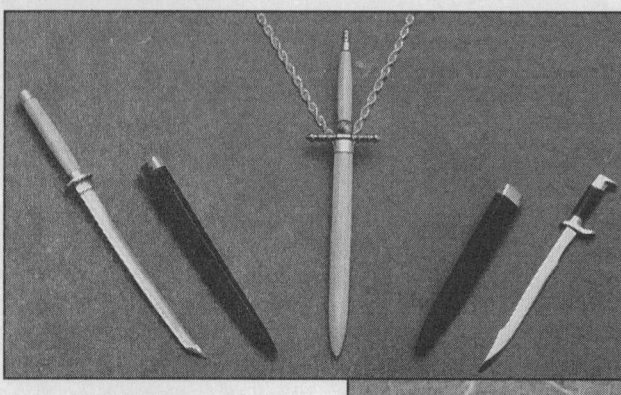

▲ *David Hesser:* Designed as pendants, these 3 1/2-inch miniatures are fitted in sterling.

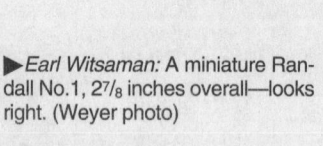

▶ *Earl Witsaman:* A miniature Randall No.1, 2 7/8 inches overall—looks right. (Weyer photo)

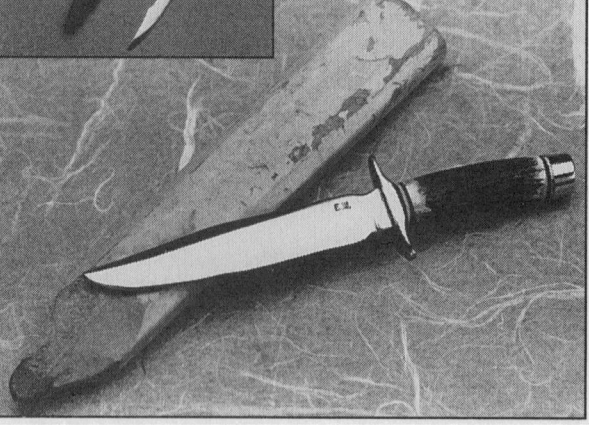

▲ *Al Eaton:* It's under 3 inches long, with Rados Damascus and turned stainless steel and ivory.

THE WORLD OF REALLY SMALL

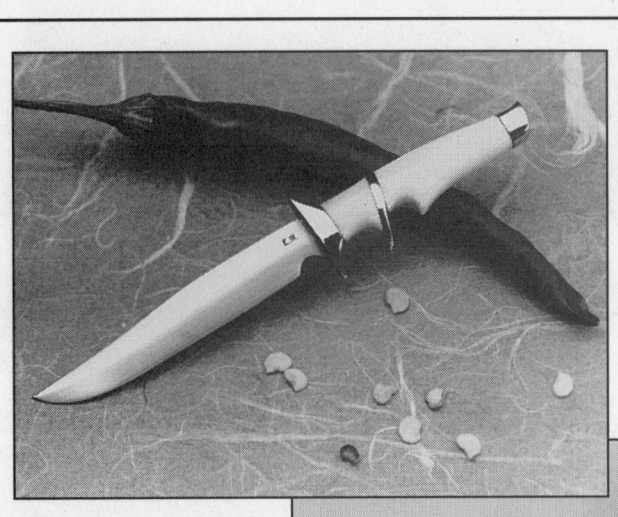

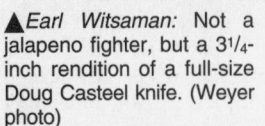

▲*Earl Witsaman:* Not a jalapeno fighter, but a 3 1/4-inch rendition of a full-size Doug Casteel knife. (Weyer photo)

▼*Al Eaton:* At 1 7/16 inches, this dagger is getting way down there in scale.

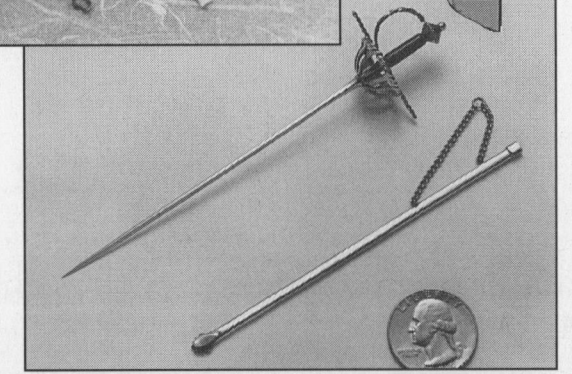

▶*Stewart Grossman:* The cup hilt rapier is handsome; the sheath is unbelievable. It's O1 steel with silver and gold.

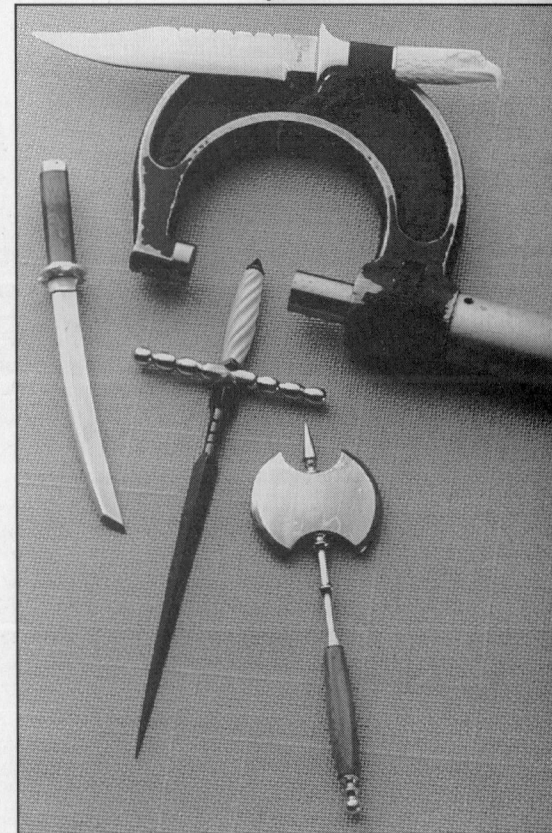

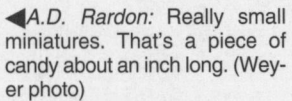

▲*Michael D. Anderson:* Amber and ivory for handles, silver mounted no doubt.

◀*A.D. Rardon:* Really small miniatures. That's a piece of candy about an inch long. (Weyer photo)

▲*Yves Côté:* A wide array of miniature fighters, from battle-axe to Bowie. (Weyer photo)

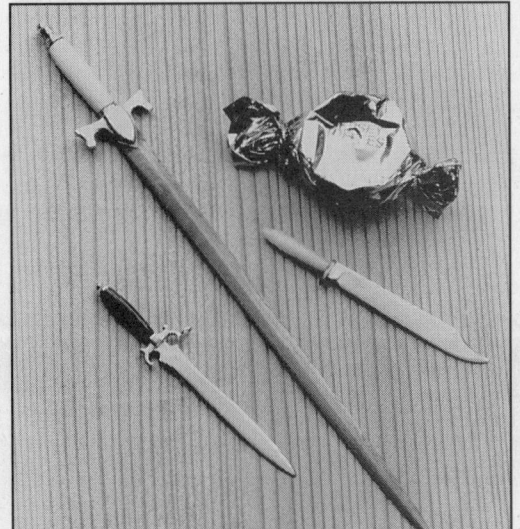

◀*Stewart Grossman:* This is the head of a halberd just 6 3/16 inches long overall—very authentic.

FIFTEENTH EDITION **87**

TRENDS

BIG KNIVES

THE SPECIAL PROBLEMS of the large knife include weight. No matter the intended function of a big design, ounces are the enemies of the maker.

Ounces are ounces, right? No big deal—just tote the load if you like a large knife, right? Well, not exactly.

Say we're talking camp knife here. Not *practical* camp cutlery, as some say, but a big knife to carry a long way if you have a long way to go, and which you can expect to handle tough stuff if you run into some. In the end, by the way, such a tool could prove to be *very* practical. There ain't nothing like inches when the brown stuff hits the rotating air-movement device.

However, if those inches are *heavy*, think again. If you have to swing it fast, it won't; an extra 4-6 ounces (easy on a big blade with a big grip) all the livelong day is noticeable; the only way to get a heavy knife balanced is to make it *all* heavy.

A really heavy camp knife is not, in fact, a knife. It is a strangely shaped handaxe, perhaps a cleaver.

OK. We can admit that big people in excellent muscle tone find heavy to be manageable. That's all, though—Superman himself cannot move a 2-pound knife as quickly as a 1-pound knife. And then there are those of us who have given up being supermen.

One of the reasons many big knives are heavier than desirable is that in some respects heavy is easier than lighter. A guy who wants a light big knife has to keep grinding, keep forging, put in tapers—it's work.

Then there's the customer. There are a *lot* of them that like heavy. It has meaning to them. Handmade knives seem superior to such people because they can be heavily constructed. It is pretty rare to find an overweight commercial knife, so a heavy knife must be better.

So what can we say? It's not right to call such people dumb. They are, after all, smart enough to buy handmade knives. Still...well, more on that later.

Years ago—maybe a half-dozen years before most of the knifemakers now making knives started—I used to hang around Bill Moran's shop. I remember a lot of things; we learned a lot. If you can imagine it, we're talking *before Damascus*.

My thoughts on *weight*, however, stem from one particular Moran knife of that period. It was a customer design—*very* specific. It had, as I recall, about a 17-inch blade, coin-silver D-guard, ivory slabs and $3/8$-inch steel.

Honest, it weighed *7 pounds*, and it terrorized us. It was the Moran kind of sharp when finished. We had to handle it for photos and such, and our every contact was tempered by the sure and certain knowledge that if dropped it would hit one or another foot, and when it did 7 pounds behind that edge would not make a wound, it would create an amputation.

That one knife embodied all the bad aspects of heavy. It was gorgeous, mind you, but it was not a great knife.

The sad fact about heavy knives from the viewpoint of this publication is that weight doesn't photograph. So it could be that some of the big knives you see here are heavy, heavy and heavy.

Big knives are not all problems, of course. It's easy to paint smoothly on a big canvas. The knifemaker has a lot of scope at big knife scale. The lines have to be straight and all that, like any knife, but the work is there, where you can get at it.

Most fantastical knives are pretty big, you'll notice. Unconventional shapes—double and triple blades, double-ended designs and such—bite. W.W. Cronk told this reporter once, proudly, that his newest creation "only bit me twice." When they're bigger there's more room to work and more time to dodge.

One of the most interesting things about big knives is that some people profess to disdain them. "What in the world...?" and stuff like that is what they say. That's a definite minority.

The rest of us, whether they're Bowies or fighters or daggers or camp and trail and hunters' designs, like 'em. A lot. And here are a bunch to see.

Ken Warner

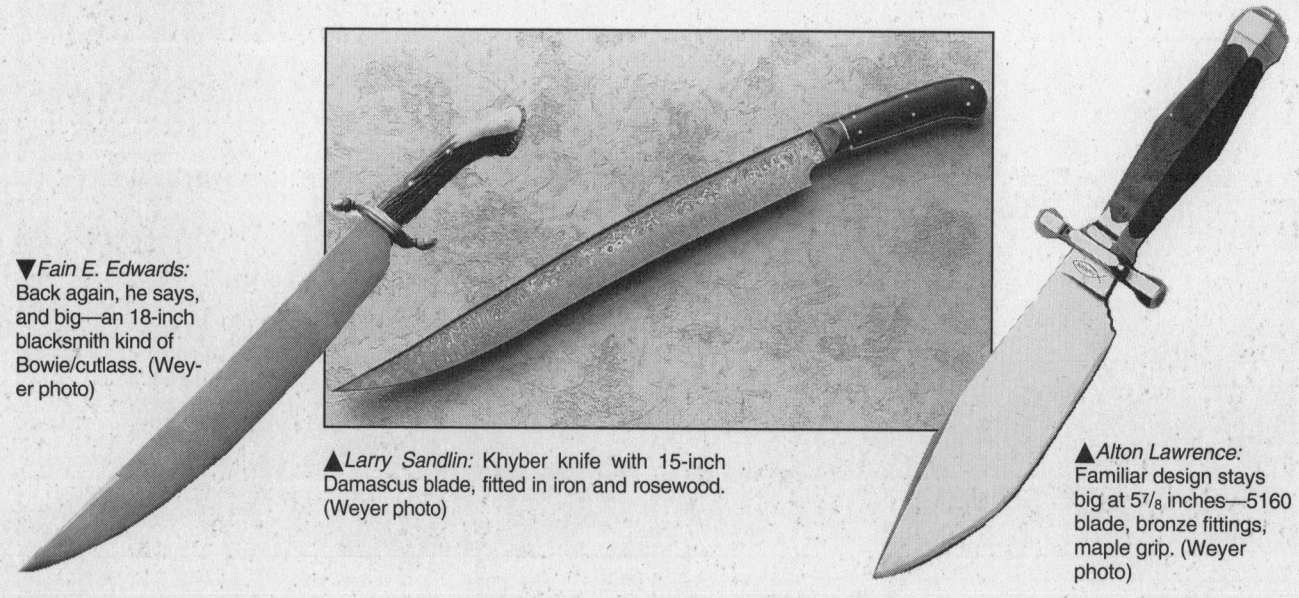

▼*Fain E. Edwards:* Back again, he says, and big—an 18-inch blacksmith kind of Bowie/cutlass. (Weyer photo)

▲*Larry Sandlin:* Khyber knife with 15-inch Damascus blade, fitted in iron and rosewood. (Weyer photo)

▲*Alton Lawrence:* Familiar design stays big at $5^{7}/_{8}$ inches—5160 blade, bronze fittings, maple grip. (Weyer photo)

BIG KNIVES

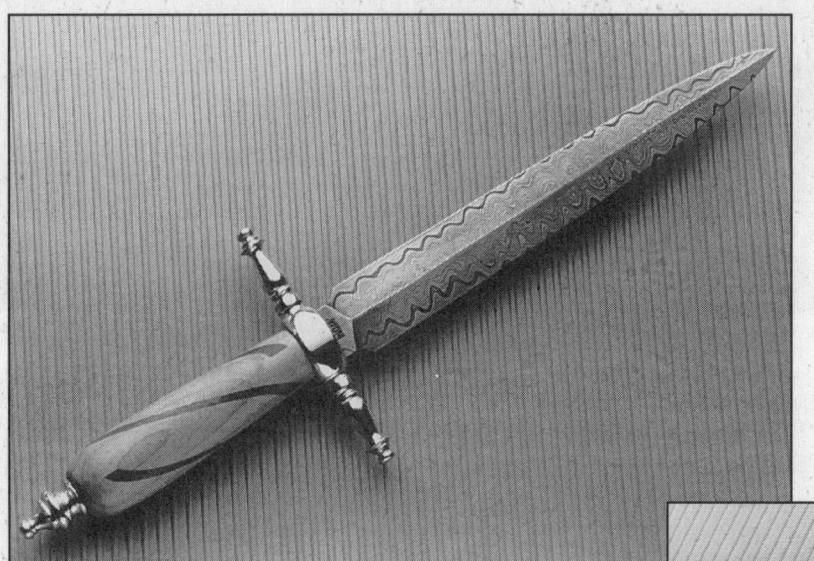

◀ *Wm. Dean Mitchell:* Quillon dagger, cherry handle inlaid with walnut, has lace Damascus blade and brass fittings. (Weyer photo)

▼ *Roger M. Green:* Sterling cutlery-style handle and 7 1/2 inches of 440C with royal blue leather sheath. (Weyer photo)

▼ *Alan W. Ray:* Camp knife/hunter with stout 7-inch blade and burl maple handle. (Weyer photo)

▲ *Kim Thomas:* Ballock dagger with steel-iron-nickel-copper, maple grip, silver-trimmed. (Long photo)

◀ *Robert J. McDonald:* Six-inch dagger has a red coral spacer, carved blackwood grip. (Weyer photo)

▶ *Andrew Frankland:* Tanto at 8 inches, handle is wrapped elephant hide.

TRENDS

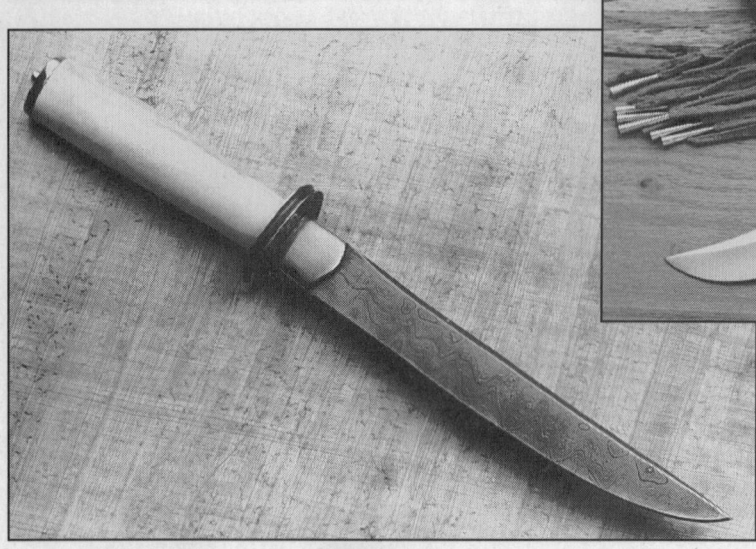

▲ *Ed Stokes:* Kabar-style combat knife—7 inches of 440C and turned linen Micarta handle.

◄ *Jarrell D. Lambert:* Tanto in Damascus at 8½ inches, handled in axis deer antler. (Weyer photo).

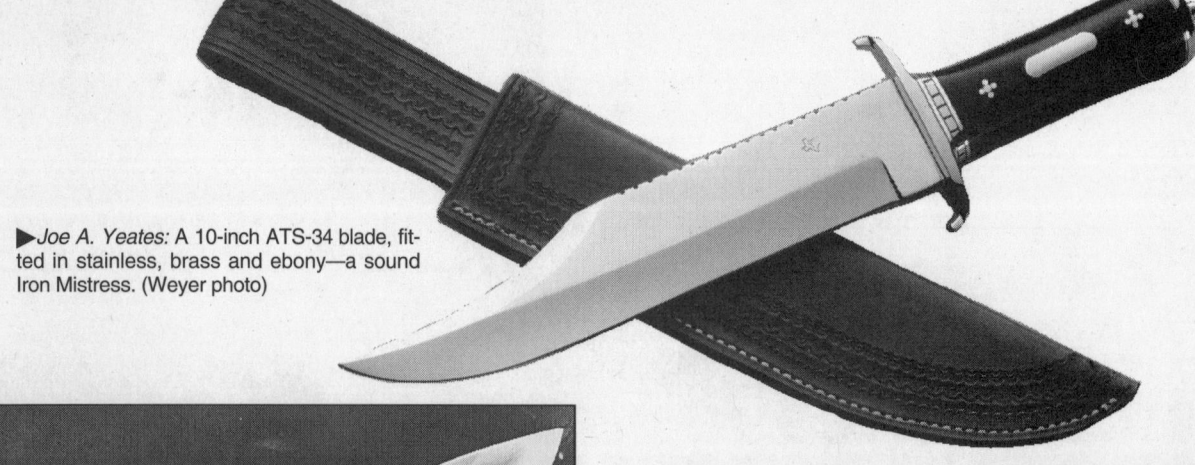

► *Joe A. Yeates:* A 10-inch ATS-34 blade, fitted in stainless, brass and ebony—a sound Iron Mistress. (Weyer photo)

▲ *Ed A. Fowler:* The maker calls this a short camp knife; it has a 6¾-inch blade forged of a ball bearing and the traditional Fowler sheephorn handle.

▲ *Tom Bullard:* Eight-inch ATS-34 blade and worked phenolic handle—it went to Somalia, the maker says.

◄ *Mike Sakmar:* Future-class fighter in ATS-34, 416 stainless, ivory—carefully sculpted.

BIG KNIVES

▲*Don R. Broughton:* Simple broad-bladed 6½-inch hunter, handled in ebony. (Weyer photo)

▼*F. Terry Callahan:* Big 5-inch hunter, forged in 1095 and gripped in ironwood. (Weyer photo)

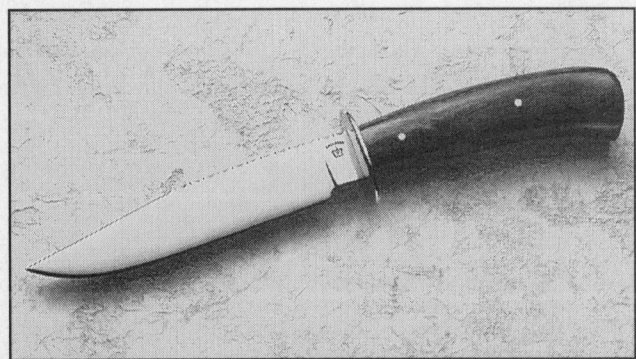

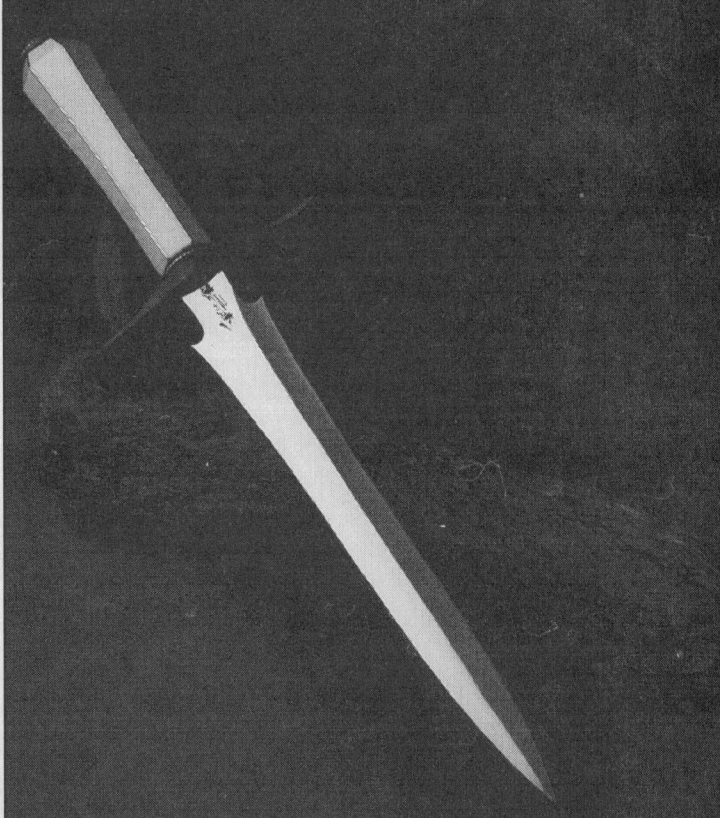

▲*Andrew Frankland:* Ivory gripped, trimmed in titanium and nickel silver, this one has a 10-inch 440C blade.

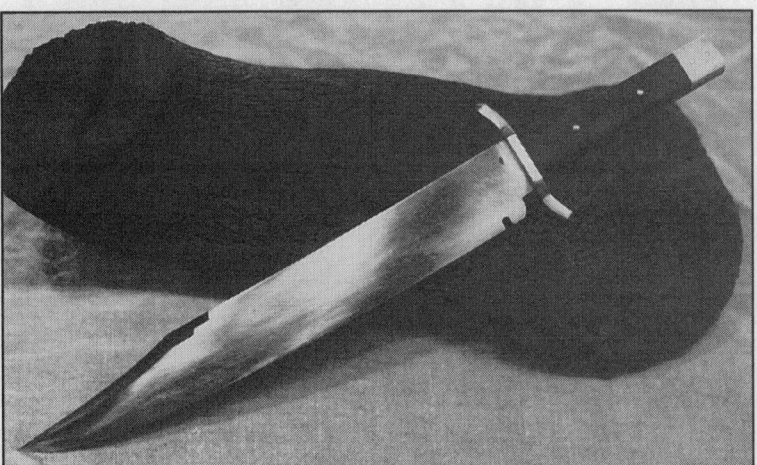

▲*Charles Robinson:* Small forged fighter in 5160 has temper line and trim good looks. (Weyer photo)

▲*James A. Rubley:* Frontier-style size and feel from a maker who is at home in the 18th century.

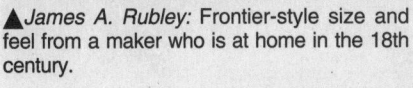

▲*Keith Kilby:* Utility in layered random Damascus, full-forged in stag—an all-purpose knife. (Long photo)

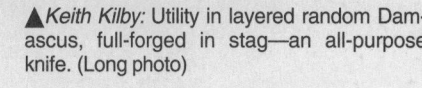

FIFTEENTH EDITION 91

TRENDS

▲ *Bill Wolf:* Big, flat fighter—in ebony and coral and nickel silver and ATS-34—has a 12-inch blade.

▲ *Gordon R. Chard:* Ten-inch dagger in ATS-34, fully embellished, Carter-style. (Weyer photo)

▶ *Phillip Baldwin:* Classy chef knife at 8¾ inches created on the anvil. (Weyer photo)

▲ *Rodney Rogers:* Scagel-style camp knife combines ATS-34 and nickel silver with ivory, oosic and stag. (Weyer photo)

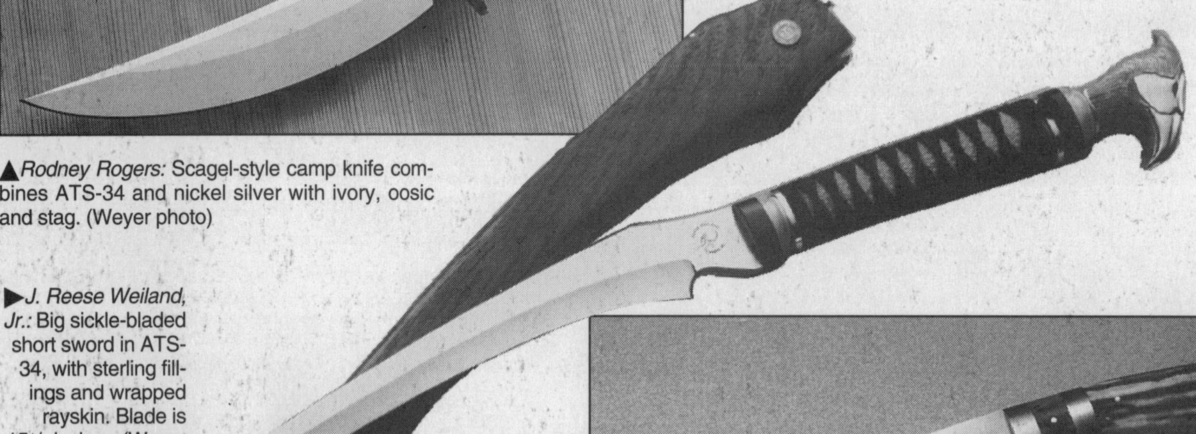

▶ *J. Reese Weiland, Jr.:* Big sickle-bladed short sword in ATS-34, with sterling fillings and wrapped rayskin. Blade is 15½ inches. (Weyer photo)

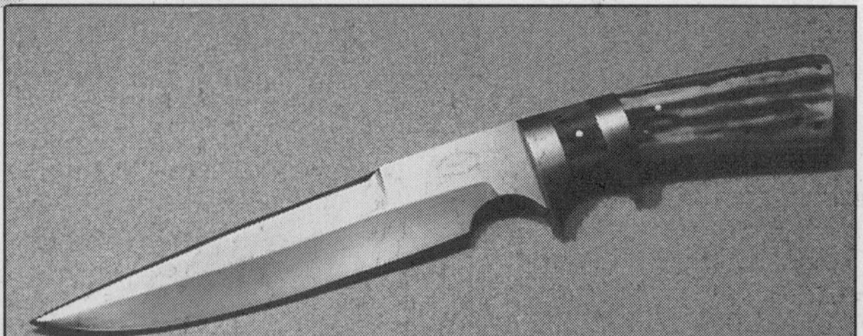

▲ *Frank J. Dilluvio:* Sub-hilt fighter has 8-inch ATS-34 blade and a handful of stag.

BIG KNIVES

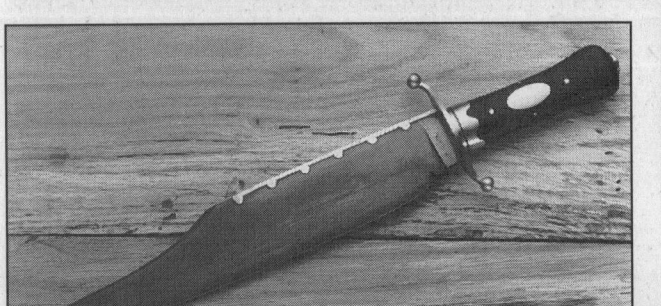

◀ *John Greco:* Eight-inch tanto-style knife—very classy, not very Japanese. (Weyer photo)

▼ *Keith Batts:* Comfortable-looking camp knife, forged to a nice curve. (Weyer photo)

◀ *David Anders:* Slim figher sheathed by Rowe, done up in Damascus and ironwood. (Weyer photo)

▲ *Roger Clark:* A more primitive Iron Mistress pattern—foot-long blade is forged 5160; grip is persimmon; trim is brass. (Box photo)

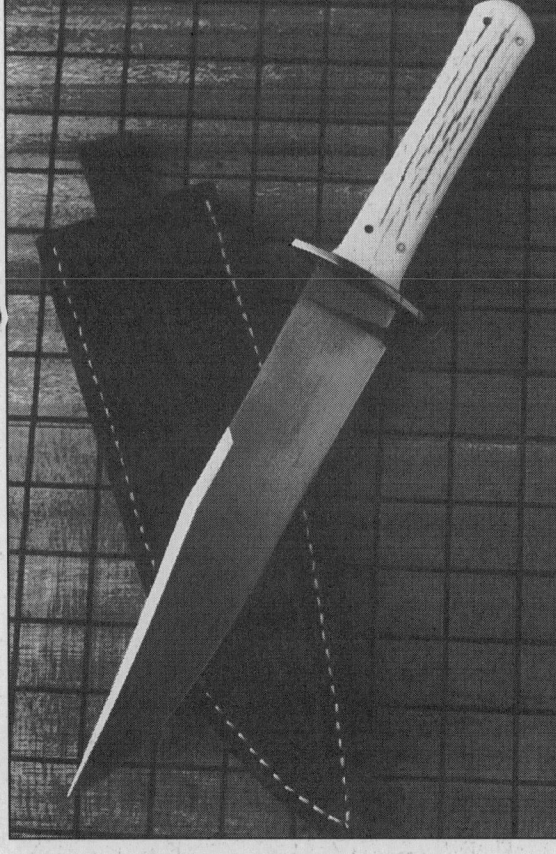

▲ *Jimmy Lile:* Made in 1989, this is the Iron Mistress Bowie style from the hand of the guy who knew how. (Weyer photo)

▲ *Robert A. Defeo:* Foot-long ATS-34 blade, ground Sheffield-style, has bark ivory slabs.

TRENDS

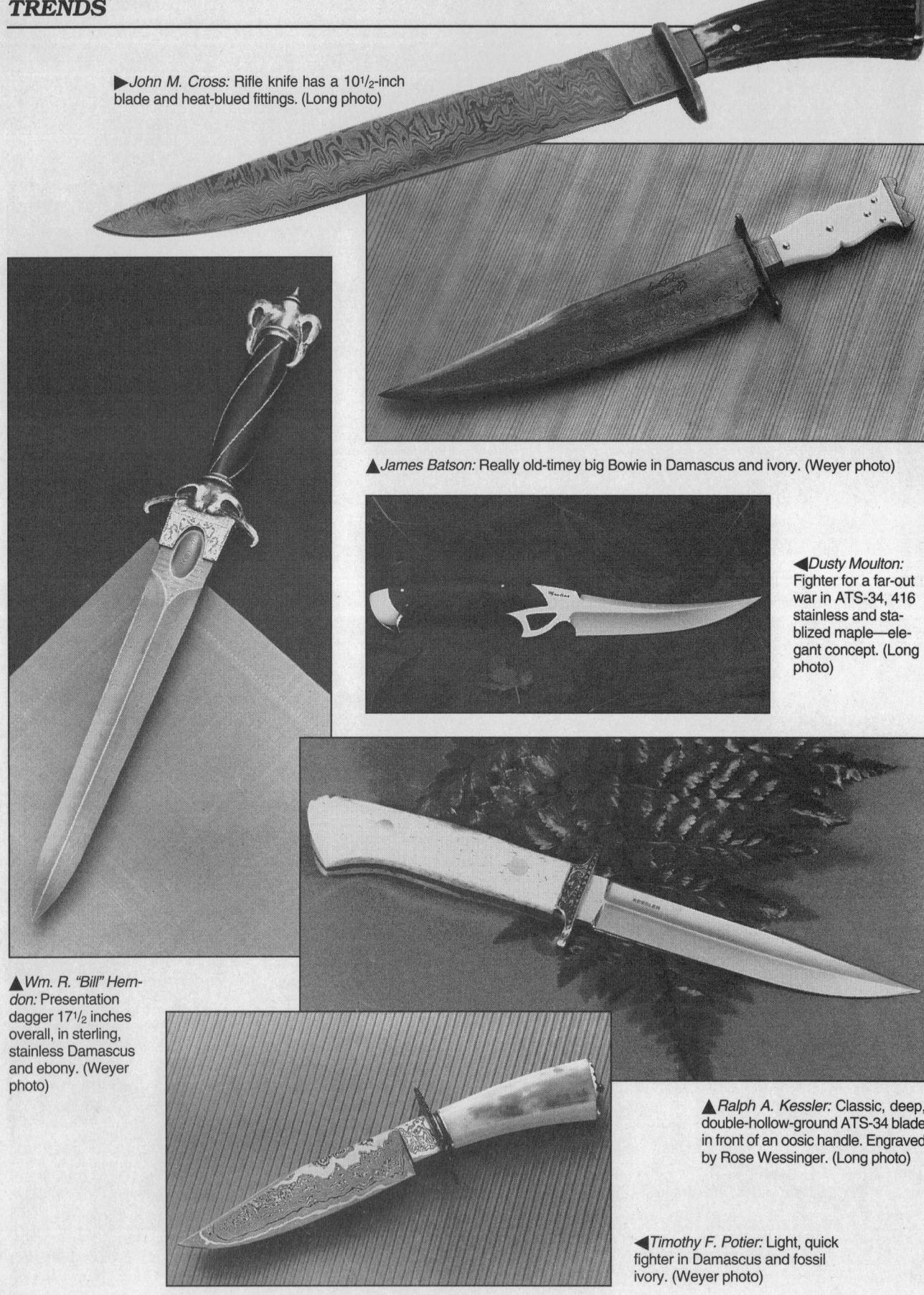

▶ *John M. Cross:* Rifle knife has a 10½-inch blade and heat-blued fittings. (Long photo)

▲ *James Batson:* Really old-timey big Bowie in Damascus and ivory. (Weyer photo)

◀ *Dusty Moulton:* Fighter for a far-out war in ATS-34, 416 stainless and stablized maple—elegant concept. (Long photo)

▲ *Wm. R. "Bill" Herndon:* Presentation dagger 17½ inches overall, in sterling, stainless Damascus and ebony. (Weyer photo)

▲ *Ralph A. Kessler:* Classic, deep, double-hollow-ground ATS-34 blade in front of an oosic handle. Engraved by Rose Wessinger. (Long photo)

◀ *Timothy F. Potier:* Light, quick fighter in Damascus and fossil ivory. (Weyer photo)

BIG KNIVES

◀ *Brian Lyttle:* At 13½ inches overall, this all-steel dagger is in the grand tradition, including floral gold inlay. (Weyer photo)

▼ *Edward N. Kalfayan:* Dramatic curves in 15 inches of dagger, set up with subhilt. (Weyer photo)

▲ *David Anders:* Light fighter in 5160 and rosewood is just 10½ inches overall and has a nice S-guard. (Weyer photo)

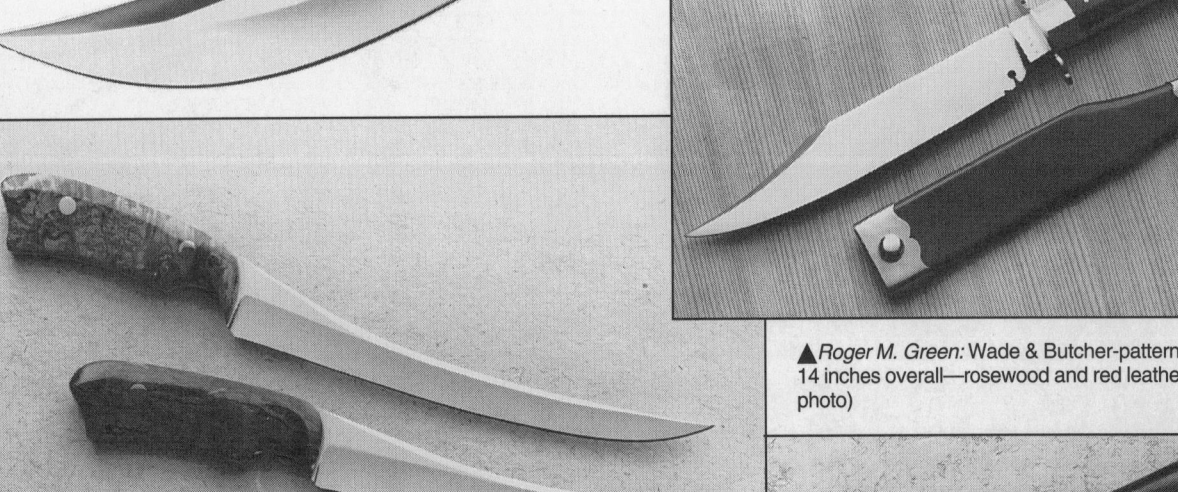

▲ *Roger M. Green:* Wade & Butcher-pattern Bowie at 14 inches overall—rosewood and red leather. (Weyer photo)

▲ *Don Zaccagnino:* Great grips on 7- and 9-inch Atlantic Coast fillet knives. (Weyer photo)

▶ *Charles F. Ochs:* Fighting Bowie in black Micarta and forged 52100 has 7½-inch blade. (Weyer photo)

FIFTEENTH EDITION 95

TRENDS

▶ *Douglas Casteel:* Big all the way around, dressy Bowie has jade handle and an 11-inch blade. (Weyer photo)

◀ *Willie Rigney:* Spanish Bowie with a few extra touches—ivory grips—Skaggs engraved. (Weyer photo)

▲ *Paul M. Jarvis:* Meier Damascus and a good deal of work in a richly embellished royal-class dagger. (Weyer photo)

▶ *Fred Duvall and Marvin Solomon:* Long camp knife in forged 5160 has Rowe sheath. (Weyer photo)

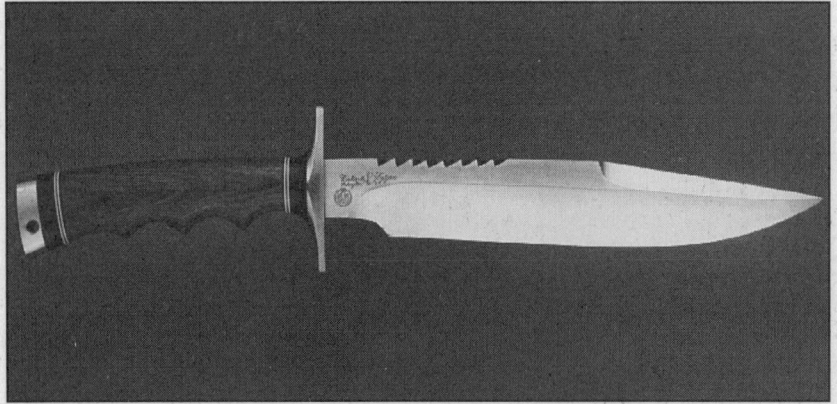

▲ *Richard G. Batson:* Foot-long Ranger Knife in brush-finished O1, differentially tempered. The sawteeth are hard.

▶ *Ronald E. Hancock:* Rifle knife for fellow named Barnes, for whom the maker wishes: "May his eyes be as sharp as his knife."

BIG KNIVES

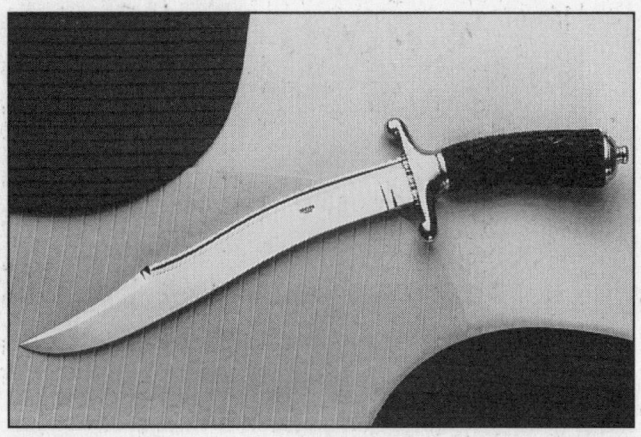

▲*Charles L. Weiss:* Yet another 17½-inch entry in the Jos. Rodgers Bowie Sweepstakes—very nice looking. (Weyer photo)

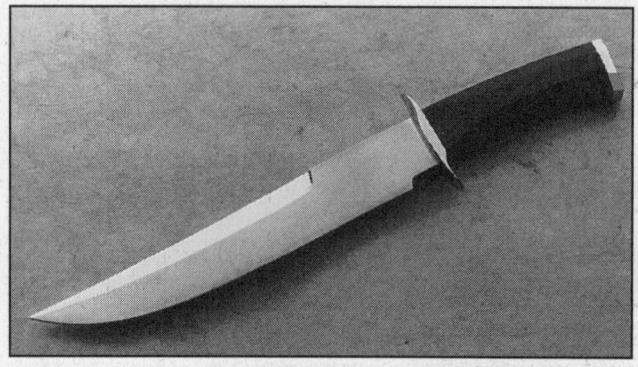

▲*Bernard Garner:* Really clean conception for a long, tall Bowie. (Weyer photo)

▲*Ed Halligan:* Fighter with a difference in Damascus, springbuck horn, turquoise and copper. (Weyer photo)

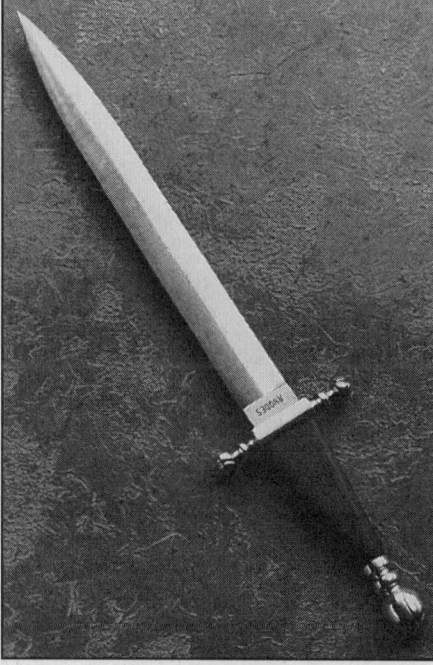

▲*James D. Rhodes:* Quillon dagger with a workmanlike attitude in Damascus, purple heart and brass—15 inches overall. (Weyer photo)

▶*Scott Richter:* Chef knives, short and long, cleanly ground with a low point. (Weyer photo)

◀*E. Jay Hendrickson:* Classic fighter in the Moran style—inlaid and sheathed handsomely. (Weyer photo)

TRENDS

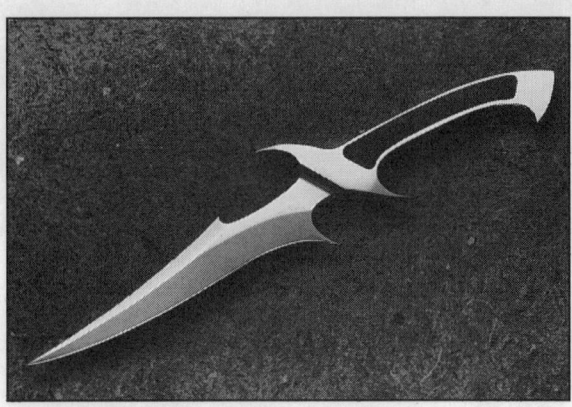

◀ *Philip L. Hagen:* At 14 inches overall, this deeply hollow-ground dagger seems to have a hollow-ground sheath. (Weyer photo)

▶ *John Rahn:* Named "Smilodon," this dagger/fighter is just over a foot long and is inlaid with malachite. (Weyer photo)

▲ *Dan Maragni:* Part of a series, this *hocho* Japanese cooking knife is serenely classy. (Weyer photo)

◀ *C. Robbin Hudson:* Bowie with a 3-D Damascus blade, walnut and Damascus-trimmed. (Weyer photo)

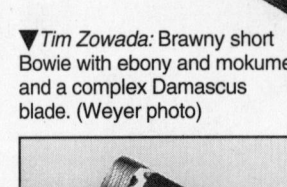

▼ *Tim Zowada:* Brawny short Bowie with ebony and mokume and a complex Damascus blade. (Weyer photo)

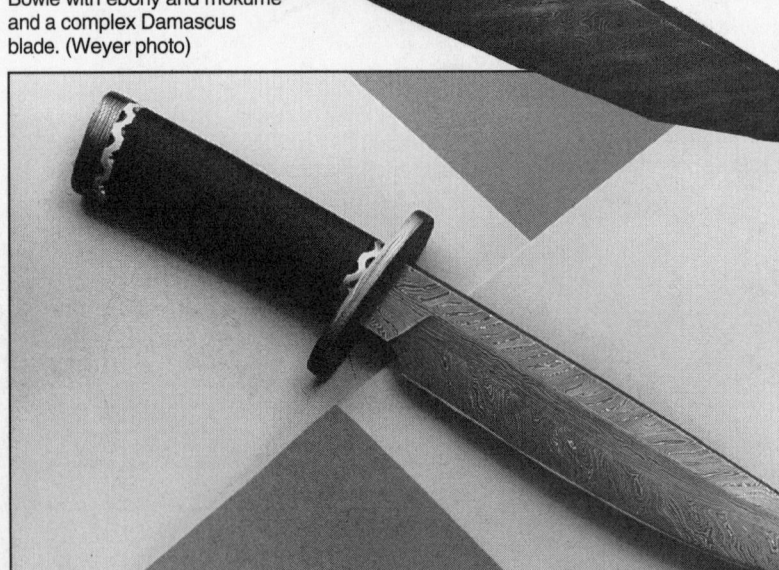

▲ *Billy Mace Imel:* Black beauty just over a foot long in A2 and blackwood; gold inlaid by Ron Skaggs. (Weyer photo)

98 KNIVES '95

BIG KNIVES

◀ *Mickey L. Ames:* Real Bowie flavor with a 10¼-inch 5160 blade and a whitetail antler grip. (Weyer photo)

▼ *Robert J. McDonald:* Persian fighter with nifty grinds, strong point and Blesbock handle. (Long photo)

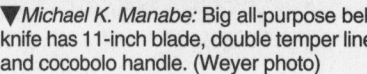

▼ *Michael K. Manabe:* Big all-purpose belt knife has 11-inch blade, double temper line and cocobolo handle. (Weyer photo)

▲ *Leonard Williams:* Forged L6 big hunter with rosewood grip on the full tang, a heavyweight belt knife.

◀ *Joe Flournoy:* New classic Bowie, sharply pointed with blued furniture and fossil ivory grips. (Weyer photo)

▶ *Fain E. Edwards:* Giant 16-inch-bladed toothpick, with crown stag handle, from his own hand. (Weyer photo)

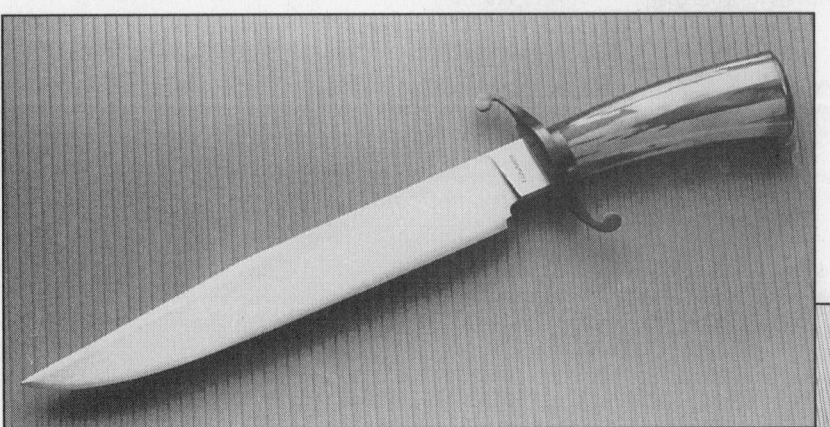

TRENDS

THE ELEGANT KNIFE

SERIOUSLY CLASSY GOOD looks are not a function of size or decoration or intent. Elegance is the creature of rightness of line and form and finish. And of concept.

So here you see elegant knives of all descriptions—plain and fancy, long and short, folding and straight, high-priced and low.

It ain't, you can see, only a question of the absence of fussy detail. It does seem that more clean and simple knives carry elegant potential than do knives with a few bells and whistles, but there are elaborate elegant knives.

Guards and quillons and bolsters and fancy ricassos and thongholes and finger-placement features *shouldn't* affect the good looks of a knife. However, there are a lot of swell blades and handles out there more than a little cluttered up with such helpful features.

All the decisions made here about the elegance of these particular knives is made on the basis of photography. That's the only basis we have, save for a few score knives handled at shows. Happily, we have thousands of brand-new photos, so we're pretty sure we've seen most of the new stuff. Of course, a good photographer selects the best angle, but that's OK.

Working from photos doesn't permit many calculated estimates of weight and feel. Therefore, we have to accept that some of this handsome cutlery, by the nature of things, falls into the clunk category once in the hand. We can't help that.

Over the years, it's worth noting, good-looking knives have seemed less often clunky than ugly knives have.

Talking (or writing) about a visual and tactile phenomenom is difficult to the point of being a waste of time. When it comes to elegance, you shouldn't try to discuss what it's not, either. Maybe, however, there's a little profit in talkng *around* it. There are some interesting landmarks in the neighborhood of elegance.

For instance, a fellow who makes one elegant knife generally makes *most* of his knives with a classy look. Also, it seems that more daggers get to elegance than most other shapes, possibly because symmetry is a *big* factor. And only the most assured stylist gets elegance out of big, bold strokes; more often the subtle and understated gets the prize.

There aren't very many showy elegant knives, but there are some such—bright and conspicuous, but still elegant. There are, for one sort, some tantos, both classical Japanese and derivative, that are very showy *and* quite elegant.

Finally, at each end of the elegance spectrum, it's mostly in the eye of the beholder. In the middle ground, we can reasonably be sure we see elegance—restrained opulence, refined grace, tasteful effect.

Ken Warner

▲ *Billy Mace Imel:* With Skaggs engraving and gold inlays, the immaculate lines of this integral dagger practically define elegance. (Weyer photo)

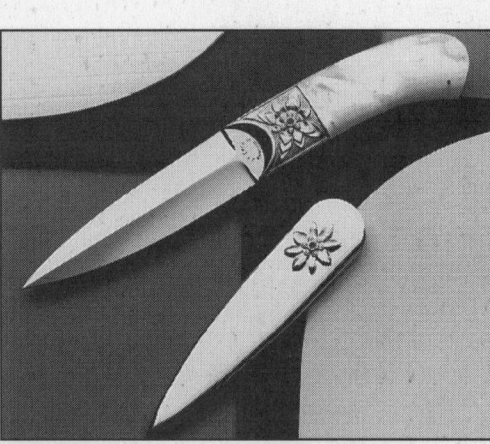

▲ *Jim Ence:* This 10-inch creation is a one-author work in pearl and gold and nickel silver.

▲◄ *Wolfgang Loerchner:* Slim short dagger or blossom-like push dagger, both with pearl inlays, demonstrate the dagger advantage in symmetry. (Weyer photo)

THE ELEGANT KNIFE
Folders

▲ *Jay Harris:* Pure lines make this folding dagger a classic, a very creative classic. Engraving is by Harry Mendenhall. (Weyer photo)

▲ *Phil Boguszewski:* This classy textured dagger in blackwood and stainless is a J.W. Townsend design called Pit Viper. (Weyer photo)

► *Robert Rupert:* Highly styled primitive folder in elegant proportion at total length of 6¾ inches. (Weyer photo)

▲ *Ken Steigerwalt:* With Howard Clark Damascus, this 19th century folding dirk is in the grand tradition. (Weyer photo)

► *Eldon G. Peterson:* At 8 inches overall length, this is an all stainless—with tool steel inlays—folding dagger engraved by Jere Davidson.

◄ *Tim Herman/Wolfgang Loerchner:* It's a small folding knife with a 416 stainless case by Herman, sculpting by Loerchner. (Weyer photo)

▲ *Bertie Rietveld:* South African puts a button lock in a Damascus blade, handled in pearl-inlaid stainless.

TRENDS

▶ *Randy Lyons:* Carefully thought-out, this one melds ironwood, nickel silver and 440C. (Box photo)

▼ *John Etzler:* Over a foot long, curved dagger is all twist Damascus and ivory. (Weyer photo)

▼ *Ed Halligan:* Small dagger in Damascus and carved ebony—9 inches overall. (Weyer photo)

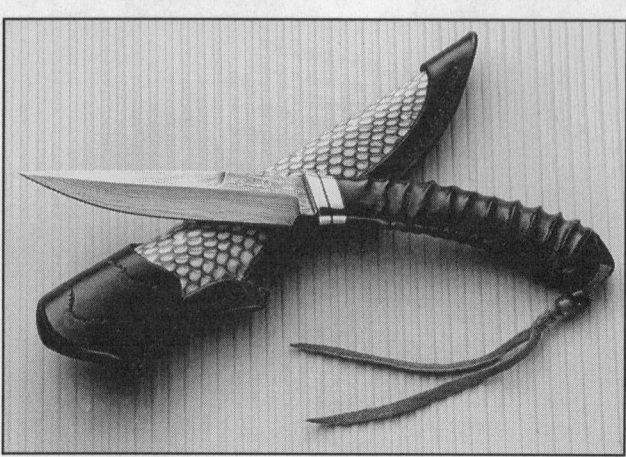

THE ELEGANT KNIFE
Curved Designs

▲ *Joseph Szilaski:* Skinner with a 3-inch D2 steel blade, and horn handle. (Weyer photo)

▶ *John Rahn:* Nine inches overall, all 440C, obsidian inlay.

▼ *Larry Turcotte:* Ebony and nickel silver in a handsome curved statement. (Long photo)

▲ *Dante Gottage:* Complex shape in stainless, brass and whale tooth still holds clean proportions, tip to pommel. (Weyer photo)

102 KNIVES '95

THE ELEGANT KNIFE

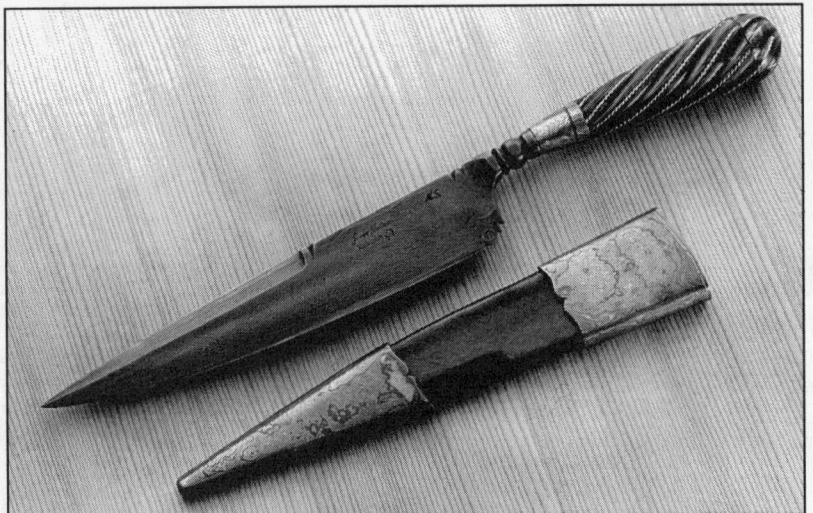

▲ *James Batson:* Mediterranean dirk, with 8-inch blade, offers rosewood, silver wire and, naturally, Damascus. (Weyer photo)

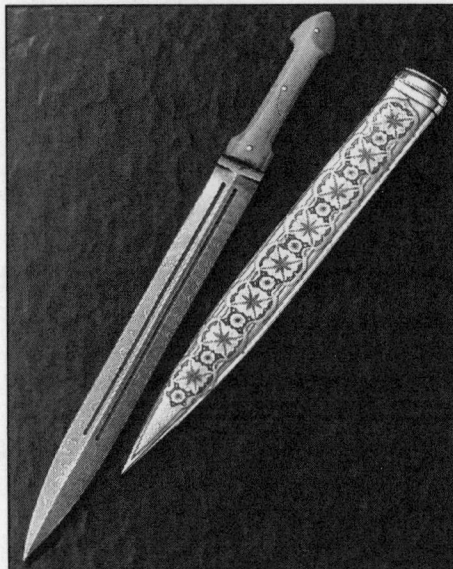

▲ *Jerry Fisk/Anatoly Bogachov:* All-out Cossack kinjal with a foot-long blade, ivory handle, etched and engraved sheath, Fisk steel. (Weyer photo)

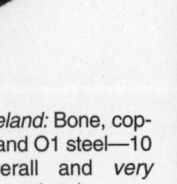

▶ *Paul M. Jarvis:* Aikuchi, at 9 inches overall, stunning in rosewood, Damascus and sterling silver. (Weyer photo)

THE ELEGANT KNIFE
Ethnic Specials

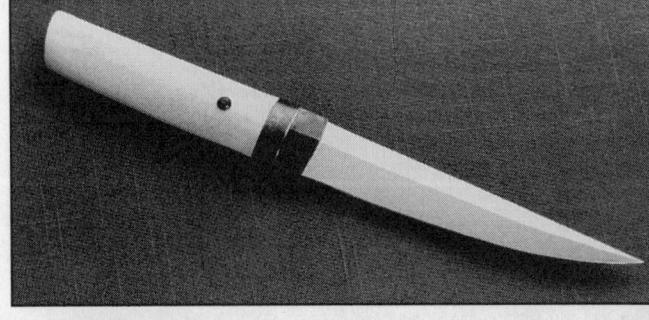

▶ *Steve Leland:* Bone, copper, nickel and O1 steel—10 inches overall and *very* clean. (Weyer photo)

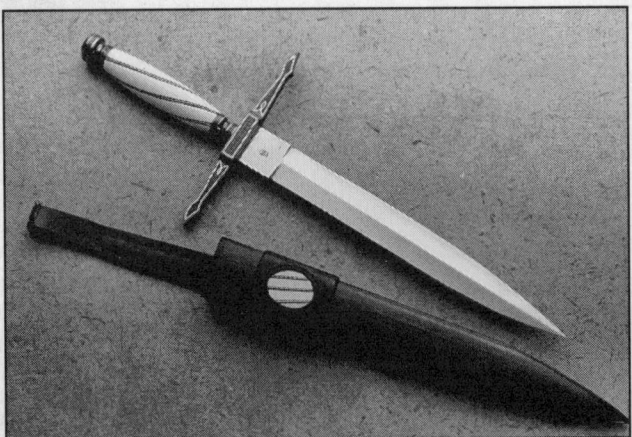

▲ *Webster Wood:* Big and fancy Middle Ages dagger, blued and inlaid fittings. (Weyer photo)

▲ *Al Eaton:* Constructed traditionally, this tanto doesn't carry *all* the stuff possible, but it's loaded.

TRENDS

▼ *Werner Kaluza:* This group shows high style, exceptional design, Fritz Oberdorfer embellishment. (Weyer photo)

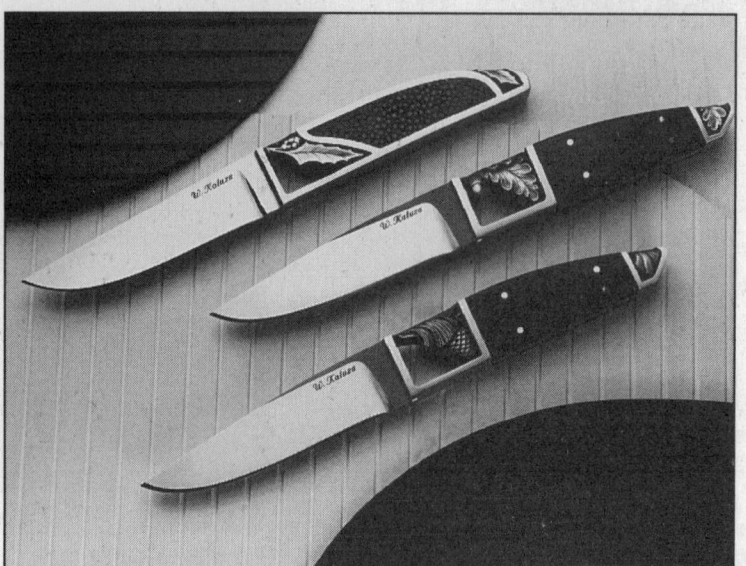

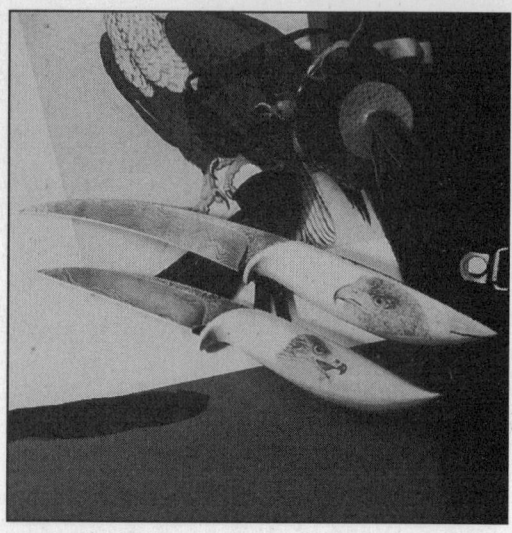

▲ *Mick Russell:* Impeccable lines in a pair of talon-style blades, scrimmed with raptors.

THE ELEGANT KNIFE
Design Groups

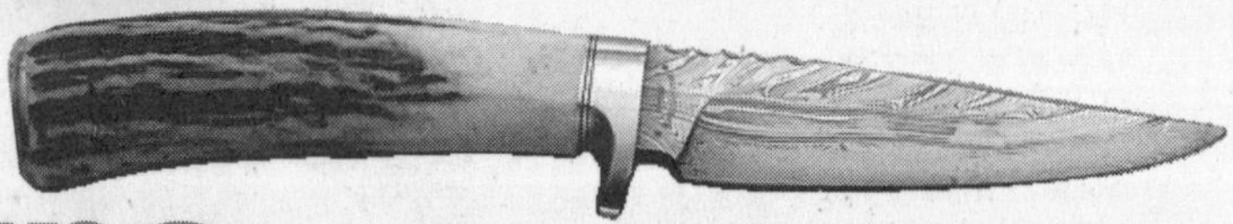

▲▼ *William Behnke:* Stag and Damascus hunters show remarkable lines. (Weyer photo)

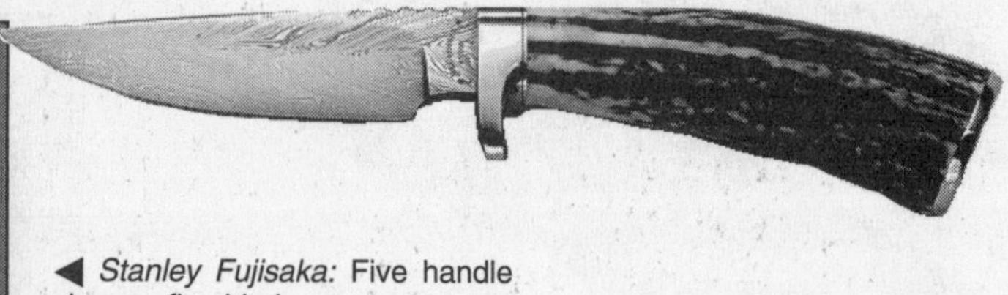

◄ *Stanley Fujisaka:* Five handle shapes, five blades, every assembly elegant. (Weyer photo)

▼ *Brian Lyttle:* Variations on a 9-inch boot theme—steel and mokume handles. (Weyer photo)

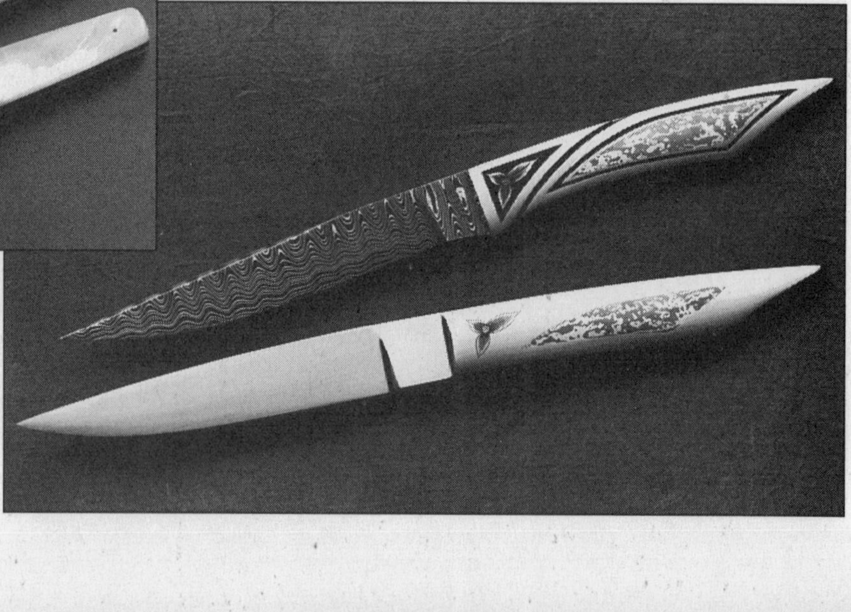

THE ELEGANT KNIFE
Field Designs

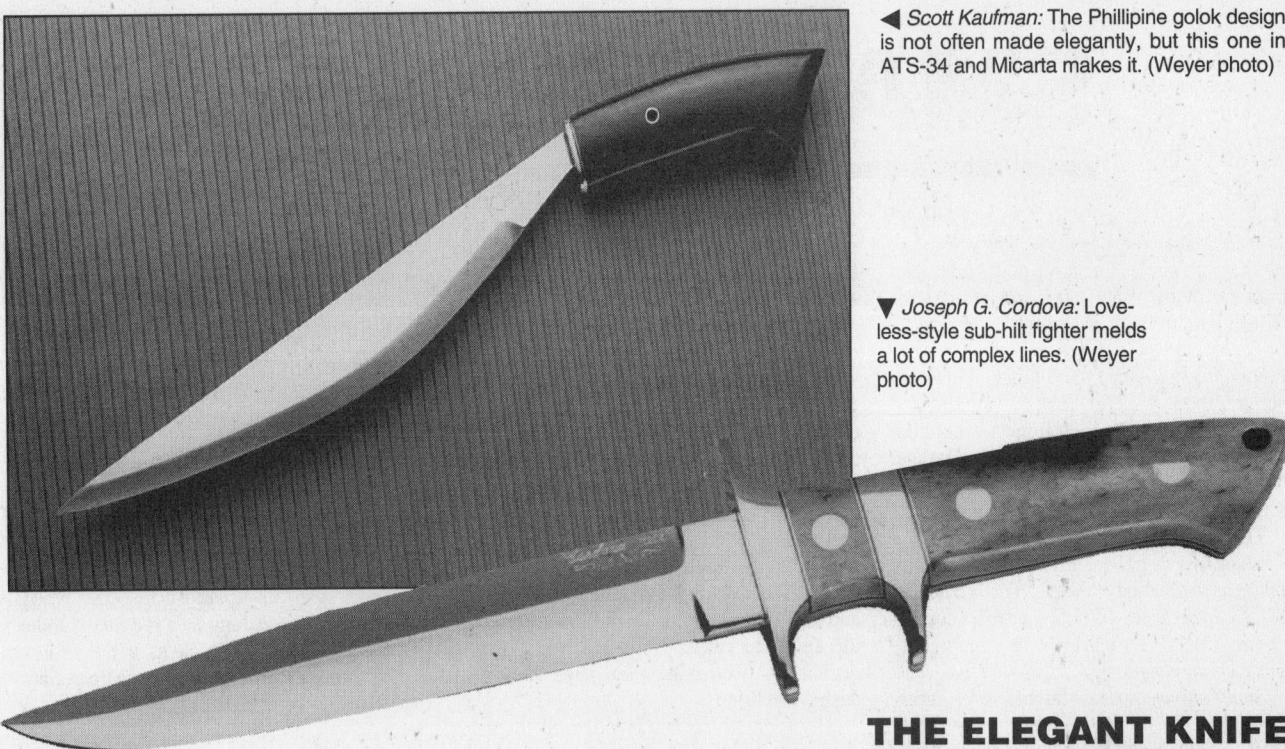

◀ *Scott Kaufman:* The Phillipine golok design is not often made elegantly, but this one in ATS-34 and Micarta makes it. (Weyer photo)

▼ *Joseph G. Cordova:* Loveless-style sub-hilt fighter melds a lot of complex lines. (Weyer photo)

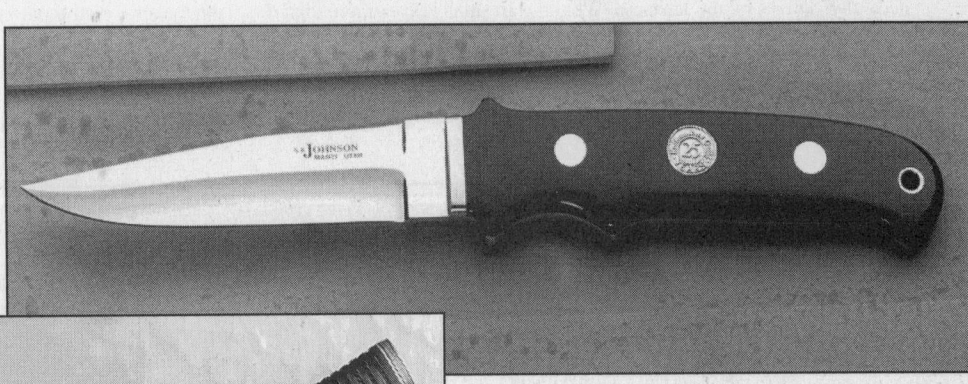

▶ *Steven R. Johnson:* Loveless-style hideout has buffalo grip and 25th Anniversary Guild button. (Weyer photo)

▼ *J.D. Smith:* Big dagger impeccably ground and fitted with carved ebony and bronze furniture. (Weyer photo)

▲ *Loyd A. McConnell Jr:* Titanium-nitrided 5-inch blade, carefully worked Micarta—unusual treatment. (Weyer photo)

TRENDS

SMALL KNIVES

MAKING SUCCESSFUL SMALL knives takes more than quitting early. The woods are full of small knives that have only size to recommend them. What's needed, besides the built-in portability, is usability.

To make a 6-inch object, which is very sharp along one end, fit and function in hands that are about 4 inches across the palm and have all those 3- to 4-inch fingers is not simple. There is, of course, a *lot* of precedent and many previous examples to go by; still, designers fail.

They also succeed. And when they do, everyone knows it. Instantly. There's the knife and there's somebody saying, "That's cute." In these circumstances, as in few others, "cute" is a compliment. It means *cunning, elegantly contrived, a neat possession, a good tool.*

Small knives means straight knives, mostly. Folders, in the main, are already pretty small. A folder with a 3-inch blade is a fairly large folder. Bigger than that and we're talking *big* folder.

Here, lately, small knives have been categorized. Little tools of a certain elegance have been called "city" knives by the Japanese. We have a whole class of little users called "danglers" or "twisters" or "swivel" knives. There's a growing tendency toward necklace knives, worn on thongs or chains about the neck. In hunting circles, small knives have long been called "capers," since their presumed use is to do fieldwork—called caping—on trophy heads. "Trout and bird" knives are another small category, generally slim and pointed.

The better a designer/maker strips unnecessary parts off a small knife, the better his small knife is. Guards, for instance, generally go early. Bolsters and pommels follow. Those functions are often carried on by handle profile and contour when the concept requires them.

There is one inescapable ratio for the designer of small knives, which in general are knives shorter than a dollar bill—sometimes a couple inches shorter, sometimes a bit longer. That's the relative lengths of the blade and the grip or handle—long blade/short handle and vice versa. The availability of this decision is what makes the wide variety of design solutions.

How attractively and intelligently this ratio is managed determines how quick the knife sells and how well it works. Profiles—both blade and handle—are important, of course, but mostly in relation to the ratio of handle length to blade length.

In small knives more than most, the maker who selects toward handle length makes a relatively broad blade; while blades seem to get slimmer on short-handled knives. We're speak-ing of general-purpose designs, not whittling tools.

Feel is the only factor governing knife weight in small knives. There are 2-ounce working knives at 5-inch length and there are 6-ounce knives just 4 inches long.

Sometimes small knives are specialized. Perhaps the working blade that got about as small as can be was Jack Crockford's trout and bird knife—bird in this case meant ruffed grouse, mostly—of a dozen years ago. This little thing was just big enough to gut the trout of mountain streams and had a handle corner shaped to scrape fishy abdomens. Its blade had a blunt back edge for cracking grouse leg joints, and the blade that gutted trout would certainly open up upland birds. The whole thing was about as long as a big man's index finger and about as thick as a house key. Crockford generally used ivory Micarta and scrimmed one panel with a grouse feather or trout fly.

Any number of makers provide special small knives besides the standard stuff. And some people specialize in small ones—a hunter with a 3½-inch blade is the biggest several guys offer, for instance—because they sell well, because they can be priced lower, even because the maker believes there's no point in bigger knives.

There is, of course, but not right here, not on these few pages where smaller is better.

Ken Warner

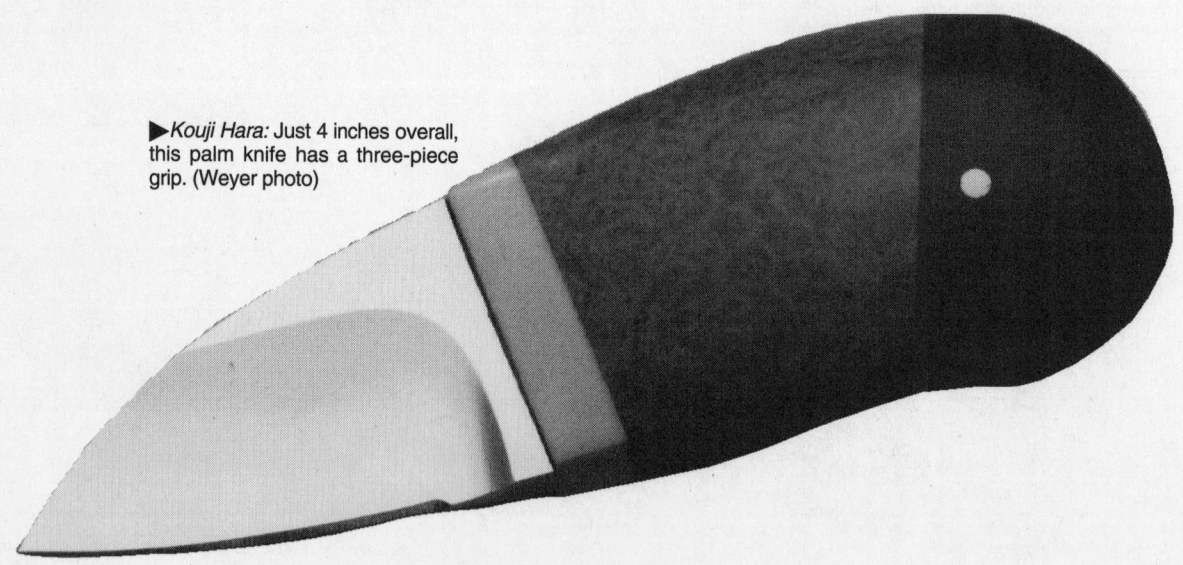

▶*Kouji Hara:* Just 4 inches overall, this palm knife has a three-piece grip. (Weyer photo)

SMALL KNIVES

▶*Edward P. Brandsey:* Pointy skinner in Pakkawood and ATS-34 has 3¼-inch blade. (Scadlock photo)

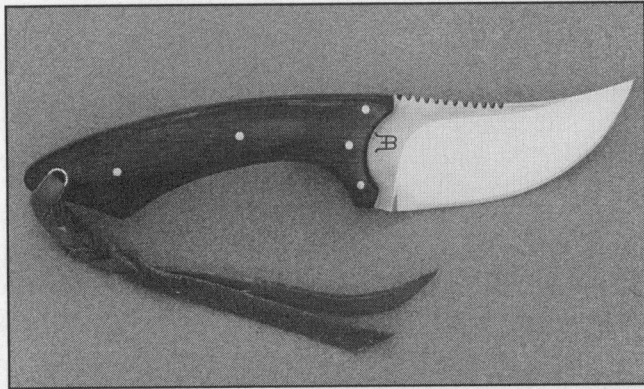

▼*Anthony I. Graffeo:* Palm skinner with 3-inch blade offers forefinger placement aids.

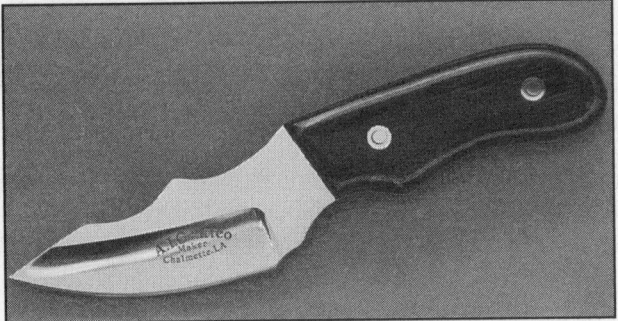

▲*Randy Lee:* Just 6 inches of Sidekick here, in ATS-34 and elk antler. (Weyer photo)

◀*William W. Hampton:* Just 4 inches of three-finger fighter has chisel edge and a pocket sheath.

▲*Chuck Ward:* Tough work or rope knife in 440C, brass and Corian.

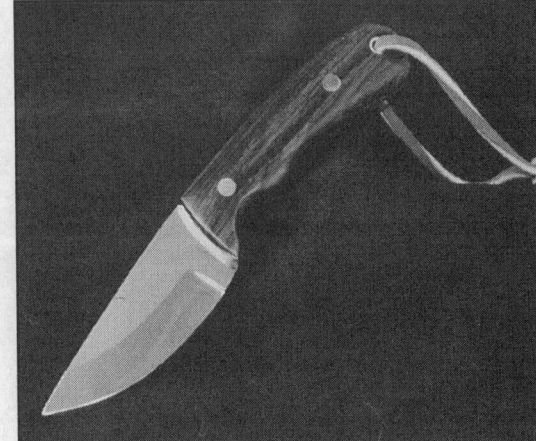

▶*Charley L. Webb, Jr.:* Longish handle in cocobolo for a 3-inch blade—called the Model K.

FIFTEENTH EDITION 107

TRENDS

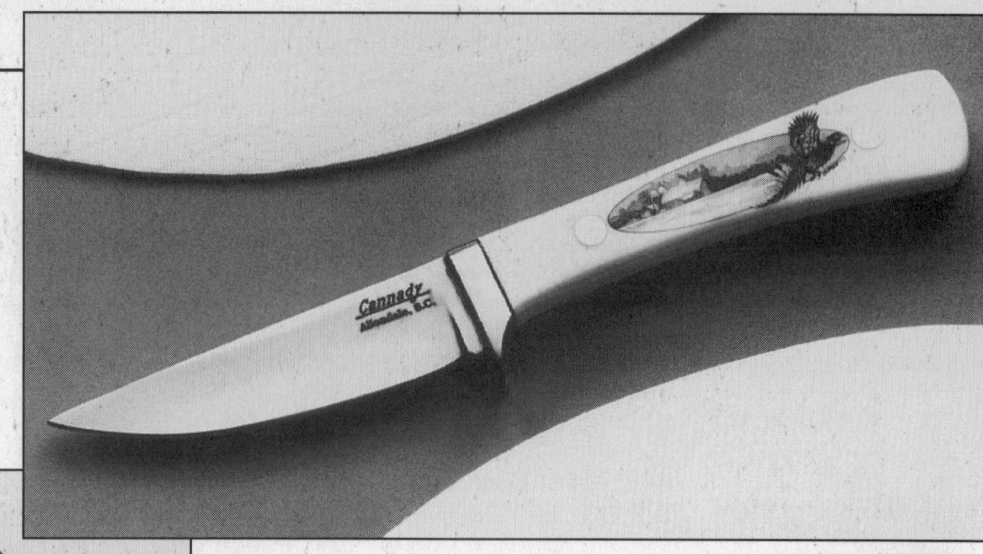

▶ *Daniel L. Cannady:* Long, but slim, with Burdette scrim, this goes 7½ inches overall. (Weyer photo)

▼ *Al Polkowski:* Necklace sheaths for knives with 3½- and 2-inch blades called Hang Tights. (Weyer photo)

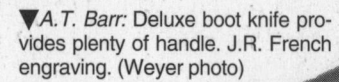

▼ *A.T. Barr:* Deluxe boot knife provides plenty of handle. J.R. French engraving. (Weyer photo)

▲ *Leonard Williams:* Tiny forged utility knife works fine and rides in a thonged sheath.

◀ *Russ Peagler:* Two-edged boot has 3¼-inch blade and 3¾-inch mastodon ivory handle. (Long photo)

▶ *Robert Patrick:* Called the B.C. Trout Knife in ATS-34 and Diamondwood. (Durant photo)

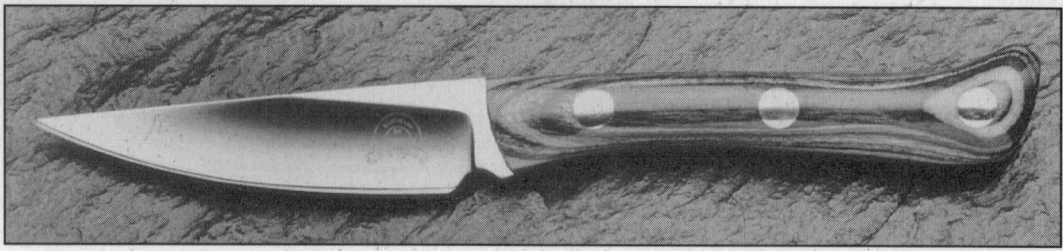

SMALL KNIVES

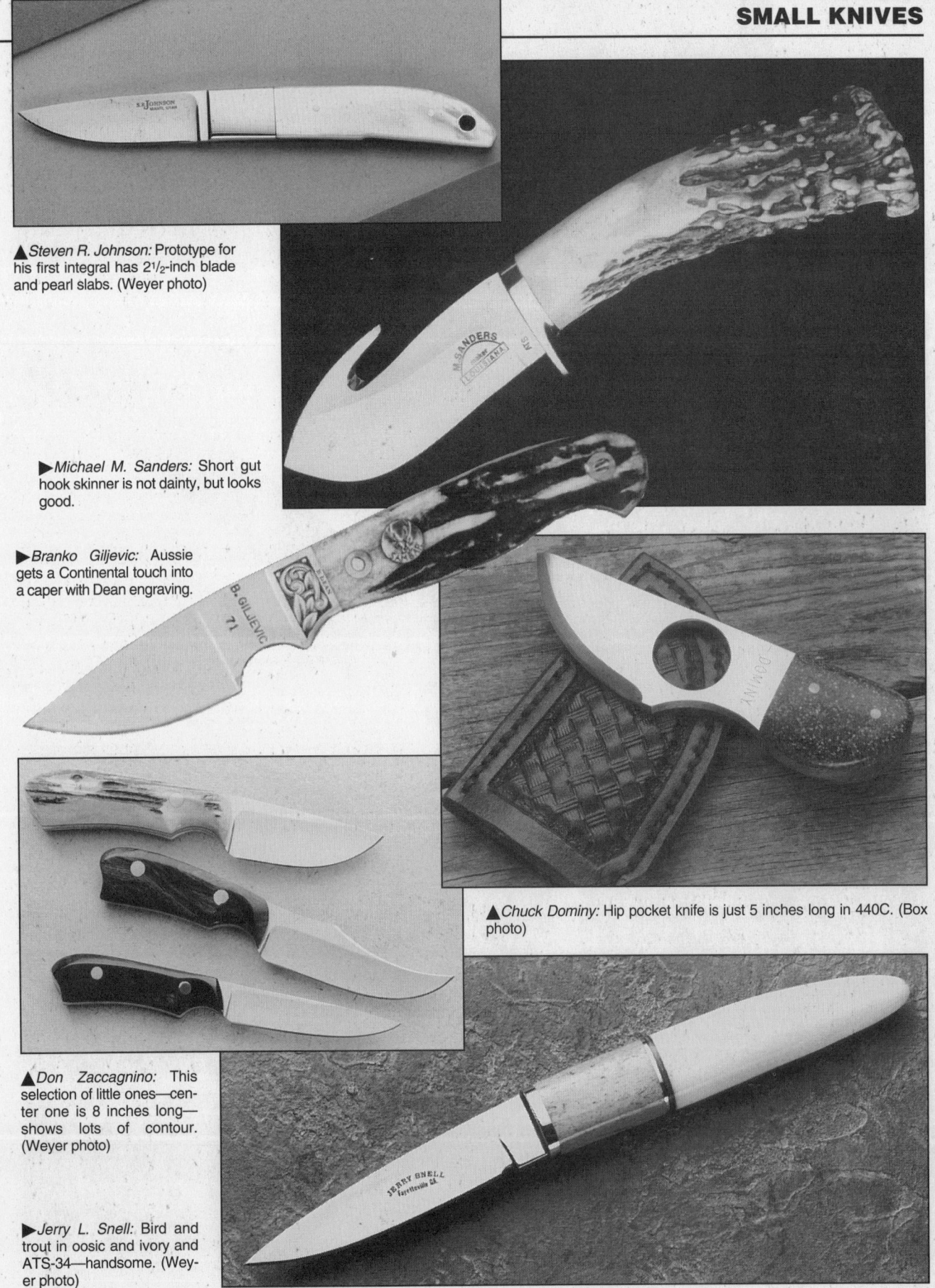

▲*Steven R. Johnson:* Prototype for his first integral has 2½-inch blade and pearl slabs. (Weyer photo)

▶*Michael M. Sanders:* Short gut hook skinner is not dainty, but looks good.

▶*Branko Giljevic:* Aussie gets a Continental touch into a caper with Dean engraving.

▲*Chuck Dominy:* Hip pocket knife is just 5 inches long in 440C. (Box photo)

▲*Don Zaccagnino:* This selection of little ones—center one is 8 inches long—shows lots of contour. (Weyer photo)

▶*Jerry L. Snell:* Bird and trout in oosic and ivory and ATS-34—handsome. (Weyer photo)

TRENDS

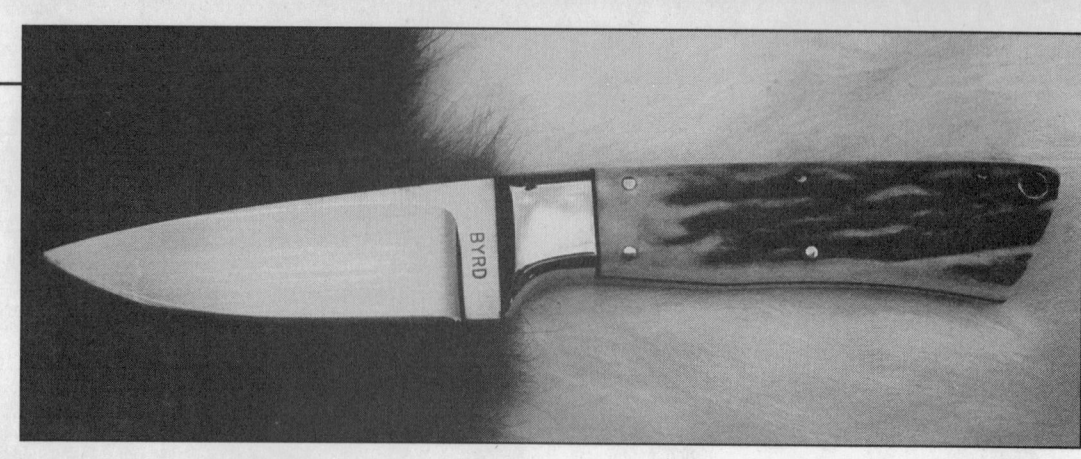

▶ *Don E. Byrd:* Little straightforward hunter with brushed finish and dropped-point.

▼ *John W. Walker:* The "Delicate Inquiry" in Damascus, sterling silver and ironwood.

▲ *Russel J. Rizzi:* Boot knife just tops folder—a nice pair in pearl. (Weyer photo)

▼ *Dominick W. Spano:* Two knife set in ATS-34 and Corian—a caper and a skinner.

▼ *Mike Wilson:* Little workers in stag and ebony—one with, one without bolster.

▶ *James F. Downs:* Blade is just 2 inches long; handle is abalone. (Ross photo)

TRENDS

THE PRIMITIVE EDGE

OF COURSE, THE ultimate primitive edge is made of stone, if we're firmly in historical reverse gear. And, in fact, there are more stone knives readily available than there used to be.

However, as with our other arbitrary and subjective categories, "Primitive" really means "sort of primitive" or "primitive looking." And by primitive, we don't mean either aboriginal or prehistoric. We really mean "backwoods knives," at least most of the time.

So, whether it's Bill Cheatham making ATS-34 blades that look like chipped flint, or Tim Herman's stainless blades cast from a genuine file-made knife, or Errett Callahan's neolithic obsidian daggers, or Dan Winkler's backwoods Bowies—it's all grist to this primitive mill. Primitive means, in this sense, non-modern, nearly anything non-modern.

Thus, we have blades made of obsidian in shapes familiar in the Stone Age and in shapes the Stone Age never saw; we have knives crafted in fully equipped shops to look like something laboriously turned out by a campfire with a rock for an anvil. We got Bowies and rifle knives and daggers and patch knives. We have bearjaw stabbers. We got variety.

Most all of them are OK cutting instruments and some are more than OK. As with all other knives, it depends on the maker.

And who buys these? Collectors aside, the main market is the buckskinner, the personal recreator of times long gone, of the glories of life in the Shining Mountains or the incredible days in the canebrakes of Kentucky when white men met red men on even terms in the Dark and Bloody Ground.

Our primitive knives are not the only modern edges that reach back. There are those who make knives for the Alamo fight, others who craft daggers for the Viking Age. Primitive knives are just North American—*old* North American.

Ken Warner

▶ *Gregory Nunn:* Dinosaur bone handle and a stone blade make a 9¾-inch knife.

▲ *Gary (Wolf) Rua:* This is a large scroll folder, with 5-inch forged blade and maple grips. (Dailey photo)

▶ *Michael W. Thourot:* Blackfoot Bear Cult dag has a flinted O1 steel blade, Jim Frey sheath and authentic assembly. (Weyer photo)

▶ *Errett Callahan:* Over 10 inches long, this one-piece dagger was flaked from rainbow obsidian.

FIFTEENTH EDITION 111

TRENDS

Daniel Winkler: The varieties of patch knives and hunting bag knives are endless, as are friction folders. Sheaths are by Karen Shook. (Weyer photos)

▼ *Mudd Sharrigan:* Buckskinner #1, the maker calls it, in 1095, forge-finished, and the right look.

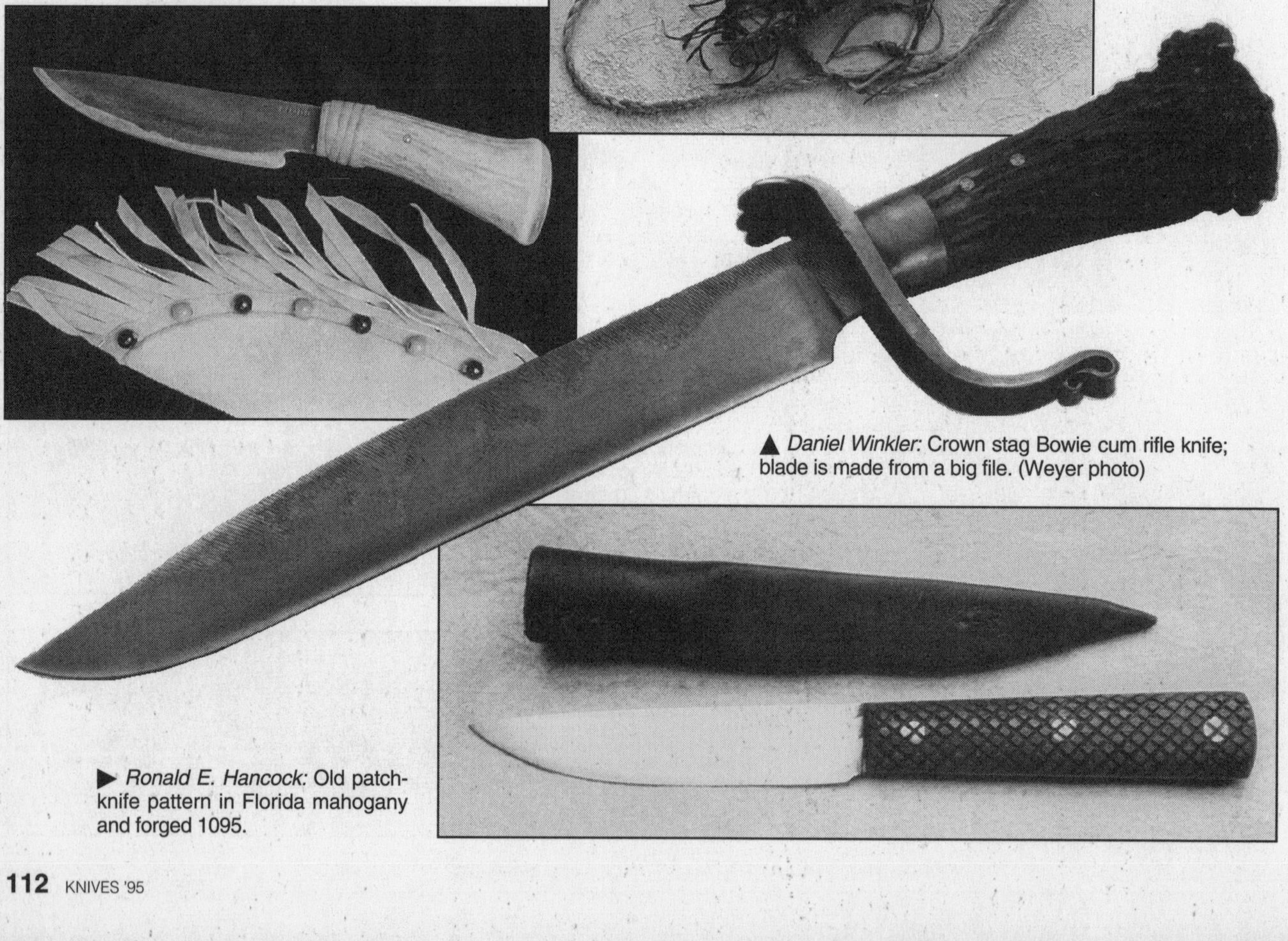

▲ *Daniel Winkler:* Crown stag Bowie cum rifle knife; blade is made from a big file. (Weyer photo)

▶ *Ronald E. Hancock:* Old patch-knife pattern in Florida mahogany and forged 1095.

THE PRIMITIVE EDGE

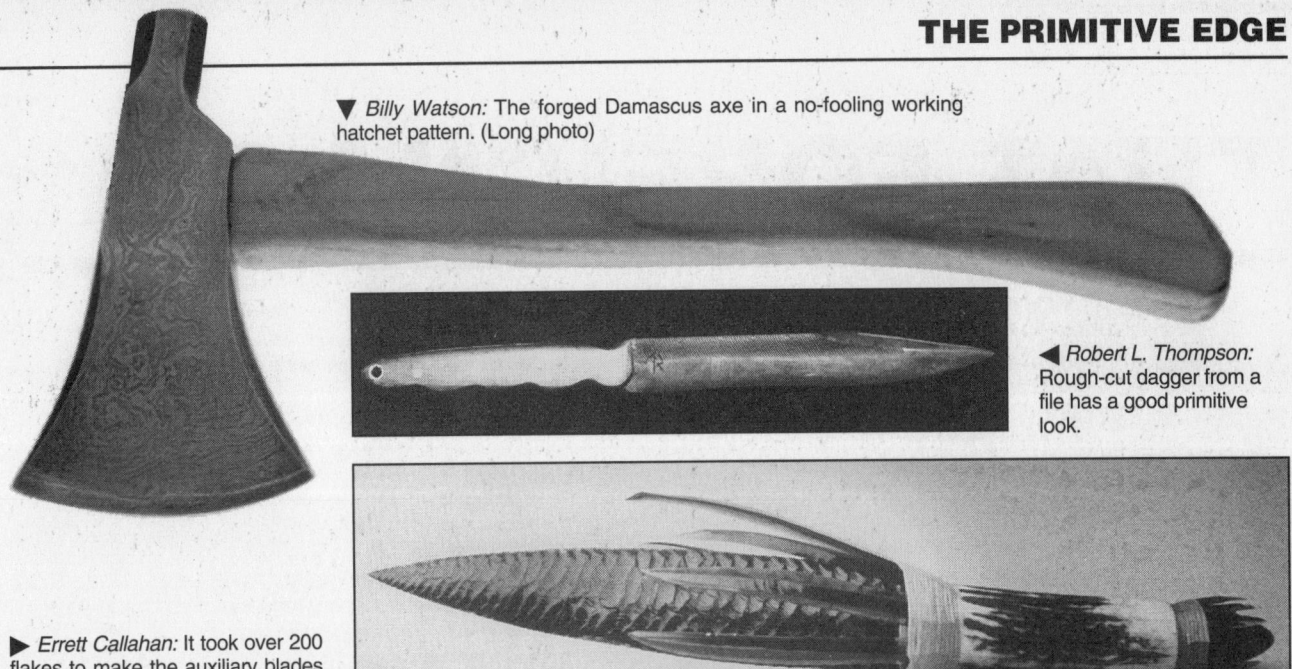

▼ *Billy Watson:* The forged Damascus axe in a no-fooling working hatchet pattern. (Long photo)

◀ *Robert L. Thompson:* Rough-cut dagger from a file has a good primitive look.

▶ *Errett Callahan:* It took over 200 flakes to make the auxiliary blades on this dagger called the Snapdragon. It's 17 inches long and very fierce and fragile. (Graves photo)

◀ *Alan W. Patterson:* The knife is a "mountain fighter" and looks it; the axe has a lot of sturdy. (Weyer photo)

▲ *Joseph E. Knuth & George W. Werth:* Forged fancy bag knives in Damascus and ivory—show pieces. (Weyer photo)

▲ *Robert Rupert:* Typical primitive surfaces in a couple of sophisticated knives. (Weyer photo)

FIFTEENTH EDITION **113**

TRENDS

THAT FOREIGN LOOK

MOSTLY, THIS YEAR'S crop of knives overseas are spread around in the various categories. A lot of them are right in the mainstream of the modern handmade knife, so that's where they belong.

Others, however, the ones you see here, are not in that mainstream. All they have in common with the mainstream are materials and fabricating technique. All they have in common with each other is their foreign look—each, of course, with a *different* foreign look.

Like every other sort of artist or artisan, knifemakers draw their ideas from diverse sources. In the Fifty States, the main body of sources is held in common—commercial knives, historical knives and other handmade knives are the three big ones. Those overseas makers who stick with patterns derived from *their* national sources produce knives that are sometimes subtly and sometimes markedly different.

We have reviewed, for instance, the knives of the Canary Islands not long ago. The national patterns of Scandinavia—relatively small, pointy, working knives—are often seen here. We are seeing Russian knives now.

It's not clear there is a U.S. market of any size for the foreign look. The knives are often stylish, very mannered, and very well made. Such knives should find new owners in any market, but they don't always.

This brief look can by no means review the whole panoply of foreign looks. But we are showing you *how* a foreign look is different.

Ken Warner

▲*Aad V. Rijswijk:* Idiosyncratic shape, grind, grip sculpturing—a mighty stylish hunter.

▶*Joe Zemitis:* Big knife—three piece blade, horn and stag grip—is not quite a Bowie. (O'Rourke photo)

▼*Yuri Kharlamov:* The blade is puukko-shaped; the handle reeks of Russian richness.

THAT FOREIGN LOOK

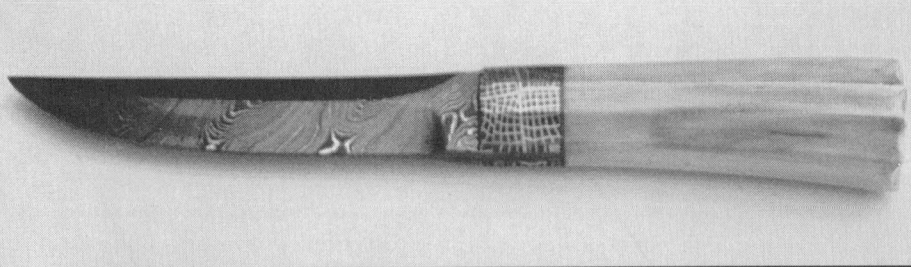

▲▼*Gerard Doursin:* A rich straight belt knife in ivory and both twist and mosaic Damascus; and an all-out opulent dagger of Napoleonic merit.

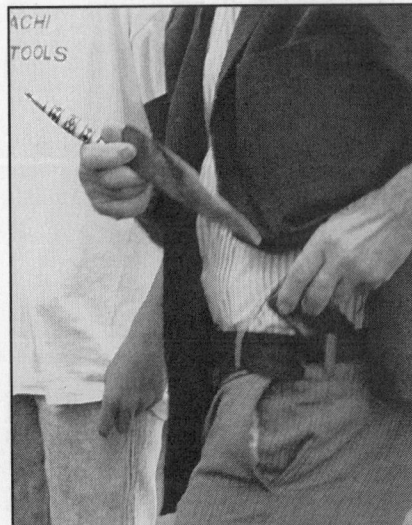

▲▼*Canary Islands:* Scenes at an ox-pull show the knife of the islands, the kind Gannaway makes. (Gannaway photos)

▲*Nestor Lorenzo Rho:* Medium knives with a big bold Argentine look in 440C, bronze and stag. (Herce photo)

▲*Laurent Doussot:* Small folding dagger has a trick lock and a distinctive medieval flavor.

TRENDS

▲*Gianluigi Simonella:* Distinctly personal renditions of the small hunter and its grinds and handles.

▲*Christian Wimpff:* Maker says this looks good closed. It's a titanium-handled liner lock and looks good open, too.

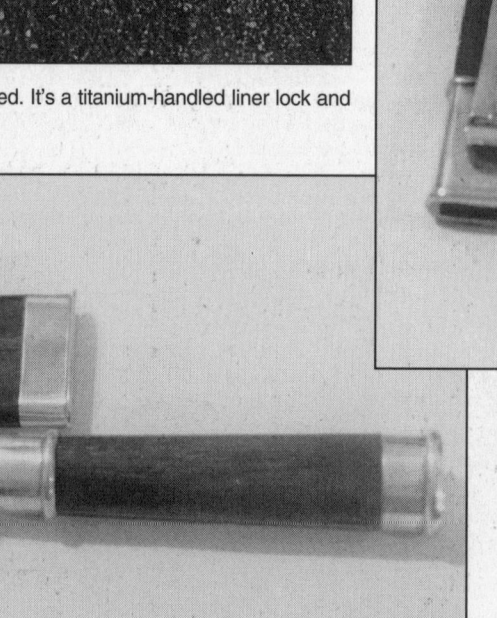

◀▲*Cristian L. Ayarragaray:* A traditional gaucho facon and a more modern short belt knife.

THAT FOREIGN LOOK

◄▲ *Marc Bjorn Carlsson:* One folder, one straight knife, one essential shape in ATS-34, sterling silver and exotic wood. (Hansen photos)

▼ *Ingemar Nordell:* Highly refined edition of the Nordic belt knife in Sandvik stainless, buckeye handle, nickel silver and coral trimmings. (Eriksson photo)

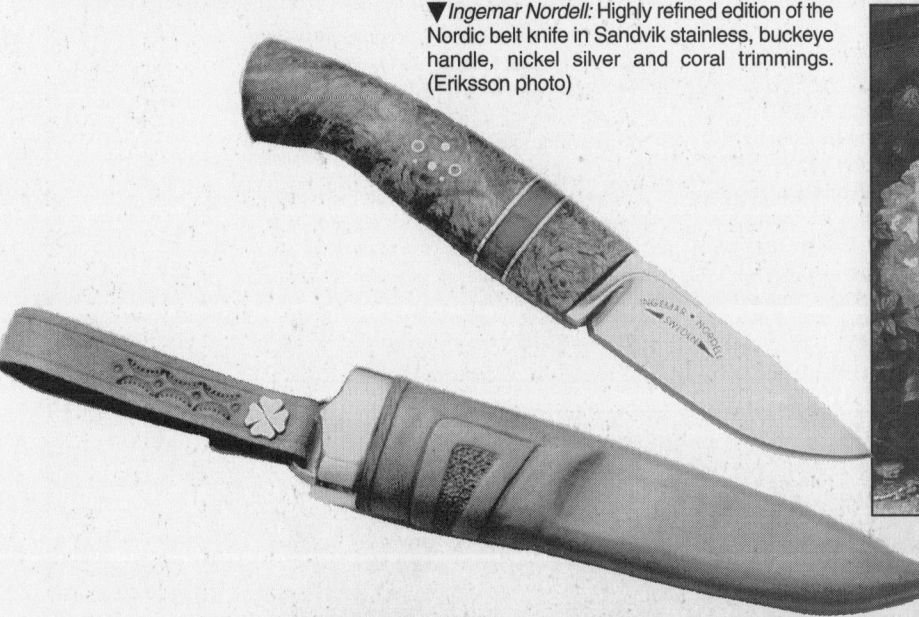

▲ *Mauro Ameri:* Heavy-duty Bowie hunter with a serious Ameri sheath.

► *Corrie Schoeman:* A general-purpose knife in ATS-34 and lignum vitae.

FIFTEENTH EDITION 117

TRENDS

THE MEDIUM KNIFE

YOU MIGHT THINK it obvious to say so, but the most important feature of the medium knife is its medium size and shape. There's nothing extreme; of most good medium knives, one can say, "If you had that'n, you wouldn't need another'n."

Most hunting knives, most general-purpose knives, and, taken together, that means most knives, are medium. A 6-inch blade is on the absolute upper end of medium; $3^{1}/_{2}$ inches is at the other end. At least that's true for our purposes and in practice at a wide variety of knife activities.

Like nearly all else related to tools (and weapons) such dimensions are related to human dimensions—largely the sizes of our hands and the lengths of our torsos. Obviously, handles have to accommodate hands; hands are very flexible, so the range of useful handle lengths goes from 3 to 6 inches. As for the torso, well, torso size determines the ease and comfort of carry for the belted knife, and for most people, a foot-long package at the belt is *big* and 5 inches is small. So your 6- to 9-inch belt package is to be considered medium.

A 5-inch blade and 4-inch handle makes it into medium; so does a 3-inch blade and a 4-inch handle. And so forth. Medium is easy to figure, though the range is not as broad as we often treat it.

Medium is useful, however. There are sound reasons for some to choose big knives and sound reasons for some to use small knives, and pure style and pure preference exist, too. Everyone else takes medium, so there is a lot of it going around.

This is curious, but it's so: People decorate and do extravagant things with big knives and little ones far more than those in between. Oh, there are a lot of engraved and/or scrimshawed medium knives, but they don't often get the full-court press.

That's probably because they are very sensible knives and attract non-extravagant people. Since we have a lot of those, there are plenty of knives in the middle sizes shown here.

Ken Warner

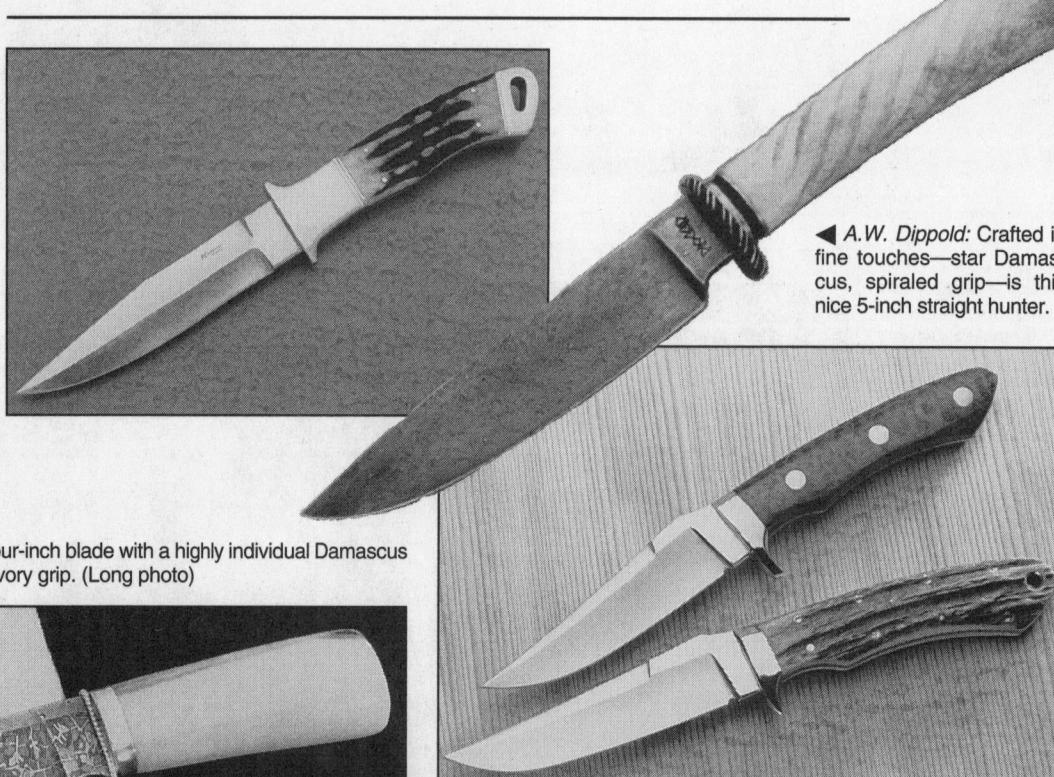

▶ *Howard Hitchmough:* Integral construction in the now-classic boot pattern, deeply hollow ground.

◀ *A.W. Dippold:* Crafted in fine touches—star Damascus, spiraled grip—is this nice 5-inch straight hunter.

▼ *Hank Knickmeyer:* Four-inch blade with a highly individual Damascus pattern and plain fossil ivory grip. (Long photo)

▲ *Michael McClure:* Gorgeous grinds in purposeful $4^{5}/_{8}$-inch hunter blades, full-tanged. (Weyer photo)

THE MEDIUM KNIFE

▲ *Steven R. Johnson:* A 4-inch handle on a 3-inch blade—on the pretty small side of medium—was a prize-winner at Blade Show. (Weyer photo)

▲ *Don E. Byrd:* Careful grind in 5/32-inch D2 with a pinned ivory grip makes a handsome defense knife.

▶ *Keith Kilby:* Double-edged boot with bark ivory and Damascus and a little trimming. (Long photo)

▲ *Charles F. Ochs:* A chute knife with more double-edge than usual in 320-layer Damascus and ivory. (Weyer photo)

▲ *Lloyd D. Pate:* Axis antler and amber for the handle and a heavy drop-point blade interestingly ground. (Box photo)

▲ *Bill Caldwell:* Taking a walk on the tame side with a 3¾-inch drop-point hunter. (Weyer photo)

▶ *Kenneth J. Onion:* A curvy chute knife in ATS-34 and ironwood. Blade is 5 inches. (Weyer photo)

TRENDS

▶ *Shane Taylor:* Handsomely shaped 4-incher in Damascus and ivory, with scrim by the maker. (Weyer photo)

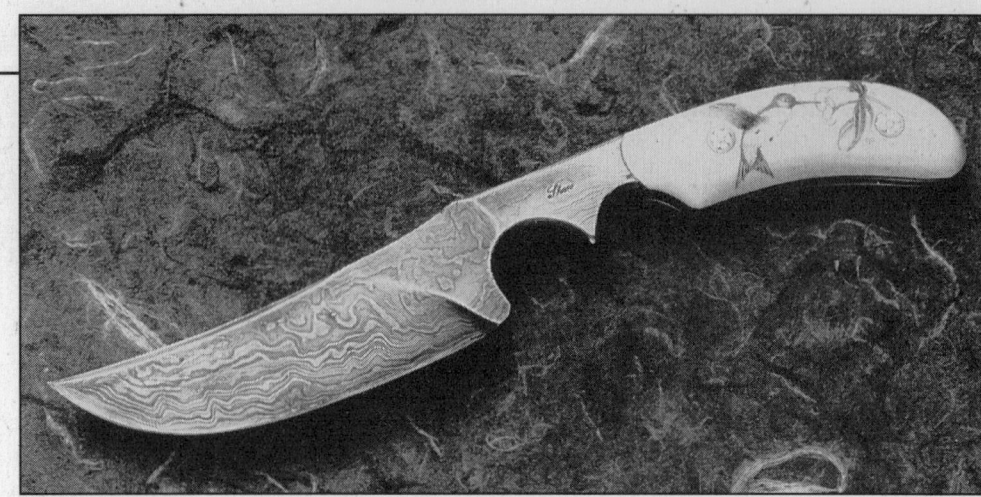

▼ *Mike Schirmer:* A lot of texture in moose-antler slabs; a lot of shape in the hollow grind.

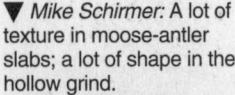

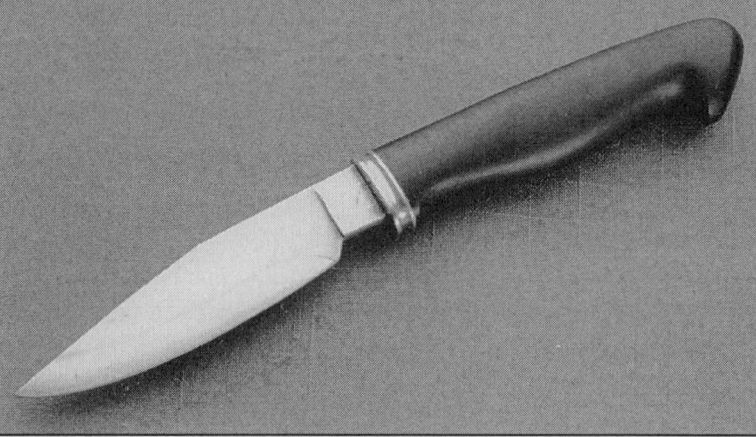

▲ *Michael K. Manabe:* Triple quenched and tempered, with ebony handle, this 4½-inch blade has a nice temper line. (Weyer photo)

▼ *Steve Likarich:* Jazzy 3¾-inch trout knife, fitted with titanium bolsters and horn handle slabs. (Weyer photo)

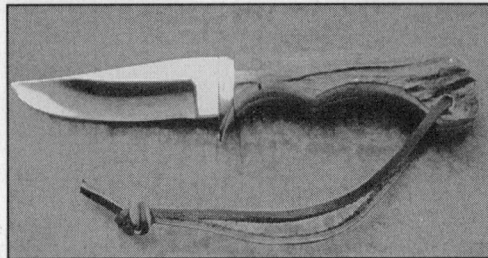

◀ *Lawrence Dungy:* Utility knife at 3¾ inches has 4½-inch Pakkawood handle. (Weyer photo)

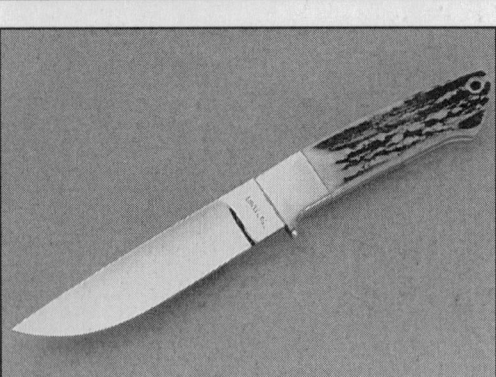

◀ *R.W. Loveless:* A new mark on a long-bolstered straight hunter. Blade is 5½ inches. (Weyer photo)

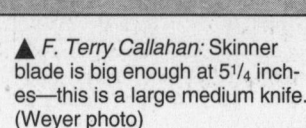

▲ *F. Terry Callahan:* Skinner blade is big enough at 5¼ inches—this is a large medium knife. (Weyer photo)

THE MEDIUM KNIFE

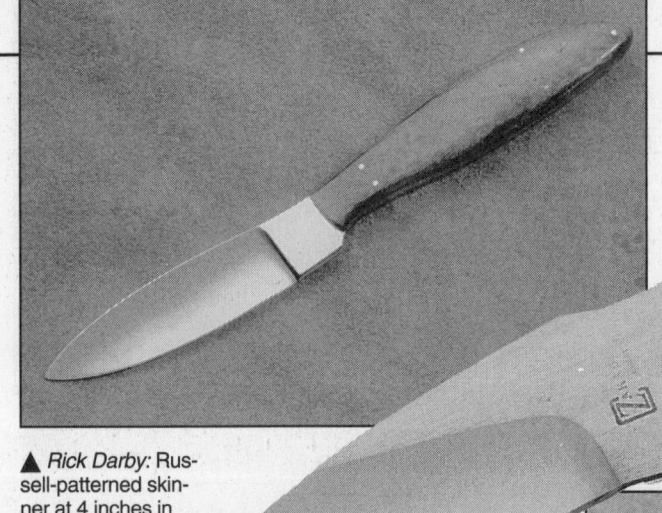

▲ *Rick Darby:* Russell-patterned skinner at 4 inches in 440C and ironwood. (Etzler photo)

◄ *Carl S. Zakabi:* Mango seed-shaped handle in Pakkawood on a 3⅝-inch 440C blade. (Long photo)

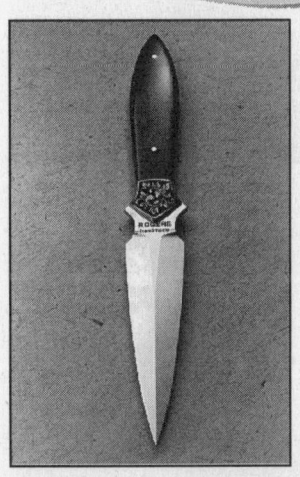

◄ *Rodney Rogers:* This triangular blade is 4½ inches long; grip is dark mastodon ivory. Robidoux engraving. (Weyer photo)

► *Clay Gault:* High-grade Texas taste in Vascowear at 3¾-inch wears Argali horn slabs. (Bibb Gault photo)

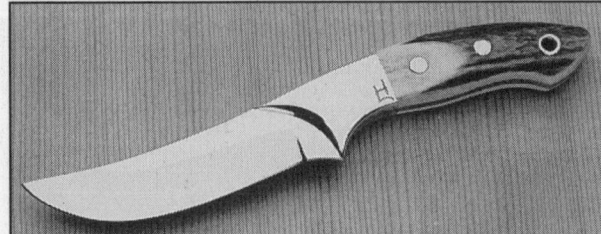

▲ *Heinz Leber:* Five-inch skinner in M2 steel carries out all its curves. (Weyer photo)

▼ *Ron Gaston:* Slim high-style dagger has 5½-inch blade and looks longer. (Weyer photo)

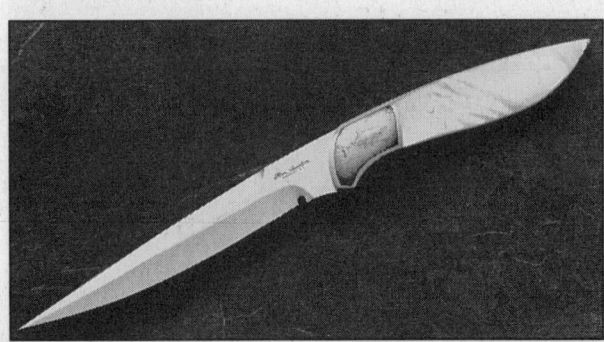

▲ *Frank Vought, Jr.:* Group of Outfitter medium knives for hunters. Blades are 4 to 4½ inches.

FIFTEENTH EDITION

TRENDS

◀ *Dal Leck:* This hunter, forged in Damascus, offers stainless trim on a maple grip. (Box photo)

▶ *Don Pavack:* Semi-skinner blade at 4 3/4 inches is 1/8-inch-thick ATS-34. Grip is ironwood.

▼ *Tim Scholl:* Slim-handled 4 1/2-inch drop-point hunter has stained maple grip. (Chiacchira photo)

▲ *Marilyn (Jimmy) Lile:* Jimmy's design for a 4 1/2-inch chute knife is in the classic mode.

▲ *William Behnke:* Pointy Damascus blade is 4 1/4 inches long—nice lines overall. (Weyer photo)

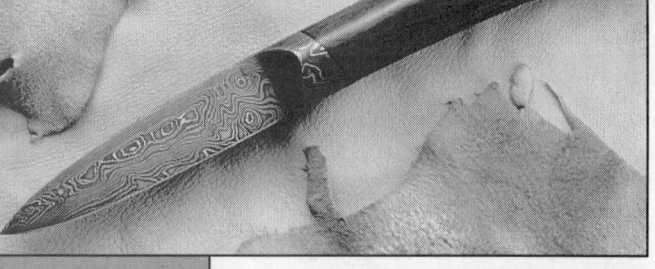

▲ *Tim Zowada:* Handsome integral hunter has cocobolo grip; blade is 4 1/2 inches. (Weyer photo)

◀ *Chris Flechtner:* This small Damascus tanto with 5 1/2-inch blade is a nice medium knife and is handsomely trimmed in blued steel, copper, horn and tulipwood. (Weyer photo)

THE MEDIUM KNIFE

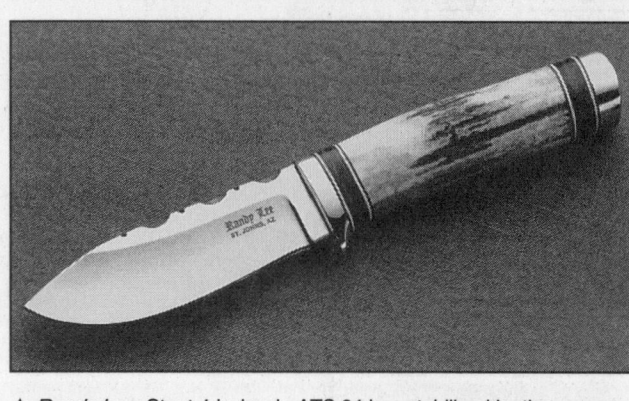

▲ *Randy Lee:* Stout 4-incher in ATS-34 has stabilized leather spacers in the stag grip.

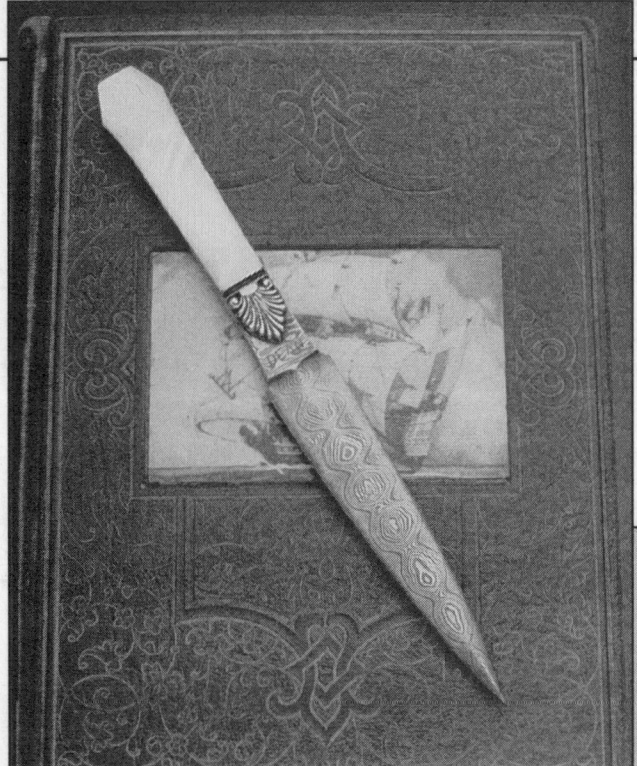

▲ *Harvey J. Dean:* Slim and serious, this 5-inch Damascus dagger is done up in nickel silver and pearl. (Box photo)

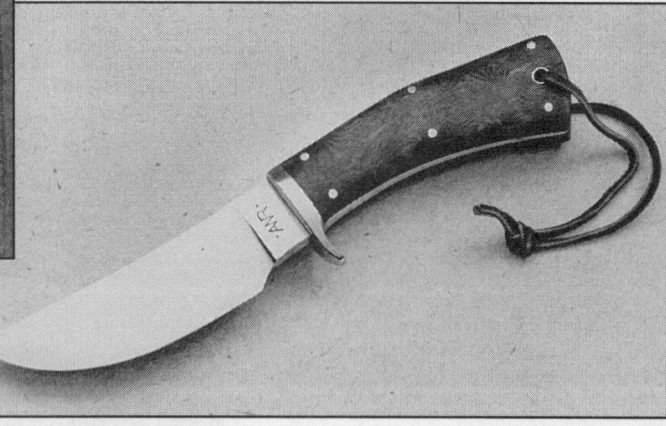

▶ *Alan W. Ray:* Forthright 4¾-inch skinner looks sturdy and has redwood burl handle slabs. (Weyer photo)

◀ *Joel Humphreys:* Curved correctly from butt to point, this little skinner should work fine. (Long photo)

◀ *Steve Dunn:* At 5¼ inches, these straight hunter blades in forged 5160 are big enough. (Weyer photo)

▲ *Randy Lyons:* Trail-point blade is 4½ inches; whole knife looks comfortable. (Box photo)

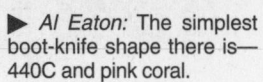

▶ *Al Eaton:* The simplest boot-knife shape there is— 440C and pink coral.

FIFTEENTH EDITION **123**

TRENDS

THE FOLDING KNIFE

BEFORE ALL THIS started, let's say, in the pre-Buck days, we customarily lumped all folding knives together and called them pocketknives. There was a basis for that, but it doesn't work anymore. The knives have sorted that out for us.

It wasn't all Buck's fault, either. There have been large locking folding hunting knives for at least seventy years. A friend of mine, annoyingly smug about it, slips a flat 5-inch folder in his pocket every deer season and upon every opportunity loudly wonders why anyone pays $20 for a good knife when his Daddy got this one in Connecticut in 1923 for $2.75. These knives have been around.

So have gent's knives, fancy gold ones, and folding dirks and, of course, a myriad of handmade-in-factories folders in hundreds of patterns. So there really aren't many new *types* of knives.

It's having all those types handmade that's the new thing. And the considerable emphasis on style and embellishment is new. There were always fancy knives if you knew where to look, but not like this.

Mechanisms, too, are proliferating. We have standard topside locking bars and liner locks and many button locks. There are several versions of the swinging blade. And the one-at-a-time fabrication of slip-joint folders with one to five blades each proceeds apace. And there's a lot of movement in the automatic-knife design sweepstakes, which is discussed elsewhere.

The two main games in handmade folders are the top locks and the liner locks. They come big and small, light and heavy, pretty inexpensive and *very* expensive. There are all sorts of both locks.

As for *how* the locking folder is constructed, the interframe is gaining ground fast. It takes a milling machine—they don't actually make them by hand, soldered, as Steve Hoel once did—so *everybody* doesn't do it, just everybody who owns a mill. A very high percentage of big-ticket folders are interframes, beginning, of course, with Ron Lake's rear-locking version.

The old-time slip-joint pocketknife, the handmade one, keeps stalling. It just hasn't made the big-time. There are gorgeous slip-joints, mind you, and their makers are top craftsmen, but there simply aren't the number of people buying like some of us predicted.

We can look for more defense-patterned big knives, it seems. The knife market will never tire of the just-in-case knife idea. That's natural. It probably wasn't very long after the knife was put to use as a tool that it became a weapon.

In sum, the idea of the handmade folder continues taking giant steps. And a number of the footprints trail across these pages, right here.

Ken Warner

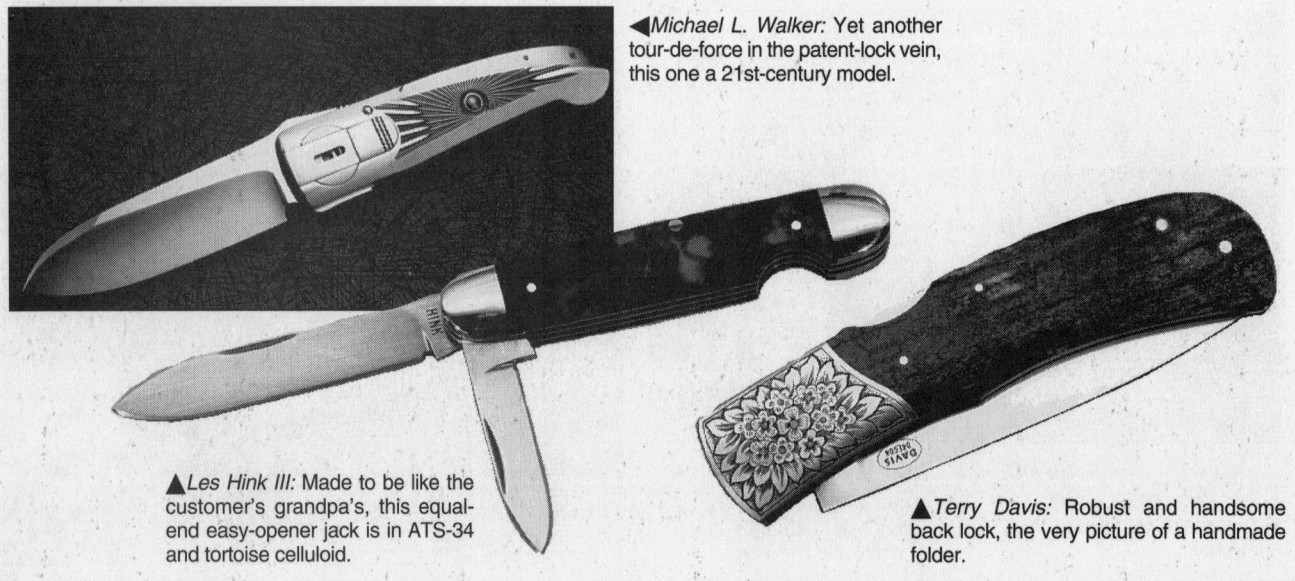

◀ *Michael L. Walker:* Yet another tour-de-force in the patent-lock vein, this one a 21st-century model.

▲ *Les Hink III:* Made to be like the customer's grandpa's, this equal-end easy-opener jack is in ATS-34 and tortoise celluloid.

▲ *Terry Davis:* Robust and handsome back lock, the very picture of a handmade folder.

THE FOLDING KNIFE

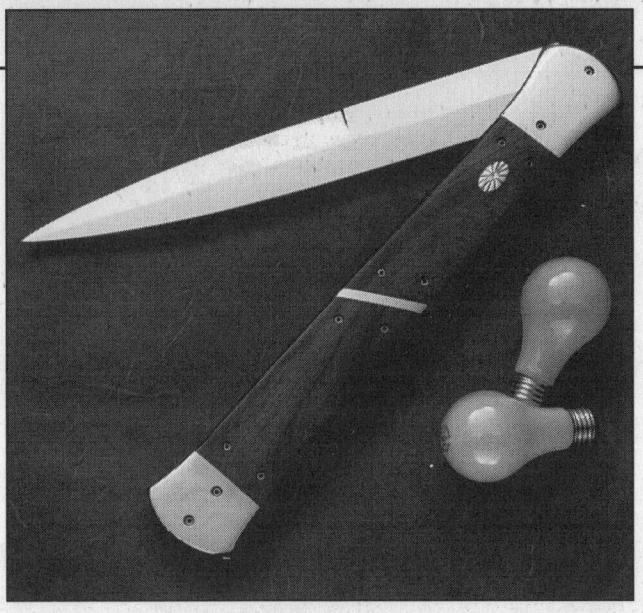

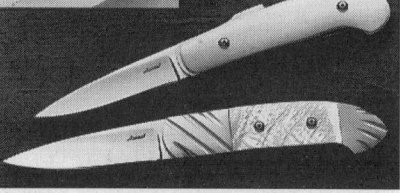

◄ *Robert Enders:* Touched up by Fred A. Harrington, this 4-inch barrel knife boasts sixteen blades. (Weyer photo)

► *Steven J. Fecas:* Too big for gent size, but gent-style lockers in ATS-34. (Weyer photo)

▲ *Arey Vallotton:* Giant folder has a 15-inch blade and what looks like a button lock. (Weyer photo)

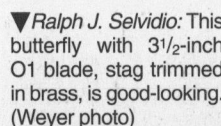

▲▼ *J.D. Clay:* Coil spring-powered, these are; hand-rubbed, too. (Long photo)

▼ *Ralph J. Selvidio:* This butterfly with 3½-inch O1 blade, stag trimmed in brass, is good-looking. (Weyer photo)

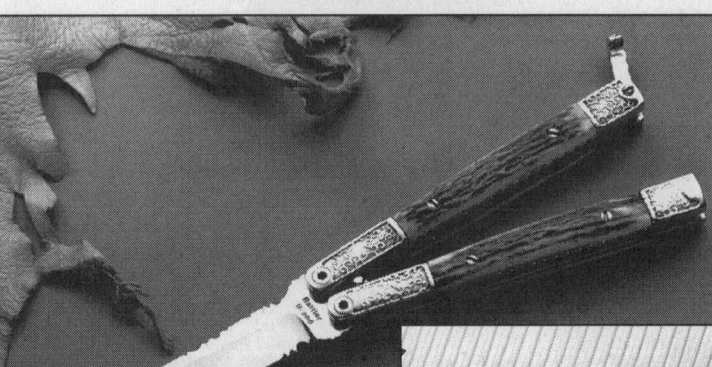

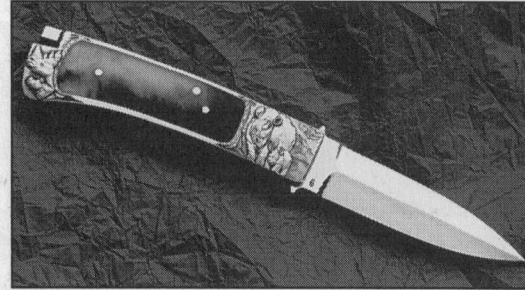

▲ *Ron Lake:* The investment-grade interframe folder of classic mien, engraved by Skaggs. (Weyer photo)

► *Roy Helton:* Called a cross lock, these handmades are like Buck's new knife—with Buck's permission. (Weyer photo)

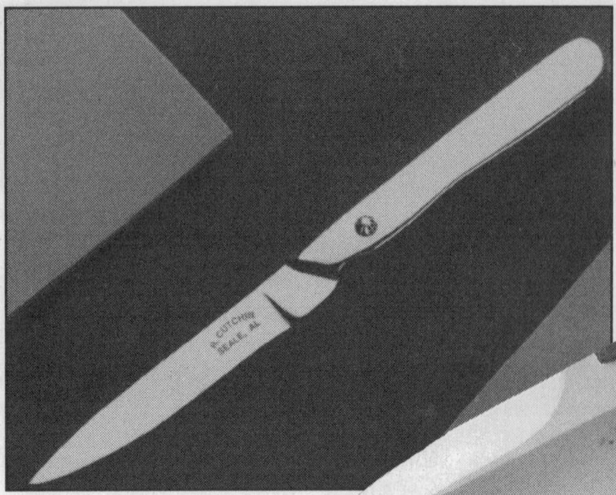

TRENDS

Roy D. Cutchin: All nickel silver and ATS-34, except for that 14-karat gold stud. (Weyer photo)

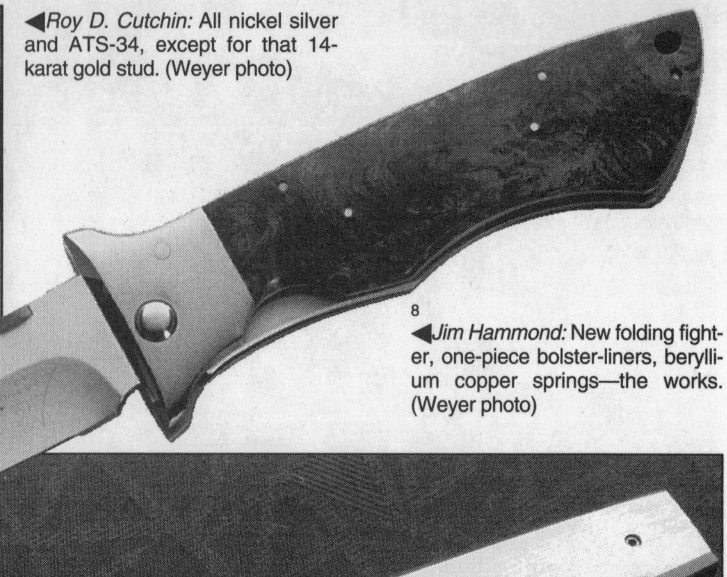

Jim Hammond: New folding fighter, one-piece bolster-liners, beryllium copper springs—the works. (Weyer photo)

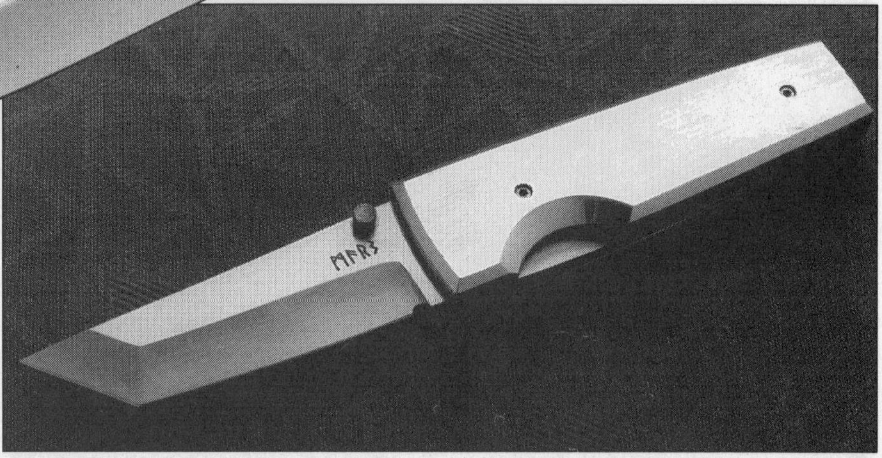

Marc Bjorn Carlsson: Solid sterling slabs and a dramatic ATS-34 tanto blade. (Hansen photo)

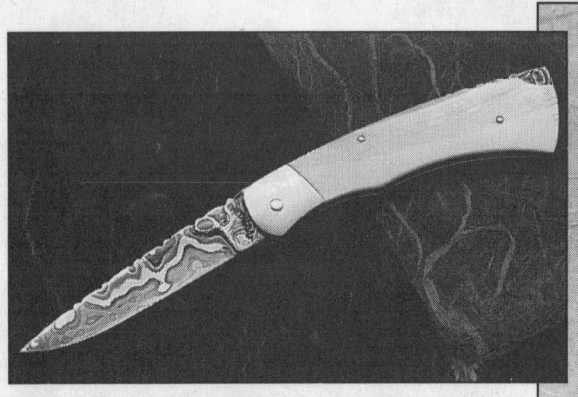

Don Hethcoat: Dramatic blade steel and a forthright rear-locker in ivory. (Weyer photo)

Raymond L. Smith: Brass and bone help with the honest old-time look of this 3-inch slip-joint knife. (Long photo)

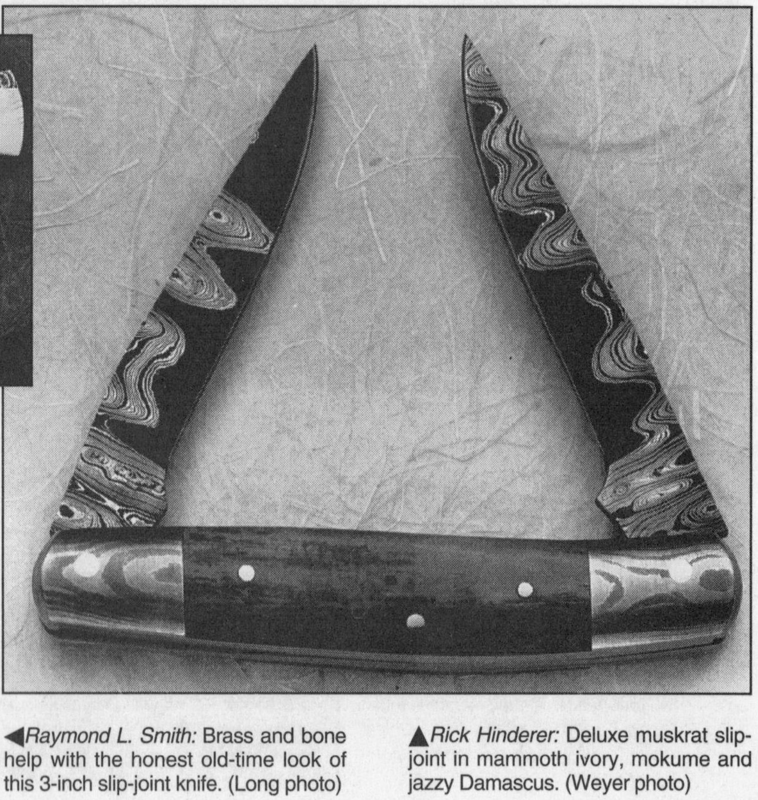

Rick Hinderer: Deluxe muskrat slip-joint in mammoth ivory, mokume and jazzy Damascus. (Weyer photo)

THE FOLDING KNIFE

▶ *Brett Laplante:* Slip-joint at 6¼ inches open—a nice pocketknife in pearl and 440C. (Weyer photo)

▼ *W.E. Ankrom:* Chubby little liner locks in pearl and ATS-34 and 416 stainless. (Weyer photo)

▼ *Frank and Tony Centofante:* Interframes all ready to engrave, hand-rubbed ATS-34 blades and all. (Weyer photo)

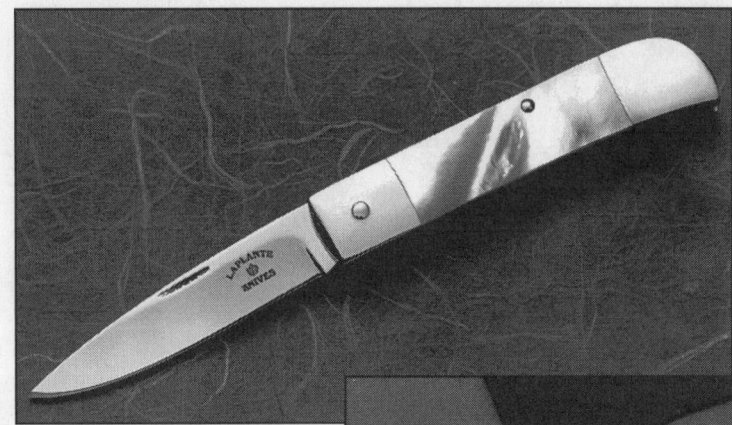

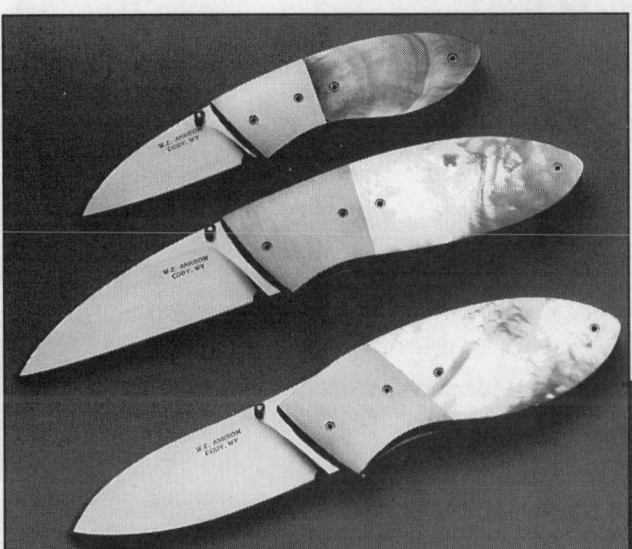

▲ *Joe Malloy:* Shadow-pattern lockback, stabilized wood slabs and very usable shape. (Weyer photo)

▼ *A.D. Rardon:* Interframe Congress pen, abalone inlaid, with the correct blade shapes. (Weyer photo)

▲ *Bob Levine:* Heavy-built liner-lock drop-point with sheephorn for slabs.

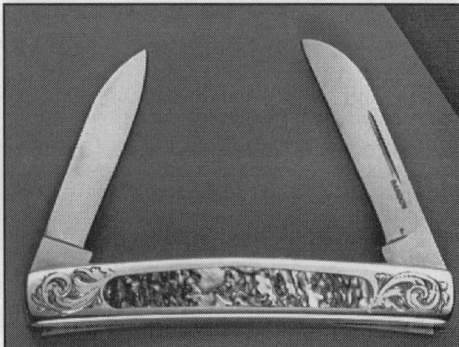

TRENDS

▲*John Holland:* Handsome stockman-pattern folder in jigged redbone and 440C—a classy knife. (Weyer photo)

▼*Allen Elishewitz:* Big in colored titanium and pearl, this is in the emergency class of folder. (Box photo)

▼*Kenneth E. Alden, Jr.:* His first folder, a rear-locker with bag handle—simple and clean. (Weyer photo)

▲*Victor Monteiro:* His first folder is a lockback with picked redbone scales, a hunter shape.

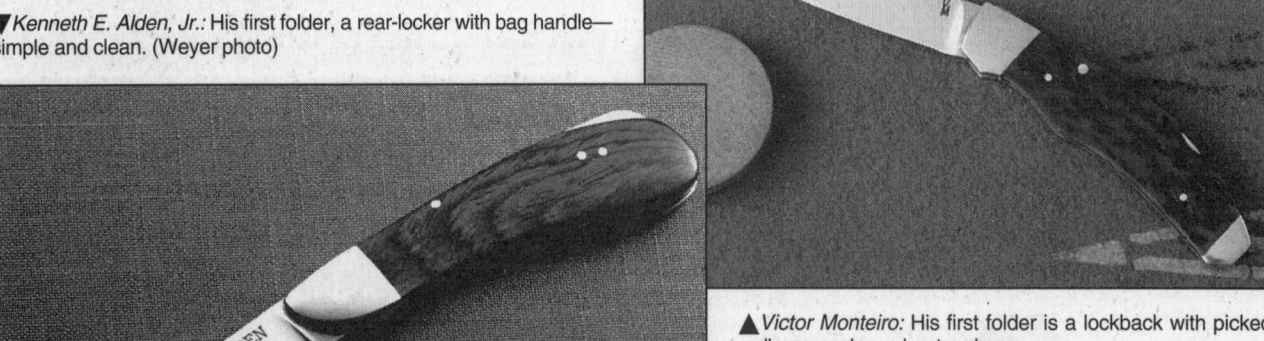

▲*Roy Helton:* Gun-blued mild steel, mastodon ivory and ATS-34 in a large liner lock called the Alaskan. (Weyer photo)

▶*Kaj Embretsen:* Small to medium interframe folders, all-Damascus, with pearl and ivory. (Weyer photo)

128 KNIVES '95

THE FOLDING KNIFE

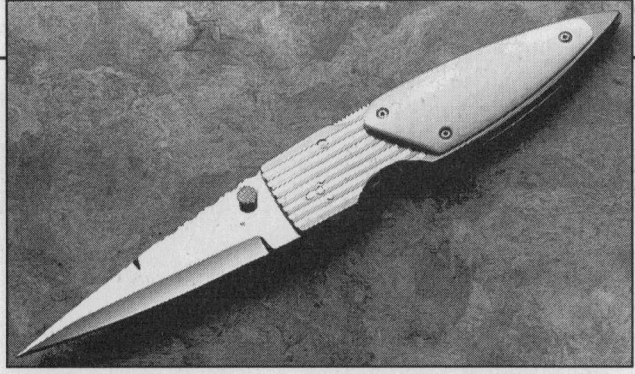

▲*Phil Boguszewski:* A Townsend design, it's also a pointed reminder in titanium, 440C and ivory—8 inches overall. (Weyer photo)

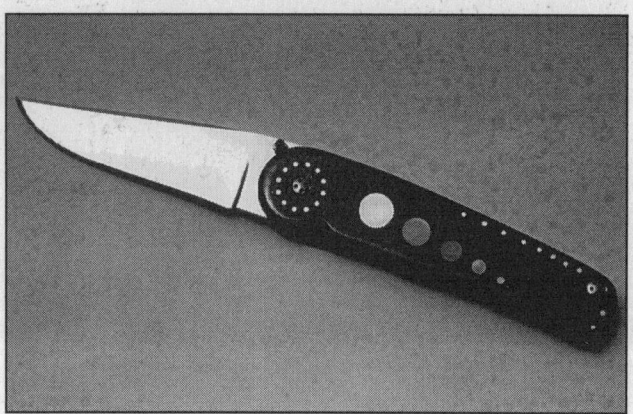

▶*Emilio Albericci:* One-hand opener, fighter styled, in ATS-34 and pearl and gold. (Vallini photo)

▼*Scot Horton:* Swingaround folder, small and useful-looking.

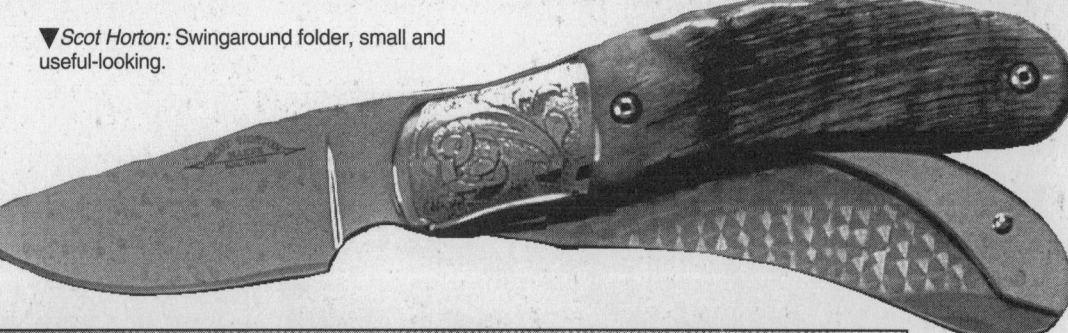

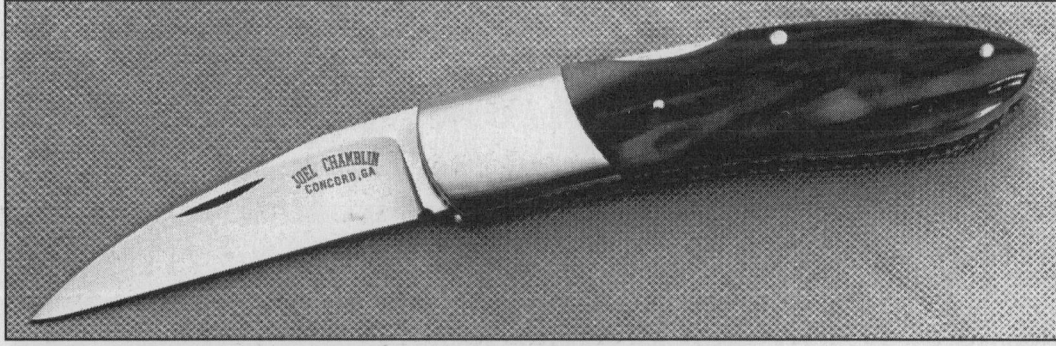

◀*Joel Chamblin:* Front-locked 2½-inch Wharncliffe blade ahead of nice mellow stag. (Long photo)

◀*Joe R. Prince:* Front-locking interframe with long clip blade, 3 inches long—a slick knife. (Weyer photo)

▲*Corbet R. Sigman:* Immaculte lines and a new handle profile around black-lip opal. (Weyer photo)

FIFTEENTH EDITION 129

TRENDS

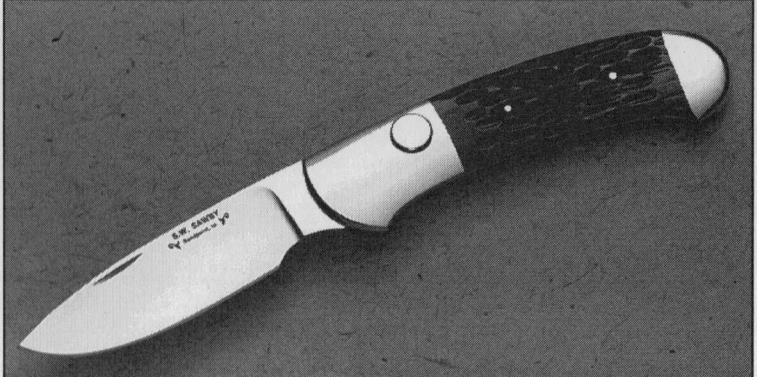

▲ *Scott Sawby:* Three inches of drop-point ahead of a button lock and jigged bone. (Weyer photo)

◄ *J.A. Harkins:* Liner lock in the tanto spirit—ray skin, cord wrap, gold menuki and all. (Slobodian photo)

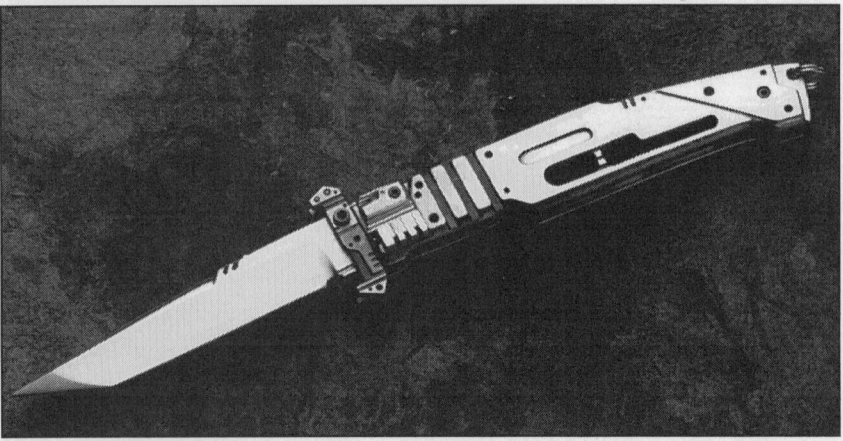

▲ *Jose C. DeBraga:* Complex assemblage of titanium in color, ATS-34 and pearl inlays. (Weyer photo)

▲ *Randall Gilbreath:* Button lock built to be slim, with pinned-on Damascus scales.

▼ *John Etzler:* Liner lock in pearl and matching Damascus—an all-purpose knife. (Weyer photo)

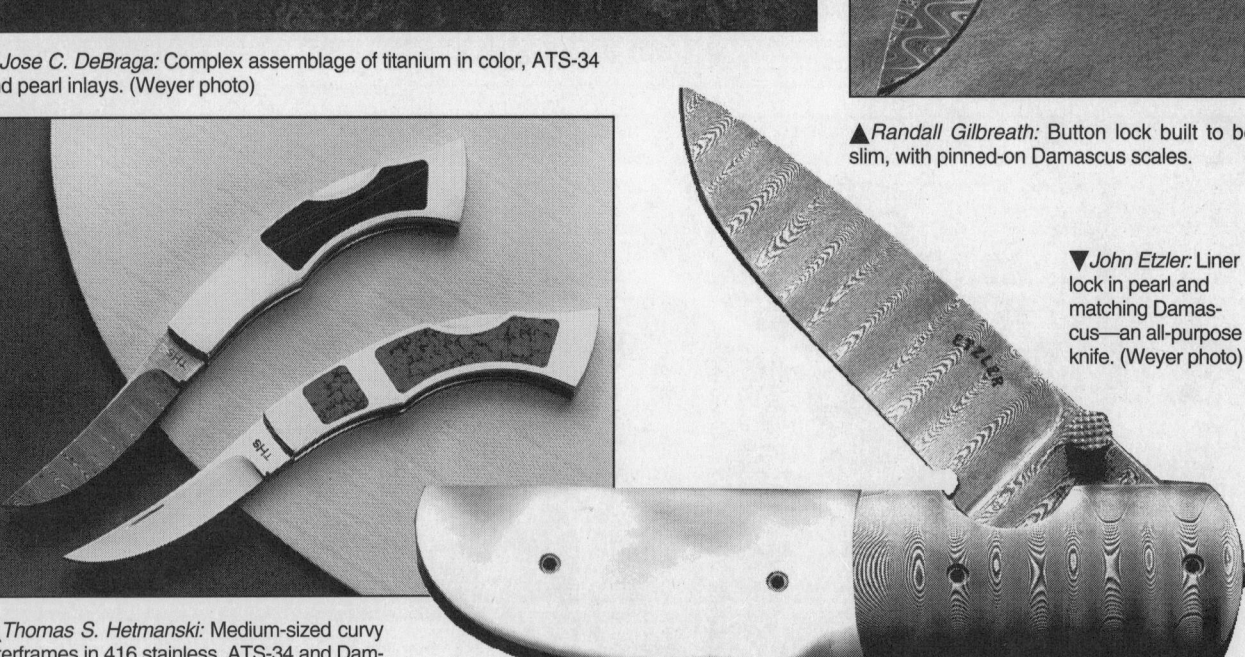

▲ *Thomas S. Hetmanski:* Medium-sized curvy interframes in 416 stainless, ATS-34 and Damascus. Inlays are malachite. (Weyer photo)

THE FOLDING KNIFE

▶ *Bill Cheatham:* Biggish interframe with smallish dinosaur-relic inlay, done in 440C. (Weyer photo)

▼ *Frank Gamble:* Button lock in redwood burl, aluminum and ATS-34 has 2½-inch blade. (Weyer photo)

▼ *Jason L. Williams:* A navaja at 4 inches with hippo-tooth scales. (Weyer photo)

▲ *Jack Davenport:* Slick liner locks with 416 stainless or mokume fittings and ATS-34 blades. (Weyer photo)

▲ *Patrick Donovan:* Little daggers with rear locks and 3-inch blades, malachite and ivory scales. (Weyer photo)

▶ *Masaki Sakakibara:* High style in smallish knives, inlaid in stag and Micarta. (Weyer photo)

TRENDS

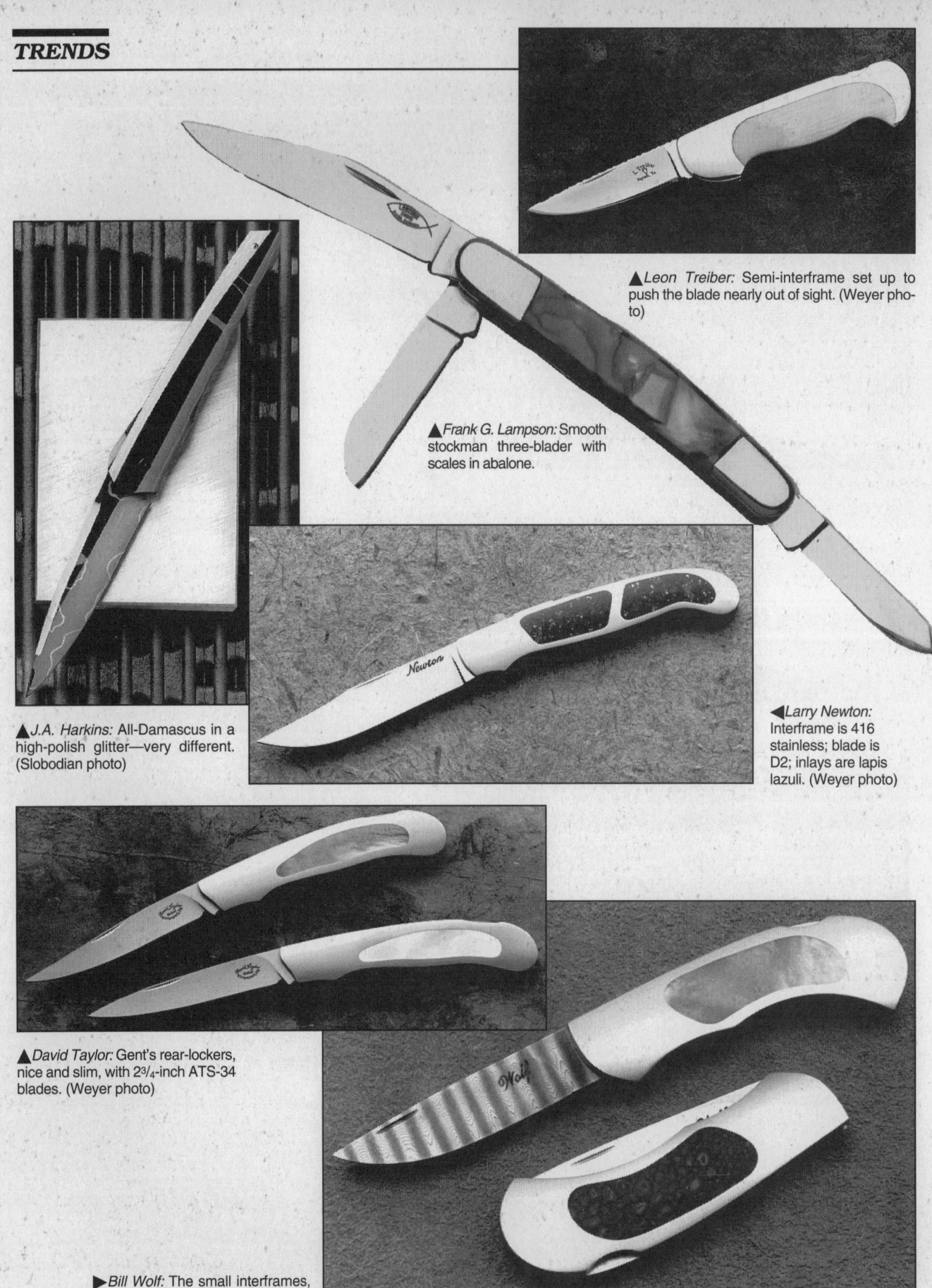

▲*Leon Treiber:* Semi-interframe set up to push the blade nearly out of sight. (Weyer photo)

▲*Frank G. Lampson:* Smooth stockman three-blader with scales in abalone.

▲*J.A. Harkins:* All-Damascus in a high-polish glitter—very different. (Slobodian photo)

◄*Larry Newton:* Interframe is 416 stainless; blade is D2; inlays are lapis lazuli. (Weyer photo)

▲*David Taylor:* Gent's rear-lockers, nice and slim, with 2³/₄-inch ATS-34 blades. (Weyer photo)

▶*Bill Wolf:* The small interframes, rear-locked, offer graceful profiles.

TRENDS

THE AUTOMATIC KNIFE

FOR SOME YEARS, we have been publishing photos of automatic folding knives. Most of the time we didn't know it. And we certainly didn't identify many of them as switchblades—that is, automatics.

Oh, your reporter was pretty sure some of the time. Nearly any nifty little Chuck Stewart knife was likely to have a surprising mechanism, for instance. We were, however, in don't ask/don't tell mode.

That's pretty silly now. On these pages there are the automatic knives of more than a dozen makers, all of whom identify their knives as automatics.

Sure there's a law. At least, in some places there's a law. And in some places there's not. And whether or not whichever law is meant to apply to one-of-a-kind $500 to $1,500 automatic knives is certainly arguable and likely not applicable—is that "commerce," for instance?

There are some experts who say having anything to do with any sort of push-button, gravity, lever-triggered automatic knife is crazy. One says that to offer one for sale through the mail is a felony. That is scary.

It is not legal to import switchblades—that's plain. Which makes one wonder why it is so easy to find brand-new, foreign-made switchblade knives for sale in the U.S. of A.

The whole discussion seems to be, from the point of view of individual knifemakers, moot. That is, their customers want them and they build them.

So here they are. It turns out there are probably more ways to make a knife open automatically, spring-powered, than there are to do it manually.

They're fun, of course. They go "click" and there's the blade. You find levers, little buttons and releases built into the decorations and sliding bolsters. There are combinations, knives that can have the spring mechanism locked out and are then slip locks or lockbacks.

The automatic is such a pervasive phenomenon in our circles, and so inconsequential in a world of crack houses and drive-by shootings and big-time violent crime, one wonders if its prohibition is just going to die on the vine. It could be that case law to come, however uncomfortable for a few automatic makers or owners, will decide the matter in favor of freedom. It is to be hoped.

Ken Warner

▲ *John LeBlanc:* These three are from a series, all benchmade and differently inlaid. (Weyer photo)

▲ *E. Blanton Cosby:* A crop of automatics in fine wood and Swedish steel—all different, you notice. (Weyer photo)

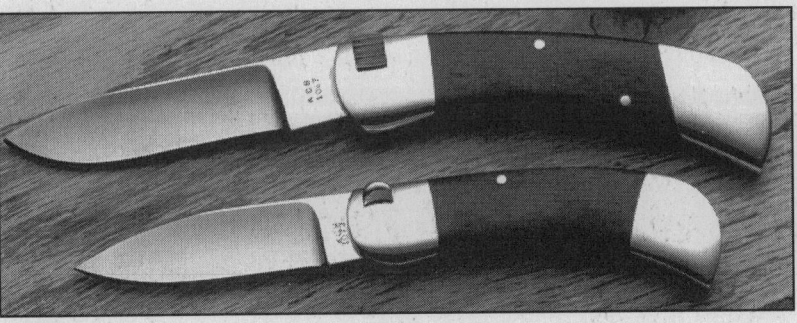

◄ *Kirby C. Bailey:* These are automatic folding hunters, sensibly provided in a choice of sizes.

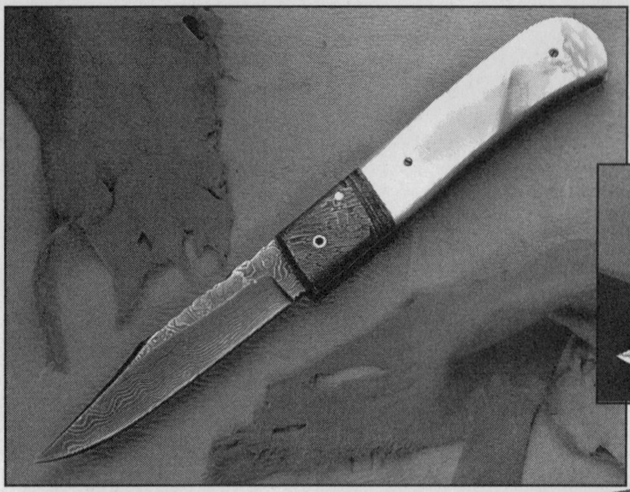

TRENDS

Ralph J. Selvidio: At 4½- and 3½-inch blade length, these two automatics don't look like automatics. (Weyer photos)

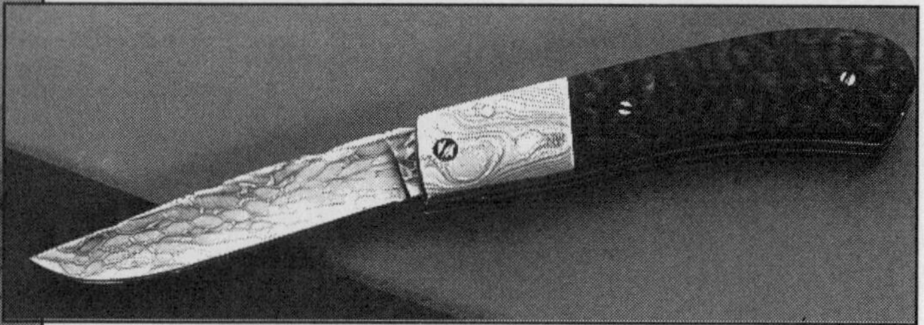

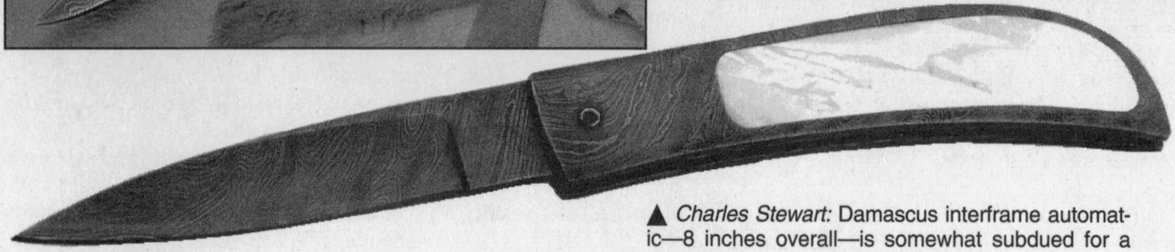

Charles Stewart: Damascus interframe automatic—8 inches overall—is somewhat subdued for a Stewart. (Weyer photo)

William James McHenry: The trio of knives offer three different mechanisms—button, rocker and bolster releases; the large handsome dirk—15½ inches overall—is another rocker release. (Weyer photos)

C.M. Dake: This fighter style has a full 4-inch blade and is called a button lock. (Box photo)

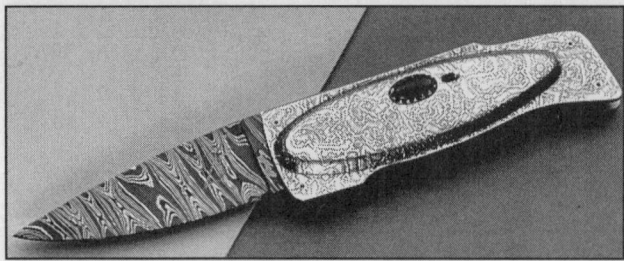

Gary L. Barnes: Textured nickel case, high-visibility Damascus, an onyx button and a four-speed auto action. (Weyer photo)

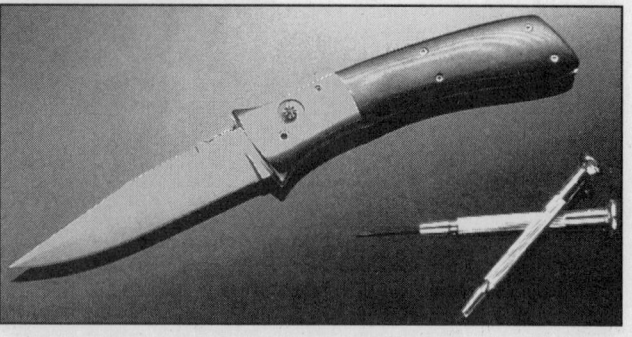

THE AUTOMATIC KNIFE

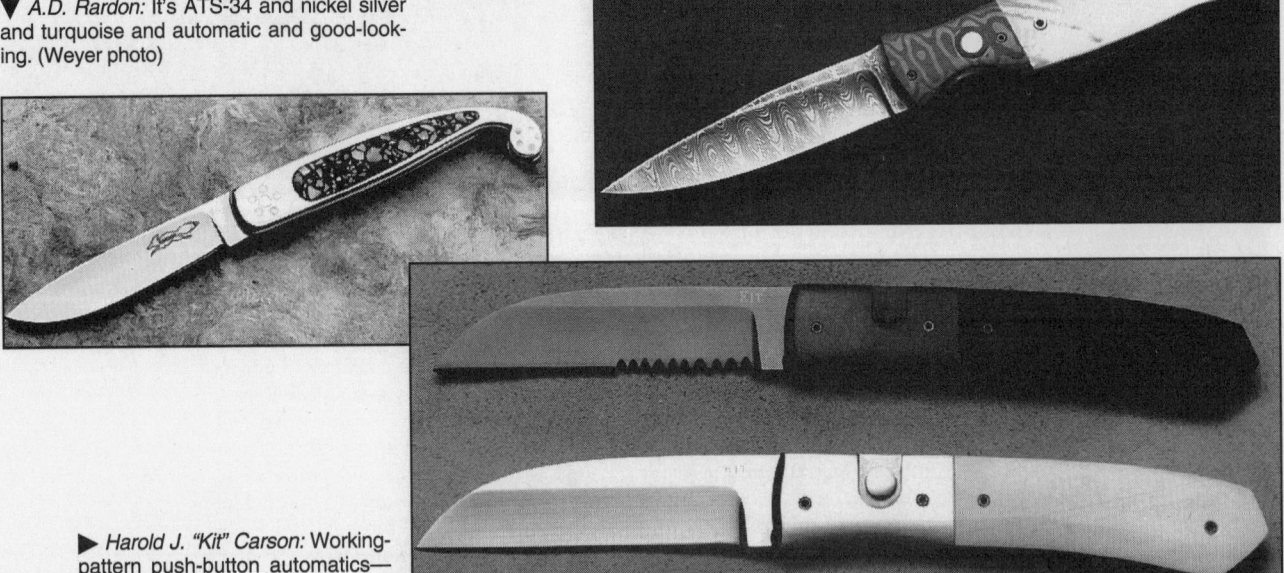

▶ *Butch Vallotton:* One of a kind with a nice button, a 3½-inch Damascus blade and welded titanium. (Weyer photo)

▼ *A.D. Rardon:* It's ATS-34 and nickel silver and turquoise and automatic and good-looking. (Weyer photo)

▶ *Harold J. "Kit" Carson:* Working-pattern push-button automatics—Carson Model 5.

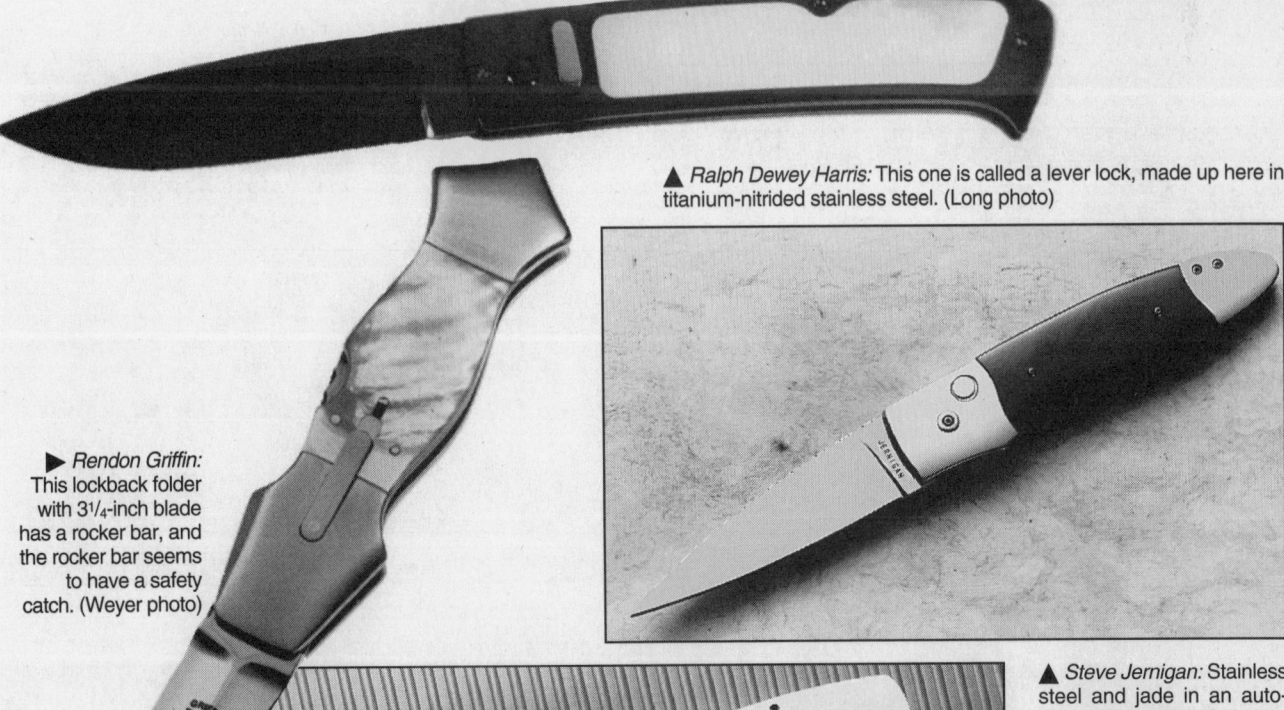

▲ *Ralph Dewey Harris:* This one is called a lever lock, made up here in titanium-nitrided stainless steel. (Long photo)

▶ *Rendon Griffin:* This lockback folder with 3¼-inch blade has a rocker bar, and the rocker bar seems to have a safety catch. (Weyer photo)

▲ *Steve Jernigan:* Stainless steel and jade in an automatic that goes 8⅜ inches overall. (Weyer photo)

◀ *Rick Hinderer:* Both these folders have what are called scale releases. The fancy pin is just that. (Weyer photo)

TRENDS

THE UPGRADED KNIFE

TAKE A STANDARD knife, a good one, and add engraving or scrimshaw or high-priced materials—you have an upgraded knife. Many people do; they're very popular.

We used to call them "fancy;" some called them "display" knives. It's always been hard to figure. One fellow's "art knife" often looked like another fellow's "fancy."

Upscale knives—over in the big investment leagues—are different. Generally, they're standard in no avoidable way, made of very expensive stuff in every respect, worked on by top-drawer talents throughout, intended for the big ticket from the start.

An upgraded knife is simpler than that. That doesn't mean tacky, mind you, just not so ambitious and not so expensive. And people are still upgrading favorite knives and/or building dream knives incrementally—the knife this year, scrimshaw next year, finally engraving.

Truth to tell, upgraded knives are very important to the marketing methods of quite a few knifemakers. It's a win-win deal: People are more attracted to the fancier knife, and there's more money in it for the seller.

And why do people buy them fancier? People buy everything fancier—basketball shoes, motorcycles, T-shirts—so why not knives? The upgraded knife is perfect that way: It's a good tool or weapon or both *and* it's something special, too. Look for yourself, right here.

Ken Warner

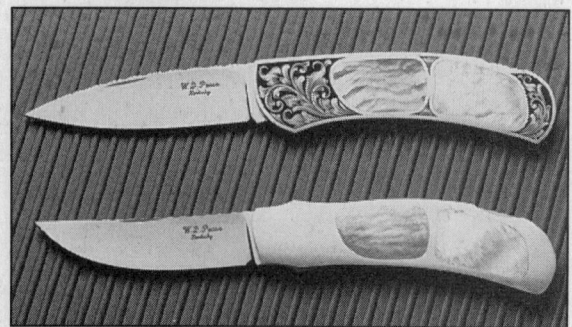

▲*W.D. Pease:* Two knives—one upgraded with Mark Waldrop engraving, the other plain. (Weyer photo)

▶*Craig Quattlebaum:* Straightforward plain fighter, ebony handled and brass-trimmed, upgraded with Damascus blade.

◀*Edmund Davidson:* Full integral knives are practically standard for this maker; the engraving upgrades them. (Armontrout photo)

▶*James D. Ragsdale:* Nice folder, a functional knife with a mild mother-of-pearl upgrade. (Weyer photo)

THE UPGRADED KNIFE

◤*Frank and Tony Centofante:* The knives are all very like; the materials and the engraving, here by Bates, make a difference.

▽*Ronald M. Lui:* Red abalone inserts were extra; Bruce Shaw engraving is a big extra. (Weyer photo)

▲*Danny Coffman:* Small knives with—and without—light touches from Billy Bates. (Weyer photo)

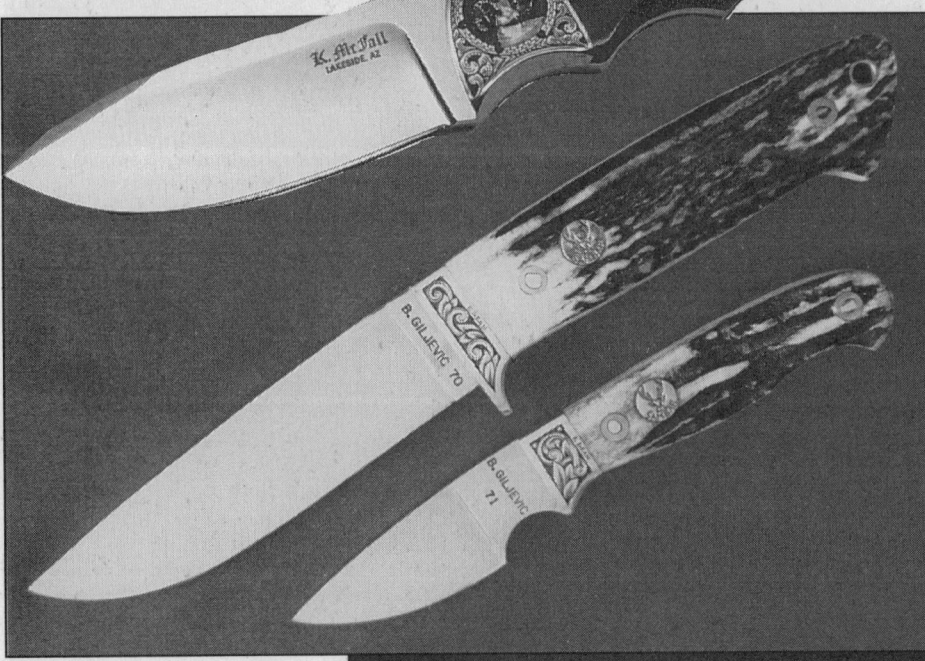

◀*Ken McFall:* Nice clipped semi-skinner; the engraved bolster is extra.

◀*Branko Giljevic:* A pair of hunters from Down Under, touched up by engraver Bruce Dean.

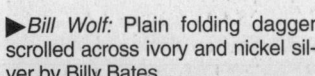

▶*Bill Wolf:* Plain folding dagger scrolled across ivory and nickel silver by Billy Bates.

FIFTEENTH EDITION **137**

TRENDS

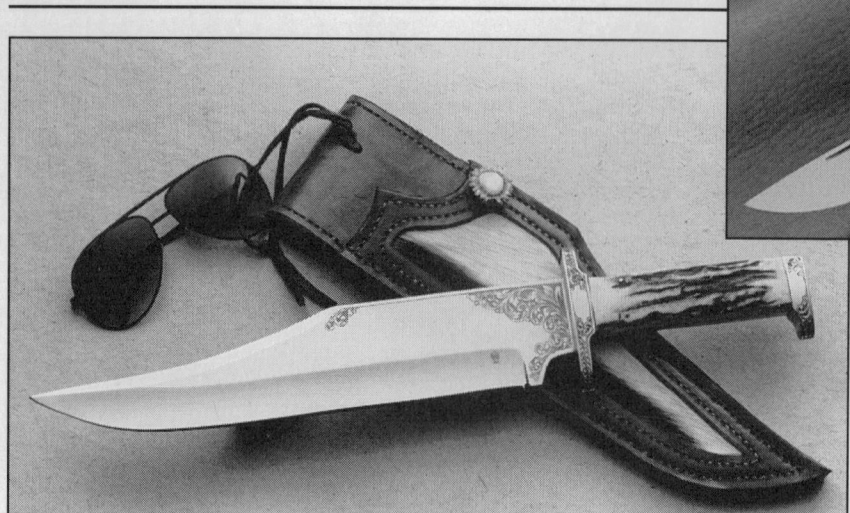

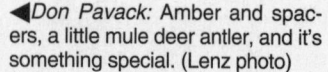

▲*John LeBlanc:* Rear-locking integral-bolstered folder with Billy Bates engraving.

◄*Webster Wood:* Massive Bowie isn't hurt by a few little touches—what would be full coverage on a small knife—by its maker. (Weyer photo)

▲*Arland (Lanny) Hartman:* Nice pins and filework, but engraved bolster gets the attention. (Weyer photo)

▼*Glenn Marshall:* Y.O. Ranch-style folder touched up by Don Henderson engraving.

◄*Don Pavack:* Amber and spacers, a little mule deer antler, and it's something special. (Lenz photo)

▶*James F. Downs:* Brawny fighter is slightly refined with Leo McCombs engraving, but still cuts. (Etzler photo)

THE UPGRADED KNIFE

◀*A.T. Barr:* J.R. French gussied up this plain boot knife's bolster. (Weyer photo)

▲*Brett Laplante:* Smallish lockback shows both Terry Theis engraving and Linda K. Karst scrim. (Weyer photo)

▶*Heinz Leber:* Cutouts *and* filework *and* an engraved guard *and* scrimshaw—all on one 9-inch Bowie. (Weyer photo)

▲*Bob Garbe:* Interframe hunter set off with scrolled backstrap and Sandra Garbe scrim.

▼*Brett Laplante:* Medium folder upgraded twice: first bark ivory, then engraved by Don Graf. (Weyer photo)

▲*C.E. "Gene" Johnson:* Mastodon ivory and some interior filework set off by a Billy Bates bolster. (Weyer photo)

FIFTEENTH EDITION 139

TRENDS

▶ *Bob Jones:* Dressed up folders in ironwood and ivory engraved by the maker. (Weyer photo)

▼ *John Holland:* Fillet knife with Dennis K. Holland scrimshaw and Bill Johns engraving. (Weyer photo)

▶ *Jim Sornberger:* Maker does this shape a lot and embellishes it differently for the upgrade. (Weyer photo)

▲ *Scot Horton:* Mild upgrade on a small hunter—sheephorn plus an engraved bolster.

▲ *Kemp King:* Ten-inch fillet knife with ivory grip and Michael Collins engraving. (Weyer photo)

▶ *Elvan Allred:* A nice shape in pearl, with bolster engraved by Scott Allred.

STATE OF THE ART

We have said before that here we deal with facts—"this is a leopard scrimmed on ivory"—and subjective facts—"this is an elegant knife." The latter means the writer is pretty sure the knife shown is extra-classy in one way or another.

As we get to them, we try to shed sufficient light on small technical matters to help the reader see them, too. Textures, surfaces and new shapes, sometimes new materials, can be revealed easily in photos and captions.

So that's what we do here. We're looking at *parts* of knives or the knifemaking process to see how they affect the knives. We have done that for fifteen years, and there are still new things to see.

So that's the other thing we do—we keep track of technical stuff. We don't *chart it*, mind you, but mostly if it's new we showed it here. It's the State of the Art, this year.

Ken Warner

Interesting Knives 142
Composite Blades for Everyman
   by Hal Davidson 148
The Ethnic Knife 150
Study of Steel and
   Shape and Stuff 152
Embellishment 158
Leatherwork 168

STATE OF THE ART
INTERESTING KNIVES

IT ISN'T ALWAYS a simple matter to figure out how or even where to talk about some knives. We want to talk about some because they're gorgeous, some because they're useful, some because they are predictable but good, some because they're improbable, whether good or bad.

So we've decided to call all the stuff that falls into these indefinable categories Interesting Knives. Often, the only things they'll have in common are that they cut and that this writer finds them interesting.

One really interesting knife is not quite a Spyderco. Some people have chosen to copy a Spyderco Clip-It, and this knock-off is out there at $10 or so. It's a line-for-line copy, except for one feature, but it's not a well-made knife. Legal steps are being taken, so in due course that will be over.

However, my personal copy of that copy interests me. It now is something special. I had sent it along to Spyderco in Golden, Colorado, and mentioned in my cover letter that it had no collector serial number as most of my other Spyderco knives had. So help me, when it came back, Spyderco had engraved the right number on it. One cannot buy class; one *has* class.

Mostly, it is hoped, the Interesting Knives will be intrinsically so, and you won't need the history to enjoy them. The faked Clip-It Celica is all the things I said, but it also has a distinction—the hole in the hump on the blade is square.

Curiously, a knife need not be way off the beaten path. There are two or three here that are interesting because they are nicely made and shaped middle-of-the-road designs. In fact, there's a Victorinox Swiss Army knife herein.

There is a place for the out-on-the-edge (Sorry.) knife and this is it. Fantasies apart, there are knives by Fogg and Kojetin and Marzitelli and Emerson that do stretch the envelope just a bit.

One hopes we'll all be surprised, now and again, by the knives that show up in this space. There will hardly be enough space to provide the mythical something for everybody, but most of you should find enough amusement to be worth the read.

Ken Warner

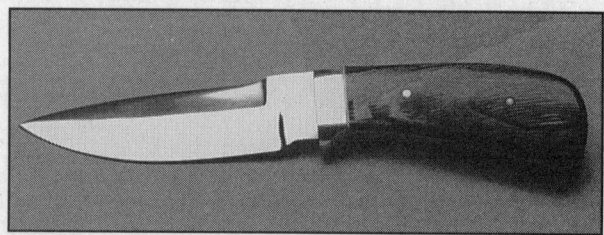

▲*Peter Bennett:* Eldon Courtney used to make a knife very like this in L6—exceptionally useful. This one's in 440C. (Venus Kondos photo)

▲*Knock-Off Artist:* Straight fake of Spyderco Celica differs from the real thing in quality and the shape of the blade aperture.

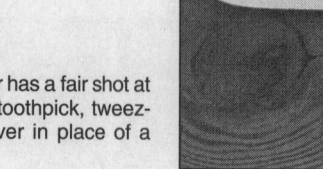

▶*Victorinox:* This new Tinker has a fair shot at "most useful" pocketknife—toothpick, tweezers and a Phillips screwdriver in place of a corkscrew.

INTERESTING KNIVES

▶ *Paul M. Jarvis:* Just 8 inches overall, this *kwaiken* is a vehicle for a *lot* of embellishment. The hippo ivory is laden with silver and gold inlays; blade steel by Meier. Rich. (Weyer photo)

▼ *Steven J. Rapp:* Bowie collector Robert Simpson has commissioned stainless replicas of historical Bowies, of which this Broomhead and Thomas is the first.

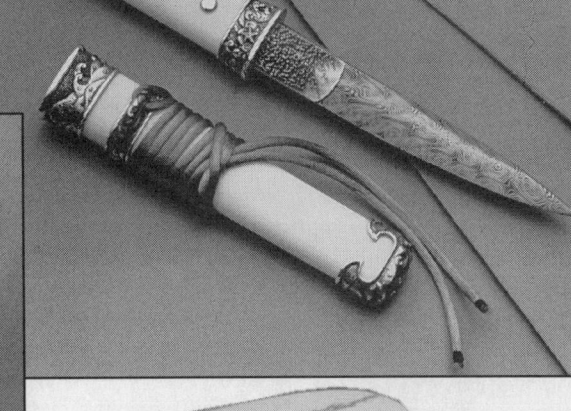

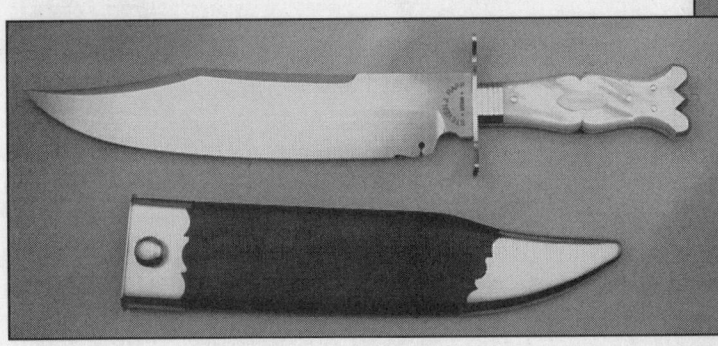

▲ *Harvey J. Dean:* Large plain folder in bark ivory with forged O1 steel blade, a classic for ordinary folks. (Box photo)

◀ *Charles F. Ochs:* A foot long and dainty, this slim rendition of a World War II design is a lively knife. (Weyer photo)

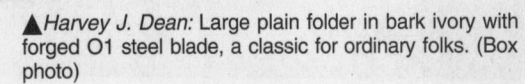

▲ *Frank G. Lampson:* Mrs. Lampson decided this is the "Axiomatic"—means sound, self-evident—and at 4½ inches in ATS-34 with those proportions, it seems to be. (Long photo)

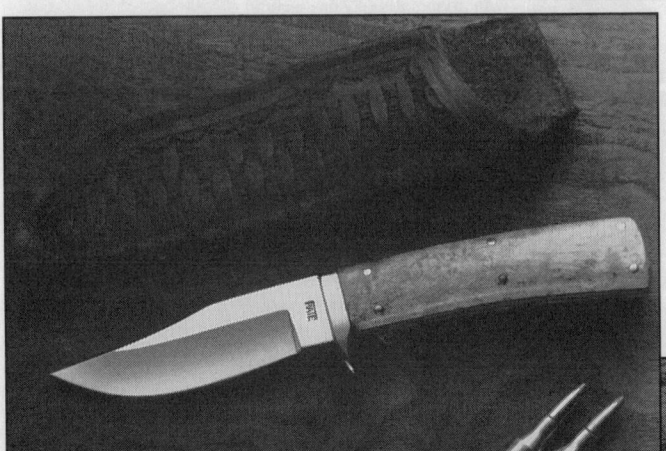

▲ *Lloyd D. Pate:* Mirror-finished 440C and maple and the sturdy hollow grind—classic middle-ground design in a hunter. (Box photo)

▶ *W. Kojetin:* Royally decorated, this unusual skinner has D2, nickel silver, sterling wire and pins, ivory and garnets in the ferrule. (Domenico photo)

FIFTEENTH EDITION 143

STATE OF THE ART

►*Peter Marzitelli:* This big claw with composite wood/antler grip is 12 inches overall and kind of menacing just laying there.

▼*Larry W. Harley:* U.S.-made small jambiya is tough, but not much like its real-life model. The difference, Harley says, is the Arab had no machinery.

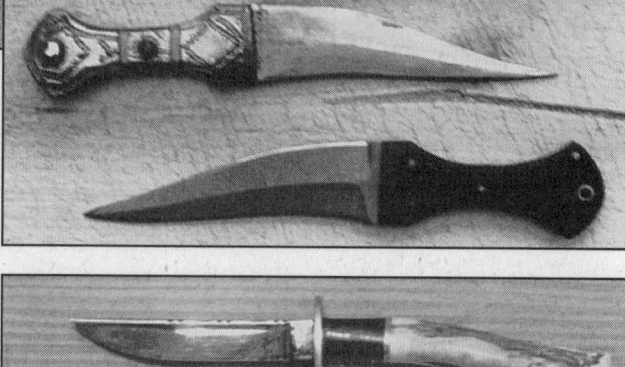

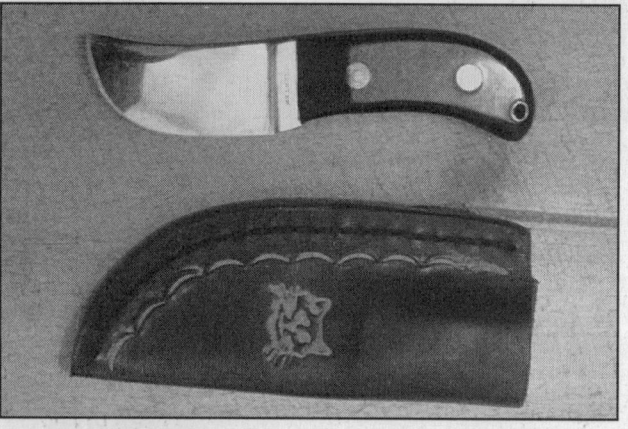

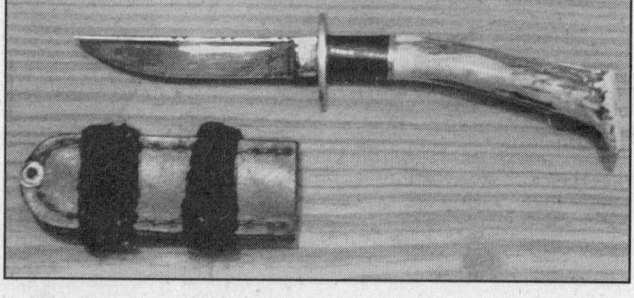

◄*Leonard Williams:* Nice shape in a heavy skinner, done up in rosewood and planer blade steel.

▲*Peter James:* Nice style in a pocket/purse knife. Makers use Solingen Blades, each with an individually crafted handle.

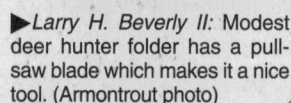

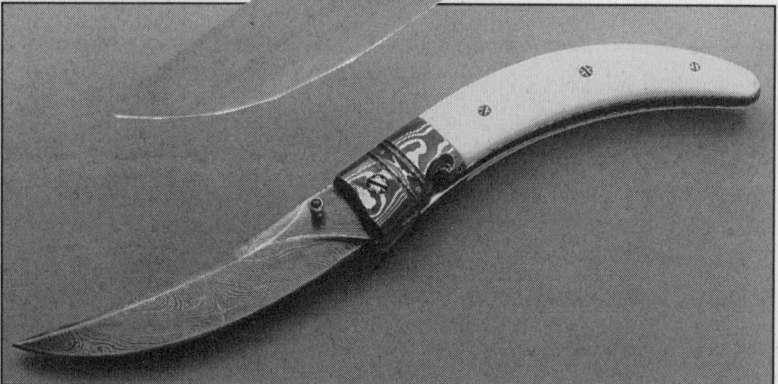

►*Larry H. Beverly II:* Modest deer hunter folder has a pull-saw blade which makes it a nice tool. (Armontrout photo)

▼*Phill Hartsfield:* Designed for a specific martial art, these are called "Chung Fu." They're A2 steel, have chisel edges and are used in pairs. (Staup photo)

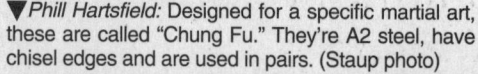

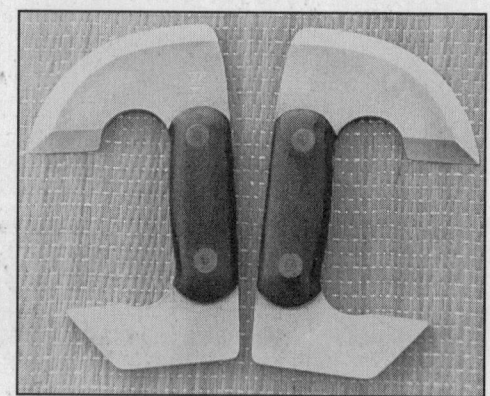

▲*Jason L. Williams:* Hippo tooth graced by a Damascus blade and bolster—and a liner-lock mechanism. (Weyer photo)

INTERESTING KNIVES

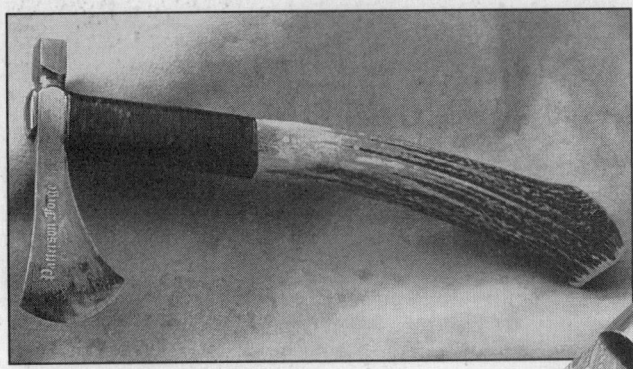

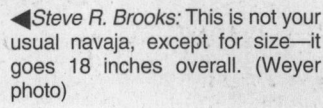

◀ *Steve R. Brooks:* This is not your usual navaja, except for size—it goes 18 inches overall. (Weyer photo)

▲ *Alan W. Patterson:* Cable Damascus hawk, handled in stacked leather and stag—pinned hidden tang—handsome ensemble. (Chiacchira photo)

▼ *Don Fogg:* Wide composite blade integral with handle and pommel—a handsome exercise.

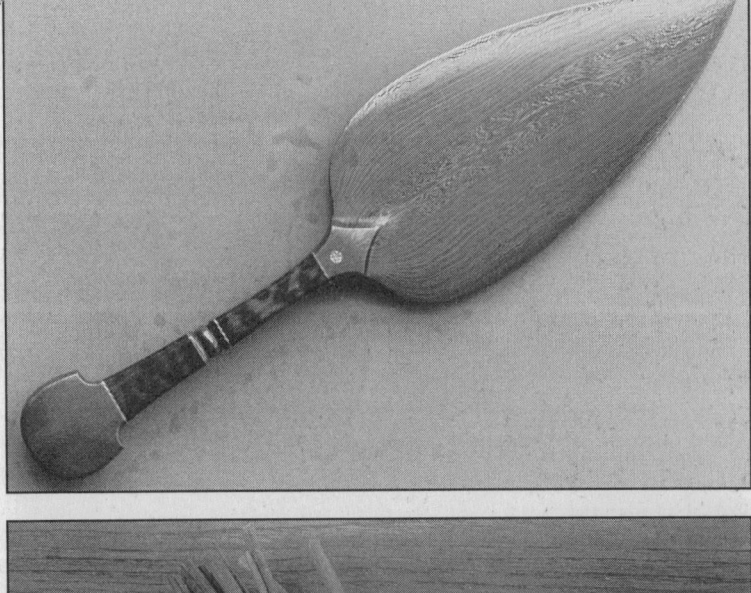

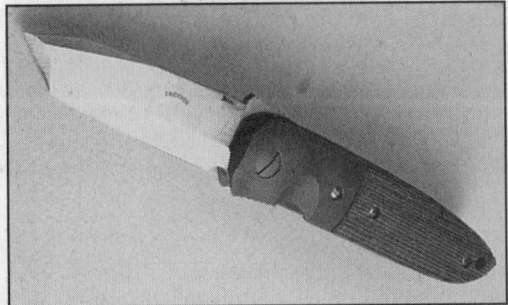

▲▼ *Ernest R. Emerson:* This blade profile with chisel edge works in both folder and straight form as a lethal instrument, the maker says.

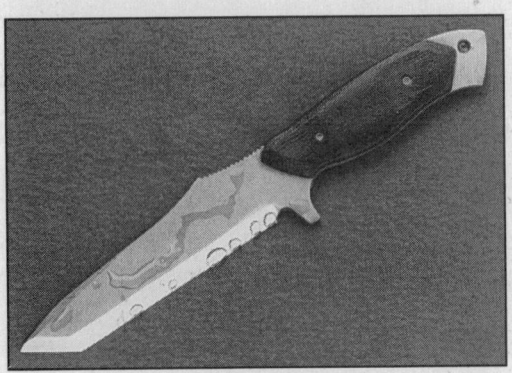

▶ *Karl Schroen:* Classy kitchen cleaver with sharpened up-front radius is "hand forged from ATS-34," sells for $500 or $600, depending on size. (Richardson photo)

FIFTEENTH EDITION 145

STATE OF THE ART

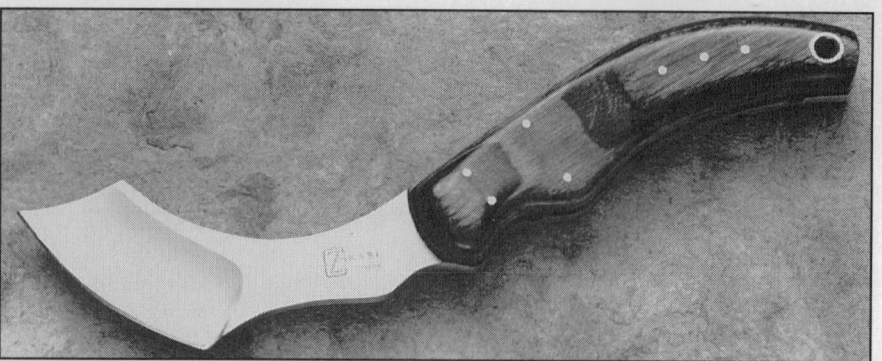

◀ *Carl S. Zakabi:* This goose-necked design with its abrupt razor blade doubtless serves an Hawaiian purpose. (Weyer photo)

▼ *Harold J. "Kit" Carson:* Called the cross lock, this interesting two-blade layout is made on license from Buck Knives. (Weyer photo)

▲ *Lee Gene Baskett:* One more good-looking example in Baskett's continuing parade of locking folders built within Colt Model 1911 grips; this one's scrimmed by Gary Williams.

◀ *Mike Lamprey:* Heavy-walled titanium case provides the liner-lock sort of latch, very like the Reeves Sebenza.

▲ *Alexander Lockachiev:* Russian knifemakers have training; however elaborate, they keep their proportions and the generally great workmanship is where you can see it. (Weyer photo)

▼ *Bob Garbe:* Straight deer-sized knife in 440C has liner-locked folding gut hook in grip—can be had with saw or vent hook.

INTERESTING KNIVES

▲ *Don Mount:* Almost normal, until you count the finger grooves and figure out how to sheath it. (Weyer photo)

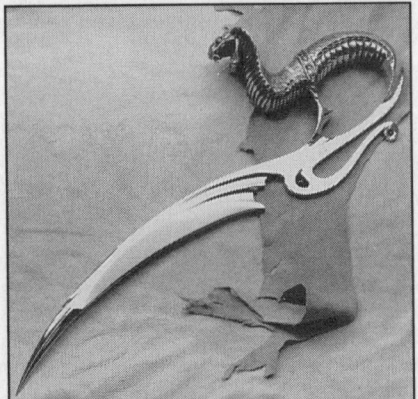

▲ *Gil Hibben:* An Ehler design called Naja, this is quite curved but rather straightforward—21 inches overall. (Weyer photo)

▲ *Gil Hibben:* Called UFO, this multi-bladed gauntlet is another Ehler idea, works out 17 1/2 inches long. (Weyer photo)

▲ *Steve Likarich:* Another push dagger in the weird mode—#6, actually—in 440C and ironwood. (Weyer photo)

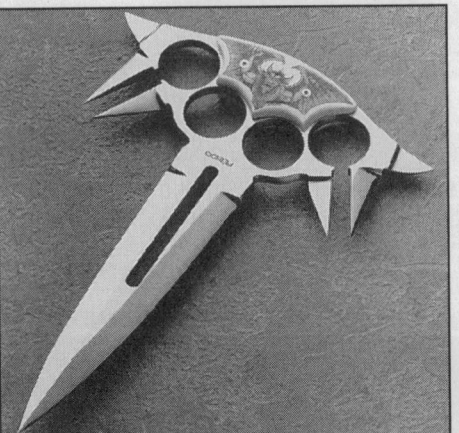

▲ *Harold Corby:* Another way to work the tough-looking push knife, this one scrimmed by Bob Burdette. (Weyer photo)

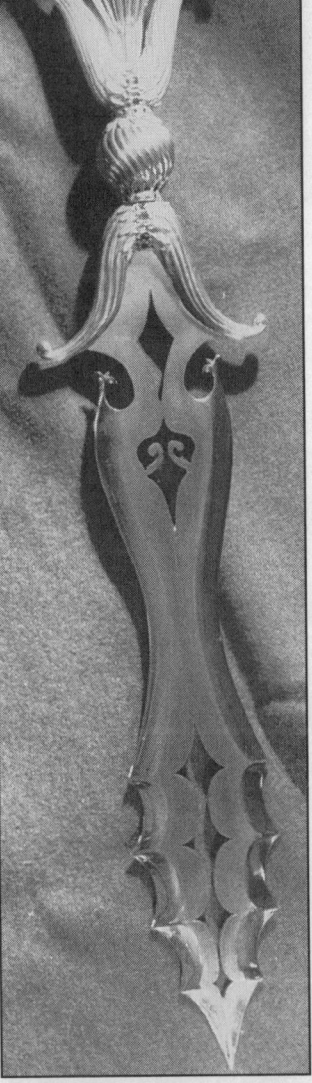

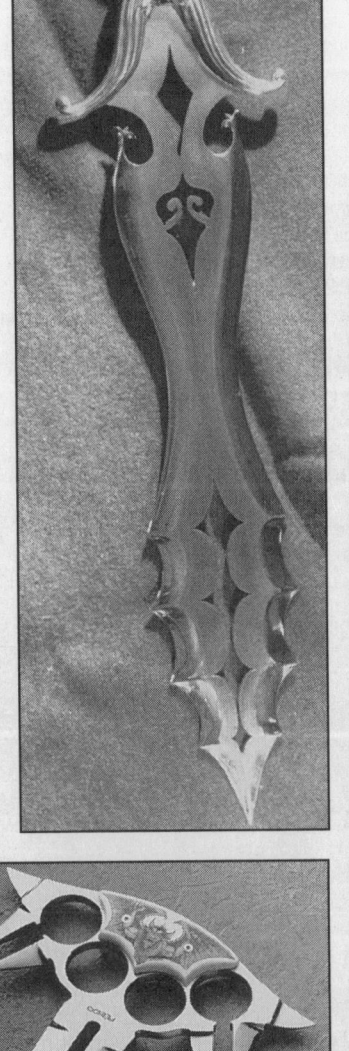

◀ *Alfredo E. Faes Scheurer:* These fantastical knife styles, we are told, have been made for a long time in Mexico.

STATE OF THE ART

COMPOSITE BLADES FOR EVERYMAN

COMPOSITE BLADES ARE made when two different materials are combined to produce a blade superior in some way to a blade made entirely from one or the other material alone. The idea is a very old one, going back to ancient times when wootz steel from India was combined with locally produced wrought iron or low carbon steel to produce a particular type of Damascus blade steel. Why were they combined? At that time, wootz was the finest steel (produced by a secret crucible process) available to bladesmiths in the Mediterranean region, found only in very small quantities at a price very near to that of gold. Only the very rich could afford a blade made entirely of wootz steel. The composite blades offered some of the qualities of wootz at a more affordable price.

More recently, Scandinavian bladesmiths have long made knives using high carbon steel for the cutting edge, laminated on either side with a layer of lower carbon steel. Until the latter part of the 19th century, the quality of the world's steel was limited by impurities in the ore, such as sulfur which weakened the steel and phosphorus which made it brittle. Swedish Dannemora ore was almost completely free of these impurities, and so the steel made from it could take and hold a better edge than most other steels of the mid-19th century. Blades of this steel could be hardened to Rc 62, which made for a wonderful cutting edge, but with some sacrifice of toughness. That didn't matter in surgical blades that were subject to negligible stress, but was undesirable in a hunter's knife. Laminating with a tougher steel solved that problem.

There are now several manufacturers of laminated steel blades in Sweden and Norway. Composite blades are also used in the Swedish wood-carving knives made by Frost and sold by Woodcraft. That company stocks five different styles and lengths of blades from 2 to $3^{7}/_{8}$ inches at $7.95 to $9.95 without sheath. The center section of these blades is "Mora" steel made from the Dannemora ore.

Three Woodcraft knives are shown here with homemade blade guards of $1/_{16}$-inch circuit board material. These are good camp and shop knives, and are a cheap way to get acquainted with composite blades. The quickest and neatest field-dressing of a wild turkey I've ever seen was done by my friend, Jim Whitlock, D.V.M., with a $2^{3}/_{4}$-inch composite blade. Woodcraft even offers a deluxe version of the $3^{7}/_{8}$-inch blade with rosewood handle and brass bolsters for $28.50 with leather sheath.

A heavier $4^{3}/_{8}$-inch hunter's blade of Mora laminated steel with handle and sheath by the author is also shown here. The handle material is white oak with a figure similar to curly maple, and the sheath is traditional Scandinavian style. We show a Norwegian knife sold by Bergans of Oslo. The $4^{1}/_{2}$-inch blade is marked "Bergans-Troll-Norway" with stamping at the bolster reading "18/8+High Carbon Edge." The 18/8 indicates the side laminations are alloy steel containing 18 percent chromium and 8 percent nickel. It is an extremely tough steel and more corrosion resistant than stainless cutlery steel, but quite

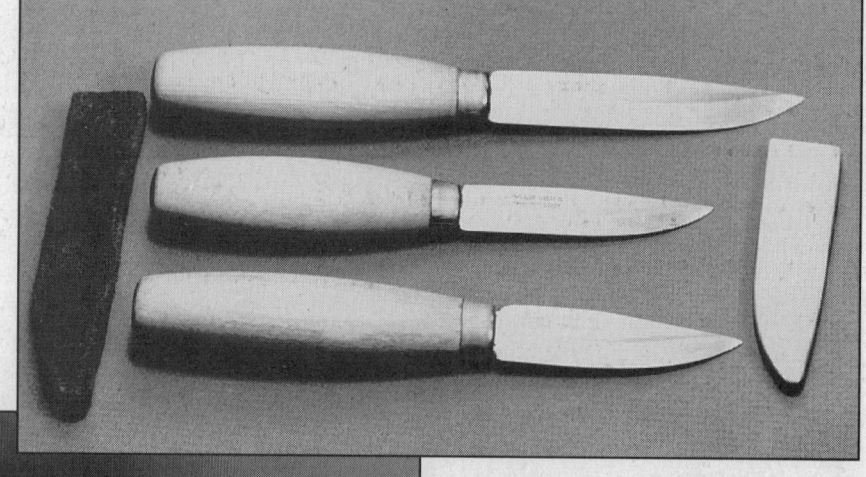

Frosts laminated blades from Woodcraft, fitted with blade guards for pocket and pouch carry.

Oak-handled by the author, this is a Helle Fabrikker blade.

COMPOSITE BLADES FOR EVERYMAN

Excellent in camp is this 6-inch Brusletto laminted blade.

This one, another Brusletto, has chestnut handle and belt-clipped sheath by the author—weighs 3 ounces and will do it all.

unsuited for a cutting edge because it is austenitic—that is, neither quench nor air-hardenable, and non-magnetic as well.

The only other stainless/high carbon blades I know of are 3½- and 4-inch blades made by Helle Fabrikker in Norway and im-ported by Atlanta Cutlery at $19.95 and $20.95. These are blades-only for the custom knifemaker and do-it-yourselfer. One 4-inch blade with figured oak handle is shown. This blade has as good a finish as I've seen on a factory-made blade.

Atlanta Cutlery also imports the Brusletto Norwegian composite blades in four lengths from 4 to 6 inches. One such blade with figure oak handle and wooden blade guard is an excellent camp and cookout knife. There's a 4-inch blade with a handle in sixty-year-old American chestnut and a blade guard with belt clip that will field-dress any of our large game and weighs only 3 ounces. Priced from $11.50 to $15.75, Brusletto blades are top quality, but not quite as finely finished as the Helle blades.

Morseth laminated blades are made to special order in Morseth patterns at Brusletto in Norway. Together with Morseth's handles and excellent sheathing, they have long had a world-class reputation.

The pluses for composite blades? They will take and hold an exceptionally fine edge (like a surgeon's scalpel) and, for their weight, are probably the toughest blades made, especially those with 18/8 lamination. The minuses? The blade stock of the Scandinavian composites is roll-welded in widths of ⅝- to ⅞-inch, which limits the range of blade shapes that can be made by grinding. Also, the blades are too short and light for knives that may be used for blazing trails or chopping brush.

Are composite steels the best for the types of blades shown in the illustrations? Everyone I know who has tried any of these blades has been impressed. In my opinion, there is no better blade material. At the same time, there are so many fine blades being made of a number of different steels, and the best only beats out next-best by a slight amount, making it of little practical importance to most knife users.

Hal Davidson

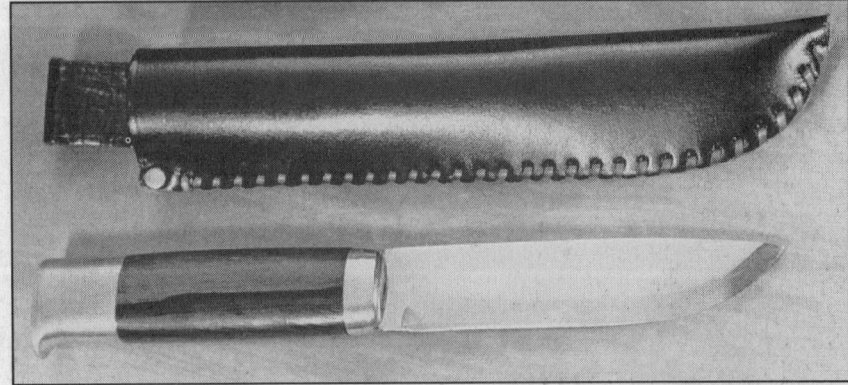

Bergans of Oslo made this one of 18/8 laminted steel—very tough.

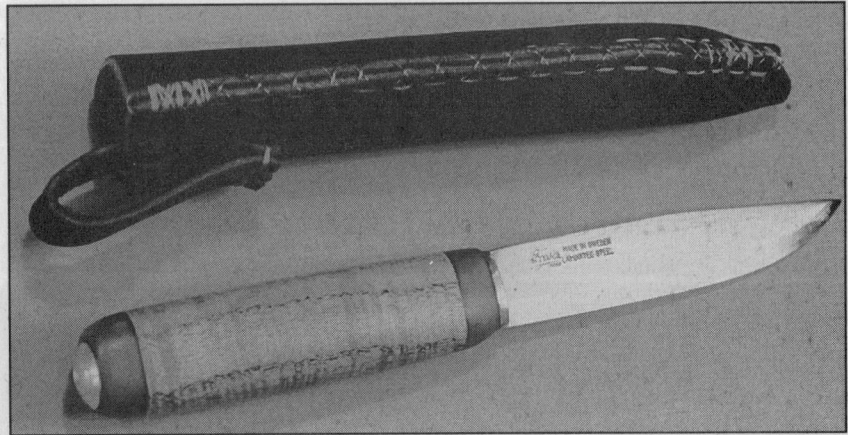

Handle and sheath by the author; blade by Frosts of Sweden.

FIFTEENTH EDITION 149

STATE OF THE ART

THE ETHNIC KNIFE

WE ARE ACCUSTOMED to Oriental and Arabic and Scandinavian and Iberian and Argentinian and Viking and Roman knives. They were around historically, and people make them today. The idea of the ethnic knife is well established.

Comes now the Jewish knife, born of the cultural heritage. And comes also a Jewish knifemaker, perhaps two. There are, of course, and have been, a lot of Jews who make knives for a living. Very few of them, however in tune with Jewish culture, make Jewish knives. Most Jews who are knifemakers make Oriental or Arabic or Viking or American frontier knives.

There is a larger story here, no doubt, and there are several smaller ones. Indeed, James K. Mattis has a story for each of his knife designs, one of which is not a knife, but a tent peg. The stories are pretty long, if vastly entertaining—"This shape could therefore be a kosher oyster knife, if you could find a kosher oyster"—so we're not printing them *in toto*.

We can tell you about them, however. The commemorative tent pegs mark the occasion the virtuous Jael slew the Canaanite Sisera by pegging his skull to the tent floor in the middle of the night. Then there is the Ibis, viewed (and marked) as a tool for people like scribes. The Chalif—the word means *change*—is a poultry slaughtering knife. It's single edged and straight and sharp and looks like a straight razor with a knife handle. The Cherev has a round nose and is sharp all around. It is a tool for a *bris*, a circumcision, and in this case, an adult circumcision.

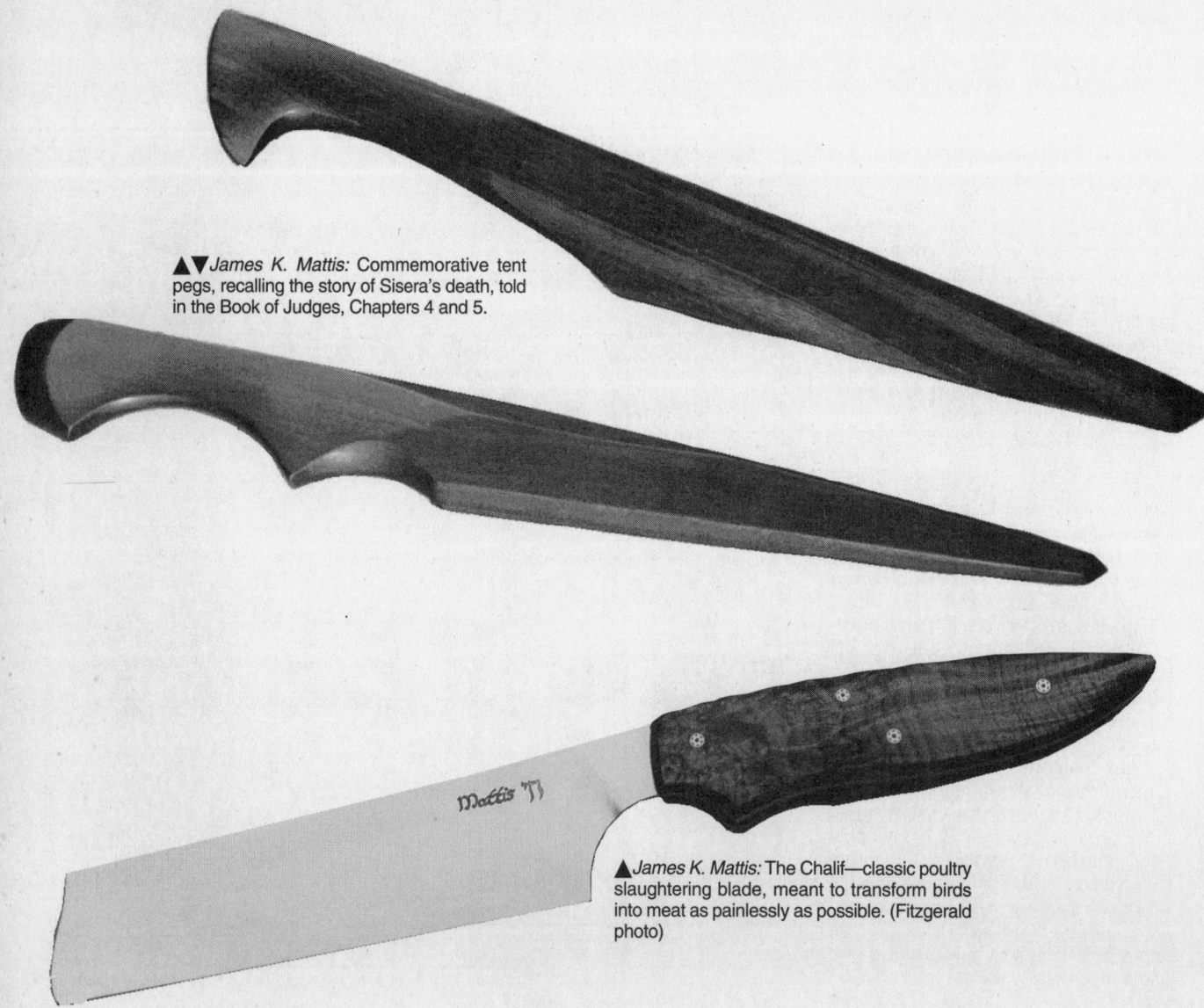

▲▼*James K. Mattis:* Commemorative tent pegs, recalling the story of Sisera's death, told in the Book of Judges, Chapters 4 and 5.

▲*James K. Mattis:* The Chalif—classic poultry slaughtering blade, meant to transform birds into meat as painlessly as possible. (Fitzgerald photo)

THE ETHNIC KNIFE

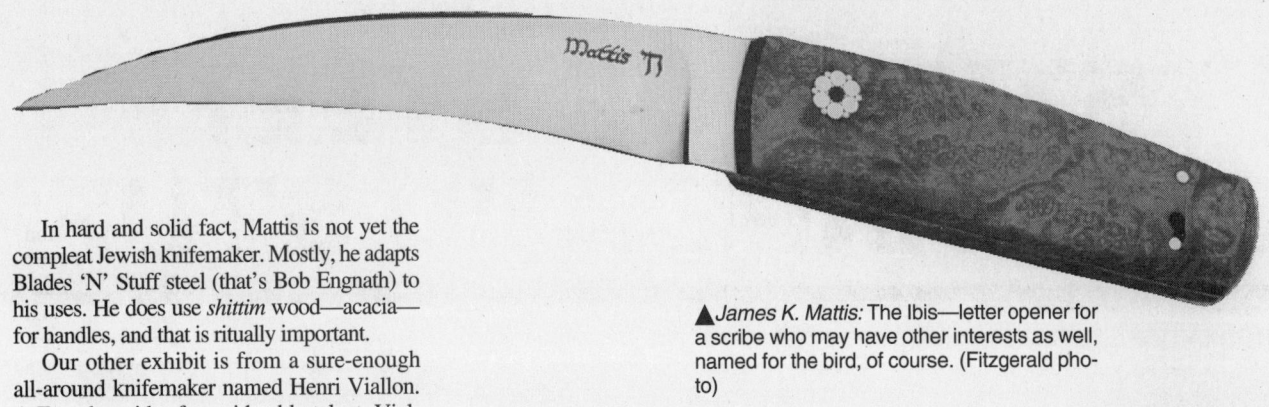

In hard and solid fact, Mattis is not yet the compleat Jewish knifemaker. Mostly, he adapts Blades 'N' Stuff steel (that's Bob Engnath) to his uses. He does use *shittim* wood—acacia—for handles, and that is ritually important.

Our other exhibit is from a sure-enough all-around knifemaker named Henri Viallon. A French smith of considerable talent, Viallon has produced the folder we show, with the Hebrew word *shalom* integral in its body. He has also furnished photos of the work in steel that made the *shalom* happen. There is hardly any more Jewish word than *shalom*, which means peace.

Taken all in all, it is obvious the ethnic knife has taken on new life. Given sufficiently scholarly reading of the Scriptures, there is probably no end to the Jewish knife potential. We await the Jewish tanto.

Ken Warner

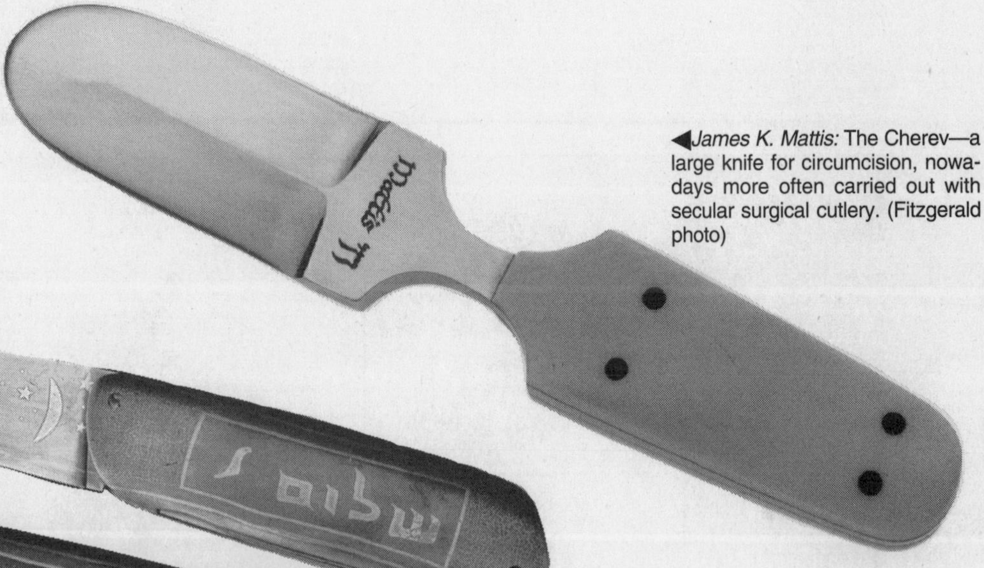

▲*James K. Mattis:* The Ibis—letter opener for a scribe who may have other interests as well, named for the bird, of course. (Fitzgerald photo)

◀*James K. Mattis:* The Cherev—a large knife for circumcision, nowadays more often carried out with secular surgical cutlery. (Fitzgerald photo)

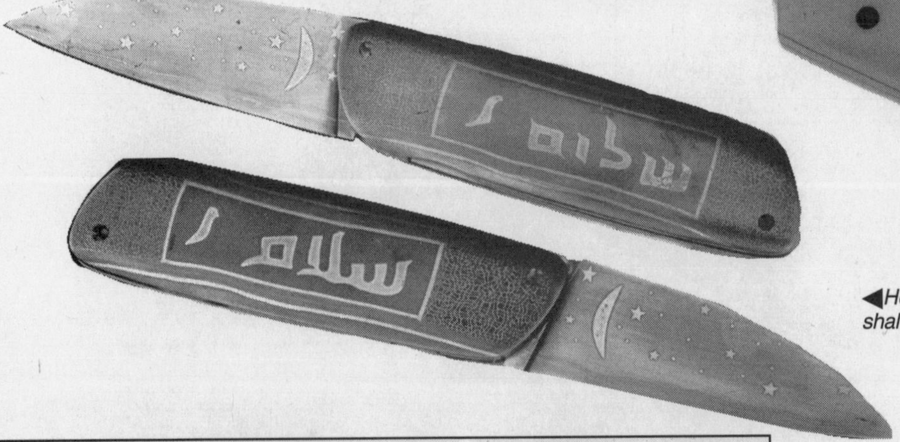

◀*Henri Viallon:* The word is *shalom*, which means peace.

◀*Henri Viallon:* Here are some hints to the fabrication of his ethnic knives.

FIFTEENTH EDITION **151**

STATE OF THE ART

STUDY OF STEEL AND SHAPE AND STUFF

▲*Hank Knickmeyer:* Five—at least—complex billets welded into one blade, fitted in cast silver and fossil ivory. (Long photo)

▲*Chuck Patrick:* Forged Damascus wedding bands—a certain symbolism there. (Long photo)

▲*Rade Hawkins:* Flint River Bowie has a stream running through it—very poetic. (Long photo)

▲*Stephen Schwarzer:* Pebble-grain Damascus, set off with deep filework. (Weyer photo)

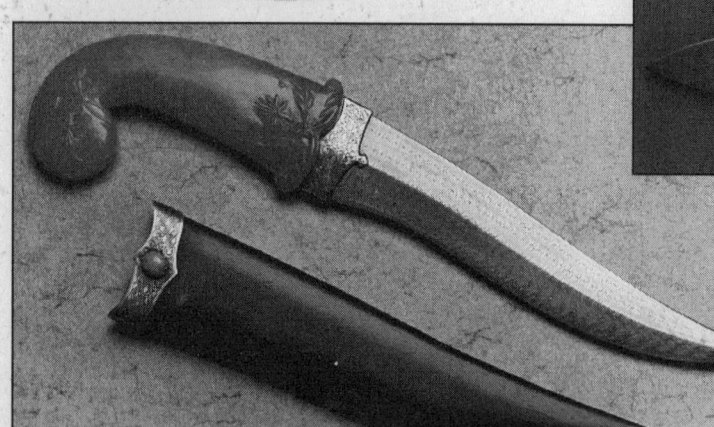

◄*Scott Slobodian:* Splendid setting of a Jerry Rados Turkish Damascus blade in jade and sterling, with ebony sheath and Frankson engraving.

STUDY OF STEEL AND SHAPE AND STUFF

▲*Charles L. Weiss:* Hunters cast in 440C—ten models next year—perhaps a harbinger.

▼*Mike Sakmar:* Inevitable, probably—here's the integral Damascus sub-hilt fighter and very nice it is. (Weyer photo)

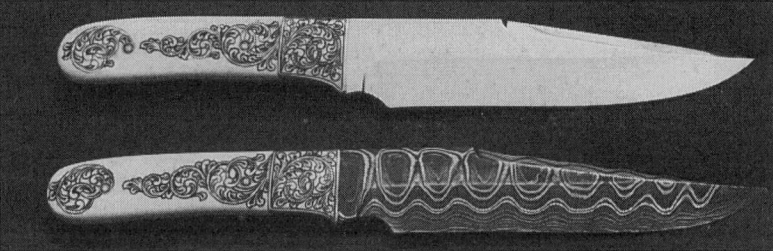

◄*Ralph Freer:* Bowies, one plain, one Damascus, Foster-engraved, demonstrate why knifemakers like Damascus.

STUDY OF STEEL AND SHAPE AND STUFF

Steel

▼*Pierre Reverdy:* Enormous intricacy in the worked surfaces of these knives, created to express the symbolism of such legends as Ouroboros—imperial indeed.

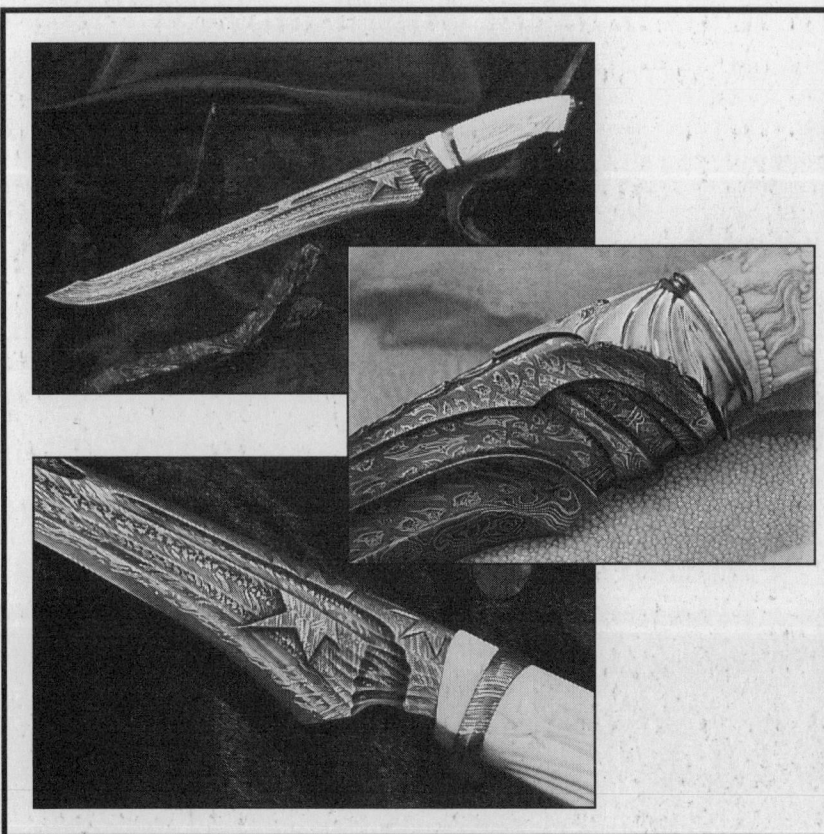

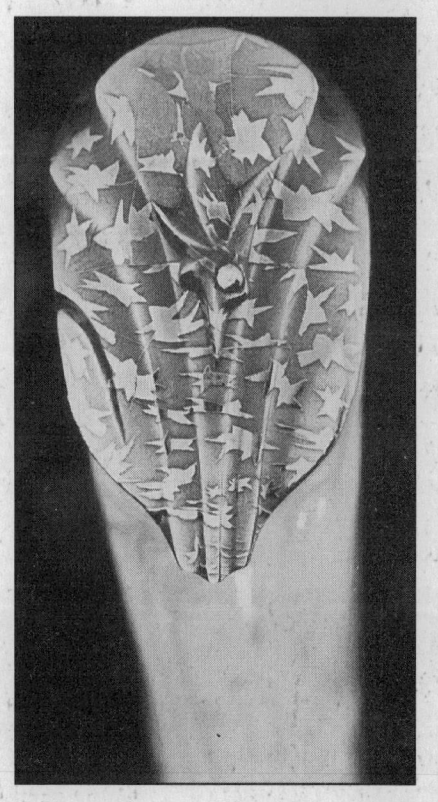

FIFTEENTH EDITION **153**

STATE OF THE ART

▲ *J.E. Parker:* It's called a 4-inch knife, a smallish handful, engraved by Shaw.

▲ *Mudd Sharrigan:* Grand old Elmer Keith shape, in forged O1, 9¼ inches overall, moose and Micarta for a handle.

◄ *William A. Werner, Jr.:* In 440C, this short knife is called "Atlantis" and looks just like it.

STUDY OF STEEL AND SHAPE AND STUFF

Shape

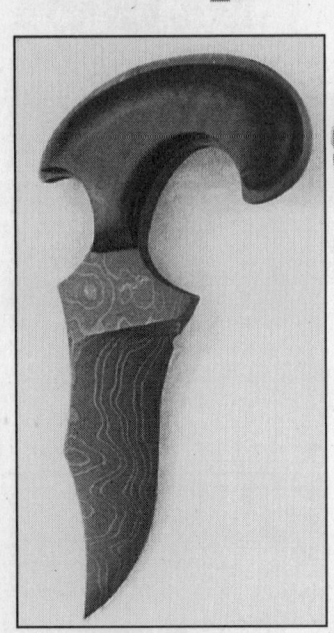

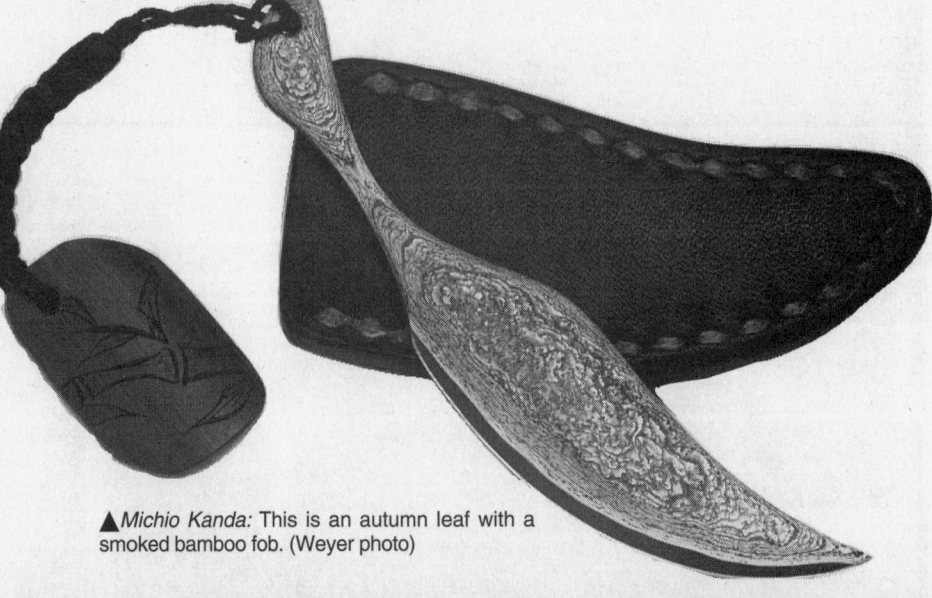

▲ *Michio Kanda:* This is an autumn leaf with a smoked bamboo fob. (Weyer photo)

▲ *John M. Smith:* A push knife far more complicated than average—hidden pin handle, for instance.

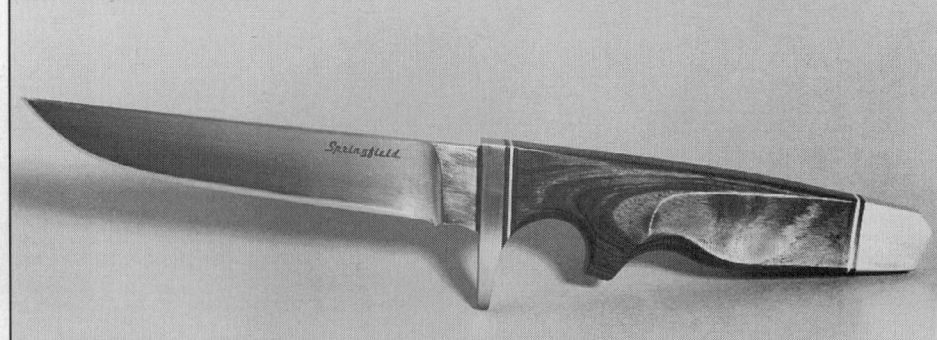

► *G.O. Greenfield:* Simple and useful blade with fully contoured grip.

154 KNIVES '95

STUDY OF STEEL AND SHAPE AND STUFF

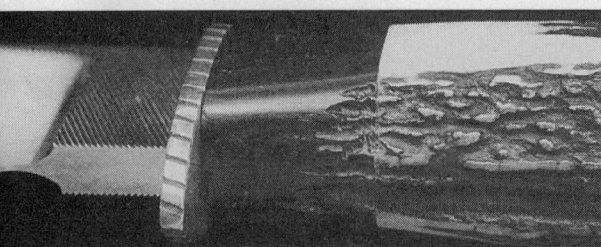
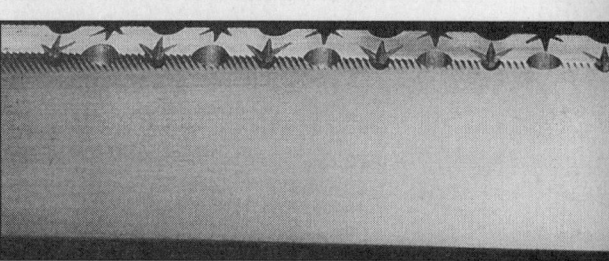

Gary L. Gaddy: File blade, and filework guard and Dremel-tool worked wood bolster, goes with the intricate filed pattern of the back of the blade.

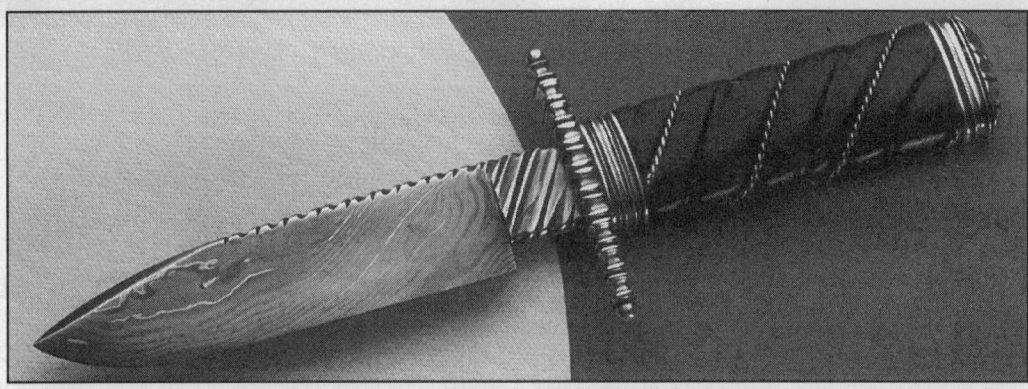

Paul Jarvis: Texture is the overall effect here—the filework, the fluting, the Damascus. (Weyer photo)

STUDY OF STEEL AND SHAPE AND STUFF

Texture

▼*Michael D. Anderson:* Malachite handle and a flinted bronze blade.

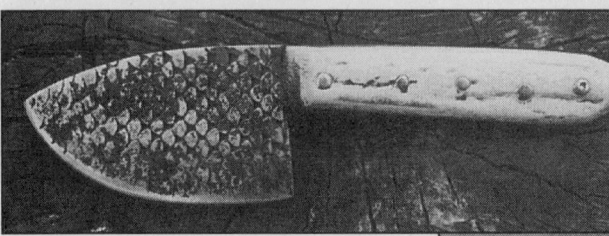

▲*Al Eaton:* Milled and polished 440C blade is really different.

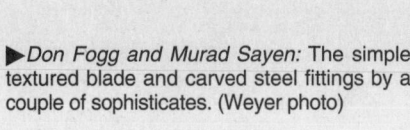

▲*Wild Bill Baker:* Shape, materials and, most of all, the file's texture—nifty old-timey knife.

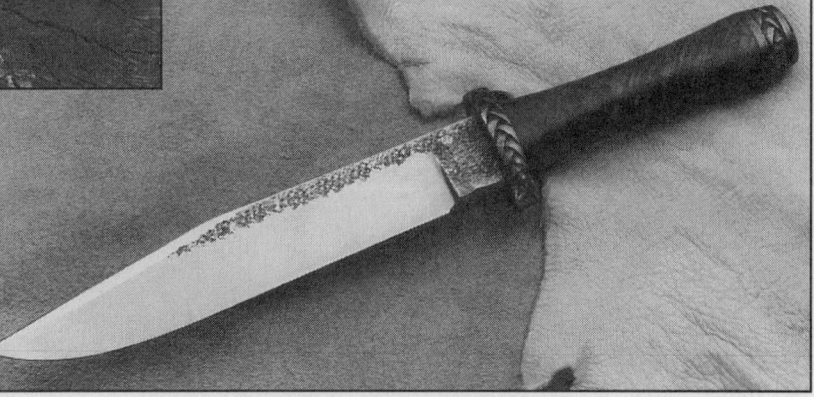

▶*Don Fogg and Murad Sayen:* The simple textured blade and carved steel fittings by a couple of sophisticates. (Weyer photo)

STATE OF THE ART

STUDY OF STEEL AND SHAPE AND STUFF

Handles

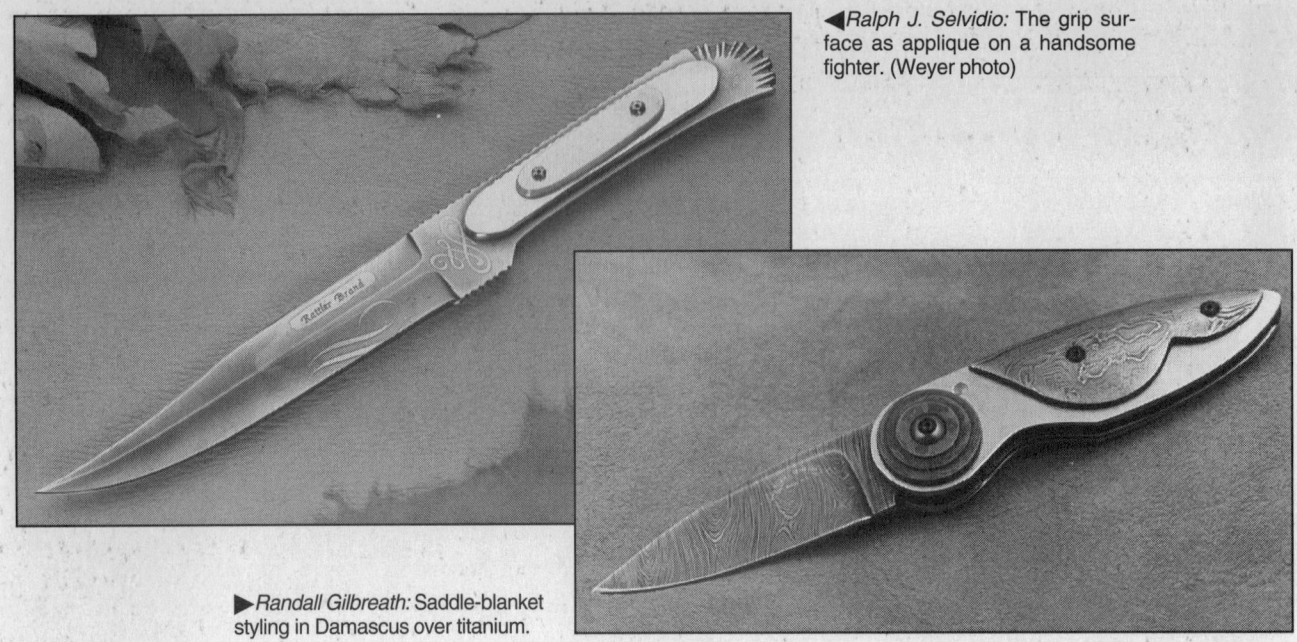

◀ *Ralph J. Selvidio:* The grip surface as applique on a handsome fighter. (Weyer photo)

▶ *Randall Gilbreath:* Saddle-blanket styling in Damascus over titanium.

▼ *George Koutsopoulos:* Back to basics with the glued leather grip on a classic fighter.

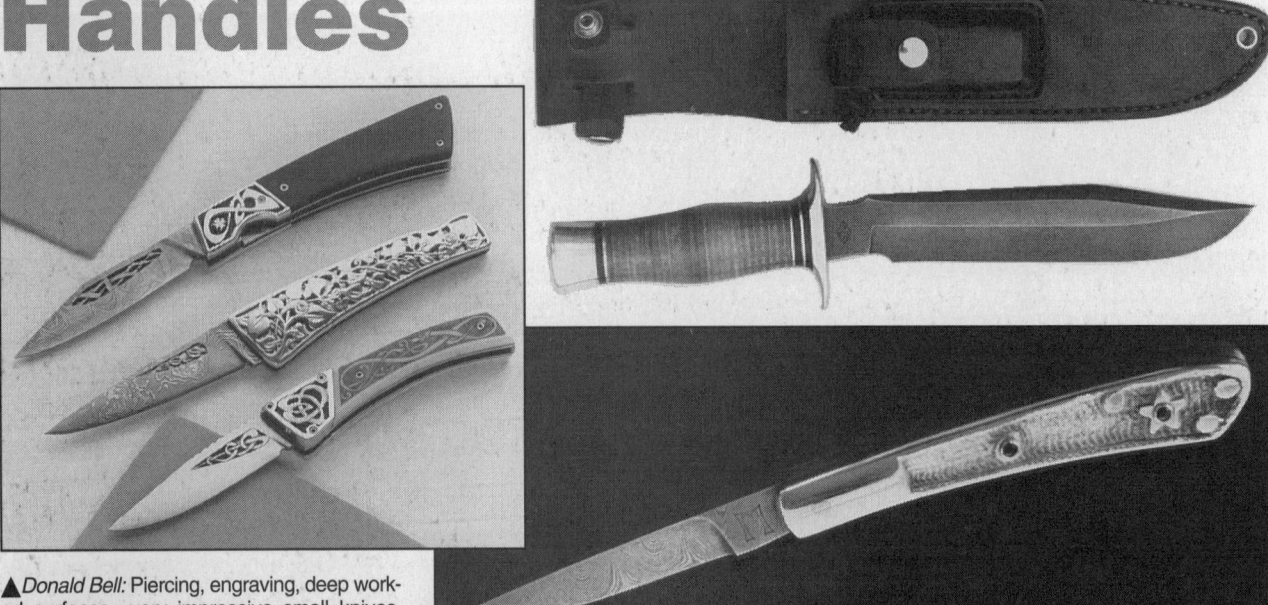

▲ *Donald Bell:* Piercing, engraving, deep worked surfaces—very impressive small knives. (Weyer photo)

▲ *Joel Ellefson:* Cast sterling silver frame, set in lapis lazuli and carnelians—classy primitive look.

◀ *Guy Hielscher:* Stacked leather on—no surprise—a brass-guarded fighter.

STUDY OF STEEL AND SHAPE AND STUFF

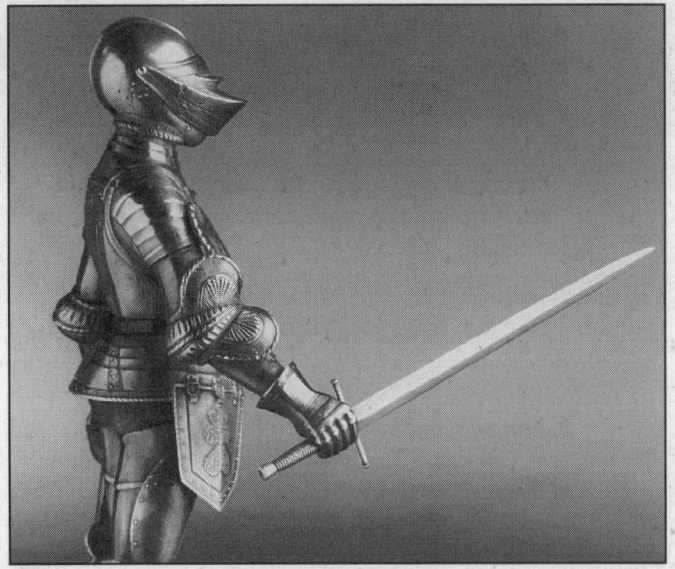

▲▶*Scott Slobodian:* The sterling silver figures are 5½ inches tall, armed appropriately with spiked war hammer and knightly sword—built to actually work for 5½-inch-tall people. (Slobodian photos)

STUDY OF STEEL AND SHAPE AND STUFF

Novelties

▶*Russians, Russians:* It seems the new capitalists are finding each other and cooperatively rendering these sorts of cutlery art—*very* Russian.

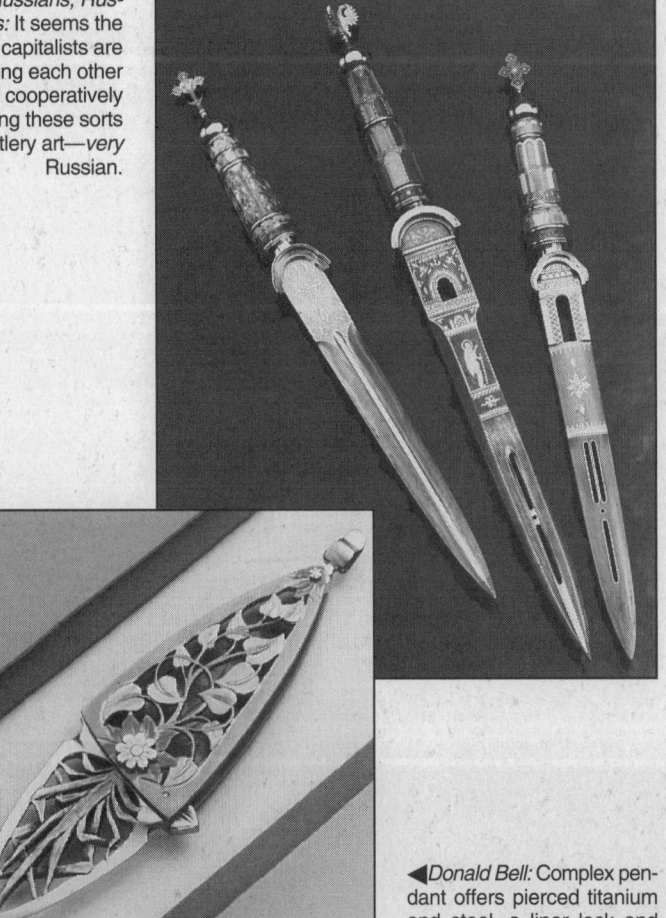

▲▼*Kazou Okaysu:* Something special in the belt buckle category—and not obviously so. (Weyer photos)

◀*Donald Bell:* Complex pendant offers pierced titanium and steel, a liner lock and color. (Weyer photo)

FIFTEENTH EDITION **157**

STATE OF THE ART

EMBELLISHMENT

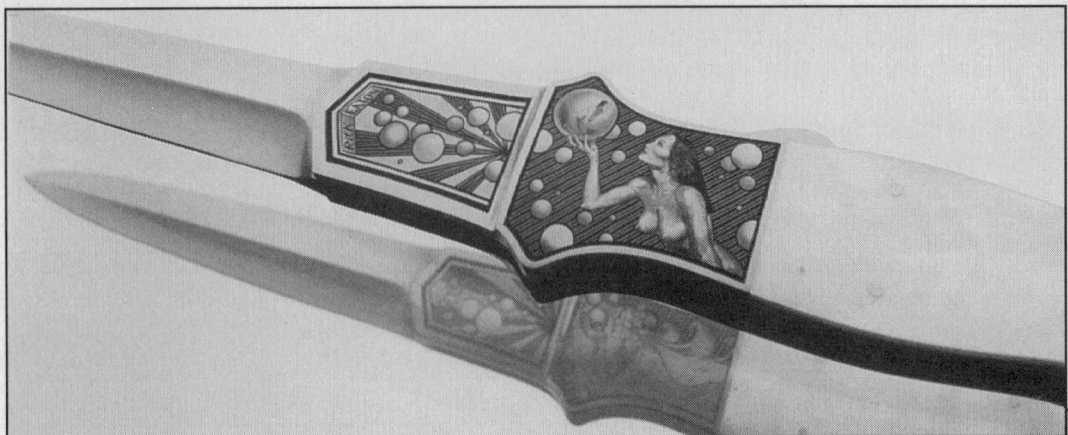

◀ *Rick Eaton:* Maker cuts a dainty lady on his own knife.

EMBELLISHMENT
Engraving

▶ *Julie Warenski:* All-out engraving on a Jim Ence Frisco-style knife. (Weyer photo)

▼ *Martin Butler:* Greatly enlarged bolster of a Warren Osborne knife shows Butler's stipple technique.

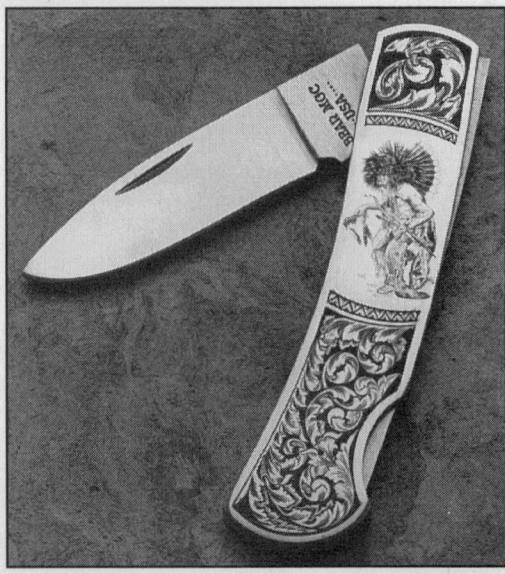

▲ *Jim Blair:* Big-time engraving on a small Bear MGC Folder. (Weyer photo)

EMBELLISHMENT
Engraving

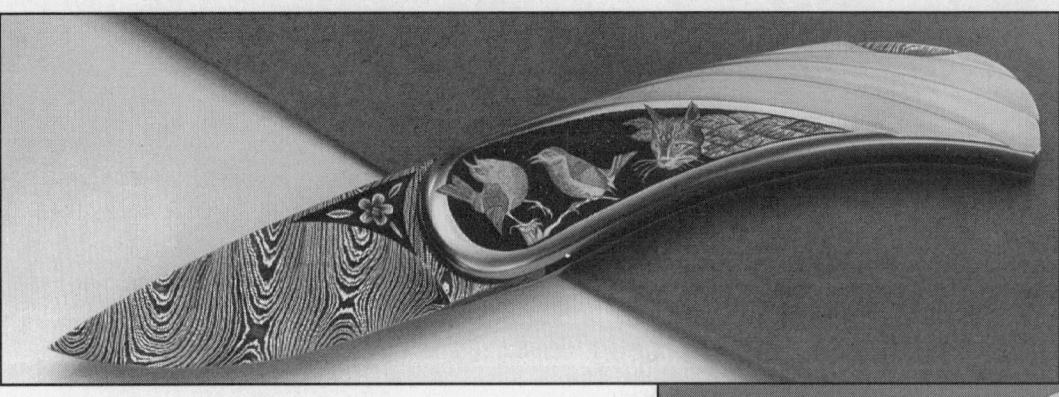

◄*Brian Lyttle:* Real action engraving by the maker on a Damascus-bladed folder. (Weyer photo)

►*Werner Kaluza:* Breakthrough style—the bolster is hollow—in an integral knife designed and made by Kaluza. (Weyer photo)

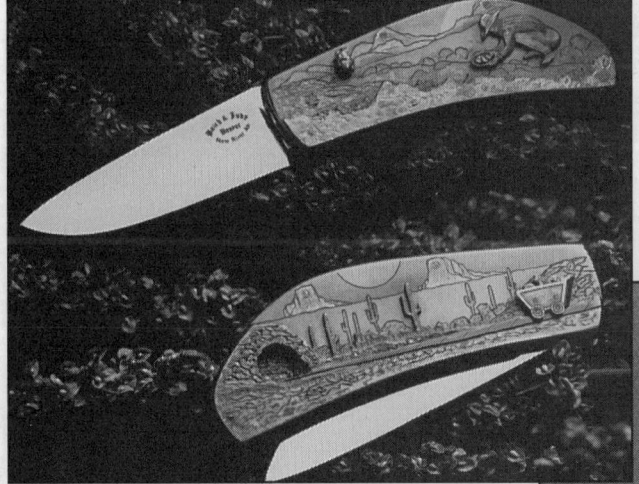

▲*Judy Beaver:* Titanium layered, engraved, anodized in color—a treasure trove of technique. (Weyer photo)

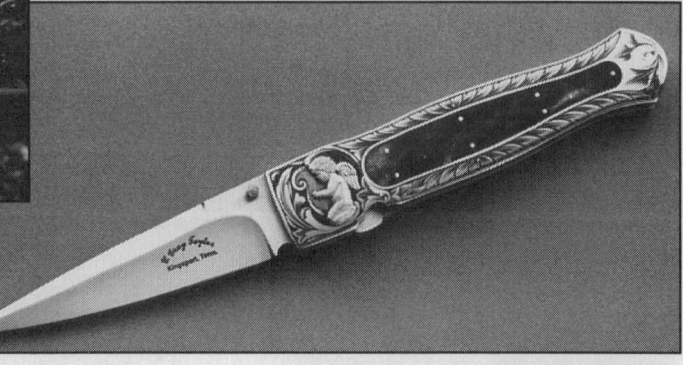

▲*R.E. Skaggs:* Marvelous layout on a liner-locked folding dagger by C. Gray Taylor. (Weyer photo)

▼*Tim George:* Classy scroll on gray metal surrounds abalone of a C. Gray Taylor interframe. (Weyer photo)

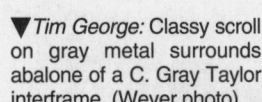

▲*Fred A. Harrington:* Bold scroll on black gives a small Judy Gottage gent's knife presence. (Weyer photo)

STATE OF THE ART

EMBELLISHMENT
Engraving

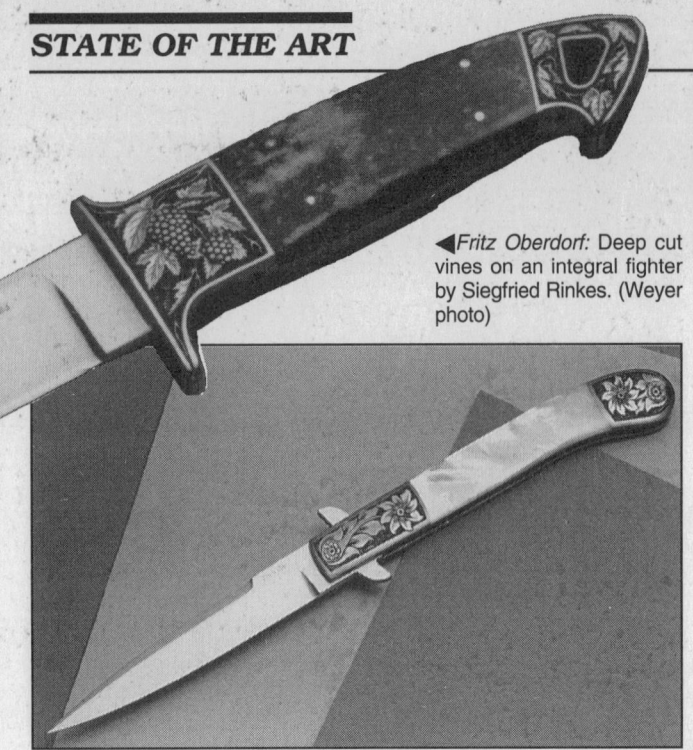

◀ *Fritz Oberdorf:* Deep cut vines on an integral fighter by Siegfried Rinkes. (Weyer photo)

▲ *Rick Eaton:* Handsome vines entwined over gray on a Jot Singh Khalsa folder.

◀ *Harry E. Mendenhall:* Nice florals on a big Jay Harris folding toothpick. (Weyer photo)

▼ *Jere Davidson:* Clean ram on the fancy bolster of an Eldon G. Peterson folder.

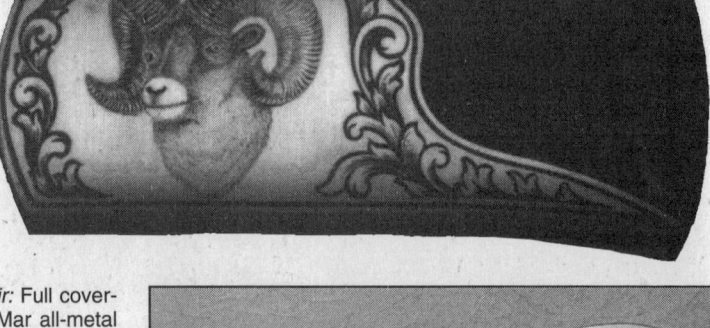

◀ *W.P. Sinclair:* Full coverage of an Al Mar all-metal folder.

▶ *David L. Perdue:* Bolsters of a Khalsa knife with engraving, 24K gold and an opal. (Weyer photo)

▲ *Scott Pilkington, Jr.:* Bold scrolls all around this interframe folder in a nice plan. (Long pho-

160 KNIVES '95

EMBELLISHMENT

▲ *Pat Holder:* Full coverage of a Bowie by D'Alton Holder, blade included. (Weyer photo)

▶ *Jim Blair:* Full coverage, grip screws included, on Kirk Rexroat knives. (Weyer photo)

▼ *Al Scott:* This maker engraved his own—all the way to the tip. (Weyer photo)

EMBELLISHMENT
Engraving

◀ *Barry Trindle:* Bold strokes by the maker on a glass-beaded background. Knife is 2¾-inch folder.

▼ *Nellie Whitener:* A boldly scrolled blade marks this Walter J. Brend commemorative—No. 4 of 25.

▲ *David A. Morton:* Small Arthur L. Summers knife, with a nicely scrolled fancy bolster.

FIFTEENTH EDITION **161**

STATE OF THE ART

EMBELLISHMENT
Scrimshaw

◀ *Rick B. Fields:* High-plains iron horse on a Centofante folder with mammoth ivory scales.

◀ *Gene Keidel:* Eagle scrimmed on black Micarta by maker.

▼ *R.W. Barrett:* Maker scrimmed his own faux ivory; plated Billy Bates engraving.

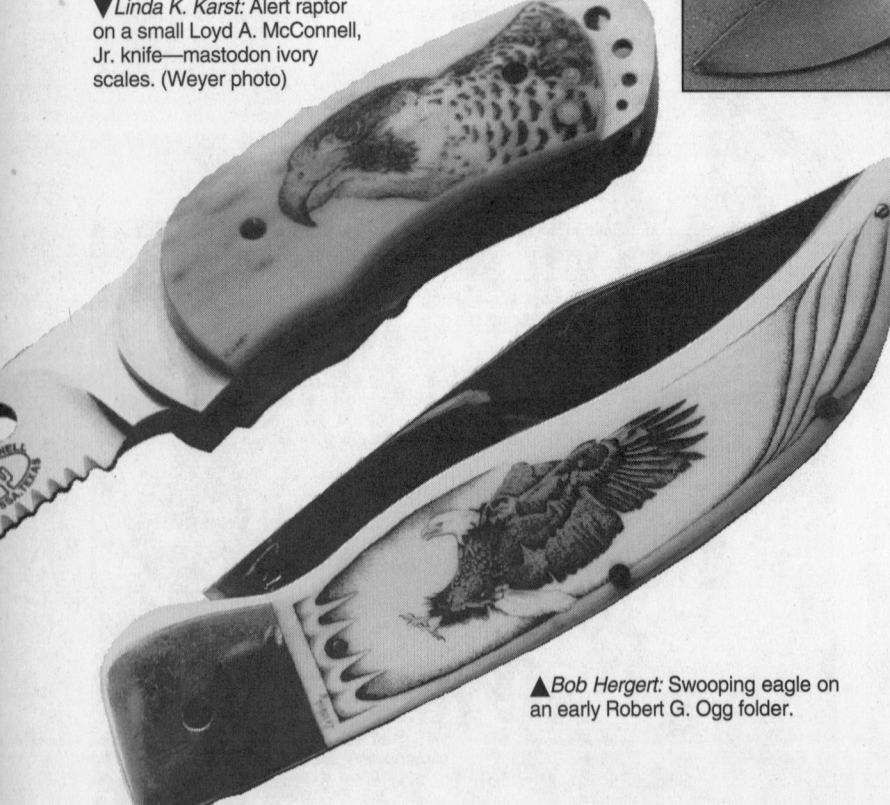

▼ *Linda K. Karst:* Alert raptor on a small Loyd A. McConnell, Jr. knife—mastodon ivory scales. (Weyer photo)

▲ *Bob Hergert:* Swooping eagle on an early Robert G. Ogg folder.

▲ *Charles Hargraves, Sr.:* Same ship, with and without sails, on a pair of Walt Stockdale knives.

EMBELLISHMENT
Scrimshaw

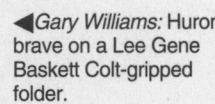

◀ *Gary Williams:* Huron brave on a Lee Gene Baskett Colt-gripped folder.

▶ *Faustina L. Mead:* Geronimo looking very tough on a buffalo-horn handle.

▲ *Rick B. Fields:* Daniel Winkler his own-self on the fossil ivory of a knife he built.

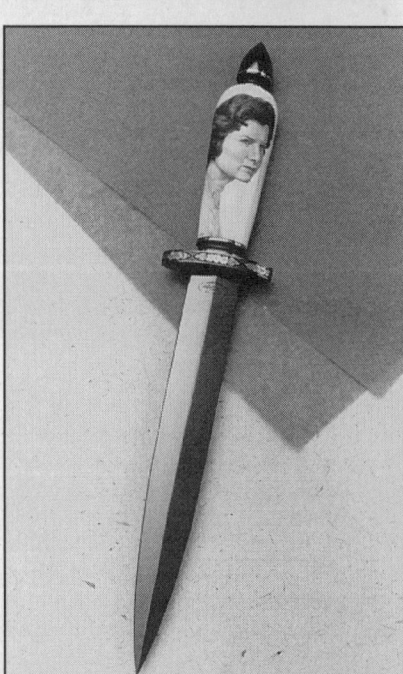
▲ *Rick B. Fields:* Portrait on a Fred Carter dagger's mastodon ivory handle. *Weyer photo)*

▶ *Rick B. Fields:* The Rose, done on the fossil ivory of a Wolfgang Loerchner dagger.

◀ *Rick B. Fields:* Classic Indian face on a Schuyler Lovestrand knife. (*Weyer photo*)

FIFTEENTH EDITION **163**

STATE OF THE ART

EMBELLISHMENT
Scrimshaw

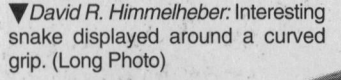

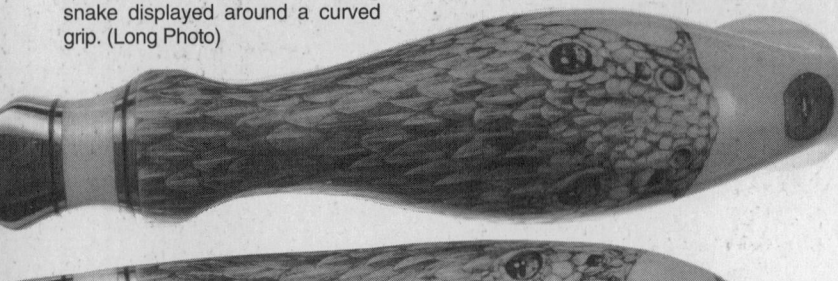
▶ *Gaetan Beauchamp:* Canadian wildlife in white on the ebony handles of two Beauchamp knives. (Weyer photo)

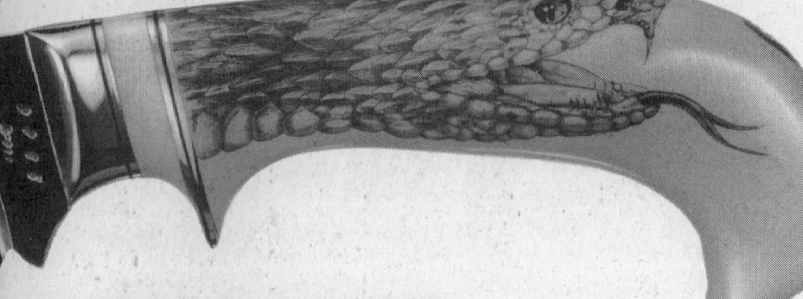
▼ *David R. Himmelheber:* Interesting snake displayed around a curved grip. (Long Photo)

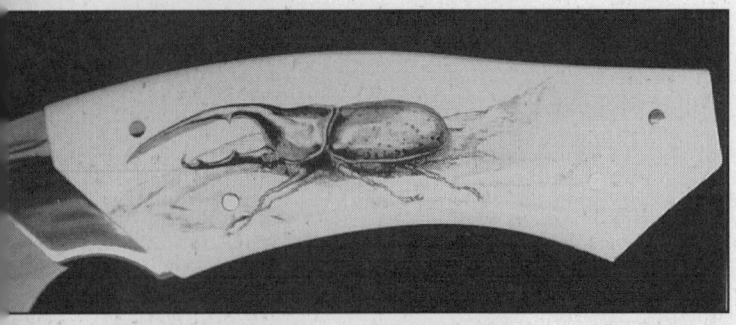
▲ *Faustina L. Mead:* Hercules beetle parades on the ivory handle of a J. Recce Weiland, Jr. knife.

◀ *Rick B. Fields:* Timber wolf on the mammoth ivory scales of a Centofante folder.

◀ *Sandra Brady:* Puma approaches from the ivory scales of an Edward N. Kalfayan Bowie. (Weyer photo)

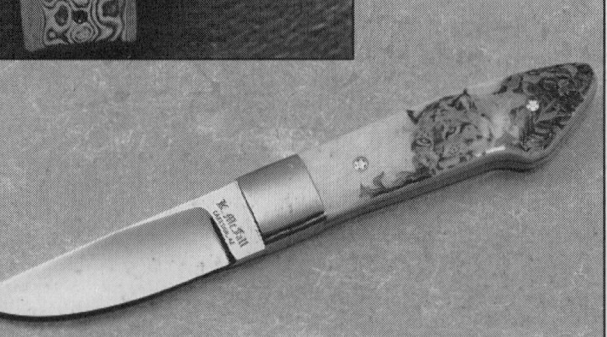
▼ *Ken McFall:* Nicely draped big cat on a working-size knife.

EMBELLISHMENT

EMBELLISHMENT
Scrimshaw

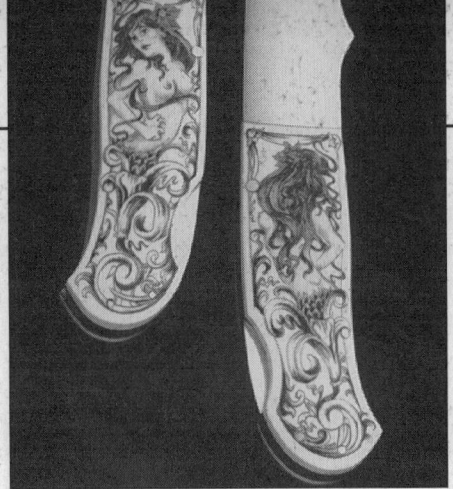

▲*Sandra Brady:* Locking folder by Andy Shinosky has a frivolous lady, both front and back. (Weyer photo)

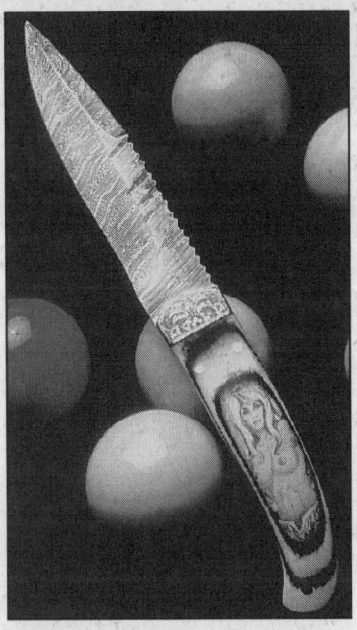

▼*Jolanta Zemitis:* Layered Micarta on a Joe Zemitis knife makes a frame for a long-haired lady.

▲*Bob Hergert:* Five female forms all at once—looks mythic.

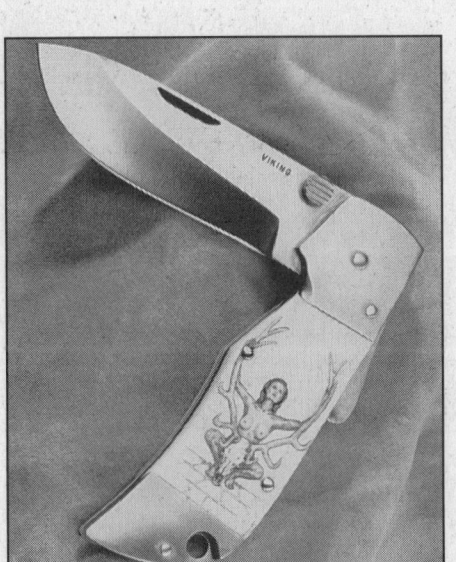

◀*Linda Karst:* Spirit lady on a James Thorlief Eriksen folder is scrimmed on ivory. (Poissenot photo)

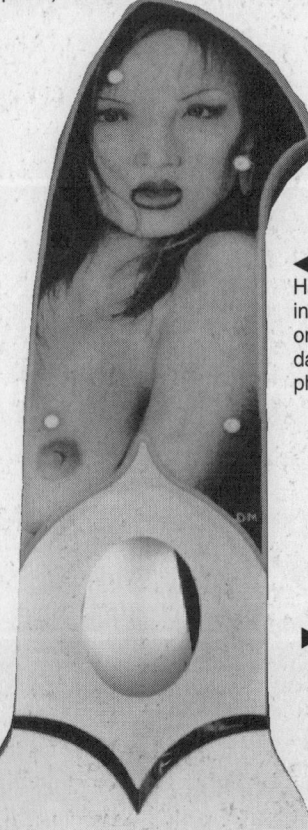

◀*Darrel Morris:* Handsome design in an unusual space on a Randy Phillips dagger. (Weyer photo)

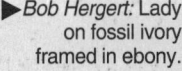

▲*Bob Hergert:* Al fresco bather with a tan line on a Gerber Silver Knight folder.

▶*Bob Hergert:* Lady on fossil ivory framed in ebony.

STATE OF THE ART

EMBELLISHMENT
Carving

Bourbeau: Dramatic curves and points in bloodwood—11 inches long. (Weyer photo)

Doug Casteel: Highly styled leaves offer both pattern and grip surface. (Weyer photo)

Paul Grussenmeyer: Jeweled eye gleam from mule deer antler crowns. (Weyer photo)

Geoff Olsen: Maximum effort on a big Wes Cannon Bowie—silver is cast, ivory is carved. (Weyer photo)

Jim D. Kelso: Rabbits can look at the moon forever on this tanto handle and scabbard.

John Greco: This may well be a self-portrait in stag. (Weyer photo)

EMBELLISHMENT

EMBELLISHMENT
Carving

▲*Paul Grussenmeyer:* Timber wolf glares from the stag pommel of a James E. Porter Bowie. (Weyer photo)

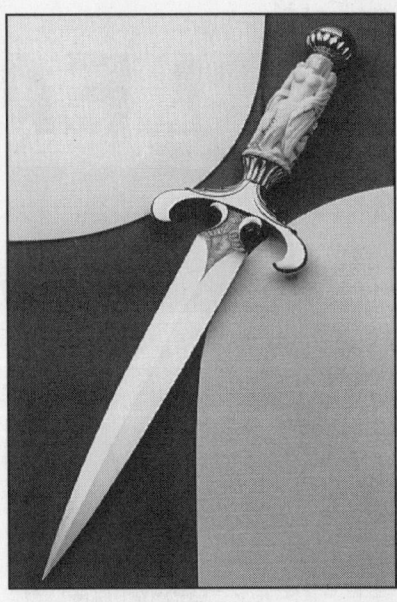

▲*Jose C. DeBraga:* Monumental ivory lady surmounts a Wolfgang Loerchner dagger engraved by Martin Butler. (Weyer photo)

◀*Joel Ellefson:* Sterling silver lake trout with a jewelled eye, 5 inches long, hides a blade.

◀*Richard DiMarzo:* A skull grins from the mouth of a snake carved from a boar's tusk. (Weyer photo)

▶*J. A. Lonewolf:* Seriously whimsical, a happy skull on a slim Lonewolf knife.

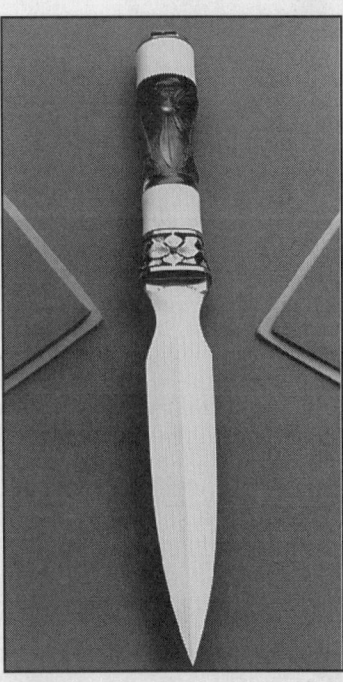

▲*Jim Sornberger:* Carved amber set off by ivory in a dagger handle. (Weyer photo)

◀*Stephen R. Burrows:* This is the pommel of a Burrows knife named Akasha.

FIFTEENTH EDITION 167

STATE OF THE ART
LEATHERWORK

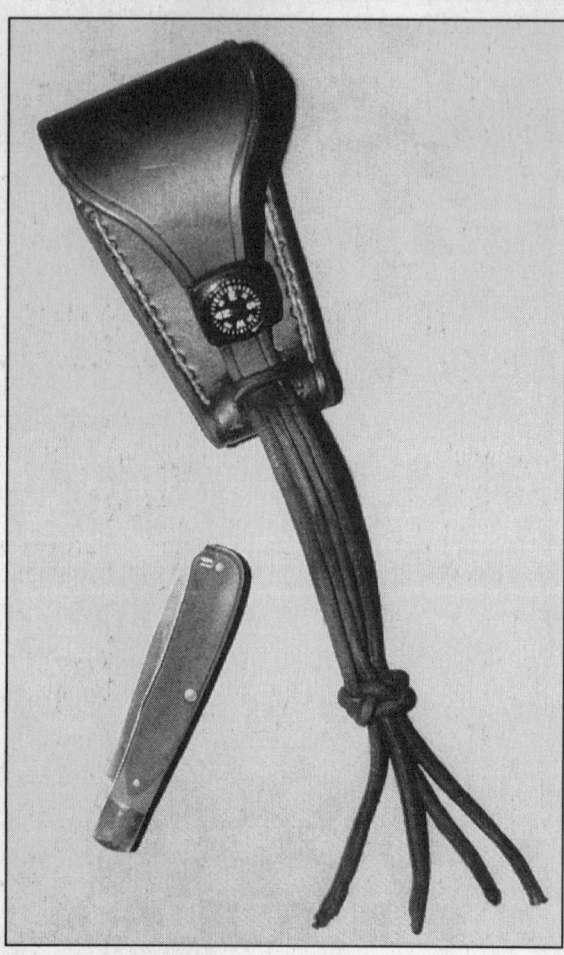

▲*Dudley Dawkins:* Wood-lined sharkskin worked out a couple of ways—nice, simple class. (Weyer photo)

▲*Barney Foley:* Simple, fancy sheath for a working-class Old Timer folding knife.

▼*Ed Halligan:* Here's a full 4-inch blade set up in Kydex for neckwear. (Weyer photo)

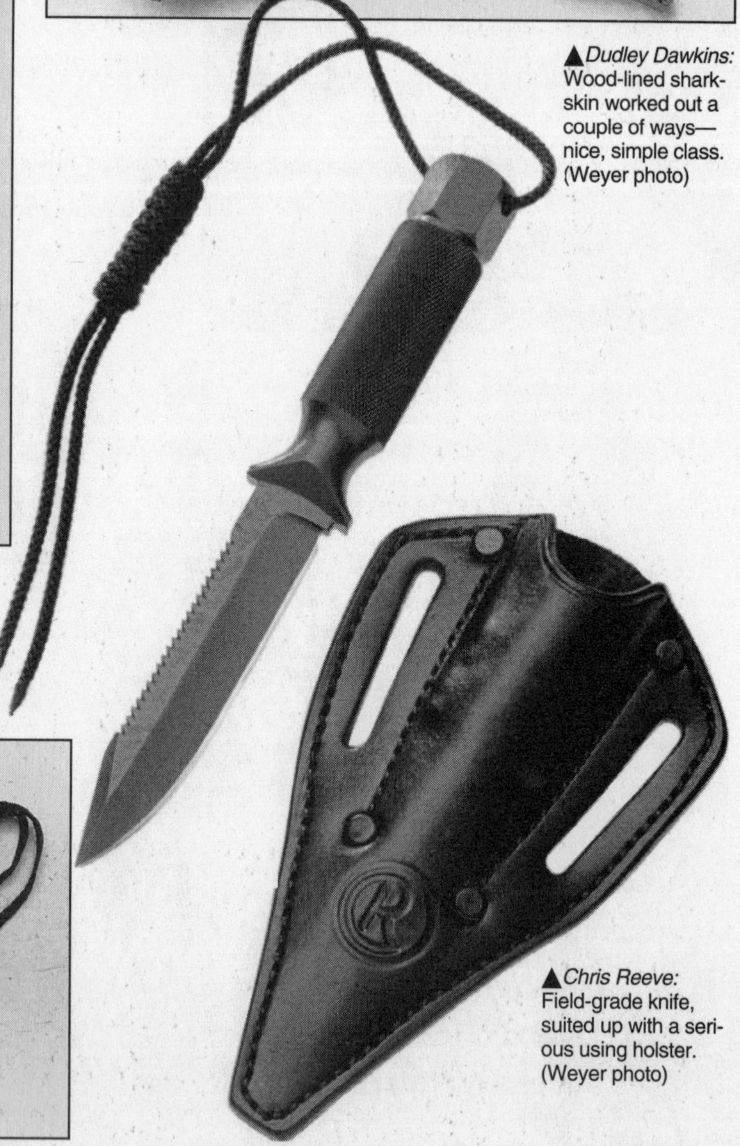

▲*Chris Reeve:* Field-grade knife, suited up with a serious using holster. (Weyer photo)

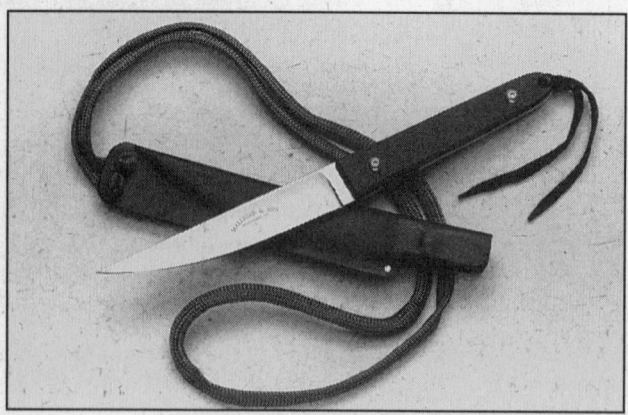

LEATHERWORK

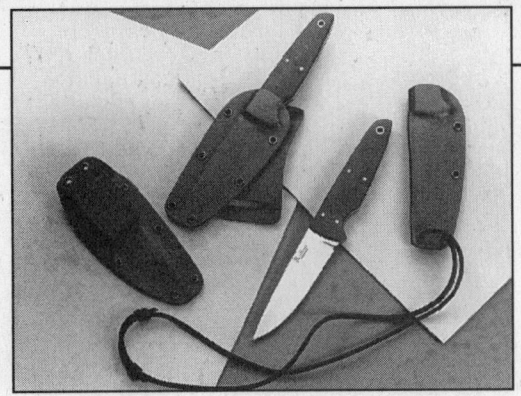

◀ *Al Polkowski:* Still furnishing utility knives with a three-sheath Kydex set. (Weyer photo)

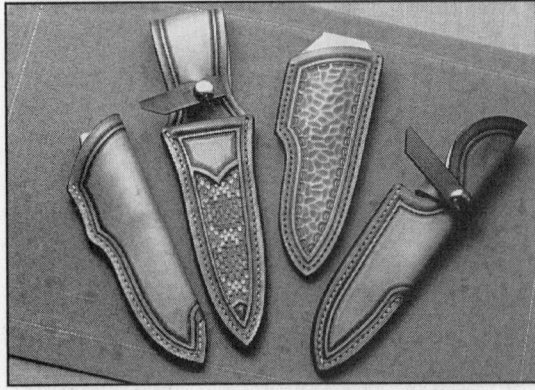

▲ *Sonja Lee:* Handsome cases with their own look and shape—obvious quality. (Weyer photo)

▲ *Melvin T. Dunn:* Neat sticker/skinner pair in an equally neat gun-holster-style sheath. (Weyer photo)

◀ *Jim Fister:* This knifemaker does not have to sit in anybody's back seat when it comes to sheaths.

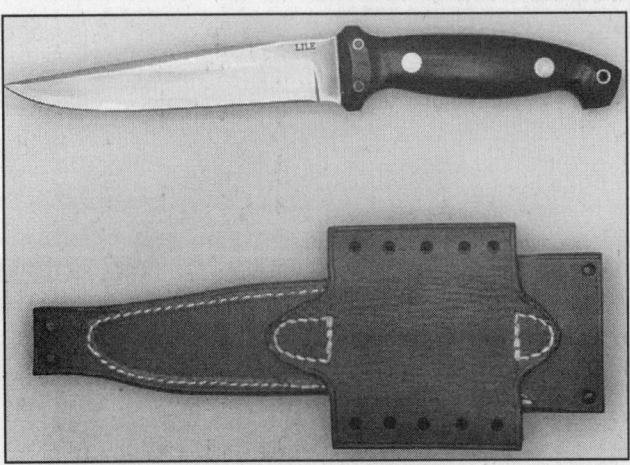

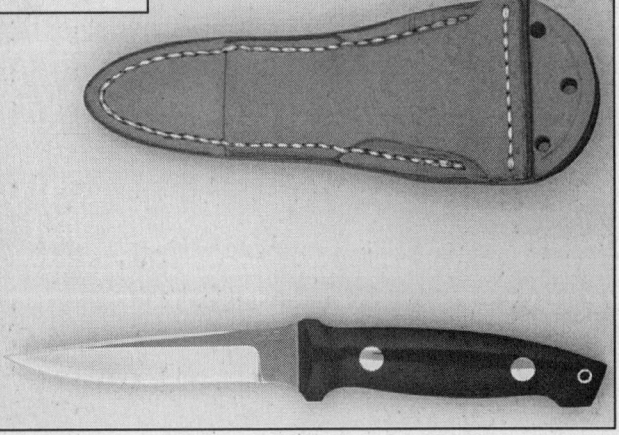

◀▲ *Jimmy Lile:* Late great maker had several slick ways to tote knives—and they're still marketed.

FIFTEENTH EDITION **169**

STATE OF THE ART

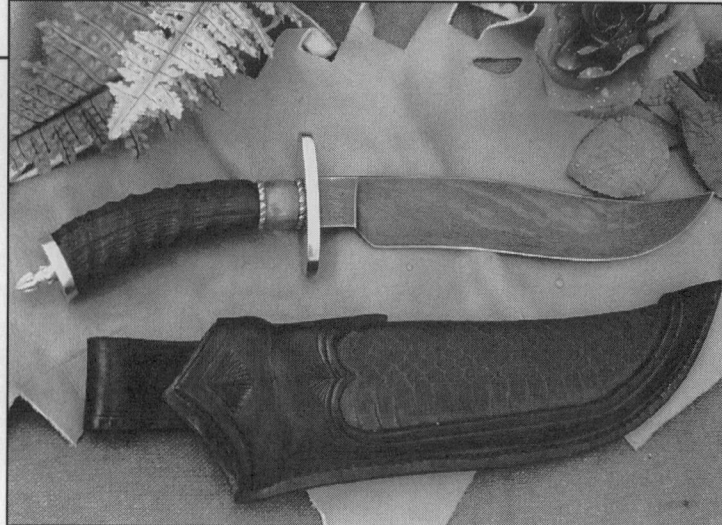

▲ *Kevin R. Cashen:* Bold, big hunter gets bold but deluxe sheath—built to last.

▲ *Robert A. Defeo:* Neither your usual pouch shape nor your ordinary tooling—from a knifemaker, yet.

▼ *Don Lozier:* Stout pouches heavily worked in big-scale traditional shapes—handsome. (Long photo)

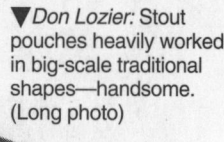

▼ *Robert G. Schrap:* Cowhide overlaid with pigskin, nicely scaled to Syslo knife with Semich artwork.

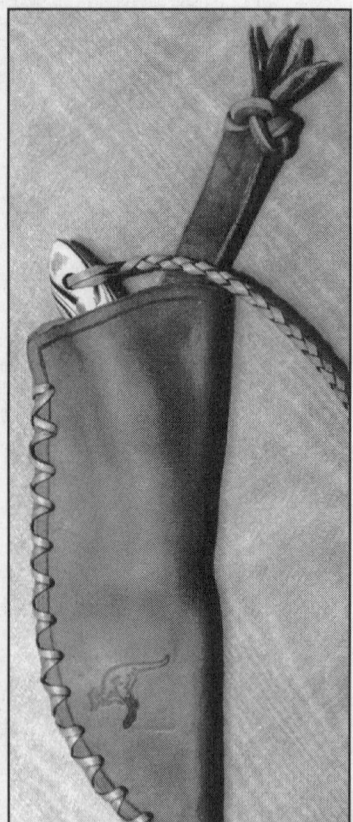

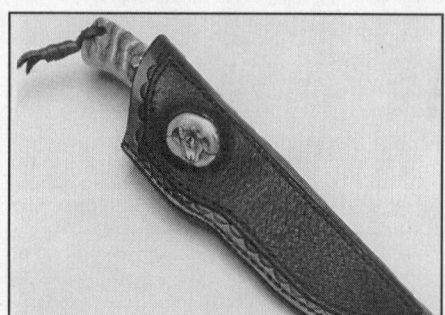

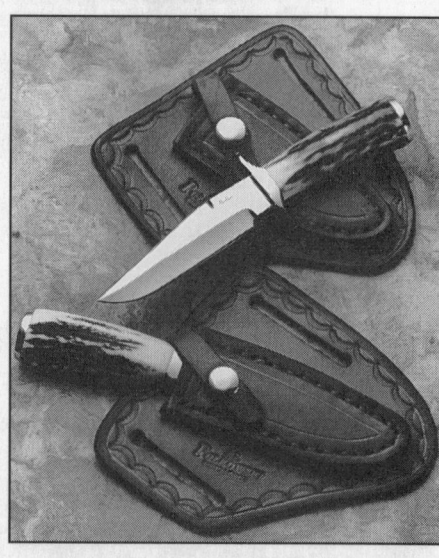

▲ *Barney Foley:* Practical pouch, deluxe thong, and a "Crown and Wall" knot. Not usual but nice.

▲ *Al Polkowski:* Working in leather, this knifemaker turns out small crossdraw sheaths for small fighters. (Weyer photo)

◄ *Kenny Rowe:* For a Fisk Bowie, this style of sheath reveals the full handle and still firmly holds the knife.

FACTORY TRENDS

Commercial cutlery tends toward the tried and true. The market needs millions of knives every year, and the market uses them up. So much of the market is replacement.

There are, however, counter-trends. That is, the marketing guys in the knife business want new stuff to talk about. And those—at least, quite a few of them—are what you see here in our "New Knives In Production" pages.

And we remark on the passing parade as well, when the commercial market displays a new direction.

Ken Warner

Tough Little Guys 172
Workers of the World 173
New Knives in Production 174

FACTORY TRENDS

TOUGH LITTLE GUYS

THEY HAVE NAMES like "Stubby," and there are a lot of them. What we're talking about are non-dainty small knives, little guys meant to stand up to heavy-duty cuts.

Spyderco has a half-dozen such designs; there have been a couple with the Fury name; Blackjack has a heavy-duty straight knife about 6 inches long of 3/16-inch stock.

And where did they come from? The trend certainly goes back to Buck's Peanuts, those many-hued little lockblades of a half-dozen years back. Others followed suit, and then it only remained to beef up those lightweights to get today's tough ones.

There will, in the fullness of time, be a full selection of small, stout folding and straight knives. For now, here are what you can buy now.

Ken Warner

▶ *Fury:* These are the variations of Uncle Bob, which weigh 2.2 ounces and are 3½ inches long.

▼ *EKA:* From Sweden, the Little Tuffy in nylon and 2¾-inch oxided carbon steel blade—"The Toughest of the Tough."

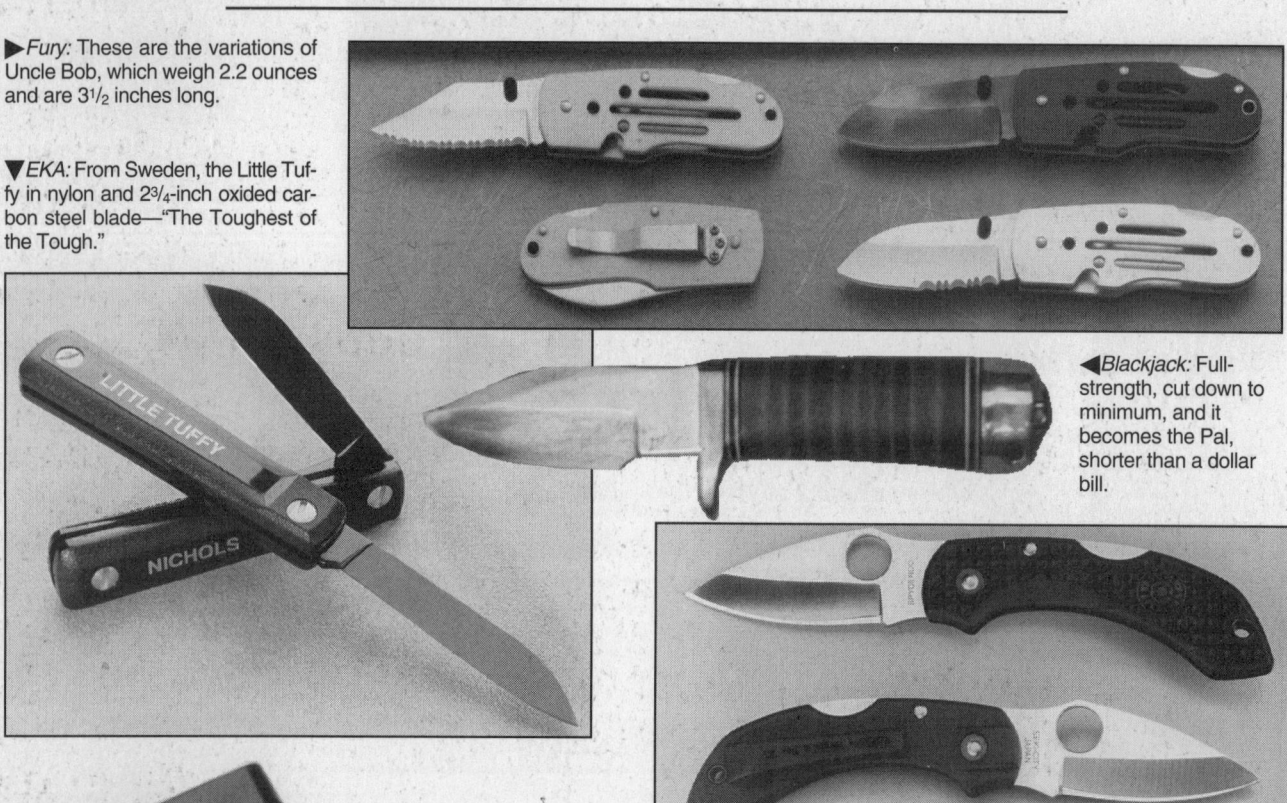

◀ *Blackjack:* Full-strength, cut down to minimum, and it becomes the Pal, shorter than a dollar bill.

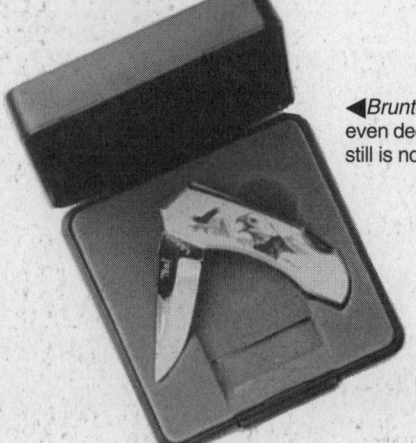

◀ *Brunton/Lakota:* Downsized, even decorated, the Lakota Teal still is no tenderfoot gent's knife.

▲ *Spyderco:* A little toughie larger than their smallest Co-Pilot turned out to be the Dragonfly.

▼ *Spyderco:* The Blackhawk is smaller than the best-seller and offers a different blade at 5½ inches.

FACTORY TRENDS

WORKERS OF THE WORLD

WHEN THE NOW-CLASSIC Leatherman tool appeared, it had two effects: First, it probably and justifiably made a lot of money, and, second, it jazzed up the whole idea of the work knife as well as the tool knife. The Leatherman has had the honor of the complete Taiwan knock-off, and the more legitimate tribute of a host of derivative—in the idea sense—competitive designs that can be found everywhere on the market.

And over on what we could call the "Swiss Army Knife" side, new designs, new approaches, are rife. Tool knives for the pocket have never been more available.

There is now a Super Leatherman, and all kind of the others. Here we show you a few of them.

Ken Warner

◄*Leatherman Tool Group, Inc.:* Here's the Super Tool—new blades, and they lock open, include both serrated and plain clip-points.

►*Colonial Knife Co., Inc.:* The TL-29 in Day-Glo colors and with a scallop-edged blade.

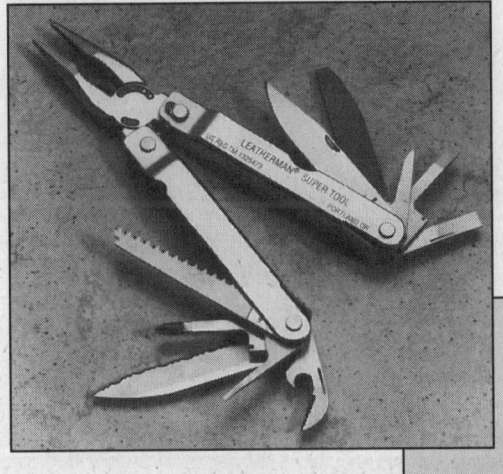

◄*Gerber Legendary Blades:* The Multi-Plier now has a file blade, and there's a tool kit to be had, full of screwdriver blades.

▼*Spyderco:* Not a Clip-It, but a Snap-It, this dangler's for those who need a work knife where they can get it quick.

◄*Coast Cutlery:* West Coast firm gets in on the good stuff with five-blade plier knife they call the Pocket Mechanic.

▼*Gerber Legendary Blades:* Slimmed down folding sport saw has lots of farm-boy and construction-job uses.

FIFTEENTH EDITION **173**

FACTORY TRENDS

NEW KNIVES IN PRODUCTION

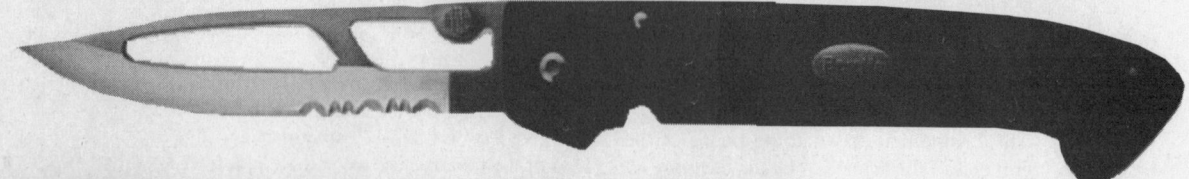

▲ *Beretta U.S.A. Corp.:* The Airlight's skeletonized blade, in choice of three serration patterns, works well—also in colors.

◀ *Spyderco:* There was a limited edition of the Police Clip-It with grey titanium handle.

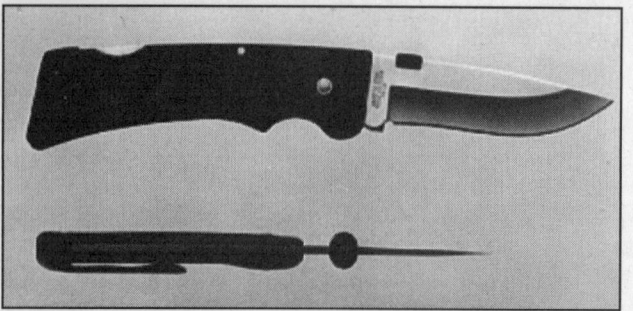

▲ *Katz Knives:* Top-mounted thumb stud and rear-mounted left-side clip—a new configuration.

▲ *Gerber Legendary Blades:* This is the E-Z-Out, pebble-grained and pocket-clipped.

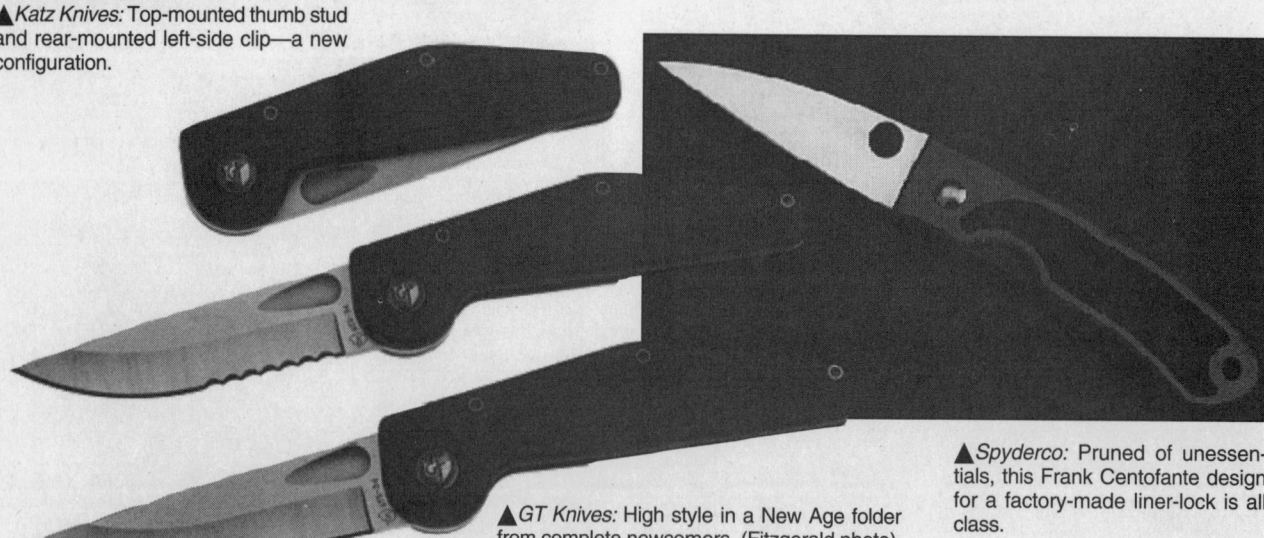

▲ *GT Knives:* High style in a New Age folder from complete newcomers. (Fitzgerald photo)

▲ *Spyderco:* Pruned of unessentials, this Frank Centofante design for a factory-made liner-lock is all class.

NEW KNIVES IN PRODUCTION

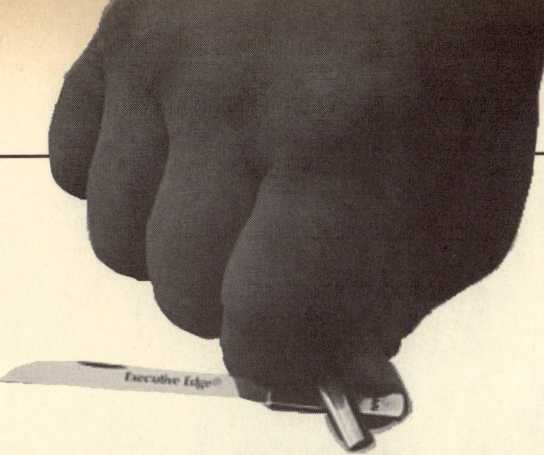
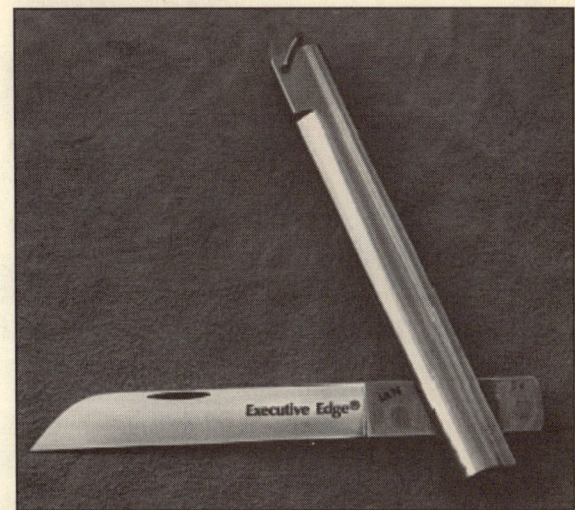

▲▶*B&D Trading Co.:* Executive Edge is, the importers say, the one design that works in the fist straight-razor style.

▼*KA-BAR:* Collector Division's Swing-Guard has all the collector touches—plus just 750 made.

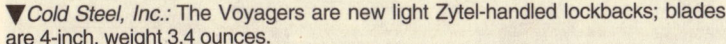

▲*Randy Thompson:* Customized Executive and Solo Spydercos with trimmings in stainless steel, brass, copper and mokume. (Weyer photo)

▼*Cold Steel, Inc.:* The Voyagers are new light Zytel-handled lockbacks; blades are 4-inch, weight 3.4 ounces.

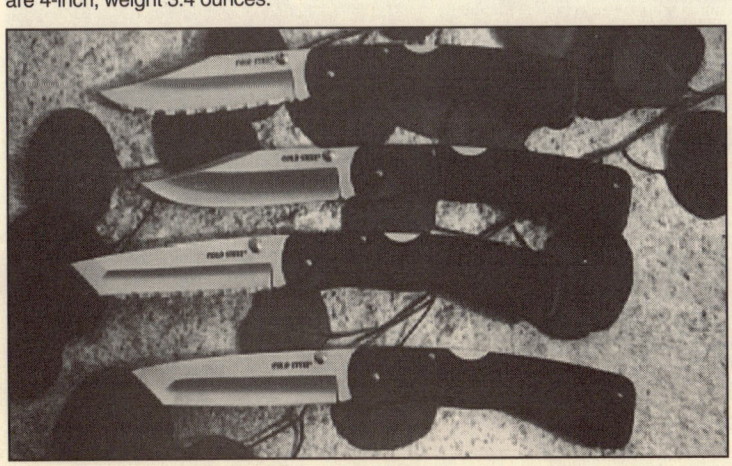

▲*EKA:* Imports by Nichols, well-made fancy gent's knives, gold-plated and etched and enameled.

FACTORY TRENDS

◀ *Buck Knives:* Two different Selector sets—one for hunter chores, the other general purpose.

▲ *Ace of Blades:* The Silent Knight, 4 1/2 inches long in 440 stainless, is this year's new one.

▼ *Boker Baumwerk:* Switchblade Optima series in four handle materials offers both 440C and ceramic blades.

▼ *Randy Lee:* Bob Karp throwers by an individual craftsman—three sizes, with or without handles. (Weyer photo)

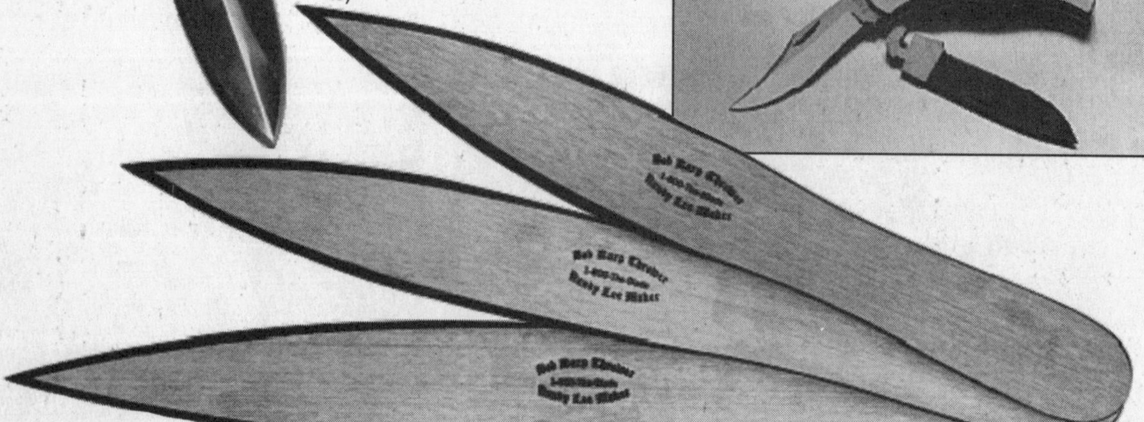

▼ *Myerchin Marine Classics:* The offshore Workman substitutes a second cutting blade for their usual marlinspike.

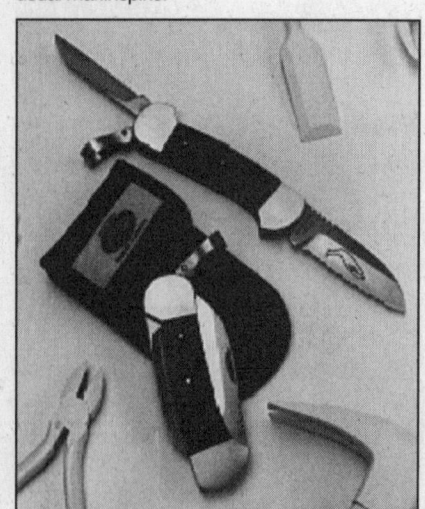

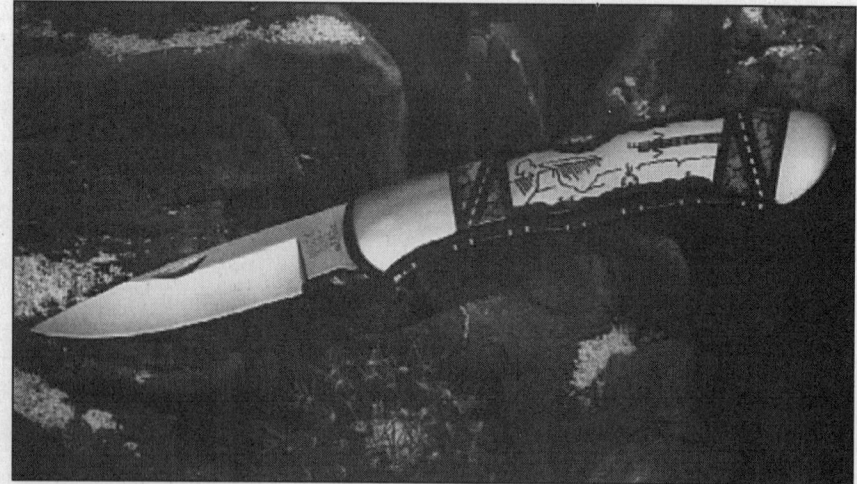

▲ *Buck Knives:* The Yellowhorse just keeps on galloping. This is the Navajo-Land, Catalog #2189.

NEW KNIVES IN PRODUCTION

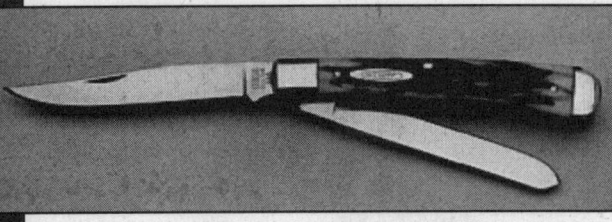

◄▲*Camillus Cutlery Co.:* New attention to the old trapper; one in 4$\frac{1}{8}$-inch length, Dura-Stag scales, stainless steel; the other 257 Roberts, much bigger in jigged bone.

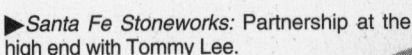

►*Santa Fe Stoneworks:* Partnership at the high end with Tommy Lee.

▼*Damascus, USA:* Replica Scagel camp knife in stag and leather and maidenhair Damascus. (Weyer photo)

▼*Giesser Messerfabrik:* German-made kitchen cutlery in very high style, the "Creative Collection" is available from Markuse Corp.

▲*Colonial Knife Co.:* Internal liner-locked Ranger three-blade Stockman, sold at the lower end.

FACTORY TRENDS

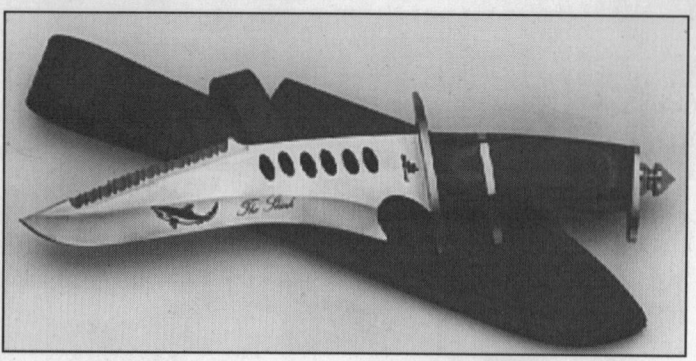

◀*Frost Cutlery Co.:* The Shark rings all the chimes in a wannabe serenade.

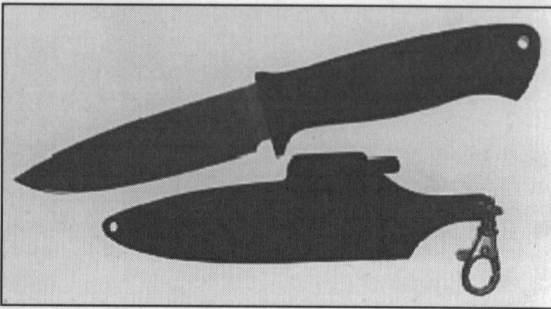

◀*A.G. Russell Co.:* Four-inch Deer Hunter as dangler— 3.3 ounces complete in Thumb-Belt locking sheath.

◀*Mission Knives, Inc.:* Titanium specialists sold the SEALS a lot of these—the MPK (Multi-Purpose Knife) is non-magnetic, won't corrode and passed a lot of tests other knives couldn't.

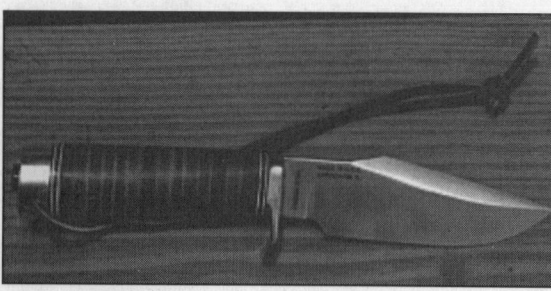

▲*Blackjack:* New Trailguide—very sharp in the traditional materials and patterns.

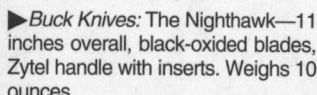

▶*Buck Knives:* The Nighthawk—11 inches overall, black-oxided blades, Zytel handle with inserts. Weighs 10 ounces.

▼*Ruana Knife Works:* Style changes in Bonner, Montana—mountain man stuff.

DIRECTORY

The only reason a maker or a source in the United States is not listed somewhere in this section is that we didn't hear of him or it, or something, went wrong. This is intended to be a complete directory for knife owners. If you know of someone who should be in this Directory and isn't, please write and tell us. If you are that someone, please write. We'll definitely appreciate it.

This is not a catalog, so there will be incomplete entries, though not many. And with probably 1,000 or more entries, it will have omissions. Very often, that will be the result of error on the part of the omitted. We tried to give everyone a chance.

The Directory is divided into different lists. The biggest is a compilation of short profiles of custom knifemakers, followed by a state-by-state list of those same knifemakers, and membership lists of professional knifemaker associations. In the knife photo index, we list all the photos of handmade knives in this edition, as well as the last five editions.

Then we list specialty cutlers; general cutlers; importers and foreign cutlers; sources for knifemaking supplies; mail-order houses that specialize in knives; knife services, which include scrimshanders, engravers, leatherworkers and several other categories. Finally, we list major organizations and publications. Those seem the most useful categories. We hope they work for you.

Ken Warner

Custom Knifemakers 180	Specialty Cutlers 292
Centerfold Knives '95 216	General Cutlers 293
Knifemakers State-By-State 274	Importers & Foreign Cutlers 293
Knifemakers Membership Lists 280	Knifemaking Supplies 295
Knife Photo Index	Mail-Order Sales 297
Knives '95 283	Knife Services 299
Knives '90-'94 285	Organizations & Publications 304

custom knifemakers

a

ABBOTT, WILLIAM M., Box 102A, RR #2, Chandlerville, IL 62627/217-458-2325
Specialties: High-grade edged weapons. **Patterns:** Locking folders, Bowies, working straight knives, kitchen cutlery, minis. **Technical:** Grinds D2, ATS-34, 440C and commercial Damascus. Heat-treats; Rockwell tests. Prefers natural handle materials. **Prices:** $100 to $1,000. **Remarks:** Part-time maker; first knife sold in 1984. **Mark:** Name.

A CUT ABOVE (See Hartsfield, Phill)

ADAMS, LES, 6413 NW 200 St., Hialeah, FL 33015/305-625-1699
Specialties: Working straight knives of his design. **Patterns:** Fighters, hunters and filet knives. **Technical:** Grinds ATS-34, 440C and D2. Offers scrimshawed handles. **Prices:** $100 to $200; some to $290. **Remarks:** Part-time maker first knife sold in 1989. **Mark:** First initial, last name, Custom Knives.

AIDA, YOSHIHITO, 26-7, Narimasu 2-chome, Itabashi-ku, Tokyo 175, JAPAN/81-3-3939-0052; FAX: 81-3-3939-0058
Specialties: High-tech working straight knives and folders of his design. **Patterns:** Bowies, lockbacks, hunters, fighters, fishing knives, boots. **Technical:** Grinds CV-134, ATS-34; buys Damascus; works in traditional Japanese fashion for some handles and sheaths. **Prices:** $300 to $700; some higher. **Remarks:** Full-time maker; first knife sold in 1978. **Mark:** Initial logo and Riverside West.

ALASKA KNIFE & SERVICE CO. (See Trujillo, Thomas A.)

ALASKAN MAID (See Kubaiko, Hank)

ALBERICCI, EMILIO, 19, via Masone, 24100, Bergamo, ITALY/01139-35-215120
Specialties: Folders and Bowies. **Patterns:** Collector knives. **Technical:** Uses stock removal with extreme lavoration accuracy; offers exotic and high-tech materials. **Prices:** Not currently selling. **Remarks:** Part-time maker. **Mark:** None.

ALDEN JR., KENNETH E., P.O. Box 1995, Ramona, CA 92065/619-789-4870; FAX: 619-788-6894
Specialties: Traditional working and using straight knives of his design and in standard patterns. **Patterns:** Bowies, fighters and hunters. **Technical:** Forges 5160 and 1095; grinds 440C. Makes own Damascus; offers filework and tooled, carved and stamped leather sheaths. **Prices:** $300 to $1,500; some to $3,000. **Remarks:** Full-time maker. Doing business as Alden Trading Co. **Mark:** Last name; first inital, last name; Lionmaker.

ALDEN TRADING CO. (See Alden Jr., Kenneth E.)

ALEXANDER, DARREL, Box 381, Ten Sleep, WY 82442/307-366-2699
Specialties: Traditional working straight knives. **Patterns:** Hunters, boots and fishing knives. **Technical:** Grinds D2, 440C, ATS-34 and 154CM. **Prices:** $75 to $120; some to $250. **Remarks:** Full-time maker; first knife sold in 1983. **Mark:** Name, city, state.

ALLEN, JOE, RR #3, Box 182, Princeton, IN 47670/812-385-8010
Specialties: Hunting and outdoor knives. **Patterns:** Bowies, working hunters, daggers and skinners. **Technical:** Grinds 440C and ATS-34. **Prices:** $125 to $300. **Remarks:** Part-time maker; first knife sold in 1976. **Mark:** Cable Joe Knives.

ALLEN, MIKE "WHISKERS", Rt. 1, Box 1080, Malakoff, TX 75148/903-489-1026
Specialties: Working and collector-quality lockbacks. **Patterns:** Hunters, tantos, Bowies, swords and miniatures. **Technical:** Forges Damascus to shape; grinds 440C and ATS-34. Engraves. **Prices:** $125 to $350. **Remarks:** Full-time maker; first knife sold in 1984. **Mark:** Whiskers and serial number.

ALLRED AND SONS (See Allred, Elvan)

ALLRED, ELVAN, 2403 Lansing Blvd., Wichita Falls, TX 76309/817-691-9563
Specialties: Fancy, high-art straight knives and folders of his design. **Patterns:** Fighters, hunters and locking folders. **Technical:** Grinds ATS-34, 440C and D2. Most knives are engraved; many have custom-fitted cases or sheaths. **Prices:** $250 to $750; some to $1,500. **Remarks:** Full-time maker; first knife sold in 1992. Doing business as Allred and Sons. **Mark:** First initial, last name, city, state.

ALSTAR (See Amoureux, A.W.)

ALVERSON, TIM (R.V.), 1158 Maple St., Klamath Falls, OR 97601/503-884-9119
Specialties: Fancy working knives to customer specs. **Patterns:** Folding lockers, miniatures, boots, fighters and hunters. **Technical:** Grinds 440C, ATS-34; buys some Damascus. **Prices:** $65 to $450. **Remarks:** Full-time maker; first knife sold in 1981. **Mark:** Rosebud or R.V.A.

AMERI, MAURO, Via Trensasco, 13a/8, 16138 Genova, ITALY/010-863035
Specialties: Working and using knives of his design. **Patterns:** Hunters, Bowies and utility/camp knives. **Technical:** Grinds 440C, ATS-34, 154CM and Damascus by C. Peterson. Handles in wood or Micarta. **Prices:** $200 to $1,200. **Remarks:** Spare-time maker; first knife sold in 1982. **Mark:** Last name, city.

AMES FORGE (See Ames, Mickey L.)

AMES, MICKEY L., P.O. Box 62, 528 Spruce, Lebo, KS 66856/316-256-6222
Specialties: Traditional working and using straight knives of his design and to customer specs. **Patterns:** Bowies, hunters and utility/camp knives. **Technical:** Forges 5160. Filework; silver wire inlay. **Prices:** $100 to $750. **Remarks:** Part-time maker; first knife sold in 1990. Doing business as Ames Forge. **Mark:** Last name.

AMOR JR., MIGUEL, 1711 White Water Rd., Lancaster, PA 17603/717-394-7590
Specialties: Working and fancy straight knives in standard patterns; some to customer specs. **Patterns:** Bowies, hunters, fighters and tantos. **Technical:** Grinds 440C, ATS-34, carbon steel and commercial Damascus; forges some in high carbon steels. **Prices:** $125 to $500; some to $1,500 and higher. **Remarks:** Part-time maker; first knife sold in 1983. **Mark:** Last name. On collectors' pieces: last name, city, state.

AMOUREUX, A.W., 3210 Woodland Pk. Dr., Anchorage, AK 99517/907-248-4442
Specialties: Heavy-duty working straight knives. **Patterns:** Bowies, fighters, camp knives and hunters for Alaska use. **Technical:** Grinds 440C, ATS-34 and 154CM. **Prices:** $80 to $2,000. **Remarks:** Part-time maker; first knife sold in 1974. **Mark:** ALSTAR.

ANDERS, DAVID, Rt. 1, Box 157, Center Ridge, AR 72027/501-893-2294
Specialties: Working straight knives of his design. **Patterns:** Bowies, fighters and hunters. **Technical:** Forges 5160, 1080 and Damascus. **Prices:** $100 to $1,200; some to $2,500. **Remarks:** Part-time maker; first knife sold in 1988. Doing business as Dutton Mountain Forge. **Mark:** Last name/JS.

ANDERSEN, HENRIK LEFOLII, Jagtvek 8, Groenholt, 3480 Fredensborg, DENMARK/4228-3026
Specialties: Hunters and matched pairs for the serious hunter. **Patterns:** Working folders for bowhunters. **Technical:** Grinds A2; uses materials native to Scandinavia. **Prices:** Start at $250. **Remarks:** Part-time maker; first knife sold in 1985. **Mark:** Initials with arrow.

ANDERSON, CHARLES B., P.O. Box 209, Lampe, MO 65681/417-779-3926
Specialties: High-tech working straight knives of his design. **Patterns:** Hunting, kitchen and fishing knives. **Technical:** Grinds 01, D2, 154CM and 440C. **Prices:** $95 to $500; exceptional knives to $1,000. **Remarks:** Full-time maker; first knife sold in 1980. **Mark:** Full name.

ANDERSON, EDWIN, c/o Glen Cove Sport Shop, 189 Forest Ave., Glen Cove, NY 11542/516-676-7120
Specialties: Hunters, fighters, boot knives and folders. **Patterns:** Standard patterns or customer designs. **Technical:** Grinds Stellite 6K, ATS-34, and 440C. Offers integral patterns. **Prices:** $200 to $500; some to $1,500. **Remarks:** Full-time gunsmith, part-time knifemaker; first knife sold in 1977. **Mark:** Name over state.

ANDERSON, GARY D., RD 2, Box 2399C, Spring Grove, PA 17362-9802/717-229-2665
Specialties: Intricate art-quality blades and folders. **Patterns:** Traditional and classic designs; customer patterns welcome. **Technical:** Forged Damascus and carbon

custom knifemakers
ANDERSON—BAILEY

steels. Offers silver inlay, mokume, filework, checkering. **Prices:** $250 to $750; some higher. **Remarks:** Full-time maker; first knife sold in 1985. **Mark:** GAND.

ANDERSON, MEL, Rt. 1, 1718 Lee Lane, Cedaredge, CO 81413/303-865-6465; FAX: 303-856-6465
Specialties: One-of-a-kind high-art and fantasy knives, full size and miniature, of his design and to customer specs. Fixed blades and folders. **Patterns:** Bowies, daggers, fighters, hunters, fillets and tantos. **Technical:** Shapes, tempers and grinds 440C, 5160, ATS-34, D2 and L6 HC; offers antler, ivory and wood carving. **Prices:** $75 to $3,000; some higher. **Remarks:** Full-time maker; first knife sold in 1987. **Mark:** Scratchy Hand.

ANDERSON, MICHAEL D., 2227 Spanish Trail, Arlington, TX 76013/817-274-3398
Specialties: Working and using straight knives of his design. **Patterns:** Hunters, Bowies, utility/camp knives and some fighters. **Technical:** Grinds D2, 01. All knives are individually ground using true North American Indian flaking styles. **Prices:** $175 to $350; some to $800. **Remarks:** Part-time maker; first knife sold in 1985. Doing business as Flint Steel Knives. **Mark:** Stylized initials.

ANDERSON, VIRGIL W., 16318 SE Taggart, Portland, OR 97236/503-761-4053
Specialties: Working straight knives of his design; fancy knives. **Patterns:** Bowies, boots, hunters and push knives. **Technical:** Grinds D2, 154CM and F8 Silvanite. **Prices:** $100 to $250; some to $500. **Remarks:** Part-time maker; first knife sold in 1984. **Mark:** Last name.

ANDRESS, RONNIE, 415 Audubon Dr. N., Satsuma, AL 36572/205-675-7604
Specialties: Traditional working and using straight knives and folders in standard patterns. **Patterns:** Hunters, kitchen knives and utility/camp knives. **Technical:** Forges 5160, cable, 440C and W2. Offers filework, hand-stitched and tooled sheaths, handrubbed satin finishes and handle inlays. **Prices:** $125 to $200; some to $350. **Remarks:** Part-time maker; first knife sold in 1983. Doing business as Andress Knives. **Mark:** Last name.

ANDREWS, DON, N. 5155 Ezy St., Coeur D'Alene, ID 83814/208-765-8844
Specialties: Plain and fancy folders and straight knives. **Technical:** Grinds D2, 440C, ATS-34; does lost wax casting for guards and pommels. **Prices:** Moderate to upscale. **Remarks:** Full-time maker; first knife sold in 1983. **Mark:** Name.

ANGEL SWORD (See Watson, Daniel)

ANKROM, W.E., 14 Marquette Dr., Cody, WY 82414/307-587-3017
Specialties: Straight working knives and folders of his design. **Patterns:** Hunters, fighters, boots; lockbacks, liner locks and interchangeables. **Technical:** Grinds ATS-34 and commercial Damascus. **Prices:** $175 to $995. **Remarks:** Full-time maker; first knife sold in 1975. **Mark:** Name, city, state.

ANTHONY, THOMAS (See Trujillo, Thomas A.)

ANTONIO JR., WILLIAM J., 14540 Stirrup Lane, Golts, MD 21637/410-755-6789
Specialties: Fancy working straight knives of his design. **Patterns:** Hunting, survival and fishing knives. **Technical:** Grinds D2, 440C and 154CM. **Prices:** $125 to $395; some to $900. **Remarks:** Part-time maker; first knife sold in 1978. **Mark:** Last name, city, state.

ANVIL HEAD FORGE (See Leone, Nick)

ANZA KNIVES (See Davis, Charlie)

APPLETON, RAY, Box 321, Byers, CO 80103/303-822-5866
Specialties: One-of-a-kind folding knives. **Patterns:** Unique multi-locks and high-tech patterns. **Technical:** All parts machined or ground; likes D2. **Prices:** Start at $500. **Remarks:** Spare-time maker; first knife sold in 1986. **Mark:** Initials connected in arrowhead, date.

ARC MOUNTAIN FORGE (See Dearing, John)

ARMORBANE (See Pagnard, Philip E.)

ARNOLD, JOE, 47 Patience Cres., London, Ont., CANADA N6E 2K7/519-686-2623
Specialties: Traditional working knives of his design and to customer specs. **Patterns:** Fighters, hunters and Bowies. **Technical:** Grinds 440C, ATS-34 and 5160. **Prices:** $75 to $500; some to $2,500. **Remarks:** Part-time maker; first knife sold in 1988. **Mark:** Last name, country.

ARROW FORGE (See Harless, Walt)

ARROWOOD, DALE, 556 Lassetter Rd., Sharpsburg, GA 30277/404-253-9672
Specialties: Fancy and traditional straight knives of his design and to customer specs. **Patterns:** Bowies, fighters and hunters. **Technical:** Grinds ATS-34 and 440C; forges high-carbon steel. Engraves and scrimshands. **Prices:** $125 to $200; some to $245. **Remarks:** Part-time maker; first knife sold in 1989. **Mark:** Anvil with an arrow through it; Old English "Arrowood Knives."

ASHBY, DOUGLAS, 10123 Deermont, Dallas, TX 75243/214-238-7531
Specialties: Traditional and fancy straight knives of his design or to customer specs. **Patterns:** Hunters, fighters, utility/camp knives. **Technical:** Grinds 440C, ATS-34 and commercial Damascus. **Prices:** $75 to $200; some to $500. **Remarks:** Part-time maker; first knife sold in 1990. **Mark:** Name, city.

ASHLEY FORGE (See Bartrug, Hugh E.)

ASHWORTH, BOYD, 3135 Barrett Ct., Powder Springs, GA 30073/404-943-4963
Specialties: Fancy straight knives and folders; working/using knives of his design and to customer specs. **Patterns:** Fighters, hunters and locking folders. **Technical:** Grinds 440C and ATS-34; forges and grinds Damascus. Scrimshaws; offers leatherwork. **Prices:** $100 to $350; some to $1,000. **Remarks:** Part-time maker; first knife sold in 1993. **Mark:** Last name.

ATHENS FORGE (See Fannin, David A.)

ATHERN FORGE (See Sanders, A.A.)

ATKINSON, DICK, General Delivery, Wausau, FL 32463/904-638-8524
Specialties: Working straight knives and folders of his design; some fancy. **Patterns:** Hunters, fighters, boots; locking folders in interframes. **Technical:** Grinds A2, 440C and 154CM. Likes filework. **Prices:** $85 to $300; some exceptional knives. **Remarks:** Part-time maker; first knife sold in 1977. **Mark:** Name, city, state.

AYARRAGARAY, CRISTIAN L., Buenos Aires 250, (3100) Parana-Entre Rios, ARGENTINA/043-231753
Specialties: Traditional working straight knives of his design. **Patterns:** Fishing and hunting knives. **Technical:** Grinds and forges carbon steel. Uses native Argentine woods and deer antler. **Prices:** $150 to $250; some to $400. **Remarks:** Full-time maker; first knife sold in 1980. **Mark:** Last name, signature.

b

BABCOCK, RAYMOND G., Rt. 1, Box 328A, Vincent, OH 45784/614-678-2688
Specialties: Fancy working straight knives and some folders of his design or to customer specs. **Patterns:** Hunters and Bowies. **Technical:** Grinds L6. **Prices:** $65 to $350. **Remarks:** Part-time maker; first knife sold in 1973. **Mark:** First initial and last name.

BACHE-WIIG, TOM, N-5966 Eivindvik, NORWAY/4757784290; FAX: 4757784122
Specialties: High-art and working knives of his design. **Patterns:** Hunters, utility knives and art knives. **Technical:** Grinds Uddeholm Elmax, powder metallurgy and tool stainless steel. Handles made of rear burls of Nordic woods stabilized with vacuum/high-pressure technique. **Prices:** $430 to $900; some to $2,300. **Remarks:** Part-time maker; first knife sold 1988. **Mark:** Etched name and eagle head.

BAGWELL, BILL, P.O. Box 265, Marietta, TX/903-835-8441
Specialties: Traditional working and using knives of his design. **Patterns:** Bowies, fighters, utility/camp knives. **Technical:** Forges 1065. Makes own Damascus. Heat-treats. **Prices:** $225 to $1,200; some to $3,000. **Remarks:** Full-time maker; first knife sold in 1968. **Mark:** Name in script or block letters.

BAILEY, JOSEPH D., 3213 Jonesboro Dr., Nashville, TN 37214/615-889-3172
Specialties: Working and using straight knives, Bowies and hunters; collector pieces. **Patterns:** Bowies, hunters, fillet knives and personal knives. **Technical:** 440C, ATS-34, Damascus and wire Damascus. Scrimshaw available through Mary

directory

BAILEY—BARRETT

Bailey. Prices: $65 to $175; some to $500. **Remarks:** Part-time maker; first knife sold in 1988. **Mark:** First and middle initials, last name—Custom Made.

BAILEY, KIRBY C., 13097 F.M. 2790 W., Lytle, TX 78052/210-772-3376
Specialties: All types of custom knives. **Patterns:** Uses all his own patterns. **Technical:** Grinds ATS-34, 440C and 01 tool steel. Offers filework on liners, backlocks and blades. Handles made with natural materials. Scrimshaws, engraves and heat-treats. **Prices:** $100 to $450. **Remarks:** Full-time maker; first knife sold 1959. Doing business as Hand Made Knives. **Mark:** Initials with serial number.

BAKER, RAY, P.O. Box 303, Sapulpa, OK 74067/918-224-8013
Specialties: High-tech working straight knives. **Patterns:** Hunters, fighters, Bowies, skinners and boots of his design and to customer specs. **Technical:** Grinds 440C, 1095 spring steel or customer request. Custom-made scabbards for any knife. **Prices:** $40 to $300, some to $1,000. **Remarks:** Full-time maker; first first knife sold in 1981. **Mark:** First initial, last name.

BAKER, VANCE, 574 Co. Rd. 675, Riceville, TN 37370/615-745-9157
Specialties: Traditional working straight knives of his design and to customer specs. Prefers drop-point hunters and small Bowies. **Patterns:** Hunters, utility and kitchen knives. **Technical:** Forges Damascus, cable, L6 and 5160. **Prices:** $75 to $175; some to $400. **Remarks:** Part-time maker, first knife sold in 1985. **Mark:** Initials connected.

BAKER, WILD BILL, Box 361, Boiceville, NY 12412/914-657-8646
Specialties: Primitive knives, buckskinners. **Patterns:** Skinners, camp knives and Bowies. **Technical:** Works with L6, files and rasps. **Prices:** $100 to $350. **Remarks:** Part-time maker; first knife sold in 1989. **Mark:** Oak leaf.

BALBACH, MARKUS, Friedrichstr. 2, 35789 Weilmunster, GERMANY/06475-8911; FAX: 06475-8911
Specialties: High-art knives and working/using knives of his design and to customer specs. Straight knives and folders. **Patterns:** Hunters and daggers. **Technical:** Forges and grinds Damascus steel. **Prices:** $250 to $600; some to $2,000. **Remarks:** Full-time maker; first knife sold in 1984. Doing business as Damastschmiede M. Balbach. **Mark:** Initials stamped inside the handle.

BALDWIN, PHILLIP, P.O. Box 563, Snohomish, WA 98290/206-334-5569
Specialties: Elegant table cutlery; exotics. **Patterns:** Contemporary and eclectic. Likes the challenge of axes and such. **Technical:** Forges W2, W1 and his own Damascus. **Prices:** From $300 to $2,500; some higher. **Remarks:** Full-time maker; first knife sold in 1973. **Mark:** Last initial marked with chisel.

BALDY MOUNTAIN FORGE (See Dunkerley, Rick)

BALL, ROBERT, 809 W. 7th Ave., Port Angeles, WA 98362/206-457-0315
Specialties: Classic straight knives; working/using knives of all designs. **Patterns:** Hunters, filets and kitchen knives. **Technical:** Grinds ATS-34 and 440C. Uses local Olympic hardwoods, stabilized woods, horn and antler. **Prices:** $150 to $350; some to $800. **Remarks:** Part-time maker; first knife sold in 1990. Doing business as Olympic Knives. **Mark:** First initial, last name.

BALLEW, DALE, P.O. Box 1277, Bowling Green, VA 22427/804-633-5701
Specialties: Miniatures only to customer specs. **Patterns:** Bowies, daggers and fighters. **Technical:** Files 440C stainless; uses ivory, abalone, exotic woods and some precious stones. **Prices:** $100 to $800. **Remarks:** Part-time maker; first knife sold in 1988. **Mark:** Initials and last name.

BANDIT BLADES (See Roberts, George A.)

BANKS, DAVID L., 99 Blackfoot Ave. #3, Riverton, WY 82501/307-856-3154
Specialties: Heavy-duty working straight knives. **Patterns:** Hunters, Bowies and camp knives. **Technical:** Forges 5160 and 52100. Handles made of horn, antlers and exotic wood. Hand-stitched harness leather sheaths. **Prices:** $200 to $500; some to $500. **Remarks:** Part-time maker. **Mark:** Initials connected.

BARBEE, JIM, Box 1173, Ft. Stockton, TX 79753/915-336-2882
Specialties: Texas-type hunter's knives. **Patterns:** Solid using patterns. **Technical:** Grinds 440C; likes stag, Micarta and ivory. **Prices:** $125 to $200; some to $500. **Remarks:** Full-time maker and heat-treater. First knife sold in the '60s. **Mark:** Name, city.

BARBER, ROBERT E., 1828 Franklin Dr., Charlottesville, VA 22901/804-295-4036
Specialties: Working straight knives and trapper pocketknives, some fancy with filework. **Patterns:** Hunters, skinners, combat knives/fighters and Bowies. **Technical:** Grinds ATS-34, 440C, D2 and A2. **Prices:** $35 to $800. **Remarks:** Part-time maker; first knife sold in 1984. **Mark:** Initials within rebel hat logo.

BARDSLEY, NORMAN P., 197 Cottage St., Pawtucket, RI 02860/401-725-9132
Specialties: Working and fantasy knives. **Patterns:** Fighters, tantos, boots in renaissance and fantasy fashion; upscale display and presentation pieces. **Technical:** Grinds 440C, ATS-34, 01 and Damascus. Uses exotic hides for sheaths. **Prices:** $100 to $6,000. **Remarks:** Full-time maker. **Mark:** Last name in script with logo.

BARE KNIVES (See Stevens, Barry B.)

BAREFOOT, JOE W., 117 Oakbrook Dr., Liberty, SC 29657
Specialties: Working straight knives of his design; mirror finishes. **Patterns:** Hunters, fighters and boots; tantos and survival knives. **Technical:** Grinds D2, 440C and ATS-34. Uses ivory and stag on customer request only. **Prices:** $50 to $160; some to $500. **Remarks:** Part-time maker; first knife sold in 1980. **Mark:** Bare footprint.

BARKER, ROBERT G., 262 Laurie Dr., Athens, GA 30605/706-546-4525
Specialties: Traditional working/using straight knives of his design. **Patterns:** Bowies, hunters and utility knives. **Technical:** Forges to shape high-carbon 5160, cable and chain. Differentially heat-treats. **Prices:** $200 to $500; some to $1,000. **Remarks:** Spare-time maker; first knife sold in 1987. **Mark:** Last name.

BARLOW, KEN, 3800 Rohner St., Fortuna, CA 95540/707-725-3106
Specialties: Working straight knives and folders, some fancy. **Patterns:** Hunters, Bowies, skinners and locking folders. **Technical:** Grinds ATS-34, 440C and D2. Heat-treats, engraves and scrimshaws. Prefers mirror finishes and hollow-grinds. **Prices:** $100 to $250; some higher. **Remarks:** Part-time maker; first knife sold in 1980. **Mark:** Stylized initials.

BARNES, AUBREY G., 10404 Bailey Rd., Hagerstown, MD 21741/301-274-8960
Specialties: Classic working and using knives of his design, to customer specs and in standard patterns. **Patterns:** Bowies, hunters and utility knives. **Technical:** Forges 5160, 9260 and 1085. Silver-wire inlays. **Prices:** $190 to $900; some to $2,500. **Remarks:** Full-time maker; first knife sold in 1992. Doing business as Falling Waters Forge. **Mark:** First and middle initials, last name.

BARNES, GARY L., 305 Church St., Box 138, New Windsor, MD 21776/410-635-6243
Specialties: High-art, high-tech working knives of his design; titanium and stainless folders. **Patterns:** Folders only. **Technical:** Mostly forges his own Damascus; uses exotic handle materials; creates unique locking mechanisms. Most knives are embellished. **Prices:** $300 to $1,500; some to $8,000. **Remarks:** Full-time maker. First knife sold in 1976. Believes in sole authorship. **Mark:** Name or an ornate last initial with a dagger.

BARNES, JACK, P.O. Box 1315, Whitefish, MT 59937-1315/406-862-6078

BARNETT, VAN, P.O. Box 1012, New Haven, WV 25265/304-882-3481
Specialties: Investor-grade one-of-a-kind daggers and fighters. **Patterns:** Folders, miniatures and hunters. **Technical:** Grinds 440C, D2, Damascus and ATS-34. **Prices:** Start at $200. **Remarks:** Full-time maker; first knife sold in 1981. **Mark:** Barnett Blades or first initial, last name.

BARR, A.T., P.O. Box 828, Nicholasville, KY 40340/606-885-1042
Specialties: Working and collector-grade straight knives and folders of his design. **Patterns:** Hunters, camp/survival knives and folders. **Technical:** Flat-and hollow-grinds ATS-34 and 01. **Prices:** Start at $115. **Remarks:** Part-time maker; first knife sold in 1979. **Mark:** Full name, city and state.

BARR CUSTOM KNIVES (See Quarton, Barr)

BARRETT, CECIL TERRY, 2514 Linda Lane, Colorado Springs, CO 80909/719-473-8325

custom knifemakers

Specialties: Working and using straight knives and folders of his design, to customer specs and in standard patterns. **Patterns:** Bowies, hunters, kitchen knives, locking folders and slip-joint folders. **Technical:** Grinds 440C, D2 and ATs-34. Wood and leather sheaths. **Prices:** $65 to $375. **Remarks:** Full-time maker. **Mark:** Stamped middle name.

BARRETT, R.W., 3214 Montrose Dr., Huntsville, AL 35805/205-539-3439
Specialties: Traditional and fancy straight knives. Makes standard patterns and one-of-a-kinds. **Patterns:** Hunters, fighters, skinners and art knives. **Technical:** Grinds 440C, ATS-34 and 01. Scrimshaws and offers photography. Prices: $150 to $250; some to $500. **Remarks:** Spare-time maker; first knife sold in 1989. **Mark:** First and middle initials, last name, city, state.

BARRETT-SMYTHE (See Howard, Durvyn M.)

BARRON, DAVID, P.O. Box 133, Etowah, NC 28729/704-692-4007
Specialties: Fancy working straight knives of his design. **Patterns:** Hunters, Bowies and using knives. **Technical:** Grinds 01, 440C and 154CM. Scrimshaws. **Prices:** $100 to $225; some to $750. **Remarks:** Full-time maker; first knife sold in 1968. **Mark:** Last name, serial number.

BARRY, JAMES J., P.O. Box 1571, West Palm Beach, FL 33402/407-832-4197
Specialties: High-art working straight knives of his design. **Patterns:** Hunters, daggers and fishing knives. **Technical:** Grinds 440C only. Prefers exotic materials for handles. Most knives embellished with filework, carving and scrimshaw. Many pieces designed to stand unassisted. **Prices:** $100 to $500; some to $5,000. **Remarks:** Part-time maker; first knife sold in 1975. Believes in sole authorship. **Mark:** Branded initials.

BARTLOW, JOHN, 111 Orchard Rd., Box 568, Norris, TN 37828/615-494-9421
Specialties: Working straight knives, some fancy. **Patterns:** Working hunters, skinners, capers, bird and trout knives, saltwater fillets. **Technical:** Grinds 440C and ATS-34; uses Tim Zowada and Jerry Rados Damascus. **Prices:** $150 to $1,500. **Remarks:** Part-time maker, first knife sold in 1979. Field-tests knives. **Mark:** Last name.

BARTRUG, HUGH E., 505 Rhodes St., Elizabeth, PA 15037/412-384-3476
Specialties: Inlaid straight knives and exotic folders; high-art knives and period pieces. **Patterns:** Hunters, Bowies and daggers; traditional patterns. **Technical:** Diffuses mokume. Forges 100 percent nickel, wrought iron, mosiac Damascus, shokeedo and 01 tool steel; grinds. **Prices:** $210 to $2,500; some to $5,000. **Remarks:** Full-time maker; first knife sold in 1980. **Mark:** Ashley Forge or name.

BASKETT, LEE GENE, P.O. Box 903, Elizabethtown, KY 42702-0903/502-862-9439
Specialties: Fancy working knives and fantasy pieces, often set up in desk stands. **Patterns:** Fighters, Bowies and survival knives; locking folders, butterflies and traditional styles. **Technical:** Grinds 01, 440C; buys Damascus. Filework provided on most knives. **Prices:** Start at $95. **Remarks:** Part-time maker; first knife sold in 1980. **Mark:** Last name.

BATSON, JAMES, 176 Brentwood Lane, Madison, AL 35758/205-837-6160
Specialties: Forged Damascus blades and fittings in collectible period pieces. **Patterns:** Integral art knives, Bowies, folders, American-styled blades and miniatures. **Technical:** Forges 52100, 5160 and his Damascus. Believes in sole authorship. **Prices:** $150 to $1,800; some to $4,500. **Remarks:** Full-time maker; first knife sold in 1978. **Mark:** Name, bladesmith with horse's head.

BATSON, RICHARD G., 6591 Waterford Rd., Rixeyville, VA 22737/703-937-5932
Specialties: Military, utility and fighting knives in working and presentation grade. **Patterns:** Daggers, combat and utility knives. **Technical:** Grinds 01. Etches and scrimshaws; offers polished, blued or Parkerized finishes. **Prices:** $175 to $350; some to $900. **Remarks:** Full-time maker. First knife sold in 1958. **Mark:** Bat in circle, hand-signed and serial numbered.

BATTS, KEITH, Rt. 1, Box 266E, Hooks, TX 75561/903-832-1140
Specialties: Working straight knives of his design or to customer specs. **Patterns:** Bowies, hunters, skinners, camp knives and others. **Technical:** Forges 5160 and his Damascus; offers filework. **Prices:** $125 to $475. **Remarks:** Part-time maker; first knife sold in 1988. **Mark:** Last name.

BAUCHOP, PETER, Germiston, SOUTH AFRICA. C/O Beck's Cutlery Specialties, 748-F E. Chatham St., Cary, N. Carolina 27511/919-460-0203
Specialties: Working straight knives and period pieces. **Patterns:** Fighters, swords and survival knives. **Technical:** Grinds 01, D2, G3, 440C and ATS-34. Scrimshaws. **Prices:** $100 to $350; some to $1,500. **Remarks:** Full-time maker; first knife sold in 1980. **Mark:** Bow and axe (BOW-CHOP).

BAUCHOP, ROBERT, P.O. Box 9821, Elsburg 1407, SOUTH AFRICA/011-824-1300; FAX: 011-824-2662
Specialties: Fantasy knives; working and using knives of his design and to customer specs. **Patterns:** Hunters, swords, utility/camp knives, diver's knives and large swords. **Technical:** Grinds Sandvick 12C27, D2, 440C. Uses South African hardwoods—red ivory, wild olive, african blackwood, etc.—on handles. **Prices:** $200 to $800; some to $2,000. **Remarks:** Full-time maker; first knife sold in 1986. Doing business as Robert Bauchop Handmade Knives. **Mark:** Viking helmet with Bauchop (bow and chopper) crest.

BEAR KNIVES (See Goode, Bear)

BEAR'S CUTLERY (See Jensen, Jr., Carl A.)

BEATTY, GORDON H., 121 Petty Rd., Seneca, SC 29678/803-882-6278
Specialties: Working straight knives, some fancy. **Patterns:** Traditional patterns, mini-skinners and letter openers. **Technical:** Grinds 440C, D2 and ATS-34; makes knives one at a time. **Prices:** $45 to $200; some to $450. **Remarks:** Part-time maker; first knife sold in 1982. **Mark:** Name.

BEAUCHAMP, GAETAN, 125, de la Riviere, Stoneham, PQ. CANADA/418-848-1914; FAX: 418-848-1035
Specialties: Working knives and folders of his design and to customer specs. **Patterns:** Hunters, fighters, fantasy knives. **Technical:** Grinds ATS-34, 440C, Damascus. Scrimshaws on ivory; specializes in buffalo horn and black backgrounds. Offers a variety of handle materials. **Prices:** Start at $125. **Remarks:** Part-time maker; first knife sold in 1992. **Mark:** Signature and year on blade.

BEAVER, D. "BUTCH" AND JUDY, 48835 N. 25 Ave. Phoenix, AZ 85027/602-465-7831; FAX: 602-465-7077
Specialties: Straight knives, daggers and "see-thru" titanium art folders. **Patterns:** No models or standard designs; prefer custom orders. **Technical:** Grind 440C and ATS-34. Most knives are embellished. **Prices:** $135 to $800; some much higher. **Remarks:** Full-time makers. First D. Beaver knife sold in 1979; first J. Beaver knife sold in 1984. **Mark:** Name, city, state, year in Roman numerals.

BEAVER, JUDY (See Beaver, D. "Butch" and Judy)

BECKER, FRANZ, Bruckbergstr. 23, 8261 Marktl/Inn, GERMANY
Specialties: Stainless steel knives in working sizes. **Patterns:** Semi- and full-integral knives; interframe folders. **Technical:** Grinds stainless steels; likes natural handle materials. **Prices:** $200 to $2,000. **Mark:** Name, country.

BEERS, RAY, 8 Manorbrook Rd., Monkton, MD 21111/410-472-2229, 813-696-3036; FAX: 410-472-9136
Specialties: Working straight knives, some fancy. **Patterns:** All fighters and tantos are popular. **Technical:** Grinds all steels; many patterns have a palm hunter handle. **Prices:** $100 to $5,000. **Remarks:** Full-time maker; first knife sold in 1976. **Mark:** Initials connected.

BEHNKE, WILLIAM, P.O. Box 174, Lake City, MI 49651/616-839-3342
Specialties: Hunters, belt knives and folders. **Patterns:** Traditional styling in moderate-sized straight and folding knives. **Technical:** Forges his own Damascus, cable, saw chain and 5160; likes brass and natural materials. **Prices:** $100 to $1,500. **Remarks:** Part-time maker. **Mark:** Name.

BELL, DONALD, 2 Division St., Bedford, Nova Scotia, B4A 1Y8 CANADA/902-835-2623
Specialties: Fancy knives; working/using straight knives and folders of his design. **Patterns:** Hunters, locking folders, jewelry knives. **Technical:** Grinds Damascus and ATS-34; forges and grinds 01. **Prices:** $150 to $650; some to $1,200. **Remarks:** Spare-time maker; first knife sold in 1993. **Mark:** Bell symbol with first initial inside.

directory

BELL, MICHAEL, Rt. 1, Box 1220, Coquille, OR 97423/503-396-3605
Specialties: Full line of traditional Japanese swords. **Patterns:** Tantos and Katanas in various styles. **Technical:** Uses own special steel; all blades forge-welded. **Prices:** $750 to $10,000. **Remarks:** Full-time maker; first knife sold in 1972. Served apprenticeship with Japanese swordmaker. Doing business as Dragonfly Forge. **Mark:** Kuni Mitsu or Dragonfly.

BENJAMIN JR., GEORGE, 3001 Foxy Lane, Kissimmee, FL 34746/407-846-7259
Specialties: Fighters in various styles to include Persian, Moro and military. **Patterns:** Daggers, skinners and one-of-a-kind grinds. **Technical:** Forges 01, D2, A2, 5160 and Damascus. Favors Pakkawood, Micarta, and mirror or Parkerized finishes. Makes unique para-military leather sheaths. **Prices:** $150 to $600; some to $1,200. **Remarks:** Doing business as The Leather Box. **Mark:** Southern Pride Knives.

BENNETT, PETER, P.O. Box 143, Engadine N.S.W. 2233, AUSTRALIA/02-520-4975
Specialties: Fancy and embellished working and using straight knives to customer specs and in standard patterns. **Patterns:** Fighters, hunters and bird/trout knives. **Technical:** Grinds 440C, ATS-34 and Damascus. Uses black coral and rare Australian desert timbers for handles. **Prices:** $90 to $500; some to $1,500. **Remarks:** Part-time maker; first knife sold in 1985. **Mark:** First and middle initials, last name; country.

BENSON, DON, 2505 Jackson St. #112, Escalon, CA 95320/209-838-7921
Specialties: Working straight knives of his design. **Patterns:** Axes, Bowies, tantos and hunters. **Technical:** Grinds 440C. **Prices:** $100 to $150; some to $400. **Remarks:** Spare-time maker; first knife sold in 1980. **Mark:** Name.

BER, DAVE, 2230 Miller Rd., San Juan Island, WA 98250/206-378-7230
Specialties: Working straight knives for the sportsman; camp knives. Welcomes customer designs. **Patterns:** Hunters, Bowies, kitchen and fishing knives. **Technical:** Forges and grinds saw blade steel, welded wire Damascus, 01, L6 and 440C. **Prices:** $100 to $200; some to $500. **Remarks:** Full-time maker; first knife sold in 1985. Doing business as Cloudy Mt. Iron Works. **Mark:** Name.

BESEDICK, FRANK E., 29 Tyler Ave., Charleroi, PA 15022/412-483-2734
Specialties: Traditional working and using straight knives of his design. **Patterns:** Hunters, utility/camp knives and miniatures; buckskinner blades and tomahawks. **Technical:** Forges and grinds 5160, 01 and Damascus. Offers filework and scrimshaw. **Prices:** $75 to $300; some to $750. **Remarks:** Part-time maker; first knife sold in 1990. **Mark:** Name or initials.

BEVERLY II, LARRY H., P.O. Box 741, Spotsylvania, VA 22553/703-898-3951
Specialties: Working straight knives, slip-joints, liner locks and miniatures. Welcomes customer designs. **Patterns:** Bowies, hunters, guardless fighters. **Technical:** Grinds 440C, A2 and 01. **Prices:** $65 to $400. **Remarks:** Part-time maker; first knife sold in 1986. **Mark:** Initials or last name in script.

BEZUIDENHOUT, BUZZ, 30 Surlingham Ave., Malvern, Queensburgh, Natal 4093, SOUTH AFRICA/031-444098; 031-3631259
Specialties: Traditional working and using straight knives of his design and to customer specs. **Patterns:** Boots, hunters, kitchen knives and utility/camp knives. **Technical:** Grinds 12C27, 440C and ATS-34. Uses local hardwoods, horn—kudu, impala, buffalo—giraffe bone and ivory for handles. **Prices:** $150 to $200; some to $1,500. **Remarks:** Spare-time maker; first knife sold in 1988. **Mark:** First name with a bee emblem.

BIGHORN KNIFEWORKS (See Padilla, Gary)

BILLY'S BLADES (See Ellis, William Dean)

BLACK, EARL, 3466 South 700 East, Salt Lake City, UT 84106/801-466-8395
Specialties: High-art straight knives and folders; period pieces. **Patterns:** Boots, Bowies and daggers; lockers and gents. **Technical:** Grinds 440C and 154CM. Buys some Damascus. Scrimshaws and engraves. **Prices:** $200 to $1,800; some to $2,500 and higher. **Remarks:** Full-time maker; first knife sold in 1980. **Mark:** Name, city, state.

BLACK, TOM, 921 Grecian NW, Albuquerque, NM 87107/505-344-2549
Specialties: Working knives to fancy straight knives of his design. **Patterns:** Drop-point skinners, folders, using knives, Bowies and daggers. **Technical:** Grinds 440C, 154CM, ATS-34, A2, D2 and Damascus. Engraves and scrimshaws. **Prices:** $125 to $1,250; some over $7,500. **Remarks:** Full-time maker; first knife sold in 1971. **Mark:** Name, city, state.

BLACK, T.J., 1507 Wayne St., Alexandria, LA 71301/318-443-6100
Specialties: Straight knives of his design or to customer specs. **Patterns:** Hunters, Bowies, skinners, utility knives and some collector pieces. **Technical:** Grinds 440C and ATS-34. Prefers natural handle materials. **Prices:** $75 to $1,000. **Remarks:** Part-time maker; first knife sold in 1987. **Mark:** First and middle initials, last name, city, state.

BLACK FOREST BLADES (See Neering, Walt and Repke, Mike)

BLACKTON, ANDREW E., 12521 Fifth Isle, Bayonet Point, FL 34667/813-869-1406
Specialties: Straight and folding knives, some fancy. **Patterns:** Hunters, Bowies and daggers. **Technical:** Grinds D2, 440C and 154CM. Offers some embellishment. **Prices:** $125 to $450; some to $2,000. **Remarks:** Full-time maker. **Mark:** Michigan state outline with knife across it and "Blackton the Great Lakes Knifemaker."

BLAKLEY II, WILLIAM E., Rt. 4, Box 106-B, Fredericksburg, VA 22405/703-775-3773
Specialties: Simple working knives. **Patterns:** Hunters and skinners; some Bowies and daggers. **Technical:** Grinds 440C; offers D2 and 01 on request. **Prices:** $75 to $300. **Remarks:** First knife sold in 1984. Not currently taking orders or going to shows. **Mark:** Initials.

BLASINGAME, ROBERT, 2906 Swanson Lane, Kilgore, TX 75662/903-983-3546
Specialties: Classic working and using straight knives and folders of his design and to customer specs. **Patterns:** Bowies, daggers, fighters and hunters; one-of-a-kind historic reproductions. **Technical:** Hand-forges P.W. Damascus, cable Damascus and chain Damascus. **Prices:** $150 to $1,000; some to $2,000. **Remarks:** Full-time maker; first knife sold in 1968. **Mark:** Large knives—last name over anvil; folders—initials.

BLAUM, ROY, 319 N. Columbia St., Covington, LA 70433/504-893-1060
Specialties: Working straight knives and folders of his design; lightweight easy-open folders. **Patterns:** Hunters, boots and fishing knives. **Technical:** Grinds A2, D2, 154CM and ATS-34. **Prices:** $75 to $200; some to $500. **Remarks:** Full-time maker; first knife sold in 1976. **Mark:** Signature engraved.

BLOMBERG, GREGG, Rt. 1, Box 1762, Lopez, WA 98261/206-468-2103
Specialties: Edged tools for carvers and sculptors. **Patterns:** Crooked knives; straight utilities; adzes. **Technical:** Forges and grinds W2, D2, 1095 and ATS-34. **Prices:** Straight knives average $160. **Remarks:** Full-time maker; first knife sold in 1978. Doing business as Kestrel Tool. **Mark:** Kestrel with flying falcon logo.

BLOOMER, ALAN T., RR 1, Box 108, Maquon, IL 61458/309-875-3583
Specialties: Working and using straight knives and folders of his design. **Patterns:** Lock-back folders and Damascus straight knives and folders. **Technical:** Grinds 440C, D2 and A2. Does own leatherwork. **Prices:** $85 to $450. **Remarks:** Part-time maker; first knife sold in 1986. **Mark:** Last name stamp.

BLUM, CHUCK, 743 S. Brea Blvd. #10, Brea, CA 92621/714-529-0484
Specialties: Art and investment daggers and Bowies. **Technical:** Flat-grinds; hollow-grinds 440C, ATS-34 on working knives. **Prices:** $125 to $8,500. **Remarks:** Part-time maker; first knife sold in 1985. **Mark:** First and middle initials and last name with sailboat logo.

BLUM, KENNETH, Rt. 6, Box 6033, Brenham, TX 77833/409-836-9577
Specialties: Traditional working straight knives of his design. **Patterns:** Camp knives, Hunters and Bowies. **Technical:** Forges 5160; grinds 440C and D2. Uses exotic woods and Micarta for handles. **Prices:** $150 to $300. **Remarks:** Part-time maker; first knife sold in 1978. **Mark:** Last name on ricasso.

BLUM, MICHEL, 1044, Chemin de St. Joseph, 83300 Draguignan, FRANCE/94 47 01 74
Specialties: Fantasy and working straight knives and folders to customer specs. **Patterns:** Hunters and fighters. **Technical:** Grinds D2 and commercial Damascus. **Remarks:** Full-time maker; first knife sold in 1988.

custom knifemakers
BLUM—BRAY

BLUM, RONALD A., 201 Masters Ct., #4, Walnut Creek, CA 94598/510-934-3381
Specialites: Miniatures only—collectible one-of-a-kind straight knives. **Patterns:** Miniature swords, fantasy and historical replicas, some battle axes. **Technical:** Files and forges 1050, 440C and commercial Damascus. **Prices:** $125 to $275; some to $400. **Remarks:** Part-time maker; first knife sold in 1988. **Mark:** None.

B-MAR KNIVES (See Mariacher, Robert R.)

BOARDMAN, GUY, 39 Mountain Ridge R., New Germany, 3619 SOUTH AFRICA/031-726-921
Specialties: American and South African styles. **Patterns:** Bowies, American and South African hunters, plus more. **Technical:** Grinds Bohler steels, some ATS-34. **Prices:** $100 to $600. **Remarks:** Part-time maker; first knife sold in 1986. **Mark:** Name, city, country.

BOB-SKY KNIVES (See Hajovsky, Robert J.)

BOCHMAN, BRUCE, 183 Howard Place, Grants Pass, OR 97526/503-471-1985
Specialties: Working straight knives in standard patterns. **Patterns:** Bowies, hunters, fishing and bird knives. **Technical:** 440C; mirror or satin finish. **Prices:** $140 to $250; some to $750. **Remarks:** Part-time maker; first knife sold in 1977. **Mark:** Custom blades by B. Bochman.

BODEN, HARRY, Via Gellia Mill, Bonsall, Matlock, Derbyshire DE4 2AJ, ENGLAND/0629-825176
Specialties: Traditional working straight knives and folders of his design. **Patterns:** Hunters, locking folders and utility/camp knives. **Technical:** Grinds Sandvik 12C27, D2 and 01. **Prices:** $70 to $150; some to $300. **Remarks:** Full-time maker; first knife sold in 1986. **Mark:** Full name.

BOGACHEV, ANATOLY (See Fisk, Jerry)

BOGUSZEWSKI, PHIL, P.O. Box 99329, Tacoma, WA 98499/206-581-7096
Specialties: Working folders—some fancy—mostly of his design. **Patterns:** Folders, slip-joints and lockers; also makes anodized titanium frame folders. **Technical:** Grinds D2, 440C and 154CM; offers filework. **Prices:** $200 to $1,500. **Remarks:** Full-time maker; first knife sold in 1979. **Mark:** Name, city and state.

BOHRMANN, BRUCE, 29 Portland St., Yarmouth, ME 04096/207-846-3385
Specialties: Straight using sport knives. **Patterns:** Hunters, fishing, camp and steak knives. **Technical:** Grinds 154CM; likes wood handles. **Prices:** $350 to $450. **Remarks:** Full-time maker; first knife sold in 1976. **Mark:** Name, city and state.

BOLTON, CHARLES B., P.O. Box 6, Jonesburg, MO 63351/314-488-5785
Specialties: Working straight knives in standard patterns. **Patterns:** Hunters, skinners, boots and fighters. **Technical:** Grinds 440C and ATS-34. **Prices:** $100 to $300; some to $600. **Remarks:** Full-time maker; first knife sold in 1973. **Mark:** Last name.

BONASSI, FRANCO, Via Superiore 14, Pordenone 33170 ITALY/434-550821
Specialties: Fancy and working one-of-a-kind straight knives of his design. **Patterns:** Hunters, skinners, boots, fighters and titanium liner locks. **Technical:** Grinds 440C, ATS-34, 154CM and commercial Damascus. Uses only titanium foreguards and pommels. **Prices:** $250 to $400; some to $800. **Remarks:** Spare-time maker; first knife sold in 1988. **Mark:** FRANK.

BOOCO, GORDON, 175 Ash St., P.O. Box 174, Hayden, CO 81639/303-276-3195
Specialties: Fancy working straight knives of his design and to customer specs. **Patterns:** Hunters and Bowies. **Technical:** Grinds 440C, D2 and A2. Heat-treats. **Prices:** $150 to $350; some $600 and higher. **Remarks:** Part-time maker; first knife sold in 1984. **Mark:** Last name with push dagger artwork.

BORGER, WOLF, Benzstrasse 8, 76670 Graben-Neudorf, GERMANY/07255-8314; FAx: 07255-6921
Specialties: High-tech working and using straight knives and folders, many with corkscrews or other tools, of his design. **Patterns:** Hunters, Bowies and folders with various locking systems. **Technical:** Grinds 440C, ATS-34 and CPM. Uses stainless Damascus. **Prices:** $250 to $900; some to $1,500. **Remarks:** Full-time maker; first knife sold in 1975. **Mark:** Howling wolf and name; first name on Damascus blades.

BOSE, TONY, RR #1, Box 340, Shelburn, IN 47879/812-397-5114
Specialties: Traditional working and using knives in standard patterns; multi-blade folders. **Patterns:** Multi-blade slip-joints. **Technical:** Grinds commercial Damascus, ATS-34 and D2. **Prices:** $225 to $800. **Remarks:** Full-time maker; first knife sold in 1975. **Mark:** First initial, last name, city and state.

BOWEN, TILTON, Rt. 1, Box 225A, Baker, WV 26801/304-897-6159
Specialties: Straight, stout working knives. **Patterns:** Hunters, fighters and boots; also offers buckskinner and throwing knives. **Technical:** Grinds D2 and 4140. **Prices:** $60 to $275. **Remarks:** Full-time maker; first knife sold in 1982-1983. Sells wholesale to dealers. **Mark:** Initials and BOWEN BLADES, WV.

BOYD, FRANCIS, 1811 Prince St., Berkeley, CA 94703/510-841-7210
Specialties: Folders and kitchen knives; Japanese swords. **Patterns:** Push-button sturdy locking folders; San Francisco-style chef's knives. **Technical:** Forges and grinds; mostly uses high-carbon steels. **Prices:** Moderate to heavy. **Remarks:** Designer. **Mark:** Name.

BOYE, DAVID, P.O. Box 1238, Dolan Springs, AZ 86441/602-767-4273
Specialties: Handsome working knives for field and kitchen. Forerunner in the use of dendritic steel for blades. **Patterns:** Chef's knives, small and large hunters, folding "pocket tool" and Boye Basics. **Technical:** Casts blades in stainless 440C; etches blade surfaces with animals, plant motifs. **Prices:** From $59 to $395. **Remarks:** Full-time maker; author of *Step-by-Step Knifemaking*; sells at craft shows. **Mark:** Name.

BRACK, DOUGLAS D., 103 Camino Ruiz #16, Camirillo, CA 93012/805-987-0490
Specialties: Working straight knives of his design. **Patterns:** Heavy-duty skinners, fighters and boots. **Technical:** Grinds 440C, ATS-34 and 5160; forges cable. **Prices:** $90 to $180; some to $300. **Remarks:** Part-time maker; first knife sold in 1984. **Mark:** "tat."

BRADBURN, GARY, 1714 Park Place, Wichita, KS 67203/316-269-4273
Specialties: Straight knives and miniatures of his design and to customer specs. **Patterns:** Bowies, fighters, hunters. **Technical:** Forges 5160 and his Damascus; Forges and grinds M2. **Prices:** $50 to $350; some to $800. **Remarks:** Part-time maker; first knife sold 1991. **Mark:** Last name or initials.

BRADLEY, DENNIS, 2410 Bradley Acres Rd., Blairsville, GA 30512/706-745-4364
Specialties: Working straight knives and folders, some high-art. **Patterns:** Hunters, boots and daggers; slip-joints and two-blades. **Technical:** Grinds ATS-34, D2, 440C and commercial Damascus. **Prices:** $100 to $500; some to $2,000. **Remarks:** Part-time maker; first knife sold in 1973. **Mark:** BRADLEY KNIVES in double heart logo.

BRADLEY, JOHN, P.O. Box 37, Pomona Park, FL 32181/904-649-4739
Specialties: Fixed-blade using knives. **Patterns:** Skinners, camp knives, fillet knives and Bowies. **Technical:** All knives forged and heat-treated by hand. Uses 52100, 1095 and own Damascus. **Prices:** $50 to $500; some higher. **Remarks:** Full-time maker; first knife sold in 1988. **Mark:** Last name.

BRANDSEY, EDWARD P., 1207 Portage Lane, Woodstock, IL 60098/815-337-6010
Specialties: Working straight knives; period pieces and art knives. **Patterns:** Hunters, fighters, Bowies and daggers, some buckskinner styles. **Technical:** Grinds ATS-34, 440C and 01. **Prices:** $125 to $250; some to $2,500. **Remarks:** Part-time maker; first knife sold in 1973. **Mark:** Initials connected.

BRANNAN, RALPH, RR1, Box 343, West Frankfort, IL 62896/618-627-2450
Specialties: Working straight knives of his design. **Patterns:** Traditional using skinners, hunters and utility knives. **Technical:** Grinds 1095, 440C and commercial Damascus. Offers filework. **Prices:** $75 to $150; some to $250. **Remarks:** Part-time maker; first knife sold in 1976. **Mark:** Initials.

BRANTON, ROBERT, 4976 Seewee Rd., Awendaw, SC 29429/803-928-3624
Specialties: Working straight knives of his design or to customer specs; throwing knives. **Patterns:** Hunters, fighters and some miniatures. **Technical:** Grinds ATS-34, A2 and 1050; forges 5160, 01. Offers hollow- or convex-grinds. **Prices:** $25 to $400. **Remarks:** Part-time maker; first knife sold in 1985. Doing business as Lowcountry Throwing Knives. **Mark:** Last name; or first and last name, city, state.

BRAY JR., W. LOWELL, 6931 Manor Beach Rd., New Port Richey, FL 34652

FIFTEENTH EDITION **185**

directory

BRAYTON—BROUGHTON

Specialties: Traditional working and using straight knives of his design. **Patterns:** Hunters, kitchen knives and utility knives. **Technical:** Grinds 440C; forges high carbon. **Prices:** $50 to $300. **Remarks:** Spare-time maker; first knife sold in 1992. **Mark:** Last name on stock removal blades; interlocking initials on forged blades.

BRAYTON, JIM, 713 Park St., Burkburnett, TX 76354/817-569-4726
Specialties: Working knives and period pieces, some fancy. **Patterns:** Bowies, hunters, fighters. **Technical:** Grinds ATS-34, delivers it at 60 Rc. **Prices:** $55 to $500; some higher. **Remarks:** Full-time maker; first knife sold in 1970. **Mark:** Initials or name.

BRAZOS FORGE (See Crawford, Larry)

BRDLIK, DAN E., 166 Campbell St. S., Prescott, WI 54021/715-262-5296
Specialties: Linerlock folders. **Patterns:** Fighters, boots, folders and Bowies; utilitarian fighter designs. **Technical:** Grinds 440C and Damascus. **Prices:** $65 to $250; some to $500. **Remarks:** Full-time maker; first knife sold in 1983. **Mark:** First name and middle initial over stylized toothpick.

BREITER, THOMAS, Rose Lane 1B, Topanga, CA 90290/310-455-2554; FAX: 310-305-1003
Specialties: Fantasy high-art knives of his design and to customer specs; dolphin knife. **Patterns:** Hunters, kitchen knives and fantasy knives. **Technical:** Grinds ATS-34, 440C and 5160. Custom makes sheaths; prefers natural handle materials. **Prices:** $80 to $500. **Remarks:** Full-time maker; first knife sold in 1987. **Mark:** Stylized initials and serial number.

BREND, WALTER J., Rt. 7, Box 224, Walterboro, SC 29488/803-538-8256; FAX: 803-538-8416
Specialties: Art and working knives. **Patterns:** Combat knives, survival knives, liner locks and Bowies. **Technical:** ATS-34. **Prices:** $425 to $1,100; some to $3,500. **Remarks:** Full-time maker; first knife sold in 1980. **Mark:** Confederate flag.

BRENNAN & SONS, JUDSON J., P.O. Box 1165, Delta Junction, AK 99737
Specialties: Period pieces. **Patterns:** All kinds of Bowies, rifle knives, daggers. **Technical:** Forges miscellaneous steels. **Prices:** Upscale, good value. **Remarks:** Muzzle-loading gunsmith; first knife sold in 1978. **Mark:** Name.

BRESHEARS, CLINT, 1261 Keats, Manhattan Beach, CA 90266/310-372-0739
Specialties: Working straight knives and folders. **Patterns:** Hunters, Bowies and survival knives. Folders are mostly hunters. **Technical:** Grinds 440C, 154CM and ATS-34; prefers mirror finishes. **Prices:** $125 to $175; some to $300. **Remarks:** Part-time maker; first knife sold in 1978. **Mark:** First name.

BREUER, LONNIE, P.O. Box 877384, Wasilla, AK 99687-7384
Specialties: Fancy working straight knives. **Patterns:** Hunters, camp knives and axes, folders and Bowies. **Technical:** Grinds 440C, AEB-L and D2; likes wire inlay, scrimshaw, decorative filing. **Prices:** $60 to $150; some to $300. **Remarks:** Part-time maker; first knife sold in 1977. **Mark:** Signature.

BRIAR KNIVES (See Ralph, Darrel)

BRIDGES, JUSTIN W., Box 974, Fish Hatchery Rd., Dubois, WY 82513/307-455-2769
Specialties: Working and using straight knives and folders in standard patterns. **Patterns:** Hunters, gent's knives and locking folders. **Technical:** Grinds 440C, ATS-34 and buys Damascus. **Prices:** $250 to $1,000; some to $3,000. **Remarks:** Full-time maker; first knife sold in 1988. Doing business as Wind River Knives. **Mark:** WRK connected; sometimes a circle with name, city and state.

BRIDWELL, RICHARD A., Rt. 2, Milford Ch. Rd., Taylors, SC 29687/803-895-1715
Specialties: Working straight knives and folders. **Patterns:** Boot and fishing knives, fighters and hunters. **Technical:** Grinds stainless steels and D2. **Prices:** $85 to $165; some to $600. **Remarks:** Part-time maker; first knife sold in 1974. **Mark:** Last name logo.

BRIGHTWELL, MARK, 21104 Creekside Dr., Leander, TX 78641/512-267-4110
Specialties: Fancy and plain folders of his design. **Patterns:** Fighters, hunters and gents, some traditional. **Technical:** Hollow- or flat- grinds ATS-34, D2, commercial Damascus; elaborate filework; heat-treats. Extensive choice of natural handle materials; no synthetics. **Prices:** $200 to $700. **Remarks:** Full-time maker. **Mark:** Last name.

BRIGNARDELLO, E.D., Rt. 2, Box 152A, Beecher, IL 60401/708-946-6609
Specialties: Working straight knives; some display pieces. **Patterns:** Hunters, fighters, boots and Bowies; some push knives. **Technical:** Grinds 440C, 154CM and ATS-34; likes mirror finishes. **Prices:** $130 to $250; some to $500. **Remarks:** Part-time maker; first knife sold in 1978. **Mark:** Name and city.

BRITTON, TIM, Rt. 1, Box 141, Kinston, NC 28501/919-523-8631
Specialties: Small and simple working knives, sgian dubhs and toggle lock folders to customer specs. **Technical:** Forges and grinds stainless steel. **Prices:** Upscale. **Remarks:** Veteran knifemaker. **Mark:** Etched signature.

BROADWELL, DAVID, P.O. Box 4314, Wichita Falls, TX 76308/817-692-1727
Specialties: One-of-a-kind pieces, especially fighters. **Patterns:** Daggers, sub-hilted fighters, Bowies, some hunters and folders of his design. **Technical:** Grinds 440C, Damascus; all hand-finished. Some embellishment. **Prices:** $200 to $2,500; some higher. **Remarks:** Full-time maker; first knife sold in 1982. **Mark:** Name, city and state.

BROCK, KENNETH L., P.O. Box 375, 207 N. Skinner Rd., Allenspark, CO 80510/303-747-2547
Specialties: Full-tang working straight knives, folders and button-lock folders. **Patterns:** Hunters, survival knives, miniatures and minis. **Technical:** Flat-grinds D2; makes own sheaths. **Prices:** $50 to $500. **Remarks:** Part-time maker; first knife sold in 1978. **Mark:** Last name, city, state and serial number.

BRONK'S CUSTOM KNIVES (See Brunckhorst, C. Lyle)

BROOKER, DENNIS, Rt. 1, Box 12A, Derby, IA 50068/515-533-2103
Specialties: Fancy straight knives and folders of his design. **Patterns:** Hunters, folders and boots. **Technical:** Forges and grinds. Full-time engraver and designer; instruction available. **Prices:** Moderate to upscale. **Remarks:** Part-time maker. Takes no orders; sells only completed work. **Mark:** Name.

BROOKS, MICHAEL, 1903 B 16th St., Lubbock, TX 79401/406-762-6413
Specialties: Working straight knives of his design or to customer specs. **Patterns:** Tantos, swords, Bowies, hunters, skinners and boots. **Technical:** Grinds 440C, D2 and ATS-34; offers wide variety of handle materials. **Prices:** $40 to $800. **Remarks:** Part-time maker; first knife sold in 1985. Does business as The Weapons Shop. **Mark:** Initials.

BROOKS, STEVE R., Box 105, Big Timber, MT 59011/406-932-5114
Specialties: Working straight knives and folders; period pieces. **Patterns:** Hunters, Bowies and camp knives; folding lockers; axes, tomahawks and buckskinner knives; swords and stilettos. **Technical:** Forges 01 and his own Damascus. Some knives come embellished. **Prices:** $100 to $350; some to $1,000. **Remarks:** Full-time maker; first knife sold in 1982. **Mark:** Lazy initials.

BROOME, THOMAS A., 1212 E. Aliak Ave., Kenai, AK 99611-8205
Specialties: Traditional working straight knives and folders. **Patterns:** Full range of straight knives and a few folders. **Technical:** Grinds D2, 440C, 440V, ATS-34 and BG42. **Prices:** $75 to $175; some to $2,000. **Remarks:** Full-time maker; first knife sold in 1979. Doing business as Thom's Custom Knives. **Mark:** Full name, city, state in logo.

BROTHERS, ROBERT L., 989 Philpott Rd., Colville, WA 99114/509-684-8922
Specialties: Traditional working and using straight knives and folders of his design and to customer specs. **Patterns:** Bowies, fighters and hunters. **Technical:** Grinds D2; forges Damascus. Makes own Damascus from saw steel wire rope and chain; part-time goldsmith and stone-setter. **Prices:** $100 to $400; some higher. **Remarks:** Part-time maker; first knife sold in 1986. **Mark:** Initials and year made.

BROUGHTON, DON R., 4690 Edwardsville-Galena Rd., Floyd Knobs, IN 47119/812-923-9222
Specialties: Traditional straight knives of his design; period pieces. Likes antiquing/aging knives. **Patterns:** Bowies, utility/camp knives and 1700- to 1800-style knives. **Technical:** Forges W2, 1095, 5160 and own Damascus. **Prices:** $150

to $450; some to $750. **Remarks:** Part-time maker; first knife sold in 1987. **Mark:** Tomahawk head, M.S.

BROWER, MAX, 2016 Story St., Boone, IA 50036/515-432-2938
Patterns: Bowies, hunters and boots. **Technical:** Grinds 440C and 154CM. **Prices:** $80 to $350. **Remarks:** Spare-time maker; first knife sold in 1981. **Mark:** Last name.

BROWN, DAVID B., 922 D St., Fairbury, NE 68352/402-729-2358
Specialties: Working straight knives and folders; some fancy. **Patterns:** Hunters, tantos and Bowies; lockers and butterflies. **Technical:** Forges and grinds W2, 440C and his own Damascus. Etches. **Prices:** $85 to $750; some to $2,000. **Remarks:** Spare-time maker; first knife sold in 1979. **Mark:** First and middle initials, last name.

BROWN, E.H., P.O. Box 40454, Grand Junction, CO 81504/303-434-4811
Specialties: Working straight knives in standard patterns; period pieces. **Patterns:** Hunters, Bowies, survival and fishing knives. **Technical:** Grinds D2 and 154CM. **Prices:** $175 to $350. **Remarks:** Full-time maker; first knife sold in 1983. **Mark:** Name, maker, city and state.

BROWN, HAROLD E., Rt. 7, Box 335, Arcadia, FL 33821/813-494-7514
Specialties: Fancy and exotic working knives. **Patterns:** Hunters, folders and fillet knives. **Technical:** Grinds D2, 440C and ATS-34. Embellishment available. **Prices:** $100 to $750; some to $1,000. **Remarks:** Full-time maker; first knife sold in 1976. **Mark:** Name and city with logo.

BROWN, PETER, 10 Island View St., Emerald Beach 2456, AUSTRALIA/02-809-0265
Specialties: Heavy-duty working knives. **Patterns:** Swords, fighters, tantos, hunting and fishing knives. **Technical:** Grinds 440C, 420 and ATS-34; makes his own Damascus steel. Heat-treats; scrimshaws. **Prices:** $135 to $500; some to $800. **Remarks:** Spare-time maker; first knife sold in 1978. **Mark:** Interlacing initials.

BROWN, ROB E., P.O. Box 15107, Emerald Hill, 6011 Port Elizabeth, SOUTH AFRICA/27-41-361086
Specialties: Contemporary-designed straight knives and period pieces. **Patterns:** Utility knives, hunters, boots, fighters and daggers. **Technical:** Grinds 440C, D2 and ATS-34. Knives mostly mirror finished; African handle materials. **Prices:** $200 to $600; some to $1,500. **Remarks:** Full-time maker; first knife sold in 1985. **Mark:** Name and city.

BROWN, TED, 7621 Firestone Blvd., Suite 104, Downey, CA 90241/213-869-9945
Specialties: Working straight knives in standard patterns. **Patterns:** Hunters, Bowies, fishing knives. **Technical:** Grinds stainless steel; some integral work. **Prices:** $100 to $350; some to $500. **Remarks:** Part-time maker; first knife sold in 1982. **Mark:** Name, address in snake logo.

BROWN, TOM, Suite 106, 5710-K High Point Rd., Greensboro, NC 27407/919-656-4955
Specialties: Classic and working straight knives of his design and in standard patterns. **Patterns:** Daggers, fighters, hunters and fish knives. **Technical:** Grinds ATS-34, 440C and D2. Some filework offered. No jigs or fixtures. **Prices:** $165 to $550. **Remarks:** Part-time maker; first knife sold in 1991. **Mark:** Brown Knives.

BROWNE, RICK, 980 West 13th St., Upland, CA 91786/714-985-1728
Specialties: High-tech working straight knives of his design. **Patterns:** Hunters, fighters and daggers. No heavy-duty knives. **Technical:** Grinds D2, 440C and ATS-34. **Prices:** $80 to $500; some to $1,500. **Remarks:** Part-time maker; first knife sold in 1975. **Mark:** Name, city, state.

BROZ KNIVES (See Meloy, Sean)

BRUMAGEN, JERRY (See Fannin, David A. and Brumagen, Jerry)

BRUNCKHORST, C. LYLE, 1450 Prospect Ave., Suite 222, Helena, MT 59601/406-449-8827
Specialties: Working straight knives and folders, some fancy. **Patterns:** Head knives, fillet knives, Bowies and backpack folders. **Technical:** ATS-34. Offers carved antler handles and scrimmed ivory. **Prices:** $85 to $3,500. **Remarks:** Full-time maker; first knife sold in 1976. Doing business as Bronk's Custom Knives. **Mark:** Bucking horse logo or BRONK.

BUCHMAN, BILL, 63312 South Rd., Bend, OR 97701/503-382-8851
Specialties: Working straight knives. **Patterns:** Hunters, Bowies, fighters, kitchen cutlery, carving sets and boots. Makes some saddlemaker knives. **Technical:** Forges 440C and Sandvik 15N20. Prefers 440C for saltwater. **Prices:** $95 to $400. **Remarks:** Part-time maker; first knife sold in 1982. **Mark:** Initials or last name.

BUCHNER, BILL, P.O. Box 73, Idleyld Park, OR 97447/503-498-2247
Specialties: Working straight knives, kitchen knives and high-art knives of his design. **Technical:** Uses W1, L6 and his own Damascus. Invented "spectrum metal" for letter openers, folder handles and jewelry. Likes sculpturing and carving in Damascus. **Prices:** $40 to $3,000; some higher. **Remarks:** Full-time maker; first knife sold in 1978. **Mark:** Signature.

BUCHOLZ, MARK A., 9197 West Parkview Terrace Loop, Eagle River, AK 99577/907-694-1037
Specialties: Working straight knives in standard patterns, some fancy. **Patterns:** Hunters, fighters and liner locks. **Technical:** Grinds 440C and ATS-34. **Prices:** $250 to $475; some to $2,500. **Remarks:** Part-time maker; first knife sold in 1976. **Mark:** Name, city and state in buffalo skull logo.

BUCKBEE, DONALD M., 42683 Jonathan Place, Clinton Township, MI 48038/313-228-2673
Specialties: Working straight knives, some fancy, in standard patterns; concentrating on kitchen knives. **Patterns:** Kitchen knives, hunters, Bowies. **Technical:** Grinds D2, 440C, ATS-34. Makes ultra-lights in hunter patterns. **Prices:** $100 to $250; some to $350. **Remarks:** Part-time maker; first knife sold in 1984. **Mark:** Antlered bee—a buck bee.

BUCKNER, JIMMIE H., P.O. Box 162, Putney, GA 31782/912-436-4182
Specialties: High-tech working straight knives and locking folders of his design or to customer specs. **Patterns:** Hunters, fighters and camp knives. **Technical:** Forges 01, 1095 and his Damascus; heat-treats. **Prices:** $100 to $300; some to $900. **Remarks:** Full-time maker; first knife sold in 1980. **Mark:** Last name over spade.

BUEBENDORF, ROBERT E., 108 Lazybrooke Rd., Monroe, CT 06468/203-452-1769
Specialties: Traditional and fancy straight knives of his design. **Patterns:** Handmakes and embellishes belt buckle knives. **Technical:** Forges and grinds 440C, 01, W2, 1095, his own Damascus and 154CM. **Prices:** $200 to $500. **Remarks:** Full-time maker; first knife sold in 1978. **Mark:** First and middle initials, last name and MAKER.

BUGDEN, JOHN, Rt. #6, Box 7, Murray, KY 42071/502-753-0305
Specialties: Working straight knives; period pieces. **Patterns:** Hunters, boots and survival knives. **Technical:** Grinds 01, 440C; buys Damascus. Offers filework. **Prices:** $125 to $500. **Remarks:** Full-time maker; first knife sold in 1975. **Mark:** Initials.

BULLARD, BILL, Rt. 5, Box 35, Andalusia, AL 36420/205-222-9003
Specialties: Traditional working and using straight knives and folders of his design. **Patterns:** Hunters, slip-joint folders and utility/camp knives. **Technical:** Forges Damascus, cable and carbon steels. Offers filework. **Prices:** $100 to $500; some to $1,500. **Remarks:** Part-time maker; first knife sold in 1974. Doing business as Five Runs Forge. **Mark:** Last name stamped on ricasso.

BULLARD, TOM, Rt. 1, Box 127-B, Comfort, TX 78013/210-995-2003
Specialties: Traditional working and using straight knives and folders of his design and to customer specs; classic knives; fancy/embellished knives. **Patterns:** Hunters, locking folders and utility knives. **Technical:** Grinds 01, 1095, ATS-34 and 440C; forges and grinds leaf springs. Heat-treats. Offers filework on blades, tangs, liners and guards. **Prices:** $100 to $250; some to $500. **Remarks:** Full-time maker; first knife sold in 1966. **Mark:** Last name.

BUMPUS, STEVE, 106 Bridle Ridge, Collinsville, IL 62234/618-345-8613
Specialties: Working straight knives of his design. **Patterns:** Hunters with gut hooks, bird and trout knives, skinners. **Technical:** Grinds L6, 440C and 154CM. **Prices:** $50 to $85; some to $225. **Remarks:** Part-time maker; first knife sold in 1981. **Marks:** Last name

BURDEN, JAMES, 405 Kelly St., Burkburnett, TX 76354

directory

BURGER—CAREY

BURGER, FRED, P.O. Munster 4278, Kwa-Zulu Natal SOUTH AFRICA/03930-92316
Specialties: Straight knives of his design. **Patterns:** Bowies, fighters and gentlemen's sword canes. **Technical:** Grinds ATS-34 and 440C. **Prices:** $200 to $400; some to $1,000. **Remarks:** Full-time maker; first knife sold in 1987. **Mark:** Last name in an oval pierced by a dagger.

BURGER, PON, 12 Glenwood Ave., Woodlands, Bulawayo, AFRICA/48628
Specialties: High-art knives—sets of two or four. **Patterns:** Fighters, locking folders of traditional styles, buckles. **Technical:** Uses 440C. African themes scrimshawed on handles. **Prices:** $750—two knives; $1,500—four knives. **Remarks:** Full-time maker; first knife sold in 1973. Doing business as Burger Products. **Mark:** Last name.

BURGER PRODUCTS (See Burger, Pon)

BURNS, DAVE, 2825 SW 5 St., Boynton Beach, FL 33435/407-734-8806
Specialties: Working straight knives of his design or to customer specs. **Patterns:** Hunters, boots, Bowies and survival knives. **Technical:** Forges and grinds 01, L6 and 1095. **Prices:** $65 to $200; some to $325. **Remarks:** Full-time maker; first knife sold in 1980. **Mark:** Last name and serial number.

BURROWS, STEPHEN R., 3532 Michigan, Kansas City, MO 64109/816-921-1573
Specialties: Fantasy straight knives of his design, to customer specs and in standard patterns; period pieces. **Patterns:** Daggers and fighters. **Technical:** Forges 5160 and 1090 high-carbon steel, 01 and his Damascus. Offers casting and lost wax bronzing of crossguards and pommels. **Prices:** $100 to $200; some to $1,000. **Remarks:** Full-time maker; first knife sold in 1983. Doing business as Gypsy Silk. **Mark:** Etched name.

BUSFIELD, JOHN, 153 Devonshire Circle, Roanoke Rapids, NC 27870/919-537-3949; FAX: 919-537-8704
Specialties: Investor-grade folders; high-grade working straight knives. **Patterns:** Original price-style and trailing-point interframe and sculpted-frame folders, drop-point hunters and semi-skinners. **Technical:** Grinds 154CM and ATS-34. Offers interframes, gold frames and inlays; uses jade, agate and lapis. **Prices:** $650 to $2,000. **Remarks:** Full-time maker; first knife sold in 1979. **Mark:** Last name and address.

BUSSE, JERRY, 11651 Co. Rd. 12, Wauseon, OH 43567/419-923-6471
Specialties: Working straight knives. **Patterns:** Heavy combat knives and camp knives. **Technical:** Grinds D2, A2, ATS-34 and 440C; hollow-grinds most blades. **Prices:** $1,100 to $3,500. **Remarks:** Full-time maker; first knife sold in 1983. **Mark:** Last name in logo.

BUZZARD'S KNOB FORGE (See Hurst, Jeff)

"BY GEORGE" (See Englebretson, George)

BYBEE, BARRY J., 795 Lock Rd. E., Cadiz, KY 42211-8615
Specialties: Working straight knives of his design. **Patterns:** Hunters, fighters, boot knives, tantos and Bowies. **Technical:** Grinds ATS-34, 440C. Likes stag and Micarta for handle materials. **Prices:** $125 to $200; some to $1,000. **Remarks:** Part-time maker; first knife sold in 1968. **Mark:** Arrowhead logo with name, city and state.

BYRD, DON E., Rt. 3, Box 223-A, Roanoke, TX 76262/817-430-1986
Specialties: Classic and working straight knives in standard patterns. **Patterns:** Fighters, hunters and utility knives. **Technical:** Grinds ATS-34, D2 and 440C. **Prices:** $85 to $225; some to $500. **Remarks:** Part-time maker; first knife sold in 1983. **Mark:** Last name.

BYWATER HOMESTEAD (See Williams, David)

CABLE JOE KNIVES (See Allen, Joe)

CACTUS CUSTOM KNIVES (See McConnell, Jr., Loyd A.)

CADILLAC BLACKSMITHING (See Pogreba, Larry)

CAFFREY, EDWARD J., 2608 Central Ave. West, Great Falls, MT 59404/406-727-9102
Specialties: Working/using knives, some collector pieces; will accept customer designs. **Patterns:** Hunters, skinners, fighters, camp knives and friction folders. **Technical:** Forges 5160, 52100, his Damascus, cable and chain Damascus. **Prices:** $100 to $750; some higher. **Remarks:** Part-time maker; first knife sold in 1989. **Mark:** Last name or engraved initials.

CALDWELL, BILL, 255 Rebecca, West Monroe, LA 71292/318-323-3025
Specialties: Straight knives and folders with machined bolsters and liners. **Patterns:** Fighters, Bowies, survival knives, tomahawks, razors and push knives. **Technical:** Owns and operates a very large, well-equipped blacksmith and bladesmith shop extant with six large forges and eight power hammers. **Prices:** $400 to $3,500; some to $10,000. **Remarks:** Full-time maker and self-styled blacksmith; first knife sold in 1962. **Mark:** Wild Bill & Sons.

CALLAHAN, ERRETT, 2 Fredonia, Lynchburg, VA 24503
Specialties: Obsidian knives. **Patterns:** Modern styles and Stone Age replicas. **Technical:** Flakes and knaps to order. **Prices:** $100 to $2,100. **Remarks:** Full-time maker; first flint blades sold in 1974. **Mark:** Blade—engraved name; handle—signed edition, year and unit number.

CALLAHAN, F. TERRY, P.O. Box 880, Boerne, TX 78006/210-981-8274; FAX: 210-981-8274
Specialties: Custom hand-forged edged knives, collectible and functional. **Patterns:** Bowies, folders, daggers, hunters, camp knives and swords. **Technical:** Forges 5160, 1095 and his own Damascus. Offers filework and handmade sheaths. **Prices:** $125 to $2,000. **Remarks:** First knife sold in 1990. **Mark:** Initials inside a keystone symbol.

CAMP, JEFF, Rt. 5, Box 3000, Ruston, LA 71270/318-255-7796
Specialties: Fancy working and using straight knives of his design and to customer specs. **Patterns:** Bowies, hunters, utility/camp knives and folders. **Technical:** Forges 5168, L6 and his Damascus. Offers filework; makes mokume. **Prices:** $260 to $1,000. **Remarks:** Part-time maker; first knife sold in 1991. **Mark:** Initials in script.

CAMPBELL, DICK, 20000 Silver Ranch Rd., Conifer, CO 80433/303-697-0150
Specialties: Fancy working straight knives and folders; period pieces. **Patterns:** Bowies, fighters, miniatures and titanium folders. **Technical:** Grinds 440C; uses titanium. Prefers natural materials. **Prices:** $130 to $750; some to $1,200. **Remarks:** Part-time maker; first knife sold in 1975. **Mark:** Name.

CANDRELLA, JOE, 1219 Barness Dr., Warminster, PA 18974/215-675-0143
Specialties: Working straight knives, some fancy. **Patterns:** Daggers, boots, Bowies. **Technical:** Grinds 440C and 154CM. **Prices:** $100 to $200; some to $1,000. **Remarks:** Part-time maker; first knife sold in 1985. Does business as Franjo. **Mark:** FRANJO with knife as J.

CANNADY, DANIEL L., Box 301, Allendale, SC 29810/803-584-2813
Specialties: Working straight knives in standard patterns. **Patterns:** Drop-point hunters, Bowies, skinners, fishing knives with concave grind, steak knives and kitchen cutlery. **Technical:** Grinds D2, 440C and ATS-34. **Prices:** $65 to $150; some to $325. **Remarks:** Full-time maker; first knife sold in 1980. **Mark:** Last name.

CANNON, RAYMOND W., 894 Mattox Ct., Homer, AK 99603/907-235-7779
Specialties: Fancy working knives, folders and swords of his design or to customer specs; many one-of-a-kind pieces. **Patterns:** Bowies, daggers and skinners. **Technical:** Forges and grinds 01, A6, 52100, 5160, his combinations for his own Damascus. **Prices:** Start at $180. **Remarks:** Full-time maker; first knife sold in 1984. **Mark:** Last name, state.

CANTER, RONALD E., 96 Bon Air Circle, Jackson, TN 38305/901-668-1780
Specialties: Traditional working knives to customer specs. **Patterns:** Beavertail skinners, Bowies, hand axes and folding lockers. **Technical:** Grinds A1, 440C and 154CM. **Prices:** $65 to $250; some $500 and higher. **Remarks:** Spare-time maker; first knife sold in 1973. **Mark:** Three last initials intertwined.

CAREY JR., CHARLES W., 1003 Minter Rd., GA 30223/404-227-6854
Specialties: Working and using knives of his design and to customer specs; period pieces. **Patterns:** Fighters, hunters, utility/camp knives and forged-to-shape miniatures. **Technical:** Forges 5160, old files and cable. Offers filework; ages some of his

knives. **Prices:** $35 to $400. **Remarks:** Part-time maker; first knife sold in 1991. **Mark:** Knife logo.

CARGILL, BOB, Rt. 1, Box 501-B, Oldfort, TN 37362/615-338-8418; FAX: 615-338-2086
Specialties: Unique multi-blade folders of his design. **Patterns:** Adaptations of traditional pocketknives in many styles. **Technical:** Grinds 1095, 440, ATS-34 and Damascus. **Prices:** Start at $500; some to $10,000. **Remarks:** Full-time maker; first knife sold in 1974. **Mark:** Cargill Knives.

CARISOLO (See Maestri, Peter A.)

CARLSSON, MARC BJORN, Sct. Hansgade 31, 4000 Roskilde, DENMARK/+45 42 35 97 24
Specialties: High-tech aluminum-handled knives. **Patterns:** Skinners, tantos, folders and art knives. **Technical:** Grinds D2 and ATS-34. **Prices:** $110 to $600; some higher. **Remarks:** Professional jeweler and knifemaker. **Mark:** First name in runic letters within Viking ship.

CAROLINA CUSTOM KNIVES (See Daniel, Travis E.; McNabb, Tommy)

CARSON, HAROLD J. "KIT", 1076 Brizendine Lane, Vine Grove, KY 40175/502-877-6300; FAX: 502-877-6338
Specialties: Military fixed blades and folders; art pieces. **Patterns:** Fighters, sidelock folders, D handles, daggers and swords. **Technical:** Grinds 440C, ATS-34, D2, 01 and Damascus. **Prices:** $250 to $750; some to $5,000. **Remarks:** Full-time maker; first knife sold in 1973. **Mark:** Name stamped or engraved.

CARTER, FRED, 5219 Deer Creek Rd., Wichita Falls, TX 76302/817-723-4020
Specialties: High-art investor-class straight knives; some working hunters and fighters. **Patterns:** Classic daggers, Bowies; interframe, stainless and blued steel folders with gold inlay. **Technical:** Grinds a variety of steels. Uses no glue or solder. Engraves and inlays. **Prices:** Generally upscale. **Remarks:** Full-time maker. Won the W.W. Cronk award in 1988, 1989. **Mark:** Signature in oval logo.

CASHEN, KEVIN R., 5615 Tyler St., Hubbardston, MI 48845/517-981-6780
Specialties: Traditional working straight knives of his design to customer specs. **Patterns:** Hunters, skinners, Bowies, fighters, tantos and utilty/camp knives. **Technical:** Forges 1095, 5160 and his own Damascus and cable; does Japanese temper lines. **Prices:** $80 to $250; some to $800. **Remarks:** Full-time maker; first knife sold in 1985. **Mark:** Old English initials and journeyman stamp.

CASTEEL, DIANNA, P.O. Box 63, Monteagle, TN 37356/615-924-2797
Specialties: Small, delicate daggers and miniatures; most knives one-of-a-kinds. **Patterns:** Daggers, boot knives, fighters and miniatures. **Technical:** Grinds 440C; makes her own Damascus. **Prices:** Start at $350; miniatures start at $250. **Remarks:** Full-time maker. **Mark:** Di in script.

CASTEEL, DOUGLAS, P.O. Box 63, Monteagle, TN 37356/615-924-2797
Specialties: One-of-a-kind collector-class period pieces. **Patterns:** Daggers, Bowies, swords and folders. **Technical:** Grinds 440C; makes his own Damascus. Offers gold and silver castings. **Prices:** Upscale. **Remarks:** Full-time maker; first knife sold in 1982. **Mark:** Last name.

CASTLE KNIVES (See Courtois, Bryan)

CELLUM, TOM S., 9 Cude Cemetary Rd., Willis, TX 77378/409-856-5937
Specialties: Working straight knives in standard patterns. **Patterns:** Bowies, camp knives, hunters. **Technical:** Forges W2, 01, 5165; makes own Damascus; prefers natural handle materials. **Prices:** Start at $100. **Remarks:** Full-time maker; first knife sold in 1982. **Mark:** Name, J.S.

CENTOFANTE, FRANK and TONY, P.O. Box 928, Madisonville, TN 37354-0928/615-442-5767
Specialties: Fancy working folders. **Patterns:** Lockers and liner locks. **Technical:** Grinds ATS-34; hand-rubbed satin finish on blades. **Prices:** $300 to $900. **Remarks:** Full-time maker; first knife sold in 1968. Son Tony is co-worker. **Mark:** Name, city, state.

CENTOFANTE, TONY (See Centofante, Frank and Tony)

CHAFFEE, JEFF L., Washington St., P.O. Box 1, Morris, IN 47033/812-934-6350
Specialties: Traditional working and using straight knives of his design or to customer specs. **Patterns:** Hunters, Bowies, fighters and kitchen knives. **Technical:** Grinds commercial Damascus, 440C, ATS-34, D2 and 01. Prefers natural handle materials. **Prices:** $25 to $250. **Remarks:** Part-time maker; first knife sold in 1988. **Mark:** First and middle initials and last name or last name only.

CHAMBERLAIN, JOHN B., 15 South Lombard, E. Wenatchee, WA 98802/509-884-6591
Specialties: Fancy working and using straight knives mainly to customer specs, though starting to make some standard patterns. **Patterns:** Hunters, Bowies and daggers. **Technical:** Grinds D2, ATS-34, M2, M4 and L6. **Prices:** $60 to $190; some to $2,500. **Remarks:** Full-time maker; first knife sold in 1943. **Mark:** Name, city, state.

CHAMBERLIN, JOHN A., 11535 Our Rd., Anchorage, AK 99516/907-346-1524; FAX: 907-562-4583
Specialties: Art and working knives. **Patterns:** Daggers and hunters; some folders. **Technical:** Grinds ATS-34, 440C, A2, D2 and Damascus. Uses Alaskan handle materials such as oosic, jade, whale jawbone, fossil ivory. **Prices:** Start at $100. **Remarks:** Full-time maker; first knife sold in 1984. **Mark:** Name over English shield and dagger.

CHAMBLIN, JOEL, 296 New Hebron Church Rd., Concord, GA 30206/706-495-9055
Specialties: Folders. **Patterns:** Fighters, hunters, locking folders and miniatures. **Technical:** Grinds ATS-34 and commercial Damascus. Offers filework. **Prices:** Start at $125. **Remarks:** Full-time maker; first knife sold in 1989. **Mark:** First and last name, city and state.

CHAMPAGNE, PAUL, 48 Brightman Rd., Mechanicville, NY 12118/518-664-4179
Specialties: Rugged, ornate straight knives in the Japanese tradition. **Patterns:** Katanas, wakizashi's, tantos and some European daggers. **Technical:** Forges and hand-finishes carbon steels and his own Damascus. Makes Tamahagane for use in traditional blades; uses traditional heat-treating techniques. **Prices:** Start at $750. **Remarks:** First knife sold in 1988. Doing business as Twilight Forge. **Mark:** Three diamonds over a stylized crown; also NOBUHIRA in Kanji.

CHAMPION, ROBERT, P.O. Box 19427, Amarillo, TX 79114/806-359-0446
Specialties: Traditional working straight knives and folders. **Patterns:** Hunters, locking and slip-joint folders; some sub-hilt fighters. **Technical:** Grinds A2, 440C, D2. **Prices:** $100 to $600. **Remarks:** Part-time maker; first knife sold in 1979. **Mark:** Last name with dagger logo, city and state.

CHAPMAN, MIKE, 907 Old Mill Ln., Houston, TX 77073/713-821-6609
Specialties: Using knives, mostly hunters. **Patterns:** Fixed blades—full and narrow tang in traditional styles; lock-back and spring-back folders—boots, fighters, camp knives, Bowies and double-edged knives. **Technical:** Grinds 440C, A2, D2, 01, ATS-34. Filework available on all styles. Heat-treats and tempers. Makes own leather sheaths, plain or tooled. **Prices:** Begin at $85. **Remarks:** Part-time maker; first knife sold in 1975. **Mark:** Cherokee Knives.

CHAPO, WILLIAM G., 45 Wildridge Rd., Wilton, CT 06897/203-544-9424
Specialties: Classic straight knives and folders of his design and to customer specs; period pieces. **Patterns:** Boots, Bowies and locking folders. **Technical:** Forges stainless Damascus. Offers filework. **Prices:** $350 to $950; some to $2,200. **Remarks:** Full-time maker; first knife sold in 1989. **Mark:** First and middle initials, last name, city, state.

CHARD, GORDON R., 104 S. Holiday Lane, Iola, KS 66749/316-365-2311
Specialties: High-tech locking folders. **Patterns:** Titanium sidelock folders, push-button locking folders, interframe lockbacks and some art knives. **Technical:** Flat- and hollow-grinds mostly ATS-34, some Damascus; hand-finishes blades. **Prices:** $300 to $2,000. **Remarks:** Part-time maker; first knife sold in 1983. **Mark:** Name, city and state in wheat logo.

CHASE, JOHN E., P.O. Drawer H, Aledo, TX 76008/817-441-8331
Specialties: Straight high-tech working knives in standard patterns or to customer specs. **Patterns:** Hunters, fighters, daggers and Bowies. **Technical:** Grinds D2, 440C; offers mostly satin finishes. **Prices:** Start at $150. **Remarks:** Part-time maker; first knife sold in 1974. **Mark:** Last name in logo.

directory

CHASTAIN—COLEMAN

CHASTAIN, WADE, Rt. 2, Box 137-A, Horse Shoe, NC 28742/704-891-4803
Specialties: Fancy fantasy and high-art straight knives of his design; period pieces. Known for unique mounts. **Patterns:** Bowies, daggers and fighters. **Technical:** Grinds 440C, ATS-34 and 01. Engraves; offers jeweling. **Prices:** $400 to $1,200; some to $2,000. **Remarks:** Full-time maker; first knife sold in 1984. Doing business as The Iron Master. **Mark:** Engraved last name.

CHEATHAM, BILL, 2930 W. Marlette, Phoenix, AZ 85017/602-242-1497
Specialties: Working straight knives and folders. **Patterns:** Hunters, fighters, boots and axes; locking folders. **Technical:** Grinds 440C. **Prices:** $150 to $350; exceptional knives to $600. **Remarks:** Full-time maker; first knife sold in 1976. **Mark:** Name, city, state.

CHELQUIST, CLIFF, P.O. Box 91, Arroyo Grande, CA 93421/805-489-8095
Specialties: Highly polished sportsman's knives. **Patterns:** Bird knives to Bowies. **Technical:** Grinds D2 and ATS-34. **Prices:** $75 to $150; some to $400. **Remarks:** Spare-time maker; first knife sold in 1983. **Mark:** Last initial.

CHEROKEE KNIVES (See Chapman, Mike)

CHURCHMAN, T.W., 8201 Lamount Dr., Amarillo, TX 79110/806-355-8507
Specialties: Fancy and traditional straight knives of his design and to customer specs. **Patterns:** Daggers, fighters and bird/trout knives. **Technical:** Grinds 440C and D2. Offers fancy filework, lined sheaths, exotic and stabilized woods, and twisted silver wire on fluted handles. **Prices:** $100 to $300; some to $1,500. **Remarks:** Part-time maker; first knife sold in 1981. Doing business as Custom Knives Churchman Made. **Mark:** Last name with dagger.

CISCO (See Syslo, Chuck)

CLAIBORNE, RON, 5416 Luttrell Rd., Knoxville, TN 37918/615-688-9268
Specialties: Working and using straight knives; period pieces. **Patterns:** Hunters, Bowies and daggers. **Technical:** Forges his own wire Damascus; grinds 440C, 01, W2 and 1095. Prefers bone and natural handle materials; some exotic woods. **Prices:** $125 to $300; some to $900. **Remarks:** Part-time maker; first knife sold in 1979. **Mark:** Last name.

CLARK, DAVE, Rt. 2, Box 2821, Live Oak, FL 32060/904-362-1671
Specialties: High-tech working and using straight knives and folders to customer specs; knives for law enforcement officers and fire fighters. **Patterns:** Daggers, swords and locking folders. **Technical:** Grinds 440C, D2 and ATS-34. **Prices:** $75 to $500; some to $750. **Remarks:** Part-time maker; first knife sold in 1988. **Mark:** Name.

CLARK, D.E. (LUCKY), Box 314, Woodlawn St. RD #1, Mineral Point, PA 15942/814-322-4725
Specialties: Working straight knives and folders to customer specs. **Patterns:** Customer designs. **Technical:** Grinds D2, 440C, 154CM. **Prices:** $100 to $200; some higher. **Remarks:** Part-time maker; first knife sold in 1975. **Mark:** Name on one side; "Lucky" on other.

CLARK, HOWARD F., RR 1, Box 74, Runnells, IA 50237/515-966-2126
Specialties: Traditional working straight knives and folders of his design or to customer specs. **Patterns:** Hunters, Bowies and utility/camp knives. **Technical:** Forges 1086, 02, L6, 52100 and his own all tool steel Damascus. Bar stock and forged blade blanks also available. **Prices:** $100 to $2,000; some higher. **Remarks:** Full-time maker; first knife sold in 1979. Doing business as Morgan Valley Forge. **Mark:** Initials connected inside anvil, M.S.

CLARK, ROGER, Rt. 1, Box 538, Rockdale, TX 76567/512-446-3388
Specialties: Traditional working and using straight knives of his design or to customer specs. **Patterns:** Hunters, Bowies and camp knives; primitive styles for blackpowder hunters. **Technical:** Forges 5168. Sheaths are extra. **Prices:** $100 to $450. **Remarks:** Full-time maker; first knife sold in 1989. **Mark:** First initial, last name.

CLAY, J.D., 5050 Hall Rd., Greenup, KY 41144/606-473-6769
Specialties: Fancy working straight knives and folders; field- and collector-grade working knives. **Patterns:** Practical hunters and locking folders. **Technical:** Grinds 01 and ATS-34; some 440C. **Prices:** $65 to $300; some to $400. **Remarks:** Full-time maker; first knife sold in 1972. **Mark:** Name on blade or in small medallion in handle.

CLAY, WAYNE, Box 474B, Pelham, TN 37366/615-467-3472
Specialties: Working straight knives and folders in standard patterns. **Patterns:** Hunters, fighters and kitchen knives; gents and hunter patterns. **Technical:** Grinds 154CM and ATS-34. **Prices:** $125 to $250; some to $1,000. **Remarks:** Full-time maker; first knife sold in 1978. **Mark:** Name.

CLOUDY MT. IRON WORKS (See Ber, Dave)

COATS, ELDON, P.O. Box 201, Bonanza, OR 97623/503-545-6960
Specialties: Plain to fancy working knives of his design or to customer specs. Will work with collectors. **Patterns:** Hunters, skinners, fighters, survival knives, Bowies, boots, fillet knives, axes and miniatures. **Technical:** Flat-grinds mostly by hand 440C, D2, 5160. Uses exotic hardwoods, Micarta and ivory for handles. Bead blasts; uses commercial heat-treater. Makes own sheaths. Scrimshaws and engraves. **Prices:** $50 to $250; miniatures start at $35; collector pieces to $1,200. **Remarks:** Full-time maker; first knife sold in 1987. **Mark:** Name, with dagger in "T."

COBB, LOWELL D., 823 Julia St., Daytona Beach, FL 32114/904-252-3514
Specialties: Working straight knives of his design or to customer specs. **Patterns:** Fighters, hunters, skinners, fillet knives and Bowies. **Technical:** Grinds 440C; embellishments available. **Prices:** $100 to $500. **Remarks:** Part-time maker; first knife sold in 1986. **Mark:** Name.

COFER, RON, 2861 Woodruff Dr., Duluth, GA 30136/404-476-5117
Specialties: Fancy working and using straight knives of his design. **Patterns:** Hunters, Bowies and fighters. **Technical:** Grinds 440C and ATS-34. Heat-treats. Some knives have carved stag handles or scrimshaw. Makes leather sheath for each knife and walnut and deer antler display stands for art knives. **Prices:** $125 to $250; some to $600. **Remarks:** Spare-time maker; first knife sold in 1991. **Mark:** Name and serial number.

COFFMAN, DANNY, 505 Angel Dr. S., Jacksonville, AL 36265/205-435-5848
Specialties: Straight knives and folders of his design. **Patterns:** Hunters, locking and slip-joint folders. **Technical:** Grinds Damascus, 440C and D2. Offers filework and engraving. **Prices:** $100 to $400; some to $800. **Remarks:** Spare-time maker; first knife sold in 1992. Doing business as Customs by Coffman. **Mark:** Last name, city, state.

COHEN, N.J. (NORM), 2408 Sugarcone Rd., Baltimore, MD 21209/410-484-3841
Specialties: Working class knives. **Patterns:** Hunters, skinners, bird knives, push daggers, boots, kitchen and practical customer designs. **Technical:** Stock removal 440C, ATS-34. Uses Micarta, Corian. Some woods in handles. **Prices:** $50 to $250. **Remarks:** Part-time maker; first knife sold in 1982. **Mark:** Etched initials or NJC MAKER.

COHEN, TERRY A., P.O. Box 406, Laytonville, CA 95454
Specialties: Working straight knives and folders. **Patterns:** Bowies to boot knives and locking folders; mini-boot knives. **Technical:** Grinds stainless; hand rubs; tries for good balance. **Prices:** $85 to $150; some to $325. **Remarks:** Part-time maker; first knife sold in 1983. **Mark:** TERRY KNIVES, city and state.

COIL, JIMMIE J., 2936 Asbury Pl., Owensboro, KY 42302/502-684-7827
Specialties: Traditional working and using straight knives of his design. **Patterns:** Hunters, Bowies and fighters. **Technical:** Grinds 440C, ATS-34 and D2. Blades are flat-ground with brush finish; most have tapered tang. Offers filework. **Prices:** $65 to $250; some to $750. **Remarks:** Spare-time maker; first knife sold in 1974. **Mark:** Name.

COLD SPRINGS FORGE (See Solomon, Marvin)

COLE, WELBORN I., 3284 Inman Dr. NE, Atlanta, GA 30319/404-261-3977
Specialties: Traditional straight knives of his design. **Patterns:** Hunters. **Technical:** Grinds 440C, ATS-34 and D2. Good wood scales. **Prices:** NA. **Remarks:** Full-time maker; first knife sold in 1983. **Mark:** Script initials.

COLEMAN, KEITH E., 13 Jardin Rd., Los Lunas, NM 87031/505-864-0024
Specialties: Affordable collector-grade straight knives and folders; some fancy. **Patterns:** Fighters, tantos, hunters and swords. **Technical:** Grinds 440C, ATS-34 and Damascus. Prefers specialty woods; offers filework. **Prices:** $150 to $700;

some to $1,500. **Remarks:** Full-time maker; first knife sold in 1980. **Mark:** Name, city and state.

COLLETT, JERRY D., P.O. Box 296, Charlotte, TX 78011/210-277-1468
Specialties: Traditional-style folders. **Patterns:** Mainly slip-joint folders. **Technical:** 440C, ATS-34, D2 anbd 01. Extensive filework offered as standard. **Prices:** $175 to $500. **Remarks:** Full-time maker; first knife sold in 1989. **Mark:** Initials or last name.

COLLINS, A.J., 9651 Elon Ave., Arleta, CA 91331/818-762-7728
Specialties: Working dress knives of his design. **Patterns:** Street survival knives, swords, axes. **Technical:** Grinds 01, 440C, 154CM. **Prices:** Start at $100. **Remarks:** Full-time maker; first knife sold in 1972. Doing business as Kustom Krafted Knives—KKK. **Mark:** Name.

COLLINS, HAROLD, 503 First St., West Union, OH 45693/513-544-2982
Specialties: Traditional using straight knives and folders of his design or to customer specs. **Patterns:** Hunters, Bowies and locking folders. **Technical:** Forges and grinds 440C, ATS-34, D2, 01 and 5160. Flat-grinds standard; filework available. **Prices:** $75 to $300. **Remarks:** Full-time maker; first knife sold in 1989. **Mark:** First initial, last name, Maker.

COLLINS, LYNN M., 138 Berkley Dr., Elyria, OH 44035/216-366-7101
Specialties: Working straight knives. **Patterns:** Field knives, boots and fighters. **Technical:** Grinds D2, 154CM and 440C. **Prices:** Start at $150. **Remarks:** Spare-time maker; first knife sold in 1980. **Mark:** Initials, asterisks.

CONKEY, TOM, 9122 Keyser Rd., Nokesville, VA 22123/703-791-3867
Specialties: Classic straight knives and folders of his design and to customer specs. **Patterns:** Boots, hunters and locking folders. **Technical:** Grinds ATS-34, 01 and commercial Damascus. Lockbacks have jeweled scales and locking bars with dovetailed bolsters. Folders utilize unique 2-piece bushing of his design and manufacture. Sheaths are handmade. Presentation boxes made upon request. **Prices:** $100 to $500. **Remarks:** Part-time maker; first knife sold in 1991. Collaborates with Dan Thomas. **Mark:** Last name with "handcrafted" underneath.

CONKLIN, GEORGE L., Box 902, Ft. Benton, MT 59442/406-622-3268; FAX: 406-622-5670
Specialties: Designer and manufacturer of the "Brisket Breaker". **Patterns:** Hunters, utility/camp knives and hatchets. **Technical:** Grinds 440C, ATS-34, D2, 1095, 154CM and 5160. Offers some forging and heat-treats for others. Offers some jeweling. **Prices:** $65 to $200, some to $1,000. **Remarks:** Full-time maker. Doing business as Rocky Mountain Knives. **Mark:** Last name in script.

CONKLIN MEADOWS FORGE (See Little, Gary M.)

CONLEY, BOB, 1013 Creasy Rd., Jonesboro, TN 37659/615-753-3302
Specialties: Working straight knives and folders. **Patterns:** Lockers, two-blades, gents, hunters, traditional styles, straight hunters. **Technical:** Grinds 440C, 154CM and ATS-34. Engraves. **Prices:** $250 to $450; some to $600. **Remarks:** Full-time maker; first knife sold in 1979. **Mark:** Full name, city, state.

CONN JR., C.T., 206 Highland Ave., Attalla, AL 35954/205-538-7688
Specialties: Working folders, some fancy. **Patterns:** Full range of folding knives. **Technical:** Grinds 02, 440C and 154CM. **Prices:** $125 to $300; some to $600. **Remarks:** Part-time maker; first knife sold in 1982. **Mark:** Name.

CONNELL, STEVE, 4204 Denniston Circle, Adamsville, AL 35005/205-674-0440
Specialties: Working and using straight knives, some one-of-a-kind. **Patterns:** Hunters, fighters, Bowies and daggers. **Technical:** Uses 440C, ATS-34, Damascus. Satin finishes. **Prices:** $75 to $500; some to $600. **Remarks:** Part-time maker; first knife sold in 1987. **Mark:** Last name in block lettering.

CONNOLLY, JAMES, P.O. Box 182, Palermo, CA 95968/916-534-5363
Specialties: Classic working and using knives of his design. **Patterns:** Boots, Bowies and daggers. **Technical:** Grinds ATS-34; forges 5160; forges and grinds 01. Engraving by George Sherwood. **Prices:** $100 to $500; some to $1,500. **Remarks:** Full-time maker; first knife sold in 1980. Doing business as Gold Rush Designs. **Mark:** First initial, last name, Handmade.

CONNOR, MICHAEL, Box 502, Winters, TX 79567/915-754-5602
Specialties: High-art straight knives and folders. **Patterns:** Hunters to camp knives to traditional locking folders. **Technical:** Forges 5168 and his own Damascus. **Prices:** $250 to $2,500. **Remarks:** Part-time maker; first knife sold in 1974. **Mark:** Last name, M.S.

CONTI, JEFFREY D., 4629 Feigley Rd. W., Port Orchard, WA 98366/206-405-0075
Specialties: Working straight knives. **Patterns:** Fighters and survival knives; hunters, camp knives and fishing knives. **Technical:** Grinds D2, 154CM and 01. Engraves. **Prices:** Start at $80. **Remarks:** Part-time maker; first knife sold in 1980. **Mark:** Initials, year, steel type, name and number of knife.

COOGAN, ROBERT, Rt. 3, Box 430, Smithville, TN 37166/615-597-6801
Specialties: One-of-a-kind knives. **Patterns:** Unique items like ooloo-style Appalachian herb knives. **Technical:** Forges; his Damascus is made from nickel steel and W1. **Prices:** Start at $100. **Remarks:** Part-time maker; first knife sold in 1979. **Mark:** Initials.

COOK, JAMES RAY, Rt. 5, Box 218B, Nashville, AR 71852/501-845-5173
Specialties: Working straight knives of his design or to customer specs. **Patterns:** Bowies, hunters and camp knives. **Technical:** Forges 5160, 01 and Damascus from 01 and 1018. **Prices:** $200 to $2,500. **Remarks:** Part-time maker; first knife sold in 1986. **Mark:** First and middle initials, last name.

COOK, LOUISE, Rt. 1, Box 104, Ozark, IL 62972/618-777-2932
Specialties: Working and using straight knives of her design and to customer specs; period pieces. **Patterns:** Bowies, hunters and utility/camp knives. **Technical:** Forges 5160. Filework; pin work; silver wire inlay. **Prices:** Start at $50/inch. **Remarks:** Part-time maker; first knife sold in 1990. Doing business as Panther Creek Forge. **Mark:** First name and journeyman stamp on one side; panther head on the other.

COOK, MIKE, Rt. 1, Box 104, Ozark, IL 62972/618-777-2932
Specialties: Traditional working and using straight knives of his design and to customer specs. **Patterns:** Bowies, hunters and utility/camp knives. **Technical:** Forges 5160. Filework; pin work. **Prices:** Start at $50/inch. **Remarks:** Spare-time maker; first knife sold in 1991. **Mark:** First initial, last name and journeyman stamp on one side; panther head on the other.

COOMBS JR., LAMONT, RFD #1, Box 1412, Bucksport, ME 04416/207-469-3057
Specialties: Classic fancy and embellished straight knives; traditional working and using straight knives. Knives of his design and to customer specs. **Patterns:** Hunters and utility/camp knives. **Technical:** Hollow-grinds ATS-34, 440C and 01; heat-treats. Offers three styles of filework. Handle embellishment available. **Prices:** With sheaths—$65 to $300; some to $1,500. **Remarks:** Part-time maker; first knife sold in 1988. **Mark:** First and middle initials, last name, Handmade with scroll.

COPELAND, GEORGE "STEVE", Star Rt., Box #36, Alpine, TN 38543/615-823-5214
Specialties: Traditional and fancy working straight knives and folders. **Patterns:** Wide range includes tomahawks, butterfly folders, camp knives, slip-joint folders. **Technical:** Grinds variety of steels. **Prices:** $60 to $350; some $1,000 and higher. **Remarks:** Part-time maker; first knife sold in 1979. **Mark:** Four-leaf clover, initials.

CORBIN KNIVES (See Newcomb, Corbin)

CORBIT, GERALD E., 1701 St. John Rd., Elizabethtown, KY 42701/502-765-7728
Specialties: Fancy and working/using straight knives and folders of all designs. **Patterns:** Daggers, hunters and locking folders. **Technical:** Grinds 440C, ATS-34 and commercial Damascus. Offers scrimshaw, engraving and filework on blades and liners. Finishes include polished, satin and bead blasted. **Prices:** $75 to $250; some to $1,000. **Remarks:** Part-time maker; first knife sold in 1991. Doing business as Corbit Custom Knives. **Mark:** Last name.

CORBY, HAROLD, 218 Brandonwood Dr., Johnson City, TN 37604/615-926-9781
Specialties: Large fighters and Bowies; self-protection knives; art knives. **Patterns:** Sub-hilt fighters and hunters. **Technical:** Grinds 154CM, ATS-34 and 440C. **Prices:** $200 to $6,000. **Remarks:** Full-time maker; first knife sold in 1969. Doing business as Knives by Corby. **Mark:** Last name.

CORDOVA, JOSEPH G., P.O. Box 977, Peralta, NM 87042/505-869-3912
Specialties: One-of-a-kind designs, some to customer specs. **Patterns:** Fighter

directory

CORKEN KNIVES—CRAWFORD

called the ``Gladiator,'' hunters, boots and cutlery. **Technical:** Forges 1095, 5160; grinds ATS-34, 440C and 154CM. **Prices:** Moderate to upscale. **Remarks:** Full-time maker; first knife sold in 1953. **Mark:** Cordova made.

CORKEN KNIVES (See Johnson, Kenneth R.)

CORRADO, JIM, 2915 Cavitt Creek Rd., Glide, OR 97443/503-496-3951
Specialties: High-tech, high-art folding knives. **Patterns:** Makes unusual and difficult pieces; follows British and Continental historical design. **Technical:** Forges mostly L6 and his own Damascus. **Prices:** $200 to $500; some to $3,000. **Remarks:** Full-time maker; first knife sold in 1974. **Mark:** Name, date and state with shield logo.

CORWIN, DON, 5064 Eber Rd., Monclova, OH 43542/419-877-5210
Specialties: Traditional-style knives to customer specs; miniatures. **Patterns:** One- to five-blade folders, slip-joints and lockers. **Technical:** Grinds 440C, ATS-34, 154CM and Damascus; makes own mokume. **Prices:** $200 to $600. **Remarks:** Part-time maker; first knife sold in 1987. **Mark:** Last name in arrowhead logo and year.

COSBY, E. BLANTON, 2954 Pierpont Ave., Columbus, GA 31904/404-323-0327
Specialties: Traditional working and using straight knives of his design. **Patterns:** Hunters, Bowies and boots. Has made a 23-inch hollow-ground machete with handguard. **Technical:** Grinds 440C, ATS-34 and commercial Damascus. **Prices:** $125 to $350; some to $550. **Remarks:** Full-time maker; first knife sold in 1988. **Mark:** First initial, last name, city, state.

COSGROVE, CHARLES G., 2112 Briarwood Dr., Amarillo, TX 79124/806-352-0334
Specialties: Traditional fixed or locking blade working knives. **Patterns:** Hunters, Bowies and locking folders. **Technical:** Stock removal using 440C, ATS-34 and D2; heat-treats. Makes heavy, hand-stitched sheaths. **Prices:** $250 to $2,500. **Remarks:** Full-time maker; first knife sold in 1968. No longer accepting customer designs. **Mark:** First initial, last name, or full name over city and state.

COSTA, SCOTT, Rt. 2, Box 503, Spicewood, TX 78669/210-693-3431
Specialties: Working straight knives. **Patterns:** Hunters, skinners, fillet knives, axes, diver's knives, custom boxed steak knives, carving sets and bar knives. **Technical:** Grinds D2, ATS-34 and 440. Heat-treats. **Prices:** $120 to $800; some to $1,400. **Remarks:** Full-time maker; first knife sold in 1985. **Mark:** Initials connected.

COTE, YVES, 1A-788 Philippe, Ste-Foy (Quebec), CANADA G1V 2R1/418-683-3285
Specialties: Classic and fancy knives in miniature. **Patterns:** Bowies, daggers and swords. **Technical:** Grinds ATS-34 and Damascus. Full-time scrimshander and carver. **Prices:** $50 to $250; some to $300. **Remarks:** Full-time maker; first knife sold in 1991. **Mark:** First name.

COTTRILL, JAMES I., 1776 Ransburg Ave., Columbus, OH 43223/614-274-0020
Specialties: Working straight knives of his design. **Patterns:** Caters to the boating and hunting crowd. **Technical:** Grinds 01, D2 and 440C. Likes filework. **Prices:** $95 to $250; some to $500. **Remarks:** Full-time maker; first knife sold in 1977. **Mark:** Name, city, state, in oval logo.

COUGHLIN, MICHAEL M., 52 Brittania Dr., Danbury, CT 06810/203-791-8580
Specialties: Edged weapons and fighters. **Patterns:** Bowies, fighters, tomahawks, utility/camp knives, concealment knives, duty knives for police/fire rescue. **Technical:** Grinds 01, D2, ATS-34 and Damascus. Offers filework; Bowies have aged blue/gray finish. **Prices:** $75 to $400; some to $600. **Remarks:** Part-time maker; first knife sold in 1985. **Mark:** Last name and year.

COURTNEY, ELDON, 2718 Bullinger, Wichita, KS 67204/316-838-4053
Specialties: Working straight knives of his design. **Patterns:** Hunters, fighters and one-of-a-kinds. **Technical:** Grinds and tempers L6, 440C and spring steel. **Prices:** $100 to $500; some to $1,500. **Remarks:** Full-time maker; first knife sold in 1977. **Mark:** Full name, city and state.

COURTOIS, BRYAN, 3 Lawn Avenue, Saco, ME 04072
Specialties: Working straight knives; prefers customer designs, no standard patterns. **Patterns:** Functional hunters; everyday knives. **Technical:** Grinds S7, 01, 440C or customer request. Hollow-grinds with a variety of finishes. Specializes in granite handles and custom skeleton knives. **Prices:** Start at $75. **Remarks:** Part-time maker; first knife sold in 1988. Doing business as Castle Knives. **Mark:** A rook chess piece machined into blade using electrical discharge process.

COUSINO, GEORGE, 7818 Norfolk, Onsted, MI 49265/517-467-4911
Specialties: Working straight knives. **Patterns:** Hunters, Bowies, buckskinners and daggers. **Technical:** Grinds D2, 440C. **Prices:** $85 to $125; some to $600. **Remarks:** Part-time maker; first knife sold in 1981. **Mark:** Last name.

COVER, RAYMOND A., Rt. 1, Box 194, Mineral Point, MO 63660/314-749-3783
Specialties: High-tech working straight knives and folders in standard patterns. **Patterns:** Bowies and boots; two-bladed folders. **Technical:** Grinds D2, 440C and 154CM. **Prices:** $135 to $250; some to $400. **Remarks:** Part-time maker; first knife sold in 1974. **Mark:** Name.

COX CALL (See Cox, Sam)

COX, COLIN J., 1609 Votaw Rd., Apopka, FL 32703/407-889-7887
Specialties: Working straight knives and folders of his design; period pieces. **Patterns:** Hunters, fighters and survival knives. Folders, two-blades, gents and hunters. **Technical:** Grinds D2, 440C, 154CM and ATS-34. **Prices:** $125 to $750; some to $4,000. **Remarks:** Full-time maker; first knife sold in 1981. **Mark:** Full name, city and state.

COX, SAM, 1756 Love Springs Rd., Gaffney, SC 29341/803-489-1892; FAX: 803-489-0403
Specialties: Classic high-art working straight knives of his design. Duck knives copyrighted. **Patterns:** Hunters, fighters and boots. **Technical:** Grinds 440C, ATS-34 and Damascus. **Prices:** $130 to $390; six-piece steak knife set $2,195. **Remarks:** Full-time maker; first knife sold in 1983. **Mark:** Cox Call and name.

C.P. KNIFEMAKER (See Pienaar, Conrad)

CRAFT III, JOHN M., Lockett Springs Ranch, P.O. Box 682, Williams, AZ 86046/602-635-2190
Specialties: High-art straight knives to customer specs; period pieces. **Patterns:** Daggers, swords and utility/camp knives. **Technical:** Forges and grinds 440C, ATS-34 and his Damascus. **Prices:** $95 to $450; some to $2,500. **Remarks:** Full-time maker; first knife sold in 1985. **Mark:** Runic M in pommel or near butt.

CRAFT, RICHARD C., 3045 Longwood Dr., Jackson, MS 39212/601-373-4046
Specialties: Fancy working knives. **Patterns:** Offers chopping knife and block for kitchen, bird knives and steak knives with presentation case. **Technical:** Grinds 01, L6 and 440C. Cases made of cherry or mahogany. **Prices:** $65 to $275; some to $600. **Remarks:** Full-time maker; first knife sold in 1985. **Mark:** Last name.

CRAIG, ROGER L., 1327 Lane, Topeka, KS 66604/913-233-3845
Specialties: Fantasy and working/using knives of his design. **Patterns:** Fighters, hunters and locking folders. **Technical:** Grinds 01 tool steel and 5160. Offers filework and cowhide sheaths colored to match the knives. **Prices:** $80 to $175; some to $450. **Remarks:** Part-time maker; first knife sold in 1991. Doing business as Craig Knives. **Mark:** Last name, sometimes with a coyote.

CRAIN, JACK W., 400 Walden Rd., Weatherford, TX 76087/817-599-6414
Specialties: Fantasy and period knives; combat and survival knives. **Patterns:** One-of-a-kind art or fantasy daggers, swords and Bowies; survival knives. **Technical:** Forges Damascus; grinds stainless steel. Carves. **Prices:** $350 to $2,500; some to $20,000. **Remarks:** Full-time maker; first knife sold in 1969. Designer and maker of the knives seen in the films *Demolition Man*, *Predator I and II*, *Commando*, *Die Hard I and II*, *Road House*, *Ford Fairlane* and *Action Jackson* and television shows *War of the Worlds*, *Air Wolf*, *Kung Fu: The Legend Cont.* and *Tales of the Crypt*. **Mark:** Annual change of registered trademark—stylized crane.

CRAWFORD, LARRY, 1810 Iris Cir. #B, Temple, TX 76502-2720/713-341-5234
Specialties: Fancy folding knives in standard patterns. **Patterns:** Locking and slip-joint folders. **Technical:** Forges 1095 and his own Damascus. Prefers exotic woods for handles; makes own mokume. **Prices:** $300 to $500; some to $1,200. **Remarks:** Part-time maker; first knife sold in 1983. Doing business as Brazos Forges. **Mark:** Last name.

CRAWFORD, PAT, 205 N. Center, West Memphis, AR 72301/501-735-4632

Specialties: High-tech working straight knives—self-defense and combat types—and folders. **Patterns:** Folding patent locks, interframes, fighters and boots. **Technical:** Grinds 440C, ATS-34, D2 and 154CM. **Prices:** $125 to $2,000. **Remarks:** Full-time maker; first knife sold in 1973. **Mark:** Last name.

CRAWLEY, BRUCE R., 16 Binbrook Dr., Croydon 3136, Victoria, AUSTRALIA
Specialties: Folders. **Patterns:** Hunters, lockback folders and Bowies. **Technical:** Grinds 440C, ATS34 and commercial Damascus. Offers filework and mirror polish. **Prices:** $160 to $850. **Remarks:** Part-time maker; first knife sold in 1990. **Mark:** Initials.

CRISP, HAROLD, 3885 Bow St. NE, Cleveland, TN 37312/615-476-8240
Specialties: Fancy working straight knives and folders. **Patterns:** Hunters to Bowies, tomahawks to miniatures. Locking folders, interframes and traditional-style knives. **Technical:** Grinds 01, D2 and 440C; forges. **Prices:** $85 to $250; some to $800. **Remarks:** Part-time maker; first knife sold in 1972. **Mark:** Initials or name.

CROCKFORD, JACK, 1859 Harts Mill Rd., Chamblee, GA 30341/404-457-4680
Specialties: Lockback folders. **Patterns:** Hunters, fishing and camp knives, traditional folders. **Technical:** Grinds A2, D2, ATS-34 and 440C. Engraves and scrimshands. **Prices:** Start at $175. **Remarks:** Part-time maker; first knife sold in 1975. **Mark:** Name.

CROSS, JOHN M., Rt. 1, Box 351, Bryceville, FL 32009/904-266-9092
Specialties: Traditional working and using straight knives of his design or to customer specs. **Patterns:** Hunters, Bowies, utility/camp knives. **Technical:** Forges his own Damascus, 01 and 1095. Prefers natural handle materials, especially buffalo bone. **Prices:** $150 to $350; some up to $750. **Remarks:** Full-time maker; first knife sold in 1985. **Mark:** A cross.

CROSSLEN, TIMOTHY J., P.O. Box 338, Grafton, WI 53024/414-375-1851
Specialties: Working knives of his design or to customer specs. **Patterns:** Hunters, utility knives, daggers and Bowies. **Technical:** Blades made of ATS-34; handles made of stabilized woods, stag, rubber and Micarta; sheaths made of leather or pigskin. **Prices:** $70 to $175. **Remarks:** Part-time maker; first knife sold in 1990. Doing business as Northern Knife Co.. **Mark:** First and middle initials, last name, city, state and a cross.

CROWDER, ROBERT, Box 1374, Thompson Falls, MT 59873/406-827-4754
Specialties: Traditional working knives to customer specs. **Patterns:** Hunters, Bowies, fighters and fillets. **Technical:** Grinds ATS-34, 154CM, 440C, Vascowear and commercial Damascus. **Prices:** $160 to $250; some to $2,500. **Remarks:** Part-time maker; first knife sold in 1985. **Mark:** Name, city and state in logo.

CROWELL, JAMES L., H.C. 74, Box 368, Mtn. View, AR 72560/501-269-4215
Specialties: Fancy period pieces and working knives to customer specs. **Patterns:** Hunters to daggers, war hammers to tantos; locking folders and slip-joints. **Technical:** Forges W2, 01 and his own Damascus. **Prices:** $250 to $1,500; some to $4,000. **Remarks:** Full-time maker; first knife sold in 1980. **Mark:** A shooting star.

CULPEPPER, JOHN, 2102 Spencer Ave., Monroe, LA 71201/318-323-3636
Specialties: Working straight knives. **Patterns:** Hunters, Bowies and camp knives in heavy-duty patterns. **Technical:** Grinds 01, D2 and 440C; hollow- grinds. **Prices:** $75 to $200; some to $300. **Remarks:** Part-time maker; first knife sold in 1970. Doing business as Pepper Knives. **Mark:** Pepper.

CULVER, STEVE, Rt. 2, Box 225A, Mayetta, KS 66509/913-966-2383
Specialties: Period pieces and working straight knives. **Patterns:** Hunters, Bowies, daggers. **Technical:** Forges his own Damascus, 01 and 5160. Fancy filework available. **Prices:** $100 to $500; some to $1000. **Remarks:** Full-time maker; first knife sold in 1989. **Mark:** Last name, J.S.

CUMMING, R.J., American Embassy Tunis, U.S. Dept. of State, Washington D.C. 20521-6360/Int'l. direct dial 216-1-741-314
Specialties: Custom designs. **Patterns:** Hunters, fighters, Bowies and one-of-a-kind straight knives. Diver's tool knife. **Technical:** Grinds D2, 440C and 154CM. **Prices:** $175 to $550; some to $2,000. **Remarks:** Part-time maker; first knife sold in 1978. **Mark:** Last name.

CUSTOM CUTLERY (See Boeckman, R. Von)

CUTCHIN, ROY D., 960 Hwy. 169 South, Seale, AL 36875/205-855-3080
Specialties: Working straight knives of his design, to customer specs and in standard patterns. **Patterns:** Hunters, boots, fighters and daggers. **Technical:** Grinds ATS-34, 440C, 01 and Damascus. **Prices:** $125 to $450; some to $700. **Remarks:** Part-time maker. **Mark:** First initial, last name, city and state.

CUTE, THOMAS, RD 4, Rt. 90, Cortland, NY 13045/607-749-4055
Specialties: Working straight knives to customer specs. **Patterns:** Hunters, Bowies and fighters. **Technical:** Grinds 01, 440C and ATS-34. **Prices:** $100 to $1,000. **Remarks:** Full-time maker; first knife sold in 1974. **Mark:** Full name.

CYPRESS BEND CUSTOM KNIVES (See Ellerbe, W.B.)

d

DACONCEICAO, JOHN M., 159 Homestead Ave., Rehoboth, MA 02769/508-252-9686
Specialties: One-of-a-kind straight knives of his design and to customer specs. **Patterns:** Boots and fighters. **Technical:** Grinds 01, 1095 and commercial Damascus. All knives come with leather sheath; cross-draw and shoulder harnesses available. **Prices:** $90 to $200; some to $500. **Remarks:** Part-time maker; first knife sold in 1993. **Mark:** JMD Blades.

DAHL, CHRIS W., Rt. 4, Box 558, Lake Geneva, WI 53147/414-248-2464
Specialties: Period pieces and high-art display knives. **Patterns:** Daggers, fighters and hunters. **Technical:** Grinds 440C and stainless steel Damascus. Works exclusively with gemstone handles on all daggers. **Prices:** $500 to $5,000; some to $10,000. **Remarks:** Full-time maker. **Mark:** Full name—maker.

DAILEY, G.E., 577 Lincoln St., Seekonk, MA 02771/508-336-5088
Specialties: Big working knives and period pieces. **Patterns:** Bowies and swords. **Technical:** Grinds 01 and 440C. **Prices:** $125 to $2,000. **Remarks:** Part-time maker. First knife sold in 1982. Likes broadswords. **Mark:** Signature or initials.

DAKE. C.M., 19759 Chef Menteur Hwy., New Orleans, LA 70129-9602/504-254-0357
Specialties: Fancy working folders. **Patterns:** Front-lock lockbacks, button-lock folders. **Technical:** Grinds ATS-34 and 440C. **Prices:** $200 to $850; some higher. **Remarks:** Full-time maker; first knife sold in 1988. **Mark:** Last name.

D'ANDREA, JOHN, 77 Pinecrest Terrace, Wayne, NJ 07470/201-839-4559
Specialties: Fancy working straight knives and folders with filework and distinctive leatherwork. **Patterns:** Hunters, fighters, daggers, folders and an occasional sword. **Technical:** Grinds ATS-34, 154CM, 440C and D2. **Prices:** $180 to $600; some to $1,000. **Remarks:** Part-time maker; first knife sold in 1986. **Mark:** First name, last initial imposed on Samurai sword.

D'ANGELO, LAURENCE, 14703 NE 17th Ave., Vancouver, WA 98686/206-576-0724
Specialties: Straight knives of his design. **Patterns:** Bowies, hunters and locking folders. **Technical:** Grinds D2, ATS-34 and 440C. Handmakes all sheaths. **Prices:** $100 to $200. **Remarks:** Full-time maker; first knife sold in 1987. **Mark:** Football logo—first and middle initials, last name, city, state, Maker.

DANIEL, TRAVIS E., 4015 Brownsboro Rd., Winston-Salem, NC 27106/919-759-0640
Specialties: Traditional working straight knives of his design or to customer specs. **Patterns:** Hunters, fighters and utility/camp knives. **Technical:** Forges and grinds ATS-34 and his own Damascus. **Prices:** $90 to $1,250; some to $2,000. **Remarks:** Part-time maker; first knife sold in 1976. **Mark:** Carolina Custom Knives.

DANIELS, ALEX, 1416 County Rd. 415, Town Creek, AL 35672/205-685-0943
Specialties: Working and using straight knives and folders; period pieces. **Patterns:** Hunters, reproduction Bowies, fishing knives, locking folders and traditional slip-joints. **Technical:** Grinds 440C and ATS-34. **Prices:** $150 to $1,000. **Remarks:** Full-time maker; first knife sold in 1963. **Mark:** First and middle initials, last name, city and state.

DANO-D. ARVEL HANDCRAFTED KNIVES (See Owens, Dan)

directory

DARBY—DEFREEST

DARBY, JED, 7878 E. Co. Rd. 50 N., Greensburg, IN 47240/812-663-2696
Specialties: Traditional working/using straight knives of his design and to customer specs. **Patterns:** Bowies, hunters and utility/camp knives. **Technical:** Grinds 440C, ATS-34 and D2. Prefers natural handle materials. **Prices:** $45 to $275; some to $400. **Remarks:** Full-time maker; first knife sold in 1992. Doing business as Darby Knives. **Mark:** Last name.

DARBY, RICK, 4026 Shelbourne, Youngstown, OH 44511/216-793-3805
Specialties: Working straight knives. **Patterns:** Boots, fighters and hunters with mirror finish. **Technical:** Grinds 440C and 154CM. **Prices:** $90 to $300. **Remarks:** Part-time maker; first knife sold in 1974. **Mark:** First and middle initials, last name.

DAUBERMANN, DESMOND P., Private Bag TO12, Tlokweng, Gaborone, Botswana SOUTH AFRICA
Specialties: Straight working knives to customer specs and in standard patterns. **Patterns:** Hunters and skinners to Bowies. **Technical:** Hollow-grinds K110 N690 and Bohler steel and forges his Damascus. Handle materials include natural woods, buffalo horn and ivory. Offers presentation cases in stinkwood or oak. **Prices:** $250 to $750. **Remarks:** part-time maker; first knife sol in 1991. **Mark:** Last name and city with dog in oval logo, or initials.

DAVENPORT, JACK, 36842 W. Center Ave., Dade City, FL 33525/904-521-4088
Specialties: Titanium linerlock folders. **Patterns:** Double-ground fighters and boot knives. **Technical:** Grinds ATS-34 and Damascus. Engraves; offers corner and screw embellishments. **Prices:** $500 to $1,500. **Remarks:** Full-time maker; first knife sold in 1986. **Mark:** Last name over U.S.A.

DAVIDSON, EDMUND, Rt. 1, Box 319, Goshen, VA 24439/703-997-5651
Specialties: Working straight knives; many integral patterns. **Patterns:** Heavy-duty skinners and camp knives. **Technical:** Grinds A2, ATS-34, S7, 440C, CPM-T-440V. **Prices:** $75 to $1,500. **Remarks:** Full-time maker; first knife sold in 1986. **Mark:** Name in deerhead or motorcycle logo.

DAVIS, BARRY L., 1875 Pittsfield Rd., Castleton, NY 12033/518-477-5036
Specialties: Collector-quality folders. **Patterns:** Traditional gentlemen's folders. **Technical:** Makes Damascus; uses only natural handle materials. **Prices:** $1,000 to $2,500; some to $6,000. **Remarks:** Part-time maker; first knife sold in 1980. **Mark:** Initials.

DAVIS, CHARLIE, P.O. Box 710806, Santee, CA 92072/619-561-9445
Specialties: Fancy and embellished working straight knives of his design. **Patterns:** Hunters, camp and utility knives. **Technical:** Grinds high-carbon files. **Prices:** $20 to $80; some to $150. **Remarks:** Full-time maker; first knife sold in 1980. **Mark:** ANZA U.S.A.

DAVIS, DIXIE, Rt. 3, Clinton, SC 29325/803-833-4964
Specialties: Working straight knives; fantasy pieces. **Patterns:** Hunters, fighters and boots. **Technical:** Grinds 440C, 154CM and ATS-34 with mirror finish. **Prices:** $85 to $140; some to $200. **Remarks:** Part-time maker; first knife sold in 1981. **Mark:** First name.

DAVIS, DON, 8415 Coyote Run, Loveland, CO 80537-9665/303-669-9016
Specialties: Working straight knives in standard patterns or to customer specs. **Patterns:** Hunters, utility knives, skinners and survival knives. **Technical:** Grinds 440C, ATS-34. **Prices:** $75 to $250. **Remarks:** Full-time maker; first knife sold in 1985. **Mark:** Signature, city and state.

DAVIS, JESSE W., Rt. 1, Box 133C, Sarah, MS 38665/601-382-7332
Specialties: Working straight knives and folders in standard patterns and to customer specs. **Patterns:** Tantos, Bowies, locking folders and hunters. **Technical:** Grinds D2, 440C and commercial Damascus. **Prices:** $125 to $300. **Remarks:** Part-time maker; first knife sold in 1977. **Mark:** Name or initials.

DAVIS, KEN, 31 S. Butler Ave. #4, Indianapolis, IN 46219/317-359-2320 days and weekends
Specialties: Classic working and using straight knives of his design and to customer specs. **Patterns:** Fighters, utility/camp knives, skinners, Bowies, chute knives. **Technical:** Hollow-grinds 440C, ATS-34 and D2; enjoys filework. **Prices:** $75 to $350; some to $500. **Remarks:** Full-time maker; first knife sold in 1985. **Mark:** Name, city in an oval, knife logo in center.

DAVIS, K.M. "TWIG", P.O. Box 267, Monroe, WA 98272/206-794-7274
Specialties: Fancy working straight knives. **Patterns:** Hunters, boots, fishing knives, Bowies and daggers. **Technical:** Grinds ATS-34, D2, 440C. **Prices:** $150 to $450; some to $600. **Remarks:** Part-time maker; first knife sold in 1979. **Mark:** Twig.

DAVIS, TERRY, Box 111, Sumpter, OR 97877/503-894-2307
Specialties: Traditional and contemporary folders. **Patterns:** Locking and slip-joint folders; multi-bladed pocketknives in contemporary and traditional patterns. **Technical:** Flat-grinds ATS-34. **Prices:** $300 to $600; some to $1,000. **Remarks:** Full-time maker; first knife sold in 1985. **Mark:** Name in logo.

DAVIS, VERNON M., 1226 LaClede, Waco, TX 76705/817-799-7671
Specialties: Presentation-grade straight knives. **Patterns:** Bowies, daggers, boots, fighters, hunters and utility knives. **Technical:** Hollow-grinds 440C, ATS-34 and D2. Grinds an aesthetic grind line near choil. **Prices:** $125 to $550; some to $5,000. **Remarks:** Part-time maker; first knife sold in 1980. **Mark:** Last name and city inside outline of state.

DAVIS, W.C., 2010 S. Madison, Raymore, MO 64083/816-331-4491
Specialties: Fancy working straight knives and folders. **Patterns:** Folding lockers and slip-joints; straight hunters, fighters and Bowies. **Technical:** Grinds 440C, A2, ATS-34. **Prices:** $80 to $200; some to $1,000. **Remarks:** Full-time maker; first knife sold in 1972. **Mark:** Name.

DAWSON, BARRY, 10A Town Plaza, Suite 303KN, Durango, CO 81301/800-356-4837; FAX: 303-385-4350
Specialties: Samurai swords, combat knives, collector daggers, folding knives and hunting knives. **Patterns:** Offers over 60 different models. **Technical:** Grinds 440C; heat-treats. **Prices:** $75 to $1,500; some to $5,000. **Remarks:** Full-time maker; first knife sold in 1975. **Mark:** Last name, USA in print or last name in script.

DAYNIA FORGE (See Saindon, R. Bill)

DEAN, HARVEY J., Rt. 2, Box 137, Rockdale, TX 76567/512-446-3111
Specialties: Collectible, functional knives. **Patterns:** Bowies, hunbters, folders, daggers, swords, battle axes, camp and combat knives. **Technical:** Forges 1095, 01, 5168 and his Damascus. **Prices:** $195 to $4,000. **Remarks:** Full-time maker; first knife sold in 1981. **Mark:** Last name and MS.

DEARING, JOHN, 1569 Flucom Rd., DeSoto, MO 63020/314-586-1772
Specialties: Traditional working and using straight knives of his design; period pieces and fancy/embellished straight knives. **Patterns:** Hunters, Bowies, fighters, skinners, utility/camp knives and buckskinner blades. **Technical:** Forges and grinds 5160, 154CM and his own Damascus. Prefers natural handle materials. **Prices:** $85 to $350. **Remarks:** Part-time maker; first knife sold in 1985. Doing business as Arc Mountain Forge. **Mark:** Initials stylized into a deer hoofprint.

DeBRAGA, JOSE C., 1519 Du Grand Bourg, Val Belair, Queb. G3J 1K4, CANADA/418-847-7855
Specialties: Art knives, fantasy pieces and working knives of his design or to customer specs. **Patterns:** Knives with sculptured or carved handles, from miniatures to full-size working knives. **Technical:** Grinds and hand-files 440C and ATS-34. A variety of steels and handle materials available. Offers lost wax casting. **Prices:** Start at $300. **Remarks:** Full-time maker; wax modeler, sculptor and knifemaker; first knife sold in 1984. **Mark:** Initials in stylized script and serial number.

DEER (See Laughlin, Don)

DEER CREEK FORGE (See Quarton, Barr)

DEFEO, ROBERT A., 403 Lost Trail Dr., Henderson, NV 89014/702-434-3717
Specialties: Working straight knives and period pieces. **Patterns:** Hunters, fighters, daggers and Bowies. **Technical:** Grinds D2, 440C and ATS-34. **Prices:** $100 to $300; some to $500. **Remarks:** Part-time maker; first knife sold in 1982. **Mark:** Last name.

DEFREEST, WILLIAM G., P.O. Box 573, Barnwell, SC 29812/803-259-7883
Specialties: Working straight knives and folders. **Patterns:** Fighters, hunters and boots; locking folders and slip-joints. **Technical:** Grinds 440C, 154CM and ATS-34;

custom knifemakers
DeGRAEVE—DOMINY

clean lines and mirror finishes. **Prices:** $100 to $700. **Remarks:** Full-time maker; first knife sold in 1974. **Mark:** GORDON.

DeGRAEVE, RICHARD, 329 Valencia St., Sebastian, FL 32958/407-589-9005
Specialties: Working straight knives of his design or to customer specs. **Patterns:** Hunters and skinners with or without gut hooks, fillets, fighters, folders, skeleton knives, mini and art knives. **Technical:** Forges and grinds 440C, ATS-34, 01, high carbon steels; scrimshaws; enjoys filework. **Prices:** $55 to $400. **Remarks:** Full-time maker; first knife sold in 1985. **Mark:** Rich

DeLONG, DICK, 17561 E. Ohio Circle, Aurora, CO 80017/303-745-2652
Specialties: Fancy working knives and fantasy pieces. **Patterns:** Hunters and small skinners. **Technical:** Grinds and files 01, D2, 440C and Damascus. Offers cocobolo and osage orange for handles. **Prices:** Start at $50. **Remarks:** Part-time maker. **Mark:** Last name; some unmarked.

DEMPSEY, GORDON S., P.O. Box 7497, N. Kenai, AK 99635/907-776-8425
Specialties: Working straight knives and folders. **Patterns:** Hunters, ooloos, harpoons. **Technical:** Forges 01. **Prices:** $80 to $250. **Remarks:** Part-time maker; first knife sold in 1974. **Mark:** Name, city and state.

DENNEHY, DAN, 13321 Hwy. 160, P.O. Box 2-F, Del Norte, CO 81132/719-657-2545
Specialties: Working knives, fighting and military knives, throwing knives. **Patterns:** Full range of straight knives, tomahawks, buckle knives. **Technical:** Forges and grinds A2, 01 and D2. **Prices:** $135 to $250; exceptional knives to $3,500. **Remarks:** Full-time maker; first knife sold in 1942. **Mark:** First name and middle initial, city, state and shamrock.

DENT, DOUGLAS M., 1208 Chestnut St., S. Charleston, WV 25309/304-768-3308
Specialties: Straight and folding sportsman's knives. **Patterns:** Hunters, boots and Bowies, interframe folders. **Technical:** Forges and grinds D2, 440C, 154CM and plain tool steels. **Prices:** $70 to $300; exceptional knives to $800. **Remarks:** Part-time maker; first knife sold in 1969. **Mark:** Last name.

DERINGER, CHRISTOPH, 207 St. Joseph, Pike River, Que. CANADA J0J 1P0/514-248-7426
Specialties: Traditional working and using straight knives of his design and to customer specs. **Patterns:** Boots, hunters, kitchen knives and utility/camp knives. **Technical:** Forges 5760, 01 and Damascus. Offers a variety of filework. **Prices:** $100 to $250; some to $750. **Remarks:** Part-time maker; first knife sold in 1989. **Mark:** Last name stamped/engraved.

DETMER, PHILLIP, 14140 Bluff Rd., Breese, IL 62230/618-526-4834
Specialties: Working knives. **Patterns:** Bowies, daggers and hunters. **Technical:** Grinds ATS-34 and D2. **Prices:** $60 to $400. **Remarks:** Part-time maker; first knife sold in 1977. **Mark:** Last name with dagger.

DeYONG, CLARENCE, 4140 Cripple Creek Way, Kennesaw, GA 30144-2165/404-928-8051
Specialties: Working and using straight knives of his design and to customer specs. **Patterns:** Hunters, fighters and boots. **Technical:** Grinds 440C, D2, ATS-34. Son Brian does scrimshaw, filework. **Prices:** $75 to $150; some to $400. **Remarks:** Part-time maker; first knife sold in 1981. **Mark:** Last name and serial number.

D'HOLDER (See Holder, D'Alton)

DICKISON, SCOTT S., 39 Bay View Ave., Portsmouth, RI 02871/401-683-7439
Specialties: Working and using straight knives and locking folders of his design. **Patterns:** Trout knives, fishing and hunting knives. **Technical:** Forges and grinds commercial Damascus and D2, 01. Uses natural handle materials. **Prices:** $200 to $600; some higher. **Remarks:** Part-time maker; first knife sold in 1989. **Mark:** Stylized initials.

DIETZEL, BILL, P.O. Box 1613, Middleburg, FL 32068/904-282-1091
Specialties: Forged straight knives and folders. **Patterns:** His interpretations. **Technical:** Forges his Damascus and other steels. **Prices:** Middle ranges. **Remarks:** Likes natural materials; uses titanium in folder liners. **Mark:** Name.

DIGANGI, JOSEPH M., Box 225, Santa Cruz, NM 87567/505-753-6414
Specialties: Kitchen and table cutlery. **Patterns:** French chef's knives, carving sets, steak knife sets, some camp knives and hunters. Holds patents and trademarks for "System II" kitchen cutlery set. **Technical:** Grinds 440C; buys Damascus. **Prices:** $150 to $450; some to $1,000. **Remarks:** Full-time maker; first knife sold in 1983. **Mark:** Last name.

DILL, DAVE, 2609 NW 33rd, Oklahoma City, OK 73112/405-943-4837
Specialties: Working straight knives of his design. **Patterns:** Bowies, various styles of hunters, skinners. **Technical:** Hand-forges 5160. Some embellishments available. **Prices:** $100 to $400. **Remarks:** Part-time maker; first knife sold in 1987. **Mark:** First initial, last name.

DILL, ROBERT, 1812 Van Buren, Loveland, CO 80538/303-667-5144; FAX: 303-667-5144
Specialties: Fancy and working knives of his design. **Patterns:** Hunters, Bowies and fighters. **Technical:** Grinds 440C and D2. Handles carved by Jim Anderson. **Prices:** $100 to $800. **Remarks:** Full-time maker; first knife sold in 1984. **Mark:** Logo stamped into blade.

DILLON, EARL E., 8908 Stanwin Ave., Arleta, CA 91331
Specialties: Fancy straight knives and folders. **Patterns:** Contemporary interpretations. **Technical:** Grinds 440C and AEB. **Prices:** $250 to $350; some over $500. **Remarks:** Part-time maker; first knife sold in 1984. Collaborates with Chuck Stapel. **Mark:** STAPEL-DILLON.

DILLUVIO, FRANK J., 13611 Joyce, Warren, MI 48093/313-775-1216
Specialties: Traditional working straight knives, some high-tech. **Patterns:** Hunters, Bowies, fishing knives, sub-hilts and miniatures. **Technical:** Grinds D2, 440C, CPM; works for precision fits—no solder. **Prices:** $95 to $450; some to $800. **Remarks:** Part-time maker; first knife sold in 1984. **Mark:** Name and state.

DINGMAN, SCOTT, 4298 Parkers Lake Rd., NE, Bemidji, MN 56601/218-751-6908
Specialties: Fancy working knives of his design. **Patterns:** Hunters, daggers, boots and camp knives. **Technical:** Forges 01, L6 and wire Damascus. Provides lost wax casting and hard cast bronze. Prefers exotic woods and high mirror finishes. **Prices:** $150 to $225; some to $500. **Remarks:** Full-time maker; first knife sold in 1983. **Mark:** Last name.

DION, GREG, 3032 S. Jackson St., Oxnard, CA 93033/805-483-1781 (evenings)
Specialties: Working straight knives, some fancy. Welcomes special orders. **Patterns:** Hunters, fighters, camp knives, Bowies, tantos and special boar knives. **Technical:** Grinds ATS-34, 154CM and 440C. **Prices:** $85 to $300; some to $600. **Remarks:** Part-time maker; first knife sold in 1985. **Mark:** Name.

DIPPOLD, A.W., RFD 3, Box 162A, Perryville, MO 63775/314-547-1119
Specialties: Embellished and working knives and folders; sopme one-of-a-kinds. **Patterns:** Hunters, Bowies, boots, fighters, file knives and folders. **Technical:** Forges and grinds carbon steels, files, own Damascus/Mosaic. Offers filework. **Prices:** $100 to $650; some higher. **Remarks:** Full-time maker; first knife sold in 1980. **Mark:** Last name in logo or weeping heart.

DIXON JR., IRA E., P.O. Box 2581, Ventura, CA 93002-2581
Specialties: Traditional working straight knives of his design. **Patterns:** Fighters, hunters, boot knives, utility knives. **Technical:** Forges and grinds 440C, ATS34 and 5160. **Prices:** $140 to $350. **Remarks:** Part-time maker; first knife sold in 1993. **Mark:** First name, Handmade.

DOC HAGEN (See Hagen, Phillip L.)

DOG KNIVES (See Dugger, Dave)

DOLAN, ROBERT L., 220—B Naalae Road, Kula, HI 96790/808-878-6406
Specialties: Working straight knives in standard patterns, his designs or to customer specs. **Patterns:** Fixed blades and potter's tools, ceramic saws. **Technical:** Grinds 01, D2, 440C and ATS-34. Heat-treats and engraves. **Prices:** Start at $75. **Remarks:** Full-time tool and knifemaker; first knife sold in 1985. **Mark:** Last name, USA.

DOMINY, CHUCK, P.O. Box 593, Colleyville, TX 76034/817-498-4527
Specialties: Traditional working and using straight knives of his design. **Patterns:** Hunters and utility/camp knives. **Technical:** Grinds 440C; heat-treats. **Prices:** $60

directory

DONOVAN—DUFF

to $200; some to $600. **Remarks:** Full-time mkaer; first knife sold in 1976. **Mark:** Last name.

DONOVAN, PATRICK, 1770 Hudson Dr., San Jose, CA 95124/408-267-9825
Specialties: Working straight knives and folders; period pieces. **Patterns:** Hunters, boots and daggers; lockers and slip-joints. **Technical:** Grinds 440C. Embellishes. **Prices:** $75 to $475; some to $1,200. **Remarks:** Full-time maker; first knife sold in 1980. **Mark:** First name.

DOOLITTLE, MIKE, 13 Denise Ct., Novato, CA 94947/415-897-3246
Specialties: Working straight knives in standard patterns. **Patterns:** Hunters and fishing knives. **Technical:** Grinds 440C, 154CM and ATS-34. **Prices:** $125 to $200; some to $750. **Remarks:** Part-time maker; first knife sold in 1981. **Mark:** Name, city and state.

DOUGLAS, DALE, 361 Mike Cooper Rd., Ponchatoula, LA 70454/504-345-6169
Specialties: Working straight knives and folders. **Patterns:** Locking folders and slip-joints; hunters, boots and camp knives. **Technical:** Grinds D2, 440C and 154CM. **Prices:** $75 to $150; some to $350. **Remarks:** Spare-time maker; first knife sold in 1980. **Mark:** Name.

DOUGLAS, JOHN J., Rt. 1, Box 379, Lynch Station, VA 24571/804-369-7196
Specialties: Fancy and traditional straight knives and folders of his design and to customer specs. **Patterns:** Locking folders, swords and sgian dubhs. **Technical:** Grinds 440C stainless, ATS-34 stainless and customer's choice. Offers newly designed non-pivot uni-lock folders. Prefers highly polished finish. **Prices:** $160 to $1,400. **Remarks:** Full-time maker; first knife sold in 1975. Doing business as Douglas Keltic. **Mark:** Stylized initial. Folders are numbered; customs are dated.

DOUGLAS KELTIC (See Douglas, John J.)

DOURSIN, GERARD, Chemin des Croutoules, F 84210 Pernes les Fontaines, FRANCE
Specialties: Period pieces. **Patterns:** Some hunters. **Technical:** Forges his own Damascus; sells commercial Damascus. **Prices:** $600 to $4,000. **Remarks:** First knife sold in 1983. **Mark:** English lion.

DOUSSOT, LAURENT, 4673 Cartier, Montreal, Quebec, CANADA H2H 1W9/514-523-3531; FAX: 514-722-1641
Specialties: Art knives; folders with "apparant lock bar,"; miniatures. **Patterns:** Utility knives, fighters and working straight knives and folders of his design or to customer specs. **Technical:** Grinds and hand files ATS-34, 01, commercial Damascus. Variety of handle materials offered from ivory to anodized titanium. **Prices:** Start at $300; miniatures start at $100. **Remarks:** Part-time maker; first knife sold in 1992. **Mark:** Engraves logo with initials.

DOVE KNIVES (See Rollert, Steve)

DOWELL, T.M., 139 NW, St. Helen's Pl., Bend, OR 97701/503-382-8924
Specialties: Integral construction in hunting knives and period pieces. Famous "Funny" folders. **Patterns:** Hunters to sword canes, price-style daggers to axes. **Technical:** Forges 1060, 5160 and 1095. Grinds BG42, D2, 440C and 154CM. Makes his own bright Damascus. **Prices:** $175 to $950; exceptional knives to $4,500. **Remarks:** Full-time maker; first knife sold in 1967. **Mark:** Initials logo.

DOWNIE, JAMES T., RR #1, Port Franks, Ont. NOM 2LO, CANADA/519-243-2290
Specialties: Serviceable straight knives and folders; period pieces. **Patterns:** Hunters, Bowies, camp knives and miniatures. **Technical:** Grinds D2, 440C and ATS-34. **Prices:** $100 to $500; some higher. **Remarks:** Part-time maker; first knife sold in 1978. **Mark:** Signature of first and middle initials, last name.

DOWNING, LARRY, Route 1, Box 387, Bremen, KY 42325/502-525-3523; FAX: 502-525-3372
Specialties: Working straight knives and folders. **Patterns:** From mini-knives to daggers, folding lockers to interframes. **Technical:** Forges and grinds 154CM, ATS-34 and his own Damascus. **Prices:** $150 to $750; some higher. **Remarks:** Part-time maker; first knife sold in 1979. **Mark:** Name in arrowhead.

DOWNING, TOM, 129 S. Bank St., Cortland, OH 44410/216-637-0623
Specialties: Working straight knives; period pieces. **Patterns:** Hunters, fighters and tantos. **Technical:** Grinds 440C, ATs-34 and CPM440V. Prefers natural handle materials. **Prices:** $100 to $400; some to $1,500. **Remarks:** Part-time maker; first knife sold in 1979. **Mark:** First and middle initials, last name.

DOWNS, JAMES F., 35 Sunset Rd., Londonderry, OH 45647/614-887-2099
Specialties: Working straight knives of his design or to customer specs. **Patterns:** Hunting and utility knives, some boots. **Technical:** Grinds 440C. Prefers stag, jigged bone, Micarta and stabilized woods. **Prices:** $65 to $720. **Remarks:** Part-time maker; first knife sold in 1981. **Mark:** Last name.

DOZIER, ROBERT LEE, P.O. Box 1941, Springdale, AR 72765
Specialties: Limited production fine knives. **Patterns:** Variety of collector-grade knives. **Technical:** Grinds 154CM. Prefers stag, bone, Micarta and stabilized woods. **Prices:** Start at $400. **Remarks:** Full-time maker; first knife sold in 1961. **Mark:** Oval etch with map of Ohio in middle.

DRAGONFLY FORGE (See Bell, Michael)

DRAGON STEEL (See Lewis, Mike)

DRAPER, BART, P.O. Box 548, Big Piney, WY 83113/307-276-3052
Specialties: Classic knives, traditional working knives, fantasy and high-art knives and period pieces. All straight knives of his design and to customer specs. **Patterns:** Boots, Bowies, daggers, fighters, hunters, kitchen knives and utility knives. **Technical:** Grinds ATS-34, 440C and CPM T 440V. Heat-treats. **Prices:** $175 to $725; some to $3,500. **Remarks:** Part-time maker; first knife sold in 1966. **Mark:** First initial, last name over city, state.

DRAPER, KENT, 23461 Highway 36, Cheshire, OR 97419/503-998-2448
Specialties: Art knives, historical and period pieces of his design. **Patterns:** Hunters, combat fighters, folding knives and swords. **Technical:** Grinds 440C and ATS-34. Heat-treats, engraves and inlays. **Prices:** $100 to $5,000; some esoteric pieces to $10,000. **Remarks:** First knife sold in 1973. **Mark:** First initial, last name, state.

DRISKILL, BERYL, P.O. Box 187, Braggadocio, MO 63826/314-757-6262
Specialties: Fancy working knives. **Patterns:** Hunting knives, fighters, Bowies, boots, daggers and lockback folders. **Technical:** Grinds 440C, ATS-34, 154CM. **Prices:** $150 to $350; some to $4,000. **Remarks:** Part-time maker; first knife sold in 1984. **Mark:** Name.

DR KNIVES (See Raymond, Donald)

DROST, MICHAEL B., Rt. 2, Box 49, French Creek, WV 26218/304-472-7901
Specialties: Working/using straight knives and folders of all designs. **Patterns:** Hunters, locking folders and utility/camp knives. **Technical:** Grinds ATS-34, D2 and CPM T440V. Offers dove-tailed bolsters and spacers, filework and scrimshaw. **Prices:** $125 to $400; some to $740. **Remarks:** Full-time maker; first knife sold in 1990. Doing business as Drost Custom Knives. **Mark:** Name, city and state.

DUBE, PAUL, P.O. Box 216, Chaska, MN 55318/612-566-9097
Specialties: Traditional working and using straight knives, high-art knives and period pieces of his design and to customer specs. **Patterns:** Fighters, Bowies, daggers, utility knives. **Technical:** Forges A2, 1050, 1095, S5, ATS-34; stock removal 01, S7 and Vascowear. **Prices:** $80 to $1,500; some to $6,000. **Remarks:** Full-time maker; first knife sold in 1988. Doing business as Troll Hammer Forge. **Mark:** Varies.

DUBLIN, DENNIS, 708 Stanley St., Box 986, Enderby, BC VOE 1V0, CANADA/604-838-6753
Specialties: Working straight knives and folders, plain or fancy. **Patterns:** Hunters and Bowies, locking hunters, combination knives/axes. **Technical:** Forges and grinds high carbon steels. **Prices:** $100 to $400; some higher. **Remarks:** Full-time maker; first knife sold in 1970. **Mark:** Name.

DUFF, BILL, P.O. Box 694, Virginia City, NV 89440/702-847-0566
Specialties: Working straight knives and folders. **Patterns:** Hunters and Bowies; locking folders and interframes. **Technical:** Grinds D2, 440C and 154CM. **Prices:** $175 to $3,500. **Remarks:** Part-time maker; first knife sold in 1976. **Mark:** Name, city, state and date.

custom knifemakers

DUFOUR, ARTHUR J., 8120 De Armoun Rd., Anchorage, AK 99516/907-345-1701 **Specialties:** Working straight knives from standard patterns. **Patterns:** Hunters, Bowies, camp and fishing knives—grinded thin and pointed. **Technical:** Grinds 440C, ATS-34, AEB-L. Tempers 57-58R; hollow-grinds. **Prices:** $135; some to $250. **Remarks:** Part-time maker; first knife sold in 1970. **Mark:** Prospector logo.

DUGGER, DAVE, 2504 West 51, Westwood, KS 66205/913-831-2382 **Specialties:** Working straight knives; fantasy pieces. **Patterns:** Hunters, boots and daggers in one-of-a-kind styles. **Technical:** Grinds D2, 440C and 154CM. **Prices:** $75 to $350; some to $1,200. **Remarks:** Part-time maker; first knife sold in 1979. Not currently accepting orders. Doing business as Dog Knives. **Mark:** DOG.

DUNGY HANDCRAFTED (See Dungy, Lawrence)

DUNGY, LAWRENCE, 8 Southmont Dr., Little Rock, AR 72209/501-568-2769 **Specialties:** Working straight knives and folders. **Patterns:** Bowies, skinners, hunters, boots, bird and trout knives. **Technical:** Grinds stainless and plain steels. **Prices:** $65 to $800. **Remarks:** Part-time maker; first knife sold in 1983. **Mark:** Dungy Handcrafted.

DUNKERLEY, RICK, Baldy Mtn. Ranch, Lincoln, MT 59639/406-362-4942 **Specialties:** Hand-forged working knives. **Patterns:** Hunters, skinners, camp knives, fighters and Bowies. **Technical:** Forges 5160 and 52100; makes his Damascus, cable Damascus and chain Damascus. Natural handle materials. **Prices:** Start at $150. **Remarks:** Full-time maker; first knife sold in 1984. **Mark:** Baldy Mountain Forge, city, state.

DUNN, CHARLES K., 17740 GA Hwy. 116, Shiloh, GA 31826/706-846-2666 **Specialties:** Fancy and working straight knives and folders of his design and to customer specs. **Patterns:** Bowies, hunters and locking folders. **Technical:** Grinds 440C and ATS34. Engraves; filework offered. **Prices:** $75 to $300. **Remarks:** Part-time maker; first knife sold in 1988. **Mark:** First initial, last name, city, state.

DUNN, MELVIN T., 5830 NW Carlson Rd., Rossville, KS 66533/913-584-6856 **Specialties:** Traditional working straight knives and folders. **Patterns:** Locking folders, straight hunters, fishing and kitchen knives. **Technical:** Grinds D2, 440C, A2 and 154CM; likes latest materials; heat-treats. **Prices:** $60 to $500. **Remarks:** Full-time maker; first knife sold in 1972. **Mark:** Name in script.

DUNN, STEVE, 376 Biggerstaff Rd., Smiths Grove, KY 42171/502-563-9830 **Specialties:** Working and using straight knives of his design; period pieces. **Patterns:** Bowies, fighters and utility/camp knives. **Technical:** Forges his Damascus, 01, 5160 and old buggy springs. Offers filework. **Prices:** Moderate to upscale. **Remarks:** Spare-time maker; first knife sold in 1990. **Mark:** Last name and JS.

DURAN, JERRY T., P.O. Box 80692, Albuquerque, NM 87198-0692/505-255-4255 **Specialties:** Working straight knives, folders and art knives. **Patterns:** Hunters, skinners, bird and trout knives, fighters. **Technical:** Grinds 440C, ATS-34. Prefers natural handle materials. **Prices:** $125 to $500; some higher. **Remarks:** Paret-time maker; influenced by Joeseph G. Cordova. **Mark:** Initials in elk rack logo.

DURIO, FRED, 289 Gulino St., Opelousas, LA 70570/318-948-4831 **Specialties:** Working straight knives; period pieces. **Patterns:** Bowies, camp knives, small hunters, fancy period pieces, miniatures. **Technical:** Forges and grinds W2, 5160, 1095 and 01. Makes own Damascus and forge-welds cable Damascus. Offers filework and tapered tangs; prefers exotic and natural materials. **Prices:** $100 to $350; some to $1,000. **Remarks:** Part-time maker; first knife sold in 1986. **Mark:** Last name and J.S.

DUTCH CREEK FORGE & FOUNDRY (See Knickmeyer, Hank)

DUTTON MOUNTAIN FORGE (See Anders, David)

DUVALL, FRED, 10715 Hwy. 190, Benton, AR 72015/501-778-9360 **Specialties:** Working straight knives and folders. **Patterns:** Locking folders, slip joints, hunters, fighters and Bowies. **Technical:** Grinds D2 and CPM 440V; forges 5160. **Prices:** $100 to $400; some to $800. **Remarks:** Part-time maker; first knife sold in 1973. **Mark:** Last name.

DUVALL, LARRY E., Rt. 3, Gallatin, MO 64640/816-663-2742 **Specialties:** Fancy working straight knives and folders. **Patterns:** Hunters to swords, minis to Bowies; locking folders. **Technical:** Grinds D2, 440C and 154CM. **Prices:** $150 to $350; some to $2,000. **Remarks:** Part-time maker; first knife sold in 1980. **Mark:** Name and address in logo.

DYESS, EDDIE, 1005 Hamilton, Roswell, NM 88201/505-623-5599 **Specialties:** Working and using straight knives in standard patterns. **Patterns:** Hunters and fighters. **Technical:** Grinds 440C, 154CM and D2 on request. **Prices:** $85 to $135; some to $250. **Remarks:** Spare-time maker; first knife sold in 1980. **Mark:** Last name.

DYRNOE, PER, Sydskraenten 10, Tulstrup, DK 3400 Hilleroed, DENMARK/+45 42287041 **Specialties:** Hand-crafted knives with zirconia ceramic blades. **Patterns:** Hunters, skinners, Norwegian-style tolleknives, most in animal-like ergonomic shapes. **Technical:** Handles of exotic hardwood, horn, fossile ivory, etc. Norwegian-style sheaths. **Prices:** Start at $500. **Remarks:** Part-time maker in cooperation with Hans J. Henriksen; first knife sold in 1993. **Mark:** Initial logo.

e

E&E EMPORIUM (See Edwards, Lynn)

EASLER, PAULA, P.O. Box 301-1025, Cross Anchor Rd., Woodruff, SC 29388/803-476-7830; FAx: 803-476-3940 **Specialties:** Traditional fancy and embellished straight knives of her design. **Patterns:** Miniatures only—hunters, fighters, tantos, razors and mini-replicas. **Technical:** Grinds ATS-34, commercial Damascus. Stainless steel pins and bolsters. Heat-treats blades, many have file-worked tapered tangs; hand-rubbed satin finish standard; natural handle materials and gems. **Prices:** $85 to $400; some to $1,000. **Remarks:** Spare-time maker; first knife sold in 1989. **Mark:** First initial, last name in block letters.

EASLER JR., RUSSELL O., P.O. Box 301, Woodruff, SC 29388/803-476-7830; FAX: 803-476-3940 **Specialties:** Working straight knives and folders. **Patterns:** Hunters, tantos and boots; locking folders and interframes. **Technical:** Grinds 440C, 154CM and ATS-34. **Prices:** $85 to $250; some to $600. **Remarks:** Part-time maker; first knife sold in 1973. **Mark:** Name or name with bear logo.

EATON, AL, P.O. Box 43, Clayton, CA 94517/510-672-5351 **Specialties:** One-of-a-kind high-art knives and fantasy knives of his design, full size and miniature. **Patterns:** Hunters, fighters, daggers. **Technical:** Grinds 440C, 154CM and ATS-34; ivory and metal carving. **Prices:** $125 to $3,000; some to $5,000. **Remarks:** Full-time maker; first knife sold in 1977. **Mark:** Full name, city and state.

EATON, RICK, 5560 Forbestown Rd., Forbestown, CA 94941/916-675-1632 **Specialties:** Straight and folding art daggers. **Patterns:** Bowies, daggers, fighters and hunters. **Technical:** Grinds 154CM, ATS-34, 440C and other maker's Damascus. Offers high-quality hand engraving, Bulino and gold inlay. **Prices:** $250 to $4,000; some higher. **Remarks:** Full-time maker; first knife sold in 1982. **Mark:** Full name and address.

ECK, LARRY A., P.O. Box 665, Terrebonne, OR 97760/503-548-7599 **Specialties:** Traditional working and using straight knives of his design, to customer specs and in standard patterns. **Patterns:** Boots, Bowies, fighters, hunters, fillets and tantos. **Technical:** Grinds ATS-34, D2, 440C and commercial Damascus. Prefers natural handle materials. Offers mirror and hand-rubbed finishes. **Prices:** $145 to $350; some to $750. **Remarks:** Part-time maker; first knife sold in 1991. **Mark:** First and middle initials, last name and state in logo.

EDGE, TOMMY, P.O. Box 156, Cash, AR 72421/501-477-5210

EDWARDS, FAIN E., 209 E. Mtn. Ave., Jacksonville, AL 36265/205-435-4994; FAX: 205-435-8499 **Specialties:** Classic and traditional knives, working/using knives and period pieces. **Patterns:** Bowies, daggers, hunters, kitchen knives, locking and slip-joint folders, swords and utility/camp knives. **Technical:** Forges Damascus and 5160. **Prices:** $500 to $2,500; some to $6,000. **Remarks:** Full-time maker; first knife sold in 1976. **Mark:** First and middle initials, last name, city and state with two bleeding hearts.

directory

EDWARDS—ENGLEBRETSON

EDWARDS, LYNN, Rt. 2, Box 614, W. Columbia, TX 77486/409-345-4080
Specialties: Traditional working and using straight knives of his design and to customer specs. **Patterns:** Bowies, hunters and utility/camp knives. **Technical:** Forges 5168 and 01; forges and grinds D2. Triple-hardens on request; offers silver wire inlay, stone inlays and spacers, filework. **Prices:** $100 to $395; some to $800. **Remarks:** Part-time maker; first knife sold in 1988. Doing business as E&E Emporium. **Mark:** Last name in script.

EK, GARY WHITNEY, 1580 NE 125th St., North Miami, FL 33161/305-891-2283
Specialties: Working straight knives of his design and to customer specs; period pieces. **Patterns:** Bowies, fighters and special-effect knives and swords. **Technical:** Grinds D2, Sandvik 13 c 26; forges and grinds 43-40 Ni Crm Moly. Offers custom refinishing and sharpening. **Prices:** $150 to $450; some to $1,200. **Remarks:** Full-time maker; first knife sold in 1971. **Mark:** Name or EKNIVES, city.

EKNIVES WORKS (See Ek, Gary Whitney)

EKLUND, ROLF, Soltappan, S-195 95 Rosersberg, SWEDEN/46-076036005
Specialties: Fishing and hunting knives of his design. **Patterns:** Swedish fishing and hunting knives. **Technical:** Forges his own laminated blades. Offers black oak handles he dived for from 17th century wreck. Traditional Swedish cowhide sheaths provided. **Prices:** $150 to $600. **Remarks:** Spare-time maker. **Mark:** Initials.

ELDRIDGE, ALLAN, 1424 Kansas Lane, Gallatin, TN 37066/615-452-6027
Specialties: Fancy classic straight knives in standard patterns. **Patterns:** Hunters, Bowies, fighters and miniatures. **Technical:** Grinds 01 and Damascus. Engraves, silver-wire inlays, pearl inlays, scrimshaws and offers filework. **Prices:** $50 to $500; some to $1,200. **Remarks:** Spare-time maker; first knife sold in 1965. **Mark:** Initials.

ELISHEWITZ, ALLEN, 6020 Richwater, Dallas, TX 75252/214-931-3746
Specialties: Collectible high-tech working straight knives and folders of his design. **Patterns:** Fighters, combat knives, skinners and utility/camp knives. **Technical:** Grinds ATS-34, D2, A2 and Vascowear. All designs drafted and field-tested. **Prices:** $200 to $500; some to $1,000. **Remarks:** Full-time maker; first knife sold in 1989. **Mark:** Initials in a box with a dragon head.

ELKINS, R. VAN, P.O. Box 156, Bonita, LA 71223/318-823-2124
Specialties: High-art Bowies, fighters, folders and period daggers; all one-of-a-kind pieces. **Patterns:** Welcomes customer designs. **Technical:** Forges his own Damascus in several patterns, 01 and 5160. **Prices:** $250 to $2,800. **Remarks:** First knife sold in 1984. **Mark:** Last name.

THE ELK RACK (See Peele, Bryan)

ELLEFSON, JOEL, 1233 Storymill Rd., Bozeman, MT 59715/406-587-5905
Specialties: Working straight knives, fancy daggers and one-of-a-kinds. **Patterns:** Hunters, daggers and some folders. **Technical:** Grinds A2, 440C and ATS-34. Makes own mokume in bronze, brass, silver and shibuishi; makes brass/steel blades. **Prices:** $75 to $500; some to $2,000. **Remarks:** Part-time maker; first knife sold in 1978. **Mark:** Stylized last initial.

ELLENBERG, WILLIAM C., 10 Asbury Ave., Melrose Park, PA 19126/215-635-1313
Specialties: Traditional working and using straight knives of his design. **Patterns:** Bowies, hunters and utility/camp knives. **Technical:** Flat-grinds 440C and ATS-34. Offers hardwood or Micarta handles. Stitches leather sheaths with stainless steel wire. **Prices:** $150 to $250; some to $450. **Remarks:** Spare-time maker; first knife sold in 1990. **Mark:** None.

ELLERBE, W.B., 3871 Osceola Rd., Geneva, FL 32732/305-349-5818
Specialties: Period and primitive knives and sheaths. **Patterns:** Bowies to patch knives, some tomahawks. Offers a line of low-priced brush-finished knives. **Technical:** Grinds Sheffield 01 and files. **Prices:** Start at $35. **Remarks:** Full-time maker; first knife sold in 1971. Doing business as Cypress Bend Custom Knives. **Mark:** Last name or initials.

ELLIOTT, J.P., 4507 Kanawha Ave., Charleston, WV 25304/304-925-5045
Specialties: Classic and traditional straight knives and folders of his design and to customer specs. **Patterns:** Hunters, locking folders and Bowies. **Technical:** Grinds ATS-34, 154CM, 01, D2 and T-440-V. All guards silver-soldered; bolsters are pinned on straight knives, spot-welded on folders. **Prices:** $80 to $265; some to $1,000. **Remarks:** Full-time maker; first knife sold in 1972. **Mark:** First and middle initials, last name, knifemaker, city, state.

ELLIOTT, MARCUS, 3 Bryn Maelgwyn, Llanrhos, Llandudno, Gwynedd, North Wales, GREAT BRITAIN/0492-584352
Specialties: Fancy working knives. **Patterns:** Boots and small hunters. **Technical:** Grinds 01, 440C and ATS-34. **Prices:** $160 to $250. **Remarks:** Spare-time maker; first knife sold in 1981. Makes only a few knives each year. **Mark:** Last name.

ELLIS, DAVID, 3505 Camino Del Rio S. #334, San Diego, CA 92108/619-285-1305 days; 619-632-7302 evenings
Specialties: Fighters and Bowies. **Patterns:** Utility knives. **Technical:** Forges and grinds 5160, 01, 1095; now working with pattern-welded Damascus. Most knives have hand-rubbed finish and single and double temper lines. All knives are double or triple hardened and triple drawn. Prefers natural handle materials. **Prices:** $250 to $450; some to $1,500. **Remarks:** Part-time maker; first knife sold in 1988. **Mark:** Last name.

ELLIS, WILLIAM DEAN, 8875 N. Barton, Fresno, CA 93720/209-299-0303
Specialties: Classic and fancy knives of his design. **Patterns:** Boots, fighters and utility knives. **Technical:** Grinds ATS34, D2 and Damascus. Offers tapered tangs and six patterns of filework; tooled multi-colored sheaths. **Prices:** $180 to $350; some to $1,300. **Remarks:** Part-time maker; first knife sold in 1991. Doing business as Billy's Blades. **Mark:** "B" in a five-point star next to "Billy", city and state within a rounded-corner rectangle.

EMBRETSEN, KAJ, P.O. Box 54, S-82821 Edsbyn, SWEDEN/46-271-20883; FAX: 46-271-22961
Specialties: Straight knives. **Patterns:** Traditional Swedish and modern hunters; folders. **Technical:** Forges Damascus. Uses only his blades; natural materials. **Prices:** Upscale. **Remarks:** Full-time maker. **Mark:** Name.

EMERSON, ERNEST R., 4142 W. 173nd St., Torrance, CA 90504/310-542-3050
Specialties: High-tech folders and combat fighters. **Patterns:** Fighters, linerlock combat folders and SPECWAR combat knives. **Technical:** Grinds ATS-34 and D2. Makes folders with titanium fittings, liners and locks. Chisel grind specialist. **Prices:** $275 to $475; some to $3,000. **Remarks:** Full-time maker; first knife sold in 1983. **Mark:** Last name or Viper.

ENCE, JIM, 145 S. 200 East, Richfield, UT 84701/801-896-6206
Specialties: High-art period pieces. **Patterns:** Daggers, art folders, fancy boot knives, fighters, Bowies and occasional hunters. **Technical:** Grinds 440C; makes his own and buys Damascus. **Prices:** $300 to $5,000; some higher. **Remarks:** Full-time maker; first knife sold in 1977. **Mark:** Name, city, state.

ENDERS, ROBERT, 3028 White Rd., Cement City, MI 49233/517-529-9667
Specialties: Pocketknives and working straight knives. **Patterns:** Traditional folders with natural materials. **Technical:** Grinds D2, 01, 440C and ATS-34. **Prices:** $125 to $300; some to $1,200. **Remarks:** Full-time maker; first knife sold in 1981. **Mark:** Name in state map logo.

ENGLAND, VIRGIL, 629 W. 15th Ave., Anchorage, AK 99501/907-274-9494
Specialties: Edged weapons and equipage, one-of-a-kind only. **Patterns:** Axes, swords, lances and body armor. **Technical:** Forges and grinds as pieces dictate. Offers stainless and Damascus. **Prices:** Upscale. **Remarks:** A veteran knifemaker. No commissions. **Mark:** Stylized initials.

ENGLE, WILLIAM, RR1, Box 58 E, Boonville, MO 65233/816-882-6277
Specialties: Traditional working and using straight knives of his design, mostly for the military. **Patterns:** Hunters, Bowies and fighters. **Technical:** Grinds 440C, ATS-34 and Damascus. **Prices:** $150 to $375; some to $700. **Remarks:** Full-time maker; first knife sold in 1982. All knives come with certificate of authenticity. Donated some knives to military special forces during Desert Storm. **Mark:** Last name in block lettering.

ENGLEBRETSON, GEORGE, 1209 NW 49th St., Oklahoma City, OK 73118/405-840-4784
Specialties: Working straight knives and period pieces. **Patterns:** Hunters, Bowies, fishing knives and axes. **Technical:** Grinds A2, D2, 440C, ATS-34 and C-350.

custom knifemakers
ENGLISH—FERDINAND

Prices: Start at $100. **Remarks:** Full-time maker; first knife sold in 1967. **Mark:** "By George," name and city.

ENGLISH, JIM, 14586 Olive Vista Dr., Jamul, CA 91935/619-669-0833
Specialties: Traditional working straight knives to customer specs. **Patterns:** Hunters, Bowies, fighters, tantos, daggers, boot and utility/camp knives. **Technical:** Grinds 440C, ATS-34, commercial Damascus and customer choice. **Prices:** $130 to $350. **Remarks:** Part-time maker; first knife sold in 1985. In addition to custom line, also does business as Mountain Home Knives. **Mark:** Double A, Double J logo.

ENGNATH, BOB, 1217 B. Crescent Dr., Glendale, CA 91205/818-241-3629
Specialties: Replica antique tantos; complete knives and swords. **Patterns:** Traditional Japanese knives; some miniatures. Kit blades also offered. **Technical:** Makes soft-back/hard-edge blades with temper lines. **Prices:** $125 to $350; some to $600. **Remarks:** Full-time maker/grinder; first knife sold in 1972. **Mark:** KODAN in Japanese script.

ENNIS, RAY W., 509 S. 3rd St., Grand Forks, ND 58201/701-775-8216/800-468-4867
Specialties: Working straight knives and folders of his design or to customer specs. **Patterns:** Hunters, fighters and locking folders. **Technical:** Grinds ATS-34, D2 and 01. **Prices:** $100 to $500; some to $1,500. **Remarks:** Full-time maker; first knife sold in 1973. **Mark:** Initials connected.

ENOS III, THOMAS M., 12302 State Rd. 535, Orlando, FL 32836/407-239-6205
Specialties: Heavy-duty working straight knives to customer specs; unusual designs. **Patterns:** Machetes, saltwater sport knives, carvers. **Technical:** Grinds 440C, D2, 154CM. **Prices:** $75 to $1,000. **Remarks:** Full-time maker; first knife sold in 1972. **Mark:** Name in knife logo and date, type of steel and serial number.

ERIKSEN, JAMES THORLIEF, 3830 Dividend Dr., Garland, TX 75042/214-494-3667; FAX: 214-238-1510
Specialties: Heavy-duty working and using straight knives and folders utilizing traditional, Viking original and customer specification patterns. Some high-tech and fancy/embellished knives available. **Patterns:** Bowies, hunters, skinners, boot and belt knives, utility/camp knives, fighters, daggers, locking folders, slip-joint folders and kitchen knives. **Technical:** Hollow-grinds 440C, D2, ASP-23, ATS-34, 154CM, Vascowear. **Prices:** $150 to $300; some to $600. **Remarks:** Full-time maker; first knife sold in 1985. Doing business as Viking Knives. **Mark:** VIKING or VIKING USA for export.

ERICKSON, CURT, 449 Washington Blvd., Ogden, UT 84404/801-782-1184
Specialties: Daggers and large knives of integral construction. **Patterns:** Period pieces; Bowies and hunting knives. **Technical:** Grinds 440C and commercial Damascus steel; sculpts and carves components. **Prices:** $240 to $1,500; some to $3,000. **Remarks:** Full-time maker; first knife sold in 1982. **Mark:** Name, state.

ERICKSON, L.M., P.O. Box 132, Liberty, UT 84310/801-745-2026
Specialties: Straight knives; period pieces. **Patterns:** Bowies, fighters, boots and hunters. **Technical:** Grinds 440C, 154CM and commercial Damascus. **Prices:** $200 to $900; some to $1,900. **Remarks:** Full-time maker; first knife sold in 1981. **Mark:** Name, city, state.

ERICKSON, WALTER E., 23883 Ada St., Warren, MI 48091/313-759-1105
Specialties: Unusual survival knives and high-tech working knives. **Patterns:** Butterflies, hunters, tantos. **Technical:** Grinds ATS-34 or customer choice. **Prices:** $150 to $500; some to $1,300. **Remarks:** Full-time maker; first knife sold in 1981. **Mark:** ERIC or last name.

ES CUSTOM KNIVES (See Shadley, Eugene W.)

ESAKI, SHUSUKE, Bl Fukoku Seimei Building, 2-4 Komatubara Cho Xitaku, Osaka City, 530 JAPAN/06-313-2525; FAX: 06-313-2626
Specialties: Classic and high-art knives of his design. **Patterns:** Bowies, daggers and fighters. **Technical:** Grinds ATS-34, Damascus and 440C. **Prices:** $200 to $3,000. **Remarks:** Spare-time maker; first knife sold in 1097. **Mark:** NA.

ESSEGIAN, RICHARD, 7387 E. Tulare St., Fresno, CA 93727/309-255-5950
Specialties: Fancy working knives of his design; art knives. **Patterns:** Bowies and some small hunters. **Technical:** Grinds A2, D2, 440C and 154CM. Engraves and inlays. **Prices:** Start at $600. **Remarks:** Part-time maker; first knife sold in 1986. **Mark:** Last name, city and state.

ETZLER, JOHN, 11200 N. Island, Grafton, OH 44044/216-748-3980
Specialties: Fancy and working straight knives and folders of his design and to customer specs. **Patterns:** Fighters, hunters, swords and utility knives. **Technical:** Forges and grinds nickel Damascus and tool steel; grinds stainless steels. Prefers exotic, natural materials. **Prices:** $175 to $300; some to $6,000. **Remarks:** Full-time maker; first knife sold in 1992. **Mark:** Name or initials.

EVANS, GRACE (See Evans, Vincent K. and Grace)

EVANS, VINCENT K. and GRACE, HCR 1, Box 5221, Keaau, HI 96749/808-966-4831
Specialties: Working straight knives; period pieces; swords. **Patterns:** Scottish patterns, clip-point using knives. **Technical:** Forges 5160 and his own Damascus. **Prices:** $50 to $300; some to $3,000. **Remarks:** Full-time maker; first knife sold in 1983. **Mark:** Bronze-filled double last initial with fish logo.

EWING, JOHN H., 3276 Dutch Valley Rd., Clinton, TN 37716/615-457-5757
Specialties: Working straight knives. **Patterns:** Hunters. **Technical:** Grinds 440C and 01; prefers forging. **Prices:** $150 to $1,000. **Remarks:** Part-time maker; first knife sold in 1985. **Mark:** First initial, last name, Handmade.

EXOTIC BLADES (See Hesser, David)

FALCON CREST FORGE (See Fowler, Charles R.)

FALLING WATERS FORGE (See Barnes, Aubrey G.)

FANNIN, DAVID A. and BRUMAGEN, JERRY, 2050 Idle Hour Center #191, Lexington, KY 40502
Specialties: High-tech classic straight knives; period pieces; traditional working knives. **Patterns:** Hunters, fighters and swords. **Technical:** Draws wire from Damascus billets for wire Damascus. High-density, migrationless and hand-smelted Sagami school Damascus steel. Offers Hamon tempering; makes mokume. **Prices:** $200 to $1,200. **Remarks:** Full-time maker; first knife sold in 1985. Doing business as Athens Forge. **Mark:** None.

FASSIO, MELVIN G., 4585 Twin Cr. Rd., Bonner, MT 59823/406-244-5208
Specialties: Working folders to customer specs. **Patterns:** Locking folders, hunters and traditional-style knives. **Technical:** Grinds 440C. **Prices:** $60 to $100; some to $200. **Remarks:** Part-time maker; first knife sold in 1975. **Mark:** Name and city, dove logo.

FAUCHEAUX, HOWARD J., P.O. Box 206, Loreauville, LA 70552/318-229-6467
Specialties: Working straight knives and folders; period pieces. **Patterns:** Traditional locking folders, hunters, fighters and Bowies. **Technical:** Forges W2, 1095 and his own Damascus. **Prices:** $165 to $500; some to $1,500. **Remarks:** Spare-time maker; first knife sold in 1969. **Mark:** Last name.

FAULKNER, ALLAN, Rt. 11, Box 161, Jasper, AL 35501/205-387-0083
Specialties: Working and fancy straight knives; kitchen cutlery. **Patterns:** Pocketknives, traditional folders, miniatures, hunters, fighters and Bowies. **Technical:** Grinds D2, 440C and 154CM; prefers natural handle materials. **Prices:** $150 to $350; some to $1,500. **Remarks:** Part-time maker, first knife sold in 1978. **Mark:** Last name.

FECAS, STEPHEN J., 1312 Shadow Lane, Anderson, SC 29625/803-287-4834
Specialties: Working straight knives in standard patterns; some period pieces. **Patterns:** Hunters to claws, folding slip-joints to buckskinners. **Technical:** Grinds D2, 440C and 154CM; most knives hand-finished to 600 grit. **Prices:** $140 to $400; some to $750. **Remarks:** Part-time maker; first knife sold in 1977. **Mark:** Last name.

FELFIDEL, RALPH, 15 Budlong Ave., Warrich, RI 02888

FERDINAND, DON, 229 Flounce Rock Dr., Prospect, OR 97536/503-560-3355

directory
FERGUSON—FORSTALL

Specialties: Working knives and period pieces; all tool steel Damascus. **Patterns:** Bowies, push knives and fishing knives. **Technical:** Forges high-carbon alloy steels—L6, D2; makes his own Damascus. **Prices:** $100 to $500. **Remarks:** Full-time maker since 1980. Does business as Wyvern. **Mark:** Initials connected.

FERGUSON, JIM, P.O. Box 40247, Downey, CA 90239/310-862-7461
Specialties: One-of-a-kind straight knives. **Patterns:** Bowies, daggers, fighters and push blades. **Technical:** Forges nickel and 1095 (twisted nickel) Damascus; grinds. **Prices:** $100 to $3,000. **Remarks:** Part-time maker; first knife sold in 1987. Doing business as Twisted Nickel Knives. **Mark:** Name.

FERGUSON, JIM, P.O. Box 764, San Angelo, TX 76902/915-651-6656
Specialties: Straight working knives and folders. **Patterns:** Working belt knives, hunters, folders, hatchets, integrals, kitchen knives. **Technical:** Grinds ATS-34, D2 and Vascowear. **Prices:** $60 to $200; some to $600. **Remarks:** Full-time maker; first knife sold in 1987. **Mark:** First and middle initials, last name.

FERGUSON, LEE, Rt. 2, Box 109, Hindsville, AR 72738/501-443-0084
Specialties: Straight working knives and folders, some fancy. **Patterns:** Hunters, daggers, swords, locking folders and slip-joints. **Technical:** Grinds D2, 440C and ATS-34; heat-treats. **Prices:** $50 to $600; some to $4,000. **Remarks:** Part-time maker; first knife sold in 1977. **Mark:** Last name.

FERRARA, THOMAS, 122 Madison Dr., Naples, FL 33942/813-597-3363; FAX: 813-597-3363
Specialties: High-art, traditional and working straight knives and folders of all designs. **Patterns:** Boots, Bowies, Daggers, Fighters and hunters. **Technical:** Grinds 440C, D2 and ATS-34; heat-treats. **Prices:** $100 to $700; some to $1,300. **Remarks:** Part-time maker; first knife sold in 1983. **Mark:** Last name.

FIELDER, WILLIAM V., 8406 Knowland Circle, Richmond, VA 23229 23229/804-750-1198
Specialties: Fancy working straight knives and folders of his design. **Patterns:** Hunters, boots and daggers; locking folders, interframes and traditional-style knives. **Technical:** Forges W2, 01 and his own Damascus; likes wire inlay. **Prices:** $25 to $500; some to $1,000. **Remarks:** Full-time maker; first knife sold in 1982. **Mark:** Last name, J.S.

FIKES, JIMMY L., P.O. Box 3457, Jasper, AL 35502/205-387-9302
Specialties: High-art working knives; artifact knives; using knives with cord-wrapped handles; swords and combat weapons. **Patterns:** Axes to buckskinners, camp knives to miniatures, tantos to tomahawks; springless folders. **Technical:** Forges W2, 01 and his own Damascus. **Prices:** $135 to $3,000; exceptional knives to $7,000. **Remarks:** Full-time maker. **Mark:** Stylized initials.

FINE CUSTOM KNIVES (See Nielson, Jeff V.)

FIORINI, BILL, 1590 Hwy. 16, LaCrescent, MN 55947/507-895-2050
Specialties: Fancy working knives and lockbacks. **Patterns:** Hunters, boots, Japanese-style knives and kitchen/utility knives. **Technical:** Forges own Damascus. **Prices:** Full range. **Remarks:** Full-time metalsmith researching pattern materials. **Mark:** W over F with Japanese lettering.

FIREPOINT KNIVES (See Renner, Terry Lee)

FISCHER, CLYDE E., HCR 40, Box 133, Nixon, TX 78140-9400/512-582-1353
Specialties: Working knives for serious and professional hunters. **Patterns:** Heavy-duty hunters and survival blades; camp knives and buckskinner knives. **Technical:** Forges and grinds L6, 01 and his own Damascus. **Prices:** $100 to $250; some to $800. **Remarks:** Full-time maker; first knife sold in 1957. **Mark:** Fish.

FISHER, JAY, 104 S. Main St., P.O. Box 267, Magdalena, NM 87825/505-854-2507
Specialties: High-art working and using straight knives of his design. **Patterns:** Hunters, daggers and high-art sculptures. **Technical:** Grinds 440C, ATS-34 and D2. Prolific maker of stone-handled knives. **Prices:** $125 to $650; some to $7,000. **Remarks:** Full-time maker; first knife sold in 1984. **Mark:** Very fine—JaFisher—Quality Custom Knives.

FISHER, THEO (TED), 8115 Modoc Lane, Montague, CA 9064/916-459-3804
Specialties: Moderately-priced working knives in carbon steel. **Patterns:** Hunters, fighters, kitchen and buckskinner knives. Damascus miniatures. **Technical:** Grinds ATS-34, L6 and 440C. **Prices:** $65 to $165; exceptional knives to $300. **Remarks:** Full-time maker; first knife sold in 1981. **Mark:** Name in banner logo.

FISK, JERRY, Rt. 1, Box 41, Lockesburg, AR 71846/501-289-3240
Specialties: Edged weapons, collectible and functional. **Patterns:** Bowies, daggers, swords, hunters, camp knives and others. **Technical:** Forges 5168 and his own Damascus. Offers filework. **Prices:** $295 to $7,000. **Remarks:** Full-time maker; first knife sold in 1980. **Mark:** Name, MS.

FISTER, JIM, 5067 Fisherville Rd., Simpsonville, KY 40067/502-834-7841
Specialties: Bowies and hunters. **Patterns:** Period pieces, buckskinners, fighters, daggers and folders. **Technical:** Forges and grinds 01, 5160, 52100, his own wire, regular and exotic Damascus and 440C. **Prices:** $100 to $900; some to $1,500. **Remarks:** Part-time maker; first knife sold in 1982. **Mark:** Last name.

FITZGERALD, DENNIS M., 4219 Alverado Dr., Fort Wayne, IN 46816-2847/219-447-1081
Specialties: Straight working knives. **Patterns:** Skinners, fighters, camp and utility knives; period pieces. **Technical:** Forges W2, 01, billet and cable-wire Damascus. Likes integral guards, bolsters and pommels. **Prices:** $100 to $500. **Remarks:** Part-time maker; first knife sold in 1985. Doing business as The Ringing Circle. **Mark:** Name and circle logo.

FIVE RUNS FORGE (See Bullard, Bill)

FLECHTNER, CHRIS, 224 St. Camille St., Fitchburg, MA 01420/508-342-4371

FLINT STEEL KNIVES (See Anderson, Michael D.)

FLOOD, JAMES (NOAH), P.O. Box 216, Chaska, MN 55318/612-448-3379
Specialties: High-art straight knives and period pieces of his design and to customer specs. **Patterns:** Bowies, daggers and fighters. **Technical:** Forges high-carbon steels; grinds 01 and Vascowear. **Prices:** $100 to $600; some to $1,500. **Remarks:** Full-time maker; first knife sold in 1989. Doing business as Troll Hammer Forge. **Mark:** Etched signature.

FLOURNOY, JOE, 5750 Lisbon Rd., El Dorado, AR 71730/501-863-7208
Specialties: Large Bowies and camp knives. **Patterns:** Hunters, Bowies, folders and daggers. **Technical:** Forges only high-carbon steel, steel cable and his own Damascus. **Prices:** $250 to $4,000. **Remarks:** Part-time maker; first knife sold in 1977. **Mark:** Last name and MS in script.

FLYNN, BRUCE, 8139 W. County Rd. 650 S, Knightstown, IN 46148-9348/317-779-4034
Specialties: Workign straight knives and folders. **Patterns:** Fighters, Bowies, daggers, skinners and hunters. **Technical:** Grinds 440C, 154CM and D2. **Prices:** Moderate. **Remarks:** Full-time maker. **Mark:** First and middle initials, last name.

FOGARIZZU, BOITEDDU, via Crispi, 6, 07016 Pattada, ITALY
Specialties: Traditional italian straight knives and folders. **Patterns:** Collectible folders. **Technical:** Forges and grinds 12C27, ATS-34 and his Damascus. **Prices:** $200 to $3,000. **Remarks:** Full-time maker; first knife sold in 1958. **Mark:** Full name and registered logo.

FOGG, DON, Rt. 6, Box 107, Alma Station Rd., Jasper, AL 35501-8813/205-483-0822
Specialties: Straight knives. **Patterns:** Bowies, stout hunters, daggers. **Technical:** Forges carbon steels, *san mai* and Damascus; all natural materials. **Prices:** $150 to $5,000. **Remarks:** Full-time maker; first knife sold in 1976. Doing business as Kemal. **Mark:** 24K gold cherry blossom.

FORD, ALLEN, 3927 Plumcrest Rd., Smyrna, GA 30080/404-432-5061
Specialties: Art knives of his design. **Patterns:** Bowies, daggers and hunters. **Technical:** Hand finishes every knife. Scrimshaws. **Mark:** First initial, last name in script.

FORSTALL, AL, 971 Walnut St., Sudell, LA 70460/504-643-6217
Specialties: Traditional working and using straight knives of his design. **Patterns:** Fighters, hunters and utility/camp knives. **Technical:** Grinds ATS-34, 440C and commercial Damascus. **Prices:** $60 to $250. **Remarks:** Spare-time maker; first knife sold in 1991. **Mark:** The number 4 with "stall" around it.

custom knifemakers
FORTHOFER—FREER

FORTHOFER, PETE, 5535 Hwy. 93S, Whitefish, MT 59937/406-862-2674
Specialties: Interframes with checkered wood inlays; working straight knives. **Patterns:** Interframe folders and traditional-style knives; hunters, fighters and Bowies. **Technical:** Grinds D2, 440C, 154CM and ATS-34. **Prices:** $250 to $1,000; some to $1,500. **Remarks:** Part-time maker; full-time gunsmith. First knife sold in 1979. **Mark:** Name and logo.

FOSTER, AL, HC 73, Box 117, Dogpatch, AR 72648/501-446-5137
Specialties: Working straight knives and folders. **Patterns:** Bowies, hunters, lockback and slip-joint folders, fishing knives; trailing-points and impala horn handles. **Technical:** Grinds D2, 440C, ATS-34 and commercial Damascus. **Prices:** $65 to $250; some to $500. **Remarks:** Full-time maker; first knife sold in 1981. **Mark:** Scorpion logo and name.

FOUST, ROGER, 1925 Vernon Ave., Modesto, CA 95351
Specialties: Period pieces; hunters and skinners. **Patterns:** One-of-a-kinds and customer designs. **Technical:** Grinds L6 and D2; spring steel. Believes in sole authorship. **Prices:** $75 to $1,000. **Remarks:** Full-time maker; first knife sold in 1980. Now accepting orders. **Mark:** Initials connected.

FOWLER, CHARLES R., Rt. 2, Box 1446 A, Ft. McCoy, FL 32134/904-467-3215
Specialties: Fancy high-art straight knives and traditional working straight knives of his design. **Patterns:** Boots, Bowies, daggers, fighters, hunters and utility knives. **Technical:** Forges L6, W2 and 5160. **Prices:** $300 to $1,200. **Remarks:** Part-time maker; first knife sold in 1986. Doing business as Falcon Crest Forge. **Mark:** Circle with falcon bust, name, bladesmith.

FOWLER FORGE KNIFEWORKS (See Fowler, Jerry)

FOWLER, ED A., Willow Bow Ranch, P.O. Box 1519, Riverton, WY 82501/307-856-9815
Specialties: Heavy-duty working and using straight knives. **Patterns:** Hunters, camp, bird and trout knives, Bowies. **Technical:** Forges 52100 and wire Damascus; multiple-quench heat-treats. Engraves all knives. All handles are domestic sheephorn, processed and aged for a minimum of four years. Makes heavy-duty, hand-stitched, waxed, harness leather pouch-type sheaths. **Prices:** $450 to $950; some over $1,500. **Remarks:** Full-time maker; first knife sold in 1962. **Mark:** Initials connected.

FOWLER, JERRY, Rt. 1, Box 107-B, Hutto, TX 78634/512-846-2860
Specialties: Using straight knives of his design. **Patterns:** A variety of hunting and camp knives, combat knives. Custom designs considered. **Technical:** Forges 5160, his own Damascus and cable Damascus. Makes sheaths. Prefers natural handle materials. **Prices:** Start at $150. **Remarks:** Part-time maker; first knife sold in 1986. Doing business as Fowler Forge Knifeworks. **Mark:** First initial, last name, date and J.S.

FOX, JACK L., 7085 Canelo Hills Dr., Citrus Heights, CA 95610/916-723-8647
Specialties: Traditional working/using straight knives of all designs. **Patterns:** Hunters, utility/camp knives and bird/fish knives. **Technical:** Grinds ATS-34, 440C and D2. **Prices:** $125 to $225; some to $350. **Remarks:** Spare-time maker; first knife sold in 1985. Doing business as Fox Knives. **Mark:** Stylized fox head.

FOX, PAUL, Rt. 3, Box 208-F Rockbarn Rd., Claremont, NC 28610/704-459-2000 evenings; 404-327-5516 days
Specialties: Unusual one-of-a-kinds of all-bolted construction; mostly folders. **Patterns:** High-tech folding fighters; straight daggers and fighters. **Technical:** Grinds 01, 154CM and commercial Damascus. **Prices:** $200 to $6,000. **Remarks:** Full-time maker; first knife sold in 1977. **Mark:** Signature.

FOX, WENDELL, 4080 S. 39th, Springfield, OR 97478/503-747-2126
Specialties: Classic and traditional straight knives and folders of his design and to customer specs. **Patterns:** Hunters, locking folders, slip-joint folders and utility/camp knives. **Technical:** Forges high-carbon steel, cable, 52100 and his own timbers steel. All carbon cable blades are differentially tempered; all sheaths are wet-moulded. **Prices:** $200 to $500. **Remarks:** Full-time maker; first knife sold in 1952. **Mark:** Name or initials.

FOX VALLEY FORGE (See Werth, George W.)

FOXWOOD FORGE (See Kilby, Keith)

FRALEY, DEREK, 430 South Ct., Dixon, CA 95620/916-678-0393
Specialties: Traditional working/using straight knives and folders of his design and in standard patterns. **Patterns:** Fighters, hunters, utility/camp knives. **Technical:** Grinds ATS-34. Offers hand-stitched sheaths. **Prices:** $100 to $400. **Remarks:** Part-time maker; first knife sold in 1990. **Mark:** First and middle initials, last name over buffalo.

FRANCE, DAN, Box 218, Cawood, KY 40815/606-573-6104
Specialties: Traditional working and using straight knives of his design. **Patterns:** Hunters, Bowies and utility/camp knives. **Technical:** Forges and grinds 01, 5160 and L6. **Prices:** $35 to $125; some to $350. **Remarks:** Spare-time maker; first knife sold in 1985. **Mark:** First name.

FRANJO (See Candrella, Joe)

FRANK, HEINRICH H., Box 984, Whitefish, MT 59937/406-862-2681
Specialties: High-art investor-class folders, handmade and engraved. **Patterns:** Folding daggers, hunter-size folders and gents. **Technical:** Grinds 07 and 01. **Prices:** $4,800 to $16,000. **Remarks:** Full-time maker; first knife sold in 1965. **Mark:** Name, address and date.

FRANKLAND, ANDREW, P.O. Box 256, Wilderness 6560, SOUTH AFRICA/0027-441-877-0260; FAX: 0027-441-745203
Specialties: Classic working and using straight knives and folders of his design and to customer specs. **Patterns:** Daggers, fighters, hunters and utility/camp knives. **Technical:** Grinds 440C, D2 and ATS-34. All double-edge knives have broad spine. **Prices:** $250 to $400; some to $1,500. **Remarks:** Part-time maker; first knife sold in 1979. **Mark:** Last name surrounded by mountain, lake, forest scene.

FRANKLIN, MIKE, 9878 Big Run Rd., Aberdeen, OH 45101/513-549-2598
Specialties: Small, lightweight hunters and boots; double-action locking folders. **Patterns:** Straight and folding knives; some period pieces. **Technical:** Grinds A2, 440C and ATS-34. **Prices:** $350 to $800. **Remarks:** Full-time maker; first knife sold in 1973. **Mark:** Last name.

FRANKS, JOEL, 6610 Quaker, Lubbock, TX 79413/806-792-7112
Specialties: Working straight knives and folders in standard patterns or to customer specs. **Patterns:** Belt knives, hunters, gut hook skinners, folders and utility knives. **Technical:** Grinds 440C, 440A and L6. Makes trophy and commemorative cases and racks to accompany his knives. Repairs and refinishes old knives. **Prices:** $35 to $300. **Remarks:** Part-time maker; first knife sold in 1973. **Mark:** Initials connected.

FRASER, GRANT, RR2 Foresters Falls, Ont., CANADA K0J 1V0/613-582-3582
Specialties: Fancy and working straight knives of his design and to customer specs. **Patterns:** Bowies, daggers and hunters. **Technical:** Forges and grinds 01 and 5160; grinds ATS-34. **Prices:** $125 to $255; some to $1,200. **Remarks:** Full-time maker; first knife sold in 1983. **Mark:** Initial tang stamp.

FRAZIER, RON, 2107 Urbine Rd., Powhatan, VA 23139/804-794-8561
Specialties: Classy working knives of his design; some high-art straight knives. **Patterns:** Wide assortment of straight knives, including miniatures and push knives. **Technical:** Grinds 440C; offers satin, mirror or sand finishes. **Prices:** $85 to $700; some to $3,000. **Remarks:** Full-time maker; first knife sold in 1976. **Mark:** Name in arch logo.

FREEMAN, ART F., 7542 Saint Philomena Way, Citrus Heights, CA 95610-2522
Specialties: Fantasy and high-art knives. **Patterns:** Hunters to Bowies, fighters to swords. **Technical:** Uses 440C, ATS-34, D2 and nickel/1095 Damascus. Customer requests. **Prices:** Start at $500. **Remarks:** Full-time maker; first knife sold in 1979. **Mark:** First initial, last name in script.

FREEMAN, JOHN, 160 Concession St., Cambridge, Ont. N1R 2H7 CANADA/519-740-2767; FAX: 519-740-2785
Specialties: Working straight knives. **Patterns:** Hunters, skinners, utilities, backpackers. **Technical:** Grinds A2 and 440C. **Prices:** Start at $125. **Remarks:** Full-time maker; first knife sold in 1985. **Mark:** Full name, city, state, Handmade.

FREER, RALPH, 3322 Orangewood Ave., Rossmoor, CA 90720/310-493-4925; FAX: 310-799-8844
Specialties: Hunters, fighters, Bowies and art pieces. **Patterns:** All his design.

directory
FREILING—GAMBLE

Technical: ATS-34, 440C, 5160, Damascus, 1060, 1095 and 01. **Prices:** $200 to $1,500. Offers custom filework. Works with natural materials, exotic woods and horn. Flawless mirror-polished or hand-rubbed satin finishes. **Remarks:** Full-time maker; first knife sold in 1991. Doing business as Freer Custom Knives. **Mark:** Last name.

FREILING, ALBERT J., 3700 Niner Rd., Finksburg, MD 21048/301-795-2880 **Specialties:** Working straight knives and folders; some period pieces. **Patterns:** Boots, Bowies, survival knives and tomahawks in 4130 and 440C; some locking folders and interframes; ball-bearing folders. **Technical:** Grinds 01, 440C and 154CM. **Prices:** $100 to $300; some to $500. **Remarks:** Part-time maker; first knife sold in 1966. **Mark:** Initials connected.

FRESE, WILLIAM R., 5374 Fernbeach, St. Louis, MO 63128/314-849-3272 **Specialties:** Unusual blade designs coupled with exotic handles. **Patterns:** Hunters, skinners and utility knives. **Technical:** Grinds D2, 440C and 01. Offers filework and scrimshaw. **Prices:** $50 to $150; miniatures range $25 to $35. **Remarks:** Part-time maker; first knife sold in 1985. Offers display stands. **Mark:** Last name.

FREY JR., W. FREDERICK, 305 Walnut St., Milton, PA 17847/717-742-9576 **Specialties:** Working straight knives and folders, some fancy. **Patterns:** Wide range—boot knives to tomahawks. **Technical:** Grinds A2, 01 and D2; hand finishes only. **Prices:** $55 to $170; some to $600. **Remarks:** Spare-time maker; first knife sold in 1983. **Mark:** Last name in script.

FRIEDLY, DENNIS E., 12 Cottontail Ln., Cody, WY 82414/307-527-6811 **Specialties:** Fancy working straight knives and daggers. **Patterns:** Hunters, fighters, short swords, minis and miniatures; new line of full-tang hunters/boots. **Technical:** Grinds 440C, ATS-34 and commercial Damascus; prefers hidden tangs. **Prices:** $135 to $900; some to $2,500. **Remarks:** Full-time maker; first knife sold in 1972. **Mark:** Name, city and state.

FRIZZELL, TED, Rt. 2, Box 326, West Fork, AR 72774/501-839-3381 **Specialties:** Heavy chopping and breaking tools. **Patterns:** Large hatchets to camp knives. **Technical:** Grinds 5160 almost exclusively—$1/4$" to $1/2$" bars—some 01 and A2 on request. All hatchets come with 8-oz. leather head covers. **Prices:** $55 to $150; some to $500. **Remarks:** Full-time maker; first knife sold in 1984. Doing business as Mineral Mountain Hatchet Works. **Mark:** A circle with line in the middle; MM and HW within the circle.

FRONEFIELD, MIKE, P.O. Box 10268, Truckee, CA 95737/916-587-3003 **Specialties:** Working straight knives in standard patterns. **Patterns:** Fly knives to remove fly hooks from fish; utility knives; some swords. **Technical:** Forges and grinds cable Damascus, 440C and L6. Scrimshaws and engraves. Makes own sheaths. **Prices:** $50 to $150; some to $500. **Remarks:** Part-time maker; first knife sold in 1986. Doing business as Truckee Knifeworks. **Mark:** Name.

FUEGEN, LARRY, RR 1, Box 279, Wiscasset, ME 04578/207-882-6391 **Specialties:** High-art folders and working straight knives. **Patterns:** Forged scroll folders in crown stag; variety of classic straight knives. **Technical:** Forges 5160 and his own Damascus. Works in exotic leather; offers elaborate filework; likes natural handle materials. **Prices:** $400 to $5,200. **Remarks:** Full-time maker; first knife sold in 1975. **Mark:** Initials connected.

FUJIKAMA, SHUN, 1157 Sawa Kaizuka, Osaka, JAPAN

FUJISAKA, STANLEY, 45-004 Holowai St., Kaneohe, HI 96744/808-247-0017 **Specialties:** Fancy working straight knives and folders. **Patterns:** Hunters, boots, personal knives, daggers, collectible art knives. **Technical:** Grinds 440C, 154CM and ATS-34; clean lines, inlays. **Prices:** $150 to $1,200; some to $3,000. **Remarks:** Full-time maker; first knife sold in 1984. **Mark:** Name, city and state.

FUKUTA, TAK, 38-Umeagae-cho, Seki-City, Gifu-Pref, JAPAN/0575-22-0264 **Specialties:** Bench-made fancy straight knives and folders. **Patterns:** Sheffield-type folders, Bowies and fighters. **Technical:** Grinds commercial Damascus. **Prices:** Start at $300. **Remarks:** Full-time maker. **Mark:** Name in knife logo.

FULLCO, INC. (See Fuller, Bruce A.)

FULLER, BRUCE A., 1305 Airhart Dr., Baytown, TX 77520/713-427-1848 **Specialties:** One-of-a-kind working/using straight knives to customer specs. **Patterns:** Bowies, hunters and utility/camp knives. **Technical:** Forges 5160, 01 and his own Damascus. Prefers El Solo Mesquite and natural materials. **Prices:** Start at $150 with sheath and case. **Remarks:** Part-time maker; first knife sold in 1991. **Mark:** Fullco, J.S.

FULLER, JACK A., 7103 Stretch Ct., New Market, MD 21774/301-831-9749 **Specialties:** Straight working knives of his design and to customer specs. **Patterns:** Fighters, camp knives, hunters and art knives. **Technical:** Forges 5160, 01, W2 and his own Damascus. Offers leatherwork; scrimshands. **Prices:** $300 to $750; some to $2,000. **Remarks:** Full-time maker; first knife sold in 1979. **Mark:** Fuller's Forge, MS.

FULLER, JOHN W., 6156 Ridge Way, Douglasville, GA 30135/404-942-1155 **Specialties:** Fancy working straight knives and folders in standard patterns. **Patterns:** Straight and folding hunters, gents, fighters. **Technical:** Grinds ATS-34, 440C and commercial Damascus. **Prices:** $75 to $300. **Remarks:** Part-time maker; first knife sold in 1978. **Mark:** Name, city, state.

FULLER'S FORGE (See Fuller, Jack A.)

FULTON, MICKEY, P.O. Box 1062, Willows, CA 95988/916-934-5780 **Specialties:** Working straight knives of his design. **Patterns:** Hunters, Bowies, kitchen and fishing knives, steak knife sets. **Technical:** Hand-filed, sanded, buffed ATS-34, 440C and A2. Uses natural handle materials. All knives mirror-finished. **Prices:** $65 to $600; some to $2,000. **Remarks:** Full-time maker; first knife sold in 1979. **Mark:** Signature.

g

GADDY, GARY LEE, 205 Ridgewood Lane, Washington, NC 27889/919-946-4359 **Specialties:** Working/using straight knives of his design; period pieces. **Patterns:** Bowies, hunters, utility/camp knives. **Technical:** Grinds ATS-34, D2 and 01. Offers filework. **Prices:** $100 to $225; some to $400. **Remarks:** Spare-time maker; first knife sold in 1991. **Mark:** Etched name and quarter moon logo.

GAETA, ROBERTO, Rua Shikazu Myai 80, 05351 Sao Paulo, S.P., BRAZIL/11-268-4626; Av. Francisco Morato, 3680, 05520, Sao Paulo, S.P., BRAZIL (shop) **Specialties:** Wide range of using knives. **Patterns:** Brazilian and North American hunting and fighting knives. **Technical:** Grinds stainless steel; likes natural handle materials. **Prices:** $100 to $250; some to $500. **Remarks:** Full-time maker; first knife sold in 1979. **Mark:** BOB'G.

GAINEY, HAL, 904 Bucklevel Rd., Greenwood, SC 29649/803-223-0225 **Specialties:** Traditional working and using straight knives and folders. **Patterns:** Hunters, slip-joint folders and utility/camp knives. **Technical:** Hollow-grinds ATS-34 and D2; makes sheaths. **Prices:** $95 to $145; some to $500. **Remarks:** Part-time maker; first knife sold in 1975. **Mark:** Eagle head and last name or last initial.

GALLAGHER, BARRY, 714 8th Ave. N., Lewistown, MT 59457/406-538-7056 **Specialties:** Traditional working/using straight knives of his design and to customer specs. **Patterns:** Bowies, fighters, hunters, fillets and hatchets. **Technical:** Grinds ATS-34, 440C and D2. Scrimshaws and engraves. **Prices:** $100 to $400; some to $850. **Remarks:** Part-time maker; first knife sold in 1993. Doing business as Gallagher Custom Knives. **Mark:** First initial, last name, city, state in football shape with "custom" in center.

GAMBLE, FRANK, P.O. Box 3687, Redwood City, CA 94064/415-368-1430 **Specialties:** Fantasy and high-art straight knives and folders of his design. **Patterns:** Daggers, fighters, hunters and special locking folders. **Technical:** Grinds 440C and ATS-34; forges Damascus/cable Damascus. Inlays; offers jeweling. **Prices:** $150 to $10,000. **Remarks:** Full-time maker; first knife sold in 1976. **Mark:** First initial, last name.

GAMBLE, ROGER, 2801 65 Way N., St. Petersburg, FL 33710/813-384-1470 **Specialties:** Traditional working/using straight knives and folders of his design. **Patterns:** Hunters and slip-joints. **Technical:** Grinds ATS-34 and Damascus. **Prices:** $50 to $150; some to $500. **Remarks:** Part-time maker; first knife sold in 1982. Doing business as Gamble Knives. **Mark:** First name in a fan of cards over last name.

custom knifemakers
GAME TRAIL KNIVES—GERUS

GAME TRAIL KNIVES (See Watson, Bert)

GAND (See Anderson, Gary D.)

GANNAWAY, WOODSON, 5402 Spicebush, Madison, WI 43714
Specialties: Traditional Spanish knives. **Patterns:** Farmers of the Canary Islands. **Technical:** Forges thin carbon and stainless steel; traditional/unique handle designs. **Prices:** $350 to $1,500; some higher. **Remarks:** Master of an ancient craft.

GANSTER, JEAN-PIERRE, 18, Rue du Vieil Hopital, F-67000 Strasbourg, FRANCE/(0033)88 32 65 61; FAX: 0033 88 22 61 94
Specialties: Fancy and high-art miniatures of his design and to customer specs. **Patterns:** Bowies, daggers, fighters, hunters, locking folders and miniatures. **Technical:** Forges and grinds stainless Damascus, ATS-34, gold and silver. **Prices:** $100 to $380; some to $1,100. **Remarks:** Part-time maker; first knife sold in 1972. **Mark:** Stylized first initials.

GARBE, BOB, 33176 Klein, Fraser, MI 48026/810-293-3664
Specialties: Folders and straight knives. **Patterns:** Hunters, locking folders and slip-joint folders. **Technical:** Grinds 440C and ATS-34. Offers filework. **Prices:** $85 to $350. **Remarks:** Full-time maker; first knife sold in 1991. **Mark:** Last name.

GARCIA JR., RAUL, P.O. Box #693, Aberdeen, MD 21001/410-272-4842; FAX: 410-272-6340
Specialties: Classic working and using knives of his design. **Patterns:** Fighters, Bowies and hunters. **Technical:** Hand forges 5160, L6 and W2; differentially heat-treats. Makes wood-lined leather sheaths. **Prices:** $150 to $500; some to $1,000. **Remarks:** Part-time maker; first knife sold in 1992. **Mark:** Last name.

GARDNER, ROB, 3828 W. Delhi Ct., Ann Arbor, MI 48103/313-996-0704
Specialties: High-art working and using knives of his design and to customer specs. **Patterns:** Daggers, hunters and ethnic-patterned knives. **Technical:** Forges Damascus, L6 and 10-series steels. Engraves and inlays. Handles and fittings may be carved. **Prices:** $175 to $500; some to $2,500. **Remarks:** Spare-time maker; first knife sold in 1987. **Mark:** Engraved initials.

GARNER, BERNARD, 11102 62nd Ave., Edmonton, Alb. CANADA T6H 1N3

GARNER JR., WILLIAM O., 2803 East DeSoto St., Pensacola, FL 32503/904-438-2009
Specialties: Working straight knives, some fancy. **Patterns:** Hunters, Bowies, fighters, double-edged daggers, folders and fishing knives. **Technical:** Grinds 440C, 154CM and ATS-34, D2 and 01 steels. **Prices:** $85 to $500. **Remarks:** Full-time maker; first knife sold in 1985. **Mark:** First and last name in oval logo or last name.

GARTMAN, M.D., Rt. 4, Box 423G, Gatesville, TX 76528/817-865-6090
Specialties: Working straight knives and folders in standard patterns. **Patterns:** A variety of folders, some Bowies and miniatures. **Technical:** Grinds D2 and ATS-34; likes unusual natural handles such as swordfish bill. **Prices:** $100 to $235. **Remarks:** Part-time maker; first knife sold in 1982. **Mark:** Last name inside arrowhead logo.

GASTON, BERT, P.O. Box 9047, North Little Rock, AR 72119/501-372-4747; 800-264-0747
Specialties: Traditional working and using straight knives of his design. **Patterns:** Hunters, Bowies and fighters. **Technical:** Forges his Damascus, 5168 and L6. Only uses natural handle materials. **Prices:** $200 to $500; some to $1,500. **Remarks:** Part-time maker; first knife sold in 1989. **Mark:** Stylized last initial and M.S.

GASTON, RON, 330 Gaston Dr., Woodruff, SC 29388/803-433-0807; FAX: 803-433-9958
Specialties: Working period pieces. **Patterns:** Hunters, fighters, tantos, boots and a variety of other straight knives; single-blade slip-joint folders. **Technical:** Grinds ATS-34. Hand-rubbed satin finish is standard. **Prices:** $100 to $350; some to $1,000. **Remarks:** Full-time maker; first knife sold in 1980. **Mark:** Name.

GAUDETTE, LINDEN L., 5 Hitchcock Rd., Wilbraham, MA 01095/413-596-4896
Specialties: Traditional working knives in standard patterns. **Patterns:** Broad-bladed hunters, Bowies and camp knives; wood carver knives; locking folders. **Technical:** Grinds ATS-34, 440C and 154CM. **Prices:** $150 to $400; some higher. **Remarks:** Full-time maker; first knife sold in 1975. **Mark:** Last name in Gothic logo; used to be initials in circle.

GAUGLER, EARL W., 44 Center Grove Rd., Randolph, NJ 07869/201-366-8524
Specialties: Traditional and fantasy straight knives and folders to customer specs. **Patterns:** Hunters, daggers and fighters. **Technical:** Forges and grinds 440C and his own Damascus. **Prices:** $125 to $250; some to $2,000. **Remarks:** Full-time maker; first knife sold in 1981. **Mark:** Brass eye in forged blades; name in stock removal blades.

GAULT, CLAY, Rt. 1, Box 287, Lexington, TX 78947/512-273-2873
Specialties: Straight and folding hunting knives. **Patterns:** Classic drop-points; traditional folding styles. **Technical:** Grinds BX-NSM 174 steel, custom rolled from billets to his specifications. **Prices:** $250 to $375; some higher. **Remarks:** Full-time maker; first knife sold in 1970. **Mark:** Name or name with cattle brand.

GEISLER, GARY R., P.O. Box 294, Clarksville, OH 45113/513-289-2469
Specialties: Traditional working straight knives. **Patterns:** English-style Bowies, drop-point hunters, and a few daggers. **Technical:** Flat-grinds A2, 440C, 01 and ATS-34. Prefers mirror finishes. **Prices:** $50 to $250; some higher. **Remarks:** Part-time maker; first knife sold in 1982. **Mark:** First and middle initials, last name and Maker in script.

GENGE, ROY E., P.O. Box 57, Eastlake, CO 80614/303-451-7991
Specialties: High-tech working knives. **Patterns:** Bowies, hatchets, hunters, survival knives, buckskinners, kukris and others. **Technical:** Forges and grinds L6, S7, W1, W2, 01, Vascowear, 154CM, ATS-34 and commercial Damascus. **Prices:** $50 to $500; embellished knives are higher. **Remarks:** Part-time maker; first knife sold in 1968. **Mark:** Name, city, state.

GENOVESE, RICK, 781 Richard St., Clarkdale, AZ 86324/602-634-2558
Specialties: Fancy and embellished folders of his design. **Patterns:** Locking folders. **Technical:** Grinds ATS-34 and J. Rados Damascus. All folders are interframes with inlays such as jade, lapis, dinosaur bone, charoite, etc. **Prices:** $800 to $1,500; some to $10,000. **Remarks:** Full-time maker; first knife sold in 1976. **Mark:** Last name.

GENSKE, JAY, 262 1/2 Elm St., Fondulac, WI 54935/414-921-6505
Specialties: Working/using knives and period pieces of his design and to customer specs. **Patterns:** Bowies, fighters, hunters. **Technical:** Grinds ATS-34 and 440C; forges and grinds Damascus and cable. Offers custom-tooled sheaths and scabbards. **Prices:** $85 to $300; some to $1,000. **Remarks:** Full-time maker; first knife sold in 1985. Doing business as Genske Knives. **Mark:** Stamped or engraved last name.

GEORGE, HARRY, 3137 Old Camp Long Rd., Aiken, SC 29801/803-649-1963
Specialties: Working straight knives of his design or to customer specs. **Patterns:** Hunters, skinners and utility knives. **Technical:** Grinds ATS-34. Prefers natural handle materials, hollow-grinds and mirror finishes. **Prices:** Start at $65. **Remarks:** Part-time maker; first knife sold in 1985. Trained under George Herron. Member SCAK. **Mark:** Name, city and state.

GEORGE, TOM, P.O. Box 1298, Magalia, CA 95954/916-873-3306
Specialties: Large Bowies and display knives. **Patterns:** Hunters, Bowies, daggers and buckskinners. **Technical:** Uses D2, 440C, ATS-34 and 154CM. **Prices:** $175 to $4,500. **Remarks:** Part-time maker; first knife sold in 1981. Accepting orders on past Glories series and broken-back jacks only. **Mark:** Name.

GEPNER, DON, 2615 E. Tecumseh, Norman, OK 73071/405-364-2750
Specialties: Traditional working and using straight knives of his design. **Patterns:** Bowies and daggers. **Technical:** Forges his Damascus, 1095 and 5160. **Prices:** $100 to $400; some to $1,000. **Remarks:** Spare-time maker; first knife sold in 1991. Has been forging since 1954; first edged weapon made at 9 years old. **Mark:** Last initial.

GERUS, GERRY, P.O. Box 2295, G.P.O. Cairns, Qld. 4870 AUSTRALIA/070-341451
Specialties: Fancy working and using straight knives of his design. **Patterns:** Hunters, Bowies and fighters. **Technical:** Uses 440C, ATS-34 and commercial

FIFTEENTH EDITION **203**

directory
GEVEDON—GOODE

Damascus. **Prices:** $275 to $600; some to $1,200. **Remarks:** Part-time maker; first knife sold in 1988. **Mark:** Last name; or last name, Hand Made, city, country.

GEVEDON, HANNERS (HANK), 1410 John Cash Rd., Crab Orchard, KY 40419-9770
Specialties: Traditional working and using straight knives. **Patterns:** Hunters, swords, utility and camp knives. **Technical:** Forges and grinds his own Damascus, 5160 and L6. Cast aluminum handles. **Prices:** $50 to $250; some to $400. **Remarks:** Part-time maker; first knife sold in 1983. **Mark:** Initials and LBF tang stamp.

G.H. KNIVES (See Hielscher, Guy)

GIBSON, JIM, RR1, Box 177F, Bunnell, FL 32110/904-437-4383

GILBREATH, RANDALL, Rt. 5, Box 823B, Dora, AL 35062/205-648-3902
Specialties: Damascus. **Patterns:** Folders and fixed blades. **Technical:** Forges Damascus and stainless steel. **Prices:** $100 to $1,500. **Remarks:** Part-time maker; first knife sold in 1979. **Mark:** Name in ribbon.

GILJEVIC, BRANKO, 35 Hayley Cresent, Queanbeyan 2620, N.S.W., AUSTRALIA/06-2977613
Specialties: Classic working straight knives and folders of his design. **Patterns:** Hunters, Bowies, skinners and locking folders. **Technical:** Grinds 440C and D2. Offers acid etching, scrimshaw and leather carving. **Prices:** $150 to $500. **Remarks:** Part-time maker; first knife sold in 1987. Doing business as Sambar Custom Knives. **Mark:** Name, serial number and sambar head logo in handle.

GILLENWATER, E.E. "DICK", 921 Dougherty Rd., Aiken, SC 29801/803-649-6787
Specialties: Straight working sportsman's knives. **Patterns:** Boot knives, hunters, fillet and steak knives. **Technical:** Grinds 154CM and ATS-34. **Prices:** $75 to $400; some to $600. **Remarks:** Part-time maker; first knife sold in 1979. **Mark:** Signature.

GILLIS, C.R. "REX", 2340 2nd Ave. SW, Great Falls, MT 59404/406-771-1082
Specialties: Working/using straight knives of all designs. **Patterns:** Fighters, hunters, Bowies. Hunting sets with hatchet or saw. **Technical:** Grinds ATS-34, 440C; forges 5160, 1060, 52100 and Damascus. Heat-treats. Offers hand-sewn leather sheaths. **Prices:** $40 to $500. **Remarks:** Full-time maker; first knife sold in 1983. Doing business as Steel Talon Cutlery. **Mark:** Eagle head and claws with a Bowie.

GLASER, KEN, Rt. #1, Box 148, Purdy, MO 65734/417-442-3371
Specialties: Working straight knives in standard patterns. **Patterns:** Hunters, bird and trout knives, boots. **Technical:** Hollow-grinds 01, D2 and 440C. **Prices:** $75 to $125; some to $250. **Remarks:** Part-time maker; first knife sold in 1983. **Mark:** Initials.

GLOVER, RON, 6775 Socialville-Foster Rd., Mason, OH 45040/513-398-7857
Specialties: High-tech working straight knives and folders. **Patterns:** Hunters to Bowies; some interchangeable blade models; unique locking mechanisms. **Technical:** Grinds 440C, 154CM; buys Damascus. **Prices:** $70 to $500; some to $800. **Remarks:** Part-time maker; first knife sold in 1981. **Mark:** Name in script.

GLUKLICK, BOB, 3129 Dufferin St., North York, Ont., CANADA M6A 2S9

GODDARD, WAYNE, 473 Durham Ave., Eugene, OR 97404/503-689-8098
Patterns: Fixed blades and folders. **Technical:** Works exclusively with wire Damascus and his own pattern-welded material. **Prices:** $250 to $4,000. **Remarks:** Full-time maker; first knife sold in 1963. Three-year backlog on orders. **Mark:** Blocked initials on forged blades; regular capital initials on stock removal.

GOERS, BRUCE, 3423 Royal Ct. S., Lakeland, FL 33813/813-647-3093, 800-392-7496
Specialties: Fancy working and using straight knives of his design and to customer specs. **Patterns:** Hunters, fighters, Bowies and fantasy knives. **Technical:** Grinds ATS-34, some Damascus. **Prices:** $195 to $600; some to $1,300. **Remarks:** Full-time maker; first knife sold in 1990. Doing business as Vulture Cutlery. **Mark:** Buzzard with initials.

GOERTZ, PAUL S., 201 Union Ave. SE, #207, Renton, WA 98059/206-228-9501
Specialties: Working straight knives of his design and to customer specs. **Patterns:** Hunters, skinners, camp, bird and fish knives, camp axes, some Bowies, fighters and boots. **Technical:** Grinds ATS-34, D2 and 440C. **Prices:** $75 to $500; some to $900. **Remarks:** Full-time maker; first knife sold in 1985. **Mark:** Signature.

GOFOURTH, JIM, 3776 Aliso Cyn. Rd., Santa Paula, CA 93060/805-659-3814
Specialties: Period pieces and working knives. **Patterns:** Bowies, locking folders, patent lockers and others. **Technical:** Grinds A2 and 154CM. **Prices:** Moderate. **Remarks:** Spare-time maker. **Mark:** Initials interconnected.

GOGUEN, SCOTT, Rt. 5, Box 746, Newport, NC 28570/919-393-6013
Specialties: Classic and traditional straight knives; working/using knives of all designs. **Patterns:** Boots, Bowies, fighters, hunters, kitchen knives, utility/camp knives, fillets. **Technical:** Grinds ATS-34 and A2; forges and grinds 01. Offers cord-wrapped handles. **Prices:** $60 to $150; some to $275. **Remarks:** Spare-time maker; first knife sold in 1988. **Mark:** Last name.

GOLD HILL KNIFE WORKS (See Scarrow, Will)

GOLDBERG, DAVID, 102-C West Germantown Pike, Norristown, PA 19401/610-239-9950
Specialties: Fancy/embellished straight knives and folders of his design or to customer specs. **Patterns:** All styles including miniatures. **Technical:** Fabricates and casts gold, platinum and silver; utilizes high-quality and Master Smith Damascus. Forges. Embellishes with precious gems and minerals. **Prices:** $100 to $1,000; some to $5,000. **Remarks:** Full-time maker; first knife sold in 1987. **Mark:** Signature, date and stamp of mountain.

GOLDENBERG, T.S., P.O. Box 238, Fairview, NC 28730
Specialties: Working straight knives and period pieces to customer specs. **Patterns:** Hunters, boots and Bowies. **Technical:** Grinds A2, 01 and 440C. **Prices:** $75 to $500; some to $700. **Remarks:** Part-time maker; first knife sold in 1975. **Mark:** Surname in mountain; some with TEDDYHAWK.

GOLDING, ROBIN, P.O. Box 267, Lathrop, CA 95330/209-982-0839
Specialties: Working knives of his design. **Patterns:** Survival knives, Bowie extractions, camp knives, diver's knives and skinners. **Technical:** Grinds 440C, 154CM and ATS-34. **Prices:** $75 to $250; some to $600. **Remarks:** Full-time maker; first knife sold in 1985. Up to 1-year waiting period on orders. **Mark:** Last name, USA.

GOLD RUSH DESIGNS (See Connolly, James)

GOLTZ, WARREN L., 802 4th Ave. E., Ada, MN 56510/218-784-7721
Specialties: Fancy working knives in standard patterns. **Patterns:** Hunters, fighters, Bowies and camp knives. **Technical:** Grinds 440C and ATS-34. **Prices:** $120 to $595; some to $950. **Remarks:** Part-time maker; first knife sold in 1984. **Mark:** Last name.

GONZALEZ, LEONARDO WILLIAMS, Ituzaingo 473, Maldonado, CP 20000, URUGUAY/(598.42)21617
Specialties: Classic high-art and fantasy straight knives; traditional working and using knives of his design, in standard patterns or to customer specs. **Patterns:** Hunters, Bowies, daggers, fighters, boots, swords and utility/camp knives. **Technical:** Forges and grinds 440C, 1095 and carbon steel. **Prices:** $100 to $900. **Remarks:** Full-time maker; first knife sold in 1985. **Mark:** None.

GOO, TAI, 3225 N. Winstel Blvd., Tucson, AZ 85716/602-721-6381; 602-325-8095
Specialties: High-art and fantasy knives; some working knives. **Patterns:** Fighters, daggers, Bowies, buckskinners, edged fetishes and sculptures. **Technical:** Forges and grinds A6, 440C and his own Damascus with iron meteorites. **Prices:** $150 to $500; some to $10,000. **Remarks:** Full-time maker; first knife sold in 1978. **Mark:** Chiseled signature; mark in spacer and tang.

GOODE, BEAR, P.O. Box 6474, Navajo Dam, NM 87419/505-632-8184
Specialties: Working/using straight knives of his design and in standard patterns. **Patterns:** Bowies, hunters and utility/camp knives. **Technical:** Grinds 440C and 1056; forges and grinds 5160. **Prices:** $45 to $125; some to $350. **Remarks:** Part-time maker; first knife sold in 1993. Doing business as Bear Knives. **Mark:** First name, or first name and year, or first name and last initial.

GORDON (See Defreest, William G.)

GORENFLO, JAMES T., 9145 Sullivan Rd., Baton Rouge, LA 70818/504-261-5868
Specialties: Traditional working and using straight knives of his design. **Patterns:** Bowies, hunters and utility/camp knives. **Technical:** Forges 5160, 1095 and 52100. **Prices:** $125 to $300. **Remarks:** Spare-time maker; first knife sold in 1992. **Mark:** Last name or initials.

GOTTAGE, DANTE, 21700 Evergreen, St. Clair Shores, MI 48082-1935/810-293-6615
Specialties: Working knives of his design or to customer specs. **Patterns:** Large and small skinners, fighters, Bowies, fillet knives and miniatures. **Technical:** Grinds 01, 440C and 154CM. **Prices:** $100 to $400; some to $500. **Remarks:** Part-time maker; first knife sold in 1975. **Mark:** Full name in script letters.

GOTTAGE, JUDY, 21700 Evergreen, St. Clair Shores, MI 48082-1935/810-293-6615; FAX: 313-293-7540
Specialties: Interframe folders of her design or to customer specs. **Patterns:** From 5 to 9 inches overall length. **Technical:** 440C, 154CM, ATS-34, Damascus. Heat-treats. **Prices:** $300 to $3,000. **Remarks:** Full-time maker; first knife sold in 1980. **Mark:** Full name or first name.

GOTTSCHALK, GREGORY J., 12 First St. (Ft. Pitt), Carnegie, PA 15106/412-279-6692
Specialties: Fancy working straight knives and folders to customer specs. **Patterns:** Hunters to tantos, locking folders to minis. **Technical:** Grinds 440C, 154CM, ATS-34. Now making own Damascus. Most knives have mirror finishes. **Prices:** Start at $75. **Remarks:** Part-time maker; first knife sold in 1977. **Mark:** Full name in crescent.

GOUKER, GARY B., P.O. Box 955, Sitka, AK 99835/907-747-3476
Specialties: Hunting knives for hard use. **Patterns:** Skinners, semi-skinners, and such. **Technical:** Likes natural materials, inlays, stainless steel. **Prices:** Moderate. **Remarks:** New Alaskan maker. **Mark:** Name.

GRAFFEO, ANTHONY I., 100 Riess Place, Chalmette, LA 70043/504-277-1428
Specialties: Traditional working and using straight knives of his design, to customer specs and in standard patterns. **Patterns:** Hunters, utility/camp knives and fishing knives. **Technical:** Hollow- and flat-grinds ATS-34, 440C and 154CM. Handle materials include Pakkawood, Micarta and sambar stag. **Prices:** $65 to $100; some to $250. **Remarks:** Part-time maker; first knife sold in 1991. Doing business as Knives by: Graf. **Mark:** First and middle initials, last name city, state, Maker.

GREBE, GORDON S., P.O. Box 296, Anchor Point, AK 99556-0296/907-235-8242
Specialties: Working straight knives and folders, some fancy. **Patterns:** Tantos, Bowies, boot fighter sets, locking folders. **Technical:** Grinds stainless steels; likes 1/4-inch stock and glass-bead finishes. **Prices:** $75 to $250; some to $2,000. **Remarks:** Full-time maker; first knife sold in 1968. **Mark:** Initials in lightning logo.

GRECO, JOHN, 4099 14th St., Bay St. Louis, MS 39520
Specialties: One-of-a-kind limited edition knives. **Patterns:** Fighters, daggers, camp knives. **Technical:** Forges and stock removes carbon steel. **Prices:** Moderate. **Remarks:** Full-time maker; first knife sold in 1986. **Mark:** Last name.

GREEN, BILL, 706 Bradfield, Garland, TX 75042/214-272-4748
Specialties: High-art and working straight knives and folders of his design and to customer specs. **Patterns:** Bowies, hunters, kitchen knives and locking folders. **Technical:** Grinds ATS34, D2 and 440V. Hand-tooled custom sheaths. **Prices:** $70 to $350; some to $750. **Remarks:** Part-time maker; first knife sold in 1990. **Mark:** Last name.

GREEN, ROGER M., 3412 Co. Rd. 1022, Joshua, TX 76058/817-641-5057
Specialties: 19th century period pieces. **Patterns:** Investor-grade Sheffield Bowies and dirks. **Technical:** Grinds 440C and D2; prefers flat-grinds; offers checkererd ivory. **Prices:** $500 to $2,500. **Remarks:** Full-time maker; first knife sold in 1984. **Mark:** First and middle initials, last name.

GREEN, WILLIAM (BILL), 46 Warren Rd., View Bank, Vic. 3084, AUSTRALIA/03-459-1529
Specialties: Traditional high-tech straight knives and folders. **Patterns:** Japanese-influenced designs, hunters, Bowies, folders and miniatures. **Technical:** Forges 01, D2 and his own Damascus. Offers lost wax castings for bolsters and pommels. Likes natural handle materials, gems, silver and gold. **Prices:** $400 to $750; some to $1,200. **Remarks:** Full-time maker. **Mark:** Initials.

GREENFIELD, G.O., POB 295, Everett, WA 98206/206-259-1672
Specialties: High-tech working straight knives and folders of his design and to customer specs. **Patterns:** Boots, daggers and hunters. **Technical:** Grinds ATS34, D2 and 440V. Makes sheaths for each knife. **Prices:** $100 to $800; some to $10,000. **Remarks:** Full-time maker; first knife sold in 1978. **Mark:** Springfield, serial number.

GREGORY, MICHAEL, 211 Calhoun Rd., Belton, SC 29627/803-338-8898
Specialties: Working straight knives and folders. **Patterns:** Hunters, tantos, locking folders and slip-joints, boots and fighters. **Technical:** Grinds 440C, 154CM and ATS-34; mirror finishes. **Prices:** $95 to $200; some to $1,000. **Remarks:** Part-time maker; first knife sold in 1980. **Mark:** Name, city in logo.

GRENIER, ROGER, 497 Chemin Paquette, Saint Jovite, P. Que. J0T 2H0, CANADA/819-425-8893
Specialties: Working straight knives. **Patterns:** Heavy-duty Bowies, fighters, hunters, swords and miniatures. **Technical:** Grinds 01, D2 and 440C. **Prices:** $70 to $225; some to $800. **Remarks:** Full-time maker; first knife sold in 1981. **Mark:** Last name on blade.

GREY, PIET, P.O. Box 1493, Silverton 0127, REPUBLIC OF SOUTH AFRICA/012-803-8206
Specialties: Fancy working and using straight knives of his design. **Patterns:** Fighters, hunters and utility/camp knives. **Technical:** Grinds ATS-34 and AEB-L; forges and grinds Damascus. Solderless fitting of guards. Engraves and scrimshaws. **Prices:** $125 to $750; some to $1,500. **Remarks:** Full-time maker; first knife sold in 1970. **Mark:** Last name.

GRIFFIN JR., HOWARD A., 14299 SW 31st Ct., Davie, FL 33330/305-474-5406
Specialties: Working straight knives and folders. **Patterns:** Hunters, Bowies, locking folders with his own push-button lock design. **Technical:** Grinds 440C. **Prices:** $100 to $200; some to $500. **Remarks:** Part-time maker; first knife sold in 1983. **Mark:** Initials.

GRIFFIN, MARK (See Griffin, Rendon and Mark)

GRIFFIN, RENDON and MARK, 9706 Cedardale, Houston, TX 77055/713-468-0436
Specialties: Working folders of their designs. **Patterns:** Standard lockers and slip-joints. **Technical:** Grind and forge 440C, 154CM and their Damascus. **Prices:** $185 to $300; some to $800. **Remarks:** Part-time makers; Rendon's first knife sold in 1966; Mark's in 1974. **Mark:** Last name logo.

GRIGSBY, BEN, 80 King George St., Batesville, AR 72501/501-251-1367
Specialties: Period pieces in steel or stone. **Patterns:** Arkansas toothpicks, Bowies and stone tools of late archaic period. **Technical:** Grinds 01, D2, 440C and native flint of Ozark Hills. **Prices:** $150 to $500; some to $1,500. **Remarks:** Spare-time maker; first knife sold in 1963. **Mark:** Initials with cache river point logo.

GRIGSBY, JOHN D. (BUTCH), 5320 Circle Rd., Corryton, TN 37721/615-933-7802
Specialties: Miniature knife pins. **Patterns:** All patterns of miniature using knives, including locking folders. **Technical:** Grinds 304 stainless and 440C. **Prices:** $10 to $100. **Remarks:** Part-time maker. **Mark:** Name.

GRINDERE OF HANDIECRAFTE CUTELLERIE (See Lozier, Don)

GRINDSTONE, THE (See Grospitch, Ernie)

GROSPITCH, ERNIE, 18440 Amityville St., Orlando, FL 32820/407-568-5438
Specialties: Working knives of his design and in standard patterns. **Patterns:** Bowies, hunters and kitchen knives. **Technical:** Grinds ATS-34, 440V and 440C. Offers dovetailed bolsters and brass space between blade and bolster. Hand-stitched sheaths. **Prices:** $140 to $180; some to $300. **Remarks:** Part-time maker; first knife sold in 1989. Doing business as The Grindstone. **Mark:** First and last name, city, state.

GROSS, W.W., 325 Sherbrook Dr., High Point, NC 27260

directory

Specialties: Working knives. **Patterns:** Hunters, boots, fighters. **Technical:** Grinds. **Prices:** Moderate. **Remarks:** Full-time maker. **Mark:** Name.

GROSSMAN, STEWART, 24 Water St. #419, Clinton, MA 01510/508-365-2291; 800-my sword
Specialties: Miniatures and full-size knives and swords. **Patterns:** One-of-a-kind miniatures—jewelry, replicas—and wire-wrapped figures. Full-size art, fantasy and combat knives, daggers and modular systems. **Technical:** Forges and grinds most metals and Damascus. Uses gems, crystals, electronics and motorized mechanisms. **Prices:** $20 to $300; some to $4,500 and higher. **Remarks:** Full-time maker; first knife sold in 1985. **Mark:** G1.

GRUBB, RICHARD E., 2759 Maplewood Dr., Columbus, OH 43231/614-882-1530
Specialties: Miniatures to Bowies. **Patterns:** Bowies, drop-point hunters, fighters, tantos and miniatures. **Technical:** Grinds 440C; likes filework; offers exotic woods, stag and Micarta, wire wrap. **Prices:** $50 to $500. **Remarks:** Part-time maker; first knife sold in 1989. **Mark:** Name.

GUIGNARD, GIB, Box 3477, Quartzsite, AZ 85359/602-927-4831
Specialties: Traditional working/using straight knives of his design and in standard patterns. **Patterns:** Bowies, hunters, kitchen knives and utility/camp knives. **Technical:** Forges 5160 and 1095; grinds 440C. Heat-treats; offers turquoise inlays in handles. **Prices:** $50 to $275; some to $400. **Remarks:** Part-time maker; first knife sold in 1989. Doing business as Cactus Forge. **Mark:** Last name.

GUESS, JACK, 12 N. Rockford, Tulsa, OK 74120/918-584-3876
Specialties: Straight hunters and working folders. **Patterns:** Hunters, utility knives, folders and boots. **Technical:** Grinds 440C, ATS-34 and 01. **Prices:** $95 to $225. **Remarks:** Part-time maker; first knife sold in 1972. **Mark:** First initial, last name.

GUESS, RAYMOND L., 7214 Salineville Rd. NE, Mechanicstown, OH 44651/216-738-2793
Specialties: Working straight knives and folders of his design or to customer specs. **Patterns:** Hunters, Bowies, fillet knives, steak and paring knife sets. **Technical:** Grinds 440C. Offers silver inlay work and mirror finishes. **Prices:** $45 to $400; some to $700. **Remarks:** Spare-time maker; first knife sold in 1985. **Mark:** First initial, last name.

THE GUN ROOM (See Shostle, Ben)

GURGANUS, CAROL, Star Rt., Box 50-A, Colerain, NC 27924/919-356-4831
Specialties: Working and using straight knives. **Patterns:** Fighters, hunters and kitchen knives. **Technical:** Grinds D2, ATS-34 and Damascus steel. Uses stag, sheephorn and exotic wood handles. **Prices:** $100 to $300. **Remarks:** Full-time maker; first knife sold in 1992. **Mark:** Female symbol, last name, city, state.

GURGANUS, MELVIN H., Star Rt., Box 50-A, Colerain, NC 27924/919-356-4831
Specialties: High-tech working folders. **Patterns:** Leaf-lock and back-lock designs, bolstered and interframe. **Technical:** D2 and 440C; makes mokume. Wife Carol scrimshaws. Heat-treats, carves and offers lost wax casting. **Prices:** $300 to $3,000. **Remarks:** Full-time maker; first knife sold in 1983. **Mark:** First initial, last name and Maker.

GUTEKUNST, RALPH, 117 SW 14th St., Richmond, IN 47374/317-966-3225
Specialties: Traditional straight knives of his design and to customer specs; period pieces. **Patterns:** Daggers, fighters and hunters. **Technical:** Forges 1084, 5160 and his own Damascus and cable. **Prices:** $35 to $300; some to $1,000. **Remarks:** Full-time maker; first knife sold in 1989. **Mark:** Rampant wolf inside shield.

GUTH, KENNETH, 8 S. Michigan, 32nd Floor, Chicago, IL 60603/312-346-1760
Specialties: One-of-a-kind ornate straight knives and folders. **Patterns:** Flemish, Japanese and African-styled knives. Also makes a few forged Damascus miniature knives with fossil ivory handles and 18K gold fittings and rivets. **Technical:** Forges and grinds high carbon and 440C. Offers brass and steel laminations, goldsmithing. **Prices:** Upscale. **Remarks:** Full-time goldsmith and knifemaker. **Mark:** Last name.

GUTHRIE, GEORGE B., 1912 Puett Chapel Rd., Bassemer City, NC 28016/704-629-3031
Specialties: Working knives of his design or to customer specs. **Patterns:** Hunters, boots, fighters, locking folders and slip-joints in traditional styles. **Technical:** Grinds D2, 440C and 154CM. **Prices:** $85 to $300; some to $450. **Remarks:** Part-time maker; first knife sold in 1978. **Mark:** Name in state.

GWOZDZ, BOB, 71 Starr Ln., Attleboro, MA 02703/508-226-7475
Specialties: Fancy working straight knives. **Patterns:** Fighters, tantos and hunters. **Technical:** Grinds 440C. **Prices:** $150 to $400; some $500 and higher. **Remarks:** Part-time maker; first knife sold in 1983. Now attending law school. Will accept phone orders during summer months only. **Mark:** Name and serial number.

GYPSY SILK (See Burrows, Stephen R.)

h

HAGEN, PHILIP L., P.O. Box 58, Pelican Rapids, MN 56572/218-863-8503
Specialties: High-tech working straight knives and folders. **Patterns:** Defense-related straight knives; wide variety of folders. **Technical:** Forges and grinds 440C and his own Damascus; Uddeholm UHB. **Prices:** $100 to $800; some to $3,000. **Remarks:** Part-time maker, first knife sold in 1975. **Mark:** DOC HAGEN in shield, knife, banner logo; or DOC.

HAGGERTY, GEORGE S., P.O. Box 88, Jacksonville, VT 05342/802-368-7437
Specialties: Working straight knives and folders. **Patterns:** Hunters, claws, camp and fishing knives, locking folders and backpackers. **Technical:** Forges and grinds W2, 440C and 154CM. **Prices:** $85 to $300. **Remarks:** Part-time maker; first knife sold in 1981. **Mark:** Initials or last name.

HAGWOOD, KELLIE, 9231 Ridgetown, San Antonio, TX 78250/210-521-8710
Specialties: Working straight knives and folders of his design or to customer specs. **Patterns:** Folders, fighters, Bowies, hunters and swords. **Technical:** Grinds 440C, ATS-34, D2 and Damascus; heat-treats. Makes leather sheaths. **Prices:** Start at $200. **Remarks:** Full-time maker; first knife sold in 1969. Exclusive maker for Texas Parks and Wildlife. Doing business as Longhorn Knife Works. **Mark:** Name, city and state in script.

HAJOVSKY, ROBERT J., P.O. Box 77, Scotland, TX 76379/817-541-2219
Specialties: Working straight knives; sub-hilted fighters. **Patterns:** Variety of straight knives. **Technical:** Grinds ATS-34 and others on request. **Prices:** $150 to $700. **Remarks:** Part-time maker; first knife sold in 1973. **Mark:** Bob-Sky Knives and name, city, state.

HALLIGAN & SON (See Halligan, Ed and Shawn)

HALLIGAN, ED and SHAWN, 14 Meadow Way, Sharpsburg, GA 30277/404-251-7720; FAX: 404-251-7720
Specialties: Working straight knives and folders, some fancy. **Patterns:** Linerlocks, hunters, skinners, boots, fighters and swords. **Technical:** Grind 440C and ATS-34; forge 5160; make cable and pattern Damascus. **Prices:** $125 to $1,200. **Remarks:** Full-time makers; first knife sold in 1985. **Mark:** Halligan & Son, city, state and USA.

HALLIGAN, SHAWN (See Halligan, Ed and Shawn)

HAMLET JR., JOHNNY, 300 Billington, Clute, TX 77531/409-265-6929
Specialties: Working straight knives and folders. **Patterns:** Hunters, fighters, fillet and kitchen knives, locking folders. Likes upswept knives and trailing-points. **Technical:** Grinds 440C, D2, ATS-34. Makes sheaths. **Prices:** $55 to $225; some to $500. **Remarks:** Part-time maker; first knife sold in 1988. **Mark:** Hamlet's Handmades in script.

HAMMERSMITH (See Smith, J.D.)

HAMMOND, JIM, P.O. Box 486, Arab, AL 35016/205-586-4151
Specialties: High-tech fighters and folders. **Patterns:** Proven-design fighters. **Technical:** Grinds 440C and ATS-34. **Prices:** $200 to $975; some to $8,500. **Remarks:** Full-time maker; first knife sold in 1977. **Mark:** Full name, city, state in shield logo.

HAMPTON, WILLIAM W., 7935 E.D. Robbins Rd., Howey in the Hills, FL 34737
Specialties: Traditional and working straight knives. **Patterns:** Bowies, fighters, tantos and skinners. **Technical:** Grinds 440C and ATS-34. **Prices:** $85 to $150; some higher. **Remarks:** Part-time maker; first knife sold in 1993. **Mark:** Last name.

custom knifemakers

HANCOCK, RONALD E., P.O. Box 402, Lecanto, FL 34460/904-628-4595
Specialties: Working knives, period pieces, bucksinners, early folder patterns, daggers, patch knives, skinners, fighters and small axes. **Patterns:** Frontlocks, backlocks, interframes and stag folders. **Technical:** Forges and grinds A2, ATS-34, 01 and own Damascus; engraves. **Prices:** $100 to $800. **Remarks:** Full-time maker; first knife sold in 1973. **Mark:** Last name.

HANCOCK, TIM, 10805 N. 83rd St., Scottsdale, AZ 85260/602-998-8849
Specialties: High-art and working straight knives and folders of his design and to customer specs. **Patterns:** Fighters, hunters and locking folders. **Technical:** Forges Damascus and 52100; grinds ATS-34. Makes Damascus. Silver-wire inlays; offers carved fittings. **Prices:** $175 to $350; some to $3,000. **Remarks:** Full-time maker; first knife sold in 1988. **Mark:** Last name or heart.

HAND, BILL, P.O. Box 773, 1103 W. 7th St., Spearman, TX 79081/806-659-2967
Specialties: Traditional working and using straight knives of his design or to customer specs. **Patterns:** Hunters, Bowies and fighters. **Technical:** Forges 5160 and Damascus. **Prices:** Start at $125. **Remarks:** Spare-time maker; first knife sold in 1988. Current delivery time six to eight weeks. **Mark:** Stylized initials.

HAND M.D., JAMES E., Rt. 1, Box 176, Gloster, MS 39638/601-225-4197
Specialties: Working and using straight knives of traditional and original patterns. **Patterns:** Hunters, fighters, combat and kitchen knives. **Technical:** Grinds ATS-34 and commercial Damascus. **Prices:** $125 to $450; some to $1,000. **Remarks:** Part-time maker; first knife sold in 1985. **Mark:** Name.

HAND MADE KNIVES (See Bailey, Kirby C.)

HANDMADE KNIVES BY MARK LUBRICH (See Lubrich, Mark)

HANGAS & SONS (See Ruana Knife Works)

HANSEN, ROBERT W., RR 2, Box 88, Cambridge, MN 55008/612-689-3242
Specialties: Working straight knives and folders. **Patterns:** From hunters to minis, camp knives to miniatures; folding lockers and slip-joints in traditional styles. **Technical:** Grinds 01, 440C and 154CM; likes filework. **Prices:** $60 to $100; some to $550. **Remarks:** Part-time maker; first knife sold in 1983. **Mark:** Fish with last initial inside.

HANSON, TRAVIS, 651 Rangeline Rd., Mosinees, WI 54455/715-693-3940
Specialties: Straight knives of his design and in standard patterns. **Patterns:** Hunters and miniatures. **Technical:** Grinds D2, 440C and Damascus. Offers scrimshaw and filework. **Prices:** $50 to $300; some to $550. **Remarks:** First knife sold in 1993. **Mark:** Name in script.

HARA, KOUJI, NO292-2 Oosugi, Seki-City Gifu-Pref JAPAN

HARDIN, ROBERT K. "FUZZY", 814 Pamela Dr., Dalton, GA 30720/404-226-3624
Specialties: Working straight knives; high-art knives of his design. **Patterns:** Bowies, skinners, Japanese short swords and using belt knives. **Technical:** Grinds 01, D2 and 154CM. Uses precious gems and ivories; engraves. **Prices:** $100 to $5,000; one has gone for $80,000. **Remarks:** Part-time maker; first knife sold in 1948. **Mark:** Name.

HARDY, SCOTT, 639 Myrtle Ave., Placerville, CA 95667/916-622-5780
Specialties: Traditional working and using straight knives of his design. **Patterns:** Bowies, hunters and utility knives. **Technical:** Grinds 01; forges W2. Offers mirror finish; differentially tempers. **Prices:** $65 to $350; some to $1,000. **Remarks:** Part-time maker; first knife sold in 1982. **Mark:** First initial, last name and Handmade with bird logo.

HARKINS, J.A., P.O. Box 6136, Crestline, CA 92325/714-338-7720
Patterns: Folders, fighters and swords. **Technical:** Grinds ATS-34 and Ferguson Damascus. Engraves; offers gem work. **Prices:** Start at $450. **Remarks:** Full-time maker and engraver; first knife sold in 1988. **Mark:** First and middle initials, last name.

HARLESS, WALT, P.O. Box 845, Stoneville, NC 27048/919-573-9768
Specialties: Traditional working straight knives. **Patterns:** Hunters, utility, combat and specialty knives; limited edition historical interpretations. **Technical:** Grinds ATS-34 and 440C; offers bone handles. **Prices:** $65 to $300; some to $1,000.

Remarks: Full-time maker; first knife sold in 1978. Doing business as Arrow Forge. **Mark:** A with arrow; name, city and state.

HARLEY, LARRY W., 348 Deerfield Dr., Bristol, TN 37620/615-878-5368 (shop); 703-466-6771 (home)
Specialties: Working knives; period pieces. **Patterns:** Full range of straight knives, tomahawks, razors, bucksinners and hog spears. **Technical:** Forges and grinds ATS-34, D2, 440, 01, L6 and his own Damascus. **Prices:** $65 to $6,500. **Remarks:** Full-time maker; first knife sold in 1983. Guides (knife only) wild boar hunts. Doing business as Lonesome Pine. **Mark:** Name, city and state in pine logo.

HARMON, JAY, 462 Victoria Rd., Woodstock, GA 30188/404-928-2734
Specialties: Working and using straight knives and folders to customer specs; collector-grade art knives. **Patterns:** Bowies, daggers, fighters, boots, camp and fishing knives and folders. **Technical:** Grinds 440C, 440V, ATS-34 and D2; heat-treats. **Prices:** Start at $185. **Remarks:** Part-time maker; first knife sold in 1984. **Mark:** Last name.

HARMON, JOE, 8014 Fisher Dr., Jonesboro, GA 30236/404-471-0024
Specialties: High-tech working and folders of his design. **Patterns:** Liner lock folders. **Technical:** Grinds 12C27 Sandvik, 440C and A2. Offers heat-treating, anodized-titanium inlays; prefers natural handle materials. **Prices:** $125 to $200. **Remarks:** Part-time maker; first knife sold in 1988. **Mark:** First name, middle initial, last name, city, state.

HARRIS, JAY, 991 Johnson St., Redwood City, CA 94061/415-366-6077
Specialties: Traditional high-tech straight knives and folders of his design. **Patterns:** Daggers, fighters and locking folders. **Technical:** Uses 440C, ATS-34 and CPM. **Prices:** $250 to $850. **Remarks:** Spare-time maker; first knife sold in 1980.

HARRIS, RALPH DEWEY, 2607 Bell Shoals Rd., Brandon, FL 33511/813-681-5293
Specialties: Collectible and working interframe locking folders. **Patterns:** Straight and folding hunters, fighters and pocketknives; backlocks, sidelocks, leverlocks and buttonlocks. **Technical:** Grinds 440C, ATS-34 and some commercial Damascus. Uses jeweled and color anodized titanium and 416SS for frames. **Prices:** $150 to $800; some to $1,000. **Remarks:** Full-time maker; first knife sold in 1978. **Mark:** Last name, or name and city.

HARSEY, WILLIAM H., 82710 N. Howe Ln., Creswell, OR 97426/503-895-4941
Specialties: High-tech kitchen and outdoor knives. **Patterns:** Folding hunters, trout and bird folders; straight hunters, camp knives and axes. **Technical:** Grinds; etches. **Prices:** $125 to $300; some to $1,500. Folders start at $350. **Remarks:** Full-time maker; first knife sold in 1979. **Mark:** Full name, state, U.S.A.

HARTMAN, ARLAN (LANNY), 340 Ruddiman, N. Muskegon, MI 49445/616-744-3635
Specialties: Working straight knives and folders. **Patterns:** Drop-point hunters, coil spring lockers, slip-joints. **Technical:** Flat-grinds D2, 440C and ATS-34. **Prices:** $125 to $250; some to $600. **Remarks:** Part-time maker; first knife sold in 1982. **Mark:** Last name.

HARTSFIELD, PHILL, P.O. Box 1637, Newport Beach, CA 92659-0637/714-722-9792; 714-636-7633
Specialties: Heavy-duty working and using straight knives. **Patterns:** Fighters, swords and survival knives, most in Japanese profile. **Technical:** Grinds A2 and M2. Believes in sole authorship. **Prices:** $350 to $20,000. **Remarks:** Full-time maker; first knife sold about 1966. Doing business as A Cut Above. **Mark:** Initials, chiseled character plus register mark.

HARVEST MOON FORGE (See Rua, Gary [Wolf])

HARVEY MOUNTAIN KNIVES (See Wahlers, Herman F.)

HARVEY, MAX, 14 Bass Rd., Bull Creek, Perth, 6155, WESTERN AUSTRALIA/09-332-7585
Specialties: Daggers, Bowies, fighters and fantasy knives. **Patterns:** Hunters, Bowies, tantos and skinners. **Technical:** Hollow- and flat-grinds 440C, ATS-34, 154CM and Damascus. Offers gem work. **Prices:** $250 to $4,000. **Remarks:** Part-time maker; first knife sold in 1981. **Mark:** First and middle initials, last name.

directory
HATCH—HENRIKSEN

HATCH, KEN, P.O. Box 82, Jensen, UT 84035/801-789-8219
Specialties: Working knives; period pieces. **Patterns:** Buckskinners, tomahawks, period Bowies. **Technical:** Forges and grinds 1095, 01, W2, ATS-34. Prefers natural handle materials. **Prices:** $60 to $250. **Remarks:** Part-time maker; first knife sold in 1977. **Mark:** Name or dragonfly stamp.

HAWK, JACK L., Rt. 1, Box 771, Ceres, VA 24318/703-624-3878, 703-624-3282
Specialties: Fancy and embellished working and using straight knives of his design or to customer specs. **Patterns:** Hunters, Bowies and daggers. **Technical:** Hollow-grinds 440C, ATS-34 and D2; likes bone and ivory handles. **Prices:** $75 to $1,200. **Remarks:** Full-time maker; first knife sold in 1982. **Mark:** Full name and initials.

HAWK, JOE, Rt. 1, Box 196, Ceres, VA 24318/703-624-3282
Specialties: Fancy working knives of his design or to customer specs. **Patterns:** Hunters, combat knives, Bowies and fighters. **Technical:** Grinds mostly ATS-34, 154CM and 440C. Scrimshaws, carves, engraves and silver inlays. **Prices:** $150 to $2,100. **Remarks:** Full-time maker; first knife sold in 1958. **Mark:** Name with tomahawk logo.

HAWK, JOEY K., Rt. 1, Box 196, Ceres, VA 24318/703-624-3282
Specialties: Working straight knives, some fancy. Welcomes customer designs. **Patterns:** Hunters, fighters, daggers, Bowies and miniatures. **Technical:** Grinds 440C or customer preference. Offers some knives with jeweling. **Prices:** $100 to $250; some to $500. **Remarks:** Part-time maker; first knife sold in 1983. **Mark:** First and middle initials, last name stamped.

HAWKINS, RADE, P.O. Box 400, Red Oak, GA 30272/404-964-1177
Specialties: Exotic steels, custom designs, one-of-a-kind knives. **Patterns:** All styles. **Technical:** Grinds CPM 10V, CPM 440V, Vascomax C-350, Stelite K6 and Damascus. **Prices:** Start at $190. **Remarks:** Part-time maker; first knife sold in 1972. **Mark:** Full name, city and state, some last name only.

HAYES, DOLORES, P.O. Box 41405, Los Angeles, CA 90041/213-258-9923
Specialties: High-art working and using straight knives of her design. **Patterns:** Art knives and miniatures. **Technical:** Grinds 440C, stainless AEB, commercial Damascus and ATS-34. **Prices:** $50 to $500; some to $2,000. **Remarks:** Spare-time maker; first knife sold in 1978. **Mark:** Last name.

HAYES, WALLY, 1024 Queen St., Orleans, Ont., CANADA K4A-3N2/613-824-9520
Specialties: Classic and fancy straight knives and folders. **Patterns:** Daggers, Bowies, fighters, tantos. **Technical:** Forges own Damascus and 01; engraves. **Prices:** $250 to $1,500; some to $4,500. **Mark:** Last name.

HAYNES, CHAP, RR #4, Tatamagouche, NS B0K 1V0, CANADA
Specialties: Ergonomic handles fitted to grips; forged carbon tools. **Patterns:** Hunters, Bowies, tomahawks, swords, miniatures. **Technical:** Forges W2, his own Damascus, and meteorite and nickel composites. **Prices:** $200 to $450; some to $1,500. **Remarks:** Part-time maker; first knife sold in 1985. **Mark:** Smith at anvil logo with HAYNES GREAT BLADES.

HAYS, MARK, 1034 Terry Way, Carrollton, TX 75006/214-242-5197
Specialties: Traditional working and using straight knives and folders in standard patterns. **Patterns:** Bowies, hunters and slip-joint folders. **Technical:** Grinds 440C. Custom sheaths by John Simon. **Prices:** $125 to $650. **Remarks:** Part-time maker; first knife sold in 1984. **Mark:** Name.

HEASMAN, H.G., 28, St. Mary's Rd., Llandudno, N. Wales U.K., LL302UB/(UK)0492-876351
Specialties: Miniatures; European daggers and military weapons. **Patterns:** Bowies, daggers and swords. **Technical:** Files from stock high-carbon and stainless steel. **Prices:** $400 to $600. **Remarks:** Part-time maker; first knife sold in 1975. Doing business as Reduced Reality. **Mark:** NA.

HEDRICK, DON, 131 Beechwood Hills, Newport News, VA 23602/804-877-8100
Specialties: Working straight knives; period pieces and fantasy knives. **Patterns:** Hunters, boots, Bowies and miniatures. **Technical:** Grinds 440C and commercial Damascus. **Prices:** $150 to $550; some to $1,200. **Remarks:** Part-time maker; first knife sold in 1982. **Mark:** First initial, last name in oval logo.

HEGWALD, J.L., 1106 Charles, Humboldt, KS 66748/316-473-3523
Specialties: Working straight knives, some fancy. **Patterns:** Makes Bowies, miniatures. **Technical:** Forges or grinds 01, L6, 440C; mixes materials in handles. **Prices:** $35 to $200; some higher. **Remarks:** Part-time maker; first knife sold in 1983. **Mark:** First and middle initials.

HEGWOOD, JOEL, Rt. 4, Box 229, Summerville, GA 30747/404-397-8187
Specialties: High-tech working knives of his design. **Patterns:** Hunters, boots and survival knives; locking folders, slip-joints and interframes. **Technical:** Grinds A2, 01 and D2; uses 7075 aluminum in lightweight folder frames. **Prices:** $65 to $125; some to $200. **Remarks:** Part-time maker; first knife sold in 1979. **Mark:** Last name.

HEHN, RICHARD KARL, Lehnm hler Str. 1, D-6531 D"rrebach GERMANY/06724 3152
Specialties: High-tech working knives. **Patterns:** Hunters, fighters, Bowies and locking folders. **Technical:** Forges and grinds 440C, CPM and his own stainless Damascus; high-tech polishing for all steels; clean grinds; deluxe natural handles. **Prices:** $350 to $4,000; some to $9,000. **Remarks:** Full-time maker; first knife sold in 1963. **Mark:** Runic last initial in logo.

HEITLER, HENRY, P.O. Box 15025, Tampa, FL 33684-5025/813-933-1645
Specialties: Traditional working and using straight knives of his design and to customer specs. **Patterns:** Fighters, hunters, utility/camp knives and fillet knives. **Technical:** Flat-grinds ATS-34; offers tapered tangs. **Prices:** $120 to $350; some to $600. **Remarks:** Part-time maker; first knife sold in 1990. **Mark:** First initial, last name, city, state circling double Hs.

HELTON, ROY, P.O. Box 26598, San Diego, CA 92196/619-578-3399
Specialties: Locking folders and straight knives in utility, fancy and interframe styles. **Patterns:** Hunters, boots, fighters, daggers and some art pieces. **Technical:** Grinds ATS-34, others on request. Likes filework; uses mostly natural handle materials. **Prices:** $100 to $525; some higher. **Remarks:** Part-time maker; first knife sold in 1975. **Mark:** Lion logo with name, city and state.

HEMBROOK, RON, P.O. Box 153, Neosho, WI 53059/414-625-3607
Specialties: Period pieces, art knives and working straight knives; enjoys customer designs. **Patterns:** Hunters, push daggers, miniatures, fighters and Bowies; lock-back folders special order only. **Technical:** Grinds 01, 440C, D2, ATS-34 and commercial hand-forged Damascus; laser-engraves handles. **Prices:** $95 to $255; some to $500. **Remarks:** Part-time maker; first knife sold in 1980. **Mark:** Last name and serial number.

HEMPHILL, JESSE, 896 Big Hill Rd., Berea, KY 40403
Specialties: Period pieces, folders and scagel reproductions. **Patterns:** Hawks, Bowies sets, fighters and utility knives. **Technical:** Forges his own Damascus, D2, 5160 and 52100. **Prices:** $50 to $300; some to $500. **Remarks:** Full-time maker; first knife sold in 1986. **Mark:** Initials or a turtle.

HENDRICKS, SAMUEL J., Star Route, Box 69, Maurertown, VA 22644/703-436-3305
Specialties: Integral hunters and skinners of thin design. **Patterns:** Boots, hunters and locking folders. **Technical:** Grinds ATS-34, 440C and D2. Integral liners and bolsters of N-S and 7075 T6 aircraft aluminium. Does leatherwork. **Prices:** $50 to $250; some to $500. **Remarks:** Full-time maker; first knife sold in 1992. **Mark:** First and middle initials, last name, city and state in football-style logo.

HENDRICKSON, E. JAY, 4204 Ballenger Creek Pike, Frederick, MD 21701/301-663-6923
Specialties: Classic collectors and working straight knives of his design. **Patterns:** Bowies, Kukri's, camp, hunters, and fighters in the Moran styles. **Technical:** Forges W2, 01, 1095, 5160; makes Damascus; does a lot of wire inlay. **Prices:** $300 to $4,000. **Remarks:** Full-time maker; first knife sold in 1975. **Mark:** Last name, M.S.

HENNON, ROBERT, 940 Vincent Lane, Ft. Walton Beach, FL 32547/904-862-9734

HENRIKSEN, HANS J., Birkegaardsvej 24, DK 3200 Helsinge, DENMARK/FAX: 45 4879 4899
Specialties: Zirconia ceramic blades. **Patterns:** Customer designs. **Technical:** Slip-cast zirconia-water mix in plaster mould; offers hidden or full tang. **Prices:** White blades start at $10/cm; colored +50 percent. **Remarks:** Part-time maker; first ceramic blade sold in 1989. **Mark:** Initial logo.

custom knifemakers
HENRY & SON—HINK

HENRY & SON, PETER, 332 Nine Mile Ride, Wokingham, Berkshire RG11 3NJ, ENGLAND/0734-734475
Specialties: Period pieces to customer specs only. **Patterns:** Period pieces only—Scottish dirks, Sgian Dubhs and Bowies, moden hunters. **Technical:** Grinds 01 and Damascus. **Prices:** $67 to $247; Damascus knives cased $975 to $1800. **Remarks:** Full-time maker; first knife sold in 1974. **Mark:** P. Henry & Son.

HENSLEY, WAYNE, P.O. Box 904, Conyers, GA 30207/404-483-8938
Specialties: Period pieces and fancy working knives. **Patterns:** Boots to Bowies, locking folders to miniatures. Large variety of straight knives. **Technical:** Grinds D2, 440C, 154CM and commerical Damascus. **Prices:** $50 to $150; some to $800. **Remarks:** Part-time maker; first knife sold in 1974. **Mark:** Last name.

HERMAN, TIM, 7721 Foster, Overland Park, KS 66204/913-649-3860; FAX: 913-649-0603
Specialties: Investment-grade folders of his design; interframes and bolster frames. **Patterns:** Boots, Bowies, daggers and push knives; high-quality folders and interframes. **Technical:** Grinds ATS-34 and A.J. Hubbard Damascus. Engraves and gold inlays with pearl, jade, lapis and Australian opal. **Prices:** $1,000 to $15,000. **Remarks:** Full-time maker; first knife sold in 1978. **Mark:** Etched signature.

HERMES, DANA E., 39594 Kona Ct., Fremont, CA 94538/415-490-0393
Specialties: Fancy and embellished classic straight knives of his design. **Patterns:** Hunters and Bowies. **Technical:** Grinds 440C and D2. **Prices:** $200 to $600; some to $1,000. **Remarks:** Spare-time maker; first knife sold in 1985. **Mark:** Last name.

HERNDON, WM. R. "BILL", 32520 Michigan St., Acton, CA 93510/805-269-5860; FAX: 805-269-4568
Specialties: Straight knives, plain and fancy. **Technical:** Carbon steel (white and blued), Damascus, stainless steels. **Prices:** NA. **Remarks:** Part-time maker; first knife sold in 1981. **Mark:** Signature and/or helm.

HERRON, GEORGE, 474 Antonio Way, Springfield, SC 29146/803-258-3914
Specialties: High-tech working and using straight knives; some folders. **Patterns:** Hunters, fighters, boots in personal styles. **Technical:** Grinds 154CM, ATS-34. **Prices:** $75 to $500; some to $750. **Remarks:** Full-time maker; first knife sold in 1963. About a seven- to eight-year (or more) backlog; will not quote a delivery date. **Mark:** Last name in script.

HESSER, DAVID, P.O. Box 1079, Dripping Springs, TX 78620/512-894-0100
Specialties: High-art straight knives of his design; period pieces. **Patterns:** Daggers, hunters, swords, battle axes, swords. **Technical:** Forges 1095 spring steel; grinds 01 and recycled tool steel. Offers custom lapidary work and stone-setting, stone handles and custom hardwood scabbards. **Prices:** $95 to $500; some to $4,000. **Remarks:** Full-time maker; first knife sold in 1989. Doing business as Exotic Blades. **Mark:** Last name, year.

HETHCOAT, DON, Box 1764, Clovis, NM 88101/505-762-5721
Specialties: Working straight knives and folders. **Patterns:** Hunters, axes, fishing knives, Bowies, boots and locking folders. **Technical:** Grinds ATS-34 and 440C. Forges some 5168 on Bowies; uses his own Damascus. **Prices:** $100 to $2,000. **Remarks:** Part-time maker; first knife sold in 1969. **Mark:** Last name and zip code on stock removal; last name on forged 5168 and Damascus.

HETMANSKI, THOMAS S., 1107 William St., Trenton, NJ 08610/609-989-9371
Specialties: Working knives, replicas, military-style knives and miniatures. **Patterns:** Hunters, boots, miniatures and some folders. **Technical:** Grinds A2, 440C, ATS-34 and commercial Damascus. **Prices:** $150 to $400; some higher. **Remarks:** Part-time maker; first knife sold in 1982. **Mark:** Initials in monogram.

HIBBEN, DARYL, P.O. Box 172, 1331 Dawkins Rd., LaGrange, KY 40031-0172/502-222-0983
Specialties: Working straight knives, some fancy to customer specs. **Patterns:** Hunters, fighters, Bowies, short sword, art and fantasy. **Technical:** Grinds 440C, ATS-34, 154CM, Damascus; prefers hollow-grinds. **Prices:** $175 to $3,000. **Remarks:** Full-time maker; first knife sold in 1979. **Mark:** Block letters.

HIBBEN, GIL, P.O. Box 13, LaGrange, KY 40031/502-222-1397
Specialties: Working knives and fantasy pieces to customer specs. **Patterns:** Full range of straight knives, including swords, axes and miniatures; some locking folders. **Technical:** Grinds D2, 440C and 154CM. **Prices:** $300 to $2,000; some to $10,000. **Remarks:** Full-time maker; first knife sold in 1957. Maker and designer of Rambo III knife; made swords for movie Marked for Death and throwing knife for movie Under Seige; made belt buckle knife and knives for movie Perfect Weapon; made knives featured in movie Star Trek VII the Next Generation. **Mark:** Hibben Knives, city and state, or signature.

HIBBEN, JOLEEN, P.O. Box 172, LaGrange, KY 40031/502-222-0983
Specialties: Miniature straight knives of her design; period pieces. **Patterns:** Hunters, axes and fantasy knives. **Technical:** Grinds Damascus, 1095 tool steel and stainless 440C or ATS-34. Uses wood, ivory, bone, feathers and claws on/for handles. **Prices:** $60 to $200. **Remarks:** Spare-time maker; first knife sold in 1991. **Mark:** Initials or first name.

HIBBEN, WESTLEY G., 14101 Sunview Dr., Anchorage, AK 99515
Specialties: Working straight knives of his design or to customer specs. **Patterns:** Hunters, fighters, daggers, combat knives and some fantasy pieces. **Technical:** Grinds 440C mostly. Filework available. **Prices:** $200 to $400; some to $3,000. **Remarks:** Part-time maker; first knife sold in 1988. **Mark:** Signature.

HIELSCHER, GUY, HC34, P.O. Box 992, Alliance, NE 69301/308-762-4318
Specialties: Traditional and working straight knives of his design, to customer specs and in standard pattersn. **Patterns:** Bowies, fighters, skinners, daggers and hunters. **Technical:** Forges his own Damascus from 0-1 and 1018 steel. **Prices:** $150 to $225; some to $850. **Remarks:** Part-time maker; first knife sold in 1988. Doing business as G.H. Knives. **Mark:** Initials in arrowhead.

HIGH, TOM, 5474 S. 112.8 Rd., Alamosa, CO 81101/719-589-2108
Specialties: Hunters, some fancy. **Patterns:** Drop-points in several shapes; some semi-skinners. Knives designed by and for top outfitters and guides. **Technical:** Grinds ATS-34; likes hollow-grinds, mirror finishes; prefers scrimmable handles. **Prices:** $100 to $5,000. **Remarks:** Full-time maker; first knife sold in 1965. Three-year backlog on all ordered knives. **Mark:** Initials connected; arrow through last name on fancy knives.

HILKER, THOMAS N., 500 Holmestead Rd., Williams, OR 97544/503-846-6461
Specialties: Traditional working straight knives and folders. **Patterns:** Folding skinner in two sizes, Bowies, fork and knife sets, camp knives and interchangeables. **Technical:** Grinds D2, 440C and ATS-34. Heat-treats. **Prices:** $50 to $350; some to $400. Doing business as Thunderbolt Artisans. Only limited production models available; not currently taking orders. **Remarks:** Full-time maker; first knife sold in 1983. **Mark:** Last name.

HILL, HOWARD E., 111 Mission Lane, Polson, MT 59860/406-883-3405
Specialties: Working knives in personal designs. **Patterns:** Fillets, fighters, Bowies, daggers and skinners. **Technical:** Grinds 440C to micro mirror finish with buffed edges. **Prices:** $110 to $300. **Remarks:** Part-time maker; first knife sold in 1981. **Mark:** Persuader.

HILL, RICK, 20 Nassau, Collinsville, IL 62234/618-288-4370
Specialties: Working knives and period pieces to customer specs. **Patterns:** Hunters, locking folders, fighters and daggers. **Technical:** Grinds D2, 440C and 154CM; forges his own Damascus. **Prices:** $75 to $500; some to $3,000. **Remarks:** Part-time maker; first knife sold in 1983. **Mark:** Full name in hill shape logo.

HILL, STEVEN E., 7814 Toucan Dr., Orlando, FL 32822/407-277-3549
Specialties: Bowies and the brass back Iron Mistress liner lock. **Patterns:** Bowies, California daggers, liner locks, fighters and hunters. **Technical:** Grinds D2 and 440C; ATS-34 and Damascus on request. Likes filework, exotic woods and hand-rubbed finishes. **Prices:** $180 to $1000; some higher. **Remarks:** Full-time maker; first knife sold in 1978. **Mark:** First initial, last name and handmade.

HINDERER, RICK, 5423 Kister Rd., Wooster, OH 44691/216-263-0962
Specialties: Working knives to one-of-a-kind Damascus straight knives and folders. **Patterns:** All. **Technical:** Grinds ATS-34 and D2; forges 01, W2 and his own nickel Damascus steel. **Prices:** $50 to $3,200. **Remarks:** Part-time maker; first knife sold in 1988. Doing business as Mustang Forge. **Mark:** Initials or first initial, last name.

HINK III, LES, 1599 Aptos Lane, Stockton, CA 95206/209-547-1292
Specialties: Traditional and contemporary folders; some straight knives to customer specs. **Patterns:** Locking and slip-joint folders, single and multi-blade. **Tech-

FIFTEENTH EDITION 209

directory
HINSON—HORNBY

nical: Grinds 440C, ATS-34 and D2. Uses natural materials for handles. **Prices:** $150 to $500. **Remarks:** Part-time maker; first knife sold in 1980. **Mark:** Last name, or last name 3.

HINSON and SON, R., 2419 Edgewood Rd., Columbus, GA 31906/706-327-6801 **Specialties:** Working straight knives and folders. **Patterns:** Locking folders, liner locks, combat knives and swords. **Technical:** Grinds 440C and commercial Damascus. **Prices:** $100 to $350; some to $1,500. **Remarks:** Part-time maker; first knife sold in 1983. Son Bob is co-worker. **Mark:** HINSON.

HINTZ, GERALD, 5402 Sahara Ct., Helena, MT 59605

HIRAM KNIVES (See Price, Joel Hiram)

HIRAYAMA, HARUMI, 4-5-13, Kitamachi, Warabi City, Saitama Pref., JAPAN/048-443-2248 **Specialties:** High-tech working knives of her design. **Patterns:** Locking folders, interframes, straight gents and slipjoints. **Technical:** Grinds 440C or equivalent; uses natural handle materials and gold. **Prices:** Start at $500. **Remarks:** Part-time maker; first knife sold in 1985. **Mark:** First initial, last name.

HITCHMOUGH, HOWARD, 3 Highland Lodge, Fox Hill, London SE 19 2UJ, ENGLAND/081-653-6166 **Specialties:** Deluxe working knives. **Patterns:** Fighters, boots, hunters, lockback folders and linerlocks. **Technical:** Grinds 440C, ATS-34 and commercial Damascus. Prefers hand-rubbed finishes and natural handle materials. **Prices:** $250 to $1,500; some to $4,000. **Remarks:** Full-time maker; first knife sold in 1967. **Mark:** Last name, country.

HOCKENSMITH, DAN, P.O. Box E, Drake, CO 80515/303-669-5404 **Specialties:** Traditional working and using straight knives of his design. **Patterns:** Hunters, Bowies, folders and utility/camp knives. **Technical:** Uses his Damascus, 5160, carbon steel and wire cable. **Prices:** $150 to $600; some to $1,000. **Remarks:** Full-time maker; first knife sold in 1987. **Mark:** Stylized initials.

HODGE, J.B., 1100 Woodmont Ave. SE, Huntsville, AL 35801/205-536-8388 **Specialties:** Fancy working folders. **Patterns:** Slipjoints. **Technical:** Grinds 154CM and ATS-34. **Prices:** Start at $175. **Remarks:** Part-time maker; first knife sold in 1978. Not currently taking orders. **Mark:** Name, city and state.

HODGE III, JOHN, 422 S. 15th St., Palatka, FL 32177/904-328-3897 **Specialties:** Fancy straight knives and folders. **Patterns:** Various. **Technical:** Pattern-welded Damascus—"Southern-style". **Prices:** To $1,000. **Remarks:** Part-time maker; first knife sold in 1981. **Mark:** JH3 logo.

HODGSON, RICHARD J., 9081 Tahoe Lane, Boulder, CO 80301/303-666-9460 **Specialties:** Straight knives and folders in standard patterns. **Patterns:** High-tech knives in various patterns. **Technical:** Grinds 440C, AEB-L and CPM. **Prices:** $850 to $2,200. **Remarks:** Part-time maker. **Mark:** None.

HOEL, STEVE, P.O. Box 283, Pine, AZ 85544/602-476-4278 **Specialties:** Investor-class folders, straight knives and period pieces of his design. **Patterns:** Folding interframes—lockers and slip-joints; straight Bowies, boots and daggers. **Technical:** Grinds 154CM, ATS-34 and commercial Damascus. **Prices:** $600 to $1,200; some to $7,500. **Remarks:** Full-time maker. **Mark:** Initial logo with name and address.

HOFFMAN, HAROLD, 7174 Hoffman Rd., San Angelo, TX 76905/915-655-5953 **Specialties:** Stout using folders. **Patterns:** Spring-back and lock-back folders only. **Technical:** Close tolerance fitting of high-strength parts; practical finishes. **Prices:** Moderate. **Remarks:** Veteran metalworker and knifemaker. **Mark:** Name.

HOFFMAN, KEVIN L., P.O. Box 5107, Winter Park, FL 32793/407-678-3124 **Specialties:** High-tech working knives. **Patterns:** Fighters, tantos, liner lock folders, claws and survival knives. **Technical:** Grinds ATS-34, 440C and D2. Tantos have polished temper lines and sandblasted finishes. Makes Kydex sheaths. **Prices:** $115 to $600; some to $1500. **Remarks:** Full-time maker; first knife sold in 1981. **Mark:** Initials.

HOFFMANN, UWE H., P.O. Box 60114, Vancouver, BC V5W 4B5 CANADA/604-572-7320 (after 5 p.m.) **Specialties:** High-tech working knives, folders and fantasy knives of his design or to customer specs. **Patterns:** Hunters, fishing knives, combat and survival knives, folders and diver's knives. **Technical:** Grinds 440C, ATS-34, D2 and commercial Damascus. **Prices:** $95 to $900; some to $2,000 and higher. **Remarks:** Full-time maker; first knife sold in 1985. **Mark:** Hoffmann Handmade Knives.

HOLDER, D'ALTON, 4412 W. Diana, Glendale, AZ 85302/602-435-9589 **Specialties:** Deluxe working knives and high-art hunters. **Patterns:** Drop-point hunters, fighters, Bowies, miniatures and locking folders. **Technical:** Grinds 440C and 154CM; uses amber and other materials in combination on stick tangs. **Prices:** $150 to $350; some to $1,000. **Remarks:** Full-time maker; first knife sold in 1970. **Mark:** D'HOLDER, city and state.

HOLLAND, DALE J., 4561 247th Place SE, Issaquah, WA 98027/206-391-4665 **Specialties:** Fancy folders. **Patterns:** Locking folders, patent locks and interframes. **Technical:** Grinds 440C, 154CM and ATS-34. **Prices:** $120 to $350; some to $450. **Remarks:** Part-time maker; first knife sold in 1980. **Mark:** Initials.

HOLLAND, JOHN H., 143 Green Meadow Lane, Calhoun, GA 30701/706-629-9622 **Specialties:** Traditional and fancy straight knives and folders. **Patterns:** Hunters, locking folders, slip-joints. **Technical:** Grinds 440V, 440C, 01. **Prices:** $200 to $500; some to $1,000. **Remarks:** Spare-time maker; first knife sold in 1988. **Mark:** First and last name, city, state.

HOLLETT, JEFF, 905 Krider Rd., P.O. Box 255, Fate, TX 75132/214-771-2014 **Specialties:** Classic, traditional, fantasy and working straight knives and folders of his design, to customer specs and in standard patterns; period pieces. **Patterns:** Bowies, fighters and hunters. **Technical:** Grinds ATS-34, 440C and D2. Heat-treats. **Prices:** $100 to $700; some to $1,000. **Remarks:** Full-time maker; first knife sold in 1989. **Mark:** Name, city, state, month and year.

HOLLOWAY, PAUL, 714 Burksdale Rd., Norfolk, VA 23518/804-588-7071 **Specialties:** Working straight knives and folders to customer specs. **Patterns:** Lockers and slip-joints; fighters and boots; fishing and push knives, from swords to miniatures. **Technical:** Grinds A2, D2, 154CM, 440C and ATS-34. **Prices:** $125 to $400; some to $1,200. **Remarks:** Part-time maker; first knife sold in 1981. **Mark:** Last name, or last name and city in logo.

HOLMES, DOC (See Holmes, Robert)

HOLMES, ROBERT, 4423 Lake Larto Circle, Baton Rouge, LA 70816/504-291-4864 **Specialties:** Using straight knives and folders of his design or to customer specs. **Patterns:** Bowies, utility hunters, camp knives, skinners, slip-joint and lock-back folders. **Technical:** Forges 1065, 1095 and L6. Makes his own Damascus and cable Damascus. Offers clay tempering. **Prices:** $150 to $1,500. **Remarks:** Part-time maker; first knife sold in 1988. **Mark:** DOC HOLMES, or anvil logo with last initial inside.

HOLUM, MORTEN, Bolerskrenten 28, 0691 Oslo, NORWAY/011-47-22-27-69-96 **Specialties:** Working straight knives. **Patterns:** Traditional Norwegian knives, hunters, fighters, axes. **Prices:** @200 to $800; some to $1,500. **Remarks:** Part-time maker; first knife sold in 1986. **Mark:** Last name.

HOMER, GLEN, P.O. Box 2702, Bloomfield, NM 87413/505-632-9615 **Specialties:** Damascus skinners. **Patterns:** Bowies, skinners, camp knives and folders. **Technical:** Forges 5160; will grind stainless on request; makes his own Damascus. **Prices:** $100 to $500. **Remarks:** Part-time maker; first knife sold in 1987. **Mark:** Name or initials.

HOOT'S HANDMADE KNIVES (See Gibson, Jim)

HORN, JESS, 87481 Rhodowood Dr., Florence, OR 97439/503-997-2593; FAX: 503-997-4550 **Specialties:** Investor-class working folders; period pieces; collectibles. **Patterns:** High-tech design and finish in folders; liner locks, traditional slip-joints. **Technical:** Grinds ATS-34, 154CM. **Prices:** Start at $500. **Remarks:** Full-time maker; first knife sold in 1968. **Mark:** Full name or last name.

HORNBY, GLEN, P.O. Box 444, Glendale, CA 91209/818-244-1354 **Specialties:** Fancy working knives. **Patterns:** Hunters, fighters, folders. **Technical:**

Grinds ATS-34, 154CM and 440C; likes bighorn sheep handles. **Prices:** $200 to $1,000. **Remarks:** Part-time maker. **Mark:** Script name under sheep horns.

HORTON, SCOT, 604 Parnell Dr., Buhl, ID 83316/208-543-4413
Specialties: Traditional working and using straight knives and folders. **Patterns:** Hunters, Bowies, fighters and skinners. **Technical:** Grinds 440C and ATS-34. Uses Rocky Mountain sheephorn, elk antler and exotic woods. Mirror finish. **Prices:** $200 to $900; some to $2,000. **Remarks:** Full-time maker; first knife sold in 1990. **Mark:** Full name in arch underlined with arrow, city, state.

HOUSE OF KOGATANA (See Rowe, Stewart G.)

HOWARD, DURVYN M., 4220 McLain St. S., Hokes Bluff, AL 35903/205-492-5720
Specialties: Collectible upscale folders; multiple patents. **Patterns:** Fine gentlemen's folders. **Technical:** Uses natural and exotic materials, precious metals and gemstones. **Prices:** $5,000 to $20,000. **Remarks:** Full-time maker; now accepting orders—purchase through Barrett-Smythe Gallery, New York, NY, exclusive agent. **Mark:** Last name etched on tang; opposite side marked Barrett-Smythe.

HOWARD, SETH, P.O. Box 65051, Baton Rouge, LA 70896

HOWELL, LEN, 550 Lee Rd. 169, Opelika, AL 36801/205-749-1942
Specialties: Traditional and working knives of his design and to customer specs. **Patterns:** Bowies, hunters and utility/camp knives. **Technical:** Forges cable Damascus, 1085 and 5160. **Prices:** $100 to $175; some to $400. **Remarks:** Full-time maker; first knife sold in 1991. **Mark:** Stamped or engraved last name.

HOWELL, ROBERT L., Rt. 3, Box 740, Hallsville, TX 75650/903-660-0423
Specialties: Straight knives and folders of his design. **Patterns:** Hunters and locking folders. **Technical:** Grinds D2 and ATS-34; forges and grinds Damascus. **Prices:** $75 to $200; some to $2,500. **Remarks:** Part-time maker; first knife sold in 1978. Doing business as Howell Knives. **Mark:** Last name.

HOWELL, TED, 1294 Wilson Rd., Wetumpka, AL 36092/205-569-2281; FAX: 205-569-1764
Specialties: Working/using straight knives and folders of his design; period pieces. **Patterns:** Bowies, fighters, hunters. **Technical:** Forges 5160, 1085 and cable. Offers light engraving and scrimshaw; filework. **Prices:** $75 to $250; some to $450. **Remarks:** Part-time maker; first knife sold in 1991. Doing business as Howell Co. **Mark:** Last name, Slapout AL.

HOWSER, JOHN C., 54 Bell Ln., Frankfort, KY 40601/502-875-3678
Specialties: Practical working knives. **Patterns:** Hunters, fighters, locking folders, fillet knives, slip-joint folders, liner locks. **Technical:** Grinds D2, 440C and 154CM; clean, crisp lines and mirror surface; natural materials. **Prices:** $85 to $200; some to $350. **Remarks:** Part-time maker; first knife sold in 1974. **Mark:** Signature or stamp.

HRISOULAS, JIM, 330 S. Decatur Ave., Suite 109, Las Vegas, NV 89107/702-566-8551
Specialties: Working straight knives; period pieces. **Patterns:** Swords, daggers and sgian dubhs. **Technical:** Double-edged differential heat treating. **Prices:** $85 to $175; some to $600 and higher. **Remarks:** Full-time maker; first knife sold in 1973. Author of *The Complete Bladesmith*, *The Pattern Welded Blade* and *The Master Bladesmith*. Doing business as Salamander Armoury. **Mark:** 8R logo and sword and salamander.

HUBBARD, ARTHUR J., 574 Cutlers Farm Road, Monroe, CT 06468/203-268-3998
Specialties: Working knives of his design or to customer specs. **Patterns:** Hunters, fighters, boots, wood carvers; traditional locking folders. **Technical:** Makes precision engineered Damascus in all-stainless steel, Mokume of copper and stainless steel, copper, brass and nickel silver, copper and brass. **Prices:** Start at $100. **Remarks:** Full-time maker; first knife sold in 1976. **Mark:** Name, city and state; first and middle initials, last name, stainless; P.E.D. stainless.

HUDSON, C. ROBBIN, 22280 Frazier Rd., Rock Hall, MD 21661/410-639-7273
Specialties: High-art working knives. **Patterns:** Hunters, Bowies, fighters and kitchen knives. **Technical:** Forges W2, nickle steel, pure nickle steel, composite and mosaic Damascus; makes knives one at a time. **Prices:** $300 to $700; some to $5,000. **Remarks:** Full-time maker; first knife sold in 1970. **Mark:** Last name and MS.

HUDSON, ROBERT, 3802 Black Cricket Ct., Humble, TX 77396/713-454-7207
Specialties: Working straight knives of his design. **Patterns:** Bowies, hunters, skinners, fighters and utility knives. **Technical:** Grinds D2, 440C, 154CM and commercial Damascus. **Prices:** $85 to $350; some to $1,500. **Remarks:** Part-time maker; first knife sold in 1980. **Mark:** Full name, handmade, city and state.

HUDSON, TOMMY, P.O. Box 2046, Monroe, NC 28110/704-283-8556
Specialties: Classic high-art straight knives and folders of his design and to customer specs. **Patterns:** Bowies, hunters and slip-joint folders; high-art golf putters. **Technical:** Grinds 440C, ATS-34. Engraves. **Prices:** $400 to $1,000; some to $2,500. **Remarks:** Part-time maker; first knife sold in 1989. **Mark:** First initial, last name or last name only.

HUEY, STEVE, 27645 Snyder Rd. #38, Junction City, OR 97448/503-689-5010
Specialties: Working straight knives, some one-of-a-kind. **Patterns:** Hunters, fighters, fishing knives and kitchen cutlery. **Technical:** Hollow- or flat-grinds 1095, L6, 440C, D2 and ATS-34. **Prices:** $75 to $600. **Remarks:** Full-time maker; first knife sold in 1981. **Mark:** Last name in rectangle.

HUGHES, DAN, 13743 Persimmon Blvd., West Palm Beach, FL 33411
Specialties: Working straight knives to customer specs. **Patterns:** Hunters, fighters, fillet knives. **Technical:** Grinds 440C and ATS-34. **Prices:** $55 to $175; some to $300. **Remarks:** Part-time maker; first knife sold in 1984. **Mark:** Initials.

HUGHES, DARYLE, 10979 Leonard, Nunica, MI 49448/616-837-6623
Specialties: Working knives. **Patterns:** Buckskinners, hunters, camp knives, kitchen and fishing knives. **Technical:** Forges and grinds W2, 01 and D2. **Prices:** $40 to $100; some to $400. **Remarks:** Part-time maker, first knife sold in 1979. **Mark:** Name and city in logo.

HUGHES, ED, 280½ Holly Lane, Grand Junction, CO 81503/303-243-8547
Specialties: Working knives and art knives. **Patterns:** Bowies, push knives; pocket-size straight knives. **Technical:** Grinds stainless steels. Engraves. **Prices:** $75 to $250; some to $600. **Remarks:** Full-time maker; first knife sold in 1978. **Mark:** Name or initials.

HUGHES, LAWRENCE, 207 W. Crestway, Plainview, TX 79072/806-293-5406
Specialties: Working and display knives. **Patterns:** Bowies, daggers, hunters, buckskinners. **Technical:** Grinds D2, 440C and 154CM. **Prices:** $125 to $300; some to $2,000. **Remarks:** Full-time maker; first knife sold in 1979. **Mark:** Name with buffalo skull in center.

HULL, MICHAEL J., 1330 Hermits Circle, Cottonwood, AZ 86326/602-634-2871
Specialties: Working knives and period pieces to customer specs. **Patterns:** Hunters, fighters, Bowies, camp and mediterranean knives, etc. **Technical:** Grinds 440C, ATS-34 and D2. **Prices:** $75 to $275; some to $700. **Remarks:** Full-time maker; first knife sold in 1983. **Mark:** Name, city, state.

HULSEY, HOYT, 5699 Pope Ave., Steele, AL 35987/205-538-6765
Specialties: Traditional working straight knives and folders of his design. **Patterns:** Hunters and utility/camp knives. **Technical:** Grinds 440C, ATS-34, 01 and A2. **Prices:** $75 to $150. **Remarks:** Part-time maker; first knife sold in 1989. **Mark:** Full name, city and state.

HUME, DON, 3511 Camino De La Cumbre, Sherman Oaks, CA 91423/818-783-5486
Specialties: Medieval theme, straight blade working and collector designed pieces. **Patterns:** Hunters, daggers and Bowies. **Technical:** Grinds Damascus, 440C, 154CM with exotic handle material. **Prices:** $180 to $1600. **Remarks:** Part-time maker; first knife sold in 1987. **Mark:** Curved D.W. HUME; first of a series of one-of-a-kinds also marked with the Fiera Madonna.

HUMENICK, ROY, P.O. Box 55, Rescue, CA 95672
Specialties: Working knives of his design. **Patterns:** Hunters, fighters, etc. **Technical:** Grinds ATS-34; forges W2 and 5160; makes Damascus. **Prices:** $200 to $600; some to $1,500. **Remarks:** First knife sold in 1984. **Mark:** Name or initials in logo.

HUMPHREYS, JOEL, Rt. 1, Box 179-B, Bowling Green, FL 33834/813-773-0439
Specialties: Traditional working/using straight knives and folders of his design and in standard patterns. **Patterns:** Hunters, locking folders, utility/camp knives. **Tech-

nical: Grinds ATS-34, D2, 440C. All knives have tapered tangs, mitered bolster/handle joints, handles of horn or bone and hand-stitched fitted sheaths. **Prices:** $135 to $225; some to $350. **Remarks:** Part-time maker; first knife sold in 1990. Doing business as Sovereign Knives. **Mark:** NA

HUNT, ALEX, 1916 Simsbury Ct., Ft. Collins, CO 80524/303-490-1065
Specialties: Fancy working straight knives. **Patterns:** Hunters, fighters and boot knives. **Technical:** Grinds 440C, ATS-34 and commercial Damascus. **Prices:** $75 to $200; some to $300. **Remarks:** Part-time maker; first knife sold in 1989. Apprenticed under Bill Amoureaux in Alaska. **Mark:** First name in knife shape.

HURST, JEFF, Rt. 1, Box 22-A, Rutledge, TN 37861/615-828-5729
Specialties: Working straight knives and folders of his design. **Patterns:** Tomahawks, hunters, boots, folders and fighters. **Technical:** Forges W2, 01 and his own Damascus. Makes mokume. **Prices:** $175 to $350; some to $500. **Remarks:** Full-time maker; first knife sold in 1984. Doing business as Buzzard's Knob Forge. **Mark:** Last name; partnered knives are marked with Newman L. Smith, handle artisan, and SH in script.

HUSIAK, MYRON, P.O. Box 238, Altona 3018, Victoria, AUSTRALIA/03-315-6752
Specialties: Straight knives and folders of his design or to customer specs. **Patterns:** Hunters, fighters, lock-back folders, skinners and boots. **Technical:** Forges and grinds his own Damascus, 440C and ATS-34. **Prices:** $200 to $900. **Remarks:** Part-time maker; first knife sold in 1974. **Mark:** First initial, last name in logo and serial number.

HYDE, JIMMY, 5094 Stagecoach Rd., Ellenwood, GA 30049/404-968-1951; FAX: 404-209-1741
Specialties: Working straight knives of any design; period pieces. **Patterns:** Bowies, hunters and utility knives. **Technical:** Grinds 440C and 5160; forges 01. Makes his own Damascus and cable Damascus. **Prices:** $75 to $200; some to $400. **Remarks:** Part-time maker; first knife sold in 1978. **Mark:** First initial, last name.

i

IIAMS, RICHARD D., P.O. Box 963, Mills, WY 82644/307-265-2435 evenings
Specialties: Using straight knives and folders. **Patterns:** camp knives, drop-point hunters, lock-back folders and skinners. **Technical:** Pattern-welded DAmascus, 52100 and mild steel. Uses filework on folders. **Prices:** $85 to $300; some higher. **Remarks:** Part-time maker; first knife sold in 1981. **Mark:** Initial logo.

IMBODEN II, HOWARD L., 620 Deauville Dr., Dayton, OH 45429/513-439-1536
Specialties: One-of-a-kind art knives with hand-carved wildlife antler handles; ivory. **Technical:** Grinds stainless and other steels; satin, bead-blasted and gun-blued blades. Uses commercial Damascus, obsidian, other maker's blades, cast sterling silver; 14K, 18K and 24K gold guards and animals. Recycles animal parts; carves handles for other knifemakers. Scrimshands and carves. **Prices:** $65 to $25,000. **Remarks:** Full-time maker; first knife sold in 1986. **Mark:** First and last initials, II.

IMEL, BILLY MACE, 1616 Bundy Ave., New Castle, IN 47362/317-529-1651
Specialties: High-art working knives, period pieces and personal cutlery. **Patterns:** Daggers, fighters, hunters; locking folders and slip-joints with interframes. **Technical:** Forges and grinds D2, 440C and 154CM. **Prices:** $200 to $2,000; some to $6,000. **Remarks:** Part-time maker; first knife sold in 1973. **Mark:** Name in monogram.

IRIE, MICHAEL L. (See Wood, Barry B. and Irie, Michael L.)

THE IRON MASTER (See Chastain, Wade)

IRON MOUNTAIN FORGE WORKS (See Small, Ed)

ISHIHARA, NOBUHIKO, 86-18 Motomachi, Sakura City, JAPAN/043-485-3208; FAX: 043-485-3208
Specialties: Fantasy straight knives and folders of his design. **Patterns:** Bowies, daggers, hunters, locking folders, utility/camp knives. **Technical:** Grinds CV134, 440C, ATS-34, D2. Engraves. **Prices:** $450 to $1,200; some to $10,000. **Remarks:** Full-time maker; first knife sold in 1987. **Mark:** Hank.

j

JACKS, JIM, 344 S. Hollenbeck Ave., Covina, CA 91723-2513/818-331-5665
Specialties: Working straight knives in standard patterns. **Patterns:** Bowies, hunters, fighters, fishing and camp knives, miniatures. **Technical:** Grinds Stellite 6K, 440C and 154CM. **Prices:** Start at $100. **Remarks:** Spare-time maker; first knife sold in 1980. **Mark:** Initials in diamond logo.

JACKSON, JIM, 10 Chantry Close, Windsor, Berkshire SL4 5EP, ENGLAND/01-930-4832
Specialties: His designs. **Patterns:** Bowies, hunters, art knives and folders. **Technical:** Forges 01, 5160 and occasionally Damascus. Offers leatherwork. **Prices:** NA. **Remarks:** Part-time maker. **Mark:** Kentucky Dreamer around last initial.

JAGED (See Smith, Gregory H.)

JARVIS, PAUL M., 30 Chalk St., Cambridge, MA 02139/617-491-2900, 617-547-4355
Specialties: High-art knives and period pieces of his design. **Patterns:** Japanese and Mid-Eastern knives. **Technical:** Grinds Myer Damascus, ATS-34, D2 and 01. Specializes in height-relief Japanese-style carving. Works with silver, gold and gems. **Prices:** $200 to $17,000. **Remarks:** Part-time maker; first knife sold in 1978.

JEAN, GERRY, 25B Cliffside Dr., Manchester, CT 06040/203-649-6449
Specialties: Historic replicas. **Patterns:** Survival and camp knives. **Technical:** Grinds A2, 440C and 154CM. Handle slabs applied in unique tongue-and-groove method. **Prices:** $125 to $250; some to $1,000. **Remarks:** Spare-time maker; first knife sold in 1973. **Mark:** Initials and serial number.

JENSEN JR., CARL A., RR #3, Box 74, Blair, NE 68008/402-426-3353
Specialties: Working knives of his design; some customer designs. **Patterns:** Hunters, fighters, boots and Bowies. **Technical:** Grinds A2, D2, 01, 440C and ATS-34; recycles old files, leaf springs; heat-treats. **Prices:** $35 to $350. **Remarks:** Part-time maker; first knife sold in 1980. **Mark:** Bear's Cutlery.

JERNIGAN, STEVE, 3082 Tunnel Rd., Milton, FL 32571/904-994-0802
Specialties: Investor-class folders. **Patterns:** Array of models and sizes in side-plate locking interframes and conventional liner construction. **Technical:** Grinds D2, ATS-34, stainless steel interframes with multiple assymetrical inlays, anodized titanium and all mokume interframes; occasional fancy dagger with "Italian Smalti" glass tiles for unique mosaic handles. **Prices:** $350 to $1,300; some to $4,000. **Remarks:** Full-time maker; first knife sold in 1982. Takes orders for folders only. **Mark:** Last name.

JETTON, CAY, P.O. Box 315, Winnsboro, TX 75494/903-342-3317

JMD BLADES (See DaConceicao, John M.)

JOBIN, JACQUES, 46 St. Dominique, Lauzon, PQ G6V 2M7, CANADA/418-833-0283; FAX: 418-833-8378
Specialties: Fancy and working straight knives and folders; miniatures. **Patterns:** Minis, fantasy knives, fighters and some hunters. **Technical:** ATS-34, some Damascus and titanium. Likes native snakewood. Heat-treats. **Prices:** Start at $150. **Remarks:** Full-time maker; first knife sold in 1986. **Mark:** Signature on blade.

JOHNS, ROB, 1423 S. Second, Enid, OK 73701/405-242-2707
Specialties: Classic and fantasy straight knives of his design or to customer specs; fighters for use at Medieval fairs. **Patterns:** Bowies, daggers and swords. **Technical:** Forges and grinds 440C, D2 and 5160. Handles of nylon, walnut or wire-wrap. **Prices:** $150 to $350; some to $2,500. **Remarks:** Full-time maker; first knife sold in 1980. **Mark:** Medieval Customs, initials.

JOHNSON, C.E. "GENE", 5648 Redwood Ave., Portage, IN 46368/219-762-5461
Specialties: Lock-back folders and springers of his design or to customer specs. **Patterns:** Hunters, Bowies, survival lock-back folders. **Technical:** Grinds D2, 440C, A18, 01, Damascus; likes filework. **Prices:** $100 to $2,000. **Remarks:** Full-time maker; first knife sold in 1975. **Mark:** "Gene," city, state and serial number.

JOHNSON, DAVID L., 9324 Westhill, Lakeside, CA 92040/907-733-2777

custom knifemakers
JOHNSON—KALUZA

Specialties: Traditional working and using straight knives. **Patterns:** Bowies, fighters and hunters; outdoor knives. **Technical:** Grinds ATS-34, D2 and 440C. **Prices:** $100 to $200; some to $450. **Remarks:** Part-time maker; first knife sold in 1979. **Mark:** Name, city and state in banner.

JOHNSON, DURRELL CARMON, P.O. Box 594, Sparr, FL 32192/904-622-5498
Specialties: Old-fashioned working straight knives and folders of his design or to customer specs. **Patterns:** Bowies, hunters, fighters, daggers, camp knives and Damascus miniatures. **Technical:** Forges 5160, his own Damascus, W2, wrought iron, nickel and horseshoe rasps. Offers filework. **Prices:** $100 to $2,000. **Remarks:** Full-time maker and blacksmith; first knife sold in 1957. **Mark:** Middle name.

JOHNSON, GORDEN W., 5426 Sweetbriar, Houston, TX 77017/713-645-8990
Specialties: Working knives and period pieces. **Patterns:** Hunters, boots and Bowies. **Technical:** Flat-grinds 440C; most knives have narrow tang. **Prices:** $60 to $90; some to $300. **Remarks:** Full-time maker; first knife sold in 1974. **Mark:** Name, city, state.

JOHNSON, HAROLD "HARRY" C., 1014 Lafayette Rd., Chickamauga, GA 30707/706-375-2321
Specialties: Working straight knives. **Patterns:** Mostly hunters, fighters and Bowies. **Technical:** Grinds ATS-34, 01 and other steels; keeps 50 woods in stock. **Prices:** $125 to $700; some $2,000 and higher. **Remarks:** Part-time maker; first knife sold in 1973. **Mark:** First initial, last name, city, state in oval logo.

JOHNSON, KENNETH R., W3565 Lockington, Mindoro, WI 54644/608-857-3035
Specialties: Hunters, clip-points, special orders. **Patterns:** Hunters, utility/camp knives and kitchen knives. **Technical:** Grinds 440C, D2 and 01. Scrimshaw by Corinne Johnson; makes sheaths. **Prices:** $65 to $500. **Remarks:** Full-time maker; first knife sold in 1990. Doing business as Corken Knives. **Mark:** CORKEN.

JOHNSON, R.B., Box 11, Clearwater, MN 55320/612-558-6128
Specialties: Automatic switch blades and lockbacks. **Patterns:** Traditional hunters and locking folders; liner locks with titanium. **Technical:** Grinds 440C, 154CM, 1095 steel and ATS-34; uses no plastic; prefers natural materials; offers mammoth ivory. **Prices:** $140 to $750. **Remarks:** Full-time maker; first knife sold in 1973. Now accepting orders. **Mark:** Signature.

JOHNSON, RUFFIN, 215 LaFonda Dr., Houston, TX 77060/713-448-4407
Specialties: Working straight knives and folders. **Patterns:** Hunters, fighters and locking folders. **Technical:** Grinds 440C and 154CM; hidden tangs and fancy handles. **Prices:** $200 to $400; some to $1,095. **Remarks:** Full-time maker; first knife sold in 1972. **Mark:** Wolf head logo and signature.

JOHNSON, RYAN M., 7320 Foster Hixson Cemetery Rd., Hixson, TN 37343/615-842-9323
Specialties: Working and using straight knives of his design and to customer specs. **Patterns:** Bowies, hunters and utiltiy/camp knives. **Technical:** Forges 5160, Damascus and files. **Prices:** $70 to $400; some to $800. **Remarks:** Full-time maker; first knife sold in 1986. **Mark:** Sledgehammer with halo.

JOHNSON, STEVEN R., 554 S. 500 E., P.O. Box 5, Manti, UT 84642/801-835-7941; FAX: 801-835-8052
Specialties: Investor-class working knives. **Patterns:** Hunters, fighters and boots in clean-lined contemporary patterns. **Technical:** Grinds ATS-34, 154CM and 440C. **Prices:** $350 to $3,500. **Remarks:** Full-time maker; first knife sold in 1972. **Mark:** Name, city, state.

JOHNSON, W.C. "BILL", 1006 Clayton Ct., New Carlisle, OH 45344/513-845-1185
Specialties: Fancy working knives to order. **Patterns:** Hunters, fighters, tantos and push knives. **Technical:** Grinds 440C and ATS-34. **Prices:** $125 to $350; some higher. **Remarks:** Full-time maker; first knife sold in 1979. **Mark:** First and middle initials, last name.

JOKERST, CHARLES, 9312 Spaulding, Omaha, NE 68134/402-571-2536
Specialties: Working knives in standard patterns. **Patterns:** Hunters, fighters and pocketknives. **Technical:** Grinds 440C, ATS-34. **Prices:** $90 to $170. **Remarks:** Spare-time maker, first knife sold in 1984. **Mark:** Early work marked RCJ; current work marked with last name and city.

JONES, BARRY M. and PHILLIP G., 221 North Ave., Danville, VA 24540/804-793-5282
Specialties: Working and using straight knives of their design and to customer specs; combat knives. **Patterns:** Bowies, fillets, fighters, wood carvers, hunters and lockback folders. **Technical:** Flat-grinds only 440C, ATS-34 and D2. All blades hand polished. **Prices:** $30 to $400, some higher. **Remarks:** Part-time makers; first knife sold in 1989. **Mark:** Jones Knives, city, state.

JONES, BOB, 6219 Aztec NE, Albuquerque, NM 87110/505-881-4472
Specialties: Fancy working knives of his design. **Patterns:** Mountainman/buckskinner-type knives; multi-blade folders, locking folders and slip-joints. **Technical:** Grinds A2, 01, 1095 and commercial Damascus; uses no stainless steel. Engraves. **Prices:** $100 to $500; some to $1,500. **Remarks:** Full-time maker; first knife sold in 1960. **Mark:** Initials on fixed blades; initials encircled on folders.

JONES, CHARLES ANTHONY, 36 Broadgate Close, Bellaire Barnstaple, No. Devon E31 4AL, ENGLAND/0271-75328
Specialties: Working straight knives. **Patterns:** Simple hunters, fighters and utility knives. **Technical:** Grinds 440C, 01 and D2; filework offered. Engraves. **Prices:** $100 to $500; engraving higher. **Remarks:** Spare-time maker; first knife sold in 1987. **Mark:** Tony engraved.

JONES, CURTIS J., 39909 176th St. E., Palmdale, CA 93591/805-264-2753
Specialties: Big Bowies, daggers, his own style of hunters. **Patterns:** Bowies, daggers, hunters, swords, boots and miniatures. **Technical:** Grinds A2, 440C and D2. Fitted guards only; does not solder. Heat-treats. Custom sheaths—hand-tooled and stitched. **Prices:** $125 to $1,500; some to $3,000. **Remarks:** Part-time maker; first knife sold in 1975. **Mark:** Stylized initials on either side of three triangles interconnected.

JONES, ENOCH, 310A Moss Ln., Warrenton, VA 22186/703-341-0292
Specialties: Fancy working straight knives. **Patterns:** Hunters, fighters, boots and Bowies. **Technical:** Forges and grinds 01, W2, 440C and Damascus. **Prices:** $100 to $350; some to $1,000. **Remarks:** Part-time maker; first knife sold in 1982. **Mark:** First name.

JONES, JOHN, 23 Sunstone St., Manly, West Brisbane 4179, AUSTRALIA/07-393-3390
Specialties: Straight knives and folders. **Patterns:** Working hunters, folding lockbacks, fancy daggers and miniatures. **Technical:** Grinds 440C, 01 and L6. **Prices:** $180 to $1200; some to $2,000. **Remarks:** Part-time maker; first knife sold in 1986. **Mark:** Jones Custom in script.

JONES, PHILLIP G. (See Jones, Barry M. and Phillip G.)

J.P.M. KNIVES (See McMahon, John P.)

J&S KNIVES (See Kitsmiller, Jerry)

k

KACZOR, TOM, 375 Wharncliffe Rd. N., Upper London, Ont., CANADA N6G 1E4/519-645-7640

KAGAWA, KOICHI, 1556 Horiyamashita Hatano-Shi, Kanagawa, JAPAN
Specialties: Fancy high-tech straight knives and folders to customer specs. **Patterns:** Hunters, locking folders and slip-joints. **Technical:** Uses 440C and ATS-34. **Prices:** $500 to $2,000; some to $20,000. **Remarks:** Part-time maker; first knife sold in 1986. **Mark:** First initial, last name-YOKOHAMA.

KALAZU, WERNER, Lochnerstr. 32, 8500 N rnberg 70, GERMANY

KALFAYAN, EDWARD N., 410 Channing, Ferndale, MI 48220/313-548-4882
Specialties: Working straight knives and folders to customer specs. **Patterns:** Bowies, toothpicks, fighters and hunters. **Technical:** Grinds 440C and ATS-34. **Prices:** $75 to $600. **Remarks:** Part-time maker; first knife sold in 1973. **Mark:** Last name.

KALUZA, WERNER, Lochnerstr. 32, 90441 Nurnberg, GERMANY/0911 666047
Specialties: Fancy high-art straight knives of his design. **Patterns:** Boots and ladies knives. **Technical:** Grinds ATS-34, CPM T 440V and Schneider Damascus.

FIFTEENTH EDITION 213

directory

KAMADA—KERSTEN

Engraving available. **Prices:** NA. **Remarks:** Part-time maker. **Mark:** First initial and last name.

KAMADA, YOSHIKAZU, B1 Fokoku Seimei Building 2-4, Komatu bara-cho kita-ku, Osaka City, 530 JAPAN/06-313-2525; FAX: 06-313-2626
Specialties: High-art working knives of his design. **Patterns:** Hunters, bush fishing knives and Japanese-style desk knives. **Technical:** Grinds D2. **Prices:** $450 to $1,800. **Remarks:** Full-time maker, first knife sold in 1953. Doing business as World Gallery Co., Ltd. **Mark:** Initials; or first initial, last name.

KANDA, MICHIO, 7-32-5 Shinzutumi-cho, Shinnanyo-shi, Yamaguehi 746 JAPAN

KATO, KIYOSHI, 4-6-4 Himonya Meguro-ku, Tokyo, 152 JAPAN
Specialties: Swords, Damascus knives, working knives and paper knives. **Patterns:** Traditional swords, hunters, Bowies and daggers. **Technical:** Forges his own Damascus and carbon steel. Grinds ATS-34. **Prices:** $260 to $700; some to $4,000. **Remarks:** Full-time maker. **Mark:** First initial, last name.

KAUFFMAN, DAVE, P.O. Box 9041, Helena, MT 59604/406-442-9328
Specialties: Fancy working straight knives of his design; also enjoys customer designs. **Patterns:** Lockblade folder interframes. **Technical:** Uses ATS-34, D2, 1095 and 203E Damascus; offers filework; heat-treats and tests. **Prices:** $65 to $500; some to $1,200. **Remarks:** Full-time maker; first knife sold in 1989. **Mark:** First and last name, Helena, MT.

KAUFMAN, SCOTT, 302 Green Meadows Cr., Anderson, SC 29624/803-231-9201
Specialties: Classic and working/using straight knives in standard patterns. **Patterns:** Fighters, hunters and utility/camp knives. **Technical:** Grinds ATS-34, 440C, 01. **Prices:** $100 to $500. **Remarks:** Part-time maker; first knife sold in 1987. **Mark:** Kaufman Knives with Bible in middle.

KAWASAKI, AKIHISA, 11-8-9 Chome Minamimach, Kobe 651-11 JAPAN

KAY, J. WALLACE, 332 Slab Bridge Rd., Liberty, SC 29657

KEESLAR, JOSEPH F., RR #1, Box 252, Almo, KY 42020/502-753-7919
Specialties: Classic Bowie reproductions and contemporary Bowies. **Patterns:** Period pieces, combat knives, hunters, daggers. Forges small working knives from files. **Technical:** Forges 5160, 52100 and his own Damascus. Decorative filework, engraving and custom leather sheaths available. **Prices:** $200 to $3,000. **Remarks:** Full-time maker; first knife sold in 1976. **Mark:** First and middle initlas, last name in hammer, knife and anvil logo.

KEESLAR, STEVEN C., 115 Lane 216, Hamilton, IN 46742/219-488-3161; FAX: 219-488-3149
Specialties: Traditional working/using straight knives of his design and to customer specs. **Patterns:** Bowies, hunters, utility/camp knives. **Technical:** Forges 5160, files, 52100. **Prices:** $100 to $600; some to $1,500. **Remarks:** Part-time maker; first knife sold in 1976. **Mark:** First initial, last name.

KEETON, WILLIAM L., 6095 Rehoboth Rd. SE, Laconia, IN 47135/812-969-2836
Specialties: Plain and fancy working knives. **Patterns:** Hunters and fighters; locking folders and slip-joints. Names patterns after Kentucky Derby winners. **Technical:** Grinds D2, ATS-34, 440C and 154CM; mirror and satin finishes. **Prices:** To $1,500; some to $5,000. **Remarks:** Full-time maker; first knife sold in 1971. **Mark:** Logo of key.

KEHIAYAN, ALFREDO, Cuzco 1455, Ing. Maschwitz, CP 1623 Buenos Aires, ARGENTINA/0321-42-212
Specialties: Functional straight knives. **Patterns:** Utility knives, skinners, hunters and boots. **Technical:** Forges and grinds SAE 52.100, SAE 6180, SAE 9260, 440C and ATS-34, titanium with nitride. All blades mirror-polished; makes leather sheaths and wood cases. **Prices:** $150 to $800; some to $3,000. **Remarks:** Full-time maker; first knife sold in 1983. **Mark:** Name.

KEIDEL, GENE W. AND SCOTT J., Rt. 2, Box 68, Dickinson, ND 58601
Specialties: Fancy/embellished and working/using straight knives of his design. **Patterns:** Bowies, hunters and miniatures. **Technical:** Grind 440C, ATS-34 and 1095. Offer scrimshaw, filework and leather tooling. **Prices:** $95 to $500. **Remarks:** Full-time makers; first knife sold in 1990. Doing business as Keidel Knives. **Mark:** Last name.

KEIDEL, SCOTT J. (See Keidel, Gene W. and Scott J.)

KELGIN KNIVES (See Largin, Ken)

KELLEY, GARY, 17485 SW Pheasant Lane, Aloha, OR 97006/503-649-7867
Specialties: Exotic miniatures with Damascus and rare materials; custom belt buckle knives, some investment-quality daggers. **Patterns:** Period and fantasy miniatures. **Technical:** Forges Damascus miniatures; casts precious metals and dendritic steel. **Prices:** $250 to $5,000. **Remarks:** Part-time maker; first knife sold in 1969. Knife consultant. Publishes *The Directory of Knifemaking Supplies*. **Mark:** Full name or initials.

KELLOGG, BRIAN R., Rt. 1, Box 357, New Market, VA 22844/703-740-4292
Specialties: Fancy and working straight knives of his design and to customer specs. **Patterns:** Fighters, hunters and utility/camp knives. **Technical:** Grinds 440C, D2 and A2. Offers filework and fancy pin and cable pin work. Prefers natural handle materials. **Prices:** $75 to $225; some to $350. **Remarks:** Part-time maker; first knife sold in 1983. **Mark:** Last name.

KELLY, LANCE, 1723 Willow Oak Dr., Edgewater, FL 32132/904-423-4933
Specialties: Investor-class straight knives and folders. **Patterns:** Kelly style in contemporary outlines. **Technical:** Grinds 01, D2 and 440C; engraves; inlays gold and silver. **Prices:** $600 to $3,500. **Remarks:** Full-time engraver and knifemaker; first knife sold in 1975. **Mark:** Last name.

KELSO, JIM, RD 1, Box 5300, Worcester, VT 05682/802-229-4254
Specialties: Fancy high-art straight knives and folders that mix Eastern and Western influences. Only uses own designs, but accepts suggestions for themes. **Patterns:** Daggers, swords and locking folders. **Technical:** Grinds only custom Damascus. Works with top Damascus bladesmiths. **Prices:** $3,000 to $8,000; some to $15,000. **Remarks:** Full-time maker; first knife sold in 1980. **Mark:** Stylized initials.

KEMAL (See Fogg, Don and Sayen, Murad)

KENNEDY JR., BILL, P.O. Box 850431, Yukon, OK 73085/405-354-9150
Specialties: Working straight knives. **Patterns:** Hunters, fighters, minis and fishing knives. **Technical:** Grinds D2, 440C and Damascus. **Prices:** $80 and higher. **Remarks:** Part-time maker; first knife sold in 1980. **Mark:** Last name and year made.

KENNEDY, JERRY, 2104 S.W.8A, Blue Springs, MO 64015/816-229-5468
Specialties: Traditional working and using knives. **Patterns:** Bowies, fighters, hunters and camp knives. **Technical:** Forges W2, 52100 and Damascus. Makes own Damascus with W2 and 203E. **Prices:** $125 to $750; some to $1,500. **Remarks:** Full-time maker; first knife sold in 1990. **Mark:** First initial, last name.

KENNEDY, KELLY S., 9894 A.W. University, Odessa, TX 79764/915-381-6165
Specialties: Traditional working and using straight knives of his design and to customer specs. **Patterns:** Bowies, hunters and utility/camp knives. **Technical:** Forges 5160, W2 and own Damascus. **Prices:** Moderate to upscale. **Remarks:** Full-time maker; first knife sold in 1991. Doing business as Noble House Armourers. **Mark:** Last name in script, J.S., A.B.S.

KENNELLEY, J.C., Box 145, Leon, KS 67074/316-745-3797
Specialties: Working straight knives; some fantasy pieces. **Patterns:** Hunters, fighters, skinners and fillet knives. **Technical:** Grinds D2 and 440C. **Prices:** $75 to $200; some to $500. **Remarks:** Part-time maker; first knife sold in 1982. **Mark:** Name logo.

KENTUCKY DREAMER (See Jackson, Jim)

KERMIT'S KNIFE WORKS (See Laurent, Kermit)

KERSTEN, MICHAEL, Borkzeile 17, 13585 Berlin, GERMANY
Specialties: Working/using straight knives and folders of his design and to customer specs. **Patterns:** Fighters, locking folders and utility/camp knives. **Technical:** Grinds 2842, 2379 and stainless steel. Handle materials include brass, hardwood and bone. Sheaths made from wood, Kydex and leather. **Prices:** $250 to $350. **Remarks:** Spare-time maker; first knife sold in 1993. **Mark:** Last initial on anvil.

custom knifemakers

KESSLER—KNOTT

KESSLER, RALPH A., P.O. Box 357, 1072 Gary Goff Rd., Marietta, SC 29661/803-438-5360
Specialties: Traditional-style knives. **Patterns:** Folders, hunters, fighters, Bowies and kitchen knives. **Technical:** Grinds D2, 01, A2 and ATS-34. **Prices:** $100 to $500. **Remarks:** Part-time maker; first knife sold in 1982. **Mark:** Last name or initials with last name.

KESTREL TOOL (See Blomberg, Gregg)

KHALSA, JOT SINGH, 368 Village St., Millis, MA 02054/508-376-8162; FAX: 508-376-8081
Specialties: Damascus-bladed/bolstered liner locks from original patterns—some engraved, some with gem handles; embellished one-of-a-kind daggers. **Patterns:** Classic with contemporary flair. Has line of knife jewelry sold through stores and dealers. **Technical:** Grinds ATS-34; forges his Damascus. **Prices:** Start at $175. **Remarks:** Full-time maker; first knife sold in 1978. **Mark:** An Adi Skakti symbol, which is crossed blades.

KHARLAMOV, YURI, Oboronnay 46, Tula, 300007 RUSSIA
Specialties: Classic, fancy and traditional knives of his design. **Patterns:** Daggers, hunters, swords. **Technical:** Forges Y13, T3, WX15, Damascus. Uses natural handle materials—engraves on metal, carves on nut-tree; silver and pearl inlays. **Prices:** $600 to $2,000; some to $2,800. **Remarks:** Full-time maker; first knife sold in 1988. **Mark:** Initials.

KI, SHIVA, 5222 Ritterman Ave., Baton Rouge, LA 70805/504-356-7274
Specialties: Fancy working straight knives and folders to customer specs. **Patterns:** Emphasis on personal defense knives, martial arts weapons. **Technical:** Forges and grinds; makes own Damascus; prefers natural handle materials. **Prices:** $135 to $850; some to $1,800. **Remarks:** Full-time maker; first knife sold in 1981. **Mark:** Name with logo.

KIEFER, TONY, 112 Chateaugay Dr., Pataskala, OH 43062/614-927-6910
Specialties: Traditional working and using straight knives in standard patterns. **Patterns:** Bowies, fighters and hunters. **Technical:** Grinds 440C and D2; forges D2. Flat-grinds Bowies; hollow-grinds drop-point and trailing-point hunters. **Prices:** $95 to $140; some to $200. **Remarks:** Spare-time maker; first knife sold in 1988. **Mark:** Last name.

KILBY, KEITH, 402 Jackson Trail Rd., Jefferson, GA 30549/706-367-9997
Specialties: Works with all designs. **Patterns:** Mostly Bowies, camp knives and hunters of his design. **Technical:** Forges 52100, 5160, 1095, Damascus and mosaic Damascus. **Prices:** $100 to $3,500. **Remarks:** Part-time maker; first knife sold in 1974. Doing business as Foxwood Forge. **Mark:** Name or fox logo.

KIMSEY, KEVIN, 1246 Woodleigh Rd., Marietta, GA 30060/404-432-0044
Specialties: Classic and working straight knives of his design. **Patterns:** Fighters, hunters and utility knives. **Technical:** Grinds 440C, ATS-34 and D2 carbon. **Prices:** $100 to $300; some to $600. **Remarks:** Part-time maker; first knife sold in 1983. Doing business as Rafter KK Custom Knives. **Mark:** Last name and year.

KING, BILL, 14830 Shaw Road, Tampa, FL 33625/813-961-3455
Specialties: Fancy working knives; locking folders and slip-joints in many varieties; liner locks in titanium; mokume bolsters. **Patterns:** Folding "Stud opener"; some Damascus folders with nickel-silver Damascus bolsters. **Technical:** ATS-34 and Damascus. **Prices:** $125 to $250; some to $500. **Remarks:** Part-time maker; first knife sold in 1976. **Mark:** Name in crown.

KING, FRED, P.O. Box 200342, Cartersville, GA 30120/404-382-8478
Specialties: Fancy and embellished working straight knives and folders. **Patterns:** Hunters, Bowies and fighters. **Technical:** Grinds 440C, ATS-34 and D2; forges 5160, L6; makes his own Damascus. Offers filework. **Prices:** $45 to $2,500. **Remarks:** Spare-time maker; first knife sold in 1984. **Mark:** Kings Edge.

KING JR., HARVEY G., 312 Walnut, Box 184, Eskridge, KS 66423-0184/913-449-2487
Specialties: Traditional working and using straight knives of his design and to customer specs. **Patterns:** Hunters, Bowies and fillet knives **Technical:** Grinds 01, A2 and D2. Prefers natural handle materials; offers leatherwork. **Prices:** $50 to $650. **Remarks:** Part-time maker; first knife sold in 1988. **Mark:** Name and serial number based on steel used, year made and number of knives made that year.

KING, KEMP, 6452 Paradise Point Rd., Flowery Branch, GA 30542/404-967-1887
Specialties: Fancy straight knives and folders in standard patterns or to customer specs. **Patterns:** Hunters, locking and slip-joint folders. **Technical:** Flat-grinds 440C, ATS-34 and D2. Hand-finish is standard. **Prices:** $250 to $750; some to $2,000. **Remarks:** Part-time maker; first knife sold in 1981. **Mark:** First name.

KING, RANDALL, 54 Mt. Carmel Rd. #12, Asheville, NC 28806/704-254-7340
Specialties: Fancy and working straight knives of his design, to customer specs and in standard patterns; movie knives, prop knives and swords. **Patterns:** Fighters, hunters and locking folders. **Technical:** Grinds ATS-34, D2 and 440C. Prefers tapered tangs. Scrimshaws. Sheaths made by Vicky King. **Prices:** $100 to $250; some to $500. **Remarks:** Part-time maker; first knife sold in 1987. **Mark:** First initial, last name, city and state.

KINGS EDGE (See King, Fred)

KIOUS, JOE, 1015 Ridge Pointe Rd., Kerrville, TX 78028/210-367-2277
Specialties: Investment-quality interframe folders. **Patterns:** Hunters, fighters, Bowies and miniatures; traditional folders. **Technical:** Grinds D2, 440C and 154CM. **Prices:** $175 to $1,000; some to $5,000. **Remarks:** Full-time maker; first knife sold in 1969. **Mark:** Last name, city and state.

KITSMILLER, JERRY, 63347 E. Juniper Rd., Montrose, CO 81401/303-249-4290
Specialties: Working straight knives in standard patterns. **Patterns:** Hunters, boots and locking folders. **Technical:** Grinds ATS-34 and 440C only. **Prices:** $75 to $200; some to $300. **Remarks:** Spare-time maker; first knife sold in 1984. **Mark:** J&S Knives.

KLIMASZEWSKI, BERNARD E., 2214 Spicewood Dr., Killeen, TX 76543/817-628-9052
Specialties: Classic working and using straight knives to customer specs. **Patterns:** Hunters, Bowies and fighters. **Technical:** Grinds 440C, 01 and commercial Damascus. Offers filework. **Prices:** $75 to $1,000; some to $2,500. **Remarks:** Part-time maker; first knife sold in 1989. **Mark:** Stylized initials.

KNEUBUHLER, W.K. (See Votaw, David P.)

KNICKMEYER, HANK, 6300 Crosscreek, Cedar Hill, MO 63016/314-285-3210
Specialties: Mosaic Damascus constructions. **Patterns:** Hunters, fighters, swords and folders. **Technical:** Mosaic Damascus with all tool steel Damascus edges. **Prices:** $450 to $1,000; some $1,500 and higher. **Remarks:** Part-time maker; first knife sold in 1989. Doing business as Dutch Creek Forge & Foundry. **Mark:** Initials connected.

KNIFECRAFT (See Wise, Donald)

KNIGHT, JIM (See Brunckhorst, C. Lyle)

KNIP CUSTOM KNIVES (See Knipschield, Terry)

KNIPSCHIELD, TERRY, 808 12th Ave. NE, Rochester, MN 55906/507-288-7829
Specialties: Working straight and some folding knives in standard patterns. **Patterns:** Lockback and slip-joint knives. **Technical:** Grinds ATS-34. **Prices:** $55 to $350; some to $600. **Remarks:** Part-time maker; first knife sold in 1986. Doing business as Knip Custom Knives. **Mark:** KNIP in Old English with shield logo.

KNIPSTEIN, R.C. (JOE), 731 N. Fielder, Arlington, TX 76012/817-265-2021
Specialties: Straight working knives in standard patterns; integral construction. **Patterns:** Hunters, Bowies, folders, fighters, utility knives. **Technical:** Grinds 440C, D2, 154CM and ATS-34. Natural handle materials and full tangs are standard. **Prices:** Start at $125. **Remarks:** Part-time maker; first knife sold in 1989. **Mark:** Name, city and state.

KNIVES BY: GRAF (See Graffeo, Anthony I.)

KNOB HILL FORGE (See Pulliam, Morris C.)

KNOTT, STEVE, 206 Academy St., Clinton, SC 29325/803-833-6348
Specialties: Fantasy working straight knives and folders of his design or to customer specs. **Patterns:** Hunters and slip-joint folders; Bowies, daggers and fighters. **Technical:** Grinds 440C, ATS-34 and commercial Damascus. Offers filework, satin and mirror finishes; will do some bluing. **Prices:** $80 to $500. **Remarks:** Full-time maker; first knife sold in 1988. **Mark:** Last name.

centerfold knives '95

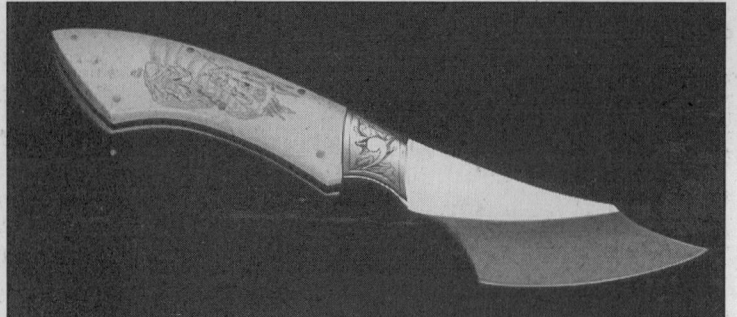
ALLRED

AIDA

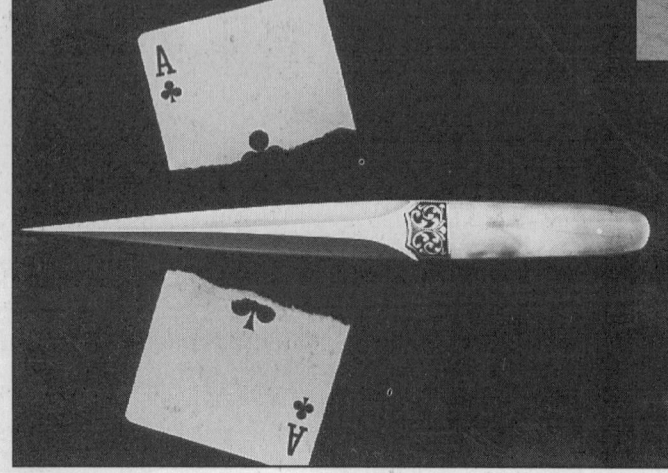
BRITTON

ARNOLD

BROOKS, S.

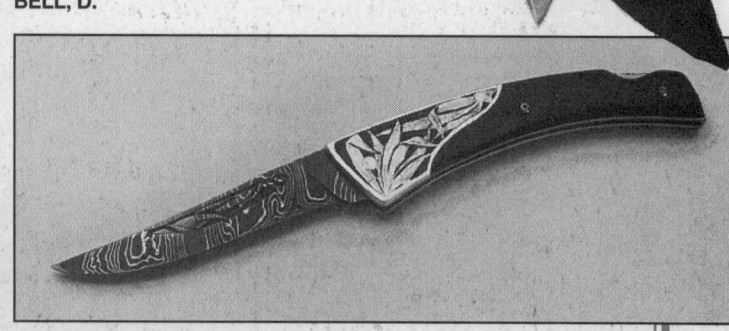
BELL, D.

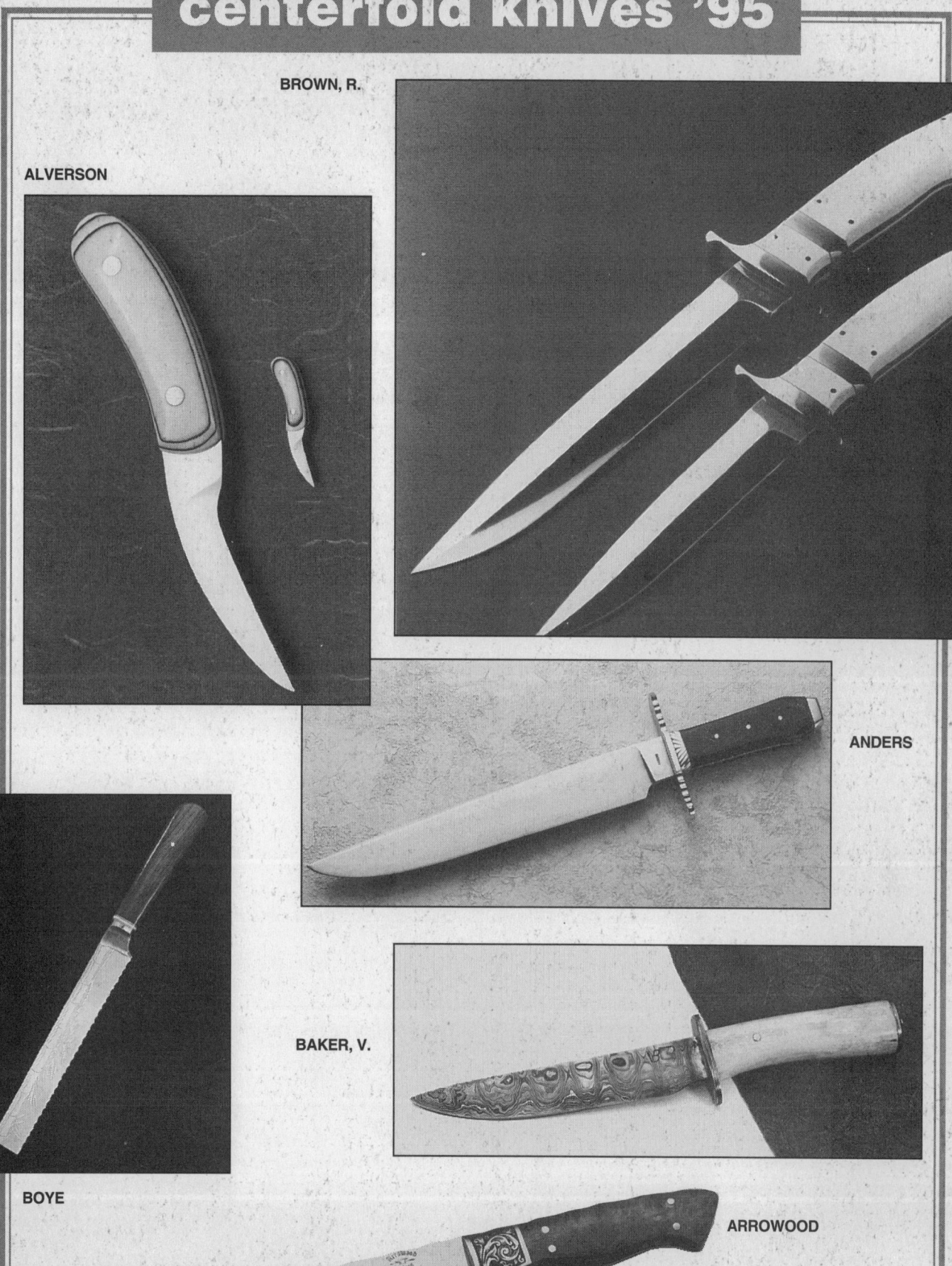

centerfold knives '95

CAREY

DION

DOUSSOT

DUNN, S.

COX, C.

DOWELL

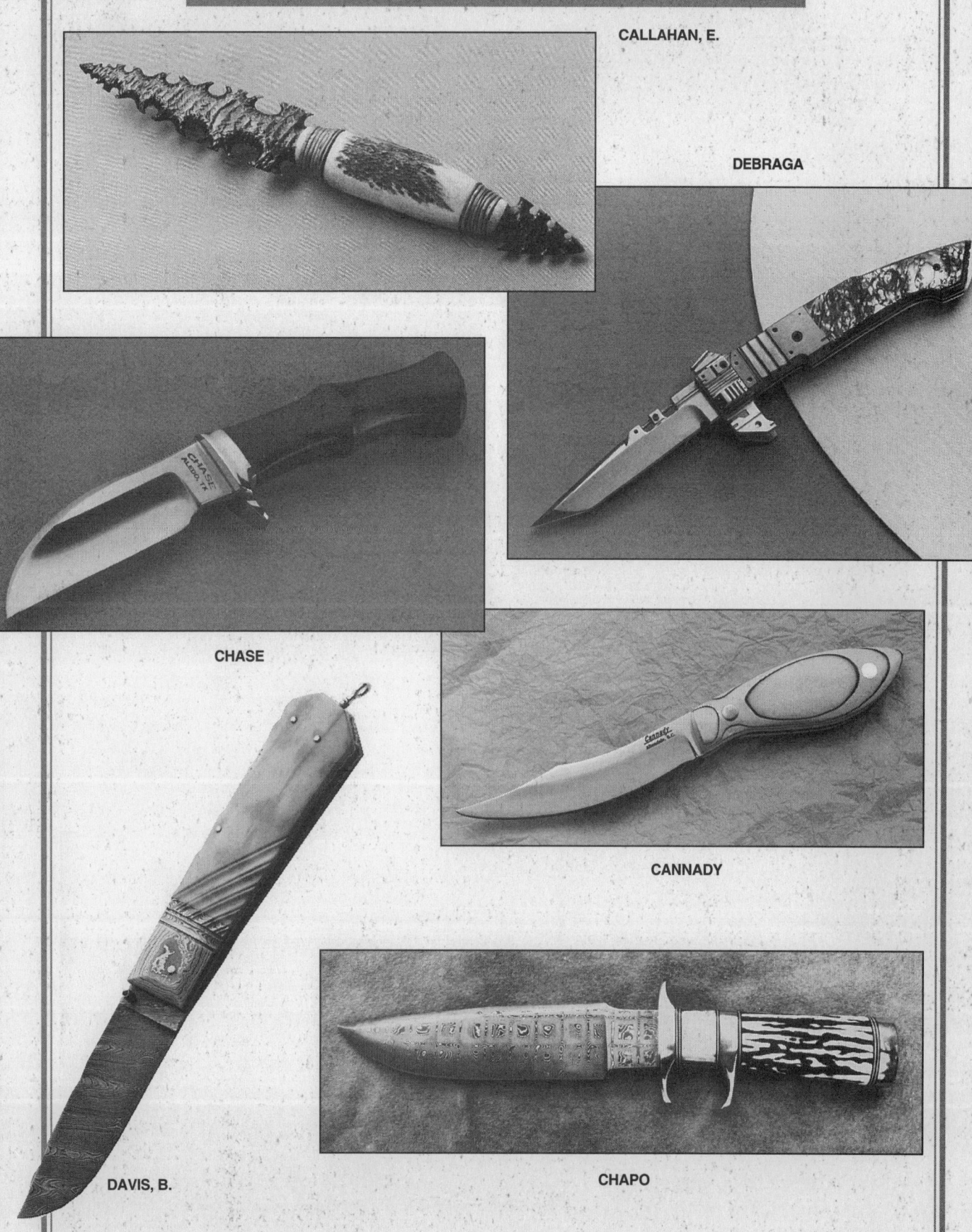

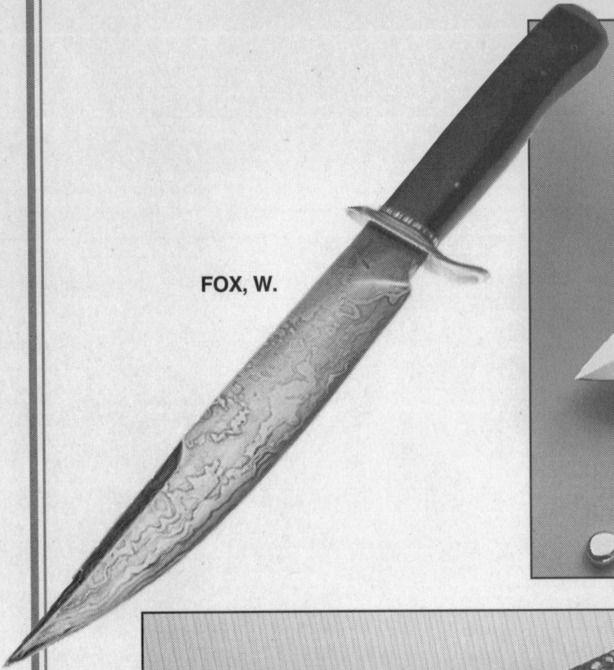

centerfold knives '95

FOX, W.

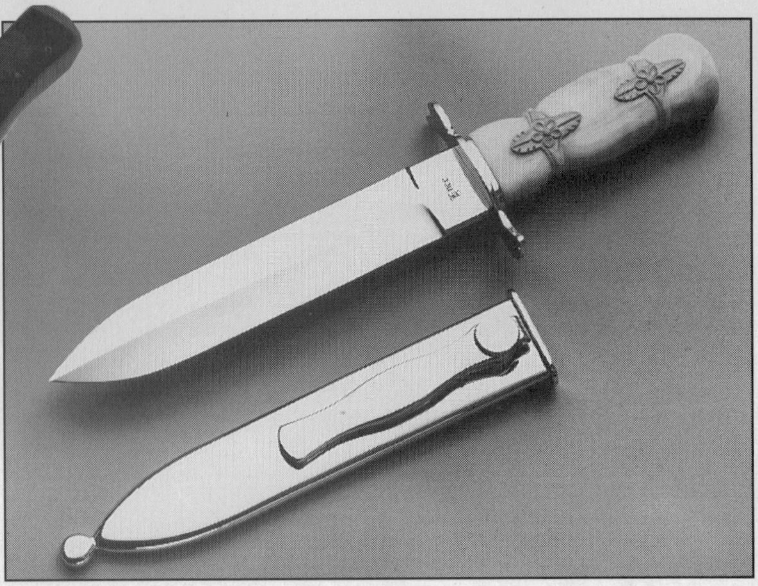

ENCE

EDWARDS, F.

ELLIS, D.

ENGLISH

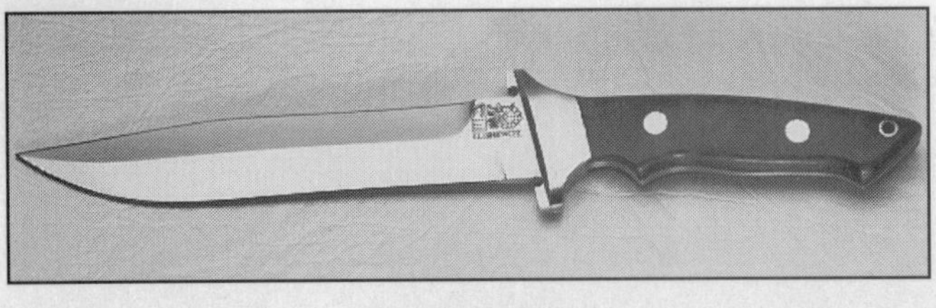

ELISHEWITZ

ENOS

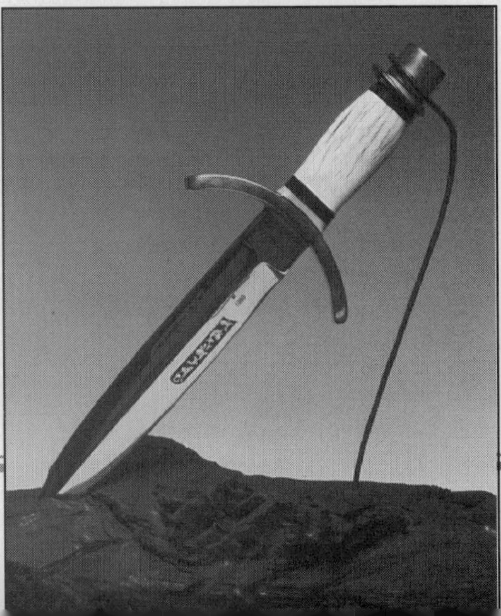

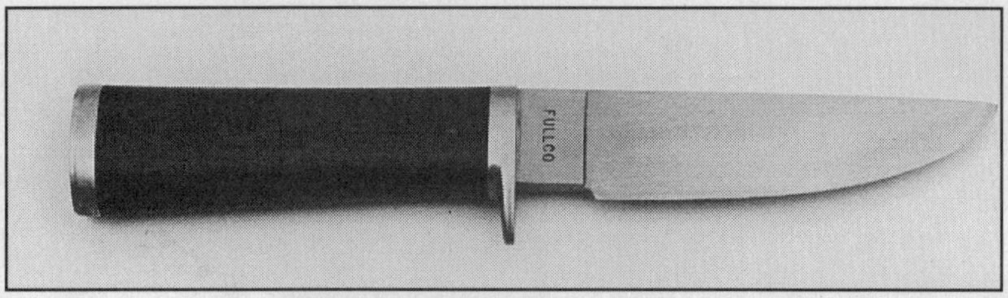

centerfold knives '95

FULLER, B.

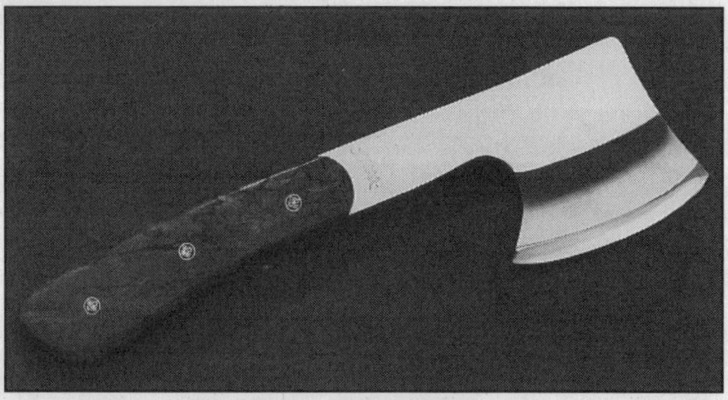

FREER

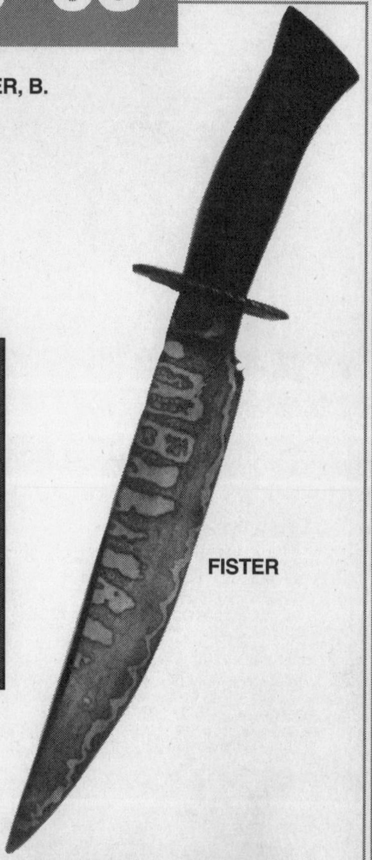

FISTER

FIORINI

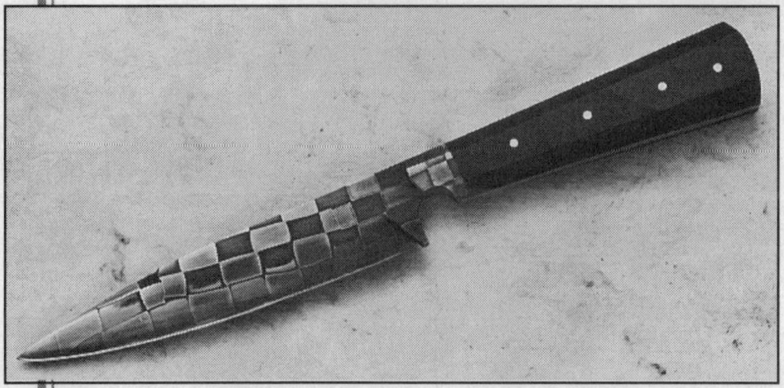

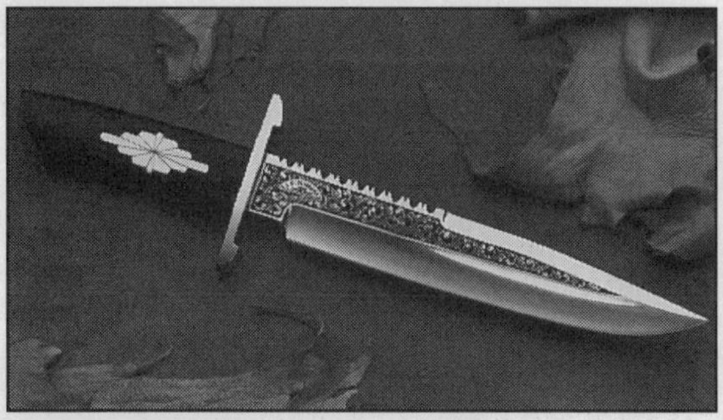

FUJISAKA

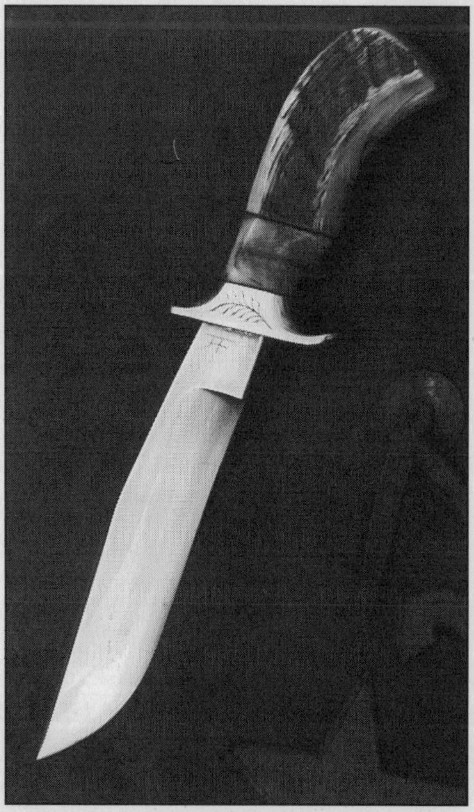

FERGUSON, JIM
CALIFORNIA

FOWLER, E.

FIFTEENTH EDITION **221**

centerfold knives '95

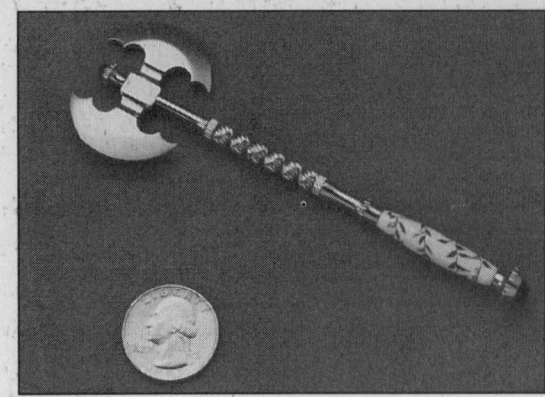

GROSSMAN

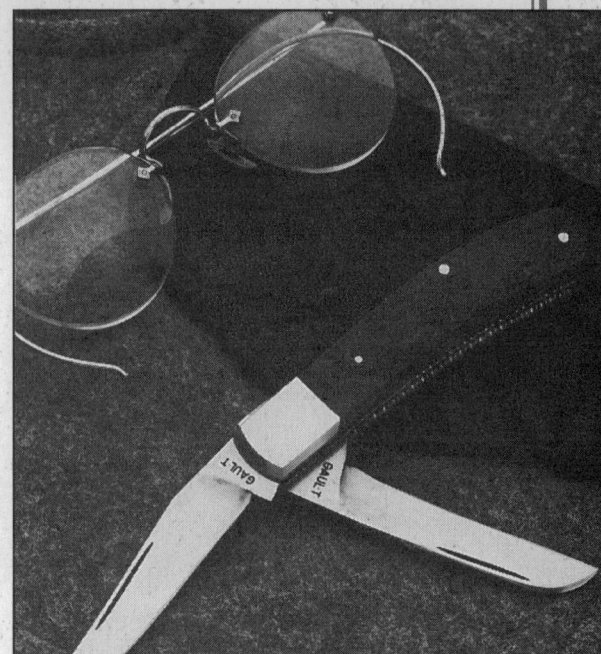

GAULT

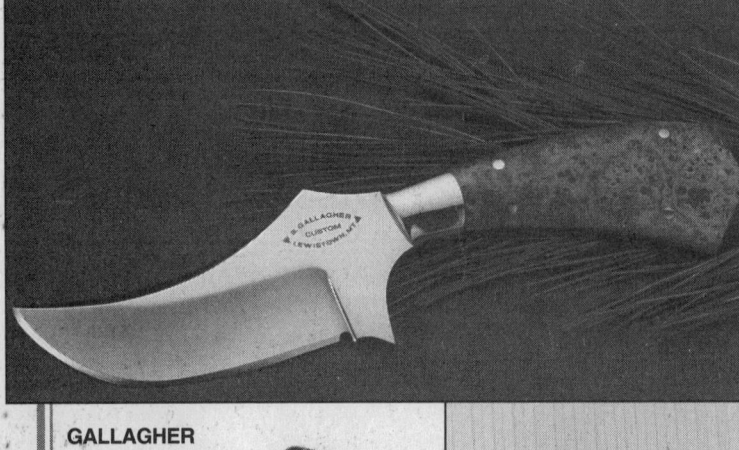

GALLAGHER

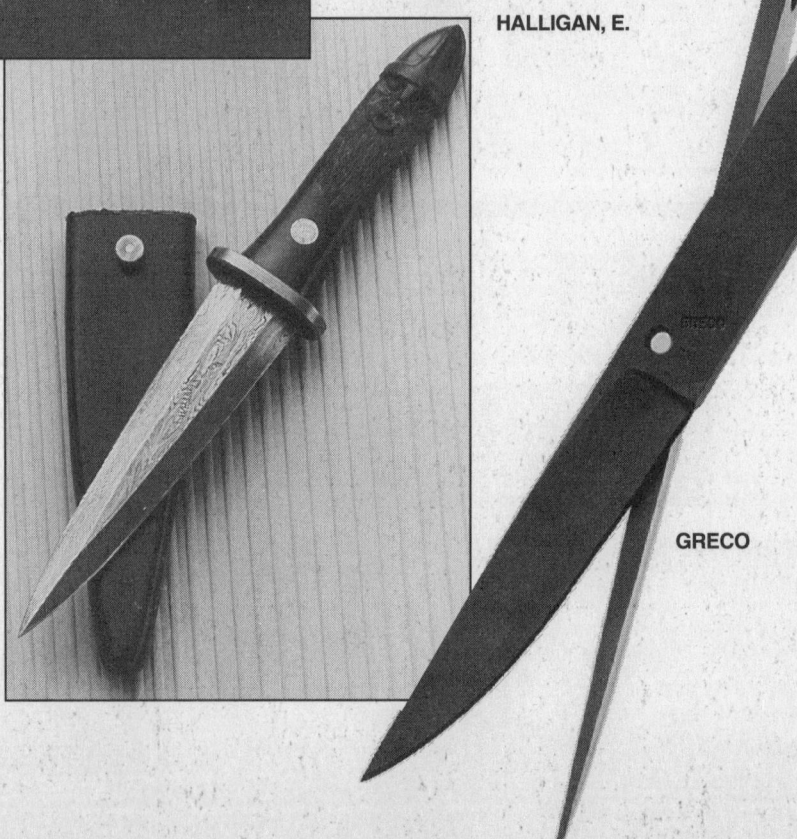

HALLIGAN, E.

GRECO

GOLDENBERG, T.S.

centerfold knives '95

GARNER, B.

HANCOCK, T.

HUGHES, E.

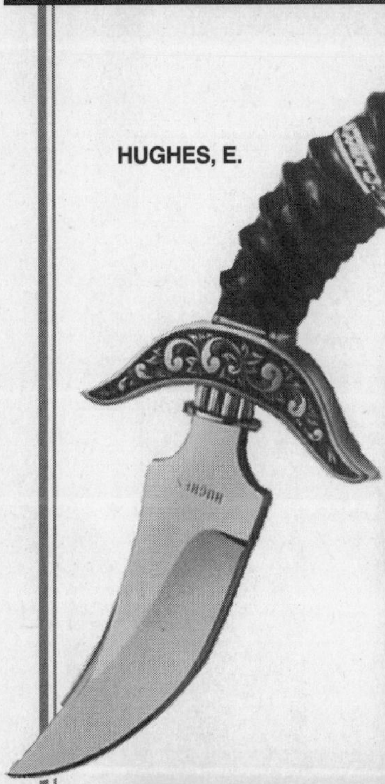

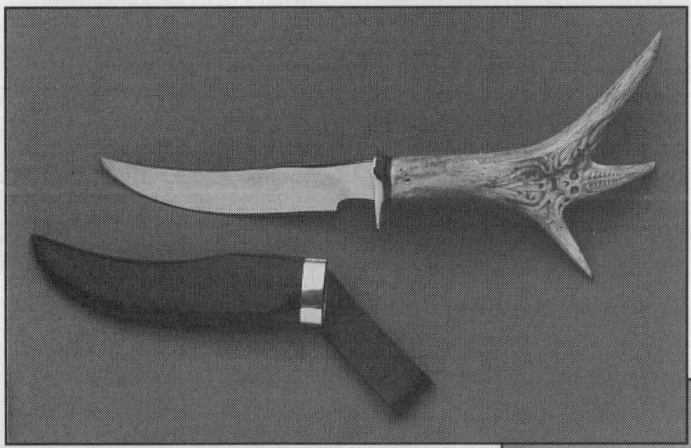

HESSER

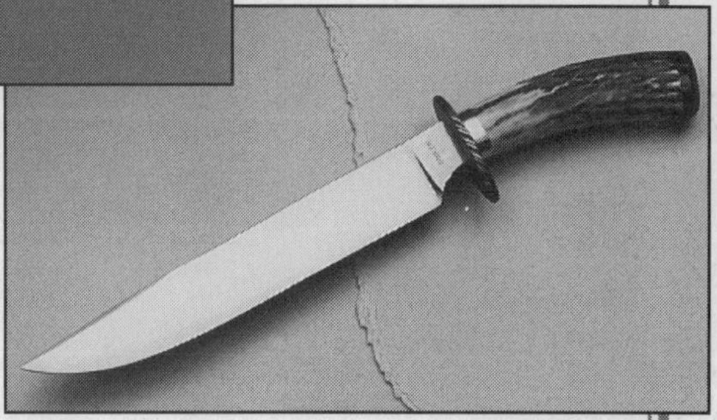

GOGUEN

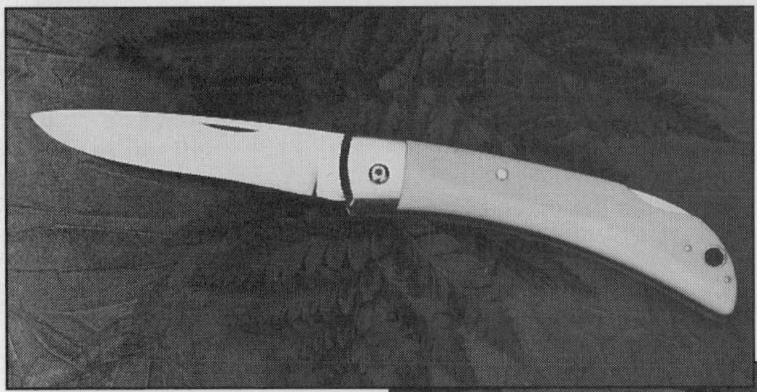

HARMON, J.

HUMPHREYS

FIFTEENTH EDITION **223**

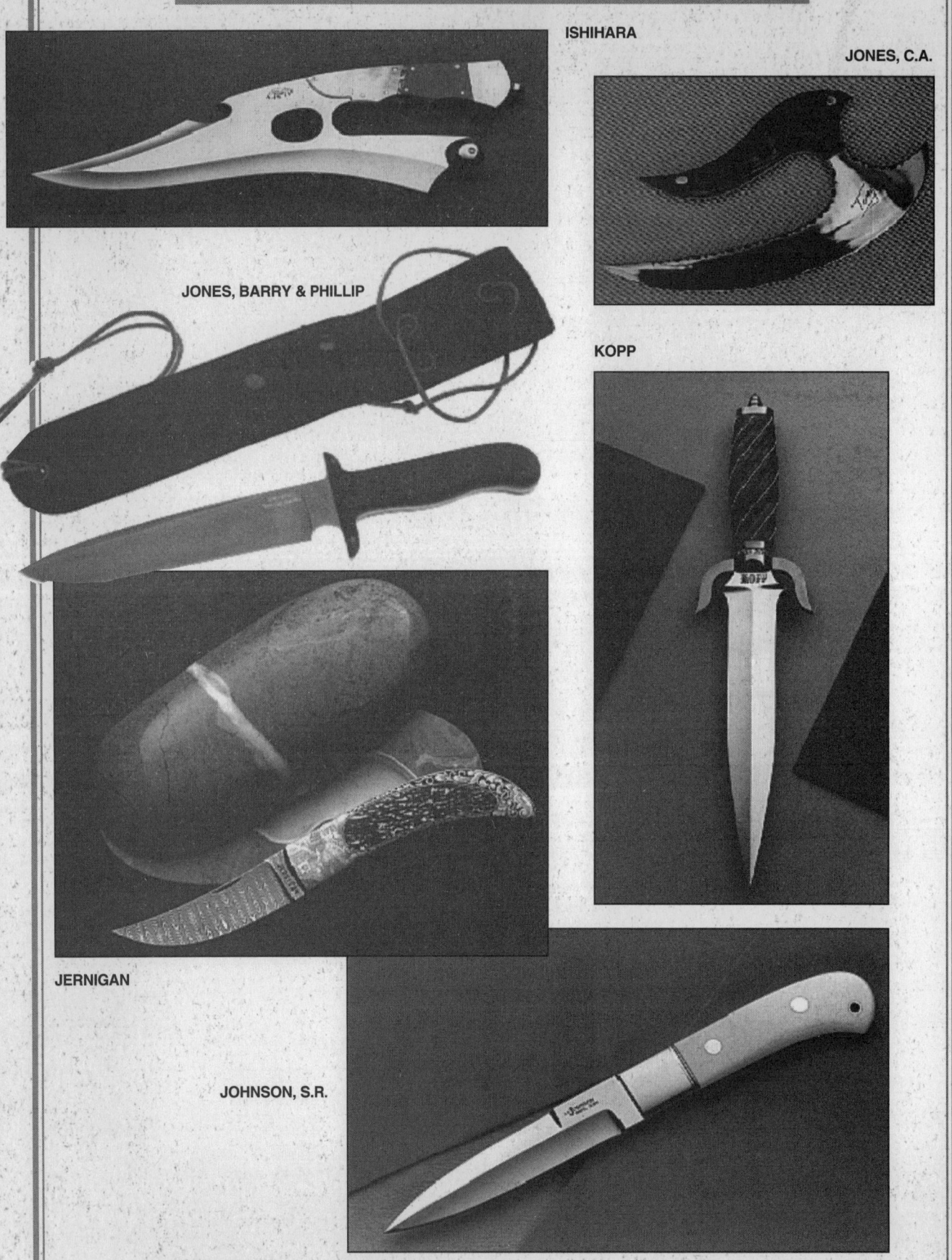

centerfold knives '95

KENNEDY, K.

KRANNING

KILBY

KALUZA

KAUFFMAN, D.

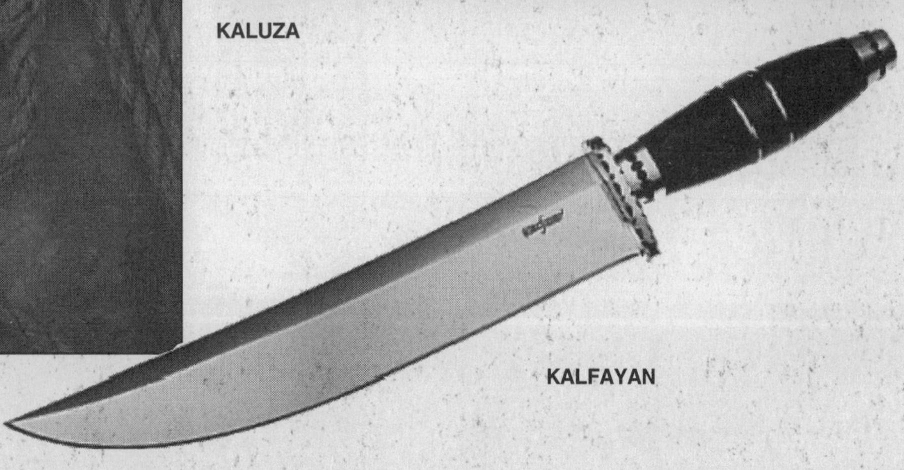

KALFAYAN

FIFTEENTH EDITION **225**

centerfold knives '95

LEACH

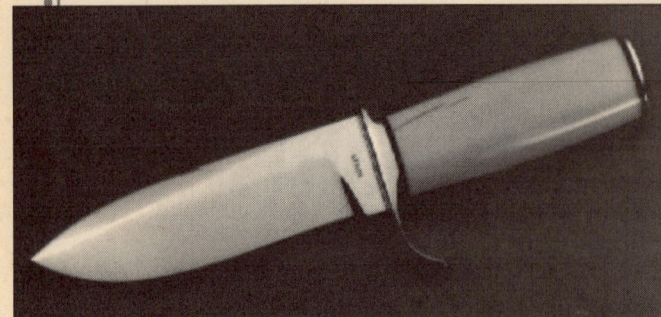

LEE, RANDY

MCDONALD

LEVINE, N.

LONG

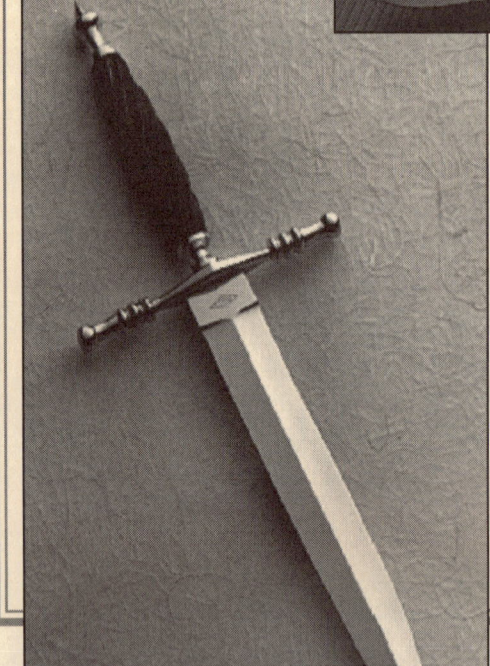

LUDWIG

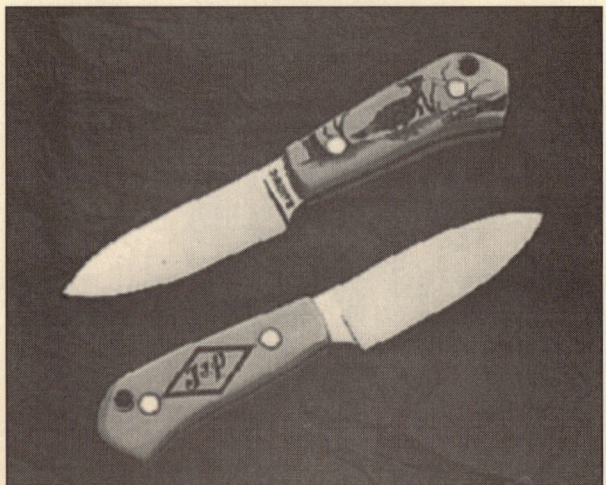

centerfold knives '95

MCCONNELL, LOYD

MACBAIN

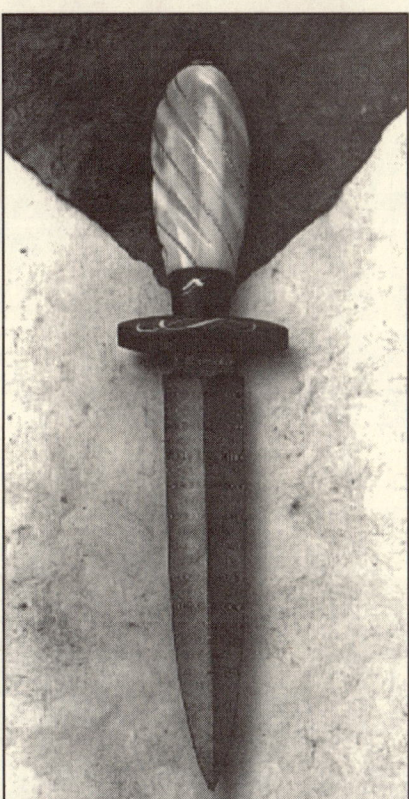

MARTRILDONNO

MINNICK

MCBURNETTE

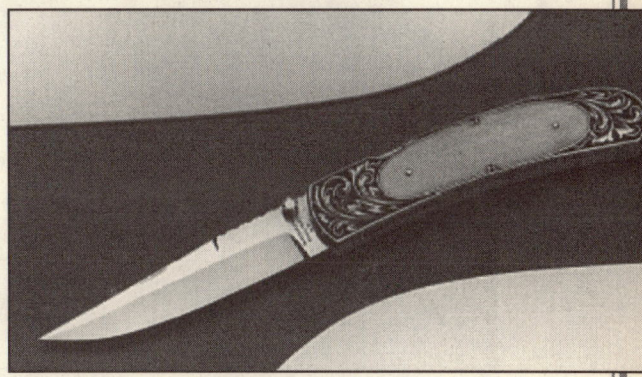

MANABE

centerfold knives '95

NEWCOMB

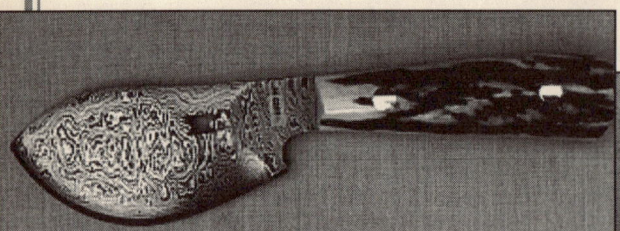

NEALY, B.

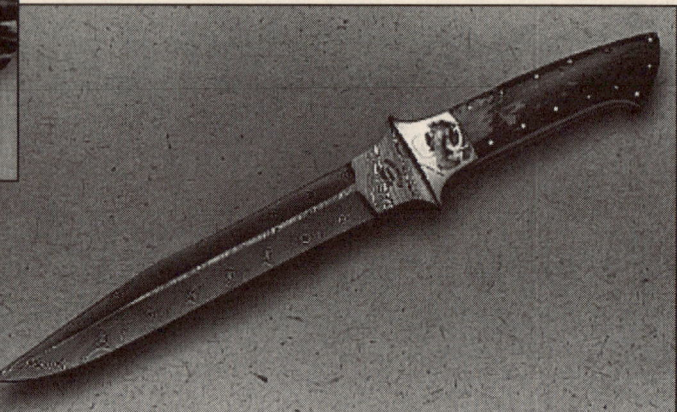

NIELSON

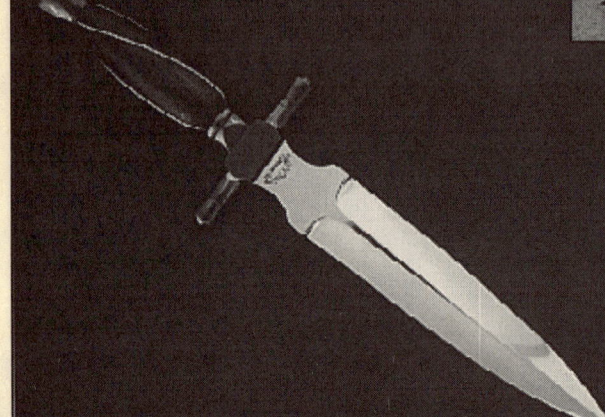

PADILLA

PETERSON, C.

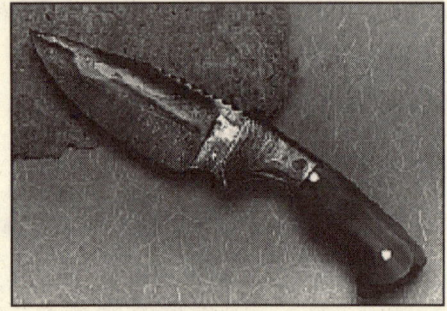

NEWTON

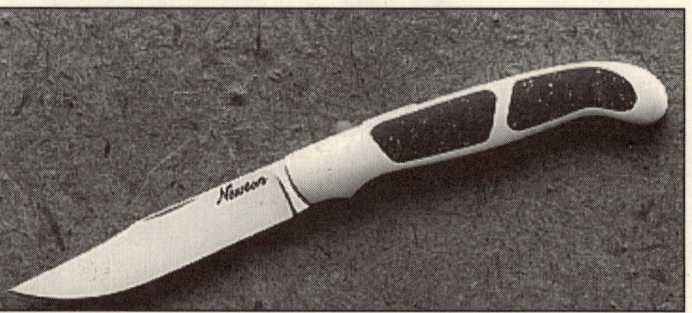

PATRICK, B.

centerfold knives '95

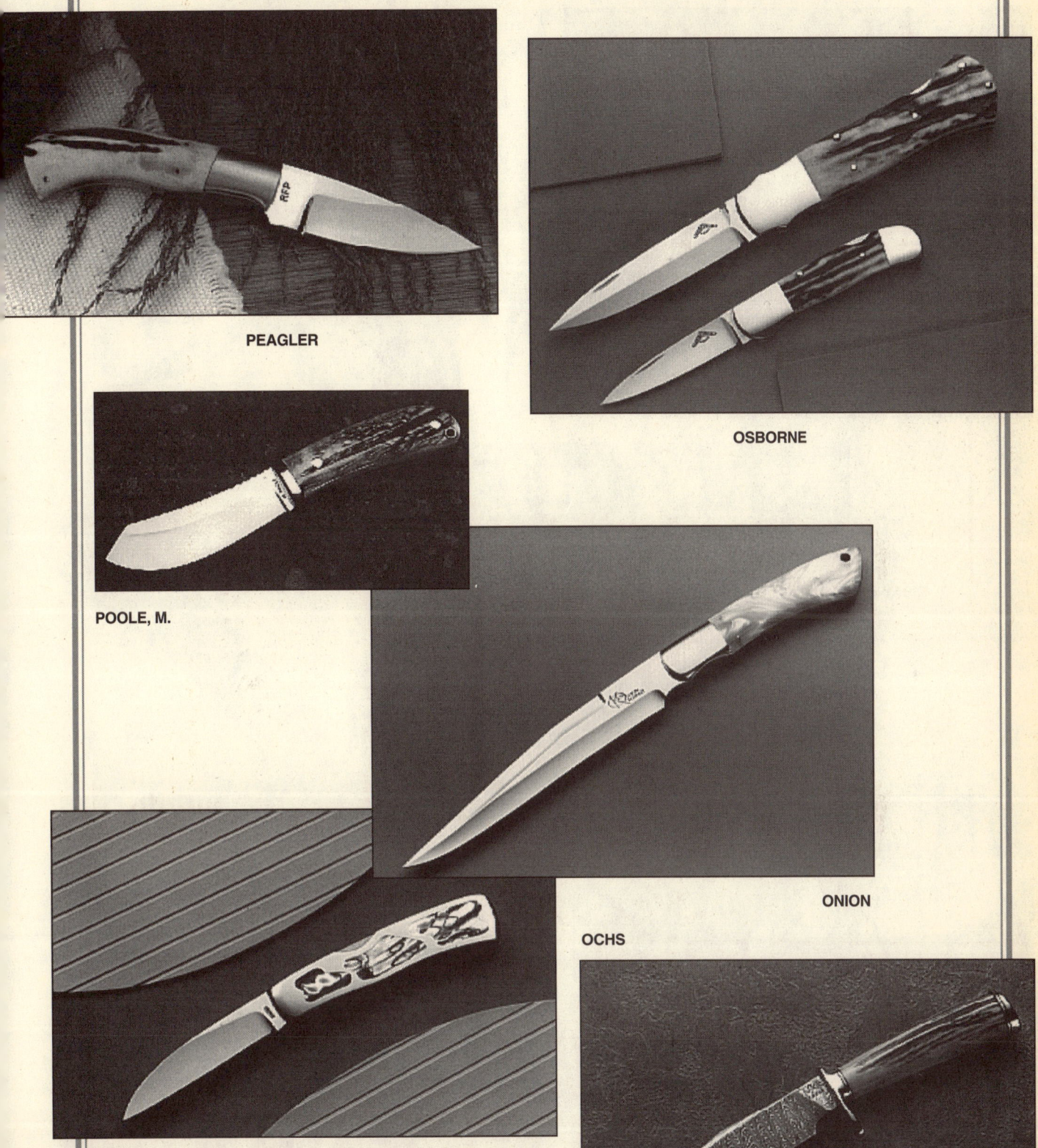

PEAGLER

OSBORNE

POOLE, M.

ONION

OCHS

PRINCE

FIFTEENTH EDITION **229**

centerfold knives '95

RARDON, A.D.

RIZZI

RINKES

REXROAT

ROBBINS

RAPP

centerfold knives '95

SLEE

SINYARD

SNELL

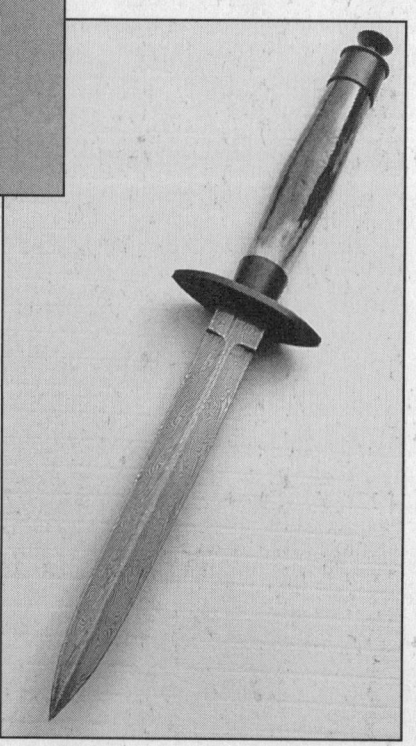
SALLEY

SCHALLER

SERAFEN

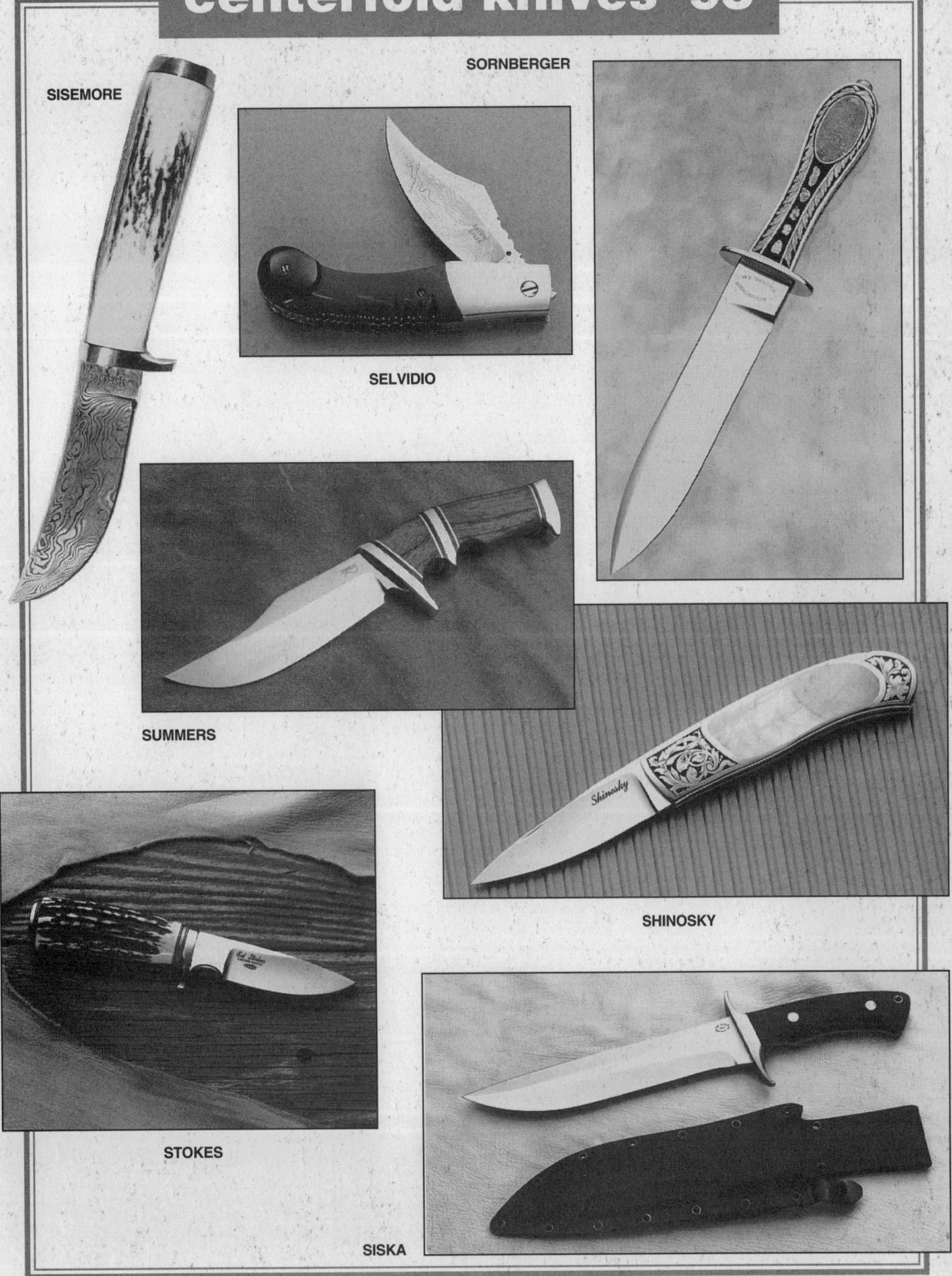

centerfold knives '95

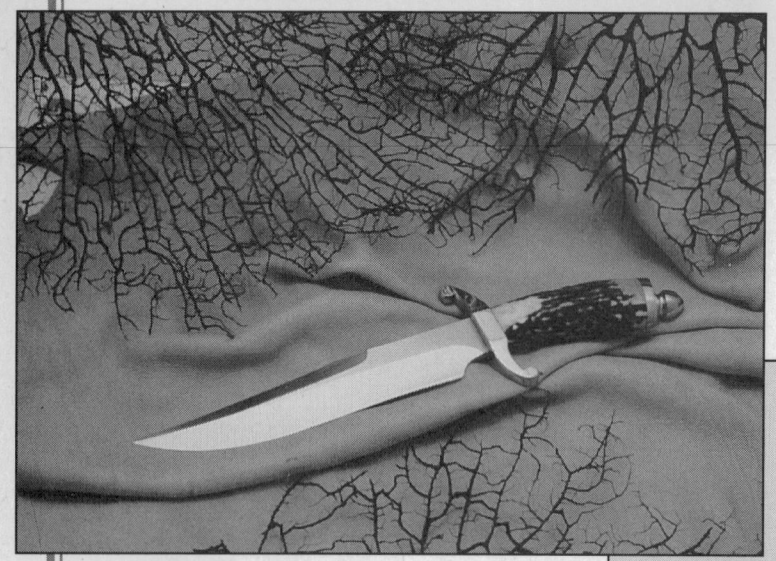
TONER

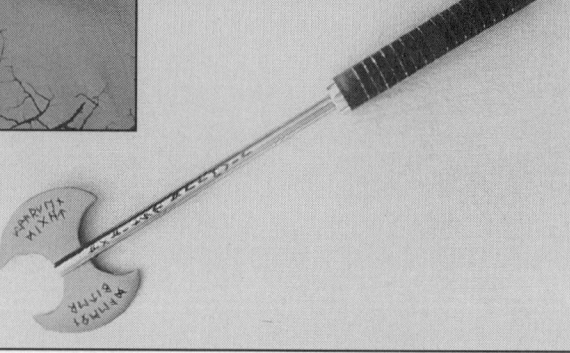
THOMPSON, R.

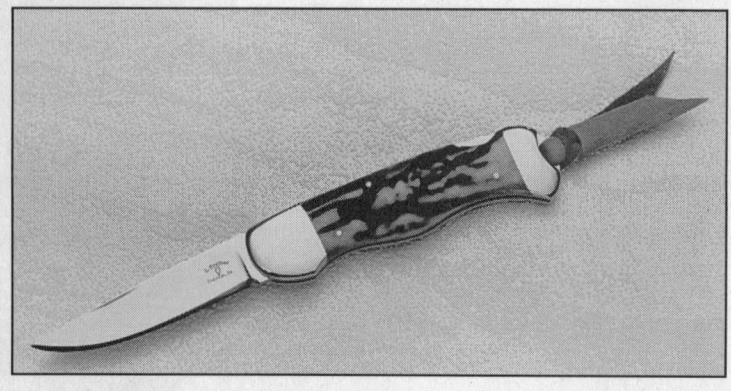
TREIBER

TOICH

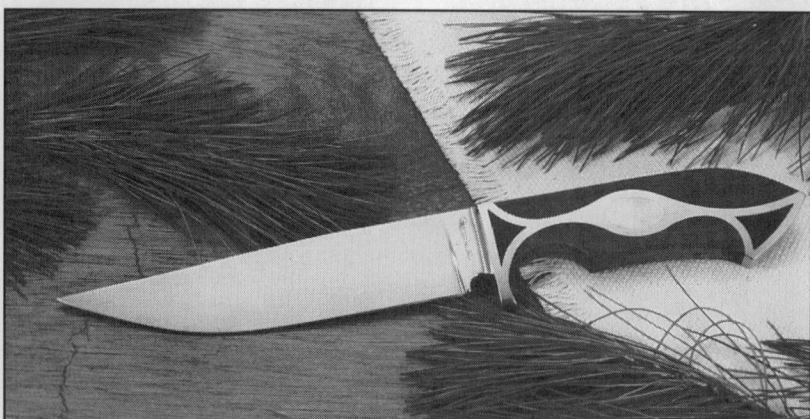
TURNBULL

centerfold knives '95

VIALLON

TOPLISS

TAYLOR, S.

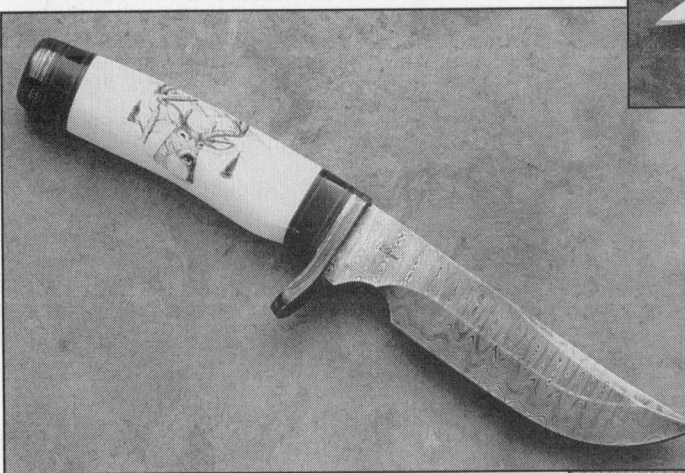

VALACHOVIC

THOMPSON, LEON

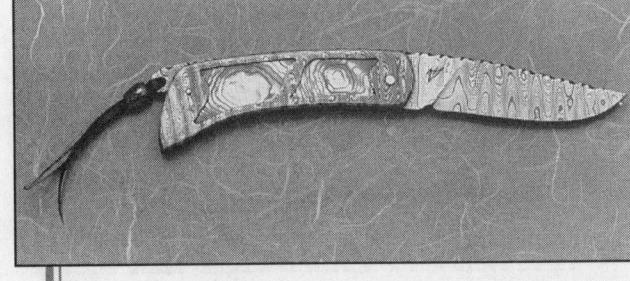

FIFTEENTH EDITION 235

centerfold knives '95

YEATES

WARDEN

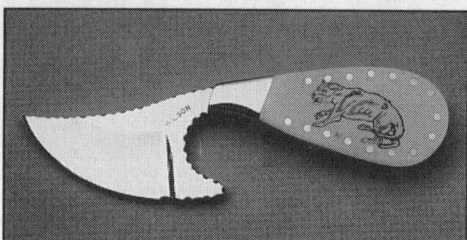

WILSON, MIKE

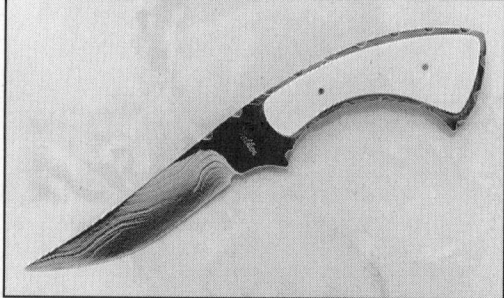

WALKER, JOHN

ZOWADA

ZEMITIS

centerfold knives '95

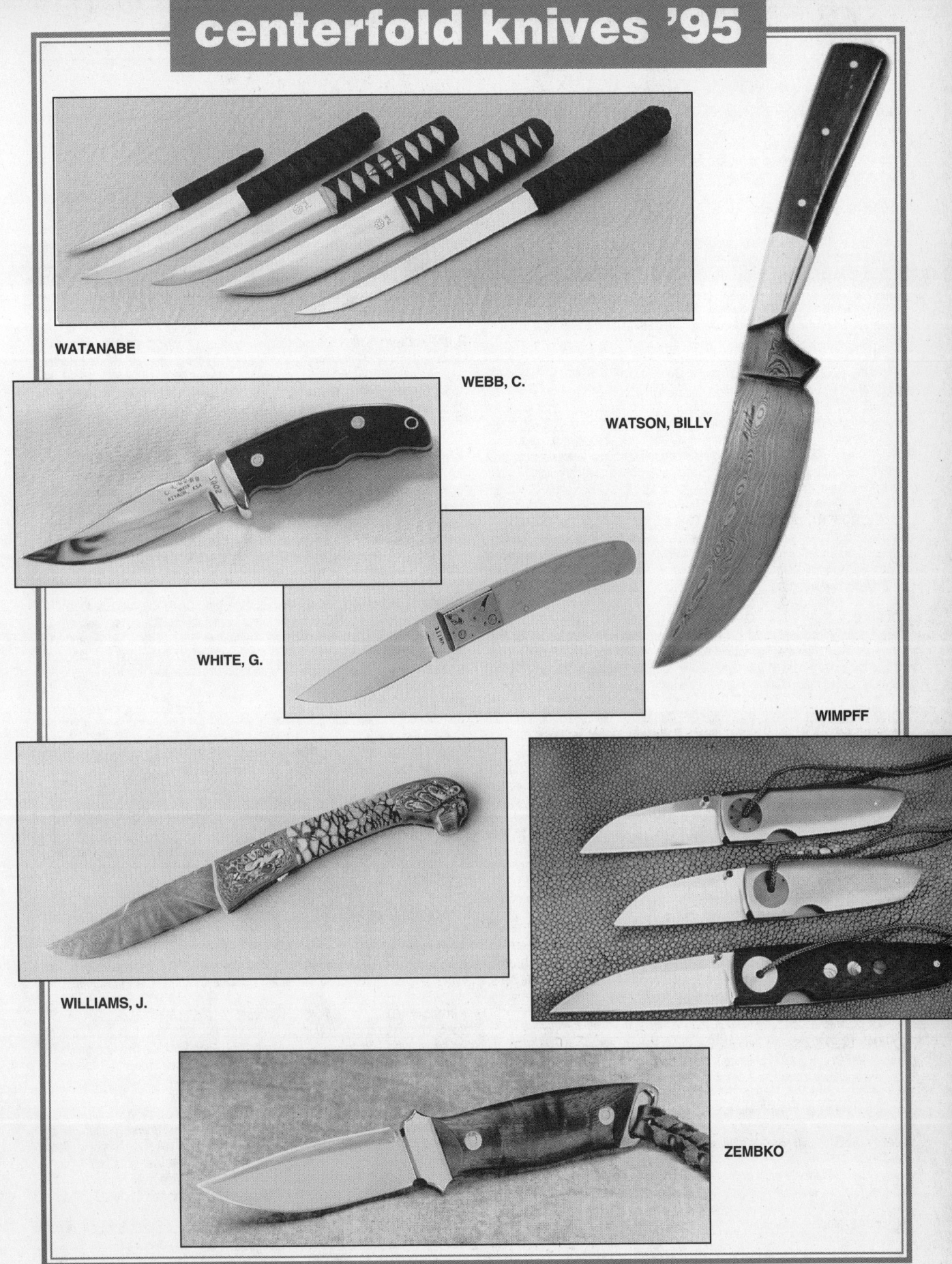

WATANABE

WEBB, C.

WATSON, BILLY

WHITE, G.

WIMPFF

WILLIAMS, J.

ZEMBKO

FIFTEENTH EDITION 237

directory
KNUTH—KUBASEK

KNUTH, JOSEPH E., 3307 Lookout Dr., Rockford, IL 61109/815-874-9597
Specialties: High-art working straight knives of his design or to customer specs. **Patterns:** Daggers, fighters and swords. **Technical:** Grinds 440C, ATS-34 and D2. **Prices:** $150 to $800; some to $2,500. **Remarks:** Full-time maker; first knife sold in 1989. **Mark:** Initials on bolster face.

KODAN (See Engnath, Bob)

KOHLER, J. MARK, 16430 Dawncrest Way, Sugarland, TX 77478
Specialties: Fancy and working straight knives and folders of his design. **Patterns:** Hunters, locking folders, gentleman's embellished folders. **Technical:** Grinds D2, ATS-34 and vascowear or 440V. Enjoys exotic handle materials—tiger coral, cape buffalo, sheephorn. Offers filework and embellished bolsters. **Prices:** $165 to $325. **Remarks:** Part-time maker; first knife sold in 1986. **Mark:** Last name in script, stamped.

KOJETIN, W., 20 Bapaume Rd., Delville, Germiston 1401 SOUTH AFRICA-011 825 6680
Specialties: High-art and working straight knives of all designs. **Patterns:** Daggers, hunters and his own Manhunter Bowie. **Technical:** Grinds D2 and ATS-34; forges and grinds 440B/C. Offers "wrap-around" pava and abalone handles, scrolled wood or ivory, stacked filework and setting of faceted semi-precious stones. **Prices:** $185 to $600; some to $11,000. **Remarks:** Spare-time maker; first knife sold in 1962. **Mark:** Billy K.

KOLITZ, ROBERT, W9342 Canary Rd., Beaver Dam, WI 53916/414-887-1287
Specialties: Working straight knives to customer specs. **Patterns:** Bowies, hunters, bird and trout knives, boots. **Technical:** Grinds 01, 440C; commercial Damascus. **Prices:** $50 to $100; some to $500. **Remarks:** Spare-time maker; first knife sold in 1979. **Mark:** Last initial.

KOPP, TODD M., P.O. Box 3474, Apache Jct., AZ 85217/602-983-6143
Specialties: Classic and traditional straight knives. **Patterns:** Bowies, boots, daggers, fighters and hunters. **Technical:** Grinds M1, ATS-34 and 4160. Some engraving and filework. **Prices:** $125 to $400; some to $800. **Remarks:** Part-time maker; first knife sold in 1989. **Mark:** Name, city and state.

KORMANIK, CHRIS, 6424 Stone Bridge Rd., Carnesville, GA 30521/706-384-4450
Specialties: Working knives and hunters. **Patterns:** Variety, including hunters, fighters and utility knives of his design or to customer specs; folders. **Technical:** Grinds and forges; prefers D2, ATS-34, cable Damascus and 5168. Heat-treats. **Prices:** $80 to $350; some higher. **Remarks:** Part-time maker; first knife sold in 1987. **Mark:** Name.

KOUTSOPOULOS, GEORGE, 41491 Biggs Rd., LaGrange, OH 44050/216-355-5013
Specialties: Heavy-duty working straight knives and folders. **Patterns:** Traditional hunters and skinners; lockbacks. **Technical:** Grinds 440C, 154CM, ATS-34. **Prices:** $75 to $275; some higher. **Remarks:** Spare-time maker; first knife sold in 1976. **Mark:** Initials in diamond logo.

KOVAL, MICHAEL T., 5819 Zarley St., New Albany, OH 43054/614-855-0777
Specialties: Working straight knives of his design; period pieces. **Patterns:** Bowies, boots and daggers. **Technical:** Grinds D2, 440C and 154CM. **Prices:** $95 to $195; some to $495. **Remarks:** Full-time knifemaker supply house; spare-time knifemaker. **Mark:** Last name.

KOVAR, EUGENE, 2626 W. 98th St., Evergreen Park, IL 60642/312-636-3724
Specialties: One-of-a-kind miniature knives only. **Patterns:** Fancy to fantasy miniature knives; knife pendants and tie tacks. **Technical:** Files and grinds nails, nickel silver and sterling silver. **Prices:** $5 to $35; some to $100. **Remarks:** Spare-time maker; first knife sold in 1987. **Mark:** GK connected.

KRAFT, ELMER, 1358 Meadowlark Lane, Big Arm, MT 59910/406-849-5086; FAX: 406-883-3056
Specialties: Traditional working/using straight knives of all designs. **Patterns:** Fighters, hunters, utility/camp knives. **Technical:** Grinds 440C, D2. Custom makes sheaths. **Prices:** $125 to $350; some to $500. **Remarks:** Part-time maker; first knife sold in 1989. **Mark:** Kraft Knives.

KRAFT, STEVE, 315 S.E. 6th, Abilene, KS 67410/913-263-2198
Specialties: Motorcycle chain Damascus with foot peg handle. **Patterns:** Hunters, boot knives and fighters. **Technical:** Forge chain Damascus and stock removal grind ATS-34. **Prices:** $150 to $1,000. **Remarks:** Part-time maker; first knife sold in 1984. **Mark:** Last name.

KRANNING, TERRY L., 1900 West Quinn, #153, Pocatello, ID 83202/208-237-9047
Specialties: Miniature and full-size fantasy and working knives of his design. **Patterns:** Miniatures and some mini straight knives including razors, tomahawks, hunters, Bowies and fighters. **Technical:** Grinds 1095, 440C, commercial Damascus and nickel silver. Uses exotic materials like meteorite. **Prices:** $20 to $100; some to $250. **Remarks:** Part-time maker; first knife sold in 1978. **Mark:** Last initial or full initials in eagle head logo.

KRAPP, DENNY, 1826 Windsor Oak Dr., Apopka, FL 32703/407-880-7115
Specialties: Fantasy and working straight knives of his design. **Patterns:** Hunters, fighters and utility/camp knives. **Technical:** Grinds ATS-34 and 440C. **Prices:** $85 to $300; some to $800. **Remarks:** Spare-time maker; first knife sold in 1988. **Mark:** Last name.

KRAUSE, ROY W., 22412 Corteville, St. Clair Shores, MI 48081/810-296-3995; FAX: 810-296-2663.
Specialties: Military and law enforcement/Japanese-style knives and swords. **Patterns:** Combat and back-up, Bowies, fighters, boot knives, daggers, tantos, wakazashis and katanas. **Technical:** Grinds ATS-34, A2, D2, 1045, 01 and commercial Damascus; differentially hardened Japanese-style blades. **Prices:** Moderate to upscale. **Remarks:** Full-time maker. **Mark:** Last name on traditional knives; initials in Japanese characters on Japanese-style knives.

KREIBICH, DONALD L., 6082 Boyd Ct., San Jose, CA 95123/408-225-4719
Specialties: Working straight knives in standard patterns. **Patterns:** Bowies, boots and daggers; camp and fishing knives. **Technical:** Grinds 440C, 154CM and ATS-34; likes integrals. **Prices:** $100 to $200; some to $500. **Remarks:** Part-time maker; first knife sold in 1980. **Mark:** First and middle initials, last name.

KREMZNER, RAYMOND L., P.O. Box 31, Stevenson, MD 21153/410-653-2657
Specialties: Working straight knives in standard patterns, some fancy. **Patterns:** Hunters, fighters, Bowies and camp knives. **Technical:** Forges 5160, 9260, W2 and his own Damascus. Offers wire inlay. **Prices:** $200 to $700; some higher. **Remarks:** Part-time maker; first knife sold in 1987. **Mark:** Last name, JS.

KRESSLER, D.F., Lochhauser Strasse 86, 8039 Puchheim, GERMANY/08134-7758; FAX: 08134-7759
Specialties: High-tech working knives. **Patterns:** Hunters, fighters, daggers. **Technical:** Grinds new state-of-the-art steels; prefers natural handle materials. **Prices:** Upscale. **Mark:** Name in logo.

KRETSINGER JR., PHILIP W., 17536 Bakersville Rd., Boonsboro, MD 21713/301-432-6771
Specialties: Fancy and traditional period pieces. **Patterns:** Hunters, Bowies, camp knives, daggers, carvers, fighters. **Technical:** Forges W2, 5160 and his own Damascus. **Prices:** Start at $200. **Remarks:** Full-time knifemaker. **Mark:** Name.

KRUSE, MARTIN, P.O. Box 487, Reseda, CA 91335/818-713-0172
Specialties: Fighters and working straight knives. **Patterns:** Full line of straight knives, swords, fighters, axes, kitchen cutlery. **Technical:** Forges and grinds 01, 1095, 5160 and Damascus; differential tempering. **Prices:** $85 to $700; some to $2,000. **Remarks:** Full-time maker; first knife sold in 1964. **Mark:** Initials.

KUBAIKO, HANK, HC01 Box 6910, Palmer, AK 99645
Specialties: Working straight knives and folders. **Patterns:** Bowies, fighters, fishing knives, kitchen cutlery, lockers, slip-joints, camp knives, axes and miniatures. **Technical:** Grinds 440C, ATS-34 and D2; will use CPM-T-440V at extra cost. Worked under Joe Cordova. **Prices:** Moderate. **Remarks:** Part-time maker in summer, full-time in winter; first knife sold in 1982. **Mark:** Alaskan Maid and name.

KUBASEK, JOHN A., 74 Northhampton St., Easthampton, MA 01027/413-527-7917
Specialties: Traditional working straight knives and folders of his design or to cus-

tomer specs. **Patterns:** Hunters, Bowies and fighters. **Technical:** Grinds 440C, ATS-34 and D2. **Prices:** $75 to $450. **Remarks:** Part-time maker; first knife sold in 1985. **Mark:** Initials.

KUNI MITSU (See Bell, Michael)

KUSTOM KRAFTED KNIVES—KKK (See Collins, A.J.)

L

LABORDE, TERRY, 230 E. Fallbrook St., Unit #11, Fallbrook, CA 92028-3381/619-723-9702
Specialties: Traditional and working straight knives of all designs. **Patterns:** Bowies, daggers and hunters. **Technical:** Forges and grinds CPMT 440V, ATS-34 and ASP-60. Barstock stainless Damascus sold by the inch. Heat-treats stainless steel. Uses stabilized woods for handles. **Prices:** $100 to $3,000; some to $5,000. **Remarks:** Part-time maker; first knife sold in 1990. **Mark:** Dragonfly over water.

LADD, JIM S., 1120 Helen, Deer Park, TX 77536/713-479-7286
Specialties: Working knives and period pieces. **Patterns:** Hunters, boots and Bowies plus other straight knives. **Technical:** Grinds D2, 440C and 154CM. **Prices:** $125 to $225; some to $550. **Remarks:** Part-time maker; first knife sold in 1965. Doing business as The Tinker. **Mark:** First and middle initials, last name.

LADD, JIMMIE LEE, 1120 Helen, Deer Park, TX 77536/713-479-7186
Specialties: Working straight knives. **Patterns:** Hunters, skinners and utility knives. **Technical:** Grinds 440C and D2. **Prices:** $75 to $225. **Remarks:** First knife sold in 1979. **Mark:** First and middle initials, last name.

LA GRANGE, FANIE, 22 Sturke Rd., Selborne, Bellville 7530, REPUBLIC OF SOUTH AFRICA/27-021-9134199; FAX: 27-021-9134199
Specialties: Fancy high-tech straight knives and folders of his design and to customer specs. **Patterns:** Daggers, hunters and locking folders. **Technical:** Grinds Sandvik 12C27 and ATS-34; forges and grinds Damascus. Engraves, enamels and anodizes bolsters. Uses rare and natural handle materials. **Prices:** $250 to $500; some higher. **Remarks:** Full-time maker; first knife sold in 1987. **Mark:** Name, town, country under Table Mountain.

LAINSON, TONY, 114 Park Ave., Council Bluffs, IA 51503/712-322-5222
Specialties: Working straight knives, locking folders, straight razors, Bowies and tantos. **Technical:** Grinds ATS-34 and 440C. Prefers mirror finishes; handle materials include Micarta, Pakkawood and bone. **Prices:** $45 to $280; some to $450. **Remarks:** Part-time maker; first knife sold in 1987; not currently taking orders. **Mark:** Name and state.

LAKE, RON, 3360 Bendix Ave., Eugene, OR 97401/503-484-2683
Specialties: High-tech working knives; inventor of the modern interframe folder. **Patterns:** Hunters, boots, etc.; locking folders. **Technical:** Grinds 154CM and ATS-34. Patented interframe with special lock release tab. **Prices:** $2,200 to $3,000; some higher. **Remarks:** Full-time maker; first knife sold in 1966. **Mark:** Last name.

LAMBERT, JARRELL D., RR1, Box 67, Granado, TX 77962/512-771-3744
Specialties: Traditional working and using straight knives of his design and to customer specs. **Patterns:** Bowies, hunters and utility/camp knives. **Technical:** Grinds ATS-34; forges W2 and his own Damascus. Makes own sheaths. **Prices:** $80 to $600; some to $1,000. **Remarks:** Part-time maker; first knife sold in 1982. **Mark:** Etched first and middle initials, last name; or stamped last name.

LAMBERT, RONALD S., 24 Vermont St., Johnston, RI 02919/401-831-5427
Specialties: Traditional working and using straight knives of his design. **Patterns:** Boots, bowies and hunters. **Technical:** Grinds 01 and 440C; forges 1070. Offers exotic wood handles; sheaths have exotic skin overlay. **Prices:** $100 to $500; some to $850. **Remarks:** Part-time maker; first knife sold in 1991. Doing business as RL Custom Knives. **Mark:** Initials; each knife is numbered.

LAMPREY, MIKE, 32 Pathfield, Great Torrington, Devon EX38 7BX ENGLAND/0805 622651
Specialties: High-tech working/using straight knives and folders of his design. **Patterns:** Fighters, locking folders, utility/camp knives. **Technical:** Grinds ATS-34, 12C27 and 440C. Offers hand-rubbed finish on blades, bead blast and anodizing on titanium and occasional engraving on bolsters, guards, etc. **Prices:** $250 to $600; some to $1,000. **Remarks:** Part-time maker; first knife sold in 1982. **Mark:** Signature.

LAMPSON, FRANK G., 2052 I Rd., Fruita, CO 81521/303-858-7292
Specialties: Working folders; one-of-a-kinds. **Patterns:** Folders, hunters, utility knives, fillet knives and Bowies. **Technical:** Grinds ATS-34, 440C and 154CM. **Prices:** $100 to $750; some to $3,500; Catalogs $2. **Remarks:** Full-time maker; first knife sold in 1971. **Mark:** Name in fish logo.

LANCASTER, C.G., P.O. Box 99, Orkney, Transvaal, SOUTH AFRICA/018-32327
Specialties: High-tech working and using knives of his design and to customer specs. **Patterns:** Hunters, locking folders and utility/camp knives. **Technical:** Grinds Sandvik 12C27, 440C and D2. Offers anodized titanium bolsters. **Prices:** $450 to $750; some to $1,500. **Remarks:** Part-time maker; first knife sold in 1990. **Mark:** Etched logo.

LANCE, BILL, P.O. Box 4427, Eagle River, AK 99577/907-694-1487
Specialties: Ooloos and working straight knives; limited issue sets. **Patterns:** Several ooloo patterns, drop-point skinners. **Technical:** Uses ATS-34, Vascomax 350; ivory, horn and high-class wood handles. **Prices:** $85 to $300; art sets to $3,000. **Remarks:** First knife sold in 1981. **Mark:** Last name over a lance.

LANDERS, JOHN, 758 Welcome Rd., Newnan, GA 30263/404-253-5719
Specialties: High-art working straight knives and folders of his design. **Patterns:** Hunters, fighters and slip-joint folders. **Technical:** Grinds 440C, ATS-34, 154CM and commercial Damascus. **Prices:** $85 to $250; some to $500. **Remarks:** Part-time maker; first knife sold in 1989. **Mark:** Last name.

LANDRUM, LEONARD "LEN", 995 Gumpond Beall Rd., Lumberton, MS 39455/601-796-4380
Specialties: Traditional working and using straight knives of his design and to customer specs. **Patterns:** Boots, Bowies, daggers, fighters, hunters, kitchen knives and utility/camp knives. **Technical:** Forges 52100, 5160 and pattern-welded steel; heat-treats. **Prices:** $100 to $500; some to $1,000. **Remarks:** Part-time maker; first knife sold in 1987. **Mark:** Handmade by Landrum.

LANE, BEN, 4802 Massie St., North Little Rock, AR 72218/501-753-8238
Specialties: Fancy straight knives of his design and to customer specs; period pieces. **Patterns:** Bowies, hunters, utility/camp knives. **Technical:** Grinds D2 and 154CM; forges and grinds 1095. Offers intricate handle work including inlays and spacers. **Prices:** $120 to $450; some to $5,000. **Remarks:** Part-time maker; first knife sold in 1989. **Mark:** Full name, city, state.

LANE, ED, 440 N. Topping, Kansas City, MO 64123/816-241-3217
Specialties: Fancy working knives to customer specs. **Patterns:** Buckskinners, hunters, fighters, tantos, fishing knives and lightweight folders under the "Kascey" line. **Technical:** Grinds 440C, 154CM, ATS-34 and commercial Damascus. Offers titanium nitride on blades. **Prices:** $65 to $350; some to $1,000. **Remarks:** Full-time maker; first knife sold in 1982. **Mark:** Signature.

LANG, KURT, 4908 S. Wildwood Dr., McHenry, IL 60050/708-516-4649
Specialties: High-art working knives. **Patterns:** Bowies, utilitarian-type knives with rough finishes. **Technical:** Forges welded steel in European and Japanese styles. **Prices:** Moderate to upscale. **Remarks:** Part-time maker. **Mark:** "Crazy Eye" logo.

LANGE, DONALD G., Rt. 1, Box 66, Pelican Rapids, MN 56572
Specialties: High-quality Damascus hunters; welcomes customer designs. **Patterns:** Hunters, fighters and Bowies. **Technical:** Forges 5160, W2, L6 and his own Damascus. **Prices:** Moderate. **Remarks:** Full-time maker; first knife sold in 1969. **Mark:** Last name, M.S.

LANGLEY, GENE H., 1022 N. Price Rd., Florence, SC 29506/803-669-3150
Specialties: Working knives in standard patterns. **Patterns:** Hunters, boots, fighters, locking folders and slip-joints. **Technical:** Grinds 440C, 154CM and ATS-34. **Prices:** $125 to $450; some to $1000. **Remarks:** Full-time maker; first knife sold in 1979. **Mark:** Name or name, city and state.

LANGLEY, MICK, 960 Bluebird Place, Qualicum Beach, B.C. CANADA V9K 1M7/604-752-5856
Specialties: Working knives; period pieces. **Patterns:** Fighters, tantos, boots,

directory

LANGSTON—LEE

Bowies and folders. **Technical:** Forges W2, 5160 and his own Damascus. **Prices:** $250 to $2,000; some to $3,500. **Remarks:** Full-time maker; first knife sold in 1977. **Mark:** Last name, M.S.

LANGSTON, BENNIE E., 3233 Ridgecrest, Memphis, TN 38127/901-357-4559
Specialties: Traditional working straight knives and folders of his design. **Patterns:** Hunters, daggers and locking folders. **Technical:** Grinds 440C. Filework; mirror-finishes. **Prices:** $50 to $100; some to $200. **Remarks:** Part-time maker; first knife sold in 1970. **Mark:** Last name and outline of state.

LANKTON, SCOTT, 8065 Jackson Rd. R-11, Ann Arbor, MI 48103/313-426-3735
Specialties: Pattern welded swords, krisses and Viking period pieces. **Patterns:** One-of-a-kind. **Technical:** Forges W2, L6 Nickel and other steels. **Prices:** $600 to $12,000. **Remarks:** Part-time bladesmith, full-time smith; first knife sold in 1976. **Mark:** Last name logo.

LAPEN, CHARLES, Box 529, W. Brookfield, MA 01585
Specialties: Fancy working straight knives. **Patterns:** camp knives, Japanese-style swords and wood working tools, hunters, Bowies and fudal European knives. **Technical:** Forges 1075, 9260 and his own Damascus. Favors narrow and Japanese tangs. **Prices:** $200 to $400; some to $2,000. **Remarks:** Full-time maker; first knife sold in 1972. **Mark:** Last name.

LAPLANTE, BRETT, 2821 Hickory Bend, Garland, TX 75044/214-414-1712
Specialties: Working straight knives and folders to customer specs. **Patterns:** Survival knives, Bowies, skinners, hunters. **Technical:** Grinds D2 and 440C. Heat-treats. **Prices:** $125 to $2500. **Remarks:** Part-time maker; first knife sold in 1987. **Mark:** Last name in Canadian maple leaf logo.

LARGIN, KEN, 23035 Pocket Rd., Batesville, IN 47006/812-934-5938
Specialties: Working knives in standard patterns. **Patterns:** Hunters, folders, miniatures and butterfly knives. **Technical:** 440-C, ATS-34; buys Damascus; offers filework. **Prices:** $99 to $250; some to $500. **Remarks:** Full-time maker; first knife sold in 1980. Doing business as KELGIN Knives. **Mark:** KELGIN or name.

LARY, ED, 651 Rangeline Rd., Mosinee, WI 54455/715-693-3940
Specialties: Entry level to embellished investment grade. **Patterns:** Hunters, interframe folders, fighters and one-of-a-kind. **Technical:** Grinds D2, 440C, ATS34 and Damascus; prefers natural handle material. Does fancy filework, scrimshaws, engraves and does matching fabricated sheaths. **Prices:** Moderate to upscale. **Remarks:** First knife sold in 1974. **Mark:** Name in script and serial numbered.

LAUGHLIN, DON, 190 Laughlin Dr., Vidor, TX 77662/409-769-3390
Specialties: Working knives of his design. **Patterns:** Hunters, fighters, Bowies, locking folders and two-blades. **Technical:** Grinds D2, 440C and 154CM. **Prices:** $75 to $200; some to $350. **Remarks:** Full-time maker; first knife sold in 1973. **Mark:** DEER or full name.

LAURENT, KERMIT, 1812 Acadia Dr., LaPlace, LA 70068/504-652-5629
Specialties: Traditional and working straight knives and folders of his design. **Patterns:** Bowies, hunters and utility knives. **Technical:** Forges 1095 and pattern-welded Damascus; grinds 440C. Specializes in altering cable patterns. Uses stabilized handle materials, especially select exotic woods. **Prices:** $75 to $200; some to $1,000. **Remarks:** Full-time maker; first knife sold in 1982. Doing business as Kermit's Knife Works. **Mark:** First name.

LAWRENCE, ALTON, Rt. 1, Box 488, De Queen, AR 71832/501-642-7643
Specialties: Classic straight knives to customer specs. **Patterns:** Bowies, hunters and utility/camp knives. **Technical:** Forges 5168, D2 and railroad spikes. **Prices:** $100 to $300. **Remarks:** Part-time maker; first knife sold in 1988. **Mark:** Last name inside fish symbol.

LAWSON, STEPHEN M., Rt. 3, Box 398 Old San Antonio Rd., Fredericksburg, TX 78624/512-997-7646
Specialties: Fancy working knives of his design or to customer specs. **Patterns:** Cleavers, Bowies, fishing and push knives; locking folders. **Technical:** Grinds 440C, 154CM and ATS-34; engraves. **Prices:** $160 to $1,500; some to $2,500. **Remarks:** Full-time maker; first knife sold in 1978. **Mark:** First initial, last name.

LAY, L.J., 602 Mimosa Dr., Burkburnett, TX 76354/817-569-1329
Specialties: Working straight knives in standard patterns; some period pieces. **Patterns:** Drop-point hunters, Bowies and fighters. **Technical:** Grinds ATS-34 to mirror finish; likes Micarta handles. **Prices:** Moderate. **Remarks:** Full-time maker; first knife sold in 1985. **Mark:** Name or name with ram head and city.

LAYTON, JIM, 2710 Gilbert Ave., Portsmouth, OH 45662

LAZO, ROBERT T., 11850 SW 181 St., Miami, FL 33177/305-232-1569
Specialties: Traditional working and using straight knives and folders in standard patterns. **Patterns:** Utility/camp knives, locking folders, fillet knives and some miniatures. **Technical:** Grinds 440C, ATS-34 and 01. All knives come with hand-tooled leather sheaths, some with fancy inlaids. **Prices:** $90 to $250; some to $500. **Remarks:** Spare-time maker; first knife sold in 1990. **Mark:** Engraved or stamped name.

LDA/LAKELL (See C-G Tay, Larry)

LEACH, MIKE J., 5377 W. Grand Blanc Rd., Swartz Creek, MI 48473/810-655-4850
Specialties: Fancy working knives. **Patterns:** Hunters, fighters, Bowies and heavy-duty knives; slip-joint folders and integral straight patterns. **Technical:** Grinds D2, 440C and 154CM; buys Damascus. **Prices:** Start at $150. **Remarks:** Full-time maker; first knife sold in 1952. **Mark:** Last name.

THE LEATHER BOX (See Benjamin, Jr., Geroge)

LEAVITT JR., EARL F., Pleasant Cove Rd., Box 306, E. Boothbay, ME 04544/207-633-3210
Specialties: 1500-1870 working straight knives and fighters; pole arms. **Patterns:** Historically significant knives, classic/modern custom designs. **Technical:** Flat-grinds 01; heat-treats. Filework available. **Prices:** $90 to $350; some to $1,000. **Remarks:** Full-time maker; first knife sold in 1981. Doing business as Old Colony Manufactory. **Mark:** Initials in oval.

LeBATARD, PAUL M., 14700 Old River Rd., Vancleave, MS 39565/601-826-4137
Specialties: Sound working knives, some fancy; lightweight folders. **Patterns:** Hunters, fillets, camp and kitchen knives, combat/survival utility knives, Bowies, toothpicks and one- and two-blade folders. **Technical:** Grinds ATS-34; forges carbon steel; machines folder frames from aircraft aluminum. **Prices:** $50 to $450. **Remarks:** Part-time maker; first knife sold in 1974. Offers knife repair, restoration and sharpening. **Mark:** Last name.

LEBER, HEINZ, Box 446, Hudson's Hope, BC VOC 1V0, CANADA/604-783-5304
Specialties: Working straight knives of his design. **Patterns:** 20 models, from capers to Bowies. **Technical:** Hollow-grinds M2 exclusively; mirror-finishes and full tang only. Likes moose, elk, stone sheep for handles. **Prices:** $135 to $1,000; 20-page color brochure $3. **Remarks:** Full-time maker; first knife sold in 1975. **Mark:** Initials connected.

LeBLANC, JOHN, Rt. 2, Box 22950, Winnsboro, TX 75494/903-629-7745

LECK, DAL, Box 390, Hayden, CO 81639/303-276-3663
Specialties: Classic, traditional and working knives of his design and in standard patterns; period pieces. **Patterns:** Boots, daggers, fighters, hunters and push daggers. **Technical:** Forges 01 and 5160; makes his own Damascus. **Prices:** $175 to $700; some to $1,500. **Remarks:** Part-time maker; first knife sold in 1990. Doing business as The Moonlight Smithy. **Mark:** Stamped initials.

LEDFORD, BRACY R., 3670 N. Sherman Dr., Indianapolis, IN 46218/317-549-1948
Specialties: Art knives and fantasy knives; working knives upon request. **Patterns:** Bowies, locking folders and hunters; coil spring action folders. **Technical:** Files and sandpapers 440C by hand; other steels available upon request; likes exotic handle materials. **Prices:** Folders start at $250; fixed blades $125 to $3,000. **Remarks:** Part-time maker; first knife sold in 1983. **Mark:** First and middle initials, last name, city and state.

LEE, RANDY, P.O. Box 1873, St. John, AZ 85936/602-337-2594
Specialties: Traditional working and using straight knives of his design. **Patterns:** Bowies, fighters, hunters and professional throwing knives and hawks. **Technical:** Grinds ATS-34, 440C and D2. Sheaths by Sonja Lee. **Prices:** $175 to $500; some to $800. **Remarks:** Part-time maker; first knife sold in 1979. **Mark:** Full name, city, state.

custom knifemakers
LEE—LISTER

LEE, TOMMY, 1011 Grassy Pond Rd., Gaffney, SC 29340/803-489-6699
Specialties: Working knives and period pieces. **Patterns:** Daggers, boots, fighters and folders. **Technical:** Forges and grinds 440C, ATS-34 and his own and commercial Damascus. **Prices:** $200 to $500; some to $2,000. **Remarks:** Full-time maker; first knife sold in 1974. **Mark:** Last name in capital block letters.

LEET, LARRY W., 2001 N. Beard, Shawnee, OK 74801/405-273-7487
Specialties: Heavy-duty working knives. **Patterns:** Hunters, tantos, camp knives and Bowies. **Technical:** Grinds stainless steels; likes filework. **Remarks:** Full-time maker; first knife sold in 1970. **Mark:** Stylized initials.

LeFONT, MARK, 3210 Oakley Dr., Hollywood, CA 90068/213-851-5940
Specialties: Classic high-art fantasy straight knives of his design. **Patterns:** Daggers and swords; chain mail armor, helmets, axes and stone knives. **Technical:** Grinds Pamir Damascus, conventional steel and non-metallic materials. **Prices:** $150 to $250; some higher. **Remarks:** Full-time maker; first knife sold in 1983. **Mark:** None.

LELAND, STEVE, P.O. Box 1173, Fairfax, CA 94978
Specialties: Traditional and working straight knives and folders of his design and to customer specs. **Patterns:** Boots, hunters and locking folders. **Technical:** Grinds 01, ATS-34 and 440C. **Prices:** $150 to $300; some to $750. **Remarks:** Part-time maker; first knife sold in 1987. Doing business as Leland Knives. **Mark:** Last name.

LEMAIRE, DENIS, 534 Verendrye St., Boucherville, P.Q. J4B 2Y1 CANADA

LEONE, NICK, 9 Georgetown, Pontoon Beach, IL 62040/618-797-1179
Specialties: Working straight knives and art daggers. **Patterns:** Bowies, skinners, hunters, camp/utility, fighters, daggers and primitive knives. **Technical:** Forges 5160, W2, 01, 1098, 52100 and his own Damascus and cable. **Prices:** $25 to $1000; some to $2500. **Remarks:** Full-time maker; first knife sold in 1987. Doing business as Anvil Head Forge. **Mark:** Last name or anvil head forge.

LEPORE, MICHAEL J., 66 Woodcutters Dr., Bethany, CT 06524/203-393-3823
Specialties: Knives of his design or to customer specs. **Patterns:** Fancy working straight knives and folders. **Technical:** Forges and grinds W2, W1 and 01; prefers natural handle materials. **Prices:** Start at $350. **Remarks:** Spare-time maker; first knife sold in 1984. **Mark:** Last name.

LETCHER, BILLY, 200 Milkyway, Fort Collins, CO 80525/303-223-9689
Specialties: Traditional working and using straight knives; fancy knives. **Patterns:** Boots, Bowies, daggers, fighters, hunters, letter openers. **Technical:** Grinds 440C, ATS-34 and D2. **Prices:** $70 to $350. **Remarks:** Part-time maker; first knife sold in 1983. **Mark:** Letcher Knives.

LEVENGOOD, BILL, 15011 Otto Rd., Tampa, FL 33624/813-961-5688
Specialties: Working straight knives and folders. **Patterns:** Hunters, Bowies, folders and collector pieces. **Technical:** Grinds ATS-34 and D2. **Prices:** $65 to $1,200. **Remarks:** Part-time maker; first knife sold in 1983. **Mark:** Last name, city, state.

LEVERETT, KEN, P.O. Box 696, Lithia, FL 33547/813-689-8578
Specialties: High-tech and working straight knives and folders of his design and to customer specs. **Patterns:** Bowies, hunters and locking folders. **Technical:** Grinds ATS-34, Damascus. **Prices:** $100 to $350; some to $1,500. **Remarks:** Part-time maker; first knife sold in 1991. **Mark:** Name, city, state.

LEVINE, BOB, 3201 Iowa Drive, Anchorage, AK 99517/907-243-3878
Specialties: Left- and Right-handed liner lock folders in titanium and ivory. **Patterns:** Full range of hunters, utility and fillet knives; miniatures. **Technical:** Grinds 440C, ATS-34 and DEBL steel; works on knife backs. Provides custom leather sheath with each knife. **Prices:** $115 to $300; some to $650. **Remarks:** Full-time maker; first knife sold in 1984. **Mark:** Name in logo.

LEVINE, NORMAN, 34582 Farm Rd., Lake Elsinore, CA 92532/909-244-0993
Specialties: Fancy art knives. **Patterns:** Hunters, boots, daggers, locking folders and slip-joints in gents and hunter patterns. **Technical:** Grinds 440C, D2 and Damascus; provides ball bearing pivot in folders. **Prices:** $135 to $5,000. **Remarks:** Full-time maker; first knife sold in 1974. **Mark:** Dragon on shield with name.

LEWIS, K.J., 374 Cook Rd., Lugoff, SC 29078/803-438-4343

LEWIS, MIKE, 111 W. Central Ave., Tracy, CA 95376/209-836-5753; 408-453-1190
Specialties: Traditional straight knives. **Patterns:** Swords and daggers. **Technical:** Grinds 440C, ATS-34 and 5160. Frequently uses cast bronze and cast nickel guards and pommels. **Prices:** $100 to $750. **Remarks:** Part-time maker; first knife sold in 1988. **Mark:** Dragon Steel and serial number.

LEWIS, RON, Box S-365, Edgewood, NM 87015/505-281-8343
Specialties: Classic straight knives. **Patterns:** Bowies, skinners, buckskinners, art and utility knives. **Technical:** Grinds and forges Damascus, 1084 and ATS-34. **Prices:** Start at $250. **Remarks:** Full-time maker; first knife sold in 1987. **Mark:** Logo with serial number.

LEWIS, TOM R., 1613 Standpipe Rd., Carlsbad, NM 88220/505-885-3616
Specialties: Traditional working straight knives. **Patterns:** Outdoor knives, hunting knives and Bowies. **Technical:** Forges and grinds ATS-34 and welded wire Damascus; forges 52100 steel. Makes Damascus. **Prices:** $75 to $400. **Remarks:** Part-time maker; first knife sold in 1980. Doing business as TRL Handmade Knives. **Mark:** Lewis family crest.

LICATA, STEVEN, 345 Concord Rd., Yonkers, NY 10710/914-779-3451; FAX: 914-779-4234
Specialties: Fantasy and high-art straight knives of his design and to customer specs. **Patterns:** Daggers, fighters and swords. **Technical:** Forges 01, 440C and Damascus. **Prices:** $200 to $1,000; some to $2,000. **Remarks:** Full-time maker; first knife sold in 1989. **Mark:** Stylized initials.

LIEBENBERT, ANDRE, 8 Hilma Rd., Bordeauxrandburg 2196, SOUTH AFRICA/011-787-2303
Specialties: High-art straight knives of his design. **Patterns:** Daggers, fighters and swords. **Technical:** Grinds 440C and 12C27. **Prices:** $250 to $500; some $4,000 and higher. Giraffe bone handles with semi-precious stones. **Remarks:** Spare-time maker; first knife sold in 1990. **Mark:** Initials.

LIEGEY, KENNETH R., 132 Carney Dr., Millwood, WV 25262/304-273-9545
Specialties: Traditional working/using straight knives of his design and to customer specs. **Patterns:** Hunters, utility/camp knives, miniatures. **Technical:** Grinds 440C. **Prices:** $75 to $150; some to $300. **Remarks:** Spare-time maker; first knife sold in 1977. **Mark:** First and middle initials, last name.

LIKARICH, STEVE, 26075 Green Acres Rd., Colfax, CA 95713/916-346-8480
Specialties: Fancy working knives; art knives of his design. **Patterns:** Hunters, fighters and art knives of his design. **Technical:** Grinds ATS-34, 154CM and 440C; likes high polishes and filework. **Prices:** $150 to $2,000; some higher. **Remarks:** Full-time maker; first knife sold in 1987. **Mark:** Name.

LILE, MARILYN (JIMMY), 2721 S. Arkansas Ave., Russellville, AR 72801/501-968-2011
Specialties: Fancy working knives. **Patterns:** Bowies, full line of straight knives, button-lock folders. **Technical:** Grinds D2 and 440C. **Prices:** $125 to $800; some higher. **Remarks:** Full-time maker; first knife sold in 1944. Creator of the original *First Blood* and *Rambo* survival knives. **Mark:** Last name with a dot between the l and L.

LINDSAY, CHRIS A., 1324 N.E. Locksley Dr., Bend, OR 97701/503-389-3875
Specialties: Working knives in standard patterns. **Patterns:** Hunters and camp knives. **Technical:** Hollow- and flat-grinds 440C and ATS-34; offers brushed finishes, tapered tangs. **Prices:** $75 to $160; knife kits $60 to $80. **Remarks:** Part-time maker; first knife sold in 1980. **Mark:** Last name, town and state in oval.

LIONMAKER (See Alden, Jr., Kenneth E.)

LISK, ARLIN J., P.O. Box 9711, Yakima, WA 98909
Specialties: Straight knives of his design. **Patterns:** Boots, hunters, utility knives and drop-point skinners. **Technical:** Uses 440C. All work done with files and sandpaper. **Prices:** $250 to $500. **Remarks:** Part-time maker; first knife sold in 1989. **Mark:** Last name.

LISTER JR., WELDON E., Rt. 1, Box 1517, Boerne, TX 78006/512-981-2210
Specialties: One-of-a-kind fancy and embellished folders. **Patterns:** Locking and slip-joint folders. **Technical:** Commercial Damascus and 01. All knives embellished.

directory

LITTLE—LUCHAK

Engraves, inlays, carves and scrimshaws. **Prices:** Upscale. **Remarks:** Spare-time maker; first knife sold in 1991. **Mark:** Last name.

LITTLE, GARY M., HC84 Box 10301, P.O. Box 156, Broadbent, OR 97414/503-572-2656
Specialties: Fancy working knives. **Patterns:** Hunters, tantos, Bowies, axes and buckskinners; locking folders and interframes. **Technical:** Forges and grinds 01, L6, 1095; makes his own Damascus; bronze fittings. **Prices:** $85 to $300; some to $2,500. **Remarks:** Full-time maker; first knife sold in 1979. Doing business as Conklin Meadows Forge. **Mark:** Name, city and state.

LITTLE, JIMMY L., P.O. Box 871652, Wasilla, AK 99687/907-373-7831
Specialties: Working straight knives; fancy period pieces. **Patterns:** Bowies, bush swords and camp knives. **Technical:** Grinds 440C, 154CM and ATS-34. **Prices:** $100 to $1,000. **Remarks:** Full-time maker; first knife sold in 1984. **Mark:** First and middle initials, last name.

LIVELY, TIM, P.O. Box 8847 CRB, Tucson, AZ 85738/602-825-0679
Specialties: Traditional and fancy straight knives and folders of his design. **Patterns:** Boots, hunters, slip-joint folders. **Technical:** Grinds ATS-34, V440T and Damascus. Uses exotic handle materials and fancy filework. **Prices:** $200 to $750; some to $5,000. **Remarks:** Full-time maker; first knife sold in 1974. **Mark:** Lively Knifeworks with broken arrow.

LIVINGSTON, ROBERT C., P.O. Box 6, Murphy, NC 28906/704-837-4155
Specialties: Art letter openers to working straight knives. **Patterns:** Minis to machetes. **Technical:** Forges and grinds his Damascus, 5160, 440C, ATS-34, L6, 1086 and most tool steels. Offers silver and gold castings and stonework—precious and semi-precious. Forges own mokume. **Prices:** $50 to $750. **Remarks:** Full-time maker; first knife sold in 1988. Doing business as Mystik Knifeworks. **Mark:** MYSTIK.

LOCKETT, STERLING, 527 E. Amherst Dr., Burbank, CA 91504/818-846-5799
Specialties: Working straight knives and folders to customer specs. **Patterns:** Hunters and fighters. **Technical:** Grinds. **Prices:** Moderate. **Remarks:** Spare-time maker. **Mark:** Name, city with hearts.

LOERCHNER, WOLFGANG, P.O. Box 255, Bayfield, Ont. N0M 1G0, CANADA/519-565-2196
Specialties: Traditional straight knives, mostly ornate. **Patterns:** Small swords, daggers and stilettos; locking folders and miniatures. **Technical:** Grinds D2, 440C and 154CM; all knives hand-filed and flat-ground. **Prices:** $300 to $5,000; some to $10,000. **Remarks:** Part-time maker; first knife sold in 1983. Often collaborates wtih engraver Martin Butler. Doing business as Wolfe Fine Knives. **Mark:** WOLFE.

LOFLIN, BOB, San Jose, Costa Rica; c/o Levi Strauss, 5979 N. West 151st St., Miami Lakes, FL 33014/011-506-799155
Specialties: Fancy working knives of his design. **Patterns:** Hunters, fighters and camp knives; locking folders. **Technical:** Grinds D2, 440C and ATS-34. **Prices:** $75 to $250; some to $700. **Remarks:** Part-time maker; first knife sold in 1983. **Mark:** Name.

LONE STAR CUSTOM KNIVES (See Richardson, Jr., Percy)

LONESOME PINE (See Harley, Larry W.)

LONEWOLF, J. AGUIRRE, Rt. 1 Box 1322A, Demorest, GA 30535/706-754-4660
Specialties: High-art working and using straight knives of his design. **Patterns:** Bowies, hunters, utility/camp knives and fint steel blades. **Technical:** Forges Damascus and high-carbon steel; grinds stainless steel. Most knives have hand-carved moose antler handles. **Prices:** $55 to $500; some to $2,000. **Remarks:** Full-time maker; first knife sold in 1980. Doing business as Lonewolf Trading Post. **Mark:** Stamp or etch.

LONEWOLF TRADING POST (See Lonewolf, J. Aguirre)

LONG, GLENN A., 3601 Catalina, Palm Beach Gardens, FL 33410/407-622-1553
Specialties: Classic working and using straight knives of his design and to customer specs. **Patterns:** Hunters, Bowies and utility/camp knives. **Technical:** Grinds ATS-34, 440C and D2. **Prices:** $65 to $200; some to $500. **Remarks:** Part-time maker; first knife sold in 1990. **Mark:** Last name inside diamond.

LONGHORN KNIFE WORKS (See Hagwood, Kellie)

LONGWORTH, DAVE, 1811 SR 774, Hamersville, OH 45130/513-876-3637
Specialties: High-tech working knives. **Patterns:** Locking folders, hunters, fighters and elaborate daggers. **Technical:** Grinds 01, ATS-34, 440C; buys Damascus. **Prices:** $125 to $600; some higher. **Remarks:** Part-time maker; first knife sold in 1980. **Mark:** Last name.

LORD (See Sontheimer, G. Douglas)

LORDITCH, CHARLES RICHARD, 7 Tollgate Rd., Johnstown, PA 15906/814-536-0579
Specialties: Using straight knives and folders of his design or to customer specs. **Patterns:** Miniatures to Bowies; slip-joints and lock-back folders. **Technical:** Forges high carbon steels and cable Damascus. Prefers natural handle materials such as corn cobs and butternuts. **Prices:** $30 to $250. **Remarks:** Full-time maker; first knife sold in 1965. **Mark:** Initials in various scripts.

LOVE, ED, 3230 Seawolf Dr., Tallahassee, FL 32312/904-385-1403
Specialties: Fancy working knives in standard patterns or to customer specs. **Patterns:** Hunters, Bowies and and one-of-a-kinds. **Technical:** Grinds ATS-34. **Prices:** $90 to $190; some to $500. **Remarks:** Part-time maker; first knife sold in 1980. **Mark:** Name in weeping heart.

LOVELESS, R.W., P.O. Box 7836, Riverside, CA 92503/909-689-7800
Specialties: Working knives, fighters and hunters of his design. **Patterns:** Contemporary hunters, fighters and boots. **Technical:** Grinds 154CM and ATS-34. **Prices:** $850 to $4950. **Remarks:** Full-time maker since 1969. **Mark:** Name in logo.

LOVESTRAND, SCHUYLER, 703 Hillcrest Dr., Dublin, GA 31021/407-889-2059
Specialties: Fancy working straight knives of his design and to customer specs; unusual fossil ivories. **Patterns:** Hunters, fighters, Bowies and fishing knives. **Technical:** Grinds ATS-34. **Prices:** $150 to $180; some higher. **Remarks:** Part-time maker; first knife sold in 1982. **Mark:** Name in logo.

LOWCOUNTRY THROWING KNIVES (See Branton, Robert)

LOZIER, DON, 5394 SE 168th Ave., Oklawaha, FL 32179/904-625-3576; FAX: 904-625-3576
Specialties: Fancy and working straight knives of his design and in standard patterns. **Patterns:** Bowies, hunters, daggers, boot knives, fishters and fillet knives. **Technical:** Grinds ATS-34, 440C and non-commercial Damascus. Most knives fileworked, custom pinned, exhibition grade handle materials. Sheaths are all hand-carved and handsewn by maker. **Prices:** Start at $165. **Remarks:** Full-time maker. Doing business as Grindere of Handiecrafte Cutellerie. **Mark:** Full name handmade purist in script.

LOZITO, JOSEPH F., 6804 Burns St., Forest Hills, NY 11375/718-793-2409
Specialties: Miniatures only—highly detailed straight knives and folders. **Patterns:** Bowies, daggers, razors and antique pocketknife replicas. **Technical:** Forges commercial nickel/mild steel Damascus; grinds 01 and A2. **Prices:** $150 to $450; some higher. **Remarks:** Part-time maker; first knife sold in 1989. Sells only at shows. **Mark:** Initials.

LUBRICH, MARK, P.O. Box 122, Matthews, NC 28106-0122/704-567-7692
Specialties: Traditional working and using straight knives of his design and to customer specs. **Patterns:** Hunters and utility/camp knives. Some folding loackbacks and woodcarving sets. **Technical:** Forges and grinds 01, 5160 and 1095; using some cable; forges 440C stainless, brass and silver inlaid handles. Differentially heat-treats; makes sheaths; hardwood/stag or leather/stag handles. **Prices:** $75 to $225; some to $500. **Remarks:** Full-time maker; first knife sold in 1980. Doing business as Handmade Knives by Mark Lubrich. **Mark:** Etched last name on stock removal and folders.

LUCHAK, BOB, 15705 Woodforest Blvd., Channelview, TX 77530/713-452-1779
Specialties: Presentation knives; start of The Survivor series. **Patterns:** Skinners, Bowies, camp axes, steak knife sets and fillet knives. **Technical:** Grinds 440C. Offers electronic etching; filework. **Prices:** $50 to $1,500. **Remarks:** Full-time maker; first knife sold in 1983. Doing business as Teddybear Knives. **Mark:** Full name, city and state with Teddybear logo.

custom knifemakers
LUCIE—MANEKER

LUCIE, JAMES R., 4191 E. Fruitport Rd., Fruitport, MI 49415/616-865-6390; FAX: 616-865-3170
Specialties: Hand-forges William Scagel-style knives. **Patterns:** Authentic Scagel-style knives and miniatures. **Technical:** Forges 5160. **Prices:** Start at $375. **Remarks:** Full-time maker; first knife sold in 1975. **Mark:** Scagel kris with name.

LUCK, GREGORY, P.O. Box 2255, Greeley, CO 80632/303-686-7223
Specialties: Forged straight knives. **Patterns:** Bowies, fighters, buckskinners and other working straight knives. **Technical:** Forges carbon steel and own cable Damascus; differential tempers; makes distinctive sheaths. **Prices:** $75 to $400; some higher. **Remarks:** Part-time maker; first knife sold in 1988. **Mark:** Three runes or last name and dragon-knot logo.

LUCKETT, BILL, 10 Amantes Lane, Weatherford, TX 76086/ 817-599-4629
Specialties: Uniquely patterned robust straight knives. **Patterns:** Fighters, Bowies, hunters. **Technical:** Grinds 440C and commercial Damascus; makes heavy knives with deep grinding. **Prices:** $375 to $800; some to $2,000. **Remarks:** Part-time maker; first knife sold in 1975. **Mark:** Last name over Bowie logo.

LUDWIG, RICHARD O., 57-63 65 St., Maspeth, NY 11378

LUI, RONALD M., 4042 Harding Ave., Honolulu, HI 96816/808-734-7746
Specialties: Working straight knives and folders in standard patterns. **Patterns:** Hunters, boots and liner locks. **Technical:** Grinds 440C and ATS-34. **Prices:** $100 to $700. **Remarks:** Spare-time maker; first knife sold in 1988. **Mark:** Initials connected.

LUM, ROBERT W., 901 Travis Ave., Eugene, OR 97404/503-688-2737
Specialties: High-art working knives of his design. **Patterns:** Hunters, fighters, tantos and folders. **Technical:** Grinds 440C, 154CM and ATS-34; plans to forge soon. **Prices:** $175 to $500; some to $800. **Remarks:** Full-time maker; first knife sold in 1976. **Mark:** Chop with last name underneath.

LUNDSTROM, JAN-AKE, Mastmostigen 8, 66010 Dals-Langed, SWEDEN/0531-41259
Specialties: Viking swords, axes and knives in cooperation with handlemakers. **Patterns:** All traditional styles, especially swords and inlaid blades. **Technical:** Forges his own Damascus and laminated steel. **Prices:** $200 to $1,000. **Remarks:** Full-time maker; first knife sold in 1985; collaborates with museums. **Mark:** Runic.

LUNN, LARRY A., 1040 Oakwood Dr., Vermilion, OH 44089/216-965-5803 or 216-967-2384. **Specialties:** Fancy art knives and swords and many one-of-a-kind of his own design. **Patterns:** Bowies, daggers, fighters, swords and fancy hunting knives. **Technical:** Forges and grinds Damascus; grinds ATS-34, 440C and carbon tool steel. Prefers natural materials; uses gold/silver. Carves handles and supplies fancy sheaths. **Prices:** Starting at $100. **Remarks:** Part-time maker; first knife sold in 1989. **Mark:** Last name in script and small Samuri helmet in a circle.

LUTES, ROBERT, 24878 U.S. #6 East (RR 1), Nappanee, IN 46550/219-773-4773
Specialties: Straight working knives of his design or to standard patterns. **Patterns:** Hunters, fighters, boots and axes. **Technical:** Grinds 440C and commercial Damascus. **Prices:** $50 to $1,500. **Remarks:** Part-time maker; first knife sold in 1980. **Mark:** Last name.

LUTZ, GREG, 149 Effie Dr., Greenwood, SC 29649/803-229-7340
Specialties: Working and using knives and period pieces of his design and to customer specs. **Patterns:** Fighters, hunters and swords. **Technical:** Forges 1095 and 01; grinds ATS-34. Differentially heat-treats forged blades; uses cryogenic treatment on ATS-34. **Prices:** $50 to $350; some to $1,200. **Remarks:** Full-time maker; first knife sold in 1986. Doing business as Scorpion Forge. **Mark:** First initial, last name.

LYLE III, ERNEST L., 4501 Meadowbrook Ave., Orlando, FL 32808/407-299-7227
Specialties: Fancy period pieces in standard patterns. **Patterns:** Arabian/Persian influenced fighters, military knives, Bowies and Roman short swords; several styles of hunters; minis and miniatures. **Technical:** Grinds D2, 440C and 154CM. Engraves. **Prices:** $250 to $800; some to $2,300. **Remarks:** Full-time maker; first knife sold in 1972. **Mark:** Last name in capital letters.

LYONS, RANDY, 572 Tannahill, Vidor, TX 77662

LYTTLE, BRIAN, Box 5697, High River, AB T1V 1M7, CANADA/403-558-3638

Specialties: Fancy working straight knives and folders; art knives. **Patterns:** Hunters, Bowies, daggers, stilettos, fighters and miniatures. **Technical:** Forges his own Damascus, cable and motorcycle chain; offers scrimshaw and forged jewelry to Damascus bits and spurs. **Prices:** $350 to $800; some to $5,000. **Remarks:** Full-time maker; first knife sold in 1983. **Mark:** Last name/country.

m

MacBAIN, KENNETH C., 30 Briarwood Ave., Norwood, NJ 07648/201-768-0652
Specialties: Fantasy straight knives and folders, some high-tech. **Patterns:** Swords, knife-rings, push daggers and some miniatures. **Technical:** Forges and grinds A2, W2 and 01. **Prices:** $200 to $500; some to $2,500. **Remarks:** Part-time maker; first knife sold in 1986. **Mark:** Initials.

MACKRILL, STEPHEN, P.O. Box 1580, Pinegowrie 2123, Johannesburg, SOUTH AFRICA/27-11-886-2893; FAX: 27-11-334-3729
Specialties: Fancy and working knives. **Patterns:** Fighters, hunters and utility/camp knives. **Technical:** N690, K110, 12C27. Silver and gold inlay on handles; wooden sheaths. **Prices:** $98 to $700; some to $1,800. **Remarks:** Full-time maker; first knife sold in 1978. **Mark:** First initial, last name.

MACRI, MIKE, Box 222, Churchill, MB R0B 0E0, CANADA/204-675-2195
Specialties: Working straight knives in standard patterns. **Patterns:** Arctic survival knives, tantos, Bowies, camp knives and locking folders. **Technical:** Grinds 440C, ATS-34 and commercial Damascus. Full-tapered tangs and hollow-grinds. **Prices:** $100 to $500; some to $2,000. **Remarks:** Full-time maker; first knife sold in 1982. **Mark:** Last name.

MADRONA KNIVES (See Rice, Adrienne)

MADSEN, JACK, 3311 Northwest Dr., Wichita Falls, TX 76305/817-322-4112
Specialties: Working straight knives in standard patterns. **Patterns:** Bowies, hunters, swords, tomahawks and heavy-duty camp knives. **Technical:** Forges W2, 01 and his own Damascus. **Prices:** $85 to $350; some to $1,000. **Remarks:** Full-time maker; first knife sold in 1975. **Mark:** Name and city.

MAESTRI BROS. (See Maestri, Peter A.)

MAESTRI, PETER A., Rt. 1, Box 111, Spring Green, WI 53588/608-546-4481
Specialties: Working straight knives in standard patterns. **Patterns:** Camp and fishing knives, utility green-river styled. **Technical:** Grinds 440C, 154CM and 440A. **Prices:** $15 to $45; some to $150. **Remarks:** Full-time maker; first knife sold in 1981. Provides professional cutler service to professional cutters. **Mark:** CARISOLO, MAESTRI BROS., or signature.

MAISEY, ALAN, P.O. Box 316, Toongabbie 2146, AUSTRALIA/Sydney 636-2183
Specialties: Daggers, especially krisses; period pieces. **Technical:** Offers finished blades only in Damascus and Nickel Damascus. **Remarks:** Part-time maker; provides complete restoration service for krisses. Trained by a Javanese kris smith. **Mark:** None, triangle in a box, or three peaks.

MALLOY, JOE, P.O. Box 156, 1039 Schwabe St., Freeland, PA 18224/717-636-2781
Specialties: Working knives; customer designs welcome. **Patterns:** Hunters, utility/camp knives, fighters Bowies, tantos and folders. **Technical:** Grinds 154CM, 440C, D2 and A2. **Prices:** $100 to $800. **Remarks:** Part-time maker; first knife sold in 1982. **Mark:** First and middle initials, last name, city and state.

MANABE, MICHAEL K., 6161 El Cajon Blvd. #176, San Diego, CA 92115/614-583-4880
Specialties: Classic and high-art straight knives of his design or to customer specs. **Patterns:** Bowies, fighters, hunters, utility/camp knives; all knives one-of-a-kind. **Technical:** Forges and grinds 52100, 5160 amd 1095. Does multiple quenching for distinctive temper lines. Each blade triple-tempered. **Prices:** Start at $200. **Remarks:** Part-time maker; first knife sold in 1994. **Mark:** First and middle initials, last name.

MANEKER, KENNETH, RR 2, Galiano Island, B.C. V0N 1P0, CANADA/604-539-2084
Specialties: Working straight knives; period pieces. **Patterns:** Camp knives and

FIFTEENTH EDITION 243

directory
MARAGNI—MAZAKI

hunters; French chef knives. **Technical:** Grinds 440C, 154CM and Vascowear. **Prices:** $50 to $200; some to $300. **Remarks:** Part-time maker; first knife sold in 1981. Doing business as Water Mountain Knives. **Mark:** Japanese Kanji of initials, plus glyph.

MARAGNI, DAN, R.D. 1, Box 106, Georgetown, NY 13072/315-662-7490
Specialties: Heavy-duty working knives, some investor class. **Patterns:** Hunters, fighters and camp knives, some Scottish types. **Technical:** Forges W2 and his own Damascus; toughness and edge-holding a high priority. **Prices:** $125 to $500; some to $1,000. **Remarks:** Full-time maker; first knife sold in 1975. **Mark:** Celtic initials in circle.

MARIACHER, ROBERT R., P.O. Box 1836, Franklin, NC 28734/704-524-2240
Specialties: Fancy miniatures, working and using straight knives of his design and to customer specs. **Patterns:** Boots, Bowies and hunters, any grind. **Technical:** Grinds D2 and ATS-34. **Prices:** $100 to $800; some to $3,600. **Remarks:** Full-time maker; first knife sold in 1989. **Mark:** B-Mar.

MARINGER, TOM, 2692 S. Powell St., Springdale, AR 72764/501-751-9220
Specialties: Investor-class high-tech and fantasy straight knives. **Patterns:** Swords, axes, daggers; state-of-the-art fighters. **Technical:** Grinds D2 and 154CM; forges. Makes wire-wrapped handles; Kydex sheaths. **Prices:** $100 to $1,000; some to $12,000. **Remarks:** Full-time maker; first knife sold in 1975. **Mark:** Full name, serial number and year.

MARKS, CHRIS, 1061 Sherwood Dr., Breaux Bridge, LA 70517/318-332-3930
Specialties: Traditional straight knives of his design; period pieces. **Patterns:** Bowies, hunters and utility/camp knives. **Technical:** Forges W2, 5160 and his own Damascus. **Prices:** NA. **Mark:** Name in anvil logo and Master Smith, ABS.

MARLOWE, DONALD, 2554 Oakland Rd., Dover, PA 17315/717-764-6055
Specialties: Working straight knives in standard patterns. **Patterns:** Bowies, fighters, boots and utility knives. **Technical:** Grinds D2 and 440C. **Prices:** $120 to $525. **Remarks:** Spare-time maker; first knife sold in 1977. **Mark:** Last name.

MARSHALL, GLENN, P.O. Box 1099 (305 Hofmann St.), Mason, TX 76856/915-347-6207
Specialties: Working knives and period pieces. **Patterns:** Straight and folding hunters, fighters and camp knives. **Technical:** Forges and grinds 01, D2 and 440C. **Prices:** $90 to $150; some to $450. **Remarks:** Full-time maker; first knife sold in 1932. **Mark:** First initial, last name, city and state with anvil logo.

MARTIN, BRUCE E., Rt. 6, Box 164-B, Prescott, AR 71857/501-887-2023
Specialties: Fancy working straight knives of his design. **Patterns:** Bowies, camp knives, skinners and fighters. **Technical:** Forges 5160, 1095 and his own Damascus. Uses natural handle materials; filework available. **Prices:** $75 to $350; some to $500. **Remarks:** Full-time maker; first knife sold in 1979. **Mark:** Name in arch.

MARTIN, RANDALL J., 1477 Country Club Rd., Middletown, CT 06457/203-347-1161
Specialties: Practical working knives. **Patterns:** Drop points, sub-hilts, boot knives, folders and chef knives. **Technical:** Grinds ATS-34, 440-C, 440-V and M2. Knives offered in working grade or presentation grade. **Prices:** Under $100. **Remarks:** Part-time maker; first knife sold in 1976. Doing business as Martinsite Knives. **Mark:** First and middle initials, last name.

MARTINSITE KNIVES (See Martin, Randall J.)

MARTRILDONNO, PAUL, P.O. Box 1501, Olivebridge, NY 12461/914-657-8580
Specialties: One-of-a-kind fantasy knives. **Patterns:** "Knifelace"—necklace with push dagger, knuckle knives, fantasy tantos, etc. **Technical:** Grinds 440C and 154CM. Reforges commercial Damascus. **Prices:** $400 to $1,500; some to $5,000. **Remarks:** Full-time maker; first knife sold in 1982. Recipient of 1991 N.Y. Foundation for the Arts Fellowship. **Mark:** PAULIE, or signature.

MARZITELLI, PETER, 19929 35A Ave., Langley, BC V3A 2R1, CANADA/604-532-8899
Specialties: High quality straight hunting and art knives. **Patterns:** Hunters, tantos, Bowies, daggers, unility and fancy art knives. Specializes in natural handle materials. **Technical:** Grinds 440C, D2, 12C27 and 01. **Prices:** $100 to $1,000. **Remarks:** Full-time maker; first knife sold in 1984. **Mark:** "Marz".

MASON, BILL, 1114 St. Louis, #33, Excelsior Springs, MO 64024/816-637-7335
Specialties: Combat knives; some folders. **Patterns:** Fighters to match knife types in book *Cold Steel*. **Technical:** Grinds 01, 440C and ATS-34. **Prices:** $115 to $250; some to $350. **Remarks:** Spare-time maker; first knife sold in 1979. **Mark:** Initials connected.

MASSEY, ROGER, RR19, Box 3300, Texarkana, AR 75502/501-779-1018
Specialties: Traditional and working straight knives and folders of his design and to customer specs. **Patterns:** Bowies, hunters and utility knives. **Technical:** Forges 5168, Damascus and 1084. Offers filework and silver wire inlay in handles. **Prices:** $125 to $500; some to $2,000. **Remarks:** Part-time maker; first knife sold in 1991. **Mark:** Last name, J.S.

MATTIS, JAMES K., 10359 Mt. Gleason Ave., Sunland, CA 91040/818-353-4734
Specialties: Working straight knives in standard patterns. **Patterns:** Hunters, kitchen knives and small utility or specialty patterns. **Technical:** Offers ATS-34, 440C and carbon; hand-rubbed finishes, hardwood handles. **Prices:** $40 to $200; some to $250. **Remarks:** Spare-time maker; first knife sold in 1990. Usually uses blades by Bob Engnath. **Mark:** Last name plus hebrew word for "life".

MAXFIELD, LYNN, 382 Colonial Ave., Layton, UT 84041/801-544-4176
Specialties: Sporting knives, some fancy. **Patterns:** Hunters, survival and fishing knives; some locking folders. **Technical:** Grinds 440C, ATS-34, D2 and Damascus. **Prices:** $150 to $350; some to $750. **Remarks:** Full-time maker; first knife sold in 1979. **Mark:** Name, city and state.

MAXWELL, DON, 4435 N. Brawley #107, Fresno, CA 93722/209-275-3460
Specialties: Fancy working and using straight knives of his design. **Patterns:** Hunters, fighters, utility/camp knives, liner lock folders and fantasy knives. **Technical:** Grinds 440C, ATS-34, D2 and commercial Damascus. **Prices:** $100 to $500; some to $2,000. **Remarks:** Full-time maker; first knife sold in 1987. **Mark:** Last name, city, state.

MAY, JAMES E., 6513 State Rd. T., Auxvasse, MO 65231/314-386-2910
Specialties: Working straight knives of his design. **Patterns:** Hunters, Bowies, fighters, camp knives, boots and folders. **Technical:** Makes own Damascus. **Prices:** $65 to $350; some to $450. **Remarks:** Spare-time maker; first knife sold in 1978. **Mark:** First initial in diamond.

MAYNARD, LARRY JOE, P.O. Box 493, Crab Orchard, WV 25827
Specialties: Fancy and fantasy straight knives. **Patterns:** Big knives; a Bowie with a full false edge; fighting knives. **Technical:** Grinds standard steels. **Prices:** $350 to $500; some to $1,000. **Remarks:** Full-time maker; first knife sold in 1986. **Mark:** Middle and last initials.

MAYNARD, WILLIAM N., 2677 John Smith Rd., Fayetteville, NC 28306/910-425-1615
Specialties: Traditional and working straight knives of all designs. **Patterns:** Bowies, fighters, hunters and utility knives. **Technical:** Grinds 440C, ATS-34 and commercial Damascus. Offers fancy filework; handmade sheaths. **Prices:** $100 to $300; some to $500. **Remarks:** Part-time maker; first knife sold in 1988. **Mark:** Last name.

MAYO JR., TOM, 67-177 Kanoulu St., Waialua, HI 96791/808-637-6560
Specialties: Working straight knives. **Patterns:** Fighters and Bowies. **Technical:** Uses ATS-34 and some D2. **Prices:** $125 to $500; some to $1,000. **Remarks:** Part-time maker; first knife sold in 1983. No longer taking orders. **Mark:** Volcano logo with name and state.

MAYVILLE, OSCAR L., 2130 E. County Rd. 910S., Marengo, IN 47140/812-338-3103
Specialties: Working straight knives; period pieces. **Patterns:** Kitchen cutlery, Bowies, camp knives and hunters. **Technical:** Grinds A2, 01 and 440C. **Prices:** $50 to $350; some to $500. **Remarks:** Full-time maker; first knife sold in 1984. **Mark:** Initials over knife logo.

MAZAKI, YOSHIO, Bl Fukoku Seimei Building 2-4, Komatu bara-cho Kita-ku, Osaka City, 530 JAPAN/06-313-2525; FAX: 06-313-2626
Specialties: Classic and working knives of his design. **Patterns:** Bowies, hunters and utility knives. **Technical:** Grinds ATS-34, Gingami 3 GO and Cowry X. **Prices:**

$250 to $1,500. **Remarks:** Part-time maker; first knife sold in 1992. Doing business as World Gallery Co., Ltd. **Mark:** NA.

McBURNETTE, HARVEY, P.O. Box 227, Eagle Nest, NM 87718/505-377-6254; FAX: 505-377-6218
Specialties: Fancy working folders; some to customer specs. **Patterns:** Front-locking folders. **Technical:** Grinds D2, 440C and 154CM; engraves. **Prices:** $450 to $3,000. **Remarks:** Full-time maker; first knife sold in 1972. **Mark:** Last name, city and state.

McCARLEY, JOHN, 562 Union Brige Rd., Union Bridge, MD 21791
Specialties: Working straight knives; period pieces. **Patterns:** Hunters, Bowies, camp knives, miniatures, throwing knives. **Technical:** Forges W2, 01 and his own Damascus. **Prices:** $150 to $300; some to $1,000. **Remarks:** Part-time maker; first knife sold in 1977. **Mark:** Initials in script.

McCARTY, HARRY, 1121 Brough Ave., Hamilton, OH 45015
Specialties: Working straight knives; period pieces. **Patterns:** Bowies, camp knives, daggers and buckskinners. **Technical:** Forges and grinds 01. **Prices:** $75 to $350; some to $600. **Remarks:** Part-time maker; first knife sold in 1977. **Mark:** Stylized initials.

McCARTY, ZOLLAN, 101½ Ave. E, Thomaston, GA 30286/404-647-6869
Specialties: Working knives; period pieces. **Patterns:** Straight knives and folders; Scagel replicas; gut hook hatchets. **Technical:** Forges and grinds 440C, 154CM and ATS-34. **Prices:** $110 to $600. **Remarks:** Full-time maker; first knife sold in 1971. Doing business as Z Custom Knives. **Mark:** First initial, last name.

McCLURE, MICHAEL, 803-17th Ave., Menlo Park, CA 94025/415-323-2596
Specialties: Working/using straight knives of his design and to customer specs. **Patterns:** Bowies, hunters, utility/camp knives. **Technical:** Grinds ATS-34, 330C, D2. Makes sheaths. **Prices:** $150 to $300; some to $500. **Remarks:** Part-time maker; first knife sold in 1991. **Mark:** Last name.

McCOLL, JOHN, 35 Green St., Stonehouse, Lanarkshire, ML9-3LW SCOTLAND/0698-792223
Specialties: Traditional working straight knives and folders of his design. **Patterns:** Hunters, Bowies and locking folders. **Technical:** Forges his Damascus; grinds 440C, D2 and 01. **Prices:** $125 to $175; some to $590. **Remarks:** Full-time maker; first knife sold in 1980. **Mark:** Full name.

McCONNELL, CHARLES R., 158 Genteel Ridge, Wellsburg, WV 26070/304-737-2015
Specialties: Working straight knives. **Patterns:** Hunters, Bowies, daggers, minis and push knives. **Technical:** Grinds 440C and 154CM; likes full tangs. **Prices:** $65 to $325; some to $800. **Remarks:** Part-time maker; first knife sold in 1977. **Mark:** Name.

McCONNELL JR., LOYD A., 1712 Royalty, Odessa, TX 79761/915-363-8344
Specialties: Working straight knives and folders, some fancy. **Patterns:** Hunters, boots, Bowies, locking folders and slip-joints. **Technical:** Grinds A2, 154CM, CPM10V and commercial Damascus. **Prices:** $175 to $900; some to $10,000. **Remarks:** Full-time maker; first knife sold in 1975. Doing business as Cactus Custom Knives. **Mark:** Name, city and state in cactus logo.

McCRACKIN and SON, V.J., 3720 Hess Rd., House Springs, MO 63051/314-677-6066
Specialties: Working straight knives in standard patterns. **Patterns:** Hunters, Bowies and camp knives. **Technical:** Forges L6, 5160, his own Damascus, cable Damascus. **Prices:** $75 to $400; some to $1,000. **Remarks:** Part-time maker; first knife sold in 1983. Son Kevin helps make the knives. **Mark:** Last name, M.S.

McDEARMONT, DAVE, 1618 Parkside Trail, Lewisville, TX 7567/214-436-4335
Specialties: Collector-grade knives. **Patterns:** Hunters, fighters, boots and folders. **Technical:** Grinds ATS-34; likes full tangs, mirror finishes. **Prices:** $200 to $1,000. **Remarks:** Part-time maker; first knife sold in 1981. **Mark:** Name.

McDONALD, ROBERT J., 2300 NW 81 Ave., Sunrise, FL 33322/305-748-5090
Specialties: Traditional working straight knives to customer specs. **Patterns:** Bowies, fighters and swords. **Technical:** Grinds 440C, ATS-34 and forges own Damascus. **Prices:** $150 to $1,000. **Remarks:** Part-time maker; first knife sold in 1988. **Mark:** Electro-etched logo.

McELHANNON, MARCUS, 14003 Kathi Lynn, Sugarland, TX 77478/713-494-1345
Specialties: Working straight knives and folders of his design and to customer specs. **Patterns:** Fighters, hunters and locking folders. **Technical:** Grinds ATS-34, 440C and 440V. **Prices:** $125 to $300; some to $1,500. **Remarks:** Spare-time maker; first knife sold in 1988. **Mark:** First name.

McFALL, KEN, P.O. Box 458, Lakeside, AZ 85929/602-537-2026
Specialties: Fancy working straight knives and some folders. **Patterns:** Daggers, boots, tantos, Bowies; some miniatures. **Technical:** Grinds D2, ATS-34 and 440C. **Prices:** $175 to $900. **Remarks:** Part-time maker; first knife sold in 1984. **Mark:** Name, city and state.

McFARLIN, ERIC E., P.O. Box 2188, Kodiak, AK 99615/907-486-4799
Specialties: Working knives of his design. **Patterns:** Bowies, skinners, camp knives and hunters. **Technical:** Flat and convex grinds 440C, A1 and AEB-L. **Prices:** Start at $130. **Remarks:** Part-time maker; first knife sold in 1989. **Mark:** Name and city in rectanglar logo.

McGILL, JOHN, P.O. Box 302, Blairsville, GA 30512/404-745-4686
Specialties: Working knives. **Patterns:** Traditional patterns; camp knives. **Technical:** Forges L6 and 9260; makes Damascus. **Prices:** $50 to $250; some to $500. **Remarks:** Full-time maker; first knife sold in 1982. **Mark:** XYLO.

McGOVERN, JIM, 31 Scenic Dr., Oak Ridge, NJ 07438/201-697-4558
Specialties: Working straight knives and folders. **Patterns:** Hunters and boots. **Technical:** Hollow-grinds 440C, ATS-34; prefers full tapered tangs. Offers filework. **Prices:** $125 to $250, some to $750; folders $175 to $450, some to $675. **Remarks:** Part-time maker; first knife sold in 1985. **Mark:** Name.

McGOWAN, FRANK E., 12629 Howard Lodge Dr., Sykesville, MD 21784/410-489-4323
Specialties: Fancy working knives to customer specs. **Patterns:** Survivor knives, fighters, fishing knives and hunters. **Technical:** Grinds and forges 01, 440C, 5160 and ATS-34. **Prices:** $75 to $500; some to $1,000. **Remarks:** Full-time maker; first knife sold in 1986. **Mark:** Last name.

McHENRY, WILLIAM JAMES, Box 67, Wyoming, RI 02898/401-539-8353
Specialties: Fancy high-tech folders of his design. **Patterns:** Locking folders with various mechanisms. **Technical:** Forges and grinds commercial Damascus and his Damascus. Most pieces disassemble and feature top-shelf materials including gold, silver and gems. **Prices:** $1,000 and $3,500. **Remarks:** Full-time maker; first knife sold in 1988. Former goldsmith. **Mark:** Last name or first and last initials.

McINTOSH, DAVID L., P.O. Box 948, Haines, AK 99827/907-766-3393
Specialties: Working straight knives and folders of all designs. **Patterns:** Boots, Bowies, fighters, hunters, locking folders and utility knives. **Technical:** Grinds ATS-34; forges pattern-welded Damascus; forges and grinds 01. Engraves; offers tooling on sheaths. **Prices:** $50 to $350; some to $800. **Remarks:** Full-time maker; first knife sold in 1984. **Mark:** Name, serial number, steel type.

McKISSACK II, TOMMY, P.O. Box 991, Sonora, TX 76950/915-387-3253
Specialties: Plain to fancy folders. **Patterns:** Swords to folders, traditional to exotic. **Technical:** Grinds and forges D2, ATS-34, Vascowear, own Damascus and mokume. **Prices:** $100 to $1,500; some to $3,500. **Remarks:** Full-time maker; first knife sold in 1980. **Mark:** Name.

McLEOD, JAMES, 941 Thermalito Ave., Oroville, CA 95965/916-533-3539
Specialties: Working knives; Scottish period pieces. **Patterns:** Dirks and sgian dubhs; buckskinners, boots and daggers. **Technical:** Grinds and files A2, 154CM and ATS-34; offers hand-sanded finishes and full or tapered tangs. **Prices:** $200 to $500; some to $2,500. **Remarks:** Spare-time maker; first knife sold in 1983. McLeod clan motto "HOLD FAST." Makes average of 20 knives per year. **Mark:** Name and clan badge.

McLUIN, TOM, 36 Fourth St., Dracut, MA 01826/508-957-4899
Specialties: Fancy and working/using straight knives of his design. **Patterns:** Boots, hunters, miniatures. **Technical:** Grinds D2, ATS-34, 440C. Offers filework, fancy pins, custom-moulded sheaths, some exotic skins. **Prices:** $50 to $250; some to $400. **Remarks:** Full-time maker; first knife sold in 1991. **Mark:** First initial, last name.

directory

McMAHON—MILLER

McMAHON, JOHN P., 44871 Santa Anita #A, Palm Desert, CA 92260/619-341-4238
Specialties: Classic working and using straight knives of his design or to customer specs. **Patterns:** Hunters, Bowies and fighters. **Technical:** Grinds 5160 spring steel for large knives and 01 tool steel for small ones. Will grind fil one order. Differentially tempers. **Prices:** $45 to $300; some to $1,000. **Remarks:** Full-time maker; first knife sold in 1989. Doing business as J.P.M. Knives. **Mark:** Initials.

McNABB, TOMMY, 4015 Brownsboro Rd., Winston-Salem, NC 27106/919-759-0640
Specialties: Working and using straight knives of his design. **Patterns:** Hunters, fighters and utility/camp knives. **Technical:** Forges and grinds ATS-34 and his Damascus. **Prices:** $100 to $550; some to $2,500. **Remarks:** Part-time maker; first knife sold in 1979. **Mark:** Carolina Custom Knives.

McWILLIAMS, SEAN, 311 Gem Lane, Bayfield, CO 81122/303-884-9854
Specialties: Stainless steel combat-survival and working knives of his own design. **Patterns:** Fighters, sub-hilts, utility and camp knives. **Technical:** Forges CPM T440V and ATS-34 stainless only. Offers high-tech Kydex-Nylon sheaths and carry systems. **Prices:** $300 to $700. Catalog $3 **Remarks:** Full-time maker; first knife sold in 1979. **Mark:** Stylized bear paw.

MECCHI, RICHARD, 4225 Gibraltar St., Las Vegas, NV 89121/702-435-7448; FAX: 702-435-7448
Specialties: Working straight knives, some fancy. **Patterns:** Hunters, daggers, Bowies and fillets. **Technical:** Grinds 440C, ATS-34 and 154CM. Exotic handle materials offered. **Prices:** $125 to $950. **Remarks:** Part-time maker; first knife sold in 1982. **Mark:** First initial, last name.

MEDIEVAL CUSTOMS (See Johns, Rob)

MEIER, DARYL, RR 4, Carbondale, IL 62901/618-549-3234
Specialties: One-of-a-kind buckskinners and swords. **Patterns:** Collaborates on blades. **Technical:** Forges his own Damascus, W1 and A203E, nickel 200 and chad steel. **Prices:** $250 to $450; some to $6,000. **Remarks:** Full-time smith and researcher since 1974; first knife sold in 1974. **Mark:** Name or circle/arrow symbol or SHAWNEE.

MELOY, SEAN, 7148 Rosemary Lane, Lemon Grove, CA 91945-2105/619-465-6757
Specialties: Traditional working straight knives of his design. **Patterns:** Bowies, fighters, swords and utility/camp knives. **Technical:** Grinds 440C, ATS-34 and D2. **Prices:** $90 to $600; some to $2,000. **Remarks:** Full-time maker; first knife sold in 1985. **Mark:** Broz Knives.

MENDENHALL, HARRY E., Ed.D., 1848 Everglades Dr., Milpitas, CA 95035/408-263-0677
Specialties: Working straight knives. **Patterns:** Hunters, boots, buckskinners and push knives. **Technical:** Grinds 440C, 154CM and ATS-34; engraves and scrimshaws. **Prices:** $150 to $3,000. **Remarks:** Full-time maker; first knife sold in 1970. Does business as Thunderbird. **Mark:** Thunderbird with logo, or signature.

MERCER, MIKE, 149 N. Waynesville Rd., Lebanon, OH 45036/513-932-2837
Specialties: Jeweled gold and ivory daggers; multi-blade folders. **Patterns:** $1^1/_4$" folders, hunters, axes, replicas. **Technical:** Uses 01 Damascus and mokume. **Prices:** $150 to $1,500. **Remarks:** Full-time maker since 1991. **Mark:** Last name in script.

MERCHANT, TED, 7 Old Garrett Ct., White Hall, MD 21161/410-343-0380
Specialties: Traditional and classic working knives. **Patterns:** Bowies, hunters, camp knives, fighters, daggers and skinners. **Technical:** Forges W2 and 5160; makes own Damascus. Makes handles with wood, stag, horn, silver and gem stone inlay; fancy filework. **Prices:** $125 to $600; some to $1,500. **Remarks:** Full-time maker; first knife sold in 1985. **Mark:** Last name.

MERZ III, ROBERT L., 20219 Prince Creek Dr., Katy, TX 77450/713-492-7337
Specialties: Working straight knives and folders, some fancy, of his design. **Patterns:** Hunters, skinners, fighters and camp knives. **Technical:** Flat-grinds 440C, D2, 01, ATS-34 and commercial Damascus. **Prices:** $125 to $300; some to $600. **Remarks:** Part-time maker; first knife sold in 1974. **Mark:** MERZ KNIVES, city and state, or last name in oval.

MESSER, DAVID T., 14 Morton Ave., Dayton, OH 45410/513-228-6561
Specialties: Fantasy period pieces, straight and folding, of his design. **Patterns:** Bowies, daggers and swords. **Technical:** Grinds 440C, 01, 06 and commercial Damascus. Likes fancy guards and exotic handle materials. **Prices:** $100 to $225; some to $375. **Remarks:** Spare-time maker; first knife sold in 1991. **Mark:** Name stamp.

METHENY, H.A. "WHITEY", 7750 Waterford Dr., Spotsylvania, VA 22553/703-582-3228
Specialties: Working and using straight knives of his design and to customer specs. **Patterns:** Hunters and kitchen knives. **Technical:** Grinds 440C. Offers filework; tooled custom sheaths. **Prices:** $125 to $200. **Remarks:** Spare-time maker; first knife sold in 1990. **Mark:** Initials or last name.

METTLER, J. BANJO, 129 S. Second St., North Baltimore, OH 45872/419-257-2210
Specialties: Fancy folders of his design. **Patterns:** Locking folders, interframes, "A-5" automatic and "L-3" lockbacks of his design, deer-foot-style lockbacks 1-inch closed. **Technical:** Grinds ATS-34, D2 and 01. **Prices:** Start at $100. **Remarks:** Part-time maker; first knife sold in 1988. **Mark:** Deer foot underlined with profile of knife.

MICK'S CUSTOM KNIVES (See Sears, Mick)

MIDDLETON, KEN, Charmichael, CA 95608/916-489-6070
Specialties: Traditional and fantasy straight knives and folders of his design. **Patterns:** Hunters, Bowies and daggers. **Technical:** Grinds 440C, ATS-34 and D2. Likes natural handle materials. **Prices:** $150 to $800; some to $3,500. **Remarks:** Spare-time maker; first knife sold in 1986. **Mark:** Last name or Middleton Custom.

MILLARD, FRED G., 5317 N. Wayne, Chicago, IL 60640/312-769-5160
Specialties: Working/using straight knives of his design or to customer specs. **Patterns:** Bowies, hunters, utility/camp knives, kitchen/steak knives. **Technical:** Grinds ATS-34, 01 and 440C. Makes sheaths. **Prices:** $90 to $225; some to $650. **Remarks:** Full-time maker; first knife sold in 1993. Doing business as Millard Knives. **Mark:** Mallard duck in flight with serial number.

MILLER, BOB, 236 Ramsey Ln., Ballwin, MO 63021/314-394-4476
Specialties: Mosaic Damascus; collector using straight knives and folders. **Patterns:** Hunters, Bowies, utility/camp knives, daggers. **Technical:** Forges own Damascus, mosaic-Damascus and 52100. **Prices:** $125 to $500. **Remarks:** Part-time maker; first knife sold in 1983. **Mark:** First and middle initials and last name, or initials.

MILLER JR., CHRIS, 3959 U.S. 27 South, Sebring, FL 33870/813-382-4402
Specialties: Fancy working straight knives. **Patterns:** Swords and large knives of all kinds. **Technical:** Grinds D2, 440C and 154CM. **Prices:** $100 to $500. **Remarks:** Full-time maker; first knife sold in 1976. **Mark:** Last initial.

MILLER, HANFORD J., Box 97, Cowdrey, CO 80434/303-723-4708
Specialties: Working knives in Moran style; period pieces. **Patterns:** Bowies, fighters, camp knives and other large straight knives. **Technical:** Forges W2, 1095, 5160 and his own Damascus; differential tempers; offers wire inlay. **Prices:** $300 to $800; some to $2,000. **Remarks:** Full-time maker; first knife sold in 1968. **Mark:** Initials or name within Bowie logo.

MILLER, JAMES P., 9024 Goeller Rd., RR 2, Box 28, Fairbank, IA 50629/319-635-2294
Specialties: All tool steel Damascus; working knives and period pieces. **Patterns:** Hunters, Bowies, camp knives and daggers. **Technical:** Forges and grinds 1095, 52100, 440C and his own Damascus. **Prices:** $100 to $350; some to $1,500. **Remarks:** Full-time maker; first knife sold in 1970. **Mark:** First and middle initials, last name with knife logo.

MILLER, LARRY, P.O. Box 3064, Missoula, MT 59806-3064/406-549-3276
Specialties: Personally designed knives. **Patterns:** Fighters, hunters and skinners. **Technical:** Grinds Damascus and 440C, fileart standard. All knives sold with sheath or displayed on walnut base. **Prices:** Damascus $850 to $1,400; 440C $250 to $600; folders $85 to $400. **Remarks:** Professional/artist maker; first knife sold in 1980. **Mark:** Buffalo skull with last name.

custom knifemakers
MILLER—MOORE

MILLER, M.A., 4131 E. 115th Place, Thornton, CO 80233/303-452-7379
Specialties: Using knives for hunting. 3½"-4" Lovless Drop-point. Made to customer specs. **Patterns:** Drop-points, fighters and Bowies. **Technical:** Grinds 440C, D2, 01 and ATS-34 Damascus miniatures. **Prices:** $225 to $275; miniatures $75. **Remarks:** Part-time maker; first knife sold in 1988. **Mark:** Last name stamped in block letters.

MILLER, MICHAEL K., 28510 Santiam Hwy., Sweet Home, OR 97386/503-367-4927
Specialties: Fancy working and using straight knives of his design or made to customer specs. **Patterns:** Hunters, utility, camp knives and kitchen knives. **Technical:** Grinds 440C and AEB-L. Does special filework/tooling, leather work, and makes carved handles. Makes custom sheaths and holsters. **Prices:** $175. **Remarks:** Full-time maker; first knife sold in 1989. **Mark:** M&M Kustom Krafts.

MILLER, R.D., 10526 Estate Lane, Dallas, TX 75238/214-348-3496
Specialties: One-of-a-kind collector-grade knives. **Patterns:** Boots, hunters, Bowies, camp and utility knives, fishing and bird knives, miniatures. **Technical:** Grinds a variety of steels to include 01, D2, 440C, 154CM and 1095. **Prices:** $65 to $300; some to $900. **Remarks:** Full-time maker; first knife sold in 1984. **Mark:** R.D. Custom Knives with date or bow and arrow logo.

MILLER, ROBERT, P.O. Box 2722, Ormond Beach, FL 32175/904-676-1193
Specialties: Working straight knives, some fancy, of his design or to customer specs. **Patterns:** Large Bowies, hunters, miniatures. **Technical:** Grinds 01, D2 and 440C. Offers inlay and fancy filework; inlayed military insignias. **Prices:** $35 to $750. **Remarks:** Full-time maker; first knife sold in 1986. **Mark:** Holly and date.

MILLER, RONALD T., 12922 127th Ave. N., Largo, FL 34644/813-595-0378 (after 5 p.m.)
Specialties: Working straight knives in standard patterns. **Patterns:** Combat knives, camp knives, kitchen cutlery, fillet knives, locking folders and butterflies. **Technical:** Grinds D2, 440C and ATS-34; offers brass inlays and scrimshaw. **Prices:** $45 to $325; some to $750. **Remarks:** Part-time maker; first knife sold in 1984. **Mark:** Name, city and state in palm tree logo.

MILLER, TED, P.O. Box 6328, Santa Fe, NM 87502/505-984-0338
Specialties: Carved antler display knives of his design. **Patterns:** Hunters, swords and miniatures. **Technical:** Grinds 440C. **Prices:** $110 to $350; some average $900. **Remarks:** Full-time maker; first knife sold in 1971. **Mark:** Initials and serial number.

MILLER, TERRY, 450 S. 1st, Seward, NE 68434/402-643-2499
Specialties: Working knives and collector pieces. **Patterns:** Hunters, fighters and Bowies. **Technical:** Grinds 440C. **Prices:** $90 to $145; some higher. **Remarks:** Part-time maker; first knife sold in 1978. **Mark:** Stylized name in knife logo.

MILLS, ANDY, 414 E. Schubert, Fredericksburg, TX 78624/512-997-8167
Specialties: Working straight knives and folders. **Patterns:** Hunters. **Technical:** Grinds 440C, D2, A2 and 154CM. Offers leatherwork, fabrication, heat-treating. **Prices:** Moderate. **Remarks:** Full-time maker; first knife sold in 1980. **Mark:** Name.

MILLS, LOUIS G., 9450 Waters Rd., Ann Arbor, MI 48103/313-668-1839
Specialties: High-art Japanese-style period pieces. **Patterns:** Traditional tantos, daggers and swords. **Technical:** Makes steel from iron; makes his own Damascus by traditional Japanese techniques. **Prices:** $900 to $2,000; some to $8,000. **Remarks:** Spare-time maker in partnership with Jim Kelso. **Mark:** Yasutomo in Japanese Kanji.

MINDS' EYE METALMASTER (See Smith, D. Noel)

MINERAL MOUNTAIN HATCHET WORKS (See Frizzell, Ted)

MINK, DAN, 4820 17 Ave. N., St. Petersburg, FL 33713/813-323-7398; FAX: 813-787-2670
Specialties: Traditional and working knives of his design. **Patterns:** Bowies, fighters and hunters. **Technical:** Grinds ATS-34, 440C and D2. Blades and tangs embellished with fancy filework. Uses natural and rare handle materials. **Prices:** $125 to $450. **Remarks:** Part-time maker; first knife sold in 1985. **Mark:** Name and star encircled by custom made, city, state.

MINNICK, JIM, 144 North 7th St., Middletown, IN 47356/317-354-4108
Specialties: Traditional working and using straight knives and folders; classic high-art and fancy/embellished knives of his design or to customer specs. **Patterns:** Hunters, Bowies, daggers, fighters, boots, art knives, locking folders and slip-joint folders. **Technical:** Grinds 440C and 154CM. Scrimshaw by wife Joyce. **Prices:** $185 to $225; some to $1,800. **Remarks:** Part-time maker; first knife sold in 1976. **Mark:** Last name.

MISSION KNIVES, INC. (See Schultz, Richard A.)

MITCHELL, WM. DEAN, P.O. Box 183, Forgan, OK 73938
Specialties: Classic and high-art knives in standard patterns. **Patterns:** Bowies, daggers and swords. **Technical:** Forges 1095, 5160; makes pattern, composite and mosaic Damascus; offers filework and elecroplating. Makes wooden display cases. **Prices:** Mid to upper scale. **Remarks:** Part-time maker; first knife sold in 1986. Doing business as Pioneer Forge & Woodshop. **Mark:** Full name or initials, MS.

MITCHELL, JAMES A., P.O. Box 4646, Columbus, GA 31904/404-322-8582
Specialties: Fancy working knives. **Patterns:** Hunters, fighters, Bowies and locking folders. **Technical:** Grinds D2, 440C and commercial Damascus. **Prices:** $100 to $400; some to $900. **Remarks:** Part-time maker; first knife sold in 1976. Sells knives in sets. **Mark:** Signature and city.

MITCHELL, MAX, DEAN AND BEN, 997 V.F.W. Rd., Leesville, LA 71446/318-239-6416
Specialties: Working knives. **Patterns:** Four-way hunter, hatchet and knife sets, Bowies. **Technical:** Grinds 01. Leatherworkers; heavy basket-weave sheaths. **Prices:** $125 to $500. **Remarks:** Part-time makers; first knife sold in 1976. **Mark:** First names in oval logo.

MITCHELL, R.W. "MITCH", 15980 Grand Ave. #T-44, Lake Elsinore, CA 92530-5621/909-678-2231
Specialties: Working straight knives with Indian influence. **Patterns:** Bowies, fighters, hunters with horseshoe guards, etc. **Technical:** Grinds 440C, 01 and ATS-34; prefers natural handle materials; heat-treats. **Prices:** $125 to $650. **Remarks:** Full-time maker; first knife sold in 1988. **Mark:** Mitch with arrow logo.

M.J.R. KNIVES (See Raymond, Mary Jane)

M&M KUSTOM KRAFTS (See Miller, Michael K.)

M&N ARTS LTD. (See Wattelet, Michael A.)

MONK, NATHAN P., 1304 4th Ave. SE, Cullman, AL 35055/205-737-0463
Specialties: Traditional working and using straight knives of his design and to customer specs; fancy knives. **Patterns:** Bowies, daggers, fighters, hunters, utility/camp knives and one-of-a-kinds. **Technical:** Grinds ATS-34, 440C and A2. Engraving by Billy Bates. **Prices:** $50 to $175. **Remarks:** Spare-time maker; first knife sold in 1990. **Mark:** First and middle initials, last name, city, state.

MONTEIRO, VICTOR, 418 Rue Engeland, 1180 Brussels, BELGIUM/322-375-49-07
Specialties: Working and fancy straight knives and folders of his design. **Patterns:** Bowies, fighters and hunters. **Technical:** Grinds ATS-34, 440C and commercial Damascus. Offers heat-treating, embellishment, filework, scrimshaw. **Prices:** $200 to $1,000, some higher. **Remarks:** Full-time maker; first knife sold in 1989. Doing business as Monteiro Knives S.C. **Mark:** Initials connected.

MONTEIRO KNIVES S.C. (See Monteiro, Victor)

MONTJOY, CLAUDE, RR 2, Box 1280, Clinton, SC 29325/803-697-6160
Specialties: Fancy working knives. **Patterns:** Hunters, boots, fighters, some art knives and folders. **Technical:** Grinds ATS-34 and 440C. Offers inlaid handle scales. **Prices:** $100 to $500. **Remarks:** Part-time maker; first knife sold in 1982. **Mark:** Last name.

THE MOONLIGHT SMITHY (See Leck, Dal)

MOORE, BILL, 879 Pinewood Rd., Leesburg, GA 31763/912-759-6521
Specialties: Working and using folders of his design and to customer specs. **Patterns:** Bowies, hunters and locking folders. **Technical:** Grinds ATS-34, forges 5168

directory

MOORE—NEALEY

and cable Damascus. Filework. **Prices:** $100 to $400. **Remarks:** Part-time maker; first knife sold in 1988. **Mark:** Moore Knives.

MOORE, JAMES B., 1707 N. Gillis, Ft. Stockton, TX 79735/915-336-2113
Specialties: Classic working straight knives and folders of his design. **Patterns:** Hunters, Bowies, daggers, fighters, boots, utility/camp knives, locking folders and slip-joint folders. **Technical:** Grinds 440C, ATS-34, D2, L6, CPM and commercial Damascus. **Prices:** $85 to $700; exceptional knives to $1,500. **Remarks:** Full-time maker; first knife sold in 1972. **Mark:** Name, city and state.

MORAN JR., WM. F., P.O. Box 68, Braddock Heights, MD 21714/301-371-7543
Specialties: High-art working knives of his design. **Patterns:** Fighters, camp knives, Bowies, daggers, axes, tomahawks, push knives and miniatures. **Technical:** Forges W2, 5160 and his own Damascus; puts silver wire inlay on most handles; uses only natural handle materials. **Prices:** $400 to $7,500; some to $9,000. **Remarks:** Full-time maker. **Mark:** First and middle initials, last name, M.S.

MORETZ, JIM, P.O. Box 2484, Brookshire Rd., Boone, NC 28607/704-262-0948
Specialties: Traditional working and using straight knives and folders. **Patterns:** Hunters, utility/camp knives and slip-joint folders. **Technical:** Forges and grinds. **Prices:** $105 to $275; some to $995. **Remarks:** Full-time maker; first knife sold in 1978. When ordering, please consider Alaska and Western big game hunting seasons. **Mark:** Stylized initials, or name, city, state.

MORGAN, JEFF, 9200 Arnaz Way, Santee, CA 92071/619-448-8430
Specialties: Fancy working straight knives. **Patterns:** Hunters, fighters, boots, miniatures. **Technical:** Grinds D2, 440C and ATS-34; likes exotic handles. **Prices:** $65 to $140; some to $500. **Remarks:** Full-time maker; first knife sold in 1977. **Mark:** Initials connected.

MORGAN, TOM, 14689 Ellett Rd., Beloit, OH 44609/216-537-2023
Specialties: Working straight knives and period pieces. **Patterns:** Hunters, boots and presentation tomahawks. **Technical:** Grinds O1, 440C and 154CM. **Prices:** $45 to $125; some to $225. **Remarks:** Part-time maker; first knife sold in 1977. **Mark:** Last name and type of steel used.

MORGAN VALLEY FORGE (See Clark, Howard F.)

MORLAN, TOM, 30635 S. Palm, Hemet, CA 92343/714-767-0543
Specialties: Fancy working knives to customer specs. **Patterns:** Bowies, tantos, fishing knives and locking folders. **Technical:** Grinds 440C, 154CM and ATS-34. **Prices:** $75 to $250; some to $3,000. **Remarks:** Part-time maker; first knife sold in 1979. **Mark:** Initials connected.

MORRIS, C.H., 828 Meadow Dr., Atmore, AL 36502/205-368-2089
Specialties: Liner lock folders. **Patterns:** Interframe liner locks. **Technical:** Grinds 440C and ATS-34. **Prices:** Start at $350. **Remarks:** Full-time maker; first knife sold in 1973. **Mark:** First and middle initials, last name.

MORRIS, DARRELL PRICE, 92 Union St., Plymouth, Devon, ENGLAND PL1 3EZ/0752 223546
Specialties: Traditional Japanese knives, large Bowies, high-art knives. **Technical:** Damascus. **Prices:** $1,000 to $4,000. **Remarks:** Part-time maker; first knife sold in 1990. **Mark:** Initials and Japanese name—Kuni Shigae.

MORSETH SPORTS EQUIPMENT CO. (See Russell, A.G.)

MOSCI, CARLOS ROBERTO, 74 St. No. 1059 (16 and 17), LaPlata, 1900, ARGENTINA/021-524029
Specialties: Unique fancy working knives. **Patterns:** Collectible display pieces to hard-working knives; Bowies to boots; folders. **Technical:** Forges and grinds manganese, carbon, tungsten and cobalt. Prefers wide bevels. Never repeats a design. **Prices:** $500 to $1,500; some to $3,000. **Remarks:** Full-time maker; first knife sold in 1955. **Mark:** C. MOSCI COLECCION ARGENTINA.

MOSSER, GARY E., 11827 NE 102nd Place, Kirkland, WA 98033-5170/206-827-2279
Specialties: Working knives. **Patterns:** Hunters, skinners, camp knives, some art knives. **Technical:** Stock removal method; prefers ATS-34. **Prices:** $100 to $250; special orders and art knives are higher. **Remarks:** Part-time maker; first knife sold in 1976. **Mark:** Name.

MOULTON, DUSTY, 11385 W. Ardyce St., Boise, ID 83704/208-323-7911
Specialties: Fancy and working straight knives. **Patterns:** Hunters, fighters, fantasy and miniatures. **Technical:** Grinds exclusively ATS-34. **Prices:** $160 to $600; some to $1,500. **Remarks:** Full-time maker; first knife sold in 1991. **Mark:** Last name, town, state.

MOUNT, DON, 387 Medill Place, Horizon City, TX 79927/314-264-1287
Specialties: High-tech working and using straight knives of his design. **Patterns:** Bowies, fighters and utility/camp knives. **Technical:** Uses 440C and ATS-34. **Prices:** $150 to $300; some to $1,000. **Remarks:** Part-time maker; first knife sold in 1985. **Mark:** Name below a woodpecker.

MOUNTAIN FORGE (See Buchman, Bill)

MOUNTAIN HOME KNIVES, P.O. Box 167, Jamul, CA 91935/619-669-0833
Specialties: High-quality working straight knives. **Patterns:** Hunters, fighters, skinners, tantos, utility and fillet knives, Bowies and *san-mai* Damascus Bowies. **Technical:** Hollow-grind 440C by hand. Feature linen Micarta handles, nickel-silver handle bolts and handmade sheaths. **Prices:** $65 to $270. **Remarks:** Company owned by Jim English. **Mark:** Mountain Home Knives.

MOYER, RUSS, 277 71st Ave. NW, Havre, MT 59501/406-265-5116
Specialties: Working knives to customer specs. **Patterns:** Hunters, Bowies and survival knives; locking folders. **Technical:** Forges W2, O1 and D2. **Prices:** $150 to $350. **Remarks:** Part-time maker; first knife sold in 1976. **Mark:** Initials in logo.

MULLIN, STEVE, 500 W. Center Valley Rd., Sandpoint, ID 83864/208-263-7492
Specialties: Damascus period pieces and folders. **Patterns:** Full range of folders, hunters and Bowies. **Technical:** Forges and grinds O1, D2, 154CM and his own Damascus. Engraves. **Prices:** $100 to $2,000. **Remarks:** Full-time maker; first knife sold in 1975. Sells line of using knives under Pack River Knife Co. **Mark:** Full name, city and state.

MURPHY, DAVE, P.O. Box 256, Gresham, OR 97030/503-665-8634
Specialties: Working knives of his design; small kitchen knives. **Patterns:** Hunters, fighters and boots. **Technical:** Grinds 440C, ATS-34 and L6; likes narrow tangs, composite handles. **Prices:** $44 to $12,500. **Remarks:** Full-time maker; first knife sold in 1940. **Mark:** Name, city and state with likeness of face on blade.

MUSTANG FORGE (See Hinderer, Rick)

M.W. KNIVES (See Wesolowski, Mike)

MYERS, MEL, 611 Elmwood Drive, Spencer, IA 51301/712-262-3383
Specialties: Working knives. **Patterns:** Hunters and small utilitarian knives. **Technical:** Uses 440C and no power tools except polisher. **Prices:** $75 to $150. **Remarks:** Spare-time maker; first knife sold in 1982. **Mark:** Signature.

MYERS, PAUL, 614 W. Airwood Dr., E. Alton, IL 62024
Specialties: Fancy working straight knives and folders. **Patterns:** Full range of folders, straight hunters and Bowies; tie tacks; knife and fork sets. **Technical:** Grinds D2, 440C, ATS-34 and 154CM. **Prices:** $100 to $350; some to $3,000. **Remarks:** Full-time maker; first knife sold in 1974. **Mark:** Initials with setting sun on front; name and number on back.

MYSTIK KNIFEWORKS (See Livingston, Robert C.)

n

NEALY, BUD, 822 Thomas St., Stroudsburg, PA 18360/717-421-4040; FAX: 717-421-2593.
Specialties: Concealment knives with designer multi-concealment sheath system. **Patterns:** Hunters, boots, combat and collector pieces. **Technical:** Grinds ATS-34. **Prices:** $150 to $1,200. **Remarks:** Full-time maker; first knife sold in 1980. **Mark:** Name, city and state.

NEALEY, IVAN F. (FRANK), Anderson Dam Rd., Box 65, HC #87, Mt. Home, ID 83647/208-587-4060
Specialties: Working straight knives in standard patterns. **Patterns:** Hunters, skinners and utility knives. **Technical:** Grinds D2, 440C and 154CM. **Prices:** $90 to

$135; some higher. **Remarks:** Part-time maker; first knife sold in 1975. **Mark:** Name.

NEELEY, VAUGHN, 666 Grand Ave., Mancos, CO 81328/303-533-7982
Specialties: High-tech working straight knives and folders. **Patterns:** High-tech approaches; locking folders and interframes. **Technical:** Grinds 440C, D2 and 154CM. **Prices:** Upscale. **Remarks:** Full-time maker; first knife sold in 1982. **Mark:** Name.

NEELY, GREG, 9605 Radio Rd., Houston, TX 77075-2238/713-991-2677
Specialties: Traditional patterns and his own patterns for work and/or collecting. **Patterns:** Hunters, Bowies and utility/camp knives. **Technical:** Forges Damascus, W2, 5160 and 5168. Selectively tempers. Prefers natural handle materials. **Prices:** $195 to $3,500. **Remarks:** Part-time maker; first knife sold in 1987. **Mark:** Last name or interlocked initials, MS.

NEERING, WALT AND REPKE, MIKE, 4191 N. Euclid Ave., Bay City, MI 48706/517-684-3111
Specialties: Traditional working and using straight knives of their design or to customer specs; classic knives; display knives. **Patterns:** Hunters, Bowies, skinners, fighters boots, axes and swords. **Technical:** Grind 440C. Offer variety of handle materials. **Prices:** $99 to $1,500. **Remarks:** Full-time makers. Doing business as Black Forest Blades. **Mark:** Knife logo.

NELSON, ROGER S., Box 294, Central Village, CT 06332/203-774-6749
Specialties: Working knives. **Patterns:** Hunters, fighters, camp knives, locking folders, butterflies. **Technical:** Grinds D2, 440C and 154CM. **Prices:** $90 to $140; some to $250. **Remarks:** Spare-time maker; first knife sold in 1975. **Mark:** First initial, last name.

NEWCOMB, CORBIN, 628 Woodland Ave., Moberly, MO 65270/816-263-4639
Specialties: Working straight knives and folders; period pieces. **Patterns:** Hunters, axes, Bowies, folders, buckskinner blades and boots. **Technical:** Hollow-grinds D2, 440C and 154CM; prefers natural handle materials. Makes own Damascus; offers cable Damascus. **Prices:** $100 to $500. **Remarks:** Full-time maker; first knife sold in 1982. Doing business as Corbin Knives. **Mark:** First name and serial number.

NEWTON, LARRY, 1758 Pronghorn Ct., Jacksonville, FL 32225/904-221-2340
Specialties: Traditional and working folders of his design. **Patterns:** Front release locking folders and interframes. **Technical:** Grinds 440C, ATS-34 and D2. **Prices:** Starting at $250. **Remarks:** Spare-time maker; first knife sold in 1989. **Mark:** Last name.

NIBARGER, CHARLIE, 4908 E. 15th St., Tulsa, OK 74112/918-749-8042
Specialties: Working straight knives in standard patterns. **Patterns:** Hunters, fighters and utility knives. **Technical:** Grinds 440C, ATS-34 and D2. **Prices:** $90 to $150. **Remarks:** Full-time maker; first knife sold in 1983. **Mark:** Last name.

NICHOLSON, R. KENT, P.O. Box 204, Phoenix, MD 21131/410-323-6925
Specialties: Large using knives. **Patterns:** Bowies and camp knives in the Moran style. **Technical:** Forges W2, 9260, 5160; makes Damascus. **Prices:** $150 to $995. **Remarks:** Part-time maker; first knife sold in 1984. **Mark:** Name.

NIELSON, JEFF V., 610 S. 200 E., P.O. Box 365, Monroe, UT 84754/801-527-4242
Specialties: Classic folders of his design and to customer specs. **Patterns:** Fighters, hunters, locking folders; miniatures. **Technical:** Grinds 440C stainless; forges Damascus. **Prices:** $80 to $500. **Remarks:** Part-time maker; first knife sold in 1991. Doing business as Fine Custom Knives. **Mark:** Name, location.

NIMO FORGE (See Sinyard, Cleston S.)

NIRO, FRANK, Box 552, Mackenzie, BC V0J 2C0, CANADA/604-997-6975
Specialties: Comfortable working straight knives and folders. **Patterns:** Hunters, Bowies, fishing knives, camp and kitchen knives. **Technical:** Grinds L6, 440C, ATS-34. Specializes in "cross cut" 440C and ATS-34. **Prices:** $40 to $450. **Remarks:** Part-time maker; first knife sold in 1983. **Mark:** Name, city, province.

NISHIUCHI, MELVIN S., 6121 Forest Park Dr., Las Vegas, NV 89115/702-438-2327
Specialties: Working straight knives; collector pieces. **Patterns:** Hunters, fighters, utility knives and some fancy personal knives. **Technical:** Grinds ATS-34; prefers exotic wood and/or stone handle materials. **Prices:** $200 to $1,000; some to $2,000. **Remarks:** Part-time maker; first knife sold in 1985. **Mark:** Circle with a line above it.

NOBLE HOUSE ARMOURERS (See Kennedy, Kelly S.)

NOLEN, GEORGE (See Nolen, R.D. and George)

NOLEN, R.D. and GEORGE, 1110 Lakeshore Dr., Estes Park, CO 80517-7113/303-586-5814
Specialties: Working knives; display pieces. **Patterns:** Wide variety of straight knives, butterflies and buckles. **Technical:** Grind D2, 440C and 154CM. Offer filework; make exotic handles. **Prices:** $100 to $800; some higher. **Remarks:** Full-time makers; first knife sold in 1968. **Mark:** NK in oval logo.

NOLFI, TIM, P.O. Box P, Chapel Hill Rd., Dawson, PA 15428/412-529-2439
Specialties: High-art straight knives and folders of his design; working and using knives. **Patterns:** Hunters, Bowies, fighters and some locking folders. **Technical:** Forges and grinds his own Damascus, 01 and 1095. Also works with wrought iron and 200 nickel. **Prices:** $125 to $1,500; some to $4,000. **Remarks:** Full-time maker; first knife sold in 1988. **Mark:** Nolfi Forge or last name alone.

NORDELL, INGEMAR, Skarpt 2103, 82041 F„rila, SWEDEN/0651-23347
Specialties: Classic working and using straight knives. **Patterns:** Hunters, Bowies and fighters. **Technical:** Forges and grinds ATS-34, D2 and Sandvik. **Prices:** $100 to $350; some to $500. **Remarks:** Part-time maker; first knife sold in 1985. **Mark:** Initials or name.

NORRIS, MIKE, 2115 Charlotte Rd., Albemarle, NC 28001/704-982-8445
Specialties: Working straight knives in standard patterns. **Patterns:** Bowies, fighters, hunters and locking folders. **Technical:** Grinds 154CM and ATS-34. **Prices:** $75 to $600; some to $1,000. **Remarks:** Part-time maker; first knife sold in 1982. **Mark:** Last name.

NORTH, DAVID and PRATER, MIKE, 105 Sharp, Chickamauga, GA 30707/706-931-2396
Specialties: Variety of horn- and stag-handled belt knives. **Patterns:** Standard patterns in large and small narrow-tang construction. **Technical:** Grind 01, D2 and Damascus. **Prices:** $165 to $10,000. **Remarks:** First knife sold in 1980. **Mark:** Names, date, serial number.

NORTHERN KNIFE CO. (See Crosslen, Timothy J.)

NORTON, DENNIS, 5334 Ashland Dr., Ft. Wayne, IN 46835/219-486-3851
Specialties: Traditional working and using straight knives of his design; martial arts weapons. **Patterns:** Bowies, fighters and utility/camp knives. **Technical:** Grinds 440C, D2 and 01. Most knives have filework and exotic hardwood handles. **Prices:** $60 to $300; some to $750. **Remarks:** Part-time maker; first knife sold in 1985. **Mark:** Initials and last name.

NORTON, DON, 3206 Aspen Dr., Farmington, NM 87401/505-327-3604
Specialties: Fancy and plain straight knives. **Patterns:** Hunters, small Bowies, tantos, boot knives, fillets. **Technical:** Prefers 440C, Micarta, exotic woods and other natural handle materials. Hollow-grinds all knives except fillet knives. **Prices:** $85 to $1,000; average is $200. **Remarks:** Full-time maker; first knife sold in 1980. **Mark:** Full name, Hsi Shugi, city, state.

NOWLAND, RICK, RR 1, Box 277, Waltonville, IL 62894/618-279-3170
Specialties: Working straight knives; collector-grade knives of his design. **Patterns:** One-of-a-kind daggers and Bowies, hunters, fighters, folders and miniatures. **Technical:** Forges 01, 5160 and Damascus. Uses some stainless steel. Makes mokume. **Prices:** $75 to $500; some to $1,000. **Remarks:** Part-time maker; first knife sold in 1986. **Mark:** Last name.

NUNN, GREGORY, CVSR Box 2107, Moab, UT 84532/801-259-8607
Specialties: High-art working and using knives of his design; new edition Emperor's Choice knife with purple sheen obsidian handle; new edition knife with handles made from Agatetized Dinosaur Bone—first ever made. **Patterns:** Flaked stone knives. **Technical:** Uses gem-quality agates, jaspers and obsidians for blades. **Prices:** $125 to $600; some to $1,000. **Remarks:** Full-time maker; first knife sold in 1989. **Mark:** Name, knife and edition numbers, year made.

directory

NYMEYER—PACKARD

NYMEYER, EARL 2802 N. Fowler, Hobbs, NM 88240/505-392-2164
Specialties: Working straight knives of his design. **Patterns:** Variations of the tanto; fighters and hunters. **Technical:** Hollow-grinds; offers filework. **Prices:** $75 to $95; some to $195. **Remarks:** Spare-time maker; first knife sold in 1983. **Mark:** Initials or first initial, last name.

o

OAKTREE FORGE (See Wagner, Dan)

OCHS, CHARLES F., 124 Emerald Lane, Largo, FL 34641/813-536-3827
Specialties: Working knives; period pieces. **Patterns:** Hunters, fighters, Bowies, buckskinners and folders. **Technical:** Forges 52100, 5160 and his own Damascus. **Prices:** $150 to $1,800; some to $2,500. **Remarks:** Full-time maker; first knife sold in 1978. **Mark:** OX Forge.

ODA, KUZAN, P.O. Box 2632, Palmer, AK 99645/907-746-3018
Specialties: High-tech Japanese-style knives; contemporary working knives. **Patterns:** Swords, fighters, hunters and folders. **Technical:** Forges and grinds BG42, 154CM, tamahagane and his own Damascus; offers traditional and authentic Japanese sword-smithing and polishing. **Prices:** $200 to $600; some to $8,000. **Remarks:** Full-time maker; first knife sold in 1957. Waiting list only. **Mark:** First name.

OGG, ROBERT G., 537 Old Dug Mtn. Rd., Paris, AR 72855/501-963-2767
Specialties: Plain and fancy working knives. **Patterns:** Folding slip-joints. **Technical:** Grinds 440C, ATS-34 and high carbon. **Prices:** Start at $120. **Remarks:** Spare-time maker; first knife sold in 1964. **Mark:** Name.

OKAYSU, KAZOU, 12-2 1 Chome Higashi Veno, Taito-Ku, Tokyo 110, JAPAN

OLD COLONY MANUFACTORY (See Leavitt, Jr., Earl F.)

OLD TOWN CUTLERY (See Ree, David)

OLIVER, ANTHONY CRAIG, 1504 Elaine Pl., Ft. Worth, TX 76106/817-625-0825
Specialties: Fancy and embellished traditional straight knives of his design. **Patterns:** Hunters, full-size folders, Bowies, daggers and miniatures in stainless and nickel Damascus with tempered blades. **Technical:** Grinds 440C and ATS-34. **Prices:** $40 to $500. **Remarks:** Part-time maker; first knife sold in 1988. **Mark:** Initials and last name.

OLSON, ROD, 110 3rd Ave. NE, High River AB, CANADA T1V 1L9/403-652-2744; FAX: 403-652-3061
Specialties: Traditional and working/using folders of his design; period pieces. **Patterns:** Locking folders. **Technical:** Grinds ATs-34. Offers filework, sculptured steel frames. **Prices:** $300 to $750. **Remarks:** Part-time maker; first knife sold in 1979. Doing business as Olson Pocket Knives. **Mark:** Last name on blade; country, serial number inside frame.

OLSON, WAYNE C., 11655 W. 35th Ave., Wheat Ridge, CO 80033/303-420-3415
Specialties: High-tech working knives. **Patterns:** Hunters to folding lockers; some integral designs. **Technical:** Grinds 440C, 154CM and ATS-34; likes hand-finishes; precision-fits stainless steel fittings—no solder, no nickel silver. **Prices:** $275 to $600; some to $3,000. **Remarks:** Full-time maker; first knife sold in 1979. **Mark:** Name, maker.

OLYMPIC KNIVES (See Ball, Robert)

ONION, KENNETH J., 91-990 Oaniani St., Kapolei, HI 96707/808-674-1300
Specialties: Fancy working straight knives and some folders. **Patterns:** Bowies, daggers, fighters, boots, hunters, utility folders, art knives. **Technical:** ATS-34, 440C, Damascus, 5160, D2. **Prices:** $110 to $800. **Remarks:** Part-time maker; first knife sold in 1991. **Mark:** NA.

ORION (See Reed, Del)

OSBORNE, WARREN, 215 Edgefield, Waxahachie, TX 75165/214-937-0899; FAX: 214-937-9004
Specialties: Working knives; fancy pieces. **Patterns:** Folders; bolstered and interframe miniatures; conventional lockers, frontlockers and backlockers; some slipjoints; some high-art pieces. **Technical:** Grinds D2, 440C and 154CM; offers serrated bolsters. **Prices:** $200 to $800; some to $2,000. Interframes $650 to $1,500. **Remarks:** Full-time maker; first knife sold in 1980. **Mark:** Last name in boomerang logo.

OSTERMAN, DANIEL E., 1644 W. 10th, Junction City, OR 97448/503-998-1503
Specialties: One-third scale copies of period pieces, investor class miniatures. **Patterns:** Antique Bowies. **Technical:** Grinds all cutlery grade steels, engraves, etches, inlays and overlays. **Prices:** Start at $600. **Remarks:** Full-time maker; first miniature knife sold in 1975. **Mark:** Initials.

OUTDOORS WEST (See Sutherland, Greg)

OUTFITTER (See Vought Jr., Frank)

OUTLAW, ANTHONY L., 4115 Gaines St., Panama City, FL 32404/904-769-7754
Specialties: Traditional working straight knives. **Patterns:** Tantos, Bowies, camp knives, etc. **Technical:** Grinds A2, W2, 01, L6, 1095 and stainless steels to mirror finish. **Prices:** $85 to $175; some to $300. **Remarks:** Part-time maker; first knife sold in 1984. **Mark:** Last name.

OVEREYNDER, T.R., 1800 S. Davis Dr., Arlington, TX 76013/817-277-4812; FAX: 817-860-5485
Specialties: Highly finished collector-grade working knives. **Patterns:** Fighters, Bowies, daggers, locking folders, slip-joints and 90 percent collector-grade interframe folders. **Technical:** Grinds D2, 440C and 154CM. Has been making titanium-frame folders since 1977. **Prices:** $500 to $1,500; some to $7,000. **Remarks:** Part-time maker; first knife sold in 1977. Doing business as TRO Knives. **Mark:** T.R. OVEREYNDER KNIVES, city and state.

OWEN, BILL, P.O. Box 161, Monterey, VA 24465/703-468-2850
Specialties: Working and using straight knives of his design. **Patterns:** Hunters, Bowies and utility/camp knives. **Technical:** Grinds D2; forges various spring steels. Heat-treats and makes sheaths. **Prices:** $85 to $250. **Remarks:** Spare-time maker; first knife sold in 1990. **Mark:** Last name.

OWENS, DAN, P.O. Box 284, Blacksburg, SC 29702/803-839-2287
Specialties: Traditional working and straight knives in standard patterns. **Patterns:** Hunters, fighters, single-edge boots, utility/camp knives. **Technical:** Grinds 440C, ATS-34, commercial Damascus, 154CM. **Prices:** $100 to $350; some to $750. **Remarks:** Full-time maker; first knife sold in 1986. Doing business as Dano-D. Arvel Handcrafted Knives. **Mark:** D. ARVEL.

OWENS, JOHN, 6513 E. Lookout Dr., Parker, CO 80134
Specialties: Contemporary working straight knives; period pieces. **Patterns:** Hunters, Bowies and camp knives. **Technical:** Grinds and forges 440C, 154CM, ATS-34 and 01. **Prices:** $125 to $350. **Remarks:** Spare-time maker. **Mark:** Last name.

OX FORGE (See Ochs, Charles F.)

OYSTER, LOWELL R., RR #1, Box 5605, Kenduskeag, ME 04450/207-884-8663
Specialties: Traditional and original designed multi-blade slip-joint folders. **Patterns:** Hunters, minis, camp and fishing knives. **Technical:** Grinds 01; heat-treats. **Prices:** $55 to $450; some to $750. **Remarks:** Full-time maker; first knife sold in 1981. **Mark:** A scallop shell.

p

PACHI, FRANCESCO, Via Albisola 97B, 16163 Genoa, ITALY/010-713050
Specialties: Fancy working knives. **Patterns:** Hunters and skinners. **Technical:** Grinds 440C. **Prices:** $200 to $500. **Remarks:** Part-time maker; first knife sold in 1991. **Mark:** Logo with last name.

PACK RIVER KNIFE CO. (See Mullin, Steve)

PACKARD, BOB, P.O. Box 311, Elverta, CA 95626/916-991-5218
Specialties: Traditional working/using straight knives of his design and to customer specs. **Patterns:** Hunters, fishing knives, utility/camp knives. **Technical:** Grinds

ATS-34, 440C; Forges 52100, 5168 and cable Damascus. **Prices:** $75 to $225. **Mark:** Engraved name and year.

PADILLA, GARY, P.O. Box 741, Weimar, CA 95736/916-637-5182
Specialties: Native American influenced working and using straight knives of his design. **Patterns:** Hunters, kitchen knives, utility/camp knives and obsidian ceremonial knives. **Technical:** Grinds 440C, ATS-34, 01 and Damascus. **Prices:** $65 to $195; some to $500. **Remarks:** Part-time maker; first knife sold in 1977. Doing business as Bighorn Knifeworks. **Mark:** Sylized initials or name over company name.

PAGE, LARRY, 165 Rolling Rock Rd., Aiken, SC 29803/803-648-0001
Specialties: Working knives of his design; period pieces. **Patterns:** Hunters, boots and fighters. **Technical:** Grinds 154CM and ATS-34. **Prices:** Start at $85. **Remarks:** Part-time maker; first knife sold in 1983. **Mark:** Name, city and state in oval.

PAGE, REGINALD, 6587 Groveland Hill Rd., Groveland, NY 14462/716-243-1643
Specialties: High-art straight knives and one-of-a-kind folders of his design. **Patterns:** Hunters, locking folders and slip-joint folders. **Technical:** Forges 01, 5160 and his own Damascus. Prefers natural handle materials but will work with Micarta. **Remarks:** Spare-time maker; first knife sold in 1985. **Mark:** First initial, last name.

PAGNARD, PHILIP E., 202 Martingale Dr., Peachtree City, GA 30269/404-487-3202
Specialties: Fantasy knives of his design; inspired by J.R.R. Tolkien. **Patterns:** Daggers, swords and axes. **Technical:** Forges his Damascus and 5160; grinds 440. Uses horn and purple heart for handles. Makes sheaths with snakeskin, leather, etc. **Prices:** $75 to $350; some to $500. **Remarks:** Part-time maker; first knife sold in 1986. Doing business as Armorbane. **Mark:** Eagle perched on a Viking helm.

PANKIEWICZ, PHILIP R., RFD #1, Waterman Rd., Lebanon, CT 06249
Specialties: Working straight knives. **Patterns:** Hunters, daggers, minis and fishing knives. **Technical:** Grinds D2, 440C and 154CM. **Prices:** $60 to $125; some to $250. **Remarks:** Spare-time maker; first knife sold in 1975. **Mark:** First initial in star.

PANTHER CREEK FORGE (See Cook, Louise and Cook, Mike)

PAPP, ROBERT, P.O. Box 29596, Parma, OH 44129/216-888-9299
Specialties: Swords—broad and fantasy; variety of display knives. **Patterns:** Integral-designed hunters, fighters, minis and boots. **Technical:** Grinds D2, 440C, 154CM, ATS-34, CPM 108 and CPM 440C. **Prices:** $95 to $10,000; some higher. **Remarks:** Full-time maker; first knife sold in 1964. **Mark:** Full name, city and state.

PARDUE, MELVIN M., Rt. 1, Box 130, Repton, AL 36475/205-248-2686
pecialties: Fancy straight knives and folders. **Patterns:** Locking and push-button folders, tantos, krisses, liner locks, fighters and boots. **Technical:** Grinds D2, 440C, 154CM and UHB-A-EBL; uses anodized titanium. Likes coffin handles. **Prices:** $140 to $350. **Remarks:** Full-time maker; first knife sold in 1974. **Mark:** Last name.

PARKER, J.E., 1300 E. Main, Clarion, PA 16214/814-226-7700

PARKS, JOHN, 3539 Galilee Church Rd., Jefferson, GA 30549/706-367-4916
Specialties: Traditional working and using straight knives of his design. **Patterns:** Trout knives, hunters and integral bolsters. **Technical:** Forges 1095 and 5168. **Prices:** $85 to $200; some to $400. **Remarks:** Part-time maker; first knife sold in 1989. **Mark:** Initials in script.

PARRISH III, GORDON A., 940 Lakloey Dr., North Pole, AK 99705/907-488-0357
Specialties: Classic high-art straight knives of his design and to customer specs.; working and using knives. **Patterns:** Bowies and hunters. **Technical:** Grinds tool steel and 440C. Uses mostly Alaskan handle materials. **Prices:** $125 to $750. **Remarks:** Spare-time maker; first knife sold in 1980. **Mark:** Last name, state.

PARRISH, ROBERT, 1922 Spartanburg Hwy., Hendersonville, NC 28739/704-692-3466
Specialties: Heavy-duty working knives of his design or to customer specs. **Patterns:** Survival and duty knives; hunters and fighters. **Technical:** Grinds 440C, D2, 01 and commercial Damascus. **Prices:** $200 to $300; some to $6,000. **Remarks:** Full-time maker; first knife sold in 1970. **Mark:** Initials connected, sometimes with city and state.

PARSONS, MICHAEL R., 1600 S. 11th St., Terre Haute, IN 47802-1722/812-234-1679
Specialties: Fancy straight knives. **Patterns:** Railroad spike knives and variety of one-of-a-kinds including files. **Technical:** Forges and hand-files scrap steel. Engraves, carves, wire inlays and offers leatherwork. **Prices:** $150 to $1,500. **Remarks:** Full-time maker; first knife sold in 1965. **Mark:** Mc with key logo.

PATE, LLOYD D., 219 Cottontail Ln., Georgetown, TX 78626/512-863-7805
Specialties: Traditional working straight knives. **Patterns:** Hunters, fighters and Bowies. **Technical:** Hollow-grinds D2, 440C and ATS-34; likes mirror-finishes. **Prices:** $75 to $350; some to $500. **Remarks:** Part-time maker; first knife sold in 1983. **Mark:** Last name.

PATRICK, CHUCK, P.O. Box 127, Brasstown, NC 28902/704-837-7627
Specialties: Hunters, daggers, tomahawks and friction folders. **Patterns:** Hunters, daggers, tomahawks, pre-Civil War folders. **Technical:** Forges all hardware, 5160, his own cable and Damascus, available in fancy pattern and mosaic. **Prices:** $150 to $1,000; some higher. **Remarks:** Full-time maker; first knife sold in 1980. **Mark:** Flying owl.

PATRICK, BOB, 4605 W. 13th Ave., Vancouver, B.C. V6R 2V6 CANADA/604-228-0770
Specialties: Working knives of his design. **Patterns:** Hunters, Bowies and specialty chisels. **Technical:** Grinds ATS-34. **Prices:** $90 to $2,000. **Remarks:** Full-time maker; first knife sold in 1987. **Mark:** Name in circle logo; British Columbia etched on other side; serial number.

PATTAY, RUDY, 20 Nevada St., Long Beach, NY 11561/516-431-0847
Specialties: Fancy and working straight knives of his design. **Patterns:** Bowies, hunters, utility/camp knives. **Technical:** Hollow-grinds ATS-34, 440C, 01. Offers stainless steel soldered guards; fabricates guard and buttcap on lathe and milling machine. Heat treats. Prefers synthetic handle materials. Offers hand-sewn sheaths. **Prices:** $100 to $350; some to $500. **Remarks:** Part-time maker; first knife sold in 1990. Doing business as Pattay Knives. **Mark:** First initial, last name in sorcerer logo.

PATTERSON, ALAN W., Rt. 3, Box 131, Hayesville, NC 28904/704-389-9103
Specialties: Working straight knives and folders of his design or to customer specs; period pieces. **Patterns:** Forged knives, swords, tomahawks and folders. **Technical:** Damascus, cable and tool steels. Some custom leatherwork; wife offers scrimshaw. **Prices:** $125 to $5,000. **Remarks:** Full-time maker; first knife sold in 1990. **Mark:** Patterson Forge.

PATTERSON, KARL, 8 Madison Ave., Silver Creek, NY 14136/716-934-2578
Specialties: Working and using straight knives of his design or to customer specs. **Patterns:** Hunters, Bowies and utility/camp knives. **Technical:** Grinds 440C, ATS-34 and 01. Prefers Micarta and pakkawood. **Prices:** $55 to $150; some to $350. **Remarks:** Spare-time maker; first knife sold in 1990. **Mark:** First name with a backward K.

PAVACK, DON, P.O. Box 318, Edgerton, WY 82635/307-437-9240; FAX: 307-437-9240
Specialties: Working straight knives. Will work with customer designs. **Patterns:** Hunters and fillet knives; folders. **Technical:** Grinds ATS-34, 440C, 154CM and Damascus steel. Prefers natural handle materials; uses Micarta and diamond wood. **Prices:** $95 to $2,000. **Mark:** Signature and initials.

PEAGLER, RUSS, P.O. Box 1314, Moncks Corner, SC 29461/803-761-1008
Specialties: Traditional working straight knives of his design and to customer specs. **Patterns:** Hunters, fighters, boots. **Technical:** Hollow-grinds 440C, ATS-34 and 01; uses Damascus steel. Prefers bone handles. **Prices:** $85 to $300; some to $500. **Remarks:** Spare-time maker; first knife sold in 1983. **Mark:** Initials.

PEASE, W.D., Rt. 2 Box 37AA, Ewing, KY 41039/606-845-0387
Specialties: Display-quality working straight knives and folders. **Patterns:** Fighters, tantos and boots; locking folders and interframes. **Technical:** Grinds 440C, 154CM and commercial Damascus; has own side-release lock system. **Prices:** $300 to $500; some to $1,500. **Remarks:** Full-time maker; first knife sold in 1970. **Mark:** First and middle initials, lst name.

PEASLEY, DAVID S., P.O. Box 604, Alamosa, CO 81101/719-589-4031

directory

PEELE—POLZIEN

Specialties: Working and using straight knives and folders of his design; period pieces. **Patterns:** Hunters, daggers and utility/camp knives; swivel knives for leatherworkers. **Technical:** Grinds 440C, D2 and commercial Damascus. **Prices:** $100 to $250; some to $450. **Remarks:** Part-time maker; first knife sold in 1981. **Mark:** Initials.

PEELE, BRYAN, 219 Ferry St., P.O. Box 1363, Thompson Falls, MT 59873/406-827-4633
Specialties: Fancy working and using knives of his design. **Patterns:** Hunters, Bowies and fighters. **Technical:** Grinds 440C, ATS-34 and commercial Damascus. **Prices:** $110 to $300; some to $900. **Remarks:** Part-time maker; first knife sold in 1985. **Mark:** The Elk Rack, full name, city, state.

PENDLETON, LLOYD, 24581 Shake Ridge Rd., Volcano, CA 95689/209-296-3353
Specialties: Contemporary working knives in standard patterns. **Patterns:** Hunters, fighters and boots. **Technical:** Grinds 154CM and ATS-34; mirror finishes. **Prices:** $300 to $700; some to $2,000. **Remarks:** Full-time maker; first knife sold in 1973. **Mark:** First initial, last name logo, city and state.

PENDRAY, ALFRED H., Rt. 2, Box 1950, Williston, FL 32696/904-528-6124
Specialties: Working straight knives and folders; period pieces. **Patterns:** Fighters and hunters, axes, camp knives and tomahawks. **Technical:** Forges Wootz steel; makes his own Damascus; makes traditional knives from old files and rasps. **Prices:** $125 to $1,000; some to $3,500. **Remarks:** Part-time maker; first knife sold in 1954. **Mark:** Last intial in horseshoe logo.

PENNINGTON, C.A., 137 Riverlea Estate Dr., Stewarts Gully, Christchurch 9, NEW ZEALAND/03-323 7292; FAX: 03-323-7292
Specialties: Classic working/using straight knives of his design. **Patterns:** Hunters, kitchen knives, utility/camp knives. **Technical:** Grinds D2, 440C, 154CM. **Prices:** $225 to $450; some to $850. **Remarks:** Full-time maker; first knife sold in 1988. **Mark:** Name, country.

PEPIOT, STEPHAN, 73 Cornwall Blvd., Winnipeg, Manitoba, CANADA R3J-1E9/204-888-1499
Specialties: Working straight knives in standard patterns. **Patterns:** Hunters and camp knives. **Technical:** Grinds 440C and industrial hacksaw blades. **Prices:** $75 to $125. **Remarks:** Spare-time maker; first knife sold in 1982. Not currently taking orders. **Mark:** PEP.

PEPPER KNIVES (See Culpepper, John)

PERSUADER (See Hill, Howard E.)

PETERSEN, DAN L., 3015 SW Clark Ct., Topeka, KS 66604
Specialties: Period pieces and forged integral hilts on hunters and fighters. **Patterns:** Texas style Bowies, boots and hunters in high carbon and Damascus steel. **Technical:** Austempers forged high-carbon blades. **Prices:** $200 to $3,000; some to $3,000. **Remarks:** First knife sold in 1978. **Mark:** Stylized initials, MS.

PETERSON, CHRIS, 2175 W. Rockyford, Box 143, Salina, UT 84654
Specialties: Working straight knives of his design. **Patterns:** Large fighters, boots, hunters and some display pieces. **Technical:** Forges 01 and meteor. Makes and sells his own Damascus. Engraves, scrimshands and inlays. **Prices:** $150 to $600; some to $1,500. **Remarks:** Full-time maker; first knife sold in 1986. **Mark:** A drop in a circle with a line through it.

PETERSON, ELDON G., 260 Haugen Hts. Rd., Whitefish, MT 59937/406-862-2204; FAX: 406-862-3103
Specialties: Fancy and working folders, any size. **Patterns:** Lockback interframes, integral bolster folders and two-bladers. **Technical:** Grinds 440C and ATS-34. Offers gold inlay work, gem stone inlays and engraving. **Prices:** $285 to $5,000. **Remarks:** Full-time maker; first knife sold in 1974. **Mark:** Name, city and state.

PHILLIPS, RANDY, 759 E. Francis St., Ontario, CA 91761/909-923-4381
Specialties: Hunters, collector-grade boots, high-art daggers, collector-grade button-release liner lock folders. **Technical:** Grinds D2, 440C and 154CM; embellishes. **Prices:** Start at $200. **Remarks:** Part-time maker; first knife sold in 1981. **Mark:** Name, city and state in eagle head.

PICKENS, SELBERT, Rt. 1, Box 216, Liberty, WV 25124/304-586-2190
Specialties: Using knives. **Patterns:** Standard sporting knives. **Technical:** Stainless steels; stock removal method. **Prices:** Moderate. **Remarks:** Part-time maker. **Mark:** Name.

PIERCE, HAROLD L., 106 Lyndon Lane, Louisville, KY 40222/502-429-5136
Specialties: Working straight knives, some fancy. **Patterns:** Big fighters and Bowies. **Technical:** Grinds D2, 440C, 154CM; likes sub-hilts. **Prices:** $150 to $450; some to $1,200. **Remarks:** Full-time maker; first knife sold in 1982. **Mark:** Last name with knife through the last initial.

PIENAAR, CONRAD, 19A Milner Rd., Bloemfontein 9300, REPUBLIC OF SOUTH AFRICA/051-314180
Specialties: Fancy working and using straight knives and folders of his design, to customer specs and in standard patterns. **Patterns:** Hunters, locking folders and utility/camp knives. **Technical:** Grinds 12C27, D2 and ATS-34. Scrimshands; engraving by Armin Winkler. Knives come with wooden box and custom-made leather sheath. **Prices:** $400 to $600. **Remarks:** Part-time maker; first knife sold in 1981. Doing business sa C.P. Knifemaker. **Mark:** Initials and serial number.

PIESNER, DEAN, 30 King St., St. Jacobs, Ont. CANADA N0B 2N0/519-664-3622; FAX: 519-664-2218
Specialties: Classic period pieces of his design and to customer specs. **Patterns:** Swingers. **Technical:** Forges 5160, steel Damascus and nickel-steel Damascus. Silver wire inlays in wood; copper-brass-silver inlays in steel. **Prices:** Start at $125. **Remarks:** Full-time maker; first knife sold in 1990. **Mark:** First initial, last name, JS.

PIONEER FORGE & WOODSHOP (See Mitchell, Wm. Dean)

PIOREK, JAMES S., P.O. Box 5032, Missoula, MT 59806/406-728-0119
Specialties: High-tech working/using straight knives of all designs. **Patterns:** Fighters, hunters, swords. **Technical:** Grinds A2. Offers ergonomically designed handles and blades. Heat treats. Kydex-lined leather sheaths available. **Prices:** $125 to $400; some higher. **Remarks:** Full-time maker; first knife sold in 1990. **Mark:** Initials with abstract cutting edge.

PITT, DAVID F., P.O. Box 1564, Pleasanton, CA 94566/415-846-9751
Specialties: Working straight knives. **Patterns:** Knives for deer and elk hunters, including hatchets and cleavers; small gut hook hunters and capers. **Technical:** Grinds A2, 440C and 154CM. **Prices:** $100 to $200; some to $450. **Remarks:** Full-time maker; first knife sold in 1972. **Mark:** Bear Paw with name.

POAG, JAMES, RR 1, Box 212A, Grayville, IL 62844/618-375-7106
Specialties: Working straight knives and folders; period pieces; of his design or to customer specs. **Patterns:** Bowies and camp knives, lockers and slip-joints. **Technical:** Forges and grinds stainless steels and others; provides serious leather; offers embellishments; scrimshaws, engraves and does leather work for other makers. **Prices:** $65 to $1,200. **Remarks:** Full-time maker; first knife sold in 1967. **Mark:** Name.

POGREBA, LARRY, Box 861, Lyons, CO 80540/303-823-6691
Specialties: Steel and Damascus lightweight hunters; kitchen knives. **Patterns:** Bird and trout knives, small hunters and kitchen knives. **Technical:** Forges/grinds his own Damascus. **Prices:** $40 to $1000. **Remarks:** Part-time maker; first knife sold in 1976. Doing business as Cadillac Blacksmithing. **Mark:** Initials.

POLK, CLIFTON, 4625 Webber Creek Rd., Van Buren, AR 72956/501-474-3828
Specialties: Fancy working straight knives and folders. **Patterns:** Locking folders, slip-joints, two-blades, straight knives. **Technical:** Offers 440C, D2 ATS-34 and Damascus. **Prices:** $150 to $3,000. **Remarks:** Full-time maker. **Mark:** Last name.

POLKOWSKI, AL, 8 Cathy Ct., Chester, NJ 07930/908-879-6030
Specialties: High-tech straight knives and folders for adventurers and professionals. **Patterns:** Fighters, side-lock folders, boots and concealment knives. **Technical:** Grinds D2 and ATS-34; features satin and bead-blast finishes; Kydex sheaths. **Prices:** Start at $100. **Remarks:** Full-time maker; first knife sold in 1985. **Mark:** Full name, Handmade.

POLZIEN, DON, 1912 Inler Suite-L, Lubbock, TX 79407/806-791-0766
Specialties: Traditional Japanese-style blades. **Patterns:** Hunters, fighters, one-of-a-kind art knives. **Technical:** 1045-1050 carbon steels, 440C, D2, ATS-34, stan-

dard and cable Damascus. **Prices:** $150 to $2,500. **Remarks:** Full-time maker. First knife sold in 1990. **Mark:** Oriental characters inside square border.

POOLE, MARVIN O., P.O. Box 5234, Anderson, SC 29623/803-225-5970
Specialties: Traditional working/using straight knives and folders of his design and in standard patterns. **Patterns:** Bowies, fighters, hunters, locking folders, bird and trout knives. **Technical:** Grinds 440C, D2, ATS-34. **Prices:** $50 to $150; some to $750. **Remarks:** Part-time maker; first knife sold in 1980. **Mark:** First initial, last name, year, serial number.

POOLE, STEVE L., 200 Flintlock Trail, Stockbridge, GA 30281/404-474-9154
Specialties: Traditional working and using straight knives and folders of his design, to customer specs and in standard patterns. **Patterns:** Bowies, fighters, hunters, utility and locking folders. **Technical:** Grinds ATS-34; buys Damascus. Heat-treats; offers leatherwork. **Prices:** $85 to $350; some to $800. **Remarks:** Spare-time maker; first knife sold in 1991. **Mark:** First and middle initials, last name and serial number.

POPLIN, JAMES L., 103 Oak St., Washington, GA 30673/404-678-2729
Specialties: Contemporary hunters. **Patterns:** Hunters and boots. **Technical:** Hollow-grinds. **Prices:** Reasonable. **Mark:** POP.

POPP SR., STEVE, 6573 Winthrop Dr., Fayetteville, NC 28311/910-822-3151
Specialties: Working straight knives. **Patterns:** Hunters, Bowies and fighters. **Technical:** Forges and grinds his own Damascus, 01, L6 and spring steel. **Prices:** $75 to $600; some to $1,000. **Remarks:** Full-time maker; first knife sold in 1984. **Mark:** Initials and last name.

PORTER, JAMES E., P.O. Box 2583, Bloomington, IN 47402/812-859-4302
Specialties: Working straight knives; period pieces. **Patterns:** Outdoor knives; Bowies and short swords. **Technical:** Forges W2 and 1095; makes pattern-welded Damascus. Prefers Damascus for blades and fittings. **Prices:** $125 to $3,000. **Remarks:** Part-time maker; first knife sold in 1986. **Mark:** Initials connected.

POSTON, ALVIN, 1197 Bass Rd., Pamplico, SC 29583/803-493-0066
Specialties: Working straight knives. **Patterns:** Hunters, Bowies and fishing knives; some miniatures. **Technical:** Grinds 154CM and ATS-34. **Prices:** Start at $100. **Remarks:** Part-time maker; first knife sold in 1979. **Mark:** Last name.

POTIER, TIMOTHY F., P.O. Box 711, Oberlin, LA 70655/318-639-2229
Specialties: Classic working and using straight knives to customer specs. **Patterns:** Hunters, Bowies and utility/camp knives. **Technical:** Forges his Damascus, 5160, L6. Offers filework. **Prices:** $200 to $1,100; some to $4,000. **Remarks:** Part-time maker; first knife sold in 1981. **Mark:** Last name.

POYTHRESS, JOHN, P.O. Box 585, 206 Freedom St., Swainsboro, GA 30401/912-237-9233; 912-237-9478
Specialties: Traditional working and using straight knives of his design or to customer specs. **Patterns:** Hunters. **Technical:** Uses 440C, ATS-34 and D2. **Prices:** $75 to $250; some to $400. **Remarks:** Spare-time maker; first knife sold in 1983. **Mark:** J.W. Poythress Handcrafted, serial number.

PRATER, MIKE (See North, David and Prater, Mike)

PRATT, CHARLEY, 1953 Fillmans Bottom Rd., Port Washington, OH 43837/614-498-5404
Specialties: Bowies, fighters, daggers and swords; kitchen knives on request. **Patterns:** Hunters, boot knives and miniatures. **Technical:** Grinds 440C, D-2, ATS-34 and commercial Damascus. **Prices:** Starting at $150. **Remarks:** Full-time maker; first knife sold in 1978. **Mark:** Last name.

PREHISTORIC EDGE, THE (See Stafford, Michael)

PRESLEY, VERN, 3803 Alston Lane, Richmond, VA 23294/804-270-4739
Specialties: Traditional working and using straight knives of his design and to customer specs. **Patterns:** Bowies, hunters and utility/camp knives. **Technical:** Grinds ATS-34, 440C amd 154CM. **Prices:** $120 to $175; some to $300. **Remarks:** Part-time maker; first knife sold in 1978. **Mark:** Stamped or etched last name.

PRESSBURGER, RAMON, 59 Driftway Rd., Howell, NJ 07731/908-363-0816
Specialties: Traditional working knives of his design. **Patterns:** Hunters and utility/camp knives. **Technical:** Uses ATS-34, D2 and BG42 amd high-carbon steels. **Prices:** $65 to $500. **Remarks:** Full-time maker; first knife sold in 1970. **Mark:** NA.

PRICE, JERRY L., P.O. Box 782, Springdale, AR 72764
Specialties: Working straight knives in standard patterns. **Patterns:** Fighters, boots and Bowies. **Technical:** Grinds A2, 440C and 154CM; matte black oxide finish on fighters. Offers Kydex sheaths. **Prices:** $60 to $200; some to $400. **Remarks:** Full-time maker; first knife sold in 1975. **Mark:** First initial, last name.

PRICE, JOEL HIRAM, RR1, Box 18GG, Interlochen, FL 32148-9709
Specialties: Working straight knives to customer specs. **Patterns:** Variety of straight knives. **Technical:** Forges and grinds W2, 01, D2 and 440C—customer choice; buys Damascus. All knives have filework. **Prices:** $50 to $250; some $750 and higher. **Remarks:** Full-time maker; first knife sold in 1984. **Mark:** Hiram Knives in script.

PRICE, STEVE, 899 Ida Lane, Kamloops, BC V2B 6V2, CANADA/604-579-8932
Specialties: Working knives and fantasy pieces of his design or to customer specs. **Patterns:** Hunters, axes, tantos, survival knives, locking folders and some miniatures. **Technical:** Grinds D2, 440C and ATS-34; buys Damascus. **Prices:** $90 to $350; some to $1,200. **Remarks:** Full-time maker; first knife sold in 1982. **Mark:** First initial, last name.

PRINCE, JOE R,, 5406 Reidville Rd., Moore, SC 29369/803-576-7479
Specialties: Traditional straight knives and folders of his design. **Patterns:** Boots and locking folders. **Technical:** Grinds ATS-34 and 154CM. **Prices:** $100 to $500. **Remarks:** Part-time maker; first knife sold in 1975. **Mark:** Last name.

PRITCHARD, RON, 613 Crawford Ave., Dixon, IL 61021/815-284-6005
Specialties: Plain and fancy working knives. **Patterns:** Variety of straight knives, locking folders, interframes and miniatures. **Technical:** Grinds 440C, 154CM and commercial Damascus. **Prices:** $100 to $200; some to $1,500. **Remarks:** Part-time maker; first knife sold in 1979. **Mark:** Name and city.

PROVENZANO, JOSEPH D., 3024 Ivy Place, Chalmette, LA 70043/504-279-3154
Specialties: Working straight knives in standard patterns. **Patterns:** Hunters with hollow-grinds, Bowies, camp and fishing knives. **Technical:** Grinds ATS-34, 440C and 154CM. **Prices:** $60 to $300; some to $500. **Remarks:** Part-time maker; first knife sold in 1980. **Mark:** Joe-Pro.

PUGH, JIM, P.O. Box 711, Azle, TX 76020/817-444-2679; FAX: 817-444-5455
Specialties: 25th Anniversary limited editions—5" fancy-filed etched Bowie with sterling silver guard, and "grizzly" head, coco bolo handle; 7" fancy-filed eched Bowie with sterling silver guard, three fancy filed spacers, "grizzly" head. Six blue/white/blue fiber spacers and ivory handle on the Deluxe model. **Patterns:** Hunters, Bowies, daggers and fighters. Makes some commemoratives and designs animal heads for buttcaps and paws or bear claws for guards. **Technical:** Grinds 440C and ATS-34; casts guards and buttcaps in bronze, synthetic gold, silver and 14K gold, all engraving by wife Raymonde. **Prices:** $500 to $5,500; some to $20,000. **Remarks:** Full-time maker; first knife sold in 1970. **Mark:** Last name.

PULLEN, MARTIN, 813 Broken Bow WHH, Granbury, TX 76049/817-573-1784
Specialties: Working straight knives; period pieces. **Patterns:** Fighters, Bowies and daggers; locking folders. **Technical:** Grinds D2, 440C, ATS-34 and 154CM. **Prices:** Start at $150. **Remarks:** Spare-time maker; first knife sold in 1978. **Mark:** Last name.

PULLIAM, MORRIS C., 560 Jeptha Knob Rd., Shelbyville, KY 40065/502-633-2261; FAX: 502-633-5294.
Specialties: Working knives; period pieces. **Patterns:** Hunters, tomahawks, buckskinners, Bowies. Makes slip-joint folders only by request. **Technical:** 01, L6, 1095, 52100, 5160 and nickel-sheet and bar Damascus. **Prices:** $165 to $1,200. **Remarks:** Full-time maker; first knife sold in 1974. Doing business as Knob Hill Forge. **Mark:** Last name or last initial with JS.

PURSLEY, AARON, Box 1037, Big Sandy, MT 59520/406-378-3200
Specialties: Fancy working knives. **Patterns:** Locking folders, straight hunters and daggers, personal wedding knives and letter openers. **Technical:** Grinds 01 and 440C; engraves. **Prices:** $300 to $600; some to $1,500. **Remarks:** Full-time maker; first knife sold in 1975. **Mark:** Initials connected with year.

directory

PUTNAM, DONALD S., 590 Wolcott Hill Rd., Wethersfield, CT 06109/203-563-0721; FAX: 203-563-9718
Specialties: Working knives for the hunter and fisherman. **Patterns:** His design or to customer specs. **Technical:** Uses stock removal method, 01, W2, D2, ATS-34, 154CM; stainless steel Damascus on request. **Prices:** NA. **Remarks:** Full-time maker; first knife sold in 1985. **Mark:** Last name with a knife outline.

q

QUALITY CUSTOM KNIVES (See Fisher, Jay)

QUARTON, BARR, P.O. Box 4335, McCall, ID 83638/208-634-3641
Specialties: Plain and fancy working knives; period pieces. **Patterns:** Hunters, tantos and swords. **Technical:** Forges and grinds 154CM, ATS-34 and his own Damascus. **Prices:** $180 to $450; some to $4,500. **Remarks:** Full-time maker; first knife sold in 1978. Doing business as Barr Custom Knives and Deer Creek Forge. **Mark:** First name with bear logo.

QUATTLEBAUM, CRAIG, P.O. Box 983, Searcy, AR 72145-0983
Specialties: Traditional working straight knives, fancy Bowies and one-of-a-kind knives of his design or to customer specs. **Patterns:** Hunters, Bowies and fighters; period pieces. **Technical:** Forges 5168, 52100 and own Damascus. **Prices:** $100 to $600. **Remarks:** Part-time maker; first knife sold in 1988. **Mark:** Stylized initials.

r

RADOS, JERRY F., P.O. Box 531, Grant Park, IL 60940/815-472-3350; FAX: 815-472-3944
Specialties: Deluxe period pieces. **Patterns:** Hunters, fighters, locking folders, daggers and camp knives. **Technical:** Forges and grinds his own Damascus which he sells commercially; makes pattern-welded Turkish Damascus. **Prices:** Start at $900. **Remarks:** Full-time maker; first knife sold in 1981. **Mark:** Last name.

RAFTER KK CUSTOM KNIVES (See Kimsey, Kevin)

RAGSDALE, JAMES D., 3002 Arabian Woods Dr., Lithonia, GA 30038/404-482-6739
Specialties: Fancy and embellished working knives of his design or to customer specs. **Patterns:** Hunters, folders and fighters. **Technical:** Grinds 440C, ATS-34 and A2. **Prices:** $100 to $350; some to $800. **Remarks:** Full-time maker; first knife sold in 1984. **Mark:** Initials connected with fish symbol.

RAHN, JOHN, 323 Concordia Cres, Waterloo, Ont., N2K 2M2 CANADA/519-886-7109
Specialties: Fancy and fantasy straight knives of his design. **Patterns:** Boots, daggers and fighters. **Technical:** Flat-grinds 440C, ATS-34 and 420. Hand files; uses natural handle materials including semi-precious and precious stone inlays. Heat-treats. **Prices:** $200 to $1,000; some to $2,000. **Remarks:** Part-time maker; first knife sold in 1990. **Mark:** First initial, last name.

RAINVILLE, RICHARD, 126 Cockle Hill Rd., Salem, CT 06420/203-859-2776
Specialties: Traditional working straight knives. **Patterns:** Outdoor knives, including fishing knives. **Technical:** Grinds 01, L6, 400C, ATS-34, 154CM. Custom fits handles. **Prices:** $85 to $600. **Remarks:** Part-time maker; first knife sold in 1982. **Mark:** Name, city, state in oval logo.

RALPH, DARREL, 7032 E. Livingston Ave., Renoldsburg, OH 43068/614-577-1040; FAX: 614-252-0173
Specialties: Fancy, high-art and fantasy knives of his design and to customer specs; straight knives and folders. **Patterns:** Boots, Bowies, daggers, fighters, hunters, locking folders, swords, collectibles. **Technical:** Forges Damascus, 01, D2; grinds 440C, ATS-34. Hand-finishes all blades. Offers filework, scrimshaw, engraving. Likes pearl and abolone handle materials; uses stones and jewels. **Prices:** $190 to $900; some to $10,000. **Remarks:** Part-time maker; first knife sold in 1986. Doing business as Briar Knives. **Mark:** Briar Custom Made.

RAMBO, J.T., 113 Weber T.R.V., Rock Springs, WY 82901/307-382-6912
Specialties: Working straight knives and folders of his design or to customer specs.
Patterns: Hunters, Bowies, fighters, skinners, fillets and sword canes. **Technical:** Stock removal method. Grinds 440C and commercial Damascus; uses other steels on request. Prefers natural handle materials. **Prices:** $150 to $1,000; some to $2,500. **Remarks:** First knife sold in 1986. **Mark:** First and middle initials, last name logo.

RAMEY, MARSHALL F., P.O. Box 2589, West Helena, AR 72390/501-572-1831
Specialties: Traditional working knives. **Patterns:** Designs military combat knives; makes butterfly folders, camp knives and miniatures. **Technical:** Grinds D2 and 440C. **Prices:** $100 to $200; some to $300. **Remarks:** Full-time maker; first knife sold in 1978. **Mark:** Name with ram's head.

RANDALL MADE KNIVES, P.O. Box 1988, Orlando, FL 32802/407-855-8075
Specialties: Working straight knives. **Patterns:** Hunters, fighters and Bowies. **Technical:** Forges and grinds 01 and 440C. **Prices:** $65 to $250; some to $450. **Remarks:** Full-time maker; first knife sold in 1937. **Mark:** Randall, city and state in scimitar logo.

RANKL, CHRISTIAN, Possenhofenerstr. 33, 81476 München, GERMANY/089-7594442; FAX: 089-7594442
Specialties: Tail-lock knives. **Patterns:** Fighters, hunters and locking folders. **Technical:** Grinds ATS-34, 4034 and stainless Damascus by F. Schneider. **Prices:** $450 to $950; some to $2,000. **Remarks:** Full-time maker; first knife sold in 1989. **Mark:** Electrochemical etching on blade.

RAPP, STEVEN J., 3437 Crestfield Dr., Salt Lake City, UT 84119/801-966-5595
Specialties: Fancy straight hunters; period pieces. **Patterns:** Gold Rush-era cutlery. **Technical:** Grinds 440C and Damascus bars. **Prices:** $200 to $3,500. **Remarks:** Part-time maker; first knife sold in 1981. **Mark:** Name and state.

RAPPAZZO, RICHARD, 142 Dunsbach Ferry Rd., Cohoes, NY 12047/518-783-6843
Specialties: Damascus locking folders and straight knives. **Patterns:** Folders, dirks, fighters and tantos in original and traditional designs. **Technical:** Hand-forges all blades; specializes in Damascus; uses only natural handle materials. **Prices:** $400 to $1,500. **Remarks:** Part-time maker; first knife sold in 1985. **Mark:** Name, date, serial number.

RARDON, A.D., Rt. 1, Box 79, Polo, MO 64671/816-354-2330
Specialties: Working knives, mostly folders. **Patterns:** Hunters, buckskinners, Bowies and daggers. **Technical:** Grinds 01, D2, 440C and ATS-34. **Prices:** $100 to $500; some to $1,000. **Remarks:** Part-time maker; first knife sold in 1954. **Mark:** Name, address in running fox logo.

RARDON, ARCHIE F., Rt. 1, Box 79, Polo, MO 64671/816-354-2330
Specialties: Working knives. **Patterns:** Hunters, Bowies and miniatures. **Technical:** Grinds 01, D2, 440C, ATS-34, cable and Damascus. **Prices:** $50 to $500. **Remarks:** Part-time maker. **Mark:** Name and address in razor-back hog logo.

RATTLER BRAND KNIVES (See Selvidio, Ralph J.)

RAY, ALAN W., P.O. Box 479, Lovelady, TX 75851/409-636-2301
Specialties: Working straight knives and folders of his design. **Patterns:** Hunters, camp knives, folders, steak knives and carving sets. **Technical:** Forges L6 and 5160 for straight knives; grinds D2 and 440C for folders and kitchen cutlery. **Prices:** $200 to $500. **Remarks:** Full-time maker; first knife sold in 1989. **Mark:** Stylized initials.

RAYMOND, DONALD, P.O. Box 1141, Groveton, TX 75845/409-642-1707
Specialties: Traditional working and using straight knives and folders of his design and to customer specs. **Patterns:** Fighters, hunters, kitchen knives and locking folders. **Technical:** Grinds 440C and D2; forges his own Damascus. **Prices:** $150 to $550; some to $850. **Remarks:** Full-time maker; first knife sold in 1988. Doing business as DR Knives. **Mark:** Stylized initials.

RAYMOND, MARY JANE, P.O. Box 1141, Groveton, TX 75845/408-642-1707
Specialties: Traditional working and using straight knives and folders of her design. **Patterns:** Hunters, locking folders and slip-joint folders. **Technical:** Grinds 440C, D2 and Donald Raymond Damascus. Makes sheaths. **Prices:** $150 to $400; some to $600. **Remarks:** Full-time maker; first knife sold in 1989. Doing business as M.J.R. Knives. **Mark:** Initials or name.

custom knifemakers

R.D. CUSTOM KNIVES—RICHARDSON

R.D. CUSTOM KNIVES (See Miller, R.D.)

RECE, CHARLES V., 1949 E. Main St., Albemarle, NC 28001/704-982-1178; FAX: 704-982-1178. **Specialties:** Bowies, hunters and presentation knives. **Technical:** Grinds ATS-34, D2 and 440C. Scrimshawed handles are standard. **Prices:** $150 to $400. **Remarks:** Limited-production maker; first knife sold in 1986. Doing business as Uwharrie Rattler Knives and Wildwood Studios. **Mark:** Engraved timber rattler.

REDDIEX, BILL, 27 Galway Ave., Palmerston North, NEW ZEALAND/06-357-0383; FAX: 06-358-2910. **Specialties:** Collector-grade working straight knives. **Patterns:** Traditional-style Bowies and drop-point hunters. **Technical:** Grinds 440C, D2 and 01; offers variety of grinds and finishes. **Prices:** $130 to $750. **Remarks:** Full-time maker; first knife sold in 1980. **Mark:** Last name around kiwi bird logo.

REDUCED REALITY (See Heasman, H.G.)

REE, DAVID, 816 Main St., Van Buren, AR 72956/501-474-3198. **Specialties:** Fancy working knives. **Patterns:** Hunters, locking folders and boots. **Technical:** Grinds 01, D2 and 440C; prefers exotic and unusual handle materials. **Prices:** $125 to $400; some to $900. **Remarks:** Full-time maker; first knife sold in 1982. Doing business as Old Town Cutlery. **Mark:** Last name.

REED, DAVE, Box 132, Brimfield, MA 01010/413-245-3661. **Specialties:** Traditional styles. Makes knives from chains, rasps, gears, etc. **Patterns:** Bush swords, hunters, working minis, camp and utility knives. **Technical:** Forges 1075 and his own Damascus. **Prices:** Start at $50. **Remarks:** Part-time maker; first knife sold in 1970. **Mark:** Initials.

REED, DEL, 13765 SW Parkway, Beaverton, OR 97005. **Specialties:** Unusual configurations. **Patterns:** Swing-blade knives. **Technical:** Grinds stainless steel. **Prices:** $100 to $125. **Remarks:** First knife sold in 1988. **Mark:** ORION.

REEVE, CHRIS, 6147 Corporal Lane, Boise, ID 83704/208-375-0367. **Specialties:** Strongest working folder on the market; one-piece utility/military fixed blades. **Patterns:** Working and art folders; variety of fixed-blade shapes in one-piece design. Availability of art pieces very limited. **Technical:** Grinds folder blades of ATS-34, mostly titanium handles; A2 for fixed blades. Art knives ATS-34 or Damascus blades, titanium or exotic handle material. **Prices:** $165 to $800; some to $4,000. **Remarks:** Full-time maker; first knife sold in 1982. **Mark:** Initials connected.

REEVES, JAMES GARY, 416 Delta Ct., Gardondale, AL 35071/205-631-4861. **Specialties:** Working straight knives in his design and standard patterns. **Patterns:** Bowies, fighters and hunters. **Technical:** Grinds ATS-34; forges and grinds 5160. **Prices:** $75 to $450. **Remarks:** Part-time maker; first knife sold in 1987. **Mark:** First and middle initials, last name, city, state.

REEVES, WINFRED M., P.O. Box 300, West Union, SC 29696/803-638-6121. **Specialties:** Working straight knives; some elaborate pieces. **Patterns:** Hunters, tantos and fishing knives. **Technical:** Grinds D2, 440C and ATS-34. Does not solder joints; does not use buffer unless requested. **Prices:** $75 to $150; some to $300. **Remarks:** Part-time maker; first knife sold in 1975. **Mark:** Last name, Walhalla, state.

REMINGTON, DAVID W., 3608-17998 Syble Rd., Lincoln, AR 72744/501-846-3526. **Specialties:** Fancy and traditional straight knives of his design and to customer specs. **Patterns:** Bowies, daggers and hunters. **Technical:** Grinds ATS-34, A2 and D2. Makes own twist and random-pattern Damascus. Whole sale D-2, A-2, stag and ossic sheephorn. Rope and thorn pattern filework; tapered tangs.; heat treats. **Prices:** $65 to $250; some to $1,000. **Remarks:** Part-time maker; first knife sold in 1991. **Mark:** First and last name, Custom.

RENNER, TERRY LEE, P.O. Box 15063, Bradenton, FL 34209/813-798-3989. **Specialties:** Fancy working straight knives and folders. **Patterns:** Hunters, game sets, fillets and miniatures. **Technical:** Grinds 440C, D2 and 01. Folders have unique integral blade lock, lightest carry weight. Deep-relief carved stag handles. **Prices:** $95 to $450; some higher. **Remarks:** Part-time maker; first knife sold in 1975. Doing business as Firepoint Knives. **Mark:** Initials with star.

REPKE, MIKE (See Neering, Walt and Repke, Mike)

REVERDY, PIERRE, 21 AV Victor Hugo, 26100 Romans, FRANCE/33-75-05-10-15; FAX: 33-75-02-28-40. **Specialties:** One-of-a-kind knives. **Patterns:** Daggers, Bowies, hunters and other large patterns. **Technical:** Forges his Damascus and "poetique Damascus"; works with his own EDM machine to create any kind of pattern inside the steel with his own touch. **Prices:** $200 to $40,000. **Remarks:** Full-time maker; first knife sold in 1986. **Mark:** Initials connected.

REXROAT, KIRK, 527 Sweetwater Circle, Box 224, Wright, WY 82732/307-464-0166. **Specialties:** Traditional working/using straight knives and folders of his design and to customer specs. **Patterns:** Bowies, hunters, locking folders, utility/camp knives. **Technical:** Grinds 440C; forges cable and layered Damascus; triple quenches 52100. Offers tapered tangs and dove-tailed guards. **Prices:** $100 to $250; some to $800. **Remarks:** Part-time maker; first knife sold in 1984. Doing business as Rexroat Knives. **Mark:** First initial, last name, city, state.

REYNOLDS, DAVE, Rt. 2, Box 36, Harrisville, WV 26362/304-643-2889. **Specialties:** Working straight knives of his design. **Patterns:** Bowies, kitchen and utility knives. **Technical:** Grinds and forges L6, 1095 and 440C. Heat-treats. **Prices:** $50 to $85; some to $175. **Remarks:** Full-time maker; first knife sold in 1980. Doing business as Terra-Gladius Knives. **Mark:** Terra-Gladius over oval with mountains and sword logo.

REYNOLDS, JOHN C., #2 Andover, HC77, Gillette, WY 82716/307-682-6076. **Specialties:** Working knives, some fancy. **Patterns:** Hunters, Bowies, tomahawks and buckskinners; some folders. **Technical:** Grinds D2, 440C and commerical Damascus. Scrimshaws. **Prices:** $100 to $320; some to $3,000. **Remarks:** Spare-time maker; first knife sold in 1969. **Mark:** Last name.

RHEA, DAVID, Rt. 1, Box 272, Lynnville, TN 38472/615-363-5993. **Specialties:** High-art fantasy knives. **Patterns:** Fighters, Bowies, survival knives and locking folders. **Technical:** Grinds D2, 440C, 154CM and Damascus. Embellishes; offers precious stones, metals and ivory. **Prices:** $300 to $2,000 and higher. **Remarks:** Part-time maker; first knife sold in 1982. **Mark:** Last name.

RHO, NESTOR LORENZO, Primera Junta 589, Junin (6000), Buenos Aires, ARGENTINA/(0362) 32247/21717. **Specialties:** Classic and fancy straight knives of his design. **Patterns:** Bowies, fighters and hunters. **Technical:** Grinds 420C, 440C and 1050. Offers semi-precious stones on handles, acid etching on blades and blade engraving. **Prices:** $60 to $300 some to $1,200. **Remarks:** Full-time maker; first knife sold in 1975. **Mark:** Name.

RHODES, JAMES D., 205 Woodpoint Ave., Hagerstown, MD 21740/301-739-2657. **Specialties:** Traditional working and using straight knives of his design. **Patterns:** Bowies, fighters, hunters and kitchen knives. **Technical:** Forges 5160, 1085 and 9260; makes own Damascus. Hard edges, soft backs, dead soft tangs. Heat-treats. **Prices:** $150 to $350. **Remarks:** Part-time maker. **Mark:** Last name, JS.

RIAL, DOUGLAS, Rt. 2, Box 117A, Greenfield, TN 38230/901-235-3994. **Specialties:** Working knives to customer specs; period pieces. **Patterns:** Hunters, fighters, boots, locking folders, slip-joints and miniatures. **Technical:** Grinds D2, 440C and 154CM. **Prices:** $60 to $100; some to $250. **Remarks:** Spare-time maker; first knife sold in 1978. **Mark:** Name and city.

RICE, ADRIENNE, P.O. Box 252, Lopez Island, WA 98261. **Specialties:** Marine-oriented knives; working straight knives. **Patterns:** Full line of working knives including skinners, fillets, rigging knives and kitchen knives. Occasionally makes fighters, tantos, short swords and primitive knives. **Technical:** Grinds ATS-34, D2 and 01; forges occasionally. **Prices:** $135 to $225. **Remarks:** Full-time maker; first knife sold in 1981. Doing business as Madrona Knives. **Mark:** Initials connected in Madrona logo with date.

RICHARD, RON, 4875 Calaveras Ave., Fremont, CA 94538/510-796-9767. **Specialties:** High-tech working straight knives of his design. **Patterns:** Bowies, swords and locking folders. **Technical:** Forges and grinds ATS-34, 154CM and 440V. All folders have dead-bolt button locks. **Prices:** $650 to $850; some to $1,400. **Remarks:** Full-time maker; first knife sold in 1968. **Mark:** Full name.

RICHARDSON JR., PERCY, P.O. Box 4, Milam, TX 75959/409-625-3415

FIFTEENTH EDITION **255**

directory
RICHTER FORGE—ROLLERT

Specialties: Traditional and working straight knives and folders in customer specs and standard patterns. **Patterns:** Bowies, daggers, hunters, locking folders, slip-joints and utility/camp knives. **Technical:** Grinds ATS-34, 440C and D2. **Prices:** $125 to $600; some to $1,800. **Remarks:** Full-time maker; first knife sold in 1990. Doing business as Lone Star Custom Knives. **Mark:** Lone Star with stylized last initial.

RICHTER FORGE (See Richter, John C.)

RICHTER, JOHN C., 932 Bowling Green Trail, Chesapeake, VA 23320
Specialties: Hand-forged knives in original patterns. **Patterns:** Hunters, fighters, utility knives and other belt knives, folders, swords. **Technical:** Hand-forges high carbon and his own Damascus; makes mokume gane. **Prices:** $75 to $1,500. **Remarks:** Part-time maker. **Mark:** Richter Forge.

RICHTER, SCOTT, 31 Broadway, Watertown, MA 02172

RICKE, DAVE, 1209 Adams, West Bend, WI 53095/414-334-5739
Specialties: Working knives; period pieces. **Patterns:** Hunters, boots, Bowies; locking folders and slip-joints. **Technical:** Grinds ATS-34, A2, 440C and 154CM. **Prices:** $75 to $260; some to $500. **Remarks:** Part-time maker; first knife sold in 1976. **Mark:** Last name.

RIETVELD, BERTIE, P.O. Box 53, Magaliesburg 2805, SOUTH AFRICA/27142-771294
Specialties: Damascus fighters, art daggers and button-lock folders. **Technical:** Damascus, titanium, gold inlay and colored stainless steel. **Prices:** $350 to $2,000. **Mark:** Elephant with last name.

RIGNEY, WILLIE, 212 Allen Dr., Somerset, KY 42501/606-679-4227
Specialties: High-tech period pieces and fancy working knives. **Patterns:** Fighters, boots, daggers and push knives. **Technical:** Grinds 440C and 154CM; buys Damascus. Most knives are embellished. **Prices:** $150 to $1,500; some to $10,000. **Remarks:** Full-time maker; first knife sold in 1978. **Mark:** First initial, last name.

RIJSWIJK, AAD VAN, Oberonweg 284, 3208 PG Spijkenisse, HOLLAND/(0)1880-40334; FAX: (0)1880-40334
Specialties: High-art interframe folders of his design and in standard patterns. **Patterns:** Hunters and locking folders. **Technical:** ATS-34. Uses semi-precious stones. Handle materials include ivory, mammoth ivory, iron wood. Offers hand-made sheaths. **Prices:** $400 to $1,200; some to $2,000. **Remarks:** Full-time maker; first knife sold in 1993. **Mark:** NA.

RINGING CIRCLE, THE (See Fitzgerald, Dennis M.)

RINKES, SIEGFRIED, Am Sportpl 2, D 91459 Markterlbach, GERMANY

RIPPY, ROBERT, Box 425 (Hwy 19N), Emory, TX 75440/903-473-3690
Specialties: Combat, survival and special operations knives. **Patterns:** Hunters, fighters, utility/camp knives. **Technical:** Grinds ATS-34 and crucible S7. Embellishes. **Prices:** $300 to $750; some higher. **Remarks:** Full-time makers; first knife sold in 1980. **Mark:** Stylized last initial.

RIZZI, RUSSELL J., 6 King Arthur's Ct., E. Setauket, NY 11733/516-689-2698
Specialties: Fancy working and using straight knives and folders of his design or to customer specs. **Patterns:** Hunters, locking folders and fighters. **Technical:** Grinds 440C, D2 and commercial Damascus. **Prices:** $150 to $750; some to $2,500. **Remarks:** Part-time maker; first knife sold in 1990. **Mark:** Last name, Long Island, NY.

RL CUSTOM KNIVES (See Lambert, Ronald S.)

ROATH, DEAN, 3050 Winnipeg Dr., Baton Rouge, LA 70819/504-272-5562
Specialties: Classic working straight knives. **Patterns:** Hunters, boating/sailing and trail knives. **Technical:** Grinds 440C and ATS-34. **Prices:** $150 to $400; some to $1,500. **Remarks:** Part-time maker; first knife sold in 1978. **Mark:** Name, city and state.

ROBBINS, HOWARD P., 875 Rams Horn Rd., Moraine Rt., Estes Park, CO 80517/303-586-8755
Specialties: High-tech working knives with clean designs, some fancy. **Patterns:** Folders, hunters and camp knives. **Technical:** Grinds 440C and ATS-34. Heat-treats; likes mirror finishes. Offers leatherwork. **Prices:** $100 to $500; some to $1,000. **Remarks:** Full-time maker; first knife sold in 1982. **Mark:** Name, city and state.

ROBERTS, CHUCK, 5004 W. 92nd Ave. #207, Westminster, CA 80030/303-650-4563
Specialties: Sheffield-style Bowies. **Patterns:** Bowies, daggers and hunters. **Technical:** Grinds 440C, Damascus and ATS-34. Handles made of stag, ivory or mother-of-pearl; fittings made of nickel or sterling silver. **Prices:** Start at $350. **Remarks:** Full-time maker. **Mark:** Last initial or last name.

ROBERTS, GEORGE A., 149 Mill St., Parkhill Ontario, CANADA/519-294-0267; FAX: 519-294-6391
Specialties: Bowies with special features not offered before. **Patterns:** Bowies, hunters, locking folders and liner locks. **Technical:** Grinds 440C, Boye Dendritic, 01, mild Damascus, 440V. Liners are titanium. Etches, engraves and offers fancy filework on blades; scrimshands and carves handles; makes leather sheaths. **Prices:** $80 to $225; some to $500. **Remarks:** Full-time maker; first knife sold in 1986. Doing business as Bandit Blades. **Mark:** Bandit.

ROBERTS, MICHAEL, 605 Oakwood Dr., Clinton, MS 39056/601-924-3154
Specialties: Working and using knives in standard patterns and to customer specs. **Patterns:** Hunters, Bowies and fighters. **Technical:** Forges 5160, 01, 1095 and his own Damascus. Uses only natural handle materials. **Prices:** $145 to $500; some to $1,100. **Remarks:** Part-time maker; first knife sold in 1988. **Mark:** Last name.

ROBINSON, CHARLES, P.O. Box 221, Vega, TX 79092

ROCHFORD, MICHAEL R., Trollhaugen Ski Area, 2232 100th Ave., Dresser, WI 54009/715-755-3520
Specialties: Working straight knives in standard patterns. **Patterns:** Bowies, fishing and camp knives. **Technical:** Grinds and forges W2, 440C, 154CM and his Damascus. **Prices:** $100 to $500; some to $800. **Remarks:** Part-time maker; first knife sold in 1984. **Mark:** Name.

ROCKY MOUNTAIN KNIVES (See Conklin, George L.)

ROE JR., FRED D., 4005 Granada Dr., Huntsville, AL 35802/205-881-6847
Specialties: Highly finished working knives of his design; period pieces. **Patterns:** Hunters, fighters and survival knives; locking folders; specialty designs like divers' knives. **Technical:** Grinds 154CM, ATS-34 and Damascus. Field-tests all blades. **Prices:** $125 to $250; some to $2,000. **Remarks:** Part-time maker; first knife sold in 1980. **Mark:** Last name.

ROGERS JR., ROBERT P., 3979 South Main St., Acworth, GA 30101/404-974-9982
Specialties: Traditional working knives. **Patterns:** Hunters, 4-inch trailing-points. **Technical:** Grinds D2, 154CM and ATS-34; likes ironwood and ivory Micarta. **Prices:** $65 to $85; some to $125. **Remarks:** Spare-time maker; first knife sold in 1975. **Mark:** Name.

ROGERS, RODNEY, 602 Osceola St., Wildwood, FL 34785/904-748-6114
Specialties: Traditional straight knives. **Patterns:** Bowies, hunters, skinners, fighters and boots. **Technical:** Flat-grinds ATS-34, 440C and D2. Prefers natural materials in full or concealed tangs. **Prices:** $100 to $1,000. **Remarks:** Full-time maker; first knife sold in 1986. **Mark:** Last name, Handmade.

ROHN, FRED, W7615 Clemetson Rd., Coeur d'Alene, ID 83814/208-667-0774
Specialties: Working straight knives, some unusual. **Patterns:** Hunters, fighters, a unique Bowie design and locking folders. **Technical:** Grinds 440C and 154CM; stainless steel pins, bolsters and guards on all knives. **Prices:** $65 to $200; some to $450 and higher. **Remarks:** Part-time maker. **Mark:** Name in logo and serial number.

ROLLERT, STEVE, P.O. Box 65, Keenesburg, CO 80643-0065/303-732-4858
Specialties: Highly finished working knives. **Patterns:** Variety of straight knives; locking folders and slip-joints. **Technical:** Forges and grinds W2, 1095, ATS-34 and his pattern-welded, cable Damascus and nickel Damascus. **Prices:** $300 to $1,000; some to $3,000. **Remarks:** Full-time maker; first knife sold in 1980. Doing business as Dove Knives. **Mark:** Last name in script.

custom knifemakers

ROSS, D.L., 22 Earnscleugh Rd., Alexandra, NZ
Specialties: Hunters, working knives. **Patterns:** Plain using knives. **Technical:** Grinds 440C. **Prices:** $60 to $185. **Remarks:** Full-time maker; first knife sold in 1988. **Mark:** Last name.

ROSS, STEPHEN, P.O. Box 951, Evanston, WY 82930/307-789-7104
Specialties: Working straight knives and folders; some fantasy pieces. **Patterns:** Combat and survival knives, hunters, boots and folders. **Technical:** Grinds ATS-34, D2 and 440C. Offers Kydex sheaths, checkering on knife handles, integral guards and variety of grinds. **Prices:** $160 to $3,000. **Remarks:** Part-time maker; first knife sold in 1971. **Mark:** Last name.

ROSS, TIM, 3239 Oliver Rd., RR #17, Thunder Bay, ON P7B 6C2, CANADA/807-935-2667
Specialties: Fancy working knives of his design. **Patterns:** Fishing and hunting knives, Bowies, daggers and miniatures. **Technical:** Uses D2, Stellite 6K and 440C; forges 52100 and Damascus. Makes antler handles and sheaths; has supply of whale teeth and moose antlers for trade. Prefers natural materials only. Wife Katherine scrimshaws. **Prices:** $100 to $350; some to $2,100. **Remarks:** Part-time maker; first knife sold in 1975. **Mark:** Last name stamped on tang.

ROTELLA, RICHARD A., 643—75th St., Niagara Falls, NY 14304
Specialties: Working knives of his design. **Patterns:** Various fishing, hunting and utility knives; folders. **Technical:** Grinds ATS-34. Prefers hand-rubbed finishes. **Prices:** $65 to $450; some to $900. **Remarks:** Spare-time maker; first knife sold in 1977. **Mark:** Name and city in stylized waterfall logo.

ROWE, STEWART G., 8-18 Coreen Court, Karana Downs, Mt. Crosby, Brisbane 4306, AUSTRALIA
Specialties: Designer knives—reproduction of ancient weaponry, traditional Japanese tantos and edged tools. **Patterns:** Traditional Japanese tantos, daggers, working knives and swords. **Technical:** Forges W1, W2, D2; creates own Tamahagne steel and pattern-welded billets. **Prices:** $300 to $11,000. **Remarks:** Full-time maker; first knife sold in 1981. Doing business as House of Kogatana. **Mark:** Kogatana.

RP KNIVES (See Parrish, Robert)

RUA, GARY (WOLF), 541 Osborn St., Fall River, MA 02724/508-677-2373
Specialties: Working knives of his design; 18th and 19th century period pieces. **Patterns:** Bowies, hunters, fighters, buckskinners and patch knives. **Technical:** Forges 5160, 1095, old files; uses only natural handle materials. **Prices:** $100 to $500; some to $1,000. **Remarks:** Part-time maker. Doing business as Harvest Moon Forge. **Mark:** Last name.

RUANA KNIFE WORKS, Box 520, Bonner, MT 59823/406-258-5368
Specialties: Working knives and period pieces. **Patterns:** Variety of straight knives. **Technical:** Forges 5160 chrome alloy for Bowies and 1095. **Prices:** $60 to $240; some to $300 and higher. **Remarks:** Full-time maker; first knife sold in 1938. **Mark:** Name.

RUBLEY, JAMES A., 5765 N. 500 W., Angola, IN 46703/219-833-1255
Specialties: Working American knives and collectibles for hunters, buckskinners and re-enactment groups from Pre-Revolutionary War through the Civil War. **Patterns:** Anything authentic, barring folders. **Technical:** Iron fittings, natural materials; forges files. **Prices:** $175 to $2,500. **Remarks:** Museum consultant and blacksmith for two decades. Offers classes in beginning, intermediate and advanced traditional knifemaking. **Mark:** Lightning bolt.

RUBY MOUNTAIN KNIVES (See Schirmer, Mike)

RUPERT, ROBERT, RD 1, Box 220, Clinton, PA 15026/412-573-4569

RUPLE, WILLIAM H., P.O. Box 370, Charlotte, TX 78011/210-277-1371
Specialties: Traditional working and using straight knives and folders in standard patterns. **Patterns:** Hunters, locking folders and slip-joint folders. **Technical:** Grinds 440C, ATS-34 and D2. Offers filework on blade and spring. **Prices:** $100 to $300; some to $500. **Remarks:** Full-time maker; first knife sold in 1988. **Mark:** Last name.

RUSSELL, A.G., 1705 Hwy. 71 N., Springdale, AR 72764/501-751-7341
Specialties: Morseth knives; contemporary working knives. **Patterns:** Hunters and Bowies; personal utility knives in Morseth line, drop-points and boots in Russell line. **Technical:** Laminated blades in Morseth line; modern stainless steel in Russell line; classic shapes. **Prices:** Moderate. **Remarks:** Old name still at work. Doing business as Morseth Sports Equip. Co. **Mark:** Morseth or first and middle initials, last name.

RUSSELL, MICK, 4 Rossini Rd., Pari Park, Port Elizabeth 6070, SOUTH AFRICA
Specialties: Art knives. **Patterns:** Working and collectible bird, trout and hunting knives, defense knives and folders. **Technical:** Grinds D2, 440C, ATS-34 and Damascus. Offers mirror or satin finishes. Uses nickel silver, 303 stainless and titanium fittings and a wide variety of African hardwoods; ivory, buffalo and antelope horn and bone handle materials. **Remarks:** Full-time maker; first knife sold in 1986.

RUSSELL, TOM, 6500 New Liberty Rd., Jacksonville, AL 36265/205-492-7866
Specialties: Straight working knives of his design or to customer specs. **Patterns:** Hunters, folders, fighters, skinners, Bowies and utility knives. **Technical:** Grinds D2, 440C and ATS-34; offers filework. **Prices:** $75 to $225. **Remarks:** Part-time maker; first knife sold in 1987. Full-time tool and die maker. **Mark:** Last name with tulip stamp.

RUST, CHARLES C., P.O. Box 374, Palermo, CA 95968/916-533-9389
Specialties: Working knives, some fancy; period pieces. **Patterns:** Hunters, Bowies, buckskinners, sets. **Technical:** All work done by hand; low production. **Prices:** $125 to $2,000; some to $3,500. **Remarks:** Full-time maker; first knife sold in 1972. Not currently taking orders. **Mark:** Rustway in logo.

RUSTWAY (See Rust, Charles C.)

RV KNIVES (See Vunk, Robert)

RYAN, C.O., 902-A Old Wormley Creek Rd., Yorktown, VA 23692/804-898-7797
Specialties: Working/using knives. **Patterns:** Hunters, kitchen knives, locking folders. **Technical:** Grinds 440C and ATS-34. **Prices:** $45 to $130; some to $450. **Remarks:** Part-time maker; first knife sold in 1980. **Mark:** Name.

RYAN, J.C., Rt. 5, Box 183-A, Lexington, VA 24450/703-348-5014

RYDER, BEN M., P.O. Box 133, Copperhill, TN 37317/615-496-2750
Specialties: Working/using straight knives of his design and to customer specs. **Patterns:** Fighters, hunters, utility/camp knives. **Technical:** Grinds 440C, ATS-34, D2, commercial Damascus. **Prices:** $75 to $400. **Remarks:** Part-time maker; first knife sold in 1992. **Mark:** Full name in double butterfly logo.

S

SAINDON, R. BILL, 11 Highland View Rd., Claremont, NH 03743/603-542-9418
Specialties: Fancy folders, straight blades for work and collecting. **Patterns:** Lockbacks and boot knives of his design or to customer specs. **Technical:** Forges 01 and 1095; makes own Damascus with tool steel and nickel; fancy files original patterns. **Prices:** $200 to $500; some to $1,000. **Remarks:** Full-time maker; first knife sold in 1981. Doing business as Daynia Forge. **Mark:** Sun logo.

SAKMAR, MIKE, 1670 Morley, Rochester, MI 48307/810-852-6775
Specialties: Fancy and working straight knives of his design and to customer specs. **Patterns:** Bowies, fighters and hunters. **Technical:** Grinds ATS-34, Damascus and high-carbon tool steels. Uses mostly natural handle materials—elephant ivory, walrus, ivory stag, wildwood, oosic, etc. **Prices:** $150 to $1,500; some to $2,500. **Remarks:** Part-time maker; first knife sold in 1990. **Mark:** Last name, year.

SALAMANDER ARMOURY (See Hrisoulas, Jim)

SAKAKIBARA, MASAKI, 20-8 Sakuragaoka, 2-Chome Setagaya-ku, Tokyo 156, JAPAN/03-420-0375

SALLEY, JOHN D., 3965 Frederick-Ginghamsburg Rd., Tipp City, OH 45371/513-698-4588
Specialties: Fancy working knives and art pieces. **Patterns:** Hunters, fighters, daggers and some swords. **Technical:** Grinds ATS-34, 12C27 and W2; buys Damascus. **Prices:** $85 to $1,000; some to $6,000. **Remarks:** Part-time maker; first knife sold in 1979. **Mark:** First initial, last name.

directory
SAMBAR CUSTOM KNIVES—SCHNEIDER

SAMBAR CUSTOM KNIVES (See Giljevic, Branko)

SAMPSON, LYNN, 381 Deakins Rd., Jonesborough, TN 37659/615-348-8373
Specialties: Highly finished working knives, mostly folders. **Patterns:** Locking folders, slip-joints, interframes and two-blades. **Technical:** Grinds D2, 440C and ATS-34; offers extensive filework. **Prices:** Start at $300. **Remarks:** Full-time maker; first knife sold in 1982. **Mark:** Name and city in logo.

SANDERS, A.A., 3850 72 Ave. NE, Norman, OK 73071/405-364-8660
Specialties: Working straight knives and folders. **Patterns:** Hunters, fighters, daggers and Bowies. **Technical:** Forges his own Damascus; offers stock removal with ATS-34, 440C, A2, D2, 01, 5160 and 1095. **Prices:** $85 to $1,500. **Remarks:** Full-time maker; first knife sold in 1985. Formerly known as Athern Forge. **Mark:** Name.

SANDERS, BILL, 335 Bauer Ave., P.O. Box 957, Mancos, CO 81328/303-533-7223
Specialties: Working straight knives, some fancy and some fantasy, of his design. **Patterns:** Hunters, boots, utility knives, using belt knives. **Technical:** Grinds 440C, ATS-34 and commercial Damascus. Provides wide variety of handle materials. **Prices:** $170 to $350; some to $800. **Remarks:** Full-time maker. **Mark:** Name, city and state.

SANDERS, MICHAEL M., P.O. Box 1106, Ponchatoula, LA 70454/504-294-3601
Specialties: Working straight knives and folders, some deluxe. **Patterns:** Hunters, fighters, Bowies, daggers, large folders and deluxe Damascus miniatures. **Technical:** Grinds 01, D2, 440C, ATS-34 and Damascus. **Prices:** $75 to $650; some higher. **Remarks:** Full-time maker; first knife sold in 1967. **Mark:** Name and state.

SANDERSON, RAY, 4403 Uplands Way, Yakima, WA 98908/509-965-0128
Specialties: One-of-a-kind Buck knives; traditonal working straight knives and folders of his design. **Patterns:** Bowies, hunters and fighters. **Technical:** Grinds 440C and ATS-34. **Prices:** $200 to $750. **Remarks:** Part-time maker; first knife sold in 1984. **Mark:** Sanderson Knives in shape of Bowie.

SANDLIN, LARRY, 4580 Sunday Dr., Adamsville, AL 35005

SASSER, JIM, 926 Jackson, Pueblo, CO 81004
Specialties: Working straight knives and folders of his design. **Patterns:** Makes elk hunters' tools, axes, camp knives, a variety of folders and limited editions. **Technical:** Grinds ATS-34. **Prices:** $75 to $300; some to $800. **Remarks:** Full-time maker; first knife sold in 1970. **Mark:** Last name or full name in circle.

SAWBY, SCOTT, 400 W. Center Valley Rd., Sandpoint, ID 83864/208-263-4171
Specialties: Folders, working and fancy. **Patterns:** Locking folders, patent locking systems and interframes. **Technical:** Grinds D2, 440C, 154CM, CPM T440V and ATS-34. **Prices:** $400 to $1,000. **Remarks:** Full-time maker; first knife sold in 1974. **Mark:** Last name, city and state.

SAYEN, MURAD, P.O. Box 127, Bryant Pond, ME 04219/207-665-2224
Specialties: Carved handles. **Patterns:** Fighters, boots, Bowies, daggers and fantasy knives. **Technical:** Forges carbon and Damascus steel only. Handles carved and inlaid, some with stones. **Prices:** $750 to $5,000. **Remarks:** Full-time maker; first knife sold in 1977. Doing business as Kemal. **Mark:** Last name with date.

SCARROW, LIN, c/o L&W Mail Service, 16236 Chicago Ave., Bellflower, CA 90706/310-866-6384
Specialties: Working knives with flowing patterns. **Technical:** Grinds and forges 52100, D2, stainless steel and high-carbon metals. Offers occasional filework. **Prices:** Start at $75. **Remarks:** Part-time maker; first knife sold in 1991. **Mark:** First name, date.

SCARROW, WILL, c/o L&W Mail Service, 16236 Chicago Ave., Bellflower, CA 90706/310-866-6384
Specialties: Working straight knives in standard patterns or to customer specs. **Patterns:** Hunters, fisherman's, skinners, swords and Bowies. **Technical:** Forges and grinds W1, W2, 5160, 1095, 440C, AEB-L, ATS-34 and other steels on request; offers some filework. **Prices:** $65 to $300; some higher. **Remarks:** Part-time maker; first knife sold in 1983. Doing business as Gold Hill Knife Works. **Mark:** SC with arrow and year made.

SCHALLER, ANTHONY B., 5609 Flint Ct. NW, Albuquerque, NM 87120/505-899-0155
Specialties: Traditional working/using straight knives of his design and in standard patterns. **Patterns:** Boots, daggers, hunters. **Technical:** Grind s440C, ATS-34. Offers filework, mirror finishes and full and narrow tangs. Prefers exotic woods or Micarta for handle materials. **Prices:** $70 to $160; some to $250. **Remarks:** Part-time maker; first knife sold in 1990. **Mark:** Last name.

SCHEID, MAGGIE, 124 Van Stallen St., Rochester, NY 14621-3557
Specialties: Simple working straight knives. **Patterns:** Kitchen and utility knives; some miniatures. **Technical:** Forges 5160 high-carbon steel. **Prices:** $100 to $200. **Remarks:** Part-time maker; first knife sold in 1986. **Mark:** Full name.

SCHELL, CLYDE M., 4735 NE Elliott Circle, Corvallis, OR 97330/503-752-0235

SCHEPERS, GEORGE B., Box 83, Chapman, NE 68827/308-986-2444
Specialties: Fancy period pieces of his design. **Patterns:** Bowies, swords, tomahawks; locking folders and miniatures. **Technical:** Grinds W1, W2 and his own Damascus; etches. **Prices:** $125 to $600; some higher. **Remarks:** Full-time maker; first knife sold in 1981. **Mark:** Schep.

SCHEURER, ALFREDO E. FAES, Rincon del Sur #15-21-7, Col. Bosque Res. del Sur, C.P. 16010 MEXICO
Specialties: Fancy and fantasy knives of his design. **Patterns:** Daggers. **Technical:** Grinds stainless steel; casts and grinds silver. Sets stones in silver. **Prices:** $2,000 to $3,000. **Remarks:** Spare-time maker; first knife sold in 1989. **Mark:** Symbol.

SCHIRMER, MIKE, 28 Biltmore Rd., P.O. Box 534, Twin Bridges, MT 59754/406-684-5868
Specialties: Working straight knives of his design or to customer specs. **Patterns:** Bowies, hunters, camp, fighters and boot knives. **Technical:** Grinds 01, D2, ATS-34, A2, 440C and G. Werth Damascus. Scrimshands. **Prices:** Starting at $75. **Remarks:** Full-time maker; first knife sold in 1992. Doing business as Ruby Mountain Knives. **Mark:** Last name or signature, company name.

SCHMIDT, JAMES A., 1167 Eastern Ave., Ballston Lake, NY 12019/518-882-9322
Specialties: High-art Damascus folders and collector-quality period pieces—sole authorship. **Patterns:** Schmidt patterns in folders; variety of investor-class straight knives. **Technical:** Forges W2 and his own Damascus; offers elaborate filework and etching; uses exotic handle materials. **Prices:** $900 to $2,200; some to $5,000. **Remarks:** Full-time maker; first knife sold in 1975. **Mark:** Last name.

SCHMIDT, RICK, P.O. Box 1318, Whitefish, MT 59937/406-862-6471; 406-862-6078
Specialties: Traditional working and using straight knives and folders of his design and to customer specs. **Patterns:** Fighters, hunters, cutlery and utility knives. **Technical:** Flat-grinds D2 and ATS-34. Custom leather sheaths. **Prices:** $120 to $250; some to $1,900. **Remarks:** Full-time maker; first knife sold in 1975. **Mark:** Stylized initials.

SCHNEIDER, CRAIG M., 285 County Rd. 1400 N., Seymour, IL 61875/217-687-2651
Specialties: Traditional working straight knives of his design or to customer specs. **Patterns:** Hunters, fighters, Bowies and utility/camp knives. **Technical:** Grinds 440C, 440V, ATS-34, D2 and 01; uses various animal horns, antlers, bones, jawbones and fossil ivory for handle materials. **Prices:** $35 to $400; some to $1,000. **Remarks:** Part-time maker; first knife sold in 1985. **Mark:** Stylized initials.

SCHNEIDER, HERMAN J., 24296 Via Aquara, Laguna Niguel, CA 92677/714-495-4589; FAX: 714-495-0377
Specialties: Investor-class straight knives and fantasy pieces of his design. **Patterns:** Fully finished hunters, daggers, fighters and push knives. **Technical:** Forges and grinds 154CM, ATS-34 and his Damascus. Exotic materials are a specialty. **Prices:** $800 to $5,000; some higher. **Remarks:** Full-time maker; first knife sold in 1972. **Mark:** First and middle initials, last name.

SCHNEIDER, KARL A., 209 N. Brownleaf Rd., Newark, DE 19713/302-737-0277
Specialties: Traditional working and using straight knives of his design. **Patterns:** Hunters, kitchen and fillet knives. **Technical:** Grinds ATS-34, D2 and 154CM. Shapes handles to fit hands; uses Micarta, Pakkawood and exotic woods. Makes hand-stitched leather cases. **Prices:** $75 to $225; some to $400. **Remarks:** Part-time maker; first knife sold in 1984-85. **Mark:** Name, address.

custom knifemakers

SCHOEMAN, CORRIE, Box 573, Bloemfontein 9300, SOUTH AFRICA/051-476105; FAX: 051-476198
Specialties: Working and using knives to his or customer's designs. **Patterns:** Fighters, boots, hunters and locking folders. **Technical:** Grinds ATS-34, 12C27 and 440B. Handles made with hardwoods, horn, ivory, warthog tusks or customer request. All knives come with custom-made sheath and/or wooden display case. **Prices:** $150 to $400. **Remarks:** Part-time maker; first knife sold in 1984. **Mark:** Etched name logo in knife shape.

SCHOENFELD, MATTHEW A., RR #1, Galiano Island, B.C. V0N 1P0, CANADA/604-539-2806
Specialties: Working knives of his design. **Patterns:** Kitchen cutlery, camp knives, hunters, swords. **Technical:** Grinds 440C buys Damascus. **Prices:** $85 to $500. **Remarks:** Part-time maker; first knife sold in 1978. **Mark:** Signature, Galiano Is. B.C., and date.

SCHOLL, TIM, Rt. 3, Box 158-1A, Angie, NC 27501/910-897-2051
Specialties: Fancy and working/using straight knives and folders of his design and to customer specs. **Patterns:** Hunters, locking folders, utility/camp knives. **Technical:** Grinds ATS-34; forges carbon and tool steel and Damascus. Offers filework. **Prices:** $100 to $650; some t0 $1,500. **Remarks:** Part-time maker; first knife sold in 1990. Doing business as Tim Scholl Custom Knives. **Mark:** Last name or last initial with arrow.

SCHROEN, KARL, 4042 Bones Rd., Sebastopol, CA 95472/707-823-4057
Specialties: Using knives made to fit. **Patterns:** Sgian dubhs, carving sets, woodcarving knives, fishing knives, kitchen knives and new cleaver design. **Technical:** Forges A2, ATS-34 and D2. **Prices:** $100 to $800. **Remarks:** Full-time maker; first knife sold in 1968. Author of The Hand Forged Knife. **Mark:** Last name.

SCHULTZ, RICHARD A., P.O. Box 1616, San Juan Capistrano, CA 92693/714-661-3879
Specialties: Traditional working and using straight knives of his design, to customer specs and in standard patterns. **Patterns:** Fighters, hunters, Specwar and survival knives. **Technical:** Grinds 440C, ATS-34, tool steels and titanium. **Prices:** $75 to $250; some to $700. **Remarks:** Part-time maker; first knife sold in 1991. Manufactures specialized knives in titanium to U.S. Government Specwar teams as Mission Knives, Inc. **Mark:** First initial, last name, year.

SCHWARZER, JAMES, P.O. Box 4, Pomona Park, FL 32181/904-649-5026; FAX: 904-649-8585
Specialties: Working straight knives of his design. **Patterns:** Capers and small hunters. **Technical:** Forges high-carbon steel and Damascus. **Prices:** $50 to $300. **Remarks:** Twelve-year-old part-time maker; first knife sold in 1989. Sells only at shows. **Mark:** Last name with anvil and first name underneath.

SCHWARZER, STEPHEN, P.O. Box 4, Pomona Park, FL 32181/904-649-5026; FAX: 904-649-8585
Specialties: Mosaic Damascus. **Patterns:** Hunters, fighters, locking folders, axes and buckskinners. **Technical:** Forges W2, 01, Wootz steel and his own Damascus; all knives have carving or filework. **Prices:** $150 to $500; some to $5,000. **Remarks:** Full-time maker; first knife sold in 1976. **Mark:** Name over anvil; folders marked inside liner.

SCOFIELD, EVERETT, 2873 Glass Mill Rd., Chickamauga, GA 30707/706-861-2911
Specialties: Historic and fantasy miniatures. **Patterns:** All patterns. **Technical:** Uses only the finest tool steels and other materials. Uses only natural, precious, and semi-precious materials. **Prices:** $100 to $1,500. **Remarks:** Full-time maker; first knife sold in 1971. Doing business as Three Crowns Cutlery. **Mark:** Three Crowns logo.

SCORDIA, PAOLO, Via del Collettore Secondario 23, 00119 Ostia Antica, ROMA ITALY /06-5650717
Specialties: Plain working knives. **Patterns:** Skinners, hunters, utility and boot knives, fighters, daggers, bush swords, kitchen knives and liner lock folders. **Technical:** Grinds 420C, 440C, ATS-34; uses hardwoods and Micarta for handles, brass and nickel silver for fittings. Makes sheaths. **Prices:** $80 to $500. **Remarks:** Part-time maker; first knife sold in 1988. **Mark:** Initials with sun and moon logo.

SCORPION FORGE (See Lutz, Greg)

SCOTT, AL, 2171 Bandera Hwy., Kerrville, TX 78028

SCOTT, WINSTON, Rt. 2, Box 62, Huddleston, VA 24104/703-297-6130
Specialties: Working knives. **Patterns:** Hunting and fishing knives. **Technical:** Grinds ATS-34, 440C and 154CM; likes full and narrow tangs, natural materials, sterling silver guards. **Prices:** $100 to $200; some to $400. **Remarks:** Part-time maker; first knife sold in 1984. **Mark:** Last name.

SEA-MOUNT KNIFE WORKS (See Wilson, Philip C.)

SEARS, MICK, 214 N. Vance St., Gastonia, NC 28052/704-867-3464
Specialties: Scots and confederate reproductions; Bowies and fighters. **Patterns:** Bowies, fighters. **Technical:** Grinds 440C and 1095. **Prices:** $50 to $150; some to $300. **Remarks:** Part-time maker; first knife sold in 1975. Doing business as Mick's Custom Knives. **Mark:** First name.

SELENT, CHUCK, P.O. Box 1207, Bonners Ferry, ID 83805-1207/208-267-5807
Specialties: Period, art and fantasy miniatures; exotics; one-of-a-kinds. **Patterns:** Swords, daggers and others. **Technical:** Works in Damascus, meteorite, 440C and tool steel. Offers scrimshaw. Offers his own casting and leatherwork; uses jewelry techniques. Makes display cases for miniatures. **Prices:** $75 to $400. **Remarks:** Part-time maker; first knife sold in 1990. **Mark:** Last name and bear paw print logo scrimshawed on handles or leatherwork.

SELF, ERNIE, 21070 Alexander Ln., Porter, TX 77365/713-572-1613
Specialties: Traditional and working straight knives and folders of his design and in standard patterns. **Patterns:** Hunters, locking folders and slip-joints. **Technical:** Grinds 440C, D2, 440V and ATS-34. Offers fancy filework. **Prices:** $125 to $350; some to $500. **Remarks:** Full-time maker; first knife sold in 1982. **Mark:** Initials brand.

SELLEVOLD, HARALD, S.Kleivesmau:2, 5023 Dreggen, NORWAY/55-310682
Specialties: Norwegian styles; collaborates with other Norse craftsmen. **Patterns:** Distinctive ferrules and other mild modifications of traditional patterns; Bowies and friction folders. **Technical:** Buys Damascus blades; blacksmiths his own blades. Semi-gemstones used in handles; gemstone inlay. **Prices:** $100 to $350; some to $1,000. **Remarks:** Full-time maker; first knife sold in 1980. **Mark:** Horseshoe last initial.

SELVIDIO, RALPH J., 15 Budlong Ave., Warwick, RI 02888/401-941-0758; FAX: 401-377-1006
Specialties: Collector-grade folders with unique mechanisms; straight and folding fantasy knives of his design. **Patterns:** Locking folders, swords and fighters. **Technical:** Grinds and forges Damascus and 1095; grinds 01. Handle material is mostly ivory and pearl. Uses exotic skin overlays on cases. **Prices:** $200 to $950; some to $1,500. **Remarks:** Part-time maker; first knife sold in 1986. Doing business as Rattler Brand Knives. **Mark:** RATTLER BRAND.

SENTZ, MARK C., 4084 Baptist Rd., Taneytown, MD 21787/410-756-2018
Specialties: Fancy straight working knives of his design. **Patterns:** Hunters, fighters, utility/camp knives. **Technical:** Forges 1085, 1095, 5160, 5155 and his Damascus. Most knives come with wood-lined leather sheath or wooden presentation sheath. **Prices:** Start at $225. **Remarks:** Full-time maker; first knife sold in 1989. Doing business as M. Charles Sentz Gunsmithing, Inc. **Mark:** Last name.

SENTZ GUNSMITHING, INC., M. CHARLES (See Sentz, Mark C.)

SERAFEN, STEVEN E., P.O. Box 898, Norwich, NY 13815/607-334-3166
Specialties: Traditional working/using straight knives of his design and to customer specs. **Patterns:** Bowies, fighters, hunters. **Technical:** Grinds ATS-34, 440C, high-carbon steel. **Prices:** $175 to $600; some to $1,200. **Remarks:** Part-time maker; first knife sold in 1990. **Mark:** First and middle initial, last name in script.

SERVEN, JIM, 6153 Third St., Mayville, MI 48744/517-843-6539
Specialties: Highly finished unique folders. **Patterns:** Fancy working folders, axes, miniatures and razors; some straight knives. **Technical:** Grinds 440C; forges his own Damascus. **Prices:** $150 to $800; some to $1,500. **Remarks:** Full-time maker; first knife sold in 1971. **Mark:** Name in map logo.

SHADLEY, EUGENE W., 645 Norway Dr., Bovey, MN 55709-9508/218-245-3820
Specialties: Classic multi-blade folders. **Patterns:** Stockman, sowbelly, congress,

directory

SHADOWMAKER—SINYARD

trapper, etc. **Technical:** Grinds ATS-34, 416 frames. **Prices:** $95 to $500; some to $800. **Remarks:** Full-time maker; first knife sold in 1985. Doing business as ES Custom Knives. **Mark:** Last name.

SHADOWMAKER (See Urstadt, E.W.)

SHARP, MARGIE (See Sharp, Wes and Margie)

SHARP, WES and MARGIE, 1220 N. 18th Ave., Milton, FL 32583/904-994-3779
Specialties: Traditional and working straight knives of their design and to customer specs. **Patterns:** Bowies, hunters and fillet knives. **Technical:** Grind 440C and ATS-34. Offer filework and custom leather work. **Prices:** $75 to $300; some to $500. **Remarks:** Full-time maker; first knife sold in 1985. **Mark:** Last name.

SHARRIGAN, MUDD, RR4, 1164 Bradford Rd., Wiscasset, ME 04578-9330/207-882-9820
Specialties: Classic working/using straight knives of his design and to customer specs. **Patterns:** Daggers, fighters, hunters. **Technical:** Forges 1095, 01 and Rolls Royce steel. **Prices:** $110 to $325; some to $600. **Remarks:** Full-time maker; first knife sold in 1982. **Mark:** First name.

SHAWNEE (See Meier, Daryl)

SHEEHAN, PAUL P., P.O. Box 3544, Frederiksted, St. Croix, U.S. VIRGIN ISLANDS 00841/809-772-0569
Specialties: Working straight knives of his design or to customer specs. **Patterns:** Bowies, kukris, sub-hilts and gents' utility knives; tantos and fantasy knives. **Technical:** Hollow-grinds 440C and commercial Damascus; prefers natural materials. Filework and full tangs are standard. **Prices:** $150 to $650. **Remarks:** Part-time maker; first knife sold in 1987. **Mark:** Full name, city and state.

SHELTON, PAUL S., 17051 County Rd. 8440, Rolla, MO 65401/314-364-3151
Specialties: Fancy working straight knives of his design or to customer specs. **Patterns:** Hunters, fighters, boots and display-stand knives. **Technical:** Grinds 440C, ATS-34 and commercial Damascus; works frequently with natural materials. **Prices:** $100 to $250; some to $650. **Remarks:** Part-time maker; first knife sold in 1984. **Mark:** Last name and serial number.

SHERMAN KNIVES (See Williams, Sherman A.)

SHIKAYAMA, TOSHIAKI, 259-2 Suka Yoshikawa Machi, Kitakatushika-Gun Saitama T342, JAPAN

SHINOSKY, ANDY, 2978 Beal St. NW, Warren, OH 44485/216-898-6298
Specialties: Fancy working and using folders. **Patterns:** Gentlemen's knives, folding fighters and boots, interframes. **Technical:** Grinds ATS-34 and commercial Damascus. Prefers natural handle materials, horns, pearls, exotic woods. **Prices:** $350 to $900; some to $1,500. **Remarks:** Part-time maker; first knife sold in 1992. **Mark:** Last name.

SHOEMAKER, SCOTT, 316 S. Main St., Miamisburg, OH 45342/513-859-1935
Specialties: Twisted, wire-wrapped handles on swords, fighters and fantasy blades; new line of seven models with quick-draw, multi-carry Kydex sheaths. **Patterns:** Bowies, boots and one-of-a-kinds in his design or to customer specs. **Technical:** Grinds A6 and ATS-34; buys Damascus. Hand satin finish is standard. **Prices:** $100 to $1,500; swords to $8,000. **Remarks:** Part-time maker; first knife sold in 1984. **Mark:** Angel wings with last initial, or last name.

SHOGER, MARK O., 14780 SW Osprey Dr., Suite 345, Beaverton, OR 97007/503-644-2495
Specialties: Working and using straight knives and folders of his design; fancy and embellished knives. **Patterns:** Hunters, Bowies, daggers and locking folders. **Technical:** Forges 01, W2 and his own pattern-welded Damascus. **Remarks:** Spare-time maker. **Mark:** Last name or stamped last initial over anvil.

SHOSTLE, BEN, 1121 Burlington, Muncie, IN 47302/317-282-9073
Specialties: Fancy high-art straight knives of his design. **Patterns:** Bowies, daggers and fighters. **Technical:** Uses 440C, ATS-34 and commercial Damascus. All knives are engraved. **Prices:** $900 to $3,200; some to $4,000. **Remarks:** Full-time maker; first knife sold in 1987. Doing business as The Gun Room (T.G.R.). **Mark:** Last name.

SHUFORD, RICK, Rt. 8, Box 256A, Statesville, NC 28677/704-873-0633
Specialties: Fancy working knives to customer specs. **Patterns:** Hunters, buckskinners, camp and fishing knives and miniatures. **Technical:** Forges and grinds 01, D2 and 440C. **Prices:** $125 to $250; some to $450. **Remarks:** Part-time maker; first knife sold in 1981. **Mark:** Last name and three dots.

SIBRIAN, AARON, 4308 Dean Drive, Ventura, CA 93003/805-642-6950
Specialties: Tough working knives of his design and in standard patterns. **Patterns:** Makes a "Viper utility"—a kukri derivative—and a variety of straight using knives. **Technical:** Grinds 440C and ATS-34. Offers traditional Japanese blades; soft backs, hard edges, temper lines. **Prices:** $60 to $100; some to $250. **Remarks:** Spare-time maker; first knife sold in 1989. **Mark:** Initials in diagonal line.

SIDELINGER, ROBERT, 1365 St. Francis Rd., Bel Air, MD 21014/410-879-0963
Specialties: Folders only of his design. **Patterns:** Drop-points, trailing-points and daggers. **Technical:** Grinds ATS-34 and Damascus. Likes interframes, integral spring locks. Handle inlays made of ivory, horn, wood, coral and pearl. **Prices:** Start at $590. **Remarks:** Part-time maker; first knife sold in 1990. **Mark:** Gothic last initial inside shield.

SIGMAN, CORBET R., Rt. 1, Box 212-A, Liberty, WV 25124/304-586-9131
Specialties: Collectible working straight knives and folders. **Patterns:** Hunters, fighters, boots, camp knives and exotics such as sgian dubhs—distinctly Sigman lines; folders. **Technical:** Grinds D2, 154CM, plain carbon tool steel and ATS-34. **Prices:** $60 to $800; some to $4,000. **Remarks:** Full-time maker; first knife sold in 1970. **Mark:** Name or initials.

SIGMAN, JAMES P., 52474 Johnson Rd., Three Rivers, MI 49093/616-279-2508
Specialties: High-tech working knives of his design. **Patterns:** Daggers, hunters, fighters and folders. **Technical:** Forges and grinds L6, 01, W2 and his Damascus. **Prices:** $150 to $750. **Remarks:** Part-time maker; first knife sold in 1982. **Mark:** First initial, last name or SIG.

SIMMONDS, KURT BARNES, 1 Yeats St., Castlemaine, Vic. 3450, AUSTRALIA/054-724387
Specialties: Straight knives and folders; fancy period pieces. **Patterns:** Art daggers, traditional Bowies, fancy folders and miniatures. **Technical:** Grinds ATS-34, D2, 440C; offers filework, chisel work and inlays. **Prices:** $185 to $375; some to $2,500. **Remarks:** Full-time maker; first knife sold in 1983. **Mark:** Initials and address in Southern Cross motif.

SIMMONS, H.R., P.O. Box 176, Grantsboro, NC 28529/919-249-0094

SIMONELLA, GIANLUIGI, 15, via Rosa Brustolo, 33085 Maniago, ITALY/01139-427-730350
Specialties: Traditional and classic working/using knives of his design and to customer specs. **Patterns:** Bowies, fighters, hunters, utility/camp knives. **Technical:** Forges ATS-34, D2, 440C. **Prices:** $250 to $400; some to $1,000. **Remarks:** Full-time maker; first knife sold in 1988. **Mark:** Wilson.

SIMONICH, ROB, P.O. Box 278, Clancy, MT 59634/406-933-8274
Specialties: Working knives in standard patterns. **Patterns:** Hunters, combat knives, Bowies and small fancy knives. **Technical:** Grinds D2, ATS-34 and 440C; forges own cable Damascus. Offers filework on most knives. **Prices:** $75 to $300; some to $1,000. **Remarks:** Spare-time maker; first knife sold in 1984. Not currently taking orders. **Mark:** Last name in buffalo logo.

SIMONS, BILL, 6217 Michael Ln., Lakeland, FL 33811/813-646-3783
Specialties: Working folders. **Patterns:** Locking folders, liner locks, slip-joints in hunters; some straight camp knives. **Technical:** Grinds D2, 440C and ATS-34. **Prices:** Start at $100. **Remarks:** Full-time maker; first knife sold in 1970. **Mark:** Last name.

SIMS, BOB, P.O. Box 772, Meridian, TX 76665/817-435-6240
Specialties: Traditional working straight knives and folders in standard patterns; banana/sheepfoot blade combinations in trapper patterns. **Patterns:** Locking folders, slip-joint folders and hunters. **Technical:** Grinds D2, ATS-34 and 01. Offers filework on some knives. **Prices:** $150 to $275; some to $600. **Remarks:** Part-time maker; first knife sold in 1975. **Mark:** The division sign.

SINYARD, CLESTON S., 27522 Burkhardt Dr., Elberta, AL 36530/205-986-7984

custom knifemakers

SISEMORE—SMITH

Specialties: Working straight knives and folders of his design. **Patterns:** Hunters, buckskinners, Bowies, daggers, fighters and all-Damascus folders. **Technical:** Makes Damascus from 440C, stainless steels, D2 and regular high-carbon steel; forges "forefinger pad" into hunters and skinners. **Prices:** In Damascus $450 to $1,500; some to $2,500. **Remarks:** Full-time maker; first knife sold in 1980. Doing business as Nimo Forge. **Mark:** Last name, U.S.A. in anvil.

SISEMORE, CHARLES, HC 63, Box 5550, Hodgen, OK 74939/918-651-3321
Specialties: Traditional straight knives of his design. **Patterns:** Bowies, daggers and hunters. **Technical:** Forges 5160 and Damascus. **Prices:** $125 to $450. **Remarks:** Full-time maker; first knife sold in 1986. **Mark:** Last name.

SISKA, JIM, 6 Highland Ave., Westfield, MA 01085/413-568-9787; FAX: 413-568-6341
Specialties: Traditional working straight knives and folders. **Patterns:** Hunters, fighters, Bowies and one-of-a-kinds; folders. **Technical:** Grinds D2 and ATS-34; buys Damascus. Likes exotic woods. **Prices:** $195 to $2,500. **Remarks:** Part-time maker; first knife sold in 1983. **Mark:** Last name in Old English.

SKELLERN, DR. M.J., P.O. Munster 4278, SOUTH AFRICA/03930-92537; FAX: 03931-76513
Specialties: Fancy high-tech folders of his design. **Patterns:** Locking and slip-joint folders. **Technical:** Grinds ATS-34 and Sandvick 12C27; uses Damascus. Inlays his stainless steel integral handles; offers rare African handle materials. **Prices:** $200 to $500; some to $700. **Remarks:** Part-time maker; first knife sold in 1986. **Mark:** Last name.

SLEE, FRED, 9 John St., Morganville, NJ 07751/908-591-9047
Specialties: Working straight knives, some fancy, to customer specs. **Patterns:** Hunters, fighters, boots, fancy daggers and folders. **Technical:** Grinds D2, 440C and 154CM. **Prices:** $90 to $450; some to $1,200. **Remarks:** Part-time maker; first knife sold in 1980. **Mark:** Name in shape of knife.

SLOAN, SHANE, Rt. 1, Box 17, Newcastle, TX 76372/817-846-3290
Specialties: Working straight knives and folders, some fancy. **Patterns:** Bowies, lockers, slip-joints, fancy folders, fighters and period pieces. **Technical:** Grinds D2 and ATS-34; tempers 440C to be less brittle. Mixes mirror and satin finishes. Prefers natural handle materials. **Prices:** $150 to $1,600. **Remarks:** Full-time maker; first knife sold in 1985. **Mark:** Name in logo with eagle.

SLOBODIAN, SCOTT, 6519 Fountain Ave., Los Angeles, CA 90028/213-464-2341; FAX: 213-464-4060
Specialties: Japanese-style knives and swords, period pieces, fantasy pieces and miniatures. **Patterns:** Small kweikens, tantos, wakazashis, katanas, traditional Samurai swords. **Technical:** Flat-grinds 1045, 1060 and commercial Damascus; differentially hardens blades with fireclay. **Prices:** $800 to $3,500; some to $7,500. **Remarks:** Full-time maker; first knife sold in 1987. **Mark:** Blade signed in Japanese characters and various scripts.

SMALL, ED, Rt. 1, Box 178-A, Keyser, WV 26726/304-298-4254
Specialties: Working knives of his design; period pieces. **Patterns:** Hunters, daggers, buckskinners and camp knives; likes one-of-a-kinds. **Technical:** Forges and grinds W2, L6 and his own Damascus. Uses no solder joint at guard or spacing material. **Prices:** $150 to $1,500. **Remarks:** Part-time maker; first knife sold in 1978. Business name is Iron Mountain Forge Works. **Mark:** Script initials connected.

SMALL, JIM, P.O. Box 67, Madison, GA 30650/404-342-4707
Specialties: Fancy working knives of his design or to customer specs. **Patterns:** Bowies, camp and fishing knives, hunters and locking folders. **Technical:** Grinds D2, 440C, 154CM and ATS-34; engraves his knives and other's. **Prices:** $75 to $185; some to $1,000. **Remarks:** Full-time maker; first knife sold in 1970. **Mark:** Last name.

SMIT, GLENN, 627 Cindy Ct., Aberdeen, MD 21001/410-272-2959
Specialties: Working and using straight knives of his design or to customer specs. **Patterns:** Hunters, Bowies, daggers, fighters, utility/camp knives and miniatures. **Technical:** Grinds 440C, ATS-34, 01, A2 and commercial Damascus. **Prices:** Miniatures start at $20; full-size knives start at $40. **Remarks:** Spare-time maker; first knife sold in 1986. Doing business as Wolf's Knives. **Mark:** WOLF.

SMITH, BOBBIE D., 802 W. WHy. 90., Bonifay, FL 32425/904-547-5935
Specialties: Working straight knives and folders. **Patterns:** Bowies, hunters and slip-joints. **Technical:** Grinds 440C and ATS-34; custom sheaths for each knife. **Prices:** $75 to $250. **Remarks:** Part-time maker. **Mark:** NA.

SMITH, D. NOEL, P.O. Box 1363, Canon City, CO 81215-1363/719-275-2574
Specialties: Fantasy and high-art knives of his design. **Patterns:** Daggers, hunters and art knives. **Technical:** Grinds 01, D2 and stainless. Offers ivory and horn-carved handles; acid-etched blades; bronze-sculptured guards, buttcaps and bases. Engraves and scrimshaws. **Prices:** $400 to $3,500; some to $10,000. **Remarks:** Full-time maker; first knife sold in 1990. Doing business as Minds' Eye Metalmaster. **Mark:** Signature, date and number.

SMITH, GREGORY H., 8607 Coddington Ct., Louisville, KY 40299/502-491-7439
Specialties: Traditional working straight knives and fantasy knives to customer specs. **Patterns:** Fighters and modified Bowies; camp knives and swords. **Technical:** Grinds 01, 440C and commercial Damascus bars. **Prices:** $55 to $300. **Remarks:** Part-time maker; first knife sold in 1985. **Mark:** JAGED, plus signature.

SMITH, J.D., 46 Waltham St. #207, Boston, MA 02118/617-542-1949
Specialties: Classic working and using straight knives and folders; period pieces mainly from his design. **Patterns:** Bowies, fighters and locking folders. **Technical:** Forges and grinds ATS-34, his Damascus, 01, 1095 and wootz-pattern hammer steel. **Prices:** $200 to $800; some to $1,500. **Remarks:** Full-time maker; first knife sold in 1987. Doing business as Hammersmith. **Mark:** Last initial alone or in cartouche.

SMITH, JOHN M., RR 6, Box 52, Centralia, IL 62801/618-249-6444
Specialties: Art knives and some work knives. **Patterns:** Daggers, sub-hilt fighters, boot knives and Bowies. **Technical:** Forges 02, W2 and his Damascus; some pieces in 440C. **Prices:** $500 to $3,000. **Remarks:** Full-time maker; first knife sold in 1980. **Mark:** Etched signature.

SMITH, JOHN W., 1416 Cow Branch Rd., West Liberty, KY 41472/606-743-3599
Specialties: Fancy and working locking folders of his design or to customer specs. **Patterns:** Interframes, traditional, daggers and hunters. **Technical:** Grinds ATS-34, 440C and commercial Damascus. Offers gold inlay, hand-fitted mosaic pearl inlay and filework. Prefers hand-rubbed finish. Pearl, ivory and exotic woods available. **Prices:** $250 to $750; some to $2,000. **Remarks:** Full-time maker; first knife sold in 1980. **Mark:** First and middle initials engraved inside last name.

SMITH JR., JAMES B. "RED", Rt. 2, Box 1525, Morven, GA 31638/912-775-2844
Specialties: Folders. **Patterns:** Rotating rear-lock folders. **Technical:** Grinds ATS-34, D2 and Vascomax 350. **Prices:** Start at $350. **Remarks:** Full-time maker; first knife sold in 1985. **Mark:** GA RED in cowboy hat.

SMITH, MICHAEL J., 14802 N. Florida T308, Tampa, FL 33613/813-962-3538
Specialties: Working and using straight knives and folders of his design, to customer specs and in standard patterns; fantasy knives. **Patterns:** Daggers, fighters and utility/camp knives. **Technical:** Grinds ATS-34 and Damascus. Uses titanium on folders; silver casting and wire/silk wraps on daggers. **Prices:** $85 to $500; some to $3,000. **Remarks:** Part-time maker; first knife sold in 1989. **Mark:** Name, city, state.

SMITH, NEWMAN L., 676 Glades Rd., Shop #3, Gatlinburg, TN 37738/615-436-3322
Specialties: Working knives. **Patterns:** Hunters, slip-joint and lock-back folders, some miniatures. **Technical:** Grinds 01 and ATS-34; makes fancy sheaths. **Prices:** $110 to $450; some to $1,000. **Remarks:** Full-time maker; first knife sold in 1984. Partners part-time to handle Damascus blades by Jeff Hurst; marks these with SH connected. **Mark:** First and middle initials, last name.

SMITH, RALPH L., F21, 100 Stallings Rd., Taylors, SC 29687/803-230-5760
Specialties: Working knives. **Patterns:** Hunters, fighters and folders. **Technical:** Grinds 440C, 154CM and ATS-34. **Prices:** $100 to $225; some to $500. **Remarks:** Part-time maker; first knife sold in 1971. **Mark:** Last name in map logo.

SMITH, RAYMOND L., Box 370, Breesport, NY 14816/607-739-3126
Specialties: Working/using straight knives and folders to customer specs and in standard patterns; period pieces. **Patterns:** Bowies, hunters, slip-joints. **Technical:** Forges 5160, 52100, 1018 Damascus and wire cable Damascus. Filework. **Prices:** $55 to $225; some to $500. **Remarks:** Part-time maker; first knife sold in 1991. **Mark:** Oval with initials.

directory

SMITH—STEGALL

SMITH, W.M., 802 W. Hwy. 90, Bonifay, FL 32425/904-547-5935

SMYTHE, KEN, Box 8, Bulwer 4575, SOUTH AFRICA/033822-1340
Specialties: Working and using straight knives of his design and to customer specs. **Patterns:** Fighters and hunters. **Technical:** Grinds 12C27 and 440C. Scrimshands. **Prices:** $150 to $480. **Remarks:** Part-time maker; first knife sold in 1982. **Mark:** Sword lying on Bible.

SNARE, MICHAEL, 3352 E. Mescal St., Phoenix, AZ 85028

SNELL, JERRY L., 235 Woodsong Dr., Fayetteville, GA 30214/404-461-0586
Specialties: Working straight knives of his design and in standard patterns. **Patterns:** Hunters, boots, fighters, daggers and a few folders. **Technical:** Grinds 440C, ATS-34; buys Damascus. **Prices:** $175 to $350; some to $500. **Remarks:** Part-time maker. **Mark:** Last name, or name, city and state.

SOKOL, RICHARD, Box 90057, Indianapolis, IN 46290
Specialties: Fantasy and medieval straight knives of his design. **Patterns:** Medieval knives. **Technical:** Grinds 440C and ATS-34. **Prices:** $70 to $250. **Remarks:** Full-time maker. **Mark:** Engraved runic initials.

SOLOMON, MARVIN, 23750 Cold Springs Rd., Ferndale, AR 72122/501-821-3170
Specialties: Traditional working and using straight knives of his design and to customer specs. **Patterns:** Bowies, hunters and utility/camp knives. **Technical:** Forges 5160, 1095, 01 and random Damascus. **Prices:** $100 to $400. **Remarks:** Part-time maker; first knife sold in 1990. Doing business as Cold Springs Forge. **Mark:** Last name.

SONTHEIMER, G. DOUGLAS, 12604 Bridgeton Dr., Potomac, MD 20854/301-948-2933
Specialties: Working straight knives of his design. **Patterns:** Fighters, backpackers, claws and straightedges. **Technical:** Grinds. **Price:** $275 to $900; some to $1,500. **Remarks:** Spare-time maker; first knife sold in 1976. **Mark:** LORD.

SOPPERA, ARTHUR, Morgenalstr. 37, P.O. Box 708, CH-8038 Zurich, SWITZERLAND/1-482 86 12
Specialties: High-art, high-tech knives of his design. **Patterns:** Locking folders, daggers and boots. **Technical:** Grinds ATS-34 and commercial Damascus. Folders have push-button release. Also makes jewelry with integrated small knives. **Prices:** $350 to $900; some $2,000 and higher. **Remarks:** Full-time maker; first knife sold in 1986. **Mark:** Stylized initials, name, country.

SORNBERGER, JIM, 25126 Overland Dr., Volcano CA 95689/209-295-7819
Specialties: Collectible straight knives. **Patterns:** Fighters, daggers, Bowies; locking folders and miniatures; hunters. **Technical:** Grinds 440C, 154CM and ATS-34; engraves, carves and embellishes. **Prices:** $500 to $1,500; some to $3,500. **Remarks:** Full-time maker; first knife sold in 1970. **Mark:** First initial, last name, city and state.

SOUTHERN PRIDE KNIVES (See Benjamin, Jr., George)

SOVEREIGN KNIVES (See Humphreys, Joel)

SPANO, DOMINICK, 2726 Rice Ave., San Angelo, TX 76904/915-944-9630
Specialties: Working/using straight knives of his design and to customer specs. **Patterns:** Boots, hunters, slip-joints. **Technical:** Grinds ATS-34. Heat-treats. Makes sheaths. **Prices:** $145 to $300. **Remarks:** Part-time maker; first knife sold in 1989. Doing business as Spano Knives. **Mark:** Last name in script.

SPENCER, JOHN E., HC63 Box 267, Harper, TX 78631/512-864-4216
Specialties: Working straight knives. **Patterns:** Hunters, fighters and survival knives; locking folders; axes. **Technical:** Grinds 01, D2 and 440C; commercial Damascus. **Prices:** $60 to $300; some to $500. **Remarks:** Full-time maker; first knife sold in 1982. **Mark:** Last name.

SPINALE, RICHARD, 4021 Canterbury Ct., Lorain, OH 44053/216-282-1565
Specialties: High-art working knives of his design. **Patterns:** Hunters, fighters, daggers and locking folders. **Technical:** Grinds 440C and 07; engraves. Offers gold bolsters and other deluxe treatments. **Prices:** $125 to $800; some to $2,000. **Remarks:** Spare-time maker; first knife sold in 1976. **Mark:** Name, address, year and model number.

SPIVEY, JEFFERSON, P.O. Box 60584, Oklahoma City, OK 73146/405-282-1802
Specialties: Heavy-duty straight knives of his design. **Patterns:** Horseman's Sabertooth and similar profiles in several sizes. **Technical:** Grinds chromemoly steel. **Prices:** Start at $225. **Remarks:** First knife sold in 1977. **Mark:** Varies, but includes name and patent number.

SPRAGG, WAYNE E., P.O. Box 508, 1314 3675 East Rd., Ashton, ID 83420
Specialties: Working straight knives, some fancy. **Patterns:** Hunters, skinners, kitchen knives, Bowies and miniatures. **Technical:** Grinds ATS-34, 440C, D2, 01 and commercial Damascus. Likes filework and fancy handlework. All blades heat-treated by Paul Bos. **Prices:** $110 to $400; some higher. **Remarks:** Spare-time maker; first knife sold in 1989. **Mark:** Name, city and state with bucking horse logo.

SPRINGFIELD (See Greenfield, G.O.)

SPROUSE, TERRY, 1633 Newfound Rd., Asheville, NC 28806/704-683-3400
Specialties: Traditional and working straight knives of his design. **Patterns:** Bowies and hunters. **Technical:** Grinds ATS-34, 440C and D2. Makes sheaths. **Prices:** $85 to $125; some to $225. **Remarks:** Part-time maker; first knife sold in 1989. **Mark:** NA.

STAFFORD, MICHAEL, 3109 Todd Dr., Madison, WI 53713/608-273-3022
Specialties: Traditional and high-art stone-bladed knives of his design. **Patterns:** Bowies, daggers and fighters. **Technical:** Hand-chips Obsidian, English flint, Danish flint. Laminations and inlays on handles; specializes in stone handles. **Prices:** $80 to $225; some to $350. **Remarks:** Part-time maker; first knife sold in 1987. Doing business as The Prehistoric Edge. **Mark:** Engraved last name.

STAFFORD, RICHARD, 104 Marcia Ct., Warner Robins, GA 31088/912-923-6372
Specialties: High-tech straight knives and some folders. **Patterns:** Hunters in several patterns, fighters, boots, camp knives, combat knives and period pieces. **Technical:** Grinds ATS-34 and 440C; satin finish is standard. **Prices:** Starting at $75. **Remarks:** Part-time maker; first knife sold in 1983. **Mark:** Last name.

STAHL, JOHN, 2049 Windsor Rd., Baldwin, NY 11510/516-223-5007
Specialties: Miniatures. **Patterns:** Bowies, daggers, tantos, push daggers and unique jewelry-type miniatures. **Technical:** Uses stainless steels and commercial Damascus. Offers scrimshaw. **Prices:** $35 to $100. **Mark:** First initial inside last initial.

STALTER, HARRY L., 2509 N. Trivoli Rd., Trivoli, IL 61569/309-362-2306
Specialties: Fancy working knives of his design and in standard patterns; period pieces. **Patterns:** Hunters, fighters and Bowies; fancy daggers, miniatures—fancy swords, daggers, fantasy knives. **Technical:** Stock removal; 440C, D2, 154CM and Damascus. Currently makes 60 styles of miniatures with 440C, Damascus. **Prices:** $110 to $2,000. **Remarks:** Full-time maker; first knife sold in 1980. **Mark:** Last name.

STAPEL, CHUCK, Box 1617, Glendale, CA 91209/213-66-KNIFE
Specialties: Working knives of his design. **Patterns:** Variety of straight knives—tantos, hunters, folders and utility knives. **Technical:** Grinds D2, 440C and AEB-L. **Prices:** $185 to $3,000. **Remarks:** Full-time maker; first knife sold in 1974. **Mark:** Last name.

STAPEL, CRAIG, Box 1617, Glendale, CA 91209/213-668-2669
Specialties: Working knives. **Patterns:** Hunters, tantos and fishing knives. **Technical:** Grinds 440C and AEB-L. **Prices:** $80 to $150. **Remarks:** Spare-time maker; first knife sold in 1981. **Mark:** First and middle initials, last name.

STEELMASTER, P.O. Box 27237, San Diego, CA 92198/619-789-9658
Specialties: Working and using straight knives to customer specs; period pieces. **Patterns:** Bowies, fighters and utility/camp knives. **Technical:** Forges and grinds D2, 01, commercial Damascus and various stainless and corrosion-resistant steels. **Prices:** $120 to $275; some to $450. **Remarks:** Full-time maker; first knife sold in 1976. **Mark:** S.

STEGALL, KEITH, summer: 2101 W. 32nd, Anchorage, AK 99517/907-276-6002; winter: P.O. Box 1035, Barrow, AK 99723/907-852-7273
Specialties: Traditional working straight knives. **Patterns:** Most patterns. **Technical:** Grinds 440C and 154CM. **Prices:** $100 to $300. **Remarks:** Spare-time maker; first knife sold in 1987. **Mark:** Name and state with anchor.

STEIGER, MONTE L., Box 186, Genesee, ID 83832/208-285-1769
Specialties: Traditional working/using straight knives of all designs. **Patterns:** Hunters, utility/camp knives. **Technical:** Grinds 1095, 01, 440C. Handles of stacked leather, Micarta or Pakkawood. Each knife comes with right- or left-handed sheath. **Prices:** $70 to $220. **Remarks:** Spare-time maker; first knife sold in 1988. **Mark:** First initial, last name.

STEIGERWALT, KEN, 6 Collister Dr., Box 8, Nescopeck, PA 18635/717-379-2869
Specialties: Fancy classic folders of his design. **Patterns:** Folders—liner locks, button locks and rear locks. **Technical:** Grinds ATS-34, 440C and commercial Damascus. Experiments with unique filework. **Prices:** $200 to $600; some to $1,500. **Remarks:** Full-time maker; first knife sold in 1981. **Mark:** Initials.

STEINAU, JURGEN, Julius-Hart Strasse 44, Berlin 0-1162, GERMANY/372-6452512; FAX: 372-645-2512
Specialties: Fantasy and high-art straight knives of his design. **Patterns:** Boots, daggers and switch-blade folders. **Technical:** Grinds 440B, 2379 and X90 Cr.Mo.V. 78. **Prices:** $1,500 to $2,500; some to $3,500. **Remarks:** Full-time maker; first knife sold in 1984. **Mark:** Symbol, plus year, month, day and serial number.

STEINBERG, AL, 2499 Trenton Dr., San Bruno, CA 94066/415-583-8281
Specialties: Fancy working straight knives to customer specs. **Patterns:** Hunters, Bowies, fishing and camp knives, push knives. **Technical:** Grinds 01, 440C and 154CM. **Prices:** $60 to $125; some to $300. **Remarks:** Full-time maker; first knife sold in 1972. **Mark:** Signature, city and state.

STEKETEE, CRAIG A., 704 NE Highway 60, Billings, MO 65610/417-744-2770
Specialties: Working straight knives of his design and to customer specs; art and collector knives. **Patterns:** Bowies, daggers, toothpicks, boots, hunters, fillets, miniatures, etc. **Technical:** Forges and stock removal 01, 1095, his Damascus; heat-treats. Engraves; offers filework. Prefers exotic and natural handle materials. **Prices:** $125 to $1,200. **Remarks:** Full-time maker. **Mark:** STEK.

STEVENS, BARRY B., Rt. 6, 901 Amherst, Cridersville, OH 45806/419-221-2446
Specialties: Classic working/using straight knives and folders of his design and to customer specs; mini-hunters and fighters. **Patterns:** Fighters, hunters, locking folders. **Technical:** Grinds ATS-34, 440C, Damascus. Prefers hand-rubbed finishes and natural handle materials—horn, ivory, pearls, exotic woods. **Prices:** $160 to $400; some to $10,000. **Remarks:** Part-time maker; first knife sold in 1991. Doing business as Bare Knives. **Mark:** Name, city, state.

STEWART, CHARLES, 2128 Garrick Ave., Warren, MI 48091/810-757-4418
Specialties: Working knives of his design. **Patterns:** Exotic opening mechanisms for his folders; personally designed and patented release locks; straight knives, some fancy. **Technical:** Forges and grinds 440C, 154CM and ATS-34; offers finishes from gold to blueing. **Prices:** $250 to $11,500; some to $9,500. **Remarks:** Full-time maker; first knife sold in 1968. **Mark:** Stylized initials.

STICE, DOUGLAS, 1901 Elmhurst Dr., Norman, OK 73071/405-360-3957
Specialties: Working straight knives. **Patterns:** Hunters, Bowies, fighters, tantos and fishing knives. **Technical:** Grinds 440C, ATS-34 and D2. **Prices:** $50 to $150; some to $225. **Remarks:** Part-time maker; first knife sold in 1985. **Mark:** Name.

STIPES, DWIGHT, 8089 SE Country Estates Way, Jupiter, FL 33458/407-743-0550
AASpecialties: Traditional and working straight knives in standard patterns. **Patterns:** Boots, Bowies, daggers, hunters and fighters. **Technical:** Grinds 440C, D2 and D3 tool steel. Handles of natural materials, animal, bone or horn. **Prices:** $75 to $150. **Remarks:** Full-time maker; first knife sold in 1972. **Mark:** Last name.

STODDART, W.B. "BILL", 917 Smiley, Forest Park, OH 45240/513-851-1543
Specialties: Sportsman's working knives and multi-blade folders. **Patterns:** Hunters, camp and fish knives; multi-blade reproductions of old standards. **Technical:** Grinds A2, 440C and ATS-34; makes sheaths to match handle materials. **Prices:** $80 to $300; some to $850. **Remarks:** Part-time maker; first knife sold in 1976. **Mark:** Name, Cincinnati, state.

STOKES, ED, 22614 Cardinal Dr., Hockley, TX 77447/713-351-1319
Specialties: Working straight knives and folders of all designs. **Patterns:** Boots, Bowies, daggers, fighters, hunters and miniatures. **Technical:** Grinds ATS-34, 440C and D2. Offers decorative buttcaps, tapered spacers on handles and finger grooves, nickel silver inlays, hand-made sheaths. **Prices:** $185 to $290; some to $350. **Remarks:** Full-time maker; first knife sold in 1973. **Mark:** First and last name, Custom Knives with apache logo.

STONE BIRDS (See Thompson, Tommy)

STONE, JERRY, P.O. Box 1027, Lytle, TX 78052/512-772-4502
Specialties: Traditional working and using folders of his design and to customer specs; fancy knives. **Patterns:** Fighters, hunters, locking folders and slip-joints. **Technical:** Grinds 440C and ATS-34. Offers filework. **Prices:** $125 to $375; some to $700. **Remarks:** Full-time maker; first knife sold in 1973. **Mark:** Initials.

STOUT, JOHNNY, 1514 Devin Dr., New Braunfels, TX 78130/210-629-1011
Specialties: Working knives, some fancy. **Patterns:** Hunters, fighters, Bowies, camp knives and folders. **Technical:** Grinds stainless and carbon steels; forges own Damascus. **Prices:** $300 to $650; some to $2,500. **Remarks:** Full-time maker; first knife sold in 1983. **Mark:** Name and city in logo with serial number.

STOVER, TERRY "LEE", 1809 N. 300E., Kokomo, IN 46901/317-457-2809
Specialties: Damascus folders with filework; Damascus Bowies of his design or to customer specs. **Patterns:** Lockback folders and sheffield-style Bowies. **Technical:** Forges 1095 and own Damascus using 01. Makes mokume. Uses only natural handle materials. **Prices:** $300 to $1,700; some to $2,000. **Remarks:** Part-time maker; first knife sold in 1984. **Mark:** First and middle initials, last name in knife logo; Damascus blades marked in Old English.

STRAIGHT, DON, 3465 Gallows Rd., Falls Church, VA 22042/703-560-6331
Specialties: Traditional working straight knives of his design. **Patterns:** Hunters, Bowies and fighters. **Technical:** Grinds 440C, ATS-34 and D2. **Prices:** $75 to $125; some to $225. **Remarks:** Spare-time maker; first knife sold in 1978. **Mark:** Last name.

STRICKLAND, DALE, 1440 E. Thompson View, Monroe, UT 84754/801-896-8362
Specialties: Traditional and working straight knives and folders of his design and to customer specs. **Patterns:** Hunters, locking folders and utility knives. **Technical:** Grinds Damascus and 440C. **Prices:** $120 to $350; some to $500. **Remarks:** Part-time maker; first knife sold in 1991. **Mark:** Oval stamp of name and city.

STROHECKER, JOHN J., P.O. Box 1411, Riverton, WY 82501/307-856-4139
Specialties: Working and special-order knives. **Patterns:** Hunters and Bowies. **Technical:** Forges 5160 and 52100. Handles made of horn, antlers and exotic woods. Offers pouch-type leather sheaths. **Prices:** $200 to $500; some higher. **Remarks:** Part-time maker; first knife sold in 1984. Studying with Ed. A. Fowler. **Mark:** Stro's.

STRONG, SCOTT, 2138 Oxmoor Dr., Beavercreek, OH 45431/513-426-9290
Specialties: Working knives, some deluxe. **Patterns:** Hunters, fighters, survival and military-style knives, art knives. **Technical:** Forges and grinds 01, A2, D2, 440C and ATS-34. Uses no solder; most knives disassemble. **Prices:** $40 to $350; some to $1,500. **Remarks:** Spare-time maker; first knife sold in 1983. **Mark:** Strong Knives.

STROYAN, ERIC, Box 218, Dalton, PA 18414/717-563-2603
Specialties: Classic and working/using straight knives and folders of his design. **Patterns:** Hunters, locking folders, slip-joints. **Technical:** Forges Damascus; grinds ATS-34, D2. **Prices:** $200 to $600; some to $2,000. **Remarks:** Part-time maker; first knife sold in 1968. **Mark:** Signature or initials stamp.

SUEDMEIER, HARLAN, RFD2, Nebraska City, NE 68410/402-873-4372
Specialties: Working straight knives. **Patterns:** Hunters, fighters and Bowies. **Technical:** Grinds A2, D2, ATS-34 and 440C. **Prices:** $65 to $300; some to $750. **Remarks:** Part-time maker; first knife sold in 1982. Not currently taking orders. **Mark:** First initial, last name.

SUMMERS, ARTHUR L., 8700 Brigner Rd., Mechanicsburg, OH 43044/513-834-3776
Specialties: Hunters, Bowies and collectors in drop points, clip points or straight blades. **Patterns:** Fighters, hunters and personal knives. **Technical:** Grinds 440C, ATS-34, D2 and Damascus. **Prices:** $100 to $350; some to $2,000. **Remarks:** Part-time maker; first knife sold in 1987. **Mark:** Last name and serial number.

SUNDERLAND, RICHARD, Box 248, Quathiaski Cove, British Columbia, CANADA/V0P 1N0/604-285-3038

directory
SUN KNIFE CO.—THOMAS

Specialties: Personal and hunting knives with carved handles in oosic and ivory. **Patterns:** Hunters, Bowies, daggers, camp and personal knives. **Technical:** Grinds 440C, ATS 34 and 01. Handle materials of rosewoods, fossil mammoth ivory and oosic. **Prices:** $150 to $850. **Remarks:** Full-time maker; first knife sold in 1983. Doing business as Sun Knife Co. **Mark:** SUN.

SUN KNIFE CO. (See Sunderland, Richard)

SUTHERLAND, GREG, P.O. Box 23516, Flagstaff, AZ 86002-3516/602-774-6050
Specialties: Classic working/using straight knives of his design and in standard patterns. **Patterns:** Bowies, hunters, kitchen knives, utility/camp knives. **Technical:** Grinds ATS-34, 01. Offers occasional filework and some bronze guards and bolsters. Likes Desert Ironwood. Hunting and utility knives come with leather or Kydex sheath. **Prices:** $100 to $275. **Remarks:** Full-time maker; first knife sold in 1989. Doing business as Outdoors West. **Mark:** Last name, city, state.

SWAIN, ROD, 1020 Avon Place, South Pasadena, CA 91030/818-799-7666
Specialties: Working straight knives, some fancy, of his design and to customer specs. **Patterns:** Outdoor patterns, Bowies and push knives, utility drop-points. **Technical:** Grinds 01, 440C, AEB-L. **Prices:** $75 to $250; some to $450. **Remarks:** Part-time maker; first knife sold in 1981. **Mark:** Last name in logo.

SYSLO, CHUCK, 3418 South 116 Ave., Omaha, NE 68144/402-333-0647
Specialties: High-tech working straight knives. **Patterns:** Hunters, daggers and survival knives; locking folders. **Technical:** Flat-grinds D2, 440C and 154CM; hand polishes only. **Prices:** $175 to $500; some to $3,000. **Remarks:** Part-time maker; first knife sold in 1978. **Mark:** CISCO in logo.

SZILASKI, JOSEPH, 29 Carroll Dr., Wappingers Falls, NY 12590/914-297-5397
Specialties: Fancy and traditional straight knives of his design, to customer specs and in standard patterns. Many pieces are one-of-a-kind. **Patterns:** Bowies, daggers, fighters and hunters. **Technical:** Grinds 440C and 154CM; forges A2, D2, 01 and Damascus. **Prices:** $95 to $275; some to $2,000. **Remarks:** Full-time maker; first knife sold in 1990. **Mark:** Snake logo.

t

TAGLIENTI, ANTONIO J., P.O. Box 221, Darlington, PA 16115/412-846-5259
Specialties: Working straight knives in standard patterns. **Patterns:** Hunters—likes forefinger radius; Bowies, tantos and camp knives. **Technical:** Grinds D2, 440C and 154CM. Emphasizes full tangs; offers filework. **Prices:** $85 to $200; some to $350. **Remarks:** Part-time maker; first knife sold in 1985. **Mark:** Last name.

TAKAHASHI, HIROHIKO, 3-76-9 Mukai Cho, Turu Mi Ku, Yokohama 230, JAPAN

TAKAHASHI, MASAO, 39-3 Sekine-cho, Maebashi-shi, Gunma 371 JAPAN/0272-34-2223

TALON BLADES (See Knuth, Joseph E.)

TAMBOLI, MICHAEL, 12447 N. 49 Ave., Glendale, AZ 85304/602-978-4308
Specialties: Miniatures, some full size. **Patterns:** Miniature hunting knives to fantasy art knives. **Technical:** Grinds 440C, 154CM and Damascus. **Prices:** $75 to $500; some to $1,000. **Remarks:** Part-time maker; first knife sold in 1978. **Mark:** Initials or last name, city and state.

TASAKI, SEICHI, 24 Shizuwa, Shimotsuga-Gun, Tochigi, JAPAN/0482-55-6066
Specialties: High-tech traditional straight knives and folders. **Patterns:** Variety of hunters, miniatures, interframe folders and more. **Technical:** Forges and grinds 440C and carbon steel. **Prices:** $230 to $850; some to $5,000. **Remarks:** Full-time maker; first knife sold in 1984. **Mark:** Initials connected.

"tat" (See Brack, Douglas D.)

TAY, LARRY C-G, Siglap P.O. Box 315, Singapore 9145, REPUBLIC OF SINGAPORE/65-2419421
Specialties: Working and using straight knives and folders of his design; Marble's Safety Knife with stained or albino Asian buffalo horn and bone or rosewood handles. **Patterns:** Fighters, locking folders and utility/camp knives. **Technical:** Forges and grinds 440C; uses Damascus USA billets, truck leaf springs. **Prices:** $50 to $200; some to $500. **Remarks:** Spare-time maker; first knife sold in 1957. **Mark:** LDA/LAKELL

TAYLOR, BILLY, 10 Temple Rd., Petal, MS 39465/601-544-0041
Specialties: Straight knives of his design. **Patterns:** Bowies, skinners, hunters and utility knives. **Technical:** Flat-grinds 440C, ATS-34 and 154CM. **Prices:** $60 to $300. **Remarks:** Part-time maker; first knife sold in 1991. **Mark:** Full name, city and state.

TAYLOR, C. GRAY, 137 Lana View Dr., Kingsport, TN 37664/615-288-5969
Specialties: High-art display knives; period pieces. **Patterns:** Fighters, Bowies, daggers, locking folders and interframes. **Technical:** Grinds 440C, 154CM and ATS-34. **Prices:** $200 to $3,000; some to $7,000. **Remarks:** Part-time maker; first knife sold in 1975. **Mark:** Name, city and state.

TAYLOR, DAVID, 137 Lana View Dr., Kingsport, TN 37664/615-288-5969
Specialties: Quality interframe locking folders. **Patterns:** Slip-joint and lock-back folders, boot knives and straight knives. **Technical:** Grinds 440C, 154CM and ATS-34. **Prices:** $150 to $550; some higher. **Remarks:** Part-time maker; first knife sold in 1981. **Mark:** Name, city and state.

TAYLOR, SHANE, Rock Springs Rt., Angela, MT 59312/406-354-6551 or 406-232-7175
Specialties: Fancy and working straight knives of his design and to customer specs. **Patterns:** Bowies, daggers, hunters and miniatures. **Technical:** Forges Damascus, cable Damascus and chain. Offers wildlife scrimshaw. **Prices:** $175 to $650; some to $1,500. **Remarks:** Part-time maker; first knife sold in 1982. **Mark:** First name.

TEDDER, MICKEY, Rt. 2, Box 22, Conover, NC 28613/704-464-9002
Specialties: Working folders. **Patterns:** Locking hunters, fighters and boots. **Technical:** Grinds D2, 440C and 154CM. Makes gold miniatures as jewelry. **Prices:** $150 to $300; some to $1,500. **Remarks:** Part-time maker. **Mark:** Last name.

TEDDYBEAR KNIVES (See Luchak, Bob)

TEDDYHAWK (See Goldenberg, T.S.)

TENNESSEE KNIFE MAKER—TKM (See Ward, W.C.)

TERRA-GLADIUS KNIVES (See Reynolds, Dave)

TERRILL, STEPHEN, 21363 Rd. 196, Lindsay, CA 93247/209-562-4395
Specialties: Deluxe working straight knives and folders. **Patterns:** Fighters, tantos, boots, locking folders and axes; traditional oriental patterns. **Technical:** Forges 440C, 1084 and his Damascus. **Prices:** Moderate. **Remarks:** Part-time maker; first knife sold in 1972. **Mark:** Name, city, state in logo.

TERRY KNIVES (See Cohen, Terry A.)

TERZUOLA, ROBERT, Rt. 6, Box 83A, Santa Fe, NM 87501/505-473-1002; FAX: 505-438-8018
Specialties: Working folders of his design; period pieces. **Patterns:** High-tech utility, defense and gentleman's folders. **Technical:** Grinds ATS-34. Offers titanium handles for side-lock folders. **Prices:** $275 to $400; some to $3,000. **Remarks:** Full-time maker; first knife sold in 1980. **Mark:** Mayan dragon head, name and motto meaning "second to none".

THAYER, DANNY, 4504 W. 660 S., Lafayette, IN 47905/317-538-3105
Specialties: Traditional working and using straight knives in standard patterns and to customer specs. **Patterns:** Hunters, Bowies, daggers, utility/camp and kitchen knives. **Technical:** Forges 01, W2 and 5160. **Prices:** $150 to $1,000. **Remarks:** Spare-time maker; first knife sold in 1988. **Mark:** Last name.

THOMAS, DANIEL, 1017 Rollins Dr. SW, Leesburg, VA 22075/703-442-6877
Specialties: Traditional working and using straight knives and folders of his design. **Patterns:** Hunters, slip-joint and locking folders. **Technical:** Grinds ATS-34, D2 and commercial Damascus. Offers fixed blade and folder repair and rebuilding. **Prices:** $125 to $200; some to $350. **Remarks:** Spare-time maker; first knife sold in 1983. **Mark:** Last name, Handcrafted.

custom knifemakers
THOMAS—TOMPKINS

THOMAS, DEVIN, 2344 Moonlite Dr., Las Vegas, NV 89115/702-643-6783
Specialties: Traditional straight knives and folders in standard patterns. **Patterns:** Bowies, fighters, hunters. **Technical:** Forges stainless Damascus, nickel and 1095. Uses, makes and sells Mokume with brass, copper and nickel silver. **Prices:** $300 to $1,200. **Remarks:** Full-time maker; first knife sold in 1979. **Mark:** First and last name, city and state with anvil, or first name only.

THOMAS, KIM, 2906 Center Rd., Brunswick OH 44212/216-225-3931
Specialties: Fancy and traditional straight knives of his design and to customer specs; period pieces. **Patterns:** Boots, daggers, fighters, swords. **Technical:** Forges 5160, C1095, 5160 and 1010. Acid etches on blades. **Prices:** $135 to $1,500; some to $3,000. **Remarks:** Part-time maker; first knife sold in 1986. Doing business as Thomas Iron Works. **Mark:** Initials.

THOMAS, ROCKY, 204 Columbia Dr., Ladson, SC 29456/803-553-6843
Specialties: Traditional working and using straight knives in standard patterns. **Patterns:** Hunters and utility/camp knives. **Technical:** Grinds 440C, ATS-34 and commercial Damascus. **Prices:** $75 to $125. **Remarks:** Spare-time maker; first knife sold in 1986. **Mark:** First name in script.

THOMPSON, KENNETH, 4887 Glenwhite Dr., Duluth, GA 30136/404-446-6730
Specialties: Traditional working and using knives of his design. **Patterns:** Hunters, Bowies and utility/camp knives. **Technical:** Forges 5168, 01, 1095 and 52100. **Prices:** $75 to $350; some to $600. **Remarks:** Part-time maker; first knife sold in 1990. **Mark:** P/W; or name, P/W, city and state.

THOMPSON, LEON, 1735 Leon Drive, Forest Grove, OR 97116/503-357-2573
Specialties: Working knives. **Patterns:** Locking folders, slip-joints and liner locks. **Technical:** Grinds ATS-34, D2 and 440C. **Prices:** $200 to $600. **Remarks:** Full-time maker; first knife sold in 1976. **Mark:** First and middle initials, last name, city and state.

THOMPSON, LLOYD, P.O. Box 1664, Pagosa Springs, CO 81147/303-264-5837
Specialties: Working and collectible straight knives and folders of his design. **Patterns:** Hunter drop-points, lockbacks and hawkbills. **Technical:** Hollow-grinds ATS-34, D2 and 01. Uses sambar stag and exotic woods. **Prices:** $125 to $400. **Remarks:** Full-time maker; first knife sold in 1985. Doing business as Trapper Creek Knife Co. **Mark:** Name.

THOMPSON, ROBERT L., P.O. Box 23992, Phoenix, AZ 85063/602-846-5102
Specialties: Fantasy and working straight knives of his design; miniatures as jewelry items. **Patterns:** Daggers, fighters and utility knives. **Technical:** Forges own Damascus, cable and meteorite; grinds file and other carbon steel. **Prices:** $35 to $350; some to $2,000. **Remarks:** Full-time maker; first knife sold in 1989. **Mark:** Runic figure of initials.

THOMPSON, TOMMY, 4015 NE Hassalo, Portland, OR 97232-2607/503-235-5762
Specialties: Fancy and working knives; mostly liner lock folders. **Patterns:** Fighters, hunters and liner locks. **Technical:** Grinds ATS-34, D2 and M35 or M4. Handles are either hardwood inlayed with wood banding and stone; shell; or made of agate, jasper, petrified woods, etc. **Prices:** $75 to $500; some to $1,000. **Remarks:** Part-time maker; first knife sold in 1987. Doing business as Stone Birds. **Mark:** First and last name, city and state.

THOM'S CUSTOM KNIVES (See Broome, Thomas A.)

THOUROT, MICHAEL W., T814RR1, RD 11, Napoleon, OH 43545/419-533-6832
Specialties: Working straight knives to customer specs. Designed two-handled skinning ax and limited edition engraved knife and art print set. **Patterns:** Fishing and fillet knives, Bowies, tantos and hunters. **Technical:** Grinds 01, D2, 440C and Damascus. **Prices:** $200 to $5,000. **Remarks:** Part-time maker; first knife sold in 1969. **Mark:** Initials.

THREE CROWNS CUTLERY (See Scofield, Everett)

THUESEN, ED, 10649 Haddington, Suite 180, Houston, TX 77043/713-461-8632; FAX: 713-461-8221
Specialties: Working straight knives. **Patterns:** Hunters, fighters and survival knives. **Technical:** Grinds D2, 440C, ATS-34 and Vascowear. **Prices:** $85 to $250; some to $600. **Remarks:** Part-time maker; first knife sold in 1979. Runs knifemaker supply business. **Mark:** Last name.

THUESEN, KEVIN, 10649 Haddington, Suite 180, Houston, TX 77043/713-461-8632
Specialties: Working straight knives. **Patterns:** Hunters, including upswept skinners, and custom walking sticks. **Technical:** Grinds D2, 440C, 154CM and ATS-34. **Prices:** $85 to $125; some to $200. **Remarks:** Part-time maker; first knife sold in 1985. **Mark:** Initials on slant.

THUNDERBIRD (See Mendenhall, Harry E.)

THUNDERBOLT ARTISANS (See Hilker, Thomas N.)

TILL, CALVIN E., 405 1/2 N. Maple St., Chadron, Nebraska 69337
Specialties: Fantasy and traditional straight knives of his design and to customer specs. **Patterns:** Bowies, hunters and locking folders. **Technical:** Grinds spring steel only. Full or threaded tangs. Prefers mirror polishes. **Prices:** $80 to $120; some to $250. **Remarks:** Part-time maker; first knife sold in 1986. **Mark:** Name, date and serial number.

THE TINKER (See Ladd, Jim S.)

TINKER, CAROLYN D., P.O. Box 5123, Whittier, CA 90607/213-696-9202
Specialties: Working straight knives of her design. **Patterns:** Hunters, kitchen and fishing knives; small tools. **Technical:** Grinds D2, 440C and 154CM. **Prices:** $85 to $125. **Remarks:** Full-time maker; first knife sold in 1974. Currently not taking orders. **Mark:** Name and city in logo.

T.J.'S CUSTOM KNIVES (See Tyer, Jerry L.)

TKM—TENNESSEE KNIFE MAKER (See Ward, W.C.)

TOICH, NEVIO, Via Pisacane G, Caldogno, Vincenza, ITALY 36030/0444-985065; FAX: 0444-301254
Specialties: Fantasy and working/using straight knives of his design. **Patterns:** Hunters, skinners. **Technical:** Grinds K100, 420C, 440C, D2. Offers hand-sewn sheaths; display cases. **Prices:** $150 to $300; some to $500. **Remarks:** Spare-time maker; first knife sold in 1989. Doing business as Custom Toich. **Mark:** Initials and model number.

TOKAR, DANIEL, Box 1776, Shepherdstown, WV 25443
Specialties: Working knives; period pieces. **Patterns:** Hunters, camp knives, buckskinners, axes, swords and battle gear. **Technical:** Forges L6, 1095 and his Damascus; makes mokume, Japanese alloys and bronze daggers; restores old edged weapons. **Prices:** $25 to $800; some to $3,000. **Remarks:** Part-time maker; first knife sold in 1979. Doing business as The Willow Forge. **Mark:** Arrow over rune and date.

TOLLEFSON, BARRY A., 177 Blackfoot Trail, P.O. Box 1425, Gunnison, CO 303-641-0752
Specialties: Working straight knives, some fancy. **Patterns:** Hunters, skinners, fighters and camp knives. **Technical:** Grinds 440C, ATS-34 and D2. Likes mirror-finishes; offers some fancy filework. Handles made from elk, deer and exotic hardwoods. **Prices:** $75 to $300; some higher. **Remarks:** Part-time maker; first knife sold in 1990. **Mark:** Stylized initials.

TOMES, ANTHONY S., 8190 Loch Seaforth Ct., Jacksonville, FL 32244
Specialties: Working knives and period pieces. **Patterns:** Hunters, daggers, folders and liner locks. **Technical:** Grinds D2 and ATS-34. **Prices:** $50 to $500. **Remarks:** Part-time maker. **Mark:** Initials.

TOMES, P.J., Rt. 2, Box 78, Grottoes, VA 24441/703-249-3238
Special Note: Veteran knifemaker on sabbatical; expected to resume knifemaking during 1995.

TOMKA ARMOURY (See Kaczor, Tom)

TOMPKINS, DAN, 310 North Second St., Peotone, Illinois 60468/708-258-3620
Specialties: Working knives, some deluxe, some folders. **Patterns:** Hunters, boots, daggers and push knives. **Technical:** Grinds D2, 440C, ATS-34 and 154CM. **Prices:** $85 to $150; some to $400. **Remarks:** Part-time maker; first knife sold in 1975. **Mark:** Last name, city, state.

directory
TONER—VALACHOVIC

TONER, ROGER, 531 Lightfoot Place, Pickering, Ont. L1V 5Z8, CANADA/416-420-5555
Specialties: Fancy high-art knives of his design. **Patterns:** Bowies, daggers and fighters. **Technical:** Grinds 440C, D2 and Damascus. Scrimshaws and engraves. Silvercast pommels and guards in animal shapes; twisted silver wire inlays. Uses semi-precious stones. **Prices:** $200 to $2,000; some to $3,000. **Remarks:** Part-time maker; first knife sold in 1982. **Mark:** Last name.

TOPLISS, M.W. "IKE", 1668 Hermosa Ct., Montrose, CO 81401/303-249-4703
Specialties: Working/using straight knives of his design and to customer specs. **Patterns:** Boots, hunters, utility/camp knives. **Technical:** Grinds ATS-34, 440C, D2. Prefers natural hardwoods, antler and Micarta. All sheaths hand-made. **Prices:** $125 to $250; some to $600. **Remarks:** Part-time maker; first knife sold in 1984. **Mark:** Name, city, state.

TOWELL, DWIGHT L., Rt. 1, Box 66, Midvale, ID 83645/208-355-2419
Specialties: Solid, elegant working knives; art knives. **Patterns:** Hunters, Bowies, daggers; folders in several weights. **Technical:** Grinds 154CM; some engraving. **Prices:** $250 to $800; some $3,500 and higher. **Remarks:** Part-time maker; first knife sold in 1970. **Mark:** Last name.

TOWNSEND, J.W., 2073 Highway 200, Trout Creek, MT 59874/406-847-2667
Specialties: One-of-a-kinds. **Patterns:** Fantasy knives and fighters. **Technical:** Grinds 440C, 01, commercial Damascus and ATS-34. **Prices:** $175 to $1,200; some higher. **Remarks:** Full-time maker; first knife sold in 1985. **Mark:** First and middle initials and last name, or stylized last name.

TRABBIC, R.W., 4550 N. Haven, Toledo, OH 43612/419-478-9578
Specialties: Working knives. **Patterns:** Hunters, Bowies, locking hunters and springbacks in standard patterns. **Technical:** Grinds D2, 440C and 154CM. **Prices:** $80 to $250. **Remarks:** Part-time maker; first knife sold in 1973. **Mark:** First and middle initials, last name.

TRACY, BUD, 15500 Fawn Ln., Reno, NV 89511

TRAPPER CREEK KNIFE CO. (See Thompson, Lloyd)

TRASK RIVER CUSTOM KNIVES (See Woodcock, Dennis "Woody")

TREIBER, LEON, P.O. Box 342, Ingram, TX 78025/210-367-2246
Specialties: Folders of his design and to customer specs. **Patterns:** Locking folders. **Technical:** Grinds CPM T 440V, D2, 440C. **Prices:** $250 to $600. **Remarks:** Part-time maker; first knife sold in 1992. Doing business as Treiber Knives. **Mark:** First initial, last name, city, state.

TREML, GLENN, RR #14, Site 11-10, Thunder Bay, Ontario, CANADA P7B 5E5/807-767-1977
Specialties: Working straight knives of his design and to customer specs. **Patterns:** Hunters, kitchen knives and double-edged survival knives. **Technical:** Grinds 440C, ATS-34 and 01; stock removal method. Uses Pakkawood and Micarta for handle materials. **Prices:** $60 to $400; some higher. **Mark:** Stamped last name.

TRINDLE, BARRY, RR #2, Box 63, Earlham, IA 50072/515-462-1237
Specialties: Engraved folders. **Patterns:** Mostly small folders, classical styles and pocket knives. **Technical:** 440 only. Engraves. Handles of wood or mineral material. **Prices:** Start at $975. **Mark:** Name on tang.

TRL HANDMADE KNIVES (See Lewis, Tom R.)

TRO KNIVES (See Overeynder, T.R.)

TROLL HAMMER FORGE (See Dube, Paul and Flood, James [Noah])

TRUCKEE KNIFEWORKS (See Fronefield, Mike)

TRUJILLO, THOMAS A., 2905 Arctic Blvd., Anchorage, AK 99503/907-563-2738
Specialties: Working knives. **Patterns:** Hunters, Bowies, daggers and locking folders. **Technical:** Grinds to customer choice, including rock and commercial Damascus. **Prices:** $150 to $900; some to $6,000. **Remarks:** Full-time maker; first knife sold in 1976. Doing business as Alaska Knife & Service Co. **Mark:** Alaska Knife and/or Thomas Anthony.

TURCOTTE, LARRY, 1707 Evergreen, Pampa, TX 79065/806-665-9369, 806-669-0435
Specialties: Fancy and working/using knives of his design and to customer specs. **Patterns:** Hunters, kitchen knives, utility/camp knives. **Technical:** Grinds 440C, D2, ATS-34. Engraves, scrimshands, silver inlays. **Prices:** $150 to $350; some to $1,000. **Remarks:** Part-time maker; first knife sold in 1977. Doing business as Knives by Turcotte. **Mark:** Last name.

TURECEK, JIM, P.O. Box 882, Derby, CT 06418/203-734-8406
Specialties: Exotic folders, art knives and some using knives. **Patterns:** Trout and bird knives with split bamboo handles; hunters, skinners, Bowies and folders. **Technical:** Grinds 440C, D2, 154CM, stainless and carbon Damascus. **Prices:** $200 to $1,500; some to $3,000. **Remarks:** Full-time maker; first knife sold in 1983. **Mark:** Last initial in script, or last name.

TURNBULL, RALPH A., 5722 Newburg Rd., Rockford, IL 61108/815-398-3799
Specialties: Plain or fancy working knives. **Patterns:** Hunters, fighters, boots, folders and Bowies. **Technical:** Grinds ATS-34, 440C, 154CM, CPM and others, Damascus. Makes wood inlay handles. **Prices:** $100 to $300; some to $2,000. **Remarks:** Full-time maker; first knife sold in 1973. **Mark:** Signature or initials.

TURNER, KEVIN, 17 Hunt Ave., Montrose, NY 10548/914-739-0535
Specialties: Working straight knives of his design and to customer specs; period pieces. **Patterns:** Daggers, fighters and utility knives. **Technical:** Forges 5160 and 52100. **Prices:** $90 to $500. **Remarks:** Part-time maker; first knife sold in 1991. **Mark:** Acid-etched signed last name and year.

TWIG (See Davis, K.M. "Twig")

TWILIGHT FORGE (See Champagne, Paul)

TWISTED NICKEL KNIVES (See Ferguson, Jim [Downey, CA])

TYC, WILLIAM J., 14 Hob St., Newburgh, NY 12550/914-562-5165
Specialties: Traditional and working straight knives of all designs. **Patterns:** Bowies, fighters and utility knives. **Technical:** Grinds 440C, ATS-34 and 01. Satin finishes blades. **Prices:** $80 to $300; some to $500. **Remarks:** Spare-time maker; first knife sold in 1989. **Mark:** First and last name.

TYER, JERRY L., HC67, Box 204, Everton, AR 72633/501-427-5393
Specialties: Classic working and using straight knives of his design and to customer specs. **Patterns:** Boots, Bowies, daggers, fighters, hunters and utility/camp knives. **Technical:** Forges 5168, 1068 and 01. Heat-treats. **Prices:** $150 to $350. **Remarks:** Full-time maker; first knife was sold in 1982. Doing business as T.J.'s Custom Knives. **Mark:** Stylized initials.

U

UEDA, MASAHARU, B1 Fokuku Seimei Building 2-4, Komatu bara-cho Kita-ku, Osaka City, 530 JAPAN/06-313-2525; FAX: 06-313-2626
Specialties: High-art straight knives of his design. **Patterns:** Hunters, kitchen knives and utility knives. **Technical:** Grinds Cowry X, 440C and ATS-34. **Prices:** $900 to $7,200. **Remarks:** Part-time maker; first knife sold in 1993. Doing business as World Gallery Co., Ltd. **Mark:** NA.

UEKAMA, NOBUYUKI, 3-2-8-302 Ochiai, Tama City, Tokyo, JAPAN

UWHARRIE RATTLER KNIVES (See Rece, Charles V.)

V

VACHON, YVON, 98, Lehoux St., Robertsonville, Queb., CANADA G0N 1L0

VALACHOVIC, WAYNE, P.O. Box 4219, Kailua-Kona, HI 96745/808-325-0203; FAX: 808-325-0303
Specialties: Damascus folders in unique designs with Persian influences. **Patterns:** Collectible folders. **Technical:** Forges own Damascus; most knives have filework. **Prices:** Start at $250. **Remarks:** Full-time maker. **Mark:** Last initial with cross.

custom knifemakers

VALLOTTON—WAHLERS

VALLOTTON, BUTCH AND AREY, 621 Fawn Ridge Dr., Oakland, OR 97462/503-459-2216
Specialties: Heavy-duty folders with complicated mechanisms to customer specs. **Patterns:** Fighters, gentleman's knives and working folders. **Technical:** Grinds ATS-34, 440C, Damascus, titanium, 416 and nickel-silver. Prefers bead-blasted, mirror or anodized finishes. **Prices:** $350 to $2,500. **Remarks:** Full-time maker; first knife sold in 1981. **Mark:** Name, area and state.

VALLOTTON, RAINY D., 1377 Lower Crest Rd., Oakland, OR 97462/503-459-2216
Specialties: Folders and one-handed openers. **Patterns:** Hunters, fighters, folders and sheath knives. **Technical:** Stock removal all steels; uses titanium liners and bolsters; uses all finishes. **Prices:** $250 to $1,000. **Remarks:** Full-time maker. **Mark:** Name.

VALLOTTON, SHAWN, 621 Fawn Ridge Dr., Oakland, OR 97462/503-459-2216
Specialties: Left-hand knives. **Patterns:** All styles. **Technical:** Grinds 440C, ATS-34 and Damascus. Uses titanuim. Prefers bead-blasted or anodized finishes. **Prices:** $250 to $1,400. **Remarks:** Full-time maker. **Mark:** Name and specialty.

VALOIS, A. DANIEL, 3552 W. Lizard Ck. Rd., Lehighton, PA 18235/717-386-3636
Specialties: Big working knives; various sized lock-back folders with new safety releases. **Patterns:** Fighters in survival packs, sturdy working knives, belt buckle knives, military-style knives, swords. **Technical:** Forges and grinds A2, 01 and 440C; likes full tangs. **Prices:** $65 to $240; some to $600. **Remarks:** Full-time maker; first knife sold in 1969. **Mark:** Anvil logo with last name inside.

VANDERFORD, CARL G., Rt. 9, Box 238B, Columbia, TN 38401/615-381-1488
Specialties: Traditional working straight knives and folders of his design. **Patterns:** Hunters, Bowies and locking folders. **Technical:** Forges and grinds 440C, 01 and wire Damascus. **Prices:** $60 to $125. **Remarks:** Part-time maker; first knife sold in 1987. **Mark:** Last name.

VAN ELDIK, FRANS, Ho Flaan 3, 3632 BT Loenen, NETHERLANDS/31-02943-3095; FAX: 02940-80430
Specialties: Fancy working knives of his design. **Patterns:** Hunters, fighters, boots and folders. **Technical:** Forges and grinds D2, 154CM, ATS-34 and Damascus from Germany. **Prices:** $225 to $1,750; some to $2,500. **Remarks:** Spare-time maker; first knife sold in 1979. **Mark:** Lion with initials and Amsterdam.

VEATCH, RICHARD, 3596 Pine St., North Bend, OR 97459/503-756-0504
Specialties: Traditional working and using straight knives of his design and in standard patterns; period pieces. **Patterns:** Dagggers, hunters, swords, utility/camp knives and minis. **Technical:** Forges own Damascus and grinds L6, D2 and 1056. Prefers natural handle materials; offers leatherwork. **Prices:** $50 to $300; some to $500. **Remarks:** Full-time maker; first knife sold in 1991. **Mark:** Stylized initials.

VEIT, MICHAEL, Rt. 1, 3070 E. Fifth Rd., LaSalle, IL 61301/815-223-3538
Specialties: Period pieces—fancy straight knives and Damascus folders. **Technical:** Forges his own Turkish Damascus and 01; engraves. **Prices:** Start at $350. **Remarks:** Part-time maker; first knife sold in 1985. **Mark:** Name in script.

VENSILD, HENRIK, Storegade 29, DK-3700 Renne, DENMARK/56-954191
Specialties: Classic and traditional working and using knives of his design; Scandinavian influence. **Patterns:** Hunters and using knives. **Technical:** Forges Damascus. Hand makes handles, sheaths and blades. **Prices:** $350 to $1,000. **Remarks:** Part-time maker; first knife sold in 1967. **Mark:** Initials.

VIALLON, HENRI, Les Belins, 63300 Thiers, FRANCE/(33)-73-80-24-03
Specialties: Traditional straight knives and folders of his design. **Patterns:** Hunters, folders, boots and utility knives. **Technical:** Forges and grinds 12C27, D2, 440C, ATS-34 and his own Damascus; mosaic Damascus. **Prices:** $175 to $375; some to $1,500. **Remarks:** Full-time maker; first knife sold in 1985. **Mark:** First initial, last name.

VIELE, H.J., 88 Lexington Ave., Westwood, NJ 07675/201-666-2906
Specialties: Folding knives of distinctive shapes. **Patterns:** High-tech folders. **Technical:** Grinds 440C and ATS-34. **Prices:** Start at $500. **Remarks:** Part-time maker; first knife sold in 1973. **Mark:** Last name with Japanese crane.

VIKING KNIVES (See Eriksen, James Thorlief)

VISTNES, TOR, N-6932 Kjelhenes, NORWAY/047-57-79-5572
Specialties: Traditional and working knives of his design. **Patterns:** Hunters and utility knives. **Technical:** Grinds Uddeholm Elmax. Handles made of rear burls of different Nordic woods. **Prices:** $300 to $500. **Remarks:** Part-time maker; first knife sold in 1988. **Mark:** Etched name and deer head, style type.

VIPER (See Emerson, Ernest R.)

VON BOECKMAN, R., P.O. Box 40506, Memphis, TN 38174/800-727-0201
Specialties: Working and using knives of his design. **Patterns:** Straight knives, hunters, fighters, utility and camp knives. **Technical:** Grinds 01, 06, D2, 440C and ATS-34. **Prices:** $75 to $300; some $600 and higher. **Remarks:** Full-time maker; first knife sold in 1987. Doing business as Custom Cutlery. **Mark:** Pyramid logo with RA inside.

VOSS, BEN, 362 Clark St., Galesburg, IL 61401/309-342-6994
Specialties: Fancy working knives of his design. **Patterns:** Sub-hilt fighters, hunters, boots and folders. **Technical:** Grinds 440C, ATS-34 and D2. **Prices:** $35 to $1,200. **Remarks:** Full-time maker; first knife sold in 1986. **Mark:** Name, city and state.

VOTAW, DAVID P., Box 327, Pioneer, OH 43554/419-737-2774
Specialties: Working knives; period pieces. **Patterns:** Hunters, Bowies, camp knives, buckskinners and tomahawks. **Technical:** Grinds 01 and D2. **Prices:** $100 to $200; some to $500. **Remarks:** Part-time maker; took over for the late W.K. Kneubuhler. Doing business as W-K Knives. **Mark:** WK with V inside anvil.

VOUGHT JR., FRANK, 115 Monticello Dr., Hammond, LA 70401/504-345-0278
Specialties: Distinctive working knives and embellished collectibles. **Patterns:** Bowies, hunters, survival knives, daggers, swords and locking folders. **Technical:** Forges and grinds D2, 440C and ATS-34; has new "field-grade" Outfitter line. **Prices:** $50 to $1,500; some to $15,000. **Remarks:** Full-time maker; first knife sold in 1973. **Mark:** Signature with fleur-de-lis, or Outfitter.

VULTURE CUTLERY (See Goers, Bruce)

VUNK, ROBERT, 4408 Buckeye Ct., Orlando, FL 32804/407-628-3970
Specialties: Working knives, some fancy; period pieces. **Patterns:** Variety of tantos, fillet knives, kitchen knives, camp knives and folders. **Technical:** Grinds 01, 440C and ATS-34; provides mountings, cases, stands. **Prices:** $55 to $1,300. **Remarks:** Part-time maker; first knife sold in 1985. Doing business as RV Knives. **Mark:** Initials.

W

WADA, YASUTAKA, Bl Fukoku Seimei Building 2-4, Komatu bara-cho Kita-ku, Osaka City, 530 JAPAN/06-313-2525; FAX: 06-313-2626

WADE, JAMES M., Rt. 1, Box 56, Wade, NC 28395/919-483-3548
Specialties: Working straight knives. **Patterns:** Gut-hook hunters, boots, Bowies, fighters. **Technical:** Grinds D2, 440C, 154CM and ATS-34. **Prices:** $100 to $450; some to $1,000. **Remarks:** Spare-time maker; first knife sold in 1982. **Mark:** Name.

WAGAMAN, JOHN K., 903 Arsenal Ave., Fayetteville, NC 28305/910-485-7860
Specialties: Fancy working knives. **Patterns:** Bowies, miniatures, hunters, fighters and boots. **Technical:** Grinds D2, 440C, 154CM and commercial Damascus; inlays mother-of-pearl. **Prices:** $80 to $340; some to $2,000. **Remarks:** Part-time maker; first knife sold in 1975. **Mark:** Last name.

WAGNER, DAN, 21167 Kansas Ave., Chestertown, MD 21620/410-778-5770; 410-778-5087
Specialties: Fantasy and working/using straight knives of his design and to customer specs. **Patterns:** Daggers, fighters, hunters. **Technical:** Grinds ATS-34, 52100, CPM 440V. Offers full or tapered tangs, fancy filework. Uses expensive burls and exotic woods for handles. Offers custom leather work. **Prices:** $75 to $250; some to $650. **Remarks:** Part-time maker; first knife sold in 1991. **Mark:** Oaktree Forge or acorn.

WAHLERS, HERMAN F., Star Rt. Box 1, Austerlitz, NY 12017/518-392-3570
Specialties: Straight working knives of his design. **Patterns:** Hunters, camp knives,

FIFTEENTH EDITION **267**

directory
WAHLSTER—WATSON

miniatures and working minis. **Technical:** Grinds D2, 440C and ATS-34. **Prices:** $75 to $200; some higher. **Remarks:** Full-time maker; first knife sold in 1983. Doing business as Harvey Mountain Knives. **Mark:** Initials.

WAHLSTER, MARK DAVID, 1404 N. Second St., Silverton, OR 97381/503-873-3775
Specialties: Antique folders in standard patterns; high-tech hunters; combat knives. **Patterns:** Hunters, fillets and folders to customer specs. **Technical:** Grinds 440C, ATS-34, D2 and Damascus. **Prices:** $100 to $1,000. **Remarks:** Full-time maker; first knife sold in 1981. **Mark:** Name, city and state or last name.

WALDROP, MARK, 14562 SE 1st Ave. Rd., Summerfield, FL 34491/904-347-9034
Specialties: Period pieces. **Patterns:** Bowies and daggers. **Technical:** Uses stock removal. Engraves. **Prices:** Moderate to upscale. **Remarks:** Part-time maker; first knife sold in 1978. **Mark:** Last name.

WALKER, GEORGE A., Star Route, Alpine, WY 83128/307-883-2372
Specialties: Deluxe working knives. **Patterns:** Hunters, boots, fighters, Bowies and folders. **Technical:** Forges his own Damascus and cable; engraves, carves, scrimshaws. Makes sheaths. **Prices:** $125 to $750; some to $1,000. **Remarks:** Full-time maker; first knife sold in 1979. Partners with wife. **Mark:** Name, city and state.

WALKER, JOHN W., 10620 Moss Branch Rd., Bon Aqua, TN 37025/615-670-4754
Specialties: Straight knives and short daggers. **Patterns:** Hunters, boots, etc., some with precious stones. **Technical:** Grinds 440C, ATS-34, L6, etc. **Prices:** $100 to $450; some to $600. **Remarks:** Part-time maker; first knife sold in 1982. **Mark:** Hohenzollern Eagle emblem with name, or last name.

WALKER, MICHAEL L., Box 2343, Taos, NM 87571/505-758-0233
Specialties: High-tech folders of his design. **Patterns:** Locking folders, patent locks, interframes—engraved, scrimmed, anodized in titanium colors, furnished with rich materials. **Technical:** Grinds AEB-L, 6K and commercial Damascus. **Prices:** Start at $800. **Remarks:** Full-time maker; first knife sold in 1980. Has trademarked words "liner lock" for advertising use. Most knives a team effort with Patricia Walker. **Mark:** Walker's Lockers by M.L. Walker, or initials.

WALKER, PATRICIA (See Walker, Michael L.)

WALKER'S LOCKERS (See Walker, Michael L.)

WALLACE, ROGER L., 4902 Collins Lane, Tampa, FL 33603/813-239-3261
Specialties: Working straight knives, Bowies and camp knives to customer specs. **Patterns:** Hunters, skinners and utility knives. **Technical:** Forges high-carbon steel. **Prices:** Start at $75. **Remarks:** Part-time maker; first knife sold in 1985. **Mark:** First initial, last name.

WALTERS, A.F., 609 E. 20th St., Tifton, GA 31794/912-382-1282
Specialties: Working knives, some to customer specs. **Patterns:** Locking folders, straight hunters, fishing and survival knives. **Technical:** Grinds D2, 154CM and 13C26. **Prices:** Start at $150. **Remarks:** Part-time maker. Label: "The jewel knife." **Mark:** J in diamond and knife logo.

WANO KNIVES (See Ware, Tommy)

WARD, CHUCK, 1010 E. North St., Benton, AR 72015/501-778-4329
Specialties: Traditional working and using straight knives and folders of his design. **Technical:** Grinds 440C, D2, A2 and 01; uses natural and composite handle materials. **Prices:** $90 to $400, some higher. **Remarks:** Full-time maker; first knife sold in 1990. **Mark:** First initial, last name.

WARD, KEN, P.O. Box 6594, Auburn, CA 95604/916-885-8908
Specialties: Working knives, some to customr specs. **Patterns:** Straight and folding hunters, axes, Bowies, buckskinners and miniatures. **Technical:** Grinds ATS-34, Damascus and 6K stellite. **Prices:** $100 to $700. **Remarks:** Part-time maker; first knife sold in 1977. **Mark:** Name.

WARD, W.C., 817 Glenn St., Clinton, TN 37716/615-457-3568
Specialties: Working straight knives; period pieces. **Patterns:** Hunters, Bowies, swords and kitchen cutlery. **Technical:** Grinds 01. **Prices:** $85 to $150; some to $500. **Remarks:** Part-time maker; first knife sold in 1969. He styled the Tennessee Knife Maker. **Mark:** TKM.

WARDELL, MICK R., 85 Coneybury, White Post, Bletchingley, Surrey RH1 4PR ENGLAND/0883-742918
Specialties: Custom knives. **Patterns:** Hunters, Bowies, tantos and friction folders. **Technical:** Grinds Sandvik 12C27, D2, 01 and 9260. Heat-treats with multiple tempering, clay tempering and hardness testing. Offers filework; makes sheaths. **Prices:** œ50 to œ200; some to œ350. **Remarks:** Full-time maker; first knife sold in 1986. **Mark:** Last name or initials.

WARDEN, ROY A., Rt. 2, Box 138-2, Union, MO 63084/314-583-8813
Specialties: Working straight knives of his design and in standard patterns. **Patterns:** Hunters, bird and trout knives, camp knives. **Technical:** Forges 5160. Makes own pattern-welded steel Damascus and mosaic Damascus; Damascus billets rough-forged and patterned to order; makes cable Damascus knives and belt buckles. Heat-treats and embellishes. Makes individual knife display stands from woods, steel and horns. **Prices:** Start at $65. **Remarks:** Part-time maker; first knife sold in 1987. **Mark:** Last name.

WARE, TOMMY, Star Route 4, Box 79, Blanco, TX 78606/512-833-5235
Specialties: Working straight knives of his design or to customer specs. **Patterns:** Hunters, single-blade folding hunters, Bowies, hatchets and camp knives, miniatures. **Technical:** Grinds 440C, ATS-34 and D2; embellishes. **Prices:** $150 to $450; some to $800. **Remarks:** Full-time maker; first knife sold in 1988. **Mark:** Wano Knives, city, state and year in oval logo.

WARENSKI, BUSTER, P.O. Box 214, Richfield, UT 84701/801-896-5319
Specialties: Investor-class straight knives. **Patterns:** Daggers, swords, fighters and Bowies. **Technical:** Grinds, engraves and inlays; offers surface treatments. **Prices:** Upscale. **Remarks:** Full-time maker. Not currently taking orders. **Mark:** First or last name.

WARREN, AL, 1423 Sante Fe Circle, Roseville, CA 95678/916-784-3217
Specialties: Working straight knives, some fancy. **Patterns:** Hunters, Bowies, daggers and short swords. **Technical:** Grinds D2, ATS-34 and 440C. **Prices:** $120 to $1,250; some to $4,200. **Remarks:** Part-time maker; first knife sold in 1978. **Mark:** Name in oval logo.

WARTHER, DALE, 331 Karl Ave., Dover, OH 44622/216-343-7513
Specialties: Working knives; period pieces. **Patterns:** Kitchen cutlery, daggers, hunters and some folders. **Technical:** Forges and grinds 01, D2 and 440C. **Prices:** $100 to $350; some to $5,000. **Remarks:** Full-time maker; first knife sold in 1967. Takes orders only at shows or by personal interviews at his shop. **Mark:** Warther Originals.

WARTHER ORIGINALS (See Warther, Dale)

WARZOCHA, STANLEY, 32540 Wareham Dr., Warren, MI 48092/313-939-9344
Specialties: Working straight knives; some period pieces. **Patterns:** Hunters, buckskinners, fighters and fishing knives. **Technical:** Grinds 440C and ATS-34. **Prices:** $125 to $1,200. **Remarks:** Spare-time maker; first knife sold in 1978. **Mark:** Last name.

WATANABE, WAYNE, P.O. Box 3563, Montebello, CA 90640/213-728-6867
Specialties: Straight knives in Japanese styles. One-of-kind designs; welcomes customer designs. **Patterns:** Tantos to katanas, Bowies. **Technical:** Flat grinds A2, 01 and ATS-34. Offers hand-rubbed finishes and wrapped handles. **Prices:** Start at $100. **Remarks:** Part-time maker. **Mark:** Name in characters with flower.

WATER MOUNTAIN KNIVES (See Maneker, Kenneth)

WATSON, BERT, P.O. Box 26, Westminster, CO 80030-0026/303-426-7577
Specialties: Working/using straight knives of his design and to customer specs. **Patterns:** Fighters, hunters, utility/camp knives. **Technical:** Grinds 01, ATS-34, 440C. **Prices:** $50 to $250. **Remarks:** Full-time maker; first knife sold in 1974. Doing business as Game Trail Knives. **Mark:** GTK stamped, sometimes with first name.

WATSON, BILLY, 440 Forge Rd., Deatsville, AL 36022/205-365-1482
Specialties: Working and using straight knives and folders of his design; period pieces. **Patterns:** Hunters, Bowies and utility/camp knives. **Technical:** Forges and grinds his own Damascus, 1095, 5160 and 52100. Copper etches on Damascus. **Prices:** $20 to $900. **Remarks:** Full-time maker; first knife sold in 1970. **Mark:** Last name.

custom knifemakers
WATSON—WEST

WATSON, DANIEL, 350 Jennifer Ln., Driftwood, TX 78619/512-847-9679
Specialties: One-of-a-kind knives and swords. **Patterns:** Hunters, daggers, swords and miniatures. **Technical:** Hand-purify and carbonize his own high-carbon steel, pattern-welded Damascus, cable and carbon-induced crystalline Damascus. European and Japanese tempering. **Prices:** $90 to $4,000; swords to $25,000. **Remarks:** Full-time maker; first knife sold in 1979. **Mark:** "Angel Sword" on forged pieces; "Bright Knight" for stock removal.

WATSON, PETER, 66 Kielblock St., La Hoff 2570, SOUTH AFRICA/018-84942
Specialties: Traditional working and using straight knives and folders of his design. **Patterns:** Hunters, locking folders and utility/camp knives. **Technical:** Sandvik and 440C. **Prices:** $120 to $250; some to $1,500. **Remarks:** Part-time maker; first knife sold in 1989. **Mark:** Buffalo head with name.

WATSON, TOM, 1103 Brenau Terrace, Panama City, FL 32405/904-785-9209
Specialties: Lockback folders with coil springs-micarta and pearl inlays. **Patterns:** Folding drop point hunters and folding boot knives. **Technical:** Flat-grinds 440C, ATS-34 and A2. Heat-treats with multiple tempering and hardness testing. Prefers satin finishes. **Prices:** Starting at $150. **Remarks:** Full-time maker; first knife sold in 1978. **Mark:** Name and city.

WATT III, FREDDIE, P.O. Box 1372, Big Spring, TX 79721/915-263-6629
Specialties: Working straight knives, some fancy. **Patterns:** Hunters, fighters and Bowies. **Technical:** Grinds A2, D2, 440C and ATS-34; prefers mirror finishes. **Prices:** $150 to $350; some to $750. **Remarks:** Full-time maker; first knife sold in 1979. **Mark:** Last name, city and state.

WATTELET, MICHAEL A., P.O. Box 649, 125 Front, Minocqua, WI 54548/715-356-3069
Specialties: Working and using straight knives of his design and to customer specs; fantasy knives. **Patterns:** Daggers, fighters and swords. **Technical:** Grinds 440C and L6; forges and grinds 01. Silversmith. **Prices:** $75 to $1,000; some to $5,000. **Remarks:** Full-time maker; first knife sold in 1966. Doing business as M&N Arts Ltd. **Mark:** First initial, last name.

WATTS, WALLY, Rt. 1, Box 81, Gatesville, TX 76528/817-487-2866
Specialties: Unique traditional folders of his design. **Patterns:** One- to four-blade folders and single-blade gents in various blade shapes. **Technical:** Grinds 440C, D2 and ATS-34. **Prices:** $100 to $200; some to $300. **Remarks:** Full-time maker; first knife sold in 1986. **Mark:** Last name.

WEAPONS SHOP (See Brooks, Michael)

WEBB JR., CHARLEY L., 2326 Airline Rd., Anderson, SC 29624
Specialties: Traditional and working straight knives of his design and to customer specs. **Patterns:** Boots, Bowies, hunters, utility knives and commemoritives. **Technical:** Grinds 440C, ATS-34 and D2. Prefers mirror polish; heat-treats. Handle materials of exotic woods, Pakkawood and Micarta. **Prices:** $75 to $250; some to $600. **Remarks:** Part-time maker; first knife sold in 1991. **Mark:** Initials or name and city.

WEBB, JIM, Rt. 2, Box 435, Joplin, MO 64804/417-781-3434
Specialties: Traditional working and using straight knives and folders of his design and in standard patterns. **Patterns:** Fighters, hunters and locking folders. **Technical:** Grinds 440C. **Prices:** $200 to $375; some to $500. **Remarks:** Full-time maker; first knife sold in 1991. Served apprenticeship in shop of G.W. Stone. **Mark:** Name and serial number.

WEBER, FRED E., 517 Tappan St., Forked River, NJ 08731/609-693-0452
Specialties: Working knives in standard patterns. **Patterns:** Hunters, slip-joint and lock-back folders, Bowies and various-sized fillets. **Technical:** Grinds D2, 440V and ATS-34. **Prices:** $125 to $250; some to $500. **Remarks:** Full-time maker; first knife sold in 1973. **Mark:** First and middle initials, last name.

WEDDLE JR., DEL, 2703 Green Valley Rd., St. Joseph, MO 64505/816-364-1981
Specialties: Working knives; some period pieces. **Patterns:** Hunters, fighters, locking folders, push knives. **Technical:** Grinds D2 and 440C; can provide precious metals and set gems. Offers his own forged wire-cable Damascus in his finished knives. **Prices:** $80 to $250; some to $2,000. **Remarks:** Full-time maker; first knife sold in 1972. **Mark:** Signature with last name and date.

WEHNER, RUDY, Rt. 4, Box 364 A1, Collins, MS 39428/601-765-4997
Specialties: Reproduction antique Bowies and contemporary Bowies in full and miniature. **Patterns:** Skinners, camp knives, fighters, axes and Bowies. **Technical:** Grinds 440C, ATS-34, 154CM and Damascus. **Prices:** $100 to $500; some to $850. **Remarks:** Full-time maker; first knife sold in 1975. **Mark:** Last name on Bowies and antiques; full name, city and state on skinners.

WEILAND JR., J. REESE, 612 Superior Ave., Tampa, FL 33606/813-971-5378 (7:30 a.m.-5:00 p.m.); 813-671-0661 (after 6:00 p.m.)
Specialties: Traditional working straight knives and folders; liner locks. **Patterns:** Hunters, tantos, Bowies, fantasy knives, spears and some swords. **Technical:** Grinds ATS-34 and Damascus bars. Offers titanium hardware on his liner locks and button locks. Distinctive bird-shaped handle on some models. **Prices:** $100 to $4,000. **Remarks:** Full-time maker; first knife sold in 1983. **Mark:** RW slant.

WEILER, DONALD E., P.O. Box 11576, Yuma, AZ 85364/602-782-1159
Specialties: Working straight knives; period pieces. **Patterns:** Dirks, daggers, fighters, survival, throwing and camp knives; scramasax; buckskinner and Norse designs. **Technical:** Forges 01, W2, 5160, ATS-34 and D2. Makes own high-carbon steel Damascus. **Prices:** $70 to $1,000. **Remarks:** Full-time maker; first knife sold in 1952. **Mark:** Last name, city.

WEINAND, GEROME M., 14440 Harpers Bridge Rd., Missoula, MT 59802/406-543-0845
Specialties: Working straight knives. **Patterns:** Bowies, fishing and camp knives, large special hunters. **Technical:** Grinds 01, 440C, ATS-34, 1084 and L6; makes all-tool steel Damascus. Heat-treats. **Prices:** $30 to $100; some to $500. **Remarks:** Full-time maker; first knife sold in 1982. **Mark:** Name, city and state.

WEISS, CHARLES L., 18847 N. 13th Ave., Phoenix, AZ 85027/602-869-0425; FAX: 602-869-0425
Specialties: High-art straight knives and folders; deluxe period pieces. **Patterns:** Daggers, fighters, boots, push knives and miniatures. **Technical:** Grinds 440C, 154CM and ATS-34. **Prices:** $300 to $1,200; some to $2,000. **Remarks:** Full-time maker; first knife sold in 1975. **Mark:** Name and city.

WELCH, WILLIAM H., 8232 W. Red Snapper Dr., Kimmell, IN 46760/219-856-3577
Specialties: Working knives; deluxe period pieces. **Patterns:** Hunters, tantos, Bowies. **Technical:** Grinds ATS-34, D2 and 440C. **Prices:** $100 to $600. **Remarks:** Part-time maker; first knife sold in 1976. **Mark:** Last name.

WERNER JR., WILLIAM A., 336 Lands Mill, Marietta, GA 30067/404-988-0074
Specialties: Fantasy and working/using straight knives. **Patterns:** Bowies, daggers, fighters. **Technical:** Grinds 440C stainless, 10 series carbon and Damascus. **Prices:** $150 to $400; some to $750. **Remarks:** Part-time maker. Doing business as Werner Knives. **Mark:** Last name.

WERTH, GEORGE W., 5223 Woodstock Rd., Poplar Grove, IL 61065/815-544-4408
Specialties: Period pieces, some fancy. **Patterns:** Straight fighters, daggers and Bowies. **Technical:** Forges and grinds 01, 1095 and his Damascus, including mosaic patterns. **Prices:** $200 to $650; some higher. **Remarks:** Full-time maker. Doing business as Fox Valley Forge. **Mark:** Name in logo or initials connected.

WESCOTT, CODY, 5610 Hanger Lake Ln., Las Cruces, NM 88012/505-382-5008
Specialties: Fancy and presentation-grade working knives. **Patterns:** Hunters, locking folders and Bowies. **Technical:** Hollow-grinds D2 and ATS-34; all knives fileworked. Offers some engraving. Makes sheaths. **Prices:** $80 to $300; some to $950. **Remarks:** Full-time maker; first knife sold in 1982. **Mark:** First initial, last name.

WESOLOWSKI, MIKE, 902-A Lohrman Lane, Petaluma, CA 94952/707-762-7564
Specialties: Working knives; display Bowies. **Patterns:** Hunters, utility and using knives, miniatures. **Technical:** Flat-grinds D2, 440C and 154CM; offers finger placement coils. **Prices:** $150 to $300; some higher. **Remarks:** Part-time maker; first knife sold in 1973. Doing business as M.W. Knives. **Mark:** Initials, city and state in knife logo.

WEST, PAT, P.O. Box 9, Charlotte, TX 78011/512-277-1290
Specialties: Classic working and using straight knives and folders. **Patterns:** Hunters, kitchen knives, slip-joint folders. **Technical:** Grinds ATS-34, D2 and Vas-

FIFTEENTH EDITION **269**

directory

WESTBERG—WILLIAMS

cowear. Offers filework and decorates liners on folders. **Prices:** $300 to $600. **Remarks:** Spare-time maker; first knife sold in 1984. **Mark:** Name.

WESTBERG, LARRY, 305 S. Western Hills Dr., Algona, IA 50511/515-295-9276 **Specialties:** Traditional and working straight knives of his design and in standard patterns. **Patterns:** Bowies, hunters, utility knives and miniatures. **Technical:** Grinds 440C, D2 and 1095. Heat-treats. Uses natural handle materials. **Prices:** $85 to $600; some to $1,000. **Remarks:** Part-time maker; first knife sold in 1987. **Mark:** Last name.

WHIPPLE, WESLEY A., P.O. Box 47, Thermopolis, WY 82443/307-864-2255 **Specialties:** Working straight knives, some fancy. **Patterns:** Hunters, Bowies, camp knives, fighters. **Technical:** Forges 5168, 52100, W2; makes cable and pattern Damascus; offers silver-wire inlay. **Prices:** $125 to $450; some higher. **Remarks:** Part-time maker; first knife sold in 1989. **Mark:** Last name.

WHISKERS (See Allen, Mike "Whiskers")

WHITE, GENE E., 1015 Cross Dr., Alexandria, VA 22302/703-671-3997 **Specialties:** Small utility/gents knives. **Patterns:** Eight standard hunters; most other patterns on commission basis. Currently no swords, axes and fantasy knives. **Technical:** Stock removal 440C and D2; others on request. Mostly hollow grinds; some flat grinds. Prefers natural handle materials. Makes own sheaths. **Prices:** Start at $75. **Remarks:** Part-time maker; first knife sold in 1971. **Mark:** First and middle intials, last name.

WHITE, ROBERT J., RR 1, 641 Knox Rd. 900 N., Gilson, IL 61436/309-289-4487 **Specialties:** Working knives, some deluxe. **Patterns:** Bird and trout knives, hunters, survival knives and locking folders. **Technical:** Grinds A2, D2 and 440C; commercial Damascus. Heat-treats. **Prices:** $125 to $250; some to $600. **Remarks:** Full-time maker; first knife sold in 1976. **Mark:** Last name in script.

WHITE JR., ROBERT J. "BUTCH", RR 1, Gilson, IL 61436/309-289-4487 **Specialties:** Working straight knives and folders; some collector pieces. **Patterns:** Hunters, fighters, boots and Damascus miniatures. **Technical:** Forges and grinds D2, 440C and his own Damascus. **Prices:** $100 to $750. **Remarks:** Full-time maker; first knife sold in 1980. **Mark:** Last name in block letters; a block last initial on miniatures.

WHITEHEAD, JAMES D., 204 Cappucino Way, Sacramento, CA 95838/916-641-7309; FAX: 916-641-1941 **Specialties:** Highly detailed straight and folding miniatures. **Patterns:** Traditional and fancy. **Technical:** Forges and grinds 01 and commercial Damascus. **Prices:** $250 to $2,000. **Remarks:** Part-time maker; first knife sold in 1985. **Mark:** Initials.

WHITLEY, WAYNE, 210 E. 7th St., Washington, NC 27889/919-946-5648 **Specialties:** Working/using straight knives of his design and to customer specs. **Patterns:** Bowies, hunters, utility/camp knives. **Technical:** Grinds ATS-34, D2, 440C; forges own Damascus and cable and high-carbon tool steels. **Prices:** $65 to $650; some to $1,500. **Remarks:** Part-time maker; first knife sold in 1990. Doing business as WW Custom Knives. **Mark:** Name, city, state.

WHITLEY, WELDON G., 6316 Jebel Way, El Paso, TX 79912/915-584-2274 **Specialties:** Working knives of his design or to customer specs. **Patterns:** Hunters, folders and various double-edged knives. **Technical:** Grinds 440C, 154CM and ATS 34. **Prices:** $150 to $1250. **Mark:** Name, address, road-runner logo.

WHITMAN, JIM, HC 80, Box 5387, 21044 Salem St., Chugiak, AK 99567/907-688-4575; 907-688-4278 **Specialties:** Working straight knives; some art pieces. **Patterns:** Hunters, especially skinners, Bowies, camp knives, working fighters, swords, hatchets and extreme walking staffs. **Technical:** Grinds AEB-L Swedish, 440C, ATS-34 and commercial Damascus in full convex. Prefers natural and native handle materials—whale bone, antler, ivory and horn. **Prices:** Start at $85. **Remarks:** Part-time maker; first knife sold in 1983. **Mark:** Name, city and state.

WHITMIRE, EARL T., 725 Colonial Dr., Rock Hill, SC 29730/803-324-8384 **Specialties:** Working straight knives, some to customer specs. **Patterns:** Hunters, fighters, fishing knives and some fantasy pieces. **Technical:** Grinds D2, 440C and 154CM. **Prices:** $40 to $200; some to $250. **Remarks:** Full-time maker; first knife sold in 1967. **Mark:** Name, city, state in oval logo.

WHITTAKER, ROBERT E., P.O. Box 204, Mill Creek, PA 17060 **Specialties:** Using straight knives. Has a line of knives for buckskinners. **Patterns:** Hunters, skinners and Bowies. **Technical:** Grinds 01, A2 and D2. Offers filework. **Prices:** $35 to $100. **Remarks:** Part-time maker; first knife sold in 1980. **Mark:** Last initial or full initials.

WHITWORTH, KEN J., 41667 Tetley Ave., Sterling Heights, MI 48078/313-739-5720 **Specialties:** Working straight knives and folders. **Patterns:** Locking folders, slip-joints and boot knives. **Technical:** Grinds 440C, 154CM and D2. **Prices:** $100 to $225; some to $450. **Remarks:** Part-time maker; first knife sold in 1976. **Mark:** Last name.

WICKER, DONNIE R., 2544 E. 40th Ct., Panama City, FL 32405/904-785-9158 **Specialties:** Traditional working and using straight knives of his design or to customer specs. **Patterns:** Hunters, fighters and slip-joint folders. **Technical:** Grinds 440C, ATS-34, D2 and 154CM. Heat-treats and does hardness testing. **Prices:** $90 to $200; some to $400. **Remarks:** Part-time maker; first knife sold in 1975. **Mark:** First and middle initials, last name.

WIGGINS, HORACE, 203 Herndon, Box 152, Mansfield, LA 71502/318-872-4471 (evenings) **Specialties:** Fancy working knives. **Patterns:** Straight and folding hunters. **Technical:** Grinds 01, D2 and 440C. **Prices:** $90 to $275. **Remarks:** Part-time maker; first knife sold in 1970. **Mark:** Name, city and state in diamond logo.

WILCHER, WENDELL L., RR3, Box 3513, Palestine, TX 75801/903-549-2530 **Specialties:** Fantasy and working/using straight knives and folders of his design and to customer specs. **Patterns:** Fighters, hunters, locking folders. **Technical:** Grinds 440C, ATS-34, 01. Some filework. **Prices:** $75 to $250; some to $600. **Remarks:** Part-time maker; first knife sold in 1987. **Mark:** Initials, year, serial number.

WILD BILL & SONS (See Caldwell, Bill)

WILDWOOD STUDIOS (See Rece, Charles V.)

WILLEY, W.G., R.D. 1, Box 235-B, Greenwood, DE 19950/302-349-4070 **Specialties:** Fancy working straight knives. **Patterns:** Small game knives, Bowies and throwing knives. **Technical:** Grinds 440C and 154CM. **Prices:** $225 to $600; some to $1,500. **Remarks:** Part-time maker; first knife sold in 1975. Owns retail store. **Mark:** Last name inside map logo.

WILLIAMS, DAVID, Box 75, Berea, WV 26327/304-659-3286 **Specialties:** Working and using straight knives of his design and in Japanese patterns; period pieces. **Patterns:** Daggers, hunters and tantos. **Technical:** Grinds L6 and 01; forges 5160/wrought iron, cable Damascus and David Boye dendritic steel. Trademark look is a rough, pitted black area above the hollow-ground area. Gas forge heat-treats. **Prices:** $75 to $300; some to $500. **Remarks:** Part-time maker; first knife sold in 1980. **Mark:** Bywater Homestead, name, knifemaker.

WILLIAMS, JASON L., P.O. Box 67, Wyoming, RI 02898/401-539-8353 **Specialties:** Fancy and high-tech folders of his design. **Patterns:** Fighters, locking folders and fancy pocketknives. **Technical:** Forges Damascus and other steels by request. Uses exotic handle materials. Offers inlayed spines and gemstone thumb knobs. **Prices:** Starting at $500. **Remarks:** Full-time maker; first knife sold in 1989. **Mark:** Initials engraved inside case.

WILLIAMS, LEONARD, P.O. Box 162, Meadow Bridge, WV 25976/304-484-7742 **Specialties:** Working knives. **Patterns:** Modern and period hunters, camp and trail knives. **Technical:** Grinds or forges all steels. **Prices:** Low to moderate. **Remarks:** Part-time maker; first knife sold in 1988. **Mark:** Name or initials.

WILLIAMS, MICHAEL L., Rt. 2, Box 832, Broken Bow, OK 74728/405-584-3925 **Specialties:** Working straight knives, some fancy; folders. **Patterns:** Hunters, Bowies, camp knives. **Technical:** Forges 5160, L6, cable and his own pattern-welded steel. **Prices:** Start at $125. **Remarks:** Part-time maker; first knife sold in 1989. **Mark:** Last name.

WILLIAMS JR., RICHARD, 1440 Nancy Circle, Morristown, TN 37814/615-581-0059

Specialties: Working and using straight knives of his design or to customer specs. **Patterns:** Hunters, dirks and utility/camp knives. **Technical:** Forges 5160 and uses file steel. Hand-finish is standard; offers filework. **Prices:** $80 to $180; some to $250. **Remarks:** Spare-time maker; first knife sold in 1985. **Mark:** Last initial or full intials.

WILLIAMS, SHERMAN A., 1709 Wallace St., Simi Valley, CA 93065/805-583-3821
Specialties: Working straight knives in standard patterns. **Patterns:** Hunters, boots, utility knives, unusual trail knives. **Technical:** Forges and grinds ATS-34, 440C, 1095 and 5160. **Prices:** $45 to $500. **Remarks:** Part-time maker; first knife sold in 1983. Doing business as Sherman Knives. **Mark:** First name in crow logo.

WILLIAMSON, TONY, Rt. 3, Box 503, Siler City, NC 27344/919-663-3551
Specialties: Flint knapping—knives made of obsidian flakes and flint with wood, antler or bone for handles. **Patterns:** Skinners, daggers and flake knives. **Technical:** Blades have width/thickness ratio of at least 4 to 1. Hafts with methods available to prehistoric man. **Prices:** $58 to $160. **Remarks:** Student of Errett Callahan. **Mark:** Initials and number code to identify year and number of knives made.

WILLIAMSON II, WALT, 10231 Ashford St., Rancho Cucamonga, CA 91730/714-944-9180
Specialties: Heavy-duty working straight knives of his design. **Patterns:** Bowies, hunters, skinners, capers, bird and fish knives. **Technical:** Hollowgrinds ATS-34 and Damascus; buys Damascus. Provides leather sheaths; offers some semi-precious stones in handles; prefers mirror finishes. **Prices:** $150 to $300. **Remarks:** Full-time maker; first knife sold in 1979. **Mark:** Name, city and state.

THE WILLOW FORGE (See Tokar, Daniel)

WILSON (See Gianluigi, Simonella)

WILSONHAWK (See Wilson, James G.)

WILSON, JAMES G., P.O. Box 4024, Estes Park, CO 80517/303-586-3944
Specialties: Bronze Age knives; 37th century knives—Medieval and Scottish styles; tomahawks. **Patterns:** Bronze knives, daggers, swords, spears and battle axes; 12-inch steel Misericorde daggers, sgian dubhs, "His and Her" skinners, bird and fish knives, capers, boots and daggers. **Technical:** Casts bronze; grinds D2, 440C and ATS-34. **Prices:** $49 to $400; some to $1,300. **Remarks:** Part-time maker; first knife sold in 1975. **Mark:** WilsonHawK.

WILSON, JON J., 1826 Ruby St., Johnstown, PA 15902/814-266-6410
Specialties: Miniatures only. **Patterns:** Bowies, daggers and hunters. **Technical:** Grinds Damascus, 440C and 01. Scrimshands and carves. **Prices:** $65 to $175; some to $250. **Remarks:** Full-time maker; first knife sold in 1988. **Mark:** First and middle initials, last name.

WILSON, MIKE, 2619 Fork Creek Ln., Bowman, GA 30624/706-245-0823
Specialties: Fancy working and using straight knives of his design or to customer specs. **Patterns:** Hunters, Bowies, utility knives, gut hooks, skinners, fighters and miniatures. **Technical:** Hollow-grinds 440C, ATS-34 and D2. Mirror finishes are standard. Offers filework. **Prices:** $70 to $300. **Remarks:** Full-time maker; first knife sold in 1985. **Mark:** Last name.

WILSON, PHILIP C., 1064 Lomitas Ave., Livermore, CA 94550/510-455-9474; 510-422-0503
Specialties: Working knives; emphasis on salt water fillet knives and utility hunters of his design. **Patterns:** Fishing knives, hunters, kitchen knives. **Technical:** Grinds ATS-34, 440C, CPM440V and D2. Prefers hollow grinds and hand-rubbed satin finishes. Heat-treats. **Prices:** Start at $80. **Remarks:** Part-time maker; first knife sold in 1985. Doing business as Sea-Mount Knife Works. **Mark:** Signature.

WILSON, R.W., P.O. Box 2012, Weirton, WV 26062/304-723-2771
Specialties: Working straight knives; period pieces. **Patterns:** Bowies, tomahawks and patch knives. **Prices:** $85 to $175; some to $1,000. **Technical:** Grinds 440C; scrimshaws. **Remarks:** Part-time maker; first knife sold in 1966. Knifemaker supplier. **Mark:** Name in tomahawk.

WIMPFF, CHRISTIAN, Rosshaustr. 67, 70597 Stuttgart, 70 GERMANY/711-764324; FAX: 711-7656960
Specialties: High-tech folders of his design. **Patterns:** Boots, locking folders and liner locks. **Technical:** Grinds CPM T 440V, ATS-34 and Schneider stainless Damascus. Offers pantographing and meteorite bolsters and blades. **Prices:** $1,000 to $2,800; some to $4,000. **Remarks:** Part-time maker; first knife sold in 1984. **Mark:** First initial, last name.

WIND RIVER KNIVES (See Bridges, Justin W.)

WINE, MICHAEL, 265 S. Atlantic Ave., Cocoa Beach, FL 32931/407-784-2187
Specialties: Traditional working straight knives. **Patterns:** Fishing, hunting and kitchen knives. **Technical:** Grinds carbon, high-chrome tool steels, stellite; casts 440C. **Prices:** Start at $145. **Remarks:** Spare-time maker; first knife sold in 1971. **Mark:** First initial, last name with palm tree.

WINGO, PERRY, 22 55th St., Gulfport, MS 39507/601-863-3193
Specialties: Traditional working straight knives. **Patterns:** Hunters, skinners, Bowies and fishing knives. **Technical:** Grinds 440C. **Prices:** $75 to $1,000. **Remarks:** Full-time maker; first knife sold in 1988. **Mark:** Last name.

WINKLER, DANIEL, P.O. Box 2166, Blowing Rock, NC 28605
Specialties: Period pieces, some made to look old; buckskinner working knives. **Patterns:** Buckskinners, patch knives, daggers, folders, skinners and fighters. **Technical:** Forges and grinds 52100, L6, 01, old files and his Damascus. **Prices:** Start at $150; some to $2,500. **Remarks:** Full-time maker; first knife sold in 1984. **Mark:** Initials connected.

WINN, TRAVIS A., 558 E. 3065 S., Salt Lake City, UT 84106/801-467-5957
Specialties: Fancy working knives and knives to customer specs. **Patterns:** Hunters, fighters, boots, Bowies and fancy daggers, some miniatures, tantos and fantasy knives. **Technical:** Grinds D2 and 440C. Embellishes. **Prices:** $100 to $500; some higher. **Remarks:** Part-time maker; first knife sold in 1976. **Mark:** TRAV stylized.

WINSTON, DAVID, 1671 Red Holly St., Starkville, MS 39759/601-323-1028
Specialties: Fancy and traditional knives of his design and to customer specs. **Patterns:** Bowies, daggers, hunters, boot knives and folders. **Technical:** Grinds 440C, ATS-34 and D2. Offers filework; heat-treats. Engraving by Norvell Foster. **Prices:** $40 to $750; some higher. **Remarks:** Part-time maker; first knife sold in 1984. Offers lifetime sharpening for original owner. **Mark:** Last name.

WISE, DONALD, 304 Bexhill Rd., St. Leonardo-On-Sea, East Sussex TN3 8AL ENGLAND
Specialties: Fancy and embellished working straight knives to customer specs. **Patterns:** Hunters, Bowies and daggers. **Technical:** Grinds Sandvik 12C27, D2, D3 and 01. Srimshaws. **Prices:** $110 to $300; some to $500. **Remarks:** Full-time maker; first knife sold in 1983. **Mark:** KNIFECRAFT.

WISE, JOHN, P.O. Box 994, Winchester, OR 97495
Specialties: Classic high-art straight knives and folders to customer specs. **Patterns:** Daggers, fighters, locking folders, miniatures. **Technical:** Grinds 440C, ATS-34, commercial Damascus. **Prices:** $150 to $350; some to $1,000. **Remarks:** Part-time maker; first knife sold in 1989. **Mark:** Stylized name.

WITSAMAN, EARL, 3957 Redwing Circle, Stow, OH 44224/216-688-4208
Specialties: Straight and fantasy miniatures. **Patterns:** Wide variety—Randalls to D-guard Bowies. **Technical:** Grinds 01, 440C and 300 stainless; buys Damascus; highly detailed work. **Prices:** $70 to $200. **Remarks:** Part-time maker; first knife sold in 1974. **Mark:** Initials.

W-K Knives (See Votaw, David P.)

WOLF, BILL, 4618 N. 79th Ave., Phoenix, AZ 85033/602-846-3585
Specialties: Investor-grade folders and straight knives. **Patterns:** Lockback, slip joint and sidelock interframes. **Technical:** Grinds ATS-34 and 440C. **Prices:** $650 to $4,000. **Remarks:** Full-time maker; first knife sold in 1989. **Mark:** Name.

WOLF'S KNIVES (See Smit, Glenn)

WOLFE FINE KNIVES (See Loerchner, Wolfgang)

WOMACK, A.M. "BABE", P.O. Box 1397, Coldspring, TX 77331/409-767-8158
Specialties: Classic and traditional straight knives and folders of his design. **Pat-

directory

terns: Hunters, locking folders and utility/camp knives. **Technical:** Grinds ATS-34, 440C and D2. Sheathmaker. **Prices:** $95 to $250; some to $700. **Remarks:** Part-time maker; first knife sold in 1989. **Mark:** Name and city.

WOOD, ALAN, Intake Farm, Slaggyford, Carlisle, CA6 7NH ENGLAND/0434-382055
Specialties: High-tech working straight knives of his design. **Patterns:** Hunters, utility/camp and military knives. **Technical:** Grinds Sandvik 12C27, D2 and 01. Blades are cryogenic treated. Offers Kydex sheaths. **Prices:** $110 to $350; some to $550. **Remarks:** Full-time maker; first knife sold in 1979. **Mark:** First initial, last name and country.

WOOD, BARRY B. and IRIE, MICHAEL L., 3002 E. Gunnison St., Colorado Springs, CO 80909/719-578-9226
Specialties: High-tech working folders with patented locking system. **Patterns:** Thirty-four variations of five designs. **Technical:** Blades mainly made of ATS-34, some of commercial Damascus. Handles investment-cast in 17-4PH and beryllium-copper. **Prices:** $225 to $460; some higher. **Remarks:** Full-time makers; first knife sold in 1969. **Mark:** Two sets of initials in script with linked triangles of arcs.

WOOD, LARRY B., 6945 Fishburg Rd., Huber Heights, OH 45424/513-233-6751
Specialties: Fancy working knives of his design. **Patterns:** Hunters, buckskinners, Bowies, tomahawks, locking folders and Damascus miniatures. **Technical:** Forges 1095, file steel and his own Damascus. **Prices:** $125 to $500; some to $2,000. **Remarks:** Full-time maker; first knife sold in 1974. Doing business as Wood's Metal Studios. **Mark:** Variations of last name, sometimes with blacksmith logo.

WOOD, LEONARD J., 16 North St., Beacon, NY 12508/914-838-1637
Specialties: Traditional working/using straight knives of all designs. **Patterns:** Boots, Bowies, hunters, miniatures. **Technical:** Grinds ATS-34, 440C, commercial Damascus. **Prices:** $85 to $375; some to $450. **Remarks:** Spare-time maker; first knife sold in 1993. Doing business as Wood's Custom Knives. **Mark:** Last initial with wings.

WOOD, OWEN DALE, P.O. Box 515, Honeydew 2040 (Transvaal), SOUTH AFRICA/011-958-1789
Specialties: Fancy working knives. **Patterns:** Hunters and fighters; variety of big knives; sword canes. **Technical:** Forges and grinds 440C, 154CM and his own Damascus. Uses rare African handle materials. **Prices:** $280 to $450; some to $3,000. **Remarks:** Full-time maker; first knife sold in 1976. **Mark:** Initials.

WOOD, WEBSTER, 4726 Rosedale, Clarkston, MI 48348/313-394-0351
Specialties: Fancy working knives. **Patterns:** Hunters, survival knives, locking folders and slip-joints. **Technical:** Grinds 01, 440C and 154CM; engraves and scrimshaws. **Prices:** $100 to $500; some to $3,000. **Remarks:** Full-time maker; first knife sold in 1980. **Mark:** Initials inside shield and name.

WOOD, WILLIAM W., P.O. Box 606, Seymour, TX 76380/817-888-5832
Specialties: Exotic working knives with Middle-East flavor. **Patterns:** Fighters, boots and some utility knives. **Technical:** Grinds D2 and 440C; buys Damascus. Prefers hand-rubbed satin finishes; uses only natural handle materials. **Prices:** $300 to $600; some to $2,000. **Remarks:** Full-time maker; first knife sold in 1977. **Mark:** Name, city and state.

WOOD'S METAL STUDIOS (See Wood, Larry B.)

WOODCOCK, DENNIS "WOODY", P.O. Box 448, Nehalem, OR 97131/503-368-7511
Specialties: Working knives; miniatures. **Patterns:** Hunters, Bowies, skinners, miniatures. **Technical:** Grinds ATS-34, 154CM, D2 and 440C. Offers filework. Scrimshaws; makes sheaths. **Prices:** $45 to $475. **Remarks:** Full-time maker; first knife sold in 1982. Doing business as Knife Emporium. **Mark:** Nickname, last name, city, state.

WOODWARD, HAROLD, RR 3, Box 391, Woodbury, TN 37190-9452/615-563-4619
Specialties: Working knives; period pieces. **Patterns:** Hunters, Bowies, swords, sword canes and tomahawks. **Technical:** Grinds A2, D2 and 440C; engraves. **Prices:** $75 to $350; some higher. **Remarks:** Full-time maker; first knife sold in 1972. **Mark:** Last name.

WOODWORTH, AL, RR #1, P.O. Box 13, Plainville, IL 62365/217-656-3591
Specialties: Fantasy knives of his design. **Patterns:** Fighters and daggers. **Technical:** Grinds 440C and ATS-34. Makes polyester resin handles. **Prices:** $700 to $2,500; some to $4,000. **Remarks:** Full-time maker; first knife sold in 1987. **Mark:** Initials with cross, Libra sign.

WORKMAN JR., HUBERT L., Tyree Rd., Williamsburg, WV 24991/304-645-4815
Specialties: Working knives of his design and to customer specs; period pieces. **Patterns:** Daggers, fighters and hunters. **Technical:** Uses obsidian, flint and chert; prefers natural materials. **Prices:** $25 to $150; some to $250. **Remarks:** Part-time maker; first knife sold in 1989. **Mark:** NA.

WORLD GALLERY CO., LTD. (See Yoshio, Mazaki; Kamada, Yoshikazu; Ueda, Masaharu; Wada, Yasutaka)

WRIGHT, KEVIN, 671 Leland Valley Rd. W, Quilcene, WA 98376-9517/206-765-3589
Specialties: Fancy working knives in standard patterns or to customer specs. **Patterns:** Hunters, boots, buckskinners, miniatures. **Technical:** Forges and grinds L6, 440C and his own Damascus. **Prices:** $50 to $300; some to $1,000. **Remarks:** Part-time maker; first knife sold in 1978. **Mark:** Last initial in anvil.

WRIGHT, TIMOTHY, 4100 W. Grand Ave., Chicago, IL 60651/312-489-4436/4186
Specialties: High-tech working folders and household knives. **Patterns:** Interframe locking folders, straight hunters and special-purpose kitchen cutlery. **Technical:** Grinds A2, ATS-34, BG42 and K190; works with new steels. Makes his own mokume. Makes folders to disassemble; furnishes parts and tools. **Prices:** $75 to $1,000; some to $2,500. **Remarks:** Full-time maker; first knife sold in 1975. **Mark:** Last name.

WW CUSTOM KNIVES (See Whitley, Wayne)

WYATT, WILLIAM R., Box 237, Rainelle, WV 25962/304-438-5494
Specialties: Classic and working knives of all designs. **Patterns:** Hunters and utility knives. **Technical:** Forges and grinds saw blades, files and rasps. Prefers stagg handles. **Prices:** $45 to $95; some to $350. **Remarks:** Part-time maker; first knife sold in 1990. **Mark:** Last name in star with knife logo.

WYVERN (See Ferdinand, Don)

x, y

XYLO (See McGill, John)

YASUTOMO (See Louis G. Mills)

YEATES, JOE A., 730 Saddlewood, Spring, TX 77381/713-367-2765
Specialties: Combat knives and period pieces. **Patterns:** Bowies, toothpicks, fighters and miniatures. **Technical:** Grinds 440C, D2 and ATS-34. **Prices:** $100 to $800; some to $1,500. **Remarks:** Full-time maker; first knife sold in 1975. **Mark:** Last initial within outline of Texas; or last initial.

YORK, DAVID C., P.O. Box 1342, Crested Butte, CO 81224/303-349-5826
Specialties: Working straight knives and folders. **Patterns:** Prefers small hunters and skinners; locking folders, buckskinner and survival knives. **Technical:** Grinds D2 and 440C; buys Damascus. **Prices:** $75 to $300; some to $600. **Remarks:** Part-time maker; first knife sold in 1975. **Mark:** Last name.

YOUNG, BUD, Box 336, Port Hardy, BC V0N 2P0, CANADA/604-949-6478
Specialties: Working straight knives, some fancy. **Patterns:** Hunters from drop-points to skinners. **Technical:** Grinds 01, L6, 1095 and 5160; uses 154CM and ATS-34 when available. Likes satin and glass bead finishes and natural handle materials. **Prices:** $200 to $400; some higher. **Remarks:** Spare-time maker; first knife sold in 1985. **Mark:** Name.

YOUNG, CLIFF, RR #1, Cotnams Island, Pembroke, Ont. K8A 6W2, CANADA/613-638-6401
Specialties: Working knives; some display pieces. **Patterns:** Hunters, fighters, locking folders and fishing knives. **Technical:** Grinds mostly, though does some forging; offers D2, 440C and 154CM. **Prices:** $165 to $350; some to $800. **Remarks:** Part-time maker; first knife sold in 1980. **Mark:** Name, city and province.

YOUNG, ERROL, 4826 Storey Land, Alton, IL 62002/618-466-4707
Specialties: Traditional working straight knives and folders **Patterns:** Wide range, including tantos, Bowies, miniatures and multi-blade folders. **Technical:** Grinds D2, 440C and ATS-34. **Prices:** $75 to $650; some to $800. **Remarks:** Part-time maker; first knife sold in 1987. **Mark:** Last name with arrow.

YOUNG, PAUL A., Route 1, Box 139-A, Vilas, NC 28692/704-297-4039
Specialties: Working straight knives and folders of his design or to customer specs; some art knives. **Patterns:** Small boot knives, skinners, 18th century period pieces and folders. **Technical:** Forges 01 and file steels. Full-time embellisher—engraves, carves and scrimshaws. **Prices:** $50 to $1,000. **Remarks:** Full-time maker; first knife sold in 1978. **Mark:** Initials in logo.

YUNES, YAMIL R., P.O. Box 573, Roma, TX 78584/512-849-1001
Specialties: Traditional straight knives and folders. **Patterns:** Locking folders, slip-joints, hunters, fighters and utility knives. **Technical:** Grinds 440C, 01 and D2. Has patented cocking design for folders. **Prices:** $45 to $140; some to $300. **Remarks:** Part-time maker; first knife sold in 1975. **Mark:** Last name.

YURCO, MIKE, P.O. Box 712, Canfield, OH 44406/216-533-4928
Specialties: Working straight knives. **Patterns:** Hunters, utility knives, Bowies and fighters, push knives, claws and other hideouts. **Technical:** Grinds 440C, ATS-34 and 154CM; likes mirror and satin finishes. **Prices:** $20 to $500. **Remarks:** Part-time maker; first knife sold in 1983. **Mark:** Name, steel, serial number.

Z

Z CUSTOM KNIVES (See McCarty, Zollan)

ZACCAGNINO, DON and DON JR., P.O. Box 583, Pahokee, FL 33476/407-924-7844
Specialties: Working knives and some period pieces of their designs. **Patterns:** Heavy-duty hunters, axes, Bowies, daggers and fantasy miniatures. **Technical:** Grinds 440C and 17-4 PH—highly finished in complex handle and blade treatments. **Prices:** $150 to $500; some to $1,000. **Remarks:** Full-time maker; first knife sold in 1969. **Mark:** ZACK, city and state inside oval.

ZACK KNIVES (See Zaccagnino, Don and Don Jr.)

ZAHM, KURT, 488 Rio Casa, Indialantic, FL 32903/407-777-4860
Specialties: Working straight knives of his design or to customer specs. **Patterns:** Daggers, fancy fighters, Bowies, hunters and utility knives. **Technical:** Grinds D2, 440C; likes filework. **Prices:** $75 to $1,000. **Remarks:** Part-time maker; first knife sold in 1985. **Mark:** Last name.

ZAKABI, CARL S., P.O. Box 3161, Mililani Town, HI 96789/808-623-9661
Specialties: Working and using straight knives of his design. **Patterns:** Fighters, hunters and utility/camp knives. **Technical:** Grinds 440C and ATS-34. **Prices:** $55 to $200. **Remarks:** Spare-time maker; first knife sold in 1988. Doing business as Zakabi's Knifeworks. **Mark:** Last name and state.

ZEMBKO III, JOHN, 140 Wilks Pond Rd., Berlin, CT 06037/203-828-3503
Specialties: Working knives of his design or to customer specs. **Patterns:** Variety of working straight knives. **Technical:** Grinds ATS-34, A2 and 01; forges 01. **Prices:** $50 to $400; some higher. **Remarks:** First knife sold in 1987. **Mark:** Name.

ZEMITIS, JOE, 14 Currawong Rd., Cardiff Hts., 2285 Newcastle, AUSTRALIA/049-549907
Specialties: Traditional working straight knives. **Patterns:** Hunters, Bowies, tantos, fighters and camp knives. **Technical:** Grinds 01, D2 and 440C; makes his own Damascus. Embellishes; engraves; scrimshands. **Prices:** $150 to $3,000. **Remarks:** Full-time maker; first knife sold in 1983. **Mark:** First initial, last name and country, or last name.

ZIMA, MICHAEL F., 732 State St., Ft. Morgan, CO 80701/303-867-6078
Specialties: Working straight knives and folders. **Patterns:** Hunters; utility, locking and slip-joint folders. **Technical:** Grinds D2, 440C and ATS-34. **Prices:** $135 to $250; some higher. **Remarks:** Full-time maker; first knife sold in 1982. **Mark:** Last name.

ZINSMEISTER, PAUL D., 315 West San Antonio St., Fredericksburg, TX 78056/512-751-2221
Specialties: Traditional working and using straight knives and folders of his design. **Patterns:** Hunters, locking folders, slip-joint folders, daggers, Bowies and miniatures. **Technical:** Uses 440C and ATS-34 stainless steel. **Prices:** $85 to $250; some to $1,500. **Remarks:** Full-time maker; first knife sold in 1982. **Mark:** Handmade with stylized last initial.

ZOWADA, TIM, 14141 P. Drive North, Marshall, MI 49068/616-781-2458
Specialties: Working knives, some fancy. **Patterns:** Hunters, camp knives, boots, swords, fighters, tantos and locking folders. **Technical:** Forges 01, W2 and his own Damascus. **Prices:** $200 to $1,000; some to $4,000. **Remarks:** Full-time maker; first knife sold in 1980. **Mark:** Lower case gothic letters for initials.

ZSCHERNY, MICHAEL, 2512 "N" Ave. NW, Cedar Rapids, IA 52405/319-396-3659
Specialties: Folders and daggers. **Patterns:** Slip-joints, lock-back folders, fancy daggers. **Technical:** Grinds 440C and 154CM; prefers natural handle materials. **Prices:** $150 to $1,000; some to $1,700. **Remarks:** Part-time maker. Not currently taking orders. **Mark:** Last name.

knifemakers state-by-state

alabama

Andress, Ronnie	Satsuma
Barrett, R.W.	Huntsville
Batson, James	Madison
Bell, Frank	Huntsville
Bullard, Bill	Andalusia
Coffman, Danny	Jacksonville
Conn Jr., C.T.	Attalla
Connell, Steve	Adamsville
Cutchin, Roy D.	Seale
Daniels, Alex	Town Creek
Edwards, Fain E.	Jacksonville
Faulkner, Allan	Jasper
Fikes, Jimmy L.	Jasper
Fogg, Don	Jasper
Gilbreath, Randall	Dora
Hammond, Jim	Arab
Hodge, J.B.	Huntsville
Howard, Durvyn M.	Hokes Bluff
Howell, Len	Opelika
Howell, Ted	Wetumpka
Hulsey Jr., Hoyt	Steele
Monk, Nathan P.	Cullman
Morris, C.H.	Atmore
Pardue, Melvin M.	Repton
Reeves, James Gary	Gardendale
Roe Jr., Fred D.	Huntsville
Russell, Tom	Jacksonville
Sandlin, Larry	Adamsville
Sinyard, Cleston S.	Elberta
Watson, Billy	Peatsville

alaska

Amoureux, A.W.	Anchorage
Brennan, Judson	Delta Junction
Breuer, Wayne	Wasilla
Broome, Thomas A.	Kenai
Bucholz, Mark A.	Eagle River
Cannon, Raymond W.	Homer
Chamberlin, John A.	Anchorage
Dempsey, Gordon W.	N.Kenai
DuFour, Arthur J.	Anchorage
England, Virgil	Anchorage
Gouker, Gary B.	Sitka
Grebe, Gordon S.	Anchor Point
Hibben, Westley G.	Anchorage
Kubaiko, Hank	Palmer
Lance, Bill	Eagle River
Levine, Bob	Anchorage
Little, Jimmy L.	Wasilla
McFarlin, Eric E.	Kodiak
McIntosh, David L.	Haines
Oda, Kuzan	Palmer
Parrish III, Gordon A.	North Pole
Stegall, Keith	Anchorage
Trujillo, Thomas A.	Anchorage
Whitman, Jim	Chugiak

arizona

Beaver, Devon	Phoenix
Boye, David	Dolan Springs
Cheatham, Bill	Phoenix
Craft III, John M.	Williams
Edge, Tommy	Cash
Genovese, Rick	Clarkdale
Goo, Tai	Tucson
Guignard, Gib	Quartzsite
Hancock, Tim	Scottsdale
Hoel, Steve	Pine
Holder, D'Alton	Glendale
Hull, Michael J.	Cottonwood
Kopp, Todd M.	Apache Junction
Lee, Randy	St. Johns
Lively, Tim	Tucson
McFall, Ken	Lakeside
Oliver, Milford	Prescott
Snare, Michael	Phoenix
Sutherland, Greg	Flagstaff
Tamboli, Michael	Glendale
Thompson, Robert L. (Bob)	Phoenix
Weiler, Donald E.	Yuma
Weiss, Charles L.	Phoenix
Wolf, Bill	Pheonix

arkansas

Anders, David	Center Ridge
Bogachov, Anatoly	Lockesburg
Cook, James Ray	Nashville
Crawford, Pat	West Memphis
Crowell, James L.	Mountain View
Dozier, Robert Lee	Springdale
Dungy, Lawrence	Little Rock
DuVall, Fred	Benton
Ferguson, Lee	Hindsville
Fisk, Jerry	Lockesburg
Flournoy, Joe	El Dorado
Foster, Al	Dogpatch
Frizzell, Ted	West Fork
Gaston, Bert	N. Little Rock
Grigsby,Ben	Batesville
Hicks, Vernon G.	Bauxite
Lane, Ben	No. Little Rock
Lawrence, Alton	DeQueen
Lile, James B. (Marilyn)	Russelville
Maringer, Tom	Springdale
Martin, Bruce E.	Prescott
Massey, Roger	Texarkana
Ogg, Robert G.	Paris
Polk, Clifton	Van Buren
Price, Jerry L.	Springdale
Quattlebaum, Craig	Searcy
Ramey, Marshall F.	West Helena
Ree, David	Van Buren
Remington, David W.	Lincoln
Russell, A.G.	Springdale
Solomon, Marvin	Ferndale
Tyer, Jerry L.	Everton
Ward, Chuck	Benton

california

Alden Jr., Kenneth E.	Ramona
Barlow, Ken	Fortuna
Benson, Don	Escalon
Blum, Chuck	Brea
Blum, Ronald	Walnut Creek
Boyd, Francis	Berkeley
Brack, Douglas	Camirillo
Breshears, Clint	Manhattan Beach
Brown, Ted	Downey
Browne, Rick	Upland
Chelquist, Cliff	Arroyo Grande
Cohen, Terry A.	Laytonville
Collins, A.J.	Arleta
Connolly, James	Palermo
Davis, Charlie	Santee
Dillon, Earl E.	Arleta
Dion, Greg	Oxnard
Dixon Jr., Ira E.	Ventura
Donovan, Patrick	San Jose
Doolittle, Mike	Novato
Eaton, Al	Clayton
Eaton, Rick	Forbestown
Ellis, William Dean	Fresno
Emerson, Ernest R.	Torrance
English, Jim	Jamul
Engnath, Bob	Glendale
Essegian, Richard	Fresno
Ferguson, Jim	Acton
Ferguson, Jim	Downey
Fisher, Ted	Montague
Foust, Roger	Modesto
Fox, Jack L.	Citrus Heights
Fraley, Ierek	Dixon
Freeman, Arthur F.	Citrus Heights
Freer, Ralph	Rossmoor
Fronefield, Mike	Truckee
Fulton, Mickey	Willows
Gamble, Frank	Redwood City
George, Tom	Magalia
Gofourth, Jim	Santa Paula
Golding, Robin	Lathrop
Hardy, Scott	Placerville
Harkins, J.A.	Crestline
Harris, Jay	Redwood City
Hartsfield, Phill	Newport Beach
Hayes, Dolores	Los Angeles
Helton, Roy	San Diego
Hermes, Dana E.	Fremont
Herndon, Wm. R. Bill	Acton
Hink, Less	Stockton
Hornby, Glen	Glendale
Hume, Don	Sherman Oaks
Humenick, Roy	Rescue
Jacks, Jim	Covina
Johnson, Dave	Jamul
Johnson, David L.	Lakeside
Jones, Curtis J.	Palmdale
Kozlow, Kelly	Ridgecrest
Kreibich, Donald L.	San Jose
Kruse, Martin	Reseda
LaBorde, Terry	Fallbrook
LeFont, Mark	Hollywood
Leland, Steve	Fairfax
Levine, Norman	Lake Elsinore
Lewis, Mike	Tracy
Likarich, Steve	Colfax
Lockett, Sterling	Burbank
Loveless, R.W.	Riverside
Manabe, Michael K.	San Diego
Mattis, James K.	Sunland
Maxwell, Don	Fresno
McClure, Michael	Menlo Park
McLeod, James	Oroville
McMahon, John	Palm Dessert
Meloy, Sean	Lemon Grove
Mendenhall, Harry E.	Milpitas
Middleton, Ken	Carmichael
Mitchell, R.W.	Lake Elsinore
Morgan, Jeff	Santee
Morlan, Tom	Hemet
Packard, Bob	Elverta
Pendleton, Lloyd	Volcano
Phillips, Randy	Ontario
Pitt, David F.	Pleasanton
Richard, Ron	Fremont
Rust, Charles C.	Palermo
Scarrow, Lin	Bellflower
Scarrow, Will	Bellflower
Schneider, Herman J.	Laguna Niguel
Schroen, Karl	Sebastopol
Schultz, Richard	San Juan Capistrano
Sibrian, Aaron	Ventura
Slobodian, Scott	Los Angeles
Somberger, Jim	Volcano
Stapel, Chuck	Glendale
Stapel, Craig	Glendale
Steel, Ray	San Diego
Steinberg, Al	San Bruno
Swain, Rod	South Pasadena
Tamboli, Michael	Glendale
Terrill, Stephen	Lindsay
Tinker, Carolyn D.	Whittier
Ward, Ken	Auburn
Warren, Al	Roseville
Watanabe, Wayne	Montebello
Wesolowski, Mike	Petaluma
Whitehead, James D.	Sacramento
Williams, Sherman A.	Simi Valley
Williamson, Walt	Rancho Cucamonga
Wilson, Philip C.	Livermore

colorado

Anderson, Mel	Cedaredge
Appleton, Ray	Byers
Barrett, Cecil Terry	Colorado Springs
Booco, Gordon	Hayden
Brock, Kenneth L.	Allenspark
Brown, E.H.	Grand Junction
Campbell, Dick	Conifer
Davis, Don	Loveland
Dawson, Barry	Durango
DeLong, Dick	Aurora
Dennehy, Dan	Del Norte
Dill, Robert, Bonnie and Chris	Loveland
Genge, Roy E.	Eastlake
High, Tom	Alamoso
Hockensmith, Dan	Drake
Hodgson, Richard J.	Boulder
Hughes, Ed	Grand Junction
Hunt, Alex	Fort Collins
Kitsmiller, Jerry	Montrose
Lampson, Frank G.	Fruita
Leck, Dal	Hayden
Letcher, Billy	Fort Collins
Luck, Greg	Greeley
McWilliams, Sean	Bayfield
Miller, Hanford J.	Cowdrey
Miller , M.A.	Thornton
Neeley, Vaughn	Mancos
Nolen, R.D. and George	Estes Park
Olson, Wayne C.	Wheat Ridge
Owens, John	Parker
Peasley, David S.	Alamosa
Pogreba, Larry	Lyons
Robbins, Howard P.	Estes Park
Roberts, Chuck	Westminster
Rollert, Steve	Keenesburg

knifemakers state-by-state

Sanders, Bill	Mancos
Sasser, Jim	Pueblo
Smith, D. Noel	Canon City
Thompson, Lloyd	Pagosa Springs
Tollefson, Barry A.	Gunnison
Topliss, M.W. "Ike"	Montrose
Watson, Bert	Westminster
Wilson, James G.	Estes Park
Wood, Barry B.	Colorado Springs
York, David C.	Crested Butte
Zima, Michael F.	Ft. Morgan

connecticut

Buebendorf, Robert E.	Monroe
Chapo, William G.	Wilton
Coughlin, Michael M.	Danbury
Hubbard, Arthur J.	Monroe
Jean, Gerry	Manchester
Lepore, Michael J.	Bethany
Martin, Randall J.	Middletown
Nelson, Roger S.	Central Village
Pankiewicz, Philip R.	Lebanon
Putnam, Donald S.	Wethersfield
Rainville, Richard	Salem
Turecek, Jim	Derby
Zembko III, John	Berlin

delaware

Dugan, Brad M.	Milford
Schneider, Karl A.	Newark
Willey, W.G.	Greenwood

district of columbia

Cumming, R.J.	Washington

florida

Adams, Les	Hialeah
Atkinson, Dick	Wausau
Barry, James J.	West Palm Beach
Benjamin Jr., George	Kissimmee
Blackton, Andrew	Bayonet Point
Bradley, John	Pomona Park
Bray Jr., W. Lowell	New Port Richey
Brown, Harold E.	Arcadia
Burns, Dave	Boynton Beach
Clark, Dave	Live Oak
Cobb, Lowell D.	Daytona Beach
Cox, Colin J.	Apopka
Cross, John M.	Bryceville
Davenport, Jack	Dade City
DeGraeve, Richard	Sebastian
Dietzel, Bill	Middleburg
Ek, Gary Whitney	North Miami
Ellerbe, W.B.	Geneva
Enos III, Thomas M.	Orlando
Faulkner, Allan	St. Petersburg
Ferrara, Thomas	Naples
Fowler, Charles R.	Ft. McCoy
Gamble, Roger	St. Petersburg
Garner Jr., William O.	Pensacola
Gibson, Jim	Bunnell
Goers, Bruce	Lakeland
Griffin Jr., Howard A.	Davie
Grospitch, Ernie	Orlando
H&W Knives	Pace
Hampton, William W.	Howey In the Hills
Hancock, Ronald E.	Lecanto
Harris, Ralph Dewey	Brandon
Heitler, Henry	Tampa
Hennon, Robert	Ft. Walton Beach
Hill, Steven E.	Orlando
Hodge III, John	Palatka
Hoffman, Kevin L.	Winter Park
Hughes, Dan	West Palm Beach
Humphries, Joel	Bowling Green
Jernigan, Steve	Milton
Johnson, Durrell Carmon	Sparr
Kelly, Lance	Edgewater
King, Bill	Tampa
Krapp, Denny	Apopka
Lazo, Robert T.	Miami
Levengood, Bill	Tampa
Leverett, Ken	Lithia
Loflin, Bob	Miami Lakes
Long, Glenn A.	Palm Beach Gardens
Lozier, Don	Oklawaha
Lyle III, Ernest L.	Orlando
McDonald, Robert J.	Sunrise
Miller Jr., Chris	Sebring
Miller, Robert	Ormond Beach
Miller, Ronald T.	Largo
Mink, Dan	St. Petersburg
Ochs, Charles F.	Largo
Outlaw, Anthony L.	Panama City
Pendray, Alfred H.	Williston
Price, Joel Hiram	Palatka
Randall, Gary T.	Orlando
Renner, Terry Lee	Bradenton
Rogers, Rodney	Wildwood
Schwarzer, James	Pomona Park
Schwarzer, Stephen	Pomona Park
Sharp, Wes & Margie	Milton
Simons, Bill	Lakeland
Smith, Bobbie D.	Bonifay
Smith, Michael J.	Tampa
Smith, W.M.	Bonifay
Stipes, Dwight	Jupiter
Tomes, Anthony	Jacksonville
Vunk, Robert Bob	Orlando
Waldrop, Mark	Summerfield
Wallace, Roger L.	Tampa
Watson, Tom	Panama City
Weiland Jr., J. Reese	Tampa
Wicker, Donnie R.	Panama City
Wine, Michael	Cocoa Beach
Zaccagnino, Don & Don Jr.	Pahokee
Zahm, Kurt	Indialantic

georgia

Arrowwood, Dale	Sharpsburg
Ashworth, Boyd	Powder Springs
Barker, Robert G.	Athens
Bradley, Dennis	Blairsville
Buckner, Jimmie H.	Putney
Carey Jr., Charles W.	Griffin
Chamblin, Joel	Concord
Cofer, Ron	Duluth
Cole, Welborn I.	Atlanta
Cosby, E. Blanton	Columbus
Crockford, Jack	Chamblee
DeYong, Clarence	Kennesaw
Dunn, Charles K.	Shiloh
Ford, Allen	Smyrna
Fuller, John W.	Douglasville
Halligan, Ed and Shawn	Sharpsburg
Hardin, Robert K.	Dalton
Harmon, Jay	Woodstock
Harmon, Joe	Jonesboro
Hawkins, Rade	Red Oak
Hegedus Jr., Lou	Cave Spring
Hegwood, Joel	Summerville
Hensley, Wayne	Conyers
Hinson, R. and Son	Columbus
Holland, John	Calhoun
Hyde, Jimmy	Ellenwood
Johnson, Harold Harry C.	Chickamauga
Kilby, Keith	Jefferson
Kimsey, Kevin	Marietta
King, Fred J.	Cartersville
King, Kemp	Flowery Branch
Kormanik, Chris	Carnesville
Landers, John	Newnan
Lonewolf, J. Aguirre	Demorest
Love, Ed	Stockbridge
Lovestrand, Schuyler	Dublin
McCarty, Zollan	Thomaston
McGill, John	Blairsville
Mitchell, James A.	Columbus
Moore, Bill	Leesburg
North, David	Chickamauga
Pagnard, Philip E.	Peachtree City
Parks, John	Jefferson
Pittman, Leon	Pendergrass
Poole, Steve L.	Stockbridge
Poplin, James L.	Washington
Poythress, John	Swainsboro
Prater, Mike	Chickamauga
Ragsdale, James D. Jim	Lithonia
Rogers Jr., Robert P.	Acworth
Royal, B.M. "Red"	Helen
Scofield, Everett	Chickamauga
Small, Jim	Madison
Smith Jr., James B.	Morven
Snell, Jerry L.	Fayetteville
Stafford, Richard	Warner Robins
Thompson, Kenneth	Duluth
Walters, A.F.	Tifton
Werner, William A. Jr.	Marietta
Wilson, Robert M.	Bowman

hawaii

Dolan, Robert L.	Kula
Evans, Vincent K.	Keaau
Fujisaka, Stanley	Kaneohe
Lui, Ronald	Honolulu
Mayo Jr., Thomas H.	Waialua
Onion, Kenneth J.	Kapolei
Valachovic, Wayne	Kailua-Kona
Zakabi, Carl S.	Mililani Town

idaho

Andrews, Don	Coeur D'Alene
Horton, Scot	Buhl
Kranning, Terry L.	Pocatello
Moulton, Dusty	Boise
Mullin, Steve	Sandpoint
Nealy, Ivan F.	Mountain Home
Quarton, Barr	McCall
Reeve, Chris	Boise
Rohn, Fred	Coeur d'Alene
Sawby, Scott	Sand Point
Selent, Chuck	Bonners Ferry
Spragg, Wayne E.	Ashton
Steiger, Monte L.	Genesee
Towell, Dwight L.	Midvale

illinois

Abbott, William M.	Chandlerville
Bloomer, Allan T.	Maquon
Brandsey, Edward P.	Woodstock
Brannan, Ralph	Frankfort
Bridgnardello, E.D.	Beecher
Bulawski, Rick	Sandwich
Bumpus, Steve	Collinsville
Cook, Louise	Ozark
Cook, Mike	Ozark
Detmer, Phillip	Breese
Guth, Kenneth	Chicago
Hill, Rick	Collinsville
Knuth, Joseph E.	Rockford
Kovar, Eugene	Evergreen Park
Lang, Kurt	McHenry
Leone, Nick	Pontoon Beach
Meier, Daryl	Carbondale
Millard, Fred G.	Chicago
Myers, Paul	East Alton
Nowland, Rick	Waltonville
Poag, James	Grayville
Pritchard, Ron	Dixon
Rados, Jerry F.	Grant Park
Schneider, Craig M.	Seymour
Smith, John M.	Centralia
Stalter, Harry L.	Trivoli
Tompkins, Dan	Peotone
Turnbull, Ralph A.	Rockford
Veit, Michael	LaSalle
Voss, Ben	Galesburg
Werth, George W.	Poplar Grove
White, Robert J. Bob	Gilson
White Jr., Robert J. "Butch"	Gilson
Woodworth, Al	Plainville
Wright, Timothy	Chicago
Young, Errol	Alton

indiana

Allen, Joe	Princeton
Birt, Sid	Nashville
Bose, Tony	Shelburn
Broughton, Don R.	Floyd Knob
Chaffee, Jeff L.	Morriss
Darby, Jed	Greensburg
Davis, Ken	Indianapolis
Fitzgerald, Dennis	Fort Wayne
Flynn, Bruce	Middletown
Gutekunst, Ralph	Richmond
Imel, Billy Mace	New Castle
Johnson, C.E. Gene	Portage
Keeslar, Steven C.	Hamilton
Keeton, William L.	Laconia
Largin, Ken	Batesville
Ledford, Bracy R.	Indianapolis
Lutes, Robert	Nappanee
Mayville, Oscar	Marengo
Minnick, Jim	Middletown
Norton, Dennis G.	Fort Wayne
Parsons, Michael R.	Terre Haute
Porter, James E.	Bloomington
Rigney, Willie	Shelbyville
Rubley, James A.	Angola

FIFTEENTH EDITION **275**

directory

Shostle, Ben — Muncie
Sokol, Richard — Indianapolis
Stover, Terry "Lee" — Kokomo
Thayer, Danny — Lafayette
Welch, William H. — Kimmell

iowa

Brooker, Dennis — Derby
Brower, Max — Boone
Clark, Howard — Runnells
Lainson, Tony — Council Bluffs
Miller, James P. — Fairbank
Myers, Mel — Spencer
Trindle, Barry — Earlham
Westberg, Larry — Algona
Zscherny, Michael — Cedar Rapids

kansas

Ames, Mickey L. — Lebo
Bradburn, Gary — Wichita
Chard, Gordon R. — Iola
Courtney, Eldon — Wichita
Craig, Roger L.
Culver, Steve — Mayetta
Dugger, Dave — Westwood
Dunn, Melvin T. — Rossville
Hegwald, J.L. — Humboldt
Herman, Tim — Overland Park
Kennelley, J.C. — Leon
Kraft, Steve — Abilene
Petersen, Dan L. — Topeka

kentucky

Barr, A.T. — Nicholasville
Baskett, Lee Gene — Elizabethtown
Brumagen, Jerry — Lexington
Bugden, John — Murray
Bybee, Barry J. — Cadiz
Carson, Harold J. Kit — Vine Grove
Clay, J.D. — Greenup
Coil, Jimmie J. — Owensboro
Corbit, Gerald E. "Jerry" — Elizabethtown
Downing, Larry — Bremen
Dunn, Steve — Smiths Grove
Fannin, David A. — Lexington
Fister, Jim — Simpsonville
France, Dan — Cawood
Gevedon, Hanners — Crab Orchard
Hemphill, Jesse — Berea
Hibben, Daryl — LaGrange
Hibben, Gil — LaGrange
Hibben, Joleen — LaGrange
Howser, John C. — Frankfort
Keeslar, Joseph F. — Almo
Pease, W.D. — Ewing
Pierce, Harold L. — Louisville
Pulliam, Morris C. — Shelbyville
Smith, Gregory H. — Louisville
Smith, John W. — West Liberty
Waddle, Thomas — Louisville

louisiana

Black, Tom — Alexandria
Blaum, Roy — Covington
Caldwell, Bill — West Monroe
Camp, Jeff — Ruston
Culpepper, John — Monroe
Dake, C.M. — New Orleans
Douglas, Dale — Ponchatoula
Durio, Fred — Opelousas
Elkins, R. Van — Bonita
Faucheaux, Howard J. — Loreauville
Forstall, Al — Slidell
Gorenflo, James T. — Baton Rouge
Graffeo, Anthony I. — Chalmette
Holmes, Robert — Baton Rouge
Howard, Seth — Baton Rouge
Ki, Shiva — Baton Rouge
Laurent, Kermit — LaPlace
Marks, Chris — Breaux Bridge
Mitchell, Max and Dean — Leesville
Potier, Timothy F. — Oberlin
Provenzano, Joseph D. — Chalmette
Roath, Dean — Baton Rouge
Sanders, Michael M. — Ponchatoula
Smith, W.F. Red — Slidell
Vought Jr., Frank — Hammond
Wiggins, Horace — Mansfield

maine

Bohrmann, Bruce — Yarmouth
Coombs Jr., Lamont — Bucksport
Courtois, Bryan — Saco
Fuegen, Larry — Wiscasset
Leavitt, Earl F. — E. Boothbay
Oyster, Lowell R. — Kenduskeag
Sayen, Murad — Bryant Pond
Sharrigan, Mudd — Wiscasset

maryland

Antonio, William J. — Golts
Barnes, Aubrey G. — Hagerstown
Barnes, Gary L. — New Windsor
Beers, Ray — Monkton
Cohen, N.J. Norm — Baltimore
Freiling, Albert J. — Finksburg
Fuller, Jack A. — New Market
Hendrickson, E.J. Jay — Frederick
Hudson, Robbin C. — Rock Hall
Kremzner, Raymond L. — Stevenson
Kretsinger Jr., Philip W. — Boonsboro
McCarley, John — Union Bridge
McGowan, Frank — Sykesville
Merchant, Ted — White Hall
Moran, Wm. F. — Braddock Heights
Nicholson, Kent R. — Phoenix
Rhodes, James D. — Hagerstown
Sentz, Mark C. — Taneytown
Sidelinger, Robert — Bel Air
Smit, Glenn — Aberdeen
Sontheimer, Douglas G. — Potomac
Wagner, Dan — Chestertown

massachusetts

Dailey, G.E. — Seekonk
DaConceicao — ReHoboth
Flechtner, Chris — Fitchburg
Gaudette, Linden L. — Wilbraham
Grossman, Stewart — Clinton
Gwozdz, Bob — Attleboro
Jarvis, Paul M. — Cambridge
Khalsa, Jot Singh — Millis
Kubasek, John A. — Easthampton
Lapen, Charles — W. Brookfield
McLuin, Tom — Dracut
Reed, Dave — Brimfield
Richter, Scott — Watertown
Rua, Gary (Wolf) — Fall River
Siska, Jim — Westfield
Sloan, John — Foxboro
Smith, J.D. — Boston
Tsoulas, Jon J. — Peabody

michigan

Beckwith, Michael R. — New Baltimore
Behnke, William — Lake City
Buckbee, Donald M. — Clinton Township
Cashen, Kevin R. — Hubbardston
Cousino, George — Onsted
Dilluvio, Frank J. — Warren
Enders, Robert — Cement City
Erickson, Walter E. — Warren
Garbe, Bob — Fraser
Gardner, Rob — Ann Arbor
Gottage, Dante and Judy — St. Clair Shores
Hartman, Arlan — N. Muskegon
Hughes, Daryle — Nunica
Kalfayan, Edward N. — Ferndale
Krause, Roy W. — St. Clair Shores
Lankton, Scott — Ann Arbor
Leach, Mike J. — Swartz Creek
Lucie, James R. — Fruitport
Mills, Louis G. Yasutomo — Ann Arbor
Repke, Mike — Bay City
Sakmar, Mike — Rochester
Serven, Jim — Mayville
Sigman, James P. — Three Rivers
Stewart, Charles Chuck — Warren
Warzocha, Stanley — Warren
Whitworth, Ken J. — Sterling Heights
Wood, Webster — Clarkston
Zowada, Tim — Marshall

minnesota

Dingman, Scott — Bemidji
Dube, Paul N. — Chaska
Fiorini, Bill — LaCrescent
Flood, James Noah — Chaska
Goltz, Warren L. — Ada
Hagen, Philip L. — Pelican Rapids
Hansen, Robert W. — Cambridge
Johnson, Ronald B. — Clearwater
Knipschield, Terry — Rochester
Lange, Donald G. — Pelican Rapids
Shadley, Eugene W. — Bovey

mississippi

Craft, Richard C. — Jackson
Davis, Jesse W. — Sarah
Greco, John — Bay St. Louis
Hand, James E., M.D. — Gloster
Landrum, Leonard — Lumberton
LeBatard, Paul M. — Vancleave
Roberts, Michael — Clinton
Taylor, Billy — Petal
Wehner, Rudy — Collins
Wingo, Perry — Gulfport
Winston, David — Starkville

missouri

Anderson, Charles B. — Lampe
Bolton, Charles B. — Jonesburg
Burrows, Stephen R. — Kansas City
Cover, Raymond A. — Mineral Point
Davis, W.C. — Raymore
Dearing, John — DeSoto
Dippold, A.W. — Perryville
Driskill, Beryl — Braggadocio
Duvall, Larry E. — Gallatin
Engle, William — Boonville
Frese, William R. — St. Louis
Garcia Jr., Raul — Aberdeen
Glaser, Ken — Purdy
Kennedy, Jerry — Blue Springs
Knickmeyer, Hank — Cedar Hill
Lane, Ed — Kansas City
Mason, Bill — Excelsior Springs
May, James E. — Auxvasse
McCrackin and Son, V.J. — House Springs
Miller, Bob — Ballwin
Newcomb, Corbin — Moberly
Rardon, A.D. — Polo
Rardon, Archie F. — Polo
Shelton, Paul — Rolla
Steketee, Craig A. — Billings
Warden, Roy A. — Union
Webb, Jim — Joplin
Weddle Jr., Del — St. Joseph

montana

Barnes, Jack — Whitefish
Brooks, Steve R. — Big Timber
Brunkhorst, C. Lyle — Helena
Caffrey, Edward J. — Great Falls
Conklin, George — Fort Benton
Crowder, Robert — Thompson Falls
Dunkerley, Rick — Lincoln
Ellefson, Joel — Bozeman
Fassio, Melvin G. — Bonner
Forthofer, Pete — Whitefish
Frank, Heinrich H. — Whitefish
Gallagher, Barry — Lewistown
Gillis, C.R. "Rex" — Great Falls
Hill, Howard — Polson
Kauffman, Dave — Helena
Kraft, Elmer — Big Arm
Miller, Larry — Missoula
Moyer, Russ — Havre
Peele, Bryan — Thompson Falls
Peterson, Eldon G. — Whitefish
Piorek, James S. — Missoula
Pursley, Aaron — Big Sandy
Ruana Knife Works — Bonner
Schirmer, Mike — Twin Bridges
Schmidt, Rick — Whitefish
Simonich, Bob — Clancy
Taylor, Shane — Angela
Townsend, J.W. — Trout Creek
Weinand, Gerome W. — Missoula

nebraska

Brown, David B. — Fairbury
Hielscher, Guy — Alliance
Jensen Jr., Carl A. — Blair
Jokerst, Charles — Omaha
Miller, Terry — Seward

knifemakers state-by-state

Schepers, George B.	Chapman
Suedmeier, Harlan	Nebraska City
Syslo, Chuck	Omaha
Till, Calvin E.	Chadron

nevada

Defeo, Robert A.	Henderson
Duff, Bill	Virginia City
Hrisoulas, Jim	Las Vegas
Mecchi, Richard	Las Vegas
Nishiuchi, Melvin S.	Las Vegas
Thomas, Devin	Las Vegas
Tracy, Bud	Reno

new hampshire

Saindon, R. Bill	Claremont

new jersey

D'Andrea, John	Wayne
Gaugler, Earl W.	Randolph
Hetmanski, Thomas S.	Trenton
MacBain, Kenneth	Norwood
McGovern, Jim	Oak Ridge
Polkowski, Al	Chester
Pressburger, Ramon	Howell
Slee, Fred	Morganville
Viele, H.J.	Westwood
Weber, Fred E.	Forked River

new mexico

Black, Tom	Albuquerque
Coleman, Keith E.	Los Lunas
Cordova, Joseph G.	Peralta
Digangi, Joseph M.	Santa Cruz
Duran, Jerry T.	Albuquerque
Dyess, Eddie	Roswell
Fisher, Jay	Magdalena
Goode, Bear	Navajo Dam
Hethcoat, Don	Clovis
Homer, Glen	Bloomfield
Jones, Bob	Albuquerque
Lewis, Ron	Edgewood
Lewis, Tom R.	Carlsbad
McBurnette, Harvey	Eagle Nest
Miller, Ted	Santa Fe
Norton, Don	Farmington
Nymeyer, Earl	Hobbs
Schaller, Antony B.	Albuquerque
Terzuola, Robert	Santa Fe
Walker, Michael	Taos
Wescott, Jim	Las Cruces

new york

Anderson, Edwin	Glen Cove
Baker, Bill	Boiceville
Champagne, Paul	Mechanicville
Cute, Thomas	Cortland
Davis, Barry L.	Castleton
Licata, Steven	Yonkers
Lozito, Joseph F.	Forest Hills
Ludwig, Richard O.	Maspeth
Maragni, Dan	Georgetown
Martrildonno, Paul	Olivebridge
Page, Reginald	Groveland
Pattay, Rudy	Long Beach
Patterson, Karl	Silver Creek
Rappazzo, Richard	Cohoes
Rizzi, Russell	East Setauket
Rotella, Richard A.	Niagara Falls
Scheid, Maggie	Rochester
Schmidt, James A.	Ballston Lake
Serafen, Steven E.	Norwich
Smith, Raymond L.	Breesport
Stahl, John	Baldwin
Szilaski, Joseph	Wappingers Falls
Turner, Kevin	Montrose
Tyc, William J.	Newburgh
Wahlers, Herman F.	Austerlitz
Wood, Leonard J.	Beacon

north carolina

Barron, David	Etowah
Britton, Tim	Kinston
Brown, Tom	Greensboro
Busfield, John	Roanoke Rapids
Chastain, Wade	Horse Shoe
Daniel, Travis E.	Winston-Salem
Fox, Paul	Claremont
Gaddy, Gary Lee	Washington
Goguen, Scott	Newport
Goldenberg, T.S.	Fairview
Gross, W.W.	High Point
Gurganus, Carol	Colerain
Gurganus, Melvin H.	Colerain
Guthrie, George B.	Bessemer City
Harless, Walt	Stoneville
Hudson, Tommy	Monroe
King, Randall	Asheville
Livingston, Robert C.	Murphy
Lubrich, Mark	Matthews
Mariacher, Robert R.	Franklin
Maynard, William N. (Bill)	Fayetteville
McNabb, Tommy	Winston-Salem
Moretz, Jim	Boone
Norris, Mike	Albemarle
Parrish, Robert	Hendersonville
Patrick, Chuck	Brasstown
Patterson, Alan W.	Hayesville
Popp Sr., Steve F.	Fayetteville
Rece, Charles V.	Albemarle
Scholl, Tim	Angier
Sears, Mick	Gastonia
Shuford, Rick	Statesville
Simmons, H.R.	Grantsboro
Sprouse, Terry	Asheville
Tedder, Mickey	Conover
Wade, J.M.	Wade
Wagaman, John K.	Fayetteville
Whitley, Wayne	Washington
Williamson, Tony	Siler City
Winkler, Daniel	Boone
Young, Paul A.	Vilas

north dakota

Ennis, Ray W.	Grand Forks
Keidel, Gene W.	Dickinson
Keidel, Scott J.	Dickinson

ohio

Babcock, Raymond G.	Vincent
Busse, Jerry	Wauseon
Collins, Harold A.	West Union
Collins, Lynn M.	Elyria
Corwin, Don	Monclova
Cottrill, James I.	Columbus
Darby, Rick	Youngstown
Downing, Tom	Cortland
Downs, Jim	Londonderry
Etzler, John	Grafton
Franklin, Mike	Aberdeen
Geisler, Gary	Clarksville
Glover, Ron	Cincinnati
Grubb, Richard A.	Columbus
Guess, Raymond L.	Mechanicstown
Hinderer, R.	Wooster
Imboden II, Howard L.	Dayton
Johnson, W.C. "Bill"	Pataskala
Kiefer, Tony	LaGrange
Koutsopoulos, George	LaGrange
Koval, Michael T.	New Albany
Layton, Jim	Portsmouth
Longworth, Dave	Hamersville
Lunn, Larry A.	Vermilion
McCarty, Harry	Hamilton
Mercer, Mike	Lebanon
Messer, David T.	Dayton
Mettler, J. Banjo	No. Baltimore
Morgan, Tom	Beloit
Papp, Robert Bob	Parma
Pratt, Charles	Port Washington
Ralph, Darrel	Reynoldburg
Salley, John D.	Tipp City
Shinosky, Andy	Warren
Shoemaker, Scott	Miamisburg
Spinale, Richard	Lorain
Steven, Barry B.	Cridersville
Stoddart, W.B. Bill	Forest Park
Strong, Scott	Beaver Creek
Summers, Arthur L.	Mechanicsburg
Thomas, Kim	Brunswick
Thourot, Michael W.	Napoleon
Trabbic, R.W.	Toledo
Votaw, David P.	Pioneer
Warther, Dale	Dover
Witsaman, Earl	Stow
Wood, Larry B.	Huber Heights
Yurco, Mike	Canfield

oklahoma

Baker, Ray	Sapulpa
Dill, Dave	Oklahoma City
Englebretson, George	Oklahoma City
Gepner, Don	Norman
Guess, Jack	Tulsa
Johns, Rob	Enid
Kennedy Jr., Bill	Yukon
Leet, Larry W.	Shawnee
Mitchell, Wm. Dean	Forgan
Nibarger, Charlie	Tulsa
Sanders, Athern Al	Norman
Sisemore, Charles	Hodgen
Spivey, Jefferson	Oklahoma City
Stice, Douglas	Norman
Williams, Michael L.	Broken Bow

oregon

Alverson, Tim	Klamath Falls
Anderson, Virgil W.	Portland
Bell, Michael	Coquille
Bochman, Bruce	Grants Pass
Buchman, Bill	Bend
Buchner, Bill	Idleyld Park
Coats, Eldon M.	Beatty
Corrado, Jim	Glide
Davis, Terry	Sumpter
Dowell, T.M.	Bend
Draper, Kent	Cheshire
Eck, Larry A.	Terrebonne
Ferdinand, Don	Prospect
Fox, Wendell	Springfield
Goddard, Wayne	Eugene
Harsey, William W.	Creswell
Hilker, Thomas N.	Williams
Horn, Jess	Florence
Huey, Steve	Junction City
Kelley, Gary	Aloha
Lake, Ron	Eugene
Lindsay, Chris A.	Bend
Little, Gary M.	Broadbent
Lum, Robert W.	Eugene
Miller, Michael K.	Sweet Home
Murphy, Dave	Gresham
Osterman, Daniel E.	Junction City
Reed, Del	Beaverton
Saddle Mountain Knife	Vernonia
Schell, Clyde M.	Corvallis
Shoger, Mark O.	Beaverton
Thompson, Leon	Forest Grove
Thompson, Tommy	Portland
Vallotton, Butch	Oakland
Vallotton, Rainy D.	Oakland
Vallotton, Shawn	Oakland
Veatch, Richard	North Bend
Wahlster, Mark David	Silverton
Woodcock, Dennis "Woody"	Nehalem
Wise, John	Winchester
Zeller, Dennis J.	Gresham

pennsylvania

Amor Jr., Miguel	Lancaster
Anderson, Gary D.	Spring Grove
Bartrug, Hugh E.	Elizabeth
Besedick, Frank E.	Charleroi
Candrella, Joe	Warminster
Clark, D.E. Lucky	Mineral Point
Ellenberg, William C.	Melrose Park
Frey Jr., W. Fredrick	Milton
Goldberg, David	Norristown
Gottschalk, Gregory J.	Carnegie
Lorditch, Charles Richard	Johnstown
Malloy, Joe	Freeland
Marlowe, Donald	Dover
Nealy, Bud	Stroudsburg
Nolfi, Tim	Dawson
Parker, J.E.	Clarion
Rupert, Robert	Clinton
Steigerwalt, Ken	Levittown
Stroyan, Eric	Dalton
Taglienti, Antonio J.	Darlington
Valois, A. Daniel	Lehighton
Whittaker, Robert E.	Mill Creek
Wilson, Jon J.	Johnstown

rhode island

Bardsley, Norman P.	Pawtucket
Black, Robert	N. Kingstown
Felfidel, Ralph	Warrich

FIFTEENTH EDITION 277

directory

Lambert, Ronald S.	Johnston
McHenry, William James	Wyoming
Selvidio, Ralph	N. Kingstown
Williams, Jason L.	Wyoming

south carolina

Barefoot, Joe W.	Liberty
Beatty, Gordon H.	Seneca
Branton, Robert	Awendaw
Brend, Walter J.	Walterboro
Bridwell, Richard A.	Taylors
Cannady, Daniel L.	Allendale
Cox, Sam	Gaffney
Davis, Dixie	Clinton
Defreest, William G.	Barnwell
Easler, Paula	Woodruff
Easler Jr., Russell O.	Woodruff
Fecas, Stephen J.	Anderson
Gainey, Hal	Greenwood
Gaston, Ron	Woodruff
George, Harry	Aiken
Gillenwater, E.E. Dick	Aiken
Gregory, Michael	Belton
Herron, George	Springfield
Kaufman, Scott	Anderson
Kay, J. Wallace	Liberty
Kessler, Ralph A.	Marietta
Knott, Steve	Clinton
Langley, Gene H.	Florence
Lee, Tommy	Gaffney
Lewis, K.J.	Lugoff
Lutz, Greg	Greenwood
Montjoy, Claude	Clinton
Owens, Dan	Blacksburg
Page, Larry	Aiken
Peagler, Russ	Moncks Corner
Poole, Marvin	Anderson
Poston, Alvin	Pamplico
Prince, Joe R.	Moore
Reeves, Winfred M.	West Union
Smith, Ralph L.	Taylors
Thomas, Rocky	Ladson
Webb, Jr., Charley L.	Anderson
Whitmire, Earl T.	Rock Hill

tennessee

Bailey, Joseph D.	Nashville
Baker, Vance	Riceville
Bartlow, John	Norris
Canter, Ronald E.	Jackson
Cargill, Bob	Oldfort
Casteel, Dianna	Monteagle
Casteel, Douglas	Monteagle
Centofante, Frank and Tony	Madisonville
Claiborne, Ron	Knoxville
Clay, Wayne	Pelham
Conley, Bob	Jonesboro
Coogan, Robert	Smithville
Copeland, George A. Steve	Alpine
Corby, Harold	Johnson City
Crisp, Harold	Cleveland
Ewing, John H.	Clinton
Eldridge, Allan L.	Gallatin
Grigsby, John D. Butch	Corryton
Harley, Larry W.	Bristol
Hurst, Jeff	Rutledge
Johnson, Ryan M.	Hixson
Langston, Bennie E.	Memphis
Rhea, David	Lynnville
Rial, Douglas	Greenfield
Ryder, Ben M.	Copperhill
Sampson, Lynn	Jonesborough
Smith, Newman L.	Gatlinburg
Taylor, C. Gray	Kingsport
Taylor, David	Kingsport
Vanderford, Carl G.	Columbia
Von Boeckman, R.	Memphis
Walker, John W.	Bon Aqua
Ward, W.C.	Clinton
Williams Jr., Richard T	Morristown
Woodward, Harold E.	Woodbury
Wright, Harold C.	Centerville

texas

Allen, Mike Whiskers	Malakoff
Allred, Elvan	Wichita Falls
Anderson, Michael D.	Arlington
Ashby, Douglas	Dallas
Bagwell, Bill	Marietta
Bailey, Kirby C.	Lytle
Barbee, Jim	Ft. Stockton
Batts, Keith	Hooks
Blasingame, Robert	Kilgore
Blum, Kenneth	Brenham
Brayton, Jim	Burkburnett
Brightwell, Mark	Leander
Broadwell, David	Wichita Falls
Brooks, Michael	Lubbock
Bullard, Tom	Comfort
Burden, James M.	Burkburnett
Byrd, Don E.	Roanoke
Callahan, F. Terry	Boerne
Carter, Fred	Wichita Falls
Cellum, Tom S.	Willis
Champion, Robert	Amarillo
Chapman, Mike	Houston
Chase, John E.	Aledo
Churchman, T.W.	Amarillo
Clark, Roger	Rockdale
Collett, Jerry D.	Charlotte
Connor, Michael	Winters
Costa, Scott	Spicewood
Crain, Jack W.	Weatherford
Crawford, Larry	Rosenberg
Davis, Vernon	Waco
Dean, Harvey J.	Rockdale
Dominy, Chuck	Colleyville
Edwards, Lynn	West Columbia
Elishewitz, Allen	Dallas
Eriksen, James Thorlief	Garland
Ferguson, Jim	San Angelo
Fischer, Clyde E.	Nixon
Fowler, Jerry	Hutto
Franks, Joel	Lubbock
Fuller, Bruce A.	Baytown
Gartman, M.D.	Gatesville
Gault, Clay	Lexington
Green, Bill	Garland
Green, Roger M.	Joshua
Griffin, Rendon and Mark	Houston
Hagwood, Kellie	San Antonio
Hajovsky, Robert J.	Scotland
Hamlet Jr., Johnny	Clute
Hand, Bill	Spearman
Hays, Mark	Carrollton
Hesser, David	Dripping Springs
Hoffman, Harold	San Angelo
Hollett, Jeff	Fate
Howell, Robert L.	Hallsville
Hudson, Robert	Humble
Hueske, Chubby	Bellaire
Hughes, Lawrence	Plainview
Jetton, Cay	Winnsboro
Johnson, Gorden W.	Houston
Johnson, Ruffin	Houston
Johnson, Ryan M.	Hixson
Kennedy, Kelly S.	Odessa
Kious, Joe	Kerrville
Klimaszewski, Bernard E.	Killeen
Knipstein, Robert C.	Arlington
Kohler, J. Mark	Sugarland
Ladd, Jim	Deer Park
Ladd, Jimmie L.	Deer Park
Lambert, Jarrell D.	Ganado
LaPlante, Brett	Garland
Laughlin, Don	Vidor
Lawson, Stephen M.	Fredericksburg
Lay, L.J.	Burkburnett
LeBlanc, John	Winnsboro
Lister Jr., Weldon E.	Boerne
Luchak, Bob	Channelview
Luckett, Bill	Weatherford
Lyons, Randy	Vidor
Madsen, Jack	Wichita Falls
Marshall, Glenn	Mason
McConnell Jr., Loyd A.	Odessa
McDearmont, Dave	Lewisville
McElhannon, Marcus	Sugarland
McKissack II, Tommy	Sonora
Merz III, Robert L.	Katy
Miller, R.D.	Dallas
Mills, Andy	Fredericksburg
Neely, Greg	Houston
Moore, James B.	Ft. Stockton
Mount, Don	Horizon City
Oliver, Anthony Craig	Ft. Worth
Osborne, Warren	Waxahachie
Overeynder, T.R.	Arlington
Pate, Lloyd D.	Georgetown
Polzien, Don	Lubbock
Pugh, Jim	Azle
Pullen, Martin	Granbury
Ray, Alan W.	Lovelady
Raymond, Donald	Groveton
Raymond, Mary Jame	Groveton
Richardson Jr., Percy	Milan
Rippy, Robert and Bonnie	Emory
Robinson, Charles	Vega
Ruple, William H.	Charlotte
Scott, Al	Kerrville
Self, Ernie	Porter
Sims, Bob	Meridian
Sloan, Shane	Newcastle
Spano, Dominick	San Angelo
Spencer, John E.	Harper
Stokes, Ed	Hockley
Stone, Jerry	Lytle
Stout, Johnny	New Braunfels
Thuesen, Ed	Houston
Thuesen, Kevin	Houston
Treiber, Leon	Ingram
Turcotte, Larry	Pampa
Ware, Tommy	Blanco
Watson, Daniel	Driftwood
Watt III, Freddie	Big Spring
Watts, Wally	Gatesville
West, Pat	Charlotte
Whitley, Weldon G.	El Paso
Wilcher, Wendell L.	Palestine
Womack, A.M. "Babe"	Coldspring
Wood, William W.	Seymour
Yeates, Joe A.	Spring
Yunes, Yamil R.	Roma
Zinsmeister, Paul	Fredericksburg

u.s. virgin islands

Sheehan, Paul P.	St. Croix

utah

Black, Earl	Salt Lake City
Ence, Jim	Richfield
Erickson, Curt	Ogden
Erickson, L.M.	Liberty
Hatch, Ken	Jensen
Johnson, Steve R.	Manti
Maxfield, Lynn	Layton
Nielson, Jeff	Monroe
Nunn, Gregory R.	Moab
Peterson, Chris	Salina
Rapp, Steven J.	Salt Lake City
Strickland, Dale	Monroe
Warenski, Buster	Richfield
Winn, Travis A.	Salt Lake City

vermont

Haggerty, George S.	Jacksonville
Kelso, Jim	Worcester

virginia

Ballew, Dale	Bowling Green
Barber, Robert E.	Charlottesville
Batson, Richard G.	Rixeyville
Beverly II, Larry H.	Hartwood
Blakley II, William E.	Fredericksburg
Callahan, Errett	Lynchburg
Conkey, Tom	Nokesville
Davidson, Edmund	Goshen
Douglas, John J.	Lynch Station
Fielder, William V.	Richmond
Frazier, Ron	Powhatan
Hawk, Jack L.	Ceres
Hawk, Joe	Ceres
Hawk, Joey K.	Ceres
Hedrick, Don	Newport News
Hendricks, Samuel J.	Maurertown
Holloway, Paul	Norfolk
Jones, Barry	Danville
Jones, Enoch	Warrenton
Jones, Phillip G.	Danville
Kellogg, Brian R.	New Market
Metheny, H.A. "Whitey"	Spotsylvania
Owen, Bill	Monterey
Presley, Vern	Richmond
Richter, John C.	Chesapeake
Ryan, C.O.	Yorktown
Scott, Winston	Huddleston
Straight, Don	Falls Church
Thomas, Daniel	Leesburg
Tomes, P.J.	Grottoes
White, Gene E.	Alexandria

knifemakers state-by-state

washington
Baldwin, Phillip	Snohomish
Ball, Robert	Port Angeles
Ber, Dave	San Juan Island
Blomberg, Gregg	Lopez
Boguszewski, Phil	Tacoma
Brothers, Robert L.	Colville
Chamberlain, John B.	East Wenatchee
Conti, Jeffrey D.	Port Orchard
D'Angelo, Laurence	Vancouver
Davis, K.M. Twig	Monroe
Goertz, Paul S.	Renton
Greenfield, G.O.	Everett
Holland, Dale J.	Issaquah
Lisk, Arlin J.	Yakima
Mosser, Gary E.	Kirkland
Rice, Adrienne	Lopez Island
Sanderson, Ray	Yakima
Wright, Kevin	Quilcene

west virginia
Barnett, Van	New Haven
Bowen, Tilton	Baker
Dent, Douglas M.	South Charleston
Drost, Michael B.	French Creek
Elliott, Jerry P.	Charleston
Liegey, Kenneth R.	Millwood
Maynard, Larry Joe	Crab Orchard
McConnell, Charles R.	Wellsburg
Pickens, Selbert	Liberty
Reynolds, Dave	Harrisville
Sigman, Corbet R.	Liberty
Small, Ed	Keyser
Tokar, Daniel	Shepherdstown
Williams, David	Berea
Williams, Leonard	Meadow Bridge
Wilson, R.W.	Weirton
Workman, Jr., Hubert L.	Williamsburg
Wyatt, William R.	Rainelle

wisconsin
Brdlik, Dan E.	Prescott
Crosslen, Timothy J.	Grafton
Dahl, Cris	Lake Geneva
Gannaway, Woodson	Madison
Genske, Jay	Fond du Lac
Hanson, Travis	Mosinee
Hembrook, Ron	Neosho
Johnson, Kenneth B.	Mindoro
Kolitz, Robert	Beaver Dam
Lary, Ed	Mosinee
Maestri, Peter A.	Spring Green
Ricke, Dave	West Bend
Rochford, Michael R.	Dresser
Stafford, Michael	Madison
Wattelet, Michael A.	Minocqua

wyoming
Alexander, Darrel	Ten Sleep
Ankrom, W.E.	Cody
Banks, David L.	Riverton
Bridges, Justin W.	Dubois
Draper, Bart	Big Piney
Fowler, Ed A.	Riverton
Friedly, Dennis	Cody
Iiams, Richard D.	Mills
Pavack, Don	Edgerton
Rambo, Jay T.	Rock Springs
Rexroat, Kirk	Wright
Reynolds, John C.	Gillette
Ross, Stephen	Evanston
Strohecker, John J.	Riverton
Walker, George A.	Alpine
Whipple, Wesley A.	Thermopolis

foreign countries

africa
Burger, Pon	Zimbabwe

argentina
Ayarragaray, Cristian L.	La Paz
Kehiayan, Alfredo	Buenos Aires
Mosci, Carlos Roberto	La Plata
Rho, Nestor Lorenzo	Junin B.A.
Schonhals, Gualberto G.	Diamante

australia
Bennett, Peter	Engadine
Brown, Peter	Emerald Beach
Crawley, Bruce R.	Croydon
Gerus, Gerry	Cairns
Giljevic, Branko	Queanbeyan
Green, William	View Bank
Harvey, Max	Perth
Husiak, Myron	Altona
Jones, John	Brisbane
Maisey, Alan	Toongabbie
Rowe, Stewart G.	Mt. Crosby
Simmonds, Kurt Barnes	Castlemaine
Zemitis, Joe	Cardiff Hts.

belgium
Monteiro, Victor	Brussels

brazil
Gaeta, Roberto	Sao Paulo

canada
Arnold, Joe	Ontario
Beauchamp, Gaetan	Stoneham
Bell, Donald	Bedford
Cote, Yves	Quebec
DeBraga	Val Belair
Deringer, Christoph	Pike River
Downie, James T.	Port Franks
Dublin, Dennis	Enderby
Fraser, Grant	Foresters Falls
Freeman, John	Cambridge
Garner, Richard	Alberta
Grenier, Roger	Saint Jovite
Hayes, Wally	Orleans
Haynes, Chap	Tatamagouche
Hoffmann, Uwe H.	Vancouver
Jobin, Jacques	Lauzon
Kaczor, Tom	Ontario
Langley, Mick	Qualicum Beach
Leber, Heinz	Hudson Hope
Lemaire, Denis	Boucherville
Loerchner, Wolfgang	Bayfield
Lyttle, Brian	High River
Macri, Mike	Churchill
Maneker, Kenneth	Galiano Island
Marzitelli, Peter	Langley
Niro, Frank	Mackenzie
Olson, Rod	High River
Patrick, Robert	Vancouver
Pepiot, Stephan	Winnipeg
Piesner, Dean	Ontario
Price, Steve	Kamloops
Rahn, John	Waterloo
Roberts, George A.	Parkhill
Ross, Tim	Thunder Bay
Schoenfeld, Matthew A.	Galiano Island
Sunderland, Richard	Quathiakski Cove
Toner, Roger	Ontario
Treml, Glenn	Thunder Bay
Vachon, Yvon	Quebec
Young, Bud	Port Hardy
Young, Cliff	Pembroke

denmark
Andersen, Henrik Lefolii	Fredensborg
Carlsson, Mark	Roskilde
Dyrnoe, Per	Hilleroed
Henriksen, Hans J.	Helsinge
Vensild, Henrik	Renne

england
Boden, Harry	Bonsall
Elliott, Marcus	Llandudno
Heasman, H.G.	Llandudno
Henry, Peter and Son	Wokingham
Hitchmough, Howard	London
Jackson, Jim	Berkshire
Jones, Charles Anthony	No. Devon
Lamprey, Mike	Devon
Morris, Darrell Price	Devon
Wardell, Michael Ronald	Bletchingley
Wise, Donald	St. Leonards-On-Sea
Wood, Alan	Slaggyford

france
Blum, Michel	Draguignan
Doursin, Gerard	Pernes les Fontaines
Ganster, Jean-Pierre	Strasbourg
Reverdy, Pierre	Valence
Viallon, Henri	Thiers

germany
Balbach, Markus	Weilm nster
Becker, Franz	Marktl/Inn
Borger, Wolf	Graben-Neudorf
Hehn, Richard Karl	D"rrebach
Kaluza, Werner	Nurnberg
Kersten, Michael	Berlin
Kressler, D.F.	Puchheim
Rankl, Christian	Munich
Rinkes, Siegfrien	Markterlbach
Steinau, Jurgen	Berlin
Wimpff, Christian	Stuttgart

italy
Albericci, Emilio	Bergamo
Ameri, Mauro	Genova
Bonassi, Franco	Pordenone
Fogarizzu, Boiteddu	Pattada
Pachi, Francesco	Genoa
Scordia, Paolo	Roma
Simonella, Gianluigi	Maniago
Toich, Nevio	Vicenza

japan
Aida, Yoshihito	Tokyo
Esaki, Shusuke	Osaka City
Fujikama, Shun	Osaka
Fukuta, Tak	Seki-City
Hara, Kovji	Seki-City
Hirayama, Harumi	Warabi City
Ishihara, Nobuhiko	Sakura City
Kagawa, Koichi	Kanagawa
Kanda, Michio	Yamaguehi
Kawasaki, Akihisa	Kobi
Mazaki, Yoshio	Osaka City
Okaysu, Kazou	Tokyo
Sakakibara, Masaki	Tokyo
Shikayama, Toshiaki	Saitama
Takahashi, Hirohiko	Yokohama
Takahashi, Masao	Gunma
Tasaki, Seiichi	Tochigi
Ueda, Masaharu	Osaka City
Uekama, Nobuyuki	Tokyo

mexico
Scheurer, Alfredo Faes	Bosque

netherlands
Rijswijk, Aad V.	Spijkenisse
Van Eldik, Frans	Loenen

new zealand
Pennington, C.A.	Christchurch
Reddiex, Bill	Palmerston North
Ross, D.L. (Dave)	Alexandra

norway
Bache-Wiig, Tom	Eivindvik
Holum, Morton	Oslo
Sellevold, Harald	Dreggen
Vistnes, Tor	Kjelhenes

russia
Kharlamov, Yuri	Tula

scotland
McColl, John	Stonehouse

singapore
Tay, Larry C-G	Singapore

south africa
Bauchop, Peter	Germiston
Bauchop, Robert	Elsburg
Bezuidenhout, Buzz	Queensburgh
Boardman, Guy	New Germany
Brown, Robert E.	Port Elizabeth
Burger, Fred	Munster
Daubermann, Desmond P.	Gaborone
Frankland, Andrew	Wilderness
Grey, Piet	Silverton
Gunther, Eddie	Seaveiw
Kojetin, W.	Germiston
LaGrange, Fanie	Bellville
Lancaster, C.G.	Oakney
Liebenberg, Andre	Bordeaux
Mackrill, Stephen	Pinegowrie
Pienaar, Conrad	Bloemfontein
Rietveld, Bertie	Magaliesburg
Russell, Mick	Port Elizabeth
Schoeman, Corrie	Bloemfontein
Skellern, Dr. M.J.	Munster
Smythe, Ken	Bullwer
Watson, Peter	Klerksdorp
Wood, Owen	Honeydew

sweden
Eklund, Rolf	Rosersberg
Embretsen, Kaj	Edsbyn
Lundstrom, Jan-Ake	Dals-Langed
Nordell, Ingemar	F„rila

switzerland
Soppera, Arthur	Zurich

uruguay
Gonzales, Leonardo Williams	Maldonado

wales
Elliott, Marcus	Llandudno

FIFTEENTH EDITION

knifemakers membership lists

Not all knifemakers are organization-types, but those listed here are in good standing with these organizations.

knifemakers guild

1994 voting membership

a **William Abbott**, Yoshihito Aida, Mike "Whiskers" Allen, R.V. Alverson, W.E. Ankrom, Dick Atkinson.

b **Phillip Baldwin**, Norman Bardsley, Gary Barnes, Cecil T. Barrett, James Barry III, John Bartlow, Hugh E. Bartrug, Gene Baskett, James Batson, Butch Beaver, Judy T. Beaver, Franz Becker, Raymond Beers, Tom Black, Andrew Blackton, Chuck Blum, Michel Blum, Philip Boguszewski, Dennis Bradley, Edward Brandsey, Clint Breshears, Mark Brightwell, Tim Britton, David Broadwell, David Brown, Harold Brown, Rick Browne, John Busfield.

c **Bill Caldwell**, Ronald Canter, Bob Cargill, Harold J. "Kit" Carson, Fred Carter, Dianna Casteel, Douglas Casteel, Frank & Tony and Sue Centofante, Gordon Chard, William Cheatham, Wayne Clay, Lowell Cobb, Keith Coleman, Vernon Coleman, Alex Collins, Blackie (Walter) Collins, Bob Conley, C.T. Conn, Harold Corby, Joe Cordova, Leonard Corlee, Jim Corrado, Charles Cosgrove, George Cousino, Raymond Cover, Colin Cox, Sam Cox, John Craft III, Pat Crawford, John M. Cross, Bob Crowder, James Crowell, Dan Cruze.

d **Alex Daniels**, Jack Davenport, Barry Davis, W.C. Davis, Bill DeFreest, Richard DeGraeve, Dan Dennehy, Robert Dill, Frank Dilluvio, Patrick Donovan, T.M. Dowell, Larry Downing, Tom Downing, Beryl Driskill, Bill Duff, Melvin Dunn, Jerry Duran, Larry Duvall.

e **Paula K. Easler**, Russell Easler, Joel Ellefson, Kaj Embretsen, Jim Ence, Robert Enders, Virgil England, Robert Engnath, Walter Erickson, James T. Eriksen.

f **Stephen Fecas**, Lee Ferguson, Jay Fisher, Jerry Fisk, Joe Flournoy, Don Fogg, Pete Forthofer, Paul Fox, Henry Frank, Ron Frazier, Dennis Friedly, Larry Fuegen, Stanley Fujisaka, Tak Fukuta, John W. Fuller, Shiro Furukawa.

g **Frank Gamble**, William Garner, Ronald Gaston, Clay Gault, Roy Genge, James "Hoot" Gibson Sr., Wayne Goddard, Warren Goltz, Dante & Judith Gottage, Greg Gottchalk, Roger M. Green, Rendon & Mark Griffin, Melvin Gurganus, Kenneth Guth.

h **Philip L. "Doc" Hagen**, Kellie Hagwood, Robert Hajovsky, Ed Halligan & Son, Jim Hammond, Ronald E. Hancock, James E. Hand, M.D., Walt Harless, Larry Harley, Ralph Harris, Joe Hawk, Rade Hawkins, Richard Hehn, Henry Heitler, Roy L. Helton, Wayne Hensley, Tim Herman, George Herron, Don Hethcoat, Thomas S. Hetmanski, Daryl Hibben, Gil Hibben, Steven Hill, Howard Hill, R. Hinson & Son, Harumi Hirayama, Richard Hodgson, Steve Hoel, Kevin Hoffman, D'Alton Holder, Dale Holland, Jess Horn, Glen Hornby, Durvyn Howard, Arthur Hubbard, Rob Hudson, Steven Douglas Huey.

i Bill Imel.

j **Jim Jacks**, Steve Jernigan, Brad Johnson, Durrell C. Johnson, Gorden Johnson, Ronald Johnson, Ruffin Johnson, Steve Johnson, W.C. Johnson, Enoch D. Jones, Robert Jones.

k **Edward N. Kalfayan**, William Keeton, Jim Kelso, King Kemp, Bill Kennedy, Ralph Kessler, Jot Khalsa, Keith Kilby, Bill King, Joe Kious, Jon Kirk, Terry Knipschield, R.C. Knipstein, Mike Koval, Dennis G. Krapp, Roy Krause, D.F. Kressler.

l **Ron Lake**, Frank Lampson, Ed Lane, Gene Langley, Scott Lankton, Ken Largin, Edward Lary, Mike Leach, Tommy Lee, Bill Levengood, Norman Levine, Lile Handmade Knives, Robert C. Livingston, Wolfgang Loerchner, R.W. Loveless, Schuyler Lovestrand, William Luckett, Robert Lum, Ernest Lyle.

m **Joe Malloy**, Dan Maragni, Tom Maringer, Randall J. Martin, James May, Harvey McBurnette, Zollan McCarty, Charles McConnell, Loyd McConnell, Ken McFall, J.J. McGovern, Frank McGowan, W.J. McHenry, Tommy McKissack, Ted Merchant, Robert Merz, James Miller, Ronald T. Miller, Andy Mills, Louis Mills, Jim Minnick, James B. Moore, Jeff Morgan, C.H. Morris, Steven Mullin, Paul Myers.

n **Bud Nealy**, Corbin Newcomb, Larry Newton, R.D. & George Nolen, Mike Norris, Don Norton.

o **Charles Ochs**, Warren Osborne, T.R. Overeynder, John Owens.

p **Larry Page**, Robert Papp, Melvin Pardue, Russ Peagler, W.D. Pease, Lloyd Pendleton, Alfred Pendray, Eldon Peterson, David Pitt, Leon Pittman, Clifton Polk, Al Polkowski, Joe Prince, Jim Pugh, Martin Pullen, Morris Pulliam.

r **Jerry Rados**, James D. Ragsdale, Steven Rapp, A. D. Rardon, Bill Reddiex, Chris Reeve, Pierre Reverdy, John Reynolds, Ron Richard, David Ricke, Willie Rigney, Dean Roath, Howard Robbins, Fred Roe, Rodney Rogers, A.G. Russell.

s **Masaki Sakakibara**, John Salley, Lynn Sampson, A.A. Sanders, Scott Sawby, Murad Sayen, James Schmidt, Herman Schneider, Maurice & Alan Schrock, Steve Schwarzer, James Serven, Eugene W. Shadley, Paul Sheehan, Scott Shoemaker, Ben Shostle, Corbet Sigman, Bill Simons, Norman Simons, R.J. Sims, Cleston Sinyard, Jim Siska, Fred Slee, Scott Slobodian, Gregory H. Smith, John Smith, Ralph Smith, Red Smith, Jerry Snell, Jim Sornberger, Richard Stafford, Harry Stalter, Ken Steigerwalt, Charles Stewart, Scott Strong, Charles Syslo.

t **Seiichi Tasaki**, David A. Taylor, Gray Taylor, Mickey Tedder, Robert Terzuola, Leon Thompson, Carolyn Tinker, Pat Tomes, Dan Tompkins, Dwight Towell, Barry Trindle, Jim Turecek, Ralph Turnbull.

v **Wayne Valachovic**, Butch Vallotton, Frans Van Eldik, Michael Veit, Howard Viele, Frank Vought, Robert "Bob" Vunk.

w **Mark David Wahlster**, Mark Waldrop, George Walker, Michael Walker, Buster Warenski, Al Warren, Dale Warther, Thomas J. Watson, Reese Weiland, Charles Weiss, Mike Wesolowski, Weldon Whitley, Donnie R. Wicker, R.W. Wilson, Daniel Winkler, Webster Wood, Tim Wright.

y **Yoshindo Yoshihara**, Mike Yurco.

z **Don & Don Jr. Zaccagnino**, Tim Zowada.

probationary members, 1993-1994

Michael Anderson (93), Joe Arnold (94), Joseph Bailey (93), Wolf Borger (94), William Chapo (93), David Clark (94), Howard Clark (93), Charles Dake (93), Terry A. David (94), Edmund Davidson (93), Vernon Davis (93), Harvey Dean (94), Jose DeBraga (94), William Dietzel (93), Albert Eaton (94), Rick Eaton (94), Allen Elishewitz (94), William Engle (94), Thomas Ferrara (93), Michael Franklin (93), Richard Genovese (93), Harry George (93), Bruce Goers (93), David Goldberg (93), Kouji Hara (94), Jay Harmon (93), Earl J. Hendrickson (93), Howard Hitchmough (93), Joel Humphreys (94), Jarrell Lambert (93), John LeBlanc (93), Bob Luchak (94), Brian Lyttle (93), David McIntosh (93), Dan Mink (94), Dano-D. Arvel Owens (94), James Poplin (94), Gote Ryberg (94), Mike Sakmar (94), Mark Sentz (93), J.D. Smith (93), Michael Stafford (94), Jurgen Steinau (94), Kenneth Thompson (94), Reinhard Tschager (94), Gordon Wilson (94), Earl Witsaman (93), William Wolf (93), Wood, Irie & Co. (94), Joe Yeates (94)

knifemakers membership lists

american bladesmith society

a **Alan Adams,** Kenneth E. Alden, Jr., Eugene Alexander, Jammie C. Allen, Mickey L. Ames, Leroy Amos, David Anders, Gary D. Anderson **(MS)**, Ronnie A. Andress, Sr., Boyd Ashworth, Scott Audral

b **Bill Bagwell,** Howard E. Baker III, R.G. Baker, Vance L. Baker, Robert Ball, David L. Banks, R.G. Barker, Charles Barley, Aubrey G. Barnes, Gary Barnes **(MS)**, Marlen R. Barnes, Al Barton, Hugh E. Bartrug **(MS)**, Ronald L. Bates, James L. Batson **(MS)**, Robert K. Batts, Ray Bear, Geneo Beasley, Paul E. Beasley, Richard Paul Beasley, William H. Behnke, Michael Bell, George Benjamin, Jr., Dave Ber, Hal Bish, Scott Black, Michael S. Blue, Kenneth Blum, Leon E. Borgman, Raymond A. Boysen, Garrick A. Bradford, John C. Bradley, Robert Branton, W. Lowell Bray, Jr., Robert C. Breeden, Jack Brewer, Don Broughton **(MS)**, Michael Bubonovich, Jimmie Buckner, Bill Bullard, Greg Bullington, Jay Burger, Paul E. Burke, Thomas V. Burnham, Stephan R. Burrows, John G. Butler, Dee Button.

c **Edward J. Caffrey,** Terry F. Callahan, Robert W. Calvert, Jeff Camp, Courtenay M. Campbell, James M. Cannon, Charles W. Carey, Ron Carpenter, James Carry, Steven R. Carter, Kevin R. Cashen, Chris Cawthorne, Tom S. Cellum, Nicholas I. Chovanes, Ron Clairborne, Peter John Clapp, Howard F. Clark **(MS)**, Roger L. Clark, Harold A. Collins, Larry D. Coltrain, Roger Comar, John W. Conner, Michael L. Connor **(MS)**, James R. Cook **(MS)**, George S. Cook, Louise Cook, J. Michael Cook, Joseph G. Cordova **(MS)**, James H. Corry, Mike Corvin, Houston L. Cotton, Monty L. Crain, John M. Cross **(MS)**, James L. Crowell **(MS)**, William M. Culnon, Steven M. Culver.

d **Mark H. Dake,** Benjamin M. Daland, Ollie Dannels, Hodge David, Don Davis, Harvey J. Dean, Jr. **(MS)**, Richard J. Delotto, Mike de Punte, Christoph Deringer, Keith Diabold, Pohl Dietmar, William J. Dietzel, A.W. Dippold, Charlie Drew, Paul Dube, Brad M. Dugan, Rick Dunkerley, Steve Dunn, Fred Durio, Oliver H. Durrell.

e **Robert E. Earhart,** Donald R. Earnest, Fain E. Edwards, Jeremy Edwards, Lynn Edwards, Mitch Edwards, Ronald V. Elkins, Dave Ellis, Shawn Ellis, Kaj Embretsen, John Etzler, Morris Everett.

f **George Fant Jr.,** William E. Felton, Bill V. Fielder, Edward Finn, William R. Fiorini, Clyde E. Fischer, Jerry Fisk **(MS)**, Jim Fister, James Flood, Joe E. Flournoy, Jr.**(MS)**, Bruce Floyd, Donna Follini, Scott T. Forbes, Chris Ford, Thomas J. Ford, Jr., Charles Ronald Fowler, Ed A. Fowler **(MS)**, Jerry B. Fowler, Wendell Fox, Walter P. Framski, Chris Fry, Larry Fuegen **(MS)**, Bruce A. Fuller, Jack A. Fuller **(MS)**, Shiro Furukawa.

g **Raul Garcia, Jr.,** Mark S. Gardner, Bernard Garner, Timothy P. Garrity, Bert Gaston **(MS)**, Thomas Gerner, Ronald J. Gillory Sr., Robert Gilchrist, Logwood U. Gion, Kevin S. Givens, Wesley Glebe, Wayne L. Goddard **(MS)**, Scott K. Goguen, Jim Gofourth, Robert Golden, Phillipe Gontier, L.W. Gonzalez, James T. Gorenflo, Greg Gottschalk, Bob Gray, John T. Greco, Cris L. Green, David Green, Lance Gridley, Anthony R. Guarnera, Frank Gunn, Ralph Gutekunst.

h **Kellie Hadwood,** Philip L. Hagen, Ed Halligan, Phil Hammond, Timothy J. Hancock **(MS)**, Bill Hand, Scott Hardy, Bob L. Harper, Jeffrey A. Harris, Dennis M. Harrison, Tom Harrison, George C. Hathaway, Richard E. Hayes, Wally Hayes, Charles E. Haynes **(MS)**, Bob Dale Hays, Darryl J. Hebert, Earl J. Hendrickson **(MS)**, Shawn E. Hendrickson, Carl E. Henkle, Don Hethcoat, Kent L. Hicks, Lonny R. Hill, Rick Hinderer, Gene R. Hobart, Dan Hockensmith, Roger A. Hockwalt, David Hodge, Michael E. Hoffman, Thomas R. Hogan, Jeff Hollett, Wayne V. Holter, Glen A. Homer, Robbin C. Hudson **(MS)**, David Hufford, Bill R. Hughes, Daryle Hughes, William Hurt.

i **Richard D. Iiams,** Paul R. Inman III, Comi Ivano.

j **Jim L. Jackson,** Bob J. James, Tom January, Chester R. Johnson, Durrell C. Johnson, John R. Johnson, Randy Johnson, Ray Johnson, Robert A. Johnson, Enoch (Nick) Jones, Jacques R. Juarer.

k **Oda Kazuhide,** Michael Keeney, Joseph F. Keeslar **(MS)**, Steven C. Keeslar, Dan A. Kendrick, Jerry Kennedy, Kelly S. Kennedy, R.W. Kern, Shiva Ki, Keith Kilby **(MS)**, Fred King, Richard L. Kimberley, Hank Knickmeyer, Kurt Knickmeyer, Jimmie N. Knight, Robert R. Kodama, Christopher R. Kormanik, Bob Kramer, Raymond Kremzner, Phillip W. Kretsinger **(MS)**, Danny L. Kyle.

l **Dan Lady,** Curtis J. Lamb, Jarrell D. Lambert, Christopher M. Lander, Leonard Landrum, Donald G. Lang **(MS)**, Mick Langley **(MS)**, Pierre LaPlante, Kermit J. Laurent, Charles A. Lawless, Alton Lawrence, Dal Leck, Rick Leeson, Scott B. Lemee, Paul R. Leonard, Jr., Nick Leone III, Glen Lillibridge, Guy A. Little, Robert C. Livingston, Lowell C. Lockett, J.A. Lonewolf, Charles R. Lorditch, Eugene F. Loro, Mark Lubrich, James R. Lucie, Gregory Luck, Gerard P. Lukaszevicz, Greg Lutz, William R. Lyons.

m **Michael K. Manabe,** Ken Mankel, Dan Maragni **(MS)**, Ken Markley, Chris Marks **(MS)**, Jesse Marsh, Bruce E. Martin, Peter Martin, Paul J. Marx, Alan Robert Massey, Roger D. Massey, Charles Richard Mathews, James E. May, Oscar L. Mayville, P. Douglas Mays, Frederick L. McCoy, Kevin McCrackin, Victor J. McCrackin **(MS)**, Robert J. McDonald, Frank McGowan, Tom McKissack, Tommy McNabb, Dave McWaters, Rain R. Mederiros, Ronald I. Meekins, Ted C. Merchant, Bart Messina, Bob Miller, Hanford J. Miller **(MS)**, James P. Miller, Kent Miller, Richard Miller, Robert J. Miller Jr., Dilbert Mills, John W. Mitchell, W. Dean Mitchell **(MS)**, Billy R. Moore, Jerry Moore, William F. Moran, Jr. **(MS)**, Keith B. More, Dennis L. Morris, Everett A. Morris, Jan Muchnikoff, Dawn Mulbery, Jack W. Muse, Jan Myhre.

n **Angelo Navagato,** Gregory T. Neely **(MS)**, Bruce W. Nelson, Donald C. Newcomb, R. Kent Nicholson, Tim Nolfi.

o **Lee D. Oates,** Lee A. Oberg, Charles F. Ochs III **(MS)**, Micah Paul Ochs, Clyde O'Dell, Randy W. Ogden, Kuzuo Okayasu, Dr. Michael R. Osborne, Stephen H. Overstreet, Donald Owens.

p **Donald Page,** Reginald Page, Phil Pagnard, Stephen E. Parker, John David Parks, Jr., Chuck Patrick, Alan Patterson, Alfred H. Pendray **(MS)**, Frederic Perrin, Johnny Perry, Dan L. Peterson **(MS)**, Clay C. Peyton, Edward W. Phillips, James M. Phillips, Dean Piesner, Charles O. Piper, James P. Poling, Keith Poole, Andrew Porter, James E. Porter **(MS)**, Michael C. Porter, Timothy F. Potier, Karlis A. Povisils, Tim Proctor, Jack O. Prothro, Morris C. Pulliam, Jonathan K. Purviance.

q **Thomas C. Quakenbush,** Craig Quattlebaum.

r **Wayne R. Raley,** Richard A. Ramsey, Gary Randall, Ralph Randow, Alan W. Ray, Karen Rechberger, James D. Rhodes, John C. Richter, Steven L. Rick, David M. Rider, Janice Rivest, James D. Robarr, E. Ray Roberts, Michael Roberts, Charles R. Robinson, Michael R. Rochford II, Jerry Romig, Eric T. Rose, Gary Rua, J. Ken Rudder Jr., Al Runyon, Raymond B. Rybar Jr., Gerald Rzewnicki.

s **Richard Saindon,** Albert A. Sanders, Jeffrey T. Sanders, Margaret R. Scheid, James S. Schippnick, James A. Schmidt **(MS)**, Charles E. Schultz, Robert W. Schultz, Steven C. Schwarzer **(MS)**, Steven Schwartz, Barry Scott, James A. Scroggs, John L. Seldomridge, Mark C. Sentz, Thomas J. Sheehy, Steven Sheets, Malcolm Tiki Shewan, Tom Siess, James P. Sigman, Cleston S. Sinyard, Harland R. Simmons, Charles A. Sisemore, Ted Sketo, Roy L. Slaughter, Patrick M. Smail, J.D. Smith, John M. Smith, Raymond L. Smith, Scott E. Smith, Thomas Smith, Wil Smith, Marvin Solomon, Scott D. Sparapani, Mark Sperry, Allen Springer, Rod Staben, Chuck Stancer, Udo Stegemann, Craig Steketee, Edward L. Stewart, Johnny H. Stiles, Mark Stokeld, Johnny Stout, Howard Stover, Terry Lee Stover, Kenneth J. Straight, Frank Stratton III, Terry Stults, Harlan Suedmeier, Cynthia Ann Summers, Stephen S. Sunk, Arthur Swyhart, Mark G. Szarek, Joseph G. Szopa.

t **Darryl I. Tanaka,** Graziano Temelacchi, James L. Temple Jr., John S. Teslow, Danny Thayer, James J. Thomas, Kenneth Thompson, Fred Thynne, P.J. Tomes **(MS)**, Samuel L. Torgeson, Kenneth W. Trisler, Charles Trulove, Donna Turner, Keven Turner, Randall W. Turner, Thomas E. Turtzo, Lester A. Twigg, Jerry L. Tyer.

u **Edgar W. Urstadt,** Tim A. Utton.

v **Wayne Valachovic (MS),** Jacob Lee Valance, Kirby Van De Grick, Jonny David Vasquez, Arthur V. Velasco, Patrik Vogt, William R. Von Bergen, Jr., Lew Von Lossberg.

w **Mark W. Waldrop,** Bill Walker, James L. Walker, John Wade Walker III, Roger L. Wallace, Charles B. Ward, Michael B. Ward, Roy Warden, Dellana Warren, Billy Watson, Kenneth Whaley, Robert R. Wheeler, Ray R. Wheelington, Wesley Whipple, Daniel J. White, Lenwood W. Whitley, Randy Whittaker, Charles E. Williams, Michael L. Williams, Richard T. Williams, Wayne Willson, David L. Wilson, James R. Wilson, Daniel Winkler**(MS)**, Donald Witzler, Randy Wooton, Bill Worthen.

z **William H. Zeanon.**

directory

miniature knifemaker's society

Bill Abbott, Mel Anderson, Michael D. Anderson, Dale Ballew, Paul Charles Basch, Lee Gene Baskett, Ray Beers, Gerald Bodner, Gary F. Bradburn, Norman W. Bradley, Dianna Casteel, Joel Chamblin, George W. Connelly, Thomas A. Counts, Jose C. de Braga, T.V. Drzewicki, Sr., Paula K. Easler, Albert & Evelyn Eaton, Allan Eldridge, Theo Fisher, Gwen Flournoy, William P. Frazee, Wayne Goddard, Roger M. Green, John Green Jr., Stuart Grossman, Melvin and Carol Gurganos, Larry Harley, Jay Harmon, Ralph Dewey Harris, Don Hedrick, Charlene C. Herring, Tom Hetmanski, Daryl Hibben, Joleen Hibben, J. Wallace Kay, Gary Kelley, Shiva Ki, Terry Kranning, Kenneth Kribs, Gary Ladd, Kenneth R. Liegey, Robert C. Livingston, Henry C. Loos, Joe Lozito, Bob Luchak, Billy Lum, Ken McFall, Mike Mercer, Paul Meyers, Kevin Mitchell, Wayne & June Morrison, Mike Moskau, Allen R. Olsen, Daniel E. Osterman, Jim Pugh, Glen A. Redd, Sidney Reggio, Paul C. Sheffield, Jeffrey D. Simos, Glen Paul Smit, Harry Stalter, Mike Tamboli, Herman F. Wahlers, Rudy Wehner, Steven B. Weiss, Gene E. White, James D. Whitehead, Michael Whittingham, Wendell L. Wilcher, Jon J. Wilson, Earl Witsaman, Dennis Woodcock, Kevin Wright, Joe A. Yeates, Errol Young.

professional knifemakers association

Mel & Marylyn Anderson, Don Andrews, K.B. Armogost, Robert Blasingame, Justin Bridges, Robert L. Brothers, C. Lyle Brunckhorst, Jerry Busse, Thomas P. Calawa, Danniel L. Cannady, Raymond W. Cannon, Curt D. Childs, Howard F. Clark, David Clouse, Eldon Coats, Alex Collins, Geroge Conklin, C.M. Dake, Don Davis, Dan Dennehy, Robert Dill, Melvin T. Dunn, Rick Eaton, Ray W. Ennis, James Thorlief Eriksen, Jay Fisher, Bob Garbe, Richard Genovese, Paul S. Goertz, Jeff A. Harkins, Jesse & Dana Hemphill, Kenneth G. Henschel, Tom High, Dan Hockensmith, Scot Horton, Michael J. Hull, Robert James Hunter, R.B. Johnson, Steven R. Johnson, Jerry Kennedy, Frank Lampson, James Largent, Norman Levine, Tim Lively, Randy Lyons, Guy MacEwan, Mike Mann, Glenn Marshall, Osa & JB McDowell, David L. McIntosh, Harry E. Mendenhall, J.P. Moss, Dusty Moulton, Bud Nealy, Willard C. Patrick, Eldon G. Peterson, Dick Presley, Cecil W. Quier, Wayne A. Reno, Robert & Bonnie Rippy, Chuck Roberts, Robert Robinson, Steve Rollert, R. Bill Saindon, Michael M. Sanders, Michael J. Schirmer, Ernie Self, Eugene W. Shadley, James Sigg, Cleston Sinyard, Noel Smith, Craig Steketee, John E. Toner, John W. Townsend, Butch Vallotton, Michael A. Wattelet, Gerome M. Weinand, Charles A. West, Bill Wolf, Barry Wood-Michael L. Irie, Joe A. Yeats.

state/regional associations

midwest knifemakers association
Robert Abel, Mike Ames, Geoffrey L. Bahr, Frank Berlin, Mark Brightwell, Howard Clark, Jim P. Cornelius, Charles Cosgrove, Charlie M. Dake, Barry Dawson, Larry Duvall, William Engle, Jerry Fields, Kenneth Hart, James L. Haynes, Harvey King, Jeff Knickerbocker, Mick Koval, Mickey Kruse, Carl LeBlanc, Matt Loomis, George Martoncik, Bill Mason, James May, Steve McAfee, Guy McConnell, Stan L. McKiernan, Jim Messick, Gene Millard, J.P. Miller, William Miller, Clayton E. Morris, Corbin Newcomb, Dan L. Peterson, Rusty Raleigh, A.D. Rardon, Archie Rardon, Curtis Rosebaugh, Al Sanders, George Schepers, Max Smith, Chuck Syslo, Alan R. Tollefson, Samuel L. Torgeson, Larry Turcotte, Ralph A. Turnbull, Rusty Von Boeckman, Del Weddle, Robert Wilson.

new england bladesmiths guild
Phillip Baldwin, Gary Barnes, Paul Champagne, Jimmy Fikes, Don Fogg, Larry Fuegen, Rob Hudson, Midk Langley, Louis Mills, Dan Maragni, Jim Schmidt, Wayne Valachovic and Tim Zowada.

alaska knifemakers association
A.W. Amoureux, John Arnold, Bud Aufdermauer, Robert Ball, J.D. Biggs, Lonnie Breuer, Tom Broome, Mark Bucholz, Irvin Campbell, Virgil Campbell, Raymond Cannon, Christopher Cawthorne, John Chamberlin, Bill Chatwood, George Cubic, Bob Cunningham, Gordon S. Dempsey, J.L. Devoll, James Dick, Art Dufour, Alan Eaker, Norm Grant, Gordon Grebe, Dave Highers, Alex Hunt, Dwight Jenkins, Hank Kubaiko, Bill Lance, Bob Levine, Michael Miller, John Palowski, Gordon Parrish, Mark W. Phillips, Frank Pratt, Guy Recknagle, Ron Robertson, Steve Robertson, Red Rowell, Dave Smith, Roger E. Smith, Gary R. Stafford, Keith Stegall, Wilbur Stegner, Norm Story, Robert D. Shaw, Thomas Trujillo, Ulys Whalen, Jim Whitman, Bob Willis.

arizona knifemakers association
D. "Butch" Beaver, Bill Cheatham, Dan Dagget, Tom Edwards, Anthony Goddard, Steve Hoel, Ken McFall, Milford Oliver, Jerry Poletis, Merle Poteet, Mike Quinn, Elmer Sams, Jim Sornberger, Glen Stockton, Bruce Thompson, Sandy Tudor, Charles Weiss.

arkansas knifemakers association
Hoyt Adcock, Mickey L. Ames, David Anders, Robert Bailey, Cecil Barnes, Keith Batts, Larry Beason, James Black, Jay Black, Joel Bradford, Mike Brannan, J.C. Brown, Richard Brown, Jim Butler, Buddy Cabe, Kendall Carpenter, Alan D. Davis, Jerry Davis, Harvey Dean, Gary Wayne Dumas, Lawrence Dungy, Fred Duvall, Jack East, George Fant Jr., Lee Ferguson, Jerry Fisk, Joe Flournoy, John Fortenbury, Roger Freeze, Dewayne Funderburg, Roger George, Don Greenwaway, Arthur J. Gunn, Jr., L.B. Handly, Monica Hansen, John Heuston, Don Hicks, Dave Hooper, Nicholas Hulbert, Jerry Husbrecht, Homer Jackson, Terry Johnson, Kenneth Kling, Ben Lane, Alton Lawrence, Bruce Martin, Douglas Mays, John McKeehan, Tom McKissack, Bart Messina, Richard C. Meyer, John Perry, Cliff Polk, Alan Purifoy, Ted Quandt, Craig Quattlebaum, Tim Richardson, Scott J. Robson, Kenny Rowe, James Seale, Andy Shaw, Carroll Shoffner, William Shoffner, Charles Sisemore, Dean Slaughter, Roy Slaughter, Scott Smith, Ray Smoker, Marvin Solomon, Sherman Sparks, Don Thurman, Arthur Tycer, James Walker, Chuck Ward, Jim Watson, Steve White, Mike Williams, Randy Wooton, Jimmy Worden, George Zimmerman.

california knifemakers association
Arnie Abegg, Kenneth E. Alden, Jr., Russell Allard, Elmer Art, John Bevans, Roger Bost, John T. Brown, Melvin Ellison, Ernest Emerson, Jim Ferguson, Logwood Gion, J.H. Harkins, Curtis J. Jones, Ron Jones, John Kray, R.W. Loveless, Thomas Markey, James K. Mattis, Jim McHann, Walt Modest, Jeff Morgan, Bob Packard, Barry Evan Posner, Antony Rebamontan, Chuck Roberts, Hugh B. Sanders, Larry Shaft, Ray Shepard, Scott Slobodian, William R. Von Bergen, Jr., Al Warren, Sherman Williams, Jr., Barry B. Wood.

north carolina custom knifemakers' guild
Dr. James Batson, Tim Britton, Thomas Brown, Dr. Robert Charlton, Donald Daniel, Travis Daniel, Billy Downs, Gary Gaddy, Major Garris, Mark Gottesman, Robert Grooms, Carol & Melvin Gurganus, George Guthrie, Jack Hyer, Barry Jones, Phillip Jones, Tony Kelly, Charles Ray Knowles, Robert Livingston, Danny Masser, Bill Maynard, Tommy McNabb, Alex Moss, James Parker, Alan Patterson, Charles Rece, Ben Ryder, J.D. Sams, Ellis Sawyer, Tim Scholl, H.R. Simmons, Russel Sutton, Robert Thomas, Mike Weaver, Wayne Whitley, Michael Wise.

ohio knifemakers association
Raymond Babcock, Van Barnett, Harold A. Collins, Larry Detty, Tom Downing, Jim Downs, Patty Ferrier, Jeff Flannery, James Fray, Bob Foster, Raymond Guess, Scott Hamrie, Rick Hinderer, Curtis Hurley, Ed Kalfayan, Michael Koval, Judy Koval, Larry Lunn, Stanley Maienknecht, Dave Marlott, Mike Mercer, David Morton, Patrick McGroder, Charles Pratt, Darrel Ralph, Roy Roddy, Carroll Shoemaker, John Smith, Clifton Smith, Art Summers, Jan Summers, Donald Tess, Dale Warther, John Wallingford, Earl Witsaman, Joanne Yurco, Mike Yurco.

south carolina association of knifemakers
Robert Branton, Richard Bridwell, Dan Cannady, Charles S. Cox, William DeFreest, Paula Easler, Russell Easler, Hal Gainey, Ron Gaston, Harry George, Dick Gillenwater, Mike Gregory, Wayne Hendrix, George Herron, Jerry Hucks, Ralph Kessler, Gene Langley, Dan Owens, Larry Page, Russ Peagler, Alvin Poston, Joe Prince, Ralph Smith, Rocky Thomas.

tennessee knifemakers association
John Bartlow, Doug Casteel, Harold Crisp, Larry Harley, John W. Walker, Harold Woodward, Harold Wright.

canadian knife collectors club
Joe Arnold (London, Ont.), Gary Choppick (Simcoe, Ont.), Alex Daniels (Lynn Haven, FL), George Dmowski (Belle River, Ont.), Harald Moeller (Nanoose Bay, B.C.), Rod Olson (High River, Alb.), George Roberts (Park Hill, Ont.), Tim and Katherine Ross (ThunderBay, Ont.), Suzanne St. Amour (Hillsburgh, Ont.), R. Sunderland (Quathiaski Cove, B.C.), Tom Watson (Panama City, FL), Daniel L. Waugh (Endicott, NY), John Zaal (Kimberley, B.C.), Mike Tierney (Woodstock, Ont.), Mary W. Bailey (Lynn Haven, FL), John Comber (Milton, Ont.).

knife photo index

knives '95

Aida, Yoshihito: 216
Alden, Jr., Kenneth E.: 83,128
Allred, Elvan: 140,216
Alverson, Tim: 217
Ameri, Mauro: 117
Ames, Mickey L.: 99
Anders, David: 93,95,217
Anderson, Michael D.: 87,155
Ankrom, W.E.: 127
Arnold, Joe: 216
Arrowood, Dale: 217
Ayarragaray, Cristian L.: 116
Bailey, Kirby C.: 133
Baker, Vance: 217
Baker, Wild Bill: 155
Baldwin, Phillip: 92
Barnes, Gary L.: 134
Barr, A.T.: 83,108,139
Barrett, R.W.: 162
Baskett, Lee Gene: 163,146
Batson, James: 78,94,103
Batson, Richard G.: 96
Batts, Keith: 93
Beauchamp, Gaetan: 164
Behnke, William: 104,122
Bell, Donald: 156,157,216
Bennett, Peter: 142
Beverly II, Larry H.: 144
Bogachov, Anatoly: 103
Boguszewski, Phil: 81,101,129
Boye, David: 217
Brack, Douglas D.: 65
Brandsey, Edward P.: 107
Brend, Walter J.: 161
Brennan, Judson: 78
Britton, Tim: 216
Brooks, Steve R.: 145,216
Broughton, Don R.: 91
Brown, Rob E.: 217
Bullard, Tom: 90
Burrows, Stephen R.: 167
Byrd, Don E.: 110,119
Caldwell, Bill: 119
Callahan, Errett: 111,219
Callahan, F. Terry: 91,120
Cannady, Daniel L.: 108,219
Cannon, Wes: 166
Carey Jr., Charles W.: 218
Carlsson, Marc Bjorn: 117,126
Carson, Harold J. "Kit": Cover,135,146
Carter, Fred: 163
Casteel, Douglas: 78,96
Centofante, Frank and Tony: 127,137,162,164
Chamblin, Joel: 129
Chapo, William G.: 219
Chard, Gordon R.: 92
Chase, John E.: 219
Cheatham, Bill: 131
Clark, Roger: 93
Clay, J.D.: 83,125
Cobb, Lowell D.: 69
Coffman, Danny: 137
Corby, Harold: 147
Cordova, Joseph G.: 105
Cosby, E. Blanton: 133
Cote, Yves: 87
Cox, Colin J.: 218
Cross, John M.: 94
Cutchin, Roy D.: 126
Dake, C.M.: 134
Darby, Rick: 121
Davenport, Jack: Cover,131
Davidson, Edmund: Cover,136
Davis, Barry L.: 219
Davis, Don: 82
Davis, Ken: 81
Davis, Terry: 124
Dean, Harvey J.: 123,143
DeBraga, Jose C.: 130,219
Defeo, Robert A.: 93
Dilluvio, Frank J.: 67,92
Dion, Greg: 218
Dippold, A.W.: 118

Dominy, Chuck: 109
Donovan, Patrick: 131
Doursin, Gerard: 115
Doussot, Laurent: 115,218
Dowell, T.M.: 218
Downs, James F.: 110,138
Dungy, Lawrence: 120
Dunn, Melvin T.: 81
Dunn, Steve: 123,218
Duvall, Fred: 96
Eaton, Al: 86,87,103,123,155
Eaton, Rick: 158
Edwards, Fain E.: 88,99,220
Eldik, Frans Van: 72
Elishewitz, Allen: 80,128,220
Ellefson, Joel: 156
Ellis, David: 220
Embretsen, Kaj: 128
Emerson, Ernest R.: 145
Ence, Jim: 77,158
Enders, Robert: 125
England, Virgil: 73
English, Jim: 220
Enos III, Thomas M.: 69,220
Eriksen, James Thorlief: 165
Etzler, John: 102,130
Evans, Vincent K.: 64
Fecas, Steven J.: 125
Ferguson, Jim: 67,221
Fikes, Jimmy L.: 67
Fiorini, Bill: 221
Fisk, Jerry: 103
Fister, Jim: 221
Flechtner, Chris: 122
Flournoy, Joe: 99
Fogg, Don: 68,74,145,155
Fowler, Ed A.: 90,221
Fox, Wendell: 220
Fraley, Derek: 82
Frank, Heinrich H.: 71
Frankland, Andrew: 89,91
Freer, Ralph: 153,221
Friedly, Dennis E.: 69
Fujisaka, Stanley: 104,221
Fuller, Bruce A.: 221
Gaddy, Gary L.: 155
Gallagher, Barry: 222
Gamble, Frank: 131
Garbe, Bob: 139,146
Garner, Bernard: 97,223
Gaston, Ron: 121
Gault, Clay: 121,222
Genovese, Rick: 77
Gilbreath, Randall: 130,156
Giljevic, Branko: 109,137
Goguen, Scott: 223
Goldenberg, T.S.: 222
Gottage, Dante: 102
Gottage, Judy: 159
Graffeo, Anthony I.: 107
Greco, John: 82,93,222
Green, Roger M.: 89,95
Greenfield, G.O.: 154
Griffin, Rendon: 135
Grossman, Stewart: 87,222
Hagen, Philip L.: 67,98
Halligan, Ed: 81,97,102
Halligan, Ed and Shawn: 222
Hammond, Jim: 81,126
Hampton, William W.: 107
Hancock, Ronald E.: 96,112
Hancock, Tim: 223
Hara, Kouji: 106
Harkins, J.A.: 130,132
Harley, Larry W.: 144
Harmon, Jay: 223
Harris, Jay: 101,160
Harris, Ralph Dewey: 135
Hartman, Arland (Lanny): 138
Hartsfield, Phill: 68,69,86,144
Hawkins, Rade: 152
Helton, Roy: 125,128
Hendrickson, E. Jay: 97
Herman, Tim: 76,101
Herndon, Wm. R. "Bill": 68,94

Hesser, David: 86,223
Hethcoat, Don: 126
Hetmanski, Thomas S.: 129,130
Hibben, Gil: Inside Cover,76,147
Hielscher, Guy: 156
Hinderer, Rick: 126,135
Hink III, Les: 124
Hitchmough, Howard: 118
Hirayama, Harumi: 72
Holder, D'Alton: 161
Holland, John: 128,140
Horton, Scot: 129,140
Howell, Robert L.: 65
Hudson, C. Robbin: 98
Hughes, Ed: 223
Humphreys, Joel: 123,223
Imel, Billy Mace: 77,98,100
Ishara, Nobuhiko: 224
James, Peter: 144
Jarvis, Paul M.: 96,103,143,155
Jernigan, Steve: 135,224
Johnson, C.E. "Gene": 139
Johnson, Steven R.: 105,109,119,224
Jones, Barry M. and Phillip G.: 82,224
Jones, Bob: 140
Jones, Charles Anthony: 224
Kalfayan, Edward N.: 95,164,225
Kaluza, Werner: 104,159,225
Kanda, Michio: 154
Kauffman, Dave: 225
Kaufman, Scott: 105
Keidel, Gene: 162
Kelso, Jim: 72
Kennedy, Kelly S.: 225
Kessler, Ralph A.: 94
Khalsa, Jot Singh: 160
Kharlamov, Yuri: 114
Kilby, Keith: 91,119,225
King, Kemp: 140
Knickmeyer, Hank: Cover,118,152
Knuth, Joseph E.: 67,113
Kojetin, W.: 143
Kopp, Todd M.: 224
Koutsopoulos, George: 156
Kranning, Terry L.: 85,225
Lake, Ron: 74,125
Lambert, Jarrell D.: 90
Lamprey, Mike: 146
Lampson, Frank G.: 132,143
Laplante, Brett: 127,139
Largin, Ken: 80
Lawrence, Alton: 88
Leach, Mike J.: 226
Leber, Heinz: 121,139
LeBlanc, John: 133,138
Leck, Dal: 122
Lee, Randy: 107,123,176,226
Leland, Steve: 103
Levine, Bob: 127
Levine, Norman: 226
Lewis, Mike: 64,66
Likarich, Steve: 120,147
Lile, Marilyn (Jimmy): 93,122
Lockachiev, Alexander: 146
Loerchner, Wolfgang: 74,100,101,163,167
Lohman, Fred: 66
Lonewolf, J.A.: 167
Long, Glenn A.: 226
Loveless, R.W.: 120
Lovestrand, Schuyler: 163
Ludwig, Richard O.: 226
Lui, Ronald M.: 137
Lyons, Randy: 102,123
Lyttle, Brian: 95,104,159
MacBain, Kenneth C.: 227
Malloy, Joe: 127
Manabe, Michael K.: 99,120,227
Mar, Al: 160
Maragni, Dan: 98
Maringer, Tom: 58,59,60,62
Marshall, Glenn: 138
Martrildonno, Paul: 227

Marzitelli, Peter: 144
Mason, Joel: 66
Mattis, James K.: 150,151
Maxwell, Don: 82
McBurnette, Harvey: 77,227
McClure, Michael: 118
McConnell, Jr., Loyd A.: 79,105,162,227
McDonald, Robert J.: 89,99,226
McFall, Ken: 137
McHenry, William James: 134
Mercer, Mike: 84,86
Minnick, Jim: 227
Mitchell, Wm. Dean: 65,89
Monteiro, Victor: 128
Moran, Jr., Wm. F.: 71
Moulton, Dusty: 85,94
Mount, Don: 147
Nealy, Bud: 228
Newcomb, Corbin: 228
Newton, Larry: 132,228
Nielson, Jeff V.: 85,228
Nordell, Ingemar: 117
Nowland, Rick: 85
Nunn, Gregory: 111
Ochs, Charles F.: 95,119,143,229
Ogg, Robert G.: 162
Okaysu, Kazou: 157
Onion, Kenneth J.: 119,229
Osborne, Warren: 75,158,229
Osterman, Daniel E.: 84,85
Overeynder, T.R.: 75
Padilla, Gary: 228
Parker, J.E.: 154
Pate, Lloyd D.: 119,143
Patrick, Bob: 108,228
Patrick, Chuck: 152
Patterson, Alan W.: 66,113,145
Pavack, Don: 122,138
Peagler, Russ: 108,229
Pease, W.D.: 84,136
Peterson, Chris: 228
Peterson, Eldon G.: 76,101,160
Phillips, Randy: 165
Polkowski, Al: 108
Poole, Marvin O.: 229
Porter, James E.: 68,167
Potier, Timothy F.: 94
Charley Pratt: Cover
Prince, Joe R.: 129,229
Quattlebaum, Craig: 136,230
Ragsdale, James D.: 136
Rahn, John: 98,102
Rapp, Steven J.: 143,231
Rardon, A.D.: 87,127,135,231
Ray, Alan W.: 89,123,230
Reeve, Chris: 80,83
Reverdy, Pierre: 153
Rexroat, Kirk: 161,230,231
Rho, Nestor Lorenzo: 115
Rhodes, James D.: 97
Richter, Scott: 97
Rietveld, Bertie: 101
Rigney, Willie: 96,230
Rijiswijk, Aad Van: 72,114,230
Rinkes, Siegfried: 160,231
Rippy, Robert: 80,83
Rizzi, Russell J.: 110,231
Robbins, Howard P.: 231
Robinson, Charles: 91
Rogers, Rodney: 92,121
Rua, Gary (Wolf): 111
Rubley, James A.: 91
Rupert, Robert: 101,113
Russell, Mick: 104,230
Sakakibara, Masaki: 131
Sakmar, Mike: 90,153
Salley, John D.: 232
Sanders, Michael M.: 109
Sandlin, Larry: 88
Sawby, Scott: 75,130
Sayen, Murad: 74,155
Schaller, Anthony B.: 232
Scheurer, Alfredo E. Faes: 147
Schirmer, Mike: 120

FIFTEENTH EDITION 283

directory

Schmidt, James A.: 74
Schoeman, Corrie: 117
Scholl, Tim: 122
Schroen, Karl: 145
Schwarzer, Stephen: 152
Scott, Al: 161
Selvidio, Ralph J.: 125,134,156,233
Serafen, Steven E.: 232
Sharrigan, Mudd: 112,154
Shinosky, Andy: 165,233
Shostle, Ben: 78
Sidelinger, Charles: Cover
Sigman, Corbet R.: 129
Simonella, Gianluigi: 116
Sinyard, Cleston S.: 232
Sisemore, Charles: 233
Siska, Jim: 233
Slee, Fred: 232
Slobodian, Scott: 66,152,157

Smith, J.D.: 105
Smith, John M.: 154
Smith, Raymond L.: 126
Snell, Jerry L.: 80,109,232
Solomon, Marvin: 96
Sornberger, Jim: 140,233
Spano, Dominick W.: 83,110
Spinale, Richard: 76
Stapel, Chuck: 81
Steigerwalt, Ken: 101
Stewart, Charles: 134
Stockdale, Walt: 162
Stokes, Ed: 82,90,233
Summers, Arthur L.: 161,233
Szilaski, Joseph: 102
Taylor, C. Gray: 74,159
Taylor, David: 132
Taylor, Shane: 120,235
Terzoula, Robert: 75
Thomas, Kim: 89

Thompson, Leon: 235
Thompson, Randy: 175
Thompson, Robert L.: 113,234
Thourot, Michael W.: 111
Toich, Nevio: 234
Toner, Roger: 234
Topliss, M.W.: 235
Treiber, Leon: 132,234
Trindle, Barry: 161
Turnbull, Ralph A.: 234
Turcotte, Larry: 102
Valachovic, Wayne: 235
Vallotton, Butch: 135
Viallon, Henri: 151,235
Vought, Jr., Frank: 121
Walker, John W.: 110,236
Walker, Michael L.: 70,124
Ward, Chuck: 107
Warden, Roy A.: 236
Warenski, Buster: 69,71
Watanabe, Wayne: 237

Watson, Billy: 113,237
Webb, Jr., Charley L.: 107,237
Weiland Jr., J. Reese: 67,92,164
Weiss, Charles L.: 97,153
Werner Jr., William A.: 154
Werth, George W.: 113
White, Gene E.: 237
Whitehead, James D.: 86
Williams, Jason L.: 131,144,237
Williams, Leonard: 99,108,144
Wilson, Mike: 110,236
Wimpff, Christian: 116,237
Winkler, Daniel: 112,163
Witsaman, Earl: 86,87
Wolf, Bill: 92,132,137
Wood, Webster: 103,138
Yeates, Joe A.: 90,236
Zaccagnino, Don: 95,109
Zakabi, Carl S.: 121,146
Zembko III, John: 237
Zemitis, Joe: 114,165,236
Zowada, Tim: 98,122,236

engravers

Allred, Scott: 140
Bates, Billy: 137,138,139,162
Beaver, Judy: 159
Blair, Jim: 158,161
Butler, Martin: 74,158,167
Collins, Michael: 140
Davidson, Jere: Cover,76,101,160
Dean, Bruce: 109,137
Eaton, Rick: 158,160
French, J.R.: 108,139

George, Tim: 159
Graf, Don: 139
Harrington, Fred A.: 125,159
Henderson, Don: 138
Holder, Pat: 161
Johns, Bill: 140
Kaluza, Werner: 159
Lyttle, Brian: 159
McCombs, Leo: 138
Mendenhall, Harry E.: 101,160

Morton, David A.: 161
Oberdorfer, Fritz: 104,160
Perdue, David L.: 160
Pilkington Jr., Scott: 160
Scott, Al: 161
Shaw, Bruce: 137,154
Shostle, Ben: 76
Sinclair, W.P.: 160
Skaggs, R.E.: Inside Cover,75, 77,96,98,100,125,159

Smith, Ron: 75
Swartley, Robert D.: 75
Theis, Terry: 139
Tomlin, Lisa: 84
Trindle, Barry: 161
Waldrop, Mark: 136
Warenski, Julie: 69,77,158
Wessinger, Rose: 94
Whitener, Nellie: 161

scrimshanders

Barrett, R.W.: 162
Beauchamp, Gaetan: 164
Brady, Sandra: 164,165
Burdette, Bob: 108,147

Fields, Rick B.: 162,163,164
Garbe, Sandra: 139
Hargraves, Sr., Charles: 162
Hergert, Bob: 162,165

Himmelheber, David R.: 164
Holland, Dennis K.: 140
Karst, Linda K.: Cover,139,162,165
Keidel, Gene: 162
McFall, Ken: 164

Mead, Faustina L.: 163,164
Morris, Darrel: 165
Williams, Gary: Inside Cover,76,146,163
Zemitis, Jolanta: 165

leatherworkers/sheathmakers

Cashen, Kevin R.: 170
Davidson, Hal: 149
Dawkins, Dudley: 168
Defeo, Robert A.: 170

Dunn, Melvin T.: 169
Fister, Jim: 169
Foley, Barney: 168,170
Frey, Jim: 111

Halligan, Ed: 168
Lee, Sonja: 169
Lile, Jimmy: 169
Lozier, Don: 170

Polkowski, Al: 169,170
Reeve, Chris: 168
Rowe, Kenny: 93,96,170
Schrap, Robert G.: 170
Shook, Karen: 112

etchers/carvers

Bourbeau: 166
Burrows, Stephen R.: 167
Casteel, Doug: 166

DeBraga, Jose C.: 167
DiMarzo, Richard: 167
Ellefson, Joel: 167

Greco, John: 166
Grussenmeyer, Paul: 166,167
Kelso, Jim D.: 166

Lonewolf, J.A.: 167
Olsen, Geoff: 166
Sornberger, Jim: 167

handle artisans

Davidson, Hal: 148,149

knife photo index

knives '90-'94

The Knife Photo Index includes only the last five editions of photos.

a

Abbott, William M.: *K'91*:91,182; *K'92*:91,176
Aida, Yoshihito: *K'90*:99,108; *K'91*:54; *K'92*:63; *K'93*:65,122; *K'94*:130,200
Alden Jr., Kenneth E.: *K'94*:200,201
Allen, Joe: *K'90*:51; *K'91*:182; *K'92*:176
Allen, Mike "Whiskers": *K'90*:188; *K'94*:149
Alverson, Tim: *K'92*:119
Ameri, Mauro: *K'92*:95,142; *K'93*:124,204
Ames, Mickey L.: *K'93*:204
Amor Jr., Miguel: *K'92*:67,89,176; *K'93*:104,205; *K'94*:123
Amoureux, A.W.: *K'90*:59
Andersen, Henrik Lefolii: *K'91*:82,182
Anderson, Charles B.: *K'91*:182; *K'92*:149
Anderson, Edwin: *K'91*:182; *K'93*:205
Anderson, Gary D.: *K'90*:188; *K'92*:176
Anderson, Michael D.: *K'92*:177
Anderson, Virgil W.: *K'90*:116
Andrews, Don: *K'91*:162
Ankrom, W.E.: *K'90*:188; *K'92*:83
Antonio, Jr., William J.: *K'90*:188
Appleton, Ray: *K'90*:79,80; *K'91*:58,61; *K'92*:81,176
Arnett, Todd J.: *K'93*:109,209; *K'94*:69
Arnold, Joe: *K'94*:200
Ashby, Douglas: *K'92*:176; *K'93*:204; *K'94*:68,200
Atkinson, Dick: *K'91*:102,129; *K'92*:79,176; *K'94*:97
Ayarragaray, Cristian: *K'94*:200
Ayarragaray, Cristian L. and Vuoto, Carlos A.: *K'90*:110; *K'91*:80,81; *K'92*:97

b

Babcock, Raymond G.: *K'94*:122
Bache-Wiig, Tom: *K'94*:129
Bailey, Joseph D.: *K'92*:177,178; *K'94*:67,137
Bailey, Kirby C.: *K'94*:97
Bagwell, Bill: *K'94*:100
Baldwin, Phillip: *K'90*:165; *K'92*:155; *K'93*:68; *K'94*:79,152
Ballew, Dale: *K'90*:188; *K'91*:73,182; *K'92*:122; *K'93*:112; *K'94*:84
Barber, Robert E.: *K'92*:68; *K'94*:120,201
Bardsley, Norman P.: *K'90*:62; *K'91*:162,164; *K'92*:68,138; *K'93*:204; *K'94*:107,117
Barefoot, Joe W.: *K'91*:144
Barnes, Aubrey G.: *K'94*:201
Barnes, Gary L.: *K'90*:46,49
Barnett, Van: *K'94*:76
Barr, A.T.: *K'93*:98; *K'94*:70,142
Barrett, Cecil Terry: *K'90*:123; *K'92*:90; *K'93*:74,78
Barron, David: *K'90*:53
Barry, James J.: *K'90*:126; *K'91*:126; *K'92*:108
Bartlow, John: *K'90*:90; *K'91*:148; *K'92*:177
Barton, Almon T.: *K'94*:97
Bartrug, Hugh E.: *K'90*:97,166; *K'91*:105,107,163,183; *K'92*:Cover,108,135,176; *K'93*:67; *K'94*:77,98,100,127,136,149
Baskett, Lee Gene: *K'90*:156; *K'91*:152,155,163; *K'92*:177; *K'93*:136,145,204
Batson, James: *K'90*:53,54,189; *K'92*:85,89,109,141,177; *K'93*:134; *K'94*:112,118
Batts, Keith: *K'91*:114; *K'92*:61; *K'93*:122; *K'94*:200
Bauchop, Robert: *K'93*:141
Beaver, D.(Butch): *K'91*:164; *K'93*:153,204
Beaver, Judy: *K'93*:153,204
Beaver, D. Butch and Judy: *K'94*:Cover,67,119
Becker, Franz: *K'90*:112,113; *K'91*:82,157; *K'92*:62,96
Beers, Ray: *K'90*:Cover; *K'91*:182; *K'92*:63,69; *K'93*:81
Behnke, William: *K'90*:133,188; *K'91*:120; *K'92*:178; *K'93*:204
Bell, Michael: *K'90*:168; *K'93*:102,104,111
Benjamin Jr., George: *K'90*:89,188; *K'91*:148; *K'92*:71,85,177; *K'93*:86
Bennett, Peter: *K'93*:59,204
Benson, Don: *K'90*:58,127,189; *K'94*:107
Besedick, Frank E.: *K'94*:85
Beverly II, Larry H.: *K'90*:99; *K'92*:56,177; *K'94*:91
Birt, Sid: *K'90*:56; *K'91*:99; *K'92*:153; *K'93*:83
Black, Robert: *K'92*:177
Black, T.J.: *K'91*:118,183; *K'93*:103
Black, Tom: *K'90*:189; *K'91*:156,159; *K'92*:152,178; *K'93*:76,83
Blakley II, William E.: *K'92*:178
Blanchard, Gary: *K'91*:158,159
Bloomer, Alan T.: *K'92*:59,177
Blum, Chuck: *K'92*:178; *K'94*:144
Blum, Kenneth: *K'91*:103,112,146
Blum, Michel: *K'92*:67,95,178; *K'93*:61,83
Boardman, Guy: *K'92*:98
Boden, Harry: *K'91*:79
Bogachov, Anatoly: *K'94*:130
Boguszewski, Phil: *K'90*:46; *K'91*:Cover,67,69; *K'92*:79,80; *K'93*:79; *K'94*:117
Bolton, Charles B.: *K'93*:204
Bonassi, Franco: *K'91*:80; *K'92*:95; *K'93*:61; *K'94*:201
Booco, Gordon: *K'92*:59,179; *K'93*:82,136,205; *K'94*:71,89
Borger, Wolf: *K'92*:96,117; *K'93*:60,80; *K'94*:74,129
Bose, Tony: *K'91*:71,183; *K'93*:75,205; *K'94*:87
Bowers, Jerry: *K'90*:101
Boyd, Francis: *K'94*:103,104
Boye, David: *K'90*:69,84,90,130,142-144,161,188; *K'91*:160,183; *K'92*:62,155; *K'94*:68
Brack, Douglas D.: *K'90*:105; *K'91*:94; *K'93*:103,134
Bradley, Dennis: *K'90*:189; *K'92*:89,106,114
Bradley, John: *K'91*:123; *K'93*:133; *K'94*:114
Brady, Sandra: *K'93*:125; *K'90*:134; *K'91*:55; *K'92*:61,87; *K'93*:125
Branton, Robert: *K'92*:57,140,178
Brayton, Jim: *K'90*:54,70,170; *K'91*:85
Brdlik, Dan E.: *K'90*:46; *K'94*:90
Breckenridge, Jack: *K'91*:94
Brend, Walter J.: *K'90*:152,153
Breshears, Clint: *K'90*:52; *K'93*:107
Brewer, Jack: *K'90*:189
Brightwell, Mark: *K'91*:59; *K'93*:73
Brignardello, E.D.: *K'91*:89
Britton, Tim: *K'90*:189; *K'91*:103,183; *K'92*:71,79,82,138; *K'93*:106
Broadwell, David: *K'91*:90,100; *K'92*:101,179; *K'93*:88,205; *K'94*:93,98,118,146
Brock, Kenneth L.: *K'94*:103
Brooker, Dennis: *K'90*:73
Brooks, Michael: *K'91*:125; *K'92*:65,179
Brooks, Steve R.: *K'90*:132; *K'92*:65,141; *K'93*:30,204
Broome, Thomas A.: *K'90*:189
Broughton, Don R.: *K'93*:204
Brown, Harold E.: *K'91*:150,183; *K'92*:178; *K'93*:98
Brown, Peter: *K'91*:183; *K'93*:98,204
Brown, Rob E.: *K'92*:179
Brown, Ted: *K'90*:130
Browne, Rick: *K'90*:60
Brumagen, Jerry: *K'91*:144
Brunckhorst, C. Lyle: *K'90*:70,189; *K'91*:134; *K'93*:145; *K'94*:82
Bryd, Don E.: *K'94*:201
Buckelew, John: *K'92*: 115
Buebendorf, Robert E.: *K'90*:127
Bullard, Bill: *K'94*:200
Burger, Pon: *K'90*:114
Burrows, Stephen R.: *K'94*:117
Busfield, John: *K'90*:83,124,127; *K'91*:64,77,183; *K'92*:74,78,179; *K'93*:66,79; *K'94*:Cover,92,145,146

c

Caffrey, Edward J.: *K'93*:97
Caldwell, Bill: *K'90*:155,165,195; *K'91*:65; *K'92*:181
Callahan, Errett: *K'90*:119; *K'91*:74,109,161,188; *K'92*:Cover,118,121,155; *K'93*:140,206; *K'94*:Inside Cover,115
Candrella, Joe: *K'90*:163,194; *K'91*:117,162; *K'92*:179
Cannady, Daniel L.: *K'92*:180
Cannon, Raymond W.: *K'90*:194; *K'91*:188; *K'93*:110; *K'94*:202
Canter, Ronald E.: *K'91*:105,189
Carey Jr., Charles W.: *K'93*:116,206; *K'94*:73,203
Cargill, Bob: *K'91*:67,188; *K'92*:50; *K'93*:63,68,73
Carlsson, Marc Bjorn: *K'91*:82,162; *K'92*:26,180; *K'93*:136,206
Carson, Harold J. "Kit": *K'90*:124; *K'91*:94,119,124,152,154; *K'92*:81,153,180; *K'93*:73,88; *K'94*:90,118,151
Carter, Fred: *K'91*:101,189; *K'93*:67,149; *K'94*:94,202
Casteel, Dianna: *K'91*:189; *K'92*:90,100,149,153; *K'93*:114; *K'94*:95
Casteel, Douglas: *K'90*:56,94,122,189; *K'91*:100,188; *K'92*:112,138,180; *K'93*:72,113
Cellum, Tom S.: *K'90*:194
Centofante, Frank and Tony: *K'90*:43,46,80,81; *K'91*:160,188; *K'92*:73,74,147; *K'93*:145,146,147
Chaffee, Jeff L.: *K'91*:189
Chamberlain, John B.: *K'92*:180; *K'93*:107
Chamberlin, John A.: *K'90*:195; *K'91*:188; *K'92*:103
Chamblin, Joel: *K'94*:86,137,203
Champion, Robert: *K'90*:101,195; *K'93*:138
Chapman, Mike: *K'90*:133,194,287; *K'91*:149
Chard, Gordon R.: *K'91*:66; *K'92*: 90,179; *K'93*:79
Chase, John E.: *K'90*:101; *K'94*:69
Cheatham, Bill: *K'91*:Cover,152; *K'92*:76,134,180; *K'93*:65
Chesterman, Michael J.: *K'93*:206
Clairbourne: *K'90*:195
Clark, Dave: *K'92*:117,181
Clark, Howard F.: *K'91*:189; *K'92*:127; *K'93*:206; *K'94*:112
Clark, Roger: *K'92*:180
Clay, J.D.: *K'90*:87,98; *K'91*:86,188; *K'92*:60
Clay, Wayne: *K'90*:75,158,162,185; *K'91*:64,158; *K'93*:72
Coats, Eldon: *K'92*:102,103,126; *K'93*:206
Cobb, Lowell D.: *K'93*:86,95,97,100
Cofer, Ron: *K'92*:181
Cohen, N.J.: *K'91*:188
Coil, Jimmie J.: *K'94*:202
Coleman, Keith E.: *K'92*:181
Collett, Jerry D.: *K'94*:87
Collins, Michael: *K'90*:87
Conley, Bob: *K'90*:83; *K'91*:63; *K'92*:54,75
Connolly, James: *K'93*:82
Connor, Michael: *K'90*:106; *K'92*:64
Coogan, Robert: *K'91*:149
Cook, James Ray: *K'90*:195; *K'92*:65,181; *K'93*:95
Cooper, George J.: *K'93*:41
Cooper, J.N.: *K'92*:19,20,21
Copemam, Neil: *K'91*:126
Corby, Harold: *K'90*:62; *K'91*:93; *K'93*:90,92,206
Cordova, Joseph G.: *K'91*:88,130; *K'93*:135; *K'94*:134
Corrado, Jim: *K'92*:127; *K'94*:83,202
Corwin, Don: *K'90*:76,77,78; *K'91*:59,71,77; *K'92*:50,51,52,54,78,180; *K'93*:147; *K'94*:98
Cosgrove, Charles G.: *K'91*:148
Cottrill, James I.: *K'90*:127,194
Courtice, Lyle: *K'90*:159
Courtois, Bryan: *K'91*:93; *K'92*:180
Cover, Raymond A.: *K'93*:154

directory

Cox, Colin J.: *K'90*:84,118; *K'91*:93,189; *K'92*:122,140,181
Cox, Sam: *K'90*:152,153; *K'92*:146; *K'93*:89
Craft III, John M.: *K'91*:106; *K'92*:104
Craft, Richard C.: *K'90*:196; *K'91*:125
Crain, Jack W.: *K'90*:90; *K'91*:120,189
Crawford, Pat: *K'90*:46,47,73,120,179; *K'91*:108,189; *K'93*:85,87; *K'94*:99,102
Crockford, Jack: *K'90*:69; *K'91*:66; *K'93*:78; *K'94*:75
Cronk, W.W.: *K'90*:118
Cross, John M.: *K'90*:101,194; *K'92*:76
Cross, Tim: *K'90*:93,95
Crosslen, Timothy J.: *K'93*:206
Crowder, Robert: *K'90*:127; *K'91*:91,159; *K'92*:119,138,181
Crowell, James L.: *K'90*:82; *K'91*:Cover; *K'92*:113; *K'94*:101
Culver, Steve: *K'93*:121,122
Cumming, R.J.: *K'91*:161,189

d

Dahl, Chris W.: *K'91*:101; *K'92*:112
Dailey, George E.: *K'90*:93,195
Dake, C.M.: *K'90*:196; *K'91*:118,146,195; *K'92*:77,190; *K'93*:77; *K'94*:99,103,202
D'Andrea, John: *K'92*:94,195
Damagala, John: *K'91*:107
Daniel, Travis E.: *K'91*:115,194
Daniels, Alex: *K'90*:70; *K'91*:145,155; *K'92*:88; *K'94*:112
Darby, Rick: *K'90*:195; *K'91*:115,194
Dauberman, Desmond P.: *K'94*:123
Davenport, Jack: *K'94*:90,203
Davenport, Steve: *K'91*:194
Davidson, Edmund: *K'90*:87,170; *K'91*:103,195; *K'92*:60,87,191; *K'93*:125,148; *K'94*:67
Davidson, Rob: *K'90*:132; *K'92*:190
Davis, Barry L.: *K'91*:194; *K'92*:84; *K'93*:70,207
Davis, Bill: *K'94*:203
Davis, Terry: *K'90*:76; *K'91*:72; *K'92*:52,76; *K'93*:74; *K'94*:87,88,93
Davis, Vernon M.: *K'90*:170,196; *K'91*:145,195; *K'92*:190
Davis, W.C.: *K'90*:100,132,197; *K'91*:86; *K'93*:86
Dawson, Dane and Barry: *K'90*:46,197
Dean, Harvey J.: *K'90*:99,195; *K'91*:96,115; *K'92*:107,191; *K'93*:92,99,207; *K'94*:96,114
Dearing, John: *K'91*:195
DeBraga, Jose C.: *K'90*:161; *K'91*:Cover,59,77; *K'92*:66,139; *K'93*:69,112; *K'94*:138
DeFeo, Robert A.: *K'90*:55,197; *K'93*:92,124; *K'94*:112
DeFreest, William G.: *K'94*:106
DeGraeve, Richard: *K'92*:191
DeLong, Dick: *K'90*:118; *K'91*:194
Dempsey, Gordon S.: *K'93*:111
Dennehy, Dan: *K'91*:90; *K'93*:36
Dennehy, John D.: *K'91*:85,86; *K'93*:122,124
Detloff, Larry: *K'90*:132
DeYong, Clarence: *K'90*:134; *K'91*:113,145,194; *K'92*:56,190
Dietzel, Bill: *K'92*:143
DiGangi, Joseph M.: *K'90*:130; *K'92*:137,190
Dill, Robert: *K'92*:154; *K'93*:153
Dill, Dave: *K'90*:197
Dilluvio, Frank J.: *K'90*:197; *K'91*:195; *K'94*:79,203
DiMarzo, Richard: *K'94*:116
Dion, Greg: *K'91*:130,195; *K'93*:207; *K'94*:127,203
Dion, Malcolm: *K'90*:197; *K'92*:58,86,191
Dippold, A.W.: *K'92*:140,191; *K'94*:134
Dominy, Chuck: *K'94*:203
Donovan, Patrick: *K'91*:126,194; *K'92*:190; *K'93*:73
Doussot, Laurent: *K'93*:63,76,207
Dowell, T.M.: *K'90*:52; *K'91*:141; *K'93*:35,80,99,123,207; *K'94*:66,132
Downie, James: *K'90*:196; *K'91*:134
Downing, Larry: *K'91*:92,195; *K'92*:74,136; *K'92*:74,136; *K'93*:54,88; *K'94*:95
Downing, Tom: *K'90*:57,97; *K'91*:55,122; *K'93*:145; *K'94*:120
Downs, James F.: *K'90*:196; *K'91*:120,195; *K'92*:91; *K'93*:54,144; *K'94*:127,202
Dozier, Robert Lee: *K'90*:100,197; *K'92*:56,101,191
Draper, Bart: *K'94*:76

Draper, Kent: *K'90*:52,57,61; *K'91*:98,131,146; *K'92*:69,91,190; *K'93*:87,95,149
Driskill, Beryl: *K'91*:194; *K'92*:153; *K'93*:106
Duff, Bill: *K'90*:94,196
Dufour, Arthur J.: *K'93*:94,207
Dungy, Lawrence: *K'94*:77
Dunkerley, Rick: *K'94*:203
Dunn, Melvin T.: *K'90*:196; *K'94*:69
Dunn, Steve: *K'92*:191; *K'93*:93; *K'94*:108,113
Duran, Jerry T.: *K'90*:197; *K'91*:96; *K'92*:191; *K'93*:87
Duvall, Larry E.: *K'91*:108,195; *K'92*:139

e

Easler, Paula: *K'91*:76; *K'92*:126; *K'93*:116
Easler Jr., Russell O.: *K'90*:64,162; *K'91*:200; *K'92*:63,147,194; *K'93*:31,144; *K'94*:149,204
Eaton, Al: *K'90*:124,204; *K'91*:76,107; *K'92*:122,127; *K'93*:113
Eaton, Rick: *K'90*:56; *K'91*:159,200; *K'92*:194; *K'93*:149
Edwards, Lynn: *K'93*:101,207; *K'94*:204
Edwards, Thomas W.: *K'90*:121,123,204
Eklund, Rolf: *K'90*:113; *K'91*:83; *K'92*:23
Eldrige, Allan: *K'92*:93; *K'93*:116
Elishewitz, Allen: *K'92*:194; *K'93*:104,138
Elkins, R. Van: *K'91*:201
Ellefson, Joel: *K'90*:Cover,167; *K'91*:201; *K'92*:194; *K'93*:65; *K'94*:120
Elliott, Marcus: *K'90*:205; *K'94*:204
Ellis, David: *K'90*:204; *K'91*:200; *K'92*:194; *K'93*:95,98
Embretsen, Kaj: *K'90*:112,113; *K'91*:83,148,200; *K'92*:24,27; *K'93*:58,70,88,111,207; *K'94*:204
Emerson, Ernest R.: *K'90*:47; *K'91*:68; *K'92*:83,148; *K'93*:78; *K'94*:137
Ence, Jim: *K'91*:100; *K'92*:194; *K'94*:Cover,118
Enders, Robert: *K'90*:78; *K'91*:64,76; *K'92*:Cover,85,195; *K'93*:159; *K'94*:104,146
England, Virgil: *K'90*:65,118,157; *K'93*:96,137; *K'94*:116
Engnath, Bob: *K'90*:64,141,204; *K'91*:129,130; *K'92*:67,119,135
Enos III, Thomas M.: *K'92*:134; *K'93*:109
Erickson, Curt: *K'90*:56
Erickson, Walter E.: *K'90*:62,95; *K'92*:113,194; *K'93*:86,109
Eriksen, James Thorlief: *K'90*:55,60,103,133,205; *K'91*:54,142,145,200; *K'92*:69,78,108; *K'93*:77,101; *K'94*:121,205
Eriksen, Jan: *K'92*:23; *K'93*:121,136
Esaki, Shusuke: *K'94*:71
Essegian, Richard: *K'90*:91,163; *K'91*:90
Etzler, John: *K'94*:107,123,205
Evans, Vincent K.: *K'90*:95; *K'91*:130,200; *K'92*:105; *K'93*:69
Ewing, John H.: *K'90*:204

f

Fannin, David A.: *K'91*:144; *K'93*:124
Farrell & Crawford: *K'90*:64
Fassio, Melvin G.: *K'90*:157; *K'91*:154; *K'92*:75
Fecas, Stephen J.: *K'92*:194; *K'93*:147
Ferguson, Jim: *K'90*:126,145-147; *K'91*:121,125,141,142,201; *K'92*:89,135,195; *K'93*:154; *K'94*:204
Fields, Rick B.: *K'93*:Inside Cover
Fiorini, Bill: *K'90*:97,168,205; *K'91*:110,116,140,201; *K'92*:134,195; *K'93*:102,135
Fischer, Clyde E.: *K'93*:39
Fisher, Jay: *K'92*:140; *K'93*:124,208; *K'94*:72
Fisher, Theo (Ted): *K'91*:75; *K'92*:126,195
Fisk, Jerry: *K'90*:59,204; *K'92*:92,195; *K'93*:Cover,77,133; *K'94*:130
Fister, Jim: *K'91*:53,117; *K'92*:86; *K'93*:208; *K'94*:73,205
Fitzgerald, Dennis M.: *K'90*:116
Flournoy, Joe: *K'91*:121,201; *K'92*:Cover,93; *K'93*:84,208; *K'94*:134,204
Fogg (See Kemal),Don: *K'90*:53; *K'91*:98; *K'92*:109,141,143; *K'93*:67,84,105,152,208; *K'94*:81,132,205
Fogle, James W.: 151
Forthofer, Pete: *K'90*:83; *K'92*:62,72,195
Foster, Al: *K'93*:208
Foust, Roger: *K'90*:168

Fowler, Ed A.: *K'90*:103; *K'91*:201; *K'92*:107; *K'93*:132; *K'94*:204
Fowler, Jerry: *K'90*:116; *K'93*:101,134
Fox, Paul: *K'90*:204; *K'91*:201; *K'92*:79; *K'93*:96
Fox, Wendell: *K'94*:102
Frank, Heinrich H.: *K'90*:80,81; *K'91*:63; *K'92*:72; *K'93*:67
Frankland, Andrew: *K'90*:114; *K'93*:208; *K'94*:97,130,134
Franklin, Mike: *K'90*:73,105; *K'93*:100
Frazier, Ron: *K'90*:56,93,135,164,205
Freeman, Art F.: *K'90*:205
Freeman, John: *K'90*:70
Friedly, Dennis E.: *K'91*:108,153,201; *K'92*:149,195; *K'93*:208; *K'94*:148,205
Frizzell, Ted: *K'91*:124
Fronefield, Mike: *K'90*:126,205; *K'91*:130
Fuegen, Larry: *K'90*:85; *K'91*:Cover; *K'92*:115,154,195; *K'93*:59,76; *K'94*:100,109,138
Fujisaka, Stanley: *K'91*:159; *K'92*:82,194; *K'94*:92,205
Fuller, Bruce A.: *K'94*:205
Fuller, Jack A.: *K'91*:77,85,97,122,143,200; *K'92*:88,107,142,155,179,195; *K'93*:123
Fuller, Jim: *K'90*:152,153
Fuller, John W.: *K'91*:200; *K'93*:208; *K'94*:96,149
Fulton, Mickey: *K'90*:99,117,204
Furukawa, Shiro: *K'90*:108; *K'91*:78

g

Gaeta, Roberto: *K'90*:110,210; *K'91*:80,204
Gamble, Frank: *K'90*:85,130; *K'91*:129; *K'92*:200
Gannaway, Woodson: *K'92*:144; *K'94*:129,133
Garbe, Bob: *K'94*:105,206
Gardner, Rob: *K'90*:166; *K'92*:69,105
Garner, Jr., William O.: *K'90*:60; *K'91*:204; *K'92*:201
Gartman, M.D.: *K'90*:76,210; *K'91*:60,71,204; *K'93*:209
Gaston, Bert: *K'92*:201
Gaston, Ron: *K'90*:60,119,129; *K'91*:91,103,154,204; *K'92*:148,153,200; *K'93*:Cover,31,147; *K'94*:109,206
Gaugler, Earl W.: *K'92*:136,200; *K'93*:93,209; *K'94*:137
Gault, Clay: *K'90*:76,87; *K'92*:54,75,78,200,201; *K'93*:91
Geisler, Gary R.: *K'91*:115; *K'92*:90
Genge, Roy E.: *K'91*:131
Genovese, Rick: *K'93*:66
George, Harry: *K'91*:204; *K'92*:57,200; *K'94*:71
Gerus, Gerry: *K'92*:98,200; *K'93*:59
Gibert, Pedro: *K'91*:80,204
Gilbreath, Randall: *K'90*:47,152,153; *K'91*:204; *K'93*:80
Giljevic, Branko: *K'91*:79,205; *K'92*:98,201; *K'93*:60; *K'94*:69,75
Gillenwater, E.E. "Dick": *K'91*:110
Glaser, Ken: *K'90*:106
Glover, Ron: *K'90*:78; *K'91*:157
Glucklick, Bob: *K'93*:114
Godby, Ronald E.: *K'93*:224
Goddard, Wayne: *K'90*:85; *K'91*:144,205; *K'94*:15,20
Godfrey, Steve: *K'91*:205; *K'93*:209
Goff, Darrel W.: *K'90*:210
Goers, Bruce: *K'92*:58; *K'93*:94,209
Goertz, Paul S.: *K'91*:204; *K'94*:15,16,140
Goldberg, David: *K'91*:76; *K'92*:120,121; *K'94*:121,206
Goldenberg, T.S.: *K'91*:102; *K'92*:89,200; *K'94*:70,113
Golding, Robin: *K'90*:210
Goltz, Warren L.: *K'92*:90,201
Gonzalez, Leonardo Williams: *K'91*:80,81; *K'92*:97; *K'94*:122
Goo, Tai: *K'93*:135; *K'94*:116
Gottage, Dante and/or Judy: *K'90*:47,60,210,211; *K'91*:70,89,128,205; *K'92*:74,108; *K'93*:80,151; *K'94*:98,102,206
Gottschalk, Gregory J.: *K'90*:47
Greco, John: *K'90*:210; *K'91*:91,125,205; *K'92*:67; *K'93*:65,87,97; *K'94*:109,206
Green, Bill: *K'91*:77,79; *K'94*:72
Green, Roger M.: *K'91*:117,205; *K'92*:87; *K'93*:92; *K'94*:82,112,206
Greenwood, R.W.: *K'91*:205
Grey, Piet: *K'93*:95,209
Griffin, Rendon: *K'92*:200; *K'94*:103

knife photo index

Grossman, Stanley: *K'90*:123,211; *K'92*:201
Grossman, Stewart: *K'92*:124; *K'93*:114; *K'94*:84,85,104
Grussenmeyer, Paul: *K'94*:115
Gurganus, Melvin H.: *K'90*:105,129,210; *K'91*:108,205; *K'92*:201; *K'93*:209; *K'94*:91
Guth, Kenneth: *K'91*:141; *K'92*:201; *K'93*:102
Gwozdz, Bob: *K'90*:55

h

Hagen, Phillip L. "Doc": *K'90*:95; *K'91*:66,210; *K'92*:70,84; *K'93*:75,79,211; *K'94*:85,98
Hagwood, Kellie: *K'94*:151
Hajovsky, Robert J.: *K'91*:114
Halligan, Ed & Shawn: *K'91*:107,124,210; *K'92*:63,101,207; *K'93*:88,105,111; *K'94*:78,114
Hammond, Jim: *K'91*:88; *K'93*:86; *K'94*:109
Hamre, Johan: *K'90*:89,112
Hancock, Ronald E.: *K'90*:211; *K'92*:53
Hancock, Tim:: *K'93*:104; *K'94*:113,206
Hand, Bill: *K'92*:92; *K'94*:67
Hangas, Vic: *K'91*:24-29
Hara, Koji: *K'93*:61
Hargis, Frank L.: *K'90*:154
Harkins, J.A.: *K'90*:89; *K'92*:76,104,113; *K'93*:71; *K'94*:89
Harless, Walt: *K'91*:101,123,211; *K'92*:63,116,146,148; *K'93*:147,150
Harley, Larry W.: *K'90*:126,164; *K'91*:109,146; *K'92*:71,102,136; *K'93*:54
Harmon, Jay: *K'90*:57,213; *K'91*:99,210; *K'92*:79,101,102; *K'93*:82,107; *K'94*:137,207
Harper, D.J.: *K'90*:210
Harrington, Mike: *K'90*:211
Harris, Jay: *K'90*:47,75; *K'91*:69; *K'92*:77,108,207; *K'93*:150; *K'94*:89
Harris, Ralph Dewey: *K'90*:47,123; *K'91*:Cover,210; *K'92*:74
Harsey, William H.: *K'91*:142
Hartman, Arlan (Lanny): *K'90*:127,211; *K'91*:114,150; *K'93*:73; *K'94*:207
Hartsfield, Phill: *K'90*:148,149; *K'93*:64,103,210; *K'94*:120,207
Harvey, Max: *K'90*:94; *K'91*:79,90,100,210; *K'92*:88; *K'93*:96
Hawk, Jack L.: *K'91*:87; *K'94*:Cover
Hawk, Joe: *K'90*:66,212; *K'91*:164; *K'92*:87
Hawk, Joey K.: *K'90*:212; *K'91*:210
Hawk, Ken: *K'92*:115
Hawkins, Rade: *K'91*:107; *K'93*:106,211
Hayes, Dolores: *K'91*:55; *K'92*:139,156,207; *K'93*:63
Hayes, Wally: *K'94*:119
Haynes, Chap: *K'90*:129; *K'91*:55,128,210
Heasman, H.G.: *K'94*:85
Hedrick, Don: *K'91*:102
Hehn, Richard Karl: *K'91*:82,83,211; *K'94*:118
Heitler, Henry: *K'94*:109
Helgason, E.O.: *K'93*:79
Helton, Roy: *K'90*:99,211; *K'91*:62,94; *K'93*:74; *K'94*:91,114,206
Hembrook, Ron: *K'90*:134
Hendricks, Samuel J.: *K'94*:67,98,207 *K'92*:109,207; *K'93*:107,210
Hendrickson, E. Jay: *K'90*:56; *K'91*:97,161; *K'94*:73
Henriksen, Hans J.: *K'91*:82,83,151; *K'92*:24,26,27; *K'93*:121,136; *K'94*:130,139
Henry, D.E.: *K'91*:30,31
Henry & Son, Peter: *K'91*:161; *K'94*:129
Hensley, Wayne: *K'92*:Cover,126
Herman, Tim: *K'90*:74,213; *K'91*:70; *K'92*:73,80; *K'93*:148,210; *K'94*:95,146
Herndon, Wm. R.: *K'90*:61,65,118,124,213; *K'91*:75,89,131,154; *K'92*:136,206; *K'93*:96,136; *K'94*:137
Herron, George: *K'90*:96,134,213
Hethcoat, Don: *K'90*:87,212; *K'92*:206; *K'94*:71,207
Hetmanski, Thomas S.: *K'93*:115,117,210
Hibben, Daryl: *K'90*:211; *K'91*:110; *K'94*:148
Hibben, Gil: *K'90*:53,100,212; *K'91*:11,155; *K'92*:81,122,166,206; *K'94*:85,116,117
Hibben, Westley G.: *K'90*:212; *K'92*:122,206,207
Hicks, Vernon W.: *K'91*:211; *K'92*:51
Hill, Howard E.: *K'90*:212; *K'91*:149; *K'93*:210
Hill, Steven E.: *K'90*:117,213; *K'91*:211; *K'92*:61,115; *K'94*:90,135

Hinderer, Rick: *K'91*:210; *K'92*:207; *K'93*:Cover,132,211; *K'94*:95,100
Hink, III, Les: *K'91*:62; *K'92*:75,78; *K'93*:75,210; *K'94*:74
Hinson & Son, R.: *K'91*:68
Hintz, Gerald: *K'93*:153
Hirayama, Harumi: *K'90*:108; *K'91*:78; *K'92*:99; *K'93*:91; *K'94*:94,128
Hitchmough, Howard: *K'91*:82,211; *K'92*:94,207; *K'93*:60,71,90,211; *K'94*:77
Hodge, J.B.: *K'90*:213; *K'91*:211
Hodgson, Richard J.: *K'94*:93
Hoel, Steve: *K'90*:74,83,97; *K'91*:63; *K'92*:51,73,151,170,206; *K'93*:66,67,146; *K'94*:145
Hoffman, Kevin L.: *K'90*:91,106,116; *K'91*:211; *K'92*:183,116,152,206; *K'93*:82; *K'94*:91
Hoffmann, Uwe H.: *K'92*:68,102,119; *K'93*:61,101; *K'94*:124,156
Holder, D'Alton: *K'90*:213; *K'91*:113; *K'92*:137; *K'93*:99
Holland, Dale J.: *K'91*:211
Holmes, Robert: *K'90*:211
Homer, Glen: *K'91*:150; *K'94*:124
Hopper, Jim: *K'91*:74
Horn, Jess: *K'90*:77,80,163; *K'91*:65; *K'92*:77,151,167; *K'94*:95
Hornby, Glen: *K'91*:211; *K'92*:127,207; *K'94*:87,110
Horton, Scot: *K'92*:207; *K'93*:77; *K'94*:103
Howard, Durvyn M.: *K'90*:75,213
Howard, Seth: *K'93*:57
Howell, Robert L.: *K'94*:103
Howser, John C.: *K'90*:212; *K'92*:54,103
Hoy, Fred W.: *K'93*:42
Hrisoulas, Jim: *K'92*:165
Hubbard, Arthur J.: *K'90*:165
Hudson, C. Robbin: *K'91*:99; *K'92*:134,143; *K'93*:65,70,84
Hudson, Robert: *K'92*:207; *K'93*:210
Hudson, Tommy: *K'91*:52,77,118,150,206; *K'93*:74,210,211; *K'94*:80,207
Hueske, Chubby: *K'92*:5
Huey, Steve: *K'90*:98,212; *K'91*:91,103; *K'92*:206
Hughes, Ed: *K'90*:105,130; *K'91*:124; *K'92*:59; *K'93*:86; *K'94*:107,207
Hull, Michael J.: *K'94*:68,106
Hulsey, Hoyt: *K'92*:106; *K'93*:78
Hume, Don: *K'90*:53; *K'91*:163; *K'92*:64; *K'93*:84
Humenick, Roy: *K'90*:128; *K'92*:69
Humphreys, Joel: *K'94*:96
Husiak, Myron: *K'91*:79,210

i

Iiams, Richard D.: *K'92*:212; *K'93*:211
Imboden II, Howard L.: *K'91*:164,216
Imel, Billy Mace: *K'90*:55; *K'91*:98,217; *K'92*:105; *K'93*:72,115
Ishihara, Hank: *K'93*:61,211

j

Jackson, Jim: *K'90*:220; *K'91*:104; *K'92*:212; *K'93*:141,212
Jackson, Mark: *K'91*:85
James, Bobby: *K'93*:53
Jean, Gerry: *K'91*:84,148,216; *K'93*:80
Jernigan, Steve: *K'90*:48,220; *K'91*:67,216; *K'92*:80,117,212; *K'93*:Cover,212; *K'94*:92,209
Jobin, Jacques: *K'90*:220; *K'92*:212; *K'94*:129,138
Johns, Rob: *K'91*:107
Johnson, Brad: *K'90*:91,221; *K'92*:115,212
Johnson, C.E. "Gene": *K'91*:65,216; *K'93*:212
Johnson, Durrell Carmon: *K'90*:220; *K'91*:121,122,216; *K'92*:85,93,213; *K'93*:212; *K'94*:209
Johnson, Gorden W.: *K'94*:113
Johnson, Kenneth R.: *K'93*:141; *K'94*:209
Johnson, Richard: *K'90*:134
Johnson, R.B.: *K'90*:Cover,156; *K'91*:155,216; *K'92*:148
Johnson, Ruffin: *K'91*:150
Johnson, Ryan M.: *K'93*:133,141,213
Johnson, Steven R.: *K'90*:69,99; *K'91*:54,85,89,104,114,159; *K'92*:58,153,213; *K'93*:64,89,212; *K'94*:110,133,209
Johnson, Skip: *K'90*:91

Johnson, W.C. "Bill": *K'90*:95,220; *K'91*:216; *K'93*:212; *K'94*:84,208
Johnson, W.M.: *K'90*:161
Jones, Barry M.: *K'94*:124,208
Jones, Bob: *K'90*:77,155,169; *K'91*:72; *K'92*:54; *K'94*:88,99
Jones, Charles Anthony: *K'91*:82,83; *K'92*:51
Jones, Curtis J.: *K'90*:64,94,124,220; *K'91*:92,109,125,216; *K'92*:138,212; *K'93*:212; *K'94*:81,209
Jones, John: *K'90*:134,220; *K'91*:86,96
Jones, Paul: *K'94*:115
Jones, Phillip G.: *K'94*:124,208
Jones, Thomas L.: *K'91*:102

k

Kagawa, Koichi: *K'90*:108; *K'92*:99
Kalazu, Werner: *K'94*:130
Kalfayan, Edward N.: *K'91*:216; *K'92*:212,213; *K'93*:90,105,110,145,213; *K'94*:66,209
Kamada, Yoshikazu: *K'93*:62
Kato, Kioshi: *K'90*:64; *K'93*:58,135
Katz, Brian: *K'90*:165
Kauffman, Dave: *K'92*:53,142; *K'94*:Cover,208
Kay, J. Wallace: *K'94*:85
Keeslar, Joseph F.: *K'91*:120; *K'92*:89,92,213; *K'93*:81,112,213
Keeslar, Steven C.: *K'94*:80,208
Keeton, William L.: *K'90*:55,59; *K'91*:66,90,126; *K'92*:213
Kehiayan, Alfredo: *K'90*:111; *K'91*:80,81,146,148; *K'93*:61
Kelley, Gary: *K'90*:106; *K'91*:74; *K'92*:119; *K'93*:140
Kelly, Lance: *K'91*:101,217
Kelso, Jim: *K'90*:63,64,94; *K'93*:141; *K'94*:126
Kemal: *K'92*:70
Kennedy, Kelly S.: *K'93*:29,213
Kessler, Ralph A.: *K'93*:77; *K'94*:108
Keyes, Dan: *K'90*:120
Khalsa, Jot Singh: *K'90*:95; *K'92*:152,170; *K'93*:83,148
Kiefer, Tony: *K'93*:213
Kilby, Keith: *K'90*:102,120,221; *K'91*:97,121,217; *K'92*:92,152; *K'93*:151,213; *K'94*:101,122,147,208
Kimsey, Kevin: *K'94*:124
King, Bill: *K'90*:156; *K'91*:62
King, Fred: *K'91*:217; *K'92*:142,213; *K'94*:209
King, Kemp: *K'91*:112
King, Randall: *K'93*:90
King Jr., Harvey G.: *K'94*:77
Kious, Joe: *K'90*:163; *K'92*:73,213; *K'93*:116
Kneubuhler, W.K.: *K'94*:25
Knickmeyer, Hank: *K'92*:69; *K'93*:99,134; *K'94*:80,136
Knight, Jim: *K'94*:82
Knipschield, Terry: *K'90*:99; *K'92*:60,102; *K'94*:132
Knipstein, R.C. "Joe": *K'91*:217; *K'92*:60
Knuth, Joseph E.: *K'93*:110,134; *K'94*:81,208
Kohler, J. Mark: *K'94*:99
Kohls: *K'90*:134
Kojetin, W.: *K'94*:128
Kolitz, Robert: *K'90*:134
Kopp, Todd M.: *K'94*:208
Kormanik, Chris: *K'92*:213; *K'93*:213
Koutsopoulos, George: *K'90*:221; *K'92*:212; *K'94*:107
Kovar, Eugene: *K'90*:221
Kozlow, Kelly: *K'93*:107
Kranning, Terry L.: *K'90*:122; *K'91*:77,217; *K'94*:84,209
Krapp, Denny: *K'92*:68,69,147
Krause, Roy W.: *K'90*:69
Kravitt, Chris: *K'92*:114,116; *K'93*:120,121
Kreibich, Donald L.: *K'90*:221
Kremzner, Raymond L.: *K'90*:102,103,116,221; *K'91*:54,129,141,142; *K'93*:106
Kressler, D.F.: *K'90*:112,113; *K'92*:62
Kretsinger, Jr., Phillip W.: *K'90*:221; *K'91*:118,120,217; *K'93*:98
Kubaiko, Hank: *K'90*:72,123; *K'92*:57,213
Kubasek, John A.: *K'91*:97,120,217; *K'92*:106

FIFTEENTH EDITION **287**

directory

l

La Grange, Fanie: *K'93*:58,68,215
Lainson, Tony: *K'90*:70,226; *K'92*:59,118,219
Lake, Ron: *K'90*:81; *K'91*:63,104; *K'93*:120; *K'94*:146,147
Lambert, Jarrell D.: *K'93*:214
Lambert, Ronald S.: *K'94*:121
Lampson, Frank G.: *K'90*:77; *K'91*:222; *K'92*:78; *K'94*:77
Lance, Bill: *K'92*:118
Landrum, Leonard "Len": *K'93*:215; *K'94*:73,210
Lang, Kurt: *K'90*:117,119,165; *K'91*:110,142; *K'92*:92,118,134
Lange, Donald G.: *K'92*:86; *K'93*:215; *K'94*:211
Langley, Gene H.: *K'91*:107; *K'93*:74
Langley, Mick: *K'90*:65; *K'91*:98
Langston, Bennie E.:; *K'93*:78,215; *K'94*:210
Lankton, Scott: *K'90*:Inside Cover,32-38; *K'92*:104,219; *K'94*:81,136
Lapen, Charles: *K'90*:226; *K'93*:111
Laplante, Brett: *K'90*:226; *K'94*:74,105
Largin, Ken: *K'90*:120; *K'92*:113; *K'93*:54
Lary, Ed: *K'91*:153; *K'93*:146
Laurent, Kermit: *K'94*:66,72
Lawrence, Alton: *K'94*:76
Lay, L.J.: *K'90*:226
Lazo, Robert T. *K'92*:116,137
Leach, Mike J.: *K'90*:51; *K'91*:222; *K'93*:87; *K'94*:211
Leavitt, Jr., Earl F.: *K'90*:71,119,226; *K'91*:109,117; *K'92*:115,137,142
LeBatard, Paul M.: *K'92*:218; *K'94*:72,211
Leber, Heinz: *K'90*:227; *K'92*:58,70
LeBlanc, John: *K'92*:218; *K'93*:77,214; *K'94*:138,210
Leck, Dal: *K'94*:111
Ledford, Bracy R.: *K'90*:62,226; *K'91*:111,222; *K'92*:105,154,219
Lee, Randy: *K'92*:218; *K'93*:92; *K'94*:73,210
Lee, Tommy: *K'91*:92,99; *K'92*:114; *K'93*:69; *K'94*:151,211
LeFaucheux, J.V.: *K'92*:96
LeFont, Mark: *K'91*:75,106
Lemaire, Denis: *K'94*:103
Leone, Nick: *K'90*:227
LePore, Michael J.: *K'90*:85,161,226; *K'91*:158,223; *K'92*:218; *K'93*:72,97
Letcher, Billy: *K'93*:214
Levengood, Bill: *K'90*:53,227; *K'91*:116,122; *K'92*:59,62,116,147,149,219; *K'93*:82,93; *K'94*:90,211
Leverett, Ken: *K'94*:121
Levine, Norman: *K'90*:66,196; *K'91*:223; *K'92*:70,136,139,154,219; *K'93*:214; *K'94*:69,135,210
Lewis, K.J.:; *K'93*:130,131
Lewis, Mike: *K'91*:106,107; *K'92*:113; *K'93*:111,213; *K'94*:80
Lewis, Tom R.: *K'92*:60,218; *K'94*:76,210
Liebenbert, Andre: *K'93*:109
Likarich, Steve: *K'90*:56,62; *K'91*:129,149,222; *K'92*:71,106,139; *K'93*:96,137,214; *K'94*:116,125,133,211
Lile, Marilyn (Jimmy): *K'90*:68,88,152,153,164; *K'91*:92,118,134,150; *K'92*:5; *K'93*:38,90,125; *K'94*:70
Lister, Jr., Weldon E.: *K'90*:78; *K'91*:62; 151,218
Little, Jimmy L.: *K'90*:117; *K'91*:108
Livingston, Robert C.: *K'90*:228; *K'91*:144,223; *K'92*:218; *K'93*:215
Lockett, Sterling: *K'90*:57,228
Loerchner, Wolfgang: *K'90*:Cover; *K'91*:100,128,156; *K'92*:Inside Cover, 104,218; *K'93*:83,151,214; *K'94*:119
Lonewolf, J. Aguirre: *K'93*:153
Longworth, Dave: *K'90*:48
Lorey: *K'92*:218
Love, Ed: *K'93*:99,101,137,214
Loveless, R.W.: *K'90*:57,59,68,98,103; *K'92*:100; *K'93*:100,125; *K'94*:73,120
Lovestrand, Schuyler: *K'90*:58,103
Lovett, Mike: *K'90*:101,125,168,227; *K'91*:113,223; *K'92*:103,108,124,140
Lozito, Joseph F.: *K'90*:124; *K'91*:73,75
Lubrich, Mark: *K'94*:210
Luchak, Bob: *K'93*:94,101,137,214; *K'94*:72
Luck, Gregory: *K'90*:89; *K'91*:85; *K'92*:116,218; *K'93*:122
Luckett, Bill: *K'90*:170; *K'91*:93,123
Lui, Ronald M.: *K'92*:68; *K'94*:92
Lum, Robert W.: *K'90*:106; *K'91*:102,114,116; *K'93*:69,82
Lundstrom, Jan-Ake: *K'90*:39,40,113
Lunn, Larry A.: *K'94*:80
Lutes, Robert: *K'90*:159; *K'91*:109,116,150; *K'92*:219; *K'93*:115; *K'94*:149
Lyle III, Ernest L.: *K'91*:223; *K'92*:88; *K'94*:211
Lyttle, Brian: *K'90*:54,71,165,167,227; *K'91*:99,121,135; *K'92*:105,151,218; *K'93*:149

m

MacBain, Kenneth C.: *K'92*:118; *K'93*:85,152
Madsen, Jack: *K'90*:228
Maisey, Alan: *K'90*:6-17,109
Malloy, Joe: *K'91*:124,223; *K'92*:221; *K'94*:124m138m213
Manabe, Michael K.: *K'94*:127,212,213
Marak, George: *K'93*:97
Mariacher, Robert R.: *K'94*:212
Maringer, Tom: *K'90*:55,93,104,105,179; *K'91*:106,108,179; *K'92*:113,141; *K'93*:140,216; *K'94*:108
Marks, Chris: *K'90*:228; *K'92*:93; *K'93*:92,104
Marktl, Franz: *K'90*:52
Marshall, Glenn: *K'90*:230; *K'91*:66,90,134
Martin, Bruce E.: *K'90*:230; *K'91*:96; *K'92*:93; *K'92*:221
Martin, Randall J.: *K'90*:230; *K'93*:89,90,138,217
Martrildonno, Paul: *K'91*:59,69,76,111,131; *K'92*:67,119,156; *K'93*:80,89,116,137; *K'94*:212
Marzitelli, Peter: *K'91*:123; *K'92*:61; *K'93*:123
Mason, Arne: *K'93*:120
Maxfield, Lynn: *K'90*:159,230; *K'91*:223; *K'92*:221; *K'93*:94,217; *K'94*:212
Maxwell, Don: *K'93*:100,217; *K'94*:91
May, James E.: *K'91*:131,222; *K'94*:114
Maynard, William N.: 212
Mayo, Jr., Tom: *K'92*:63
Mayville, Oscar L.: *K'91*:119
McBain, Ken: *K'90*:95
McBurnette, Harvey: *K'91*:65,69; *K'92*:74,221; *K'93*:216; *K'94*:93
McClung, Kevin: *K'93*:139
McConnell, Jr., Loyd A.: *K'91*:92; *K'92*:89,146,148,156,220; *K'93*:71,88
McCrackin, Kevin: *K'93*:95
McCrackin and Son, V.J.: *K'90*:168; *K'91*:123; *K'92*:64,84,86,221; *K'93*:216; *K'94*:83,114,212
McDearmont, Dave: *K'90*:230
McDonald, Robert J.: *K'92*:71,91; *K'93*:216; *K'94*:79,150,151
McFall, Ken: *K'90*:69; *K'91*:145; *K'93*:148
McFarlin, Eric E.: *K'90*:230
McGovern, Jim: *K'92*:221
McGowan, Frank E.: *K'90*:231; *K'91*:223; *K'92*:154,221; *K'94*:213
McHenry, William James: *K'92*:77,79,142; *K'93*:106,108,149,216; *K'94*:101,213
McKissack II, Tommy: *K'90*:78,231; *K'91*:68,71; *K'92*:53,75,220; *K'93*:74; *K'94*:75,79
McNabb, Tommy: *K'92*:115,194
McWilliams, Sean: *K'90*:231; *K'91*:89; *K'93*:87; *K'94*:213
Mecchi, Richard: *K'90*:158,231; *K'91*:55; *K'92*:137
Meier, Daryl: *K'91*:Inside Cover; *K'92*:145
Mendenhall, Harry E.: *K'90*:97; *K'91*:94; *K'92*:150,220; *K'93*:96
Mercer, Mike: *K'90*:122; *K'91*:77,222; *K'92*:121,122,124; *K'93*:113; *K'94*:82
Merchant, Ted: *K'90*:102; *K'92*:221
Merz III, Robert L.: *K'90*:231; *K'91*:67,105,118; *K'92*:78,220; *K'93*:68; *K'94*:74,99,213
Messer, David T.: *K'92*:124
Mettler, J. Banjo: *K'90*:227; *K'91*:60; *K'92*:51
Meyers, Paul: *K'92*:219
Middleton, Ken: *K'94*:111
Millard, Fred G.: *K'94*:124
Miller, Bob: *K'90*:229; *K'91*:144; *K'92*:220; *K'93*:132,141; *K'94*:119
Miller, Clark: *K'93*:82
Miller, Hanford J.: *K'91*:98; *K'92*:64; *K'94*:141
Miller, James K.: *K'93*:217
Miller, James P.: *K'91*:95,223; *K'92*:65,106,219
Miller, Jim H.:217
Miller, Larry: *K'91*:134,222; *K'92*:220
Miller, R.D.: *K'90*:51,229; *K'92*:220; *K'94*:74
Miller, Robert: *K'93*:65,107
Miller, Ronald T.: *K'90*:229; *K'92*:82; *K'93*:94
Miller, Terry: *K'90*:229
Mills, Andy: *K'91*:64,69
Mills, Louis G.: *K'90*:63,94
Minnick, Jim: *K'91*:161; *K'92*:104; *K'93*:216; *K'94*:Cover
Mitchell, Dean: *K'94*:110,135,212
Mitchell, Max, Dean and Ben: *K'90*:229; *K'93*:84
Mitchell, R.W.: *K'90*:229
Moeller, Harald: *K'90*:65; *K'91*:108
Monteiro, Victory: *K'94*:156
Montjoy, Claude: *K'90*:Cover,59,105,229; *K'91*:62,129,154,222; *K'92*:220; *K'93*:85,106,110,150,217
Moore, James B.: *K'91*:72
Moran, Jr., Wm. F.: *K'90*:57,65,90,102,134,180; *K'91*:6,97,128,137; *K'92*:62,70,92; *K'93*:99,121,217; *K'94*:71,114
Morgan, Gerald: *K'90*
Morgan, Jeff: *K'92*:219
Morris, C.H.: *K'90*:48,228; *K'93*:216
Morseth, Harry: *K'93*:38
Mosci, Carlos Roberto: *K'91*:81
Mosci, M.: *K'90*:111
Moulton, Dusty: *K'94*:108,120,213
Mount, Don: *K'92*:138; *K'94*:117
Mullin, Steve: *K'90*:236; *K'91*:98,141; *K'93*:70
Murphy, Dave: *K'92*:43
Myers, Paul: *K'90*:76; *K'91*:152,153; *K'92*:124

n

Narikawa, Junko: *K'90*:63
Nealy, Bud: *K'90*:70,129,236; *K'91*:230; *K'92*:58,68,107,150,155; *K'93*:Cover,63
Neeley, Vaughn: *K'93*:160,161
Neely, Greg: *K'92*:92; *K'94*:141
Newcomb, Corbin: *K'91*:124
Nielson, Jeff V.: *K'93*:218; *K'94*:214
Nishiuchi, Melvin S.: *K'91*:87,230; *K'92*:229; *K'94*:107,136,214
Nolen, R.D. and George: *K'90*:160; *K'91*:160,162,164,230; *K'92*:153,156,229; *K'93*:151,154,218; *K'94*:214
Nolfi, Tim: *K'91*:144,230; *K'92*:64,136,139,228; *K'93*:85,135; *K'94*:121
Nordell, Ingemar: *K'92*:24,26; *K'93*:59,98
Norris, Mike: *K'91*:230
North, David and Prater, Mike: *K'90*:161,236; *K'91*:230; *K'92*:228
Norton, Dennis: *K'91*:125,131
Norton, Don: *K'90*:159,236; *K'91*:230; *K'92*:146,228; *K'94*:70,215
Nowland, Rick: *K'92*:228; *K'93*:218
Nunn, Gregory: *K'91*:230

o

Ochs, Charles F.: *K'90*:54,78,236; *K'91*:96,122; *K'92*:65,109,228; *K'93*:76,85; *K'94*:70,112
O'Leary, Gordon: *K'90*:236
Oliver, Anthony Craig: *K'91*:230
Olson, Wayne C.: *K'94*:70
Osborne, Warren: *K'91*:65,231; *K'92*:73,170,228; *K'93*:67; *K'94*:86
Osterman, Daniel E.: *K'93*:68,113,114,117,218; *K'94*:82,83,94
Outlaw, Anthony L.: *K'91*:231
Overeynder, T.R.: *K'91*:117; *K'92*:74,228
Owens, Dan: *K'91*:64,113; *K'93*:138,218; *K'94*:76
Oyster, Lowell R.: *K'90*:78,84; *K'91*:72,109; *K'92*:51,119; *K'93*:75; *K'94*:87,211

p

Padilla, Gary: *K'93*:219
Page, Larry: *K'93*:219
Page, Reginald: *K'90*:73; *K'91*:110
Papp, Robert: *K'90*:58; *K'91*:91
Pardue, Melvin M.: *K'90*:48; *K'91*:63,70; *K'94*:215
Parks, John: *K'92*:141; *K'93*:219
Parsons, Michael R.: *K'90*:52,89; *K'91*:111,143,158,159,231; *K'92*:150; *K'93*:149
Pate, Lloyd D.: *K'94*:215
Patrick, Chuck: *K'90*:93,237; *K'91*:60,109,231; *K'92*:85,136,229; *K'93*:63,133
Patterson, Alan W.: *K'93*:71,122; *K'94*:78
Patterson, Karl: *K'92*:57
Pavack, Don: *K'91*:231; *K'93*:219; *K'94*:215

knife photo index

Peagler, Russ: *K'91*:104; *K'92*:68
Pease, W.D.: *K'90*:75,82; *K'92*:73; *K'93*:62,72; *K'94*:95
Peele, Bryan: *K'93*:121
Pendleton, Lloyd: *K'90*:117,237; *K'91*:114; *K'94*:68,214
Pendray, Alfred H.: *K'90*:66; *K'92*:70; *K'93*:105,219; *K'94*:126
Petersen, Dan L.: *K'90*:61,120,237; *K'92*:90,92,229
Peterson, Chris: *K'90*:237; *K'94*:123,214
Peterson, Eldon G.: *K'90*:75,83,164; *K'91*:152,157,231; *K'92*:72,152; *K'93*:66,151; *K'94*:94,214
Peterson, Jack V.: *K'92*:121
Phillips, Randy: *K'91*:104,231; *K'92*:80,82; *K'94*:150
Pienaar, Conrad:; *K'93*:98,219; *K'94*:121
Pienaar, David: *K'90*:114
Pitt, David F.: *K'91*:88
Pittman, Leon: *K'90*:163; *K'91*:157
Poag, James: *K'91*:156
Pogreba, Larry: *K'90*:48,166; *K'94*:74
Polk, Clifton: *K'90*:83; *K'93*:75
Polkowski, Al: *K'90*:100,237; *K'91*:231; *K'92*:82,103; *K'93*:86,100; *K'94*:107
Poole, Marvin: *K'94*:69
Popp, Sr., Steve: *K'92*:88,126
Porter, James E.: *K'90*:93,102; *K'91*:92,95,113; *K'92*:65,103,107; *K'93*:110,125,153; *K'94*:118,214
Potier, Timothy F.: *K'92*:101,229; *K'93*:93,121; *K'94*:49,51,215
Poythress, John: *K'92*:229
Prater, Mike: *K'94*:215
Pratt, Charles: *K'92*:106,229; *K'93*:123; *K'94*:66,83,215
Price, Joel Hiram: *K'90*:237
Price, Steve: *K'90*:103; *K'91*:90; *K'92*:91; *K'93*:219
Provenzano, Joseph D.: *K'90*:237
Pugh, Jim: *K'90*:91; *K'91*:163; *K'92*:82
Pullen, Martin: *K'93*:228; *K'94*:75,95,125,134
Pulliam, Morris C.: *K'90*:58; *K'91*:96,231; *K'93*:93,121
Pursley, Aaron: *K'91*:116,158; *K'92*:77,118,229; *K'93*:219; *K'94*:94

q

Quarton, Barr: *K'92*:104,238
Quattlebaum, Craig: *K'92*:236; *K'93*:220

r

Rados, Jerry F.: *K'90*:165; *K'91*:69,105,143,154,238; *K'92*:238; *K'93*:132; *K'94*:89,216
Ragsdale, James D..; *K'93*:221; *K'94*:96,216
Rahn, John: *K'94*:110,111,134,216
Rainville, Richard: *K'90*:242
Rambo, J.T.: *K'91*:150
Randall Made Knives: *K'94*:148
Randall, W.D. and (Bo) Gary T.: *K'90*:120; *K'91*:52,112; *K'92*:87,147,156,238
Rapp, Steven J.: *K'90*:52; *K'91*:93,100,238; *K'92*:238; *K'93*:221; *K'94*:113
Rappazzo, Richard: *K'90*:71,84; *K'91*:238; *K'92*:84; *K'93*:71; *K'94*:100
Rardon, A.D.: *K'91*:72,238; *K'92*:55,77; *K'93*:69,116,220; *K'94*:87
Ray, Alan W.: *K'91*:71,240; *K'92*:55,59,107; *K'94*:81,216
Rece, Charles V.: *K'93*:144
Reddiex, Bill: *K'90*:109,242; *K'91*:79,241; *K'92*:98,127,238; *K'93*:61,221; *K'94*:216
Ree, David: *K'91*:240
Reeve, Chris: *K'91*:42,45,60,238; *K'92*:81,82,238; *K'93*:87,162
Reinhardt, Hank: *K'92*:168
Remington, David W.: *K'94*:216
Reverdy, Pierre: *K'92*:95,135
Rhea, David: *K'90*:242
Rho, Nester Lorenzo: *K'94*:123,216
Richard, Ron: *K'91*:67,238; *K'93*:109
Richardson, Jr., Percy: *K'93*:220
Richter, John C.: *K'93*:135
Ricke, Dave: *K'90*:70,134; *K'91*:238; *K'92*:56,237; *K'94*:216

Rietveld, Bertie: *K'93*:220; *K'94*:216
Rigney, Willie: *K'91*:101,238; *K'92*:146,236; *K'93*:83,220; *K'94*:216
Rippy, Robert and Bonnie (The Rippys): *K'91*:91,115; *K'92*:59,100,102,237; *K'93*:123,138,220; *K'94*:216
Rizzi, Russell J.: *K'92*:58,236; *K'93*:221
Robbins, Howard P.: *K'90*:242; *K'92*:236; *K'93*:221
Roberts, Chuck: *K'93*:138
Roe, Jr., Fred D.: *K'91*:130,240
Rogers, Rodney: *K'90*:243; *K'91*:119,155; *K'92*:63,101,109,148,236; *K'94*:148,151
Rollert, Steve: *K'92*:237
Roper, Jr., Mark H.: *K'90*:164
Ross, Tim: *K'90*:243
Rotella, Richard A.: *K'90*:243
Rowe, Kenny: *K'91*:84; *K'93*:122,125
Rua, Gary (Wolf) *K'94*:79
Ruana, Rudolph H.: *K'91*:24-29; *K'93*:25,26,27
Rubley, James A.: *K'94*:137,216
Ruple, William H.: *K'92*:55,237; *K'93*:221
Russ, Joe: *K'93*:221
Russell, A.G.: *K'92*:166; *K'94*:19
Russell, Tom: *K'90*:243
Rychetnik, Joe: *K'94*:24

s

Saindon, R. Bill: *K'94*:97,150,218
Sakmar, Mike: *K'93*:222; *K'94*:219
Salisbury, Joel: *K'93*:134
Salley, John D.: *K'90*:60,82; *K'91*:60,239; *K'93*:144; *K'94*:219
Sampson, Lynn: *K'90*:75; *K'91*:62; *K'92*:83; *K'94*:90
Sandberg, Dale: *K'93*:51
Sanders, A.A.: *K'90*:245; *K'91*:240
Sanders, Bill: *K'90*:244; *K'92*:60,150,236
Sanders, Michael M.: *K'90*:244; *K'91*:129; *K'92*:239; *K'93*:103; *K'94*:218
Sasser, Jim: *K'90*:100
Sawby, Scott: *K'90*:77,84,157; *K'91*:66; *K'93*:66,76,145; *K'94*:92,145,133
Sayen, Murad: *K'93*:105,137,152,213; *K'94*:119
Scarrow, Will: *K'90*:245; *K'91*:240
Schepers, George B.: *K'93*:133
Schirmer, Mike: *K'93*:222; *K'94*:108,120
Schmidt, James A.: *K'91*:241; *K'93*:70; *K'94*:118
Schmidt, Rick: *K'94*:69,113
Schneider, Herman J.: *K'90*:167; *K'92*:152,239; *K'93*:33,34
Schoeman, Corrie: *K'93*:76
Schoenfeld, Matthew A.: *K'90*:61; *K'91*:131,241
Schonhals, G.G.: *K'92*:97
Schwarzer, Stephen: *K'90*:85,120,165,167; *K'91*:134,239; *K'92*:84,85,135,143,239; *K'93*:134; *K'94*:136
Scordia, Paolo: *K'93*:59; *K'94*:111,219
Scullin, Ken: *K'90*:134
Selent, Chuck: *K'93*:116
Self, Ernie: *K'94*:75,98
Sellevold, Harald: *K'90*:89,112; *K'91*:87; *K'92*:22,25,27; *K'94*:129,138
Selvidio, Ralph J.: *K'93*:108; *K'94*:89,219
Semich, Peter: *K'91*:119
Sentz, Mark C.: *K'91*:97,239; *K'92*:115
Serven, Jim: *K'90*:48,55,73,82; *K'91*:60,241; *K'92*:80; *K'94*:102
Shadley, Eugene W.: *K'92*:52,64; *K'94*:88,94
Shaffer, Russell: *K'91*:110
Sheehan, Paul P.: *K'90*:126,244; *K'91*:55,126,240; *K'93*:117
Shinosky, Andy: *K'94*:93
Shoemaker, Scott: *K'91*:110; *K'92*:Cover; *K'93*:110; *K'94*:119
Shoger, Mark O.: *K'91*:95,239; *K'92*:85,239; *K'94*:219
Shostle, Ben: *K'92*:236
Sidelinger, Robert: *K'92*:53; *K'93*:222; *K'94*:219
Sigman, Corbet R.: *K'90*:69,126; *K'91*:49,62,241; *K'92*:237,239; *K'93*:37,69,222; *K'94*:92
Simmonds, Kurt Barnes: *K'90*:122; *K'93*:73,223
Simonich, Rob: *K'90*:71,95,243
Simons, Bill: *K'90*:243; *K'92*:55,83,117; *K'93*:77
Sims, Bob: *K'90*:78,245; *K'91*:64; *K'92*:52,54,55
Sinyard, Cleston S.: *K'92*:87,237; *K'93*:109,223; *K'94*:219
Siska, Jim: *K'90*:106,165,178; *K'91*:89,240; *K'92*:88,236; *K'93*:120,132,222
Slee, Fred: *K'91*:65,241; *K'94*:125

Sloan, Shane: *K'90*:122,244; *K'92*:76,91
Slobodian, Scott: *K'92*:66,67,134,239; *K'93*:103,104,109,223; *K'94*:81,83,113,126
Small, Ed: *K'90*:242; *K'91*:240
Small, Jim: *K'90*:49
Smit, Glenn: *K'90*:133,245; *K'92*:120; *K'93*:97
Smith, D. Noel: *K'94*:116
Smith, Gregory H.: *K'91*:119
Smith, J.B.: *K'92*:93
Smith, J.D.: *K'92*:105,239; *K'93*:92,105,133,223; *K'94*:79,91,101,121,126,127,141
Smith, John M.: *K'91*:121
Smith, John T.: *K'90*:126
Smith, Newman L.: *K'90*:245
Smith, W.F. (Red): *K'91*:241
Snell, Jerry L.: *K'90*:65,242; *K'91*:239; *K'92*:101,239; *K'93*:223; *K'94*:96,125,218
Sodergren, Orjan: *K'90*:113
Solomon, Marvin: *K'93*:222
Solydwood: *K'91*:106
Sonntag, Carl: *K'94*:20
Soppera, Arthur: *K'92*:94,96; *K'93*:60,64,223; *K'94*:102
Sornberger, Jim: *K'90*:82,134; *K'91*:128,158,163; *K'92*:75,236
Spencer, John E.: *K'90*:133
Spinale, Richard: *K'91*:157; *K'92*:73; *K'93*:67,223
Stafford, Michael: *K'94*:115
Stafford, Richard: *K'90*:103,243; *K'91*:114,239; *K'92*:237,238; *K'93*:140
Stahl, John: *K'90*:124
Stalter, Harry L.: *K'91*:76,94; *K'92*:125,239; *K'93*:117
Stapel, Chuck: *K'90*:51,134; *K'91*:89,113,134,239; *K'93*:108,222; *K'94*:218
Stegall, Keith: *K'90*:59,119; *K'91*:103; *K'92*:238
Steigerwalt, Ken: *K'91*:70,241; *K'93*:70,71
Steinau, Jurgen: *K'92*:96,138; *K'93*:222
Steinberg, Al: *K'90*:245; *K'92*:238
Stewart, Charles (Chuck): *K'90*:Cover,49,74,83,167; *K'91*:65,239; *K'92*:73,80; *K'93*:72,75,80; *K'94*:89,94,102
Stewart, Patrick C.: *K'92*:120,238
Stokes, Ed: *K'94*:67,77,218
Strong, Scott: *K'90*:58; *K'91*:100,116,240; *K'92*:140,237; *K'93*:85; *K'94*:72,111,218
Stuart, V. Pat: *K'92*:114
Stumpff, Jr., George: *K'90*:244; *K'91*:241
Suedmeier, Harlan: *K'90*:245; *K'91*:94; *K'93*:223
Sullivent, Loyd: *K'92*:121,237; *K'93*:54
Sunderland, Richard: *K'91*:161; *K'92*:236
Swain, Rod: *K'93*:89,138
Syslo, Chuck: *K'90*:51,66,245
Szilaski, Joseph: *K'94*:218

t

Taglienti, Antonio J.: *K'92*:93
Takahashi, Masao: *K'90*:108; *K'94*:66,68
Tamboli, Michael: *K'91*:77,246; *K'92*:127; *K'93*:73,115; *K'94*:86,220
Tanaka, Darryl: *K'90*:168
Tasaki, Seichi: *K'90*:107; *K'91*:78
Tay, Larry: *K'92*:99
Taylor, C. Gray: *K'90*:250; *K'91*:68,72; *K'92*:83; *K'94*:Cover,93
Taylor, David: *K'93*:225; *K'94*:86,221
Taylor, Shane: *K'94*:83,221
Tedder, Mickey: *K'90*:62,250
Terrill, Stephen: *K'90*:90
Terzuola, Robert: *K'91*:68; *K'92*:83,140,247; *K'94*:90,138
Thayer, Danny: *K'91*:97; *K'92*:247; *K'94*:109,221
Theis, Terry: *K'90*:66
Thomas, Daniel: *K'90*:103
Thompson, Kenneth: *K'93*:225; *K'94*:221
Thompson, Leon : *K'90*:250; *K'91*:68; *K'92*:76,246; *K'93*:225; *K'94*:87,220
Thorn, Anders: *K'90*:113
Thourot, Michael W.: *K'91*:246; *K'92*:57,61; *K'93*:225; *K'94*:68,76,221
Toich, Nevio: *K'94*:220
Tollefson, Barry A.: *K'92*:247
Tokar, Daniel: *K'93*:125,137
Tomes, Anthony S.: *K'91*:246
Tomes, P.J.: *K'90*:48,54,157; *K'91*:152,155,246; *K'92*:109; *K'93*:Cover,146; *K'94*:148
Tompkins, Dan: *K'90*:250
Toner, Roger: *K'92*:156; *K'93*:85,152,223,224
Towell, Dwight L.: *K'90*:61,83,87,158,166; *K'91*:64,246; *K'94*:75

FIFTEENTH EDITION 289

directory

Townsend, J.W.: *K'91*:94; *K'92*:88,139,246; *K'93*:108; *K'94*:117,119,136
Treiber, Leon: *K'94*:74,97
Treml, Glenn: *K'92*:246; *K'93*:94,224
Trindle, Barry: *K'90*:Cover,74; *K'91*:66,246; *K'92*:72,246; *K'93*:224
Trujillo, Thomas A.: *K'90*:60,250
Tuoteet, Lauri: *K'91*:11
Turcotte, Larry: *K'94*:220
Turecek, Jim: *K'90*:61; *K'91*:246; *K'92*:106,247; *K'93*:64; *K'94*:101,105
Turnbull, Ralph A.: *K'90*:74,82,129,167,250; *K'91*:58,88,104,144,246; *K'92*:54,126,246,247; *K'93*:224; *K'94*:96,105
Turunen, Pentti: *K'92*:25
Tyc, William J.: *K'93*:87
Tyer, Jerry L.: *K'94*:124,221

u

Ueda, Masaharu: *K'94*:104
Uekama, Nobuyuki: *K'93*:89
Ulrich, Micheal H.: *K'91*:86
Urstadt, E.W.: *K'90*:251; *K'91*:247

v

Valachovic, Wayne: *K'90*:82,154,251; *K'91*:70,247; *K'92*:84,247; *K'93*:225; *K'94*:100
Vallotton, Butch: *K'93*:224; *K'94*:134
Vallotton, Shawn: *K'93*:224
Valois, A. Daniel: *K'90*:73; *K'92*:137,246
Van Eldik, Frans: *K'90*:112; *K'91*:83,247; *K'93*:58,99; *K'94*:128,220
Van Elkins, R.: *K'92*:93
Van Wyk, Danie: *K'90*:114
Veatch, Richard: *K'93*:117
Veit, Michael: *K'90*:251; *K'91*:68,101,156; *K'92*:75,246; *K'94*:93,133,221
Vensild, Henrik: *K'92*:25
Venter, Ben: *K'90*:114
Viallon, Henri: *K'90*:112,113; *K'91*:83,247; *K'92*:94,135,149; *K'93*:60,225; *K'94*:101,129,220
Vistnes, Tor: *K'94*:133,220
Von Boeckman, R.: *K'90*:251; *K'91*:247; *K'92*:107,246
Voss, Ben: *K'90*:60,106,250; *K'91*:246; *K'92*:90,247; *K'93*:76,100,225; *K'94*:106
Vought, Jr., Frank: *K'90*:58,69,251; *K'91*:92,102,105,115,247; *K'92*:57,102,246; *K'93*:65,225; *K'94*:108
Vunk, Robert: *K'90*:93,251; *K'91*:85,130,247; *K'92*:67,105,148,149; *K'93*:103,132

w

Waddle, Thomas: *K'91*:63,250
Wagaman, John K.: *K'91*:123,145; *K'92*:253; *K'93*:227
Wahlster, Mark David: *K'90*:64,254
Waldrop, Mark: *K'92*:70
Walker, George A.: *K'91*:153
Walker, Michael L.: *K'90*:45; *K'91*:67,157; *K'92*:143,151
Wallace, Roger L.: *K'92*:253
Walters, Brian K.: *K'91*:250
Ward, Chuck: *K'94*:223
Wardell, Michael Ronald: *K'94*:122
Warden, Roy A.: *K'91*:250; *K'92*:253; *K'93*:133; *K'94*:222
Ware, J.D.: *K'90*:254
Warenski, Buster: *K'90*:80,95,97,162; *K'91*:70,99,250; *K'92*:104,152,252; *K'93*:105,151,226; *K'94*:80,76,92,147
Warren, Al: *K'91*:119,250
Watanabe, Wayne: *K'94*:126,222
Watson, Billy: *K'94*:73
Watson, Daniel and Billy: *K'92*:141; *K'93*:226
Watson, Tom: *K'91*:251; *K'92*:144; *K'93*:100,146
Wattelet, Michael A.: *K'93*:110
Watts, Wally: *K'90*:77,132,254; *K'91*:71,250; *K'92*:76; *K'93*:74,78; *K'94*:88
Webb, Jim: *K'94*:123,222
Weddle, Jr., Del: *K'90*:254
Wegner, Tim: *K'93*:123
Wehner, Rudy: *K'90*:53; *K'94*:223
Weiland, Jr., J. Reese: *K'91*:251; *K'92*:253; *K'93*:147,227; *K'94*:222
Weiler, Donald E.: *K'91*:250; *K'93*:84; *K'94*:110,127
Weinand, Gerome W.: *K'91*:251; *K'92*:64,65,253; *K'93*:105,227; *K'94*:70,146
Weiss, Charles L.: *K'90*:52,158; *K'91*:101,117,251; *K'92*:87,252; *K'93*:145
Wescott, Cody: *K'91*:251; *K'93*:150,227; *K'94*:77,99
West, Pat: *K'92*:253
Westberg, Larry: *K'93*:227
Whipple, Wesley A.: *K'92*:71
White, Gene E.: *K'94*:68,84,223
White, Robert J.: *K'90*:73,86; *K'91*:60
White, Jr., Robert J. "Butch": *K'90*:82,122; *K'91*:59; *K'92*:253
Whitehead, James D.: *K'91*:75,250; *K'92*:121; *K'93*:113,115
Whitley, Weldon G.: *K'90*:170; *K'92*:252
Wilder, Barry: *K'91*:87
Willey, W.G.: *K'91*:160
Williams, David: *K'93*:102; *K'94*:127,133
Williams, Sherman A.: *K'90*:54; *K'91*:251; *K'92*:60,103,252; *K'93*:124
Williamson, Tony: *K'90*:119
Willson III, George H.: *K'93*:226
Wilson, Jon J.: *K'94*:84
Wingo, Perry: *K'92*:253
Winkler, Daniel: *K'90*:71,132,254; *K'91*:59,86,95,153,251; *K'92*:84,252; *K'93*:140,141,154,226; *K'94*:Cover,100,112
Winn, Travis A.: *K'92*:71
Witsaman, Earl: *K'90*:123; *K'91*:75; *K'92*:122,124; *K'93*:113,117,128,226; *K'94*:83,84,222
Wolf, Bill: *K'92*:58,61,91,252; *K'93*:72,79
Wood, Alan: *K'94*:130,222
Wood, Owen Dale: *K'90*:114,118; *K'93*:59,69,137,226
Wood, Webster: *K'90*:59,90; *K'92*:252
Wood, William W.: *K'90*:66; *K'91*:157; *K'93*:106,150; *K'94*:85
Woodworth, Al: *K'90*:105,254
Workman Jr., Hubert L.: *K'94*:115
Wright, Adam: *K'94*:67
Wright, Kevin: *K'91*:76,251; *K'93*:143
Wright, Timothy: *K'90*:165; *K'92*:141
Wyatt, Alan: *K'91*:72

y

Yeates, Joe A.: *K'92*:124; *K'93*:93,115; *K'94*:110,223
Young, Bud: *K'90*:50; *K'91*:105
Young, Cliff: *K'90*:133
Young, Errol: *K'93*:114
Young, J.A.: *K'93*:75
Yurco, Mike: *K'91*:93,126,254; *K'92*:255; *K'94*:104,223

z

Zaccagnino, Don: *K'90*:49,66,123; *K'91*:119,149,254; *K'93*:94; *K'94*:71,223
Zakabi, Carl S.: *K'93*:89,136; *K'94*:222
Zemetis, Joe: *K'90*:254; *K'91*:79,254; *K'92*:98; *K'93*:93,227; *K'94*:223
Zembko III, John: *K'90*:71; *K'91*:254; *K'92*:255
Zima, Michael F.: *K'91*:254; *K'92*:55,255; *K'93*:104,227; *K'94*:86,96
Zinsmeister, Paul D.: *K'92*:255; *K'93*:79,227
Zowada, Tim: *K'92*:112,134,136,255; *K'93*:88,132; *K'94*:97
Zscherny, Michael: *K'91*:63

engravers

Alfano, Sam: *K'93*:Cover; *K'94*:120
Bates, Billy: *K'90*:164; *K'91*:102; *K'92*:50,153; *K'93*:73; *K'94*:149
Becker, Franz: *K'91*:157
Blanchard, Gary: *K'90*:75,82; *K'91*:158,159,163; *K'92*:74
Boster, A.D.: *K'91*:Cover,99; *K'92*:152; *K'93*:147,150,151; *K'94*:96,147
Butler, Martin: *K'91*:100,128,156; *K'92*:74,104,151; *K'93*:151
Carter, Fred: *K'91*:90,101; *K'93*:67,149
Churchill, Winston: *K'90*:80,163; *K'91*:63; *K'94*:145,147
Collins, David: *K'92*:170
Collins, Michael: *K'91*:112
Cover, Jr., Raymond A.: *K'93*:154; *K'94*:146
Davidson, Jere: *K'93*:148
Draper, Kent: *K'93*:149
Dubben, Michael: *K'94*:95
Dubber: *K'93*:88
Duggette: *K'90*:164
Eaton, Rick: *K'93*:149; *K'94*:145
Eldridge, Allan: *K'91*:125
Ence, Jim: *K'93*:150
Erhardt, Arnold: *K'93*:153
Flannery, Jeff: *K'91*:70,121; *K'92*:153; *K'93*:73; *K'94*:118
Fleischer, M.: *K'90*:113
Fogle, James W.: *K'93*:151
Foster, Norvell: *K'93*:73
Fracassi, Firmo: *K'93*:146
French, J.R.: *K'94*:95
Foster, Norvell: *K'91*:59
Galleazzi, A.: *K'92*:151
George, Tim and Christy: *K'92*:73; *K'93*:66,67,72
Glimm, Jerome C.: 152
Goodwin, Dan: *K'92*:72
Gournet, Geoffroy R.: *K'92*:150; *K'93*:63; *K'94*:95
Harrington, Fred A.: *K'90*:83; *K'92*:51,74,150; *K'93*:75,106,151; *K'94*:102,146
Henderson, Fred D.: *K'91*:63
Hendricks, Frank E.: *K'92*:75
Herman, Tim: *K'91*:70; *K'93*:148; *K'94*:95
Holder, Pat: *K'93*:73
Horvath, Kurt: *K'93*:66
Hudson, Tommy: *K'92*:52,150; *K'93*:74
Hurst, Ken: *K'92*:74
Jacobs, Yuri: *K'93*:90
Kelly, Lance: *K'91*:101
Kelso, Jim: *K'93*:67
Lageose, Tony: *K'90*:75,83,164; *K'92*:72; *K'93*:151
LaPage, Tony: *K'90*:97; *K'91*:116
Lee, Ray: *K'91*:103
Leschorn, Tony: *K'91*:112; *K'93*:148
Limings, Jr., Harry: *K'90*:163; *K'91*:92; *K'92*:74,126; *K'93*:145
Lindsay, Steve: *K'90*:80,83,127,162,163; *K'91*:64; *K'93*:148; *K'94*:93,146,147
Lister, Weldon: *K'91*:62,71; *K'92*:75,151; *K'93*:88
Lyttle, Brian: *K'92*:151; *K'93*:149; *K'94*:145
Lytton, Simon M.: *K'90*:83; *K'91*:159; *K'92*:63,73,94,98; *K'93*:85,150
Marek, George: *K'91*:89
McDonald, Ralph: *K'90*:162
McHenry, William James: *K'93*:149
McKenzie, Lynton: *K'92*:51,151,153; *K'93*:66,83
Mendenhall, Harry E.: *K'91*:69; *K'92*:79,108,150; *K'93*:150
Meyer, Chris: *K'91*:157
Morton, David A.: *K'94*:77,94,102
Nixon, Jim: *K'94*:149
Old Dominion Engravers: *K'90*:56,83,93,163; *K'91*:70,72,157,158,159; *K'92*:153; *K'93*:72,92
Parsons, Michael R.: *K'91*:158,159; *K'92*:150; *K'93*:149
Pederson, Rex: *K'93*:73
Pedini, Marcello: *K'93*:73
Perdue, David: *K'94*:130
Pilkington, Jr., Scott: *K'90*:82,109,162; *K'91*:62,64,158; *K'92*:73; *K'93*:72; *K'94*:146
Poag,James: *K'91*:156

knife photo index

Pursley, Aaron: *K'91*:116,158; *K'94*:94
Rabeno, Martin: *K'90*:80,163
Raftis, Andrew: *K'92*:152
Robyn, Jon: *K'90*:81; *K'91*:65,104; *K'92*:170; *K'93*:72
Rudolph, Gil: *K'92*:75
Rundell, Joe: *K'93*:105; *K'94*:102
Sanchez, Lewis B.: *K'90*:75,164; *K'91*:62,116; *K'92*:62; *K'93*:114; *K'94*:107
Scharnagel: *K'91*:82
Schmidt, R.: *K'93*:58
Scott, Alvin: *K'91*:64
Selent, Chuck: *K'92*:75
Shaw, Bruce: *K'90*:57,66,164; *K'91*:157,159; *K'92*:68; *K'93*:73,148,154
Sherwood, George: *K'91*:66,91; *K'92*:118; *K'93*:82
Shostle, Ben: *K'90*:62,163,164; *K'91*:91,163; *K'92*:150,153; *K'93*:Cover,72,89,149; *K'94*:109,144,147

Sinclair, W.P.: *K'93*:150
Skaggs, R.E.: *K'90*:52; *K'91*:64,101,156; *K'92*:152; *K'93*:66,148; *K'94*:Cover
Smith, Ron: *K'90*:80,81,163; *K'91*:117; *K'92*:170; *K'94*:144
Sornberger, Jim: *K'91*:158
Spinale, Richard: *K'91*:157; *K'93*:67; *K'94*:144
Stewart, James: *K'92*:71; *K'93*:125
Stoltz, Stanley: *K'90*:112; *K'92*:150
Takeuchi, Shigetoshi: *K'90*:108; *K'93*:58
Taylor, David: *K'94*:147
Theis, Terry: *K'90*:159,164; *K'91*:64,69; *K'93*:150
Tomlin, Lisa: *K'90*:157; *K'92*:73; *K'93*:72; *K'94*:95
Trindle, Barry: *K'91*:94
Tuscano, Tony: *K'90*:97
Usher, Jerry: *K'90*:118
Valade, Robert: *K'91*:131
Vancura: *K'92*:70
Vinnecombe: *K'91*:79

Vos, Eduard: *K'91*:83; *K'93*:58
Vos of Liege: *K'90*:112
Waldrop, Mark: *K'90*:84; *K'93*:72
Walker, Patricia: *K'90*:79,80; *K'91*:58,61,67,157; *K'92*:81,151
Warenski, Buster: *K'91*:70,99; *K'94*:144
Warenski, Julie: *K'90*:56,80,162; *K'91*:89,101,159; *K'92*:152; *K'93*:67,83,105,151; *K'94*:147
Warren, Kenneth: *K'91*:156,159; *K'92*:152; *K'93*:76
Wescott, Cody: *K'93*:150
Whitehead, James D.: *K'93*:113,115
Wilkerson, Dan: *K'93*:100; *K'94*:146
Williams, Gary: *K'93*:113
Winkler, Armin: *K'93*:58
Wood, Mel: *K'90*:83,129; *K'91*:99; *K'93*:151

scrimshanders

Bailey, Mary W.: *K'91*:155; *K'92*:148,149; *K'93*:146
Barrett, R.W.: *K'94*:149
Bellet, Connie: *K'93*:145
Bonshire, Benita: *K'90*:62,163; *K'94*:149
Bowles, Rick: *K'90*:81,157,164; *K'91*:112,152,155; *K'92*:147; *K'93*:146; *K'94*:148
Brady, Sandra: *K'90*:80,157; *K'91*:154; *K'93*:145,146,147; *K'94*:148,150,151
Burdette, Bob: *K'93*:92,147
Byrne, Mary Gregg: *K'90*:158
Clark, Chris: *K'91*:116; *K'92*:147,149
Collins, Michael: *K'91*:112
Cosimini, Rene Danielle: *K'94*:150,151
Cover, Jr., Raymond A.: *K'90*:159; *K'91*:152
Cox, Andy: *K'92*:146
Davidson, Mary E.: *K'90*:158
Dolbare, Elizabeth: *K'94*:151
Eisbacher, Johann: *K'90*:113
Engnath, Bob: *K'90*:158; *K'91*:104,152,153,154; *K'92*:149; *K'94*:148,149

Erickson, Linda: *K'92*:68
Fields, Rick B.: *K'90*:156, *K'91*:78,154,155; *K'92*:74,146,147,148; *K'93*:145,146,147; *K'94*:148
Fisk, Dale: *K'90*:158,159; *K'94*:150
Fracassi, Firmo: *K'93*:146
Gigi: *K'90*:122,159
Hargraves, Sr., Charles: *K'90*:159; *K'91*:155; *K'92*:148; *K'93*:144; *K'94*:148,151
Harless, Star: *K'92*:146,148; *K'93*:147
Hawkins, Stan: *K'90*:158
Hergert, Bob: *K'93*:114,144
Holland, Dennis K.: *K'90*:159; *K'92*:146; *K'94*:149
Karst, Linda K.: *K'91*:153; *K'92*:50,84,146,148,149; *K'93*:68,84,144,145,147
Kondrla, Denise: *K'92*:126,147; *K'93*:Cover,116,144
McGrath, Gayle: *K'90*:159; *K'91*:109,116; *K'93*:115,146; *K'94*:149
McLaran, Lou: *K'93*:73

Mead, Faustine: *K'93*:147
Minnick, Joyce: *K'91*:161
Morris, Darrel: *K'94*:150
Mueller, Linda: *K'90*:157
Ochonicky, Michelle: *K'91*:155
Petree, Linda A.: *K'91*:73; *K'92*:68
Purvis, Hilton: *K'91*:154
Rade, Mary: *K'90*:158
Rece, Charles V.: *K'92*:147; *K'93*:144; *K'94*:151
Raoux, Serge: *K'92*:149
Richardson, Will: *K'90*:159
Rizzini, Aldo: *K'92*:149
Russ, Joann: *K'93*:75
Selent, Chuck: *K'90*:157; *K'91*:154; *K'93*:116,165; *K'94*:150
Semrich, Alice: *K'91*:119
Smuck, Bruce: *K'93*:85
Talley, Mary Austin: *K'91*:152,153; *K'92*:124
Walker, Karen: *K'91*:153; *K'92*:149,252
Williams, Gary: *K'90*:124,156; *K'91*:75,77,94,152,154; *K'93*:136,144,145; *K'94*:83,151
Young, Mary: *K'93*:114

etchers/carvers

Anderson, Jim: *K'93*:153
Bartrug, Hugh E.: *K'93*:152
Beaver, Judy: *K'91*:164; *K'93*:153
Boye, David: *K'92*:155
Cover, Jr., Raymond A.: *K'93*:154
DeBraga, Jose C.: *K'93*:152
DiMarzo, Richard: *K'92*:126,154; *K'94*:116
Eubanks, Mary Ann: *K'91*:164
Evans, Dale: *K'93*:154
Ferguson, Jim: *K'92*:154; *K'93*:154; *K'94*:152
Fuegen, Larry: *K'92*:154
Fuller, Jack A.: *K'92*:155
Grussenmeyer, Paul;: *K'93*:152,153,154; *K'94*:115,152

Harrison, Lou: *K'93*:96
Hayes, Dolores: *K'92*:156
Hoffman, Kevin L.: *K'93*:153
Hudson, C. Robbin: *K'94*:152
Imboden II, Howard L.: *K'91*:164; *K'92*:155; *K'93*:154
Kalyna, Greg: *K'93*:152
Kelso, Jim: *K'92*:155; *K'94*:152
Lefaucheux, Jean-Victor: *K'90*:161
Leibowitz, Leonard: *K'91*:158,160; *K'92*:156; *K'93*:72; *K'94*:152
Leschorn, Tom: *K'92*:156
Lonewolf, J. Aguirre: *K'93*:153; *K'94*:152
MacBain, Ken: *K'93*:152

Martrildonno, Paul: *K'92*:156
McConnell, Loyd: *K'92*:156
Meyers, Ron: *K'92*:154
Myers, Ron;: *K'93*:148; *K'94*:152
Nealy, Bud: *K'92*:155
Nolfi, Tim: *K'93*:154
Quarton, Barr: *K'92*:154
Ramsey, Dale: *K'92*:154
Rothenburger Waffeneck: *K'91*:83
Russell, Michael: *K'92*:154
Smith, Glen: *K'90*:161
Toner, Roger: *K'92*:156

leatherworkers/sheathmakers

Barnett, Jack: *K'94*:25
Barr, A.T.: *K'94*:142
Dawkins, Dudley: *K'94*:141
Dennehy, John D.: *K'94*:141
Layton, Jim: *K'94*:20

Polkowski, Al: *K'94*:142
Potier, Timothy: *K'94*:51
Rippys, The: *K'94*:142
Row, Kenny: *K'94*:141
Schrap, Robert G.: *K'94*:141

Sellevold, Harald: *K'94*:142
Stuart, Pat: *K'94*:141
Tierney, Mike: *K'94*:141
Turner, Kevin: *K'94*:142
Wegner, Tim: *K'94*:19,20,140
Weiler, Donald E.: *K'94*:142

handle artisans

Crosslen, T.J.: *K'92*:169
DiMarzo, Richard: *K'90*:161; *K'91*:163
Eubanks, Mary Ann: *K'92*:156
Hirayama, Harumi: *K'92*:170
Holder, Pat: *K'93*:115

Jones, Paul: *K'94*:115
Katz, Brian: *K'92*:141
Kelso, Jim: *K'94*:79,152
Lane, Tom: *K'94*:97
Marvis, Paul M.: *K'93*:105

Miller, Robert: *K'93*:105
Myers, Ron: *K'92*:156
Paranto, Craig: *K'93*:153
Rardon, A.D.: *K'93*:116
Sayen, Murad: *K'93*:152

specialty cutlers

The firms listed here are special in the sense that they make or market special kinds of knives made in facilities they own or control either in the U.S. or overseas. Or they are special because they make knives of unique design or function.

ACE OF BLADES
P.O. Box 3336
Fairfax, VA 22038
Phone: 703-904-8629
Specialties: Discreet personal defense cutlery by John Mitchell, owner and designer.

ADAMS INTERNATIONAL KNIFEWORKS
(See Importers & Foreign Cutlers)

AMERICAN WILDERNESS
P.O. Box 25208
Colorado Springs, CO 80936
Phone: 719-574-4462
FAX: 719-574-4462
Specialties: Multi-functional survival tools.

ANZA FILE KNIVES (See Blair Blades & Accessories—Mail-Order Sales)

B&D TRADING CO.
3935 Fair Hill Rd.
Fair Oaks, CA 95628
Phone: 916-967-9366;800-334-3790
FAX: 916-967-4873
Specialties: Carries the full line of Executive Edge—Brazil's locking folders.

BARTEAUX MACHETES, INC.
P.O. Box 66464
Portland, OR 97290
Phone: 503-665-2577
Specialties: Machetes of high-carbon and stainless steel. Line greatly expanded of late.

BECKER KNIFE and TOOL CO.
(See Blackjack Knives)

BENCHMADE KNIFES, INC.
15875-G SE 114th St.
Clackamas, OR 97015
Phone: 503-655-6004
FAX: 503-655-6223
Specialties: Balisong knives, tactical patterns in axes and big knives. U.S. production.

BENCHMARK KNIVES (See Gerber Legendary Blades—General Cutlers)

BERETTA U.S.A. CORP.
17601 Beretta Dr.
Accokeek, MD 20607
Phone: 301-283-2191
Specialties: A variety of Beretta-only designs, including several lockblade duty daggers.

BLACKJACK KNIVES
Also Condor Sport Knives, Becker Knife and Tool Co., Ek Commando Knive Co., Cripple Creek Knives
1307 W. Wabash Ave.
Effingham, IL 62401
Phone: 217-347-7700
FAX: 217-347-7737
Specialties: High-tech self-defense and adventure patterns with names like Mamba, Panga, Machax; also high-end hunters and a variety of specialty patterns. Has own factory in Effingham.

BLUE GRASS CUTLERY CORP.
304 W. 2nd St.
Manchester, OH 45144
Phone: 513-549-2709
FAX: 513-549-2602
Specialties: Re-creating great old patterns with the great names—Winchester, Primble and more.

BROWNING
Rt. 1
Morgan, UT 84050
Phone: 800-333-3288
Specialties: Has its own name on sports knives of all kinds, all in Browning finish.

BRUNTON/LAKOTA U.S.A.
620 E. Monroe St.
Riverton, WY 82501-4997
Phone: 307-856-6559
FAX: 307-856-1840
Specialties: Heavy-duty sports knives, straight and folding, on a distinctive design theme.

COLD STEEL, INC.
2128 Knoll Dr., Unit D
Ventura, CA 93003
Phone: 805-656-5191
FAX: 805-642-9727
Specialties: Variety of urban survival instruments—big in tantos. Outdoorsman series, Bowie and Hunter; several new and exclusive specialty designs.

CONDOR SPORT KNIVES
(See Blackjack Knives)

CRIPPLE CREEK KNIVED
(See Blackjack Knives)

EK COMMANDO KNIFE CO.
(See Blackjack Knives)

EQUIP USA
666 Grand Ave.
Mancos, CO 81328
Phone: 303-533-7982
Specialties: Vaughan Neely designs, such as the Timberlite, plus Timberline knives.

F&H MARKETING, INC.
3165 S. A-2 Campbell
Springfield, MO 65807
Phone: 417-886-2888
Specialties: Manufacturer of the Honeycomb.

GT KNIVES
7716 Arsons Dr.
San Diego, CA 92126
Phone: 619-566-1511
FAX: 619-530-0734

HANDMADE CLASSICS
P.O. Box 578373
Chicago, IL 60657
Phone: 312-944-4307
Specialties: Authentic hand-forged replicas of period pieces, currently doing Scagel, Bowie, and Early File knife. Brochure $1.

H&B FORGE CO.
Rt. 2, Geisinger Rd.
Shiloh, OH 44878
Phone: 419-895-1856
Specialties: Tomahawks and throwing knives.

IRON MOUNTAIN KNIFE CO.
P.O. Box 2146
Sparks, NV 89432
Phone: 702-356-3631
Specialties: Line of fixed-blade hunters based on special patented handle shape.

KAI CUTLERY CO.
(See Kershaw/KAI Cutlery Co.)

KATZ KNIVES, INC.
P.O. Box 730
Chandler, AZ 85224
Phone: 602-786-9334
FAX: 602-786-9338

KERSHAW/KAI CUTLERY CO.
25300 SW Parkway
Wilsonville, OR 97070
Phone: 503-682-1966
Specialties: Former Gerber designer's heavy-duty sports knives made overseas; also smaller "pocket jewelry"; handsome scrimshaw; new designs in using knives.

KNIVES OF ALASKA
P.O. Box 675
Cordova, AK 99574
Phone: 800-572-0980
FAX: 903-463-7165
Specialties: Husky edged tools for big game hunting and fishing.

LAKOTA U.S.A. (See Brunton/Lakota U.S.A.)

LEATHERMAN TOOL GROUP, INC.
P.O. Box 20595
Portland, OR 97220
Phone: 503-253-7826
FAX: 800-367-1355
Specialties: All-in-one pocket tool in two sizes.

MAR KNIVES, INC., AL
5755 SW Jean Rd., Suite 101
Lake Oswego, OR 97035
Phone: 503-635-9229
Specialties: Founded by the late Al Mar, a designer, the company continues to market Mar's designs under the direction of Ann Mar.

MISSION KNIVES, INC.
P.O. Box 1616
San Juan Capistrano, CA 92693
Phone: 714-661-3879
Specialties: Titanium blade knives and all titanium folders. Currently supplying certified non-magnetic SPECWAR knives to the U.S. Navy SEALS and EOD teams.

MORTY THE KNIFE MAN, INC.
60 Otis St.
West Babylon, NY 11704
Phone: 516-491-5764/800-247-2511
Specialties: Everything for the fish trade; own and make both U.S. and import brands; includes many working knives not easily found, as well as chain mesh protection gloves and aprons.

MUSEUM REPLICAS LTD.
2143 Gees Mill Rd., Box 840XZ
Conyers, GA 30207
Phone: 404-922-3703
Specialties: Authentic edged weapons of the ages, battle-ready—over 50 models; subsidiary of Atlanta Cutlery; catalog $2.

MYERCHIN MARINE CLASSICS
P.O. Box 911
Rialto, CA 92376
Phone: 714-875-3592
FAX: 909-874-6058
Specialties: The Myerchin Offshore System—a quality cutlery package for the yachtsman or deep water sailor; supplier to the U.S. Navy and Coast Guard.

ORION KNIFE CO., INC.
13765 SW Parkway
Beaverton, OR 97005
Phone: 503-643-2719
Specialties: Two-blade designs—the Orion Swing Blade and the Northwest Trader.

OUTDOOR EDGE CUTLERY CORP.
2888 Bluff St., Suite 130
Boulder, CO 80301
Phone: 303-652-8212
FAX: 303-652-8238
Specialties: All-in-one tools for preparing game and all-purpose field use.

PILTDOWN PRODUCTIONS
Errett Callahan
Cliffside
2 Fredonia Ave.
Lynchburg, VA 24503
Phone: 804-528-3444
Specialties: Makes obsidian scalpels and knives; replicates Stone Age tools and weapons—all types—for museums and academia. $3 for catalog.

REMINGTON ARMS CO., INC.
1007 Market St.
Wilmington, DE 19898
Phone: 302-773-5292
Specialties: Old and new patterns in the Remington style and more to come.

SANTA FE STONEWORKS
3790 Cerrillos Rd.
Santa Fe, NM 87501
Phone: 505-471-3953
FAX: 505-471-0036
Specialties: Embellished personal and gift cutlery and desk accessories.

SOG SPECIALTY KNIVES, INC.
P.O. Box 1024
Edmonds, WA 98020
Phone: 206-771-6230
Specialties: High-quality folding and combat knives, and a multi-tool, as well.

SOQUE RIVER KNIVES
P.O. Box 880
Clarksville, GA 30523
Phone: 706-754-8500
FAX: 706-754-7263
Specialties: Manufacturers of uniquely designed folding knives, beginning with the Lev-R-Lok, a quick-opener.

general cutlers

SPORT BLADES
447 E. Gardena Blvd.
Gardena, CA 90248
Phone: 310-538-9561
FAX: 310-538-9560
Specialties: The patented deer skinner once the Cal-Mont is now the Skinmaster; there are other edged items like broadheads; all are made overseas.

SPYDERCO, INC.
P.O. Box 800
Golden, CO 80402-0800
Phone: 303-279-8383, 800-525-7770

FAX: 303-278-2229
Specialties: Clipit folding knives; sharpening gear. Has kitchen and diving knives and new stuff every year.

TRU-BALANCE KNIFE CO.
2155 Tremont Blvd., NW
Grand Rapids, MI 49504
Phone: 616-453-3679
Specialties: The late Harry McEvoy's full line of throwers—a design for any throwing job. Can provide custom-made throwing knives. Catalog and throwing instructions can be had with a SASE.

WENOKA SEA STYLE
P.O. Box 10969
Riviera Beach, FL 33419-0969
Phone: 407-845-6155
FAX: 407-842-4247
Specialties: First a full line of divers' knives; now a beefy folder.

WYOMING KNIFE CORP.
101 Commerce Dr.
Ft. Collins, CO 80524
Phone: 303-224-3454
Specialties: A tool for dealing with game animals—gutting and skinning. Also makes a short folding saw, and the Powder River folders.

general cutlers

These are, plain and simple, knife factories. Some are giants; some not so big; some are a century old; some just two decades in existence. All market very complete lines of knives, generally through standard mercantile channels.

ALCAS CUTLERY CORP. (See Cutco Cutlery)

AMERICAN CONSUMER PRODUCTS, INC.
(See Ka-Bar Knives)

BEAR MGC CUTLERY
1 O'Connell St. SW
Jacksonville, AL 36265
Phone: 205-435-2227
FAX: 205-435-9348
Specialties: General line of traditional folders and belt knives—wide range of patterns.

BUCK KNIVES
1900 Weld Blvd.
El Cajon, CA 92020
Phone: 619-449-1100
Specialties: Creators of the belt folder syndrome; sturdy, solid working knives widely sold.

CAMILLUS CUTLERY CO.
54 Main St.
Camillus, NY 13031
Phone: 315-672-8111; 800-344-0456
FAX: 315-672-8832
Specialties: Long-time competitor in all phases of cutlery; military knife contractor; some neat pocketknife designs. Makes and markets Western knives.

CASE & SONS CUTLERY CO., W.R.
Owens Way
Bradford, PA 16701
Phone: 814-368-4123
FAX: 814-362-4877
Specialties: At the same old stand producing the good base patterns, and widely advertised these days.

CHICAGO CUTLERY CO.
1536 Beech St.
Terre Haute, IN 47804

Phone: 800-457-2665
Specialties: Solid utility knives; a full line of kitchen cutlery; owned by General Housewares Corp.

COAST CUTLERY (See Importers & Foreign Cutlers)

COLONIAL KNIFE CO., INC.
287 Agnes at Magnolia St.
Providence, RI 02909-0327
Phone: 401-421-1600; 800-556-7824
FAX: 401-421-2047
Specialties: Commercial pocketknives for competitive pricing; some belt knives.

CUTCO CUTLERY
P.O. Box 810
Olean, NY 14760
Phone: 716-372-3111
Specialties: Kitchen cutlery—American-made shears, steak knife sets, some sportsman knives. Parent company—Alcas Cutlery Corp.

FISKARS (See Gerber Legendary Blades)

GERBER LEGENDARY BLADES
14200 SW 72nd Ave.
Portland, OR 97281
Phone: 503-639-6161
FAX: 503-684-7008
Specialties: Well-known sports and dining cutlery line, plus Fiskars cutlery and Benchmark specialty knives.

IMPERIAL SCHRADE CORP.
99 Madison Ave.
New York, NY 10016
Phone: 212-889-5700
FAX: 212-799-7699
Specialties: Probably the biggest; owns Imperial and Schrade. Sells many labels in several brands, U.S.-made and imported.

KA-BAR KNIVES
Ka-Bar Knives, Collectors Division
31100 Solon Rd.
Solon, OH 44139
Phone: 216-248-7000; 800-321-9316 (Ext. 329)
FAX: 216-348-8051
Specialties: Sells working sports cutlery. Made the first WWII Marine Corps knife, a design still in service. Imports Sabre knives. Collectors division specializes in commemoratives and special models. A division of American Consumer Products, Inc.

ONTARIO KNIFE CO.
P.O. Box 145
Franklinville, NY 14737
Phone: 716-676-5535; 800-222-5233
FAX: 716-676-5535
Specialties: Some pocketknives; many styles of utility knives for household and restaurant use. Brands, both Hickory and Colonial Forge. Excellent values.

QUEEN CUTLERY
P.O. Box 500
Franklinville, NY 14737
Phone: 800-222-5233, 716-676-5535
FAX: 716-676-5535
Specialties: Old name. The line is growing, moving toward collector appeal.

SCHRADE (See Imperial Schrade Corp.)

UTICA CUTLERY CO.
820 Noyes St.
Utica, NY 13503
Phone: Outside NY 800-888-4223; 315-733-4663
FAX: 315-733-6602
Specialties: Nice line of pocketknives, including Barlows and hunters and working pattern knives. Brands: Kutmaster, Walco.

WESTERN CUTLERY (See Camillus Cutlery Co.)

importers & foreign cutlers

Knives are imported by almost every sort of commercial cutler, but the names here are those whose specialty is importing, whether it be their brand, famous overseas brands, or special knives for special purposes best made overseas. Every effort is made to keep the list updated, but importing is sometimes an uncertain endeavor.

A&D ASSOCIATES IMPORT/EXPORT
P.O. Box 52089
Philadelphia, PA 19115
Phone: 215-677-9007
Specialties: Imports variety of folding and straight knives for sale at medium to low prices.

ADAMS INTERNATIONAL KNIFEWORKS
8710 Rosewood Hills
Edwardsville, IL 62025
Phone: NA
Specialties: Llarge dealer in Linder-Solingen hunting knives. Also carries Muela, Al Mar, Kershaw and Commando. Catalog $3.

AITOR-CUCHILLERIA DEL NORTE, S.A.
P.O. Box No. 1; Izelaieta 17
48260 Ermua (Vizcaya)
SPAIN

Phone: 943-17.08.50; Intl.: 34-43-170850
FAX: 943-17.00.01; Intl.: 34-43-17001
Specialties: Full range of Aitor products from jungle knives to folding pocketknives.

ARISTOCRAT (See Degen Knives, Inc.)

ATLANTA CUTLERY CORP.
2143 Gees Mill Rd., Box 839XZ
Conyers, GA 30207
Phone: 404-922-3700
Specialties: Carefully chosen inventory from all over the world; selected Indian, Pakistani, Spanish, Japanese, German, English and Italian knives; often new ideas—a principal source for kukris.

B&D TRADING CO.
3935 Fair Hill Rd.
Fair Oaks, CA 95628

Phone: 916-967-9366/800-334-3790
FAX: 916-967-4873
Specialties: The Executive Edge, folders made in Brazil.

BAILEY'S
P.O. Box 550
Laytonville, CA 95454
Specialties: Importers of Tuatahi brand axes from New Zealand.

BAKER, B.W.
Smith Rd., RD 2
Waiuku, South Auckland
NEW ZEALAND
Phone: 0064-9-2358846
Specialties: New Zealand private cutler makes belt knives and commercial knives.

FIFTEENTH EDITION **293**

directory

BOKER USA, INC.
14818 W. 6th Ave. #10A
Golden, CO 80401-5045
Phone: 303-279-5997
FAX: 303-279-5919
Specialties: Tree Brand knives and a host of new knives in the Boker USA label.

C.A.S. IBERIA, INC./MUELA
5900 Cassandra Smith Rd.
Hixson, TN 37343-3318
Phone: 615-842-6311
Specialties: Knives made in Spain by people with an eye on U.S. custom makers.

CATOCTIN CUTLERY
P.O. Box 188; 17 S. Main St.
Smithsburg, MD 21783
Phone: 301-824-7416
FAX: 301-824-6138
Specialties: Full line of Aitor knives from Spain, others from Italy, Germany, the Philippines; wholesale only. Has own brands—Fox and Konceptm, the latter U.S.-made.

COAST CUTLERY
609 SE Ankeny St.
Portland, OR 97214
Phone: 503-234-4545
FAX: 503-234-4422
Specialties: Long-time large wholesaler now national Puma reps; exclusive Puma importer.

COLUMBIA PRODUCT CO.
P.O. Box 1333
Sialkot 51310
PAKISTAN
Phone: 011-92-432-86921/432-562009
FAX: 011-92-432-558417
Specialties: See **Columbus Prods. Int'l.**

COLUMBIA PRODUCTS INT'L.
P.O. Box 8243
New York, NY 10116-8243
Phone: 201-854-8504
FAX: 201-854-7058 (U.S. Branch Office)
Specialties: Lockblade and slip-joint folders in old and new U.S.-style patterns; heavy-duty belt knives; low prices.

COMPASS INDUSTRIES, INC.
104 E. 25th St.
New York, NY 10010
Phone: 212-473-2614; 800-221-9904
Specialties: Imports for dealer trade from all over at many price and quality levels; two hot brands are Silver Falcon and Sportster.

CONFEDERATE STATES ARMORY
2143 Gees Mill Rd.
Box 839XZ
Conyers, GA 30207
Phone: 800-241-3664
Specialties: Replicas of Confederate arms of the Civil War.

CONSOLIDATED CUTLERY CO., INC.
696 NW Sharpe St.
Port St. Lucie, FL 34983
Phone: 407-878-6139/800-288-6288
Specialties: Hunting knives, wood-carving tools, stag-handled steak/carving sets, camping axes, knife sharpening steels.

CRAZY CROW TRADING POST
P.O. Box 314-K'95
Denison, TX 75020
Phone: 903-463-1366
FAX: 903-463-7734
Specialties: Mountain man cutlery and fixings.

DEGEN KNIVES, INC.
9608 Van Nuys Blvd. #104
Panorama City, CA 91402
Phone: 818-892-6534; 800-433-4367
FAX: 818-830-7333
Specialties: Imports two knife lines—Degen, a variety of lock-back folding knives and multi-function knives for the outdoorsman; Aristocrat, a premium cutlery line made in Seki, Japan, uniquely styled, competitively priced.

EKA (See Nichols Co.)

EMPIRE CUTLERY CORP.
12 Kruger Ct.
Clifton, NJ 07013
Phone: 201-472-5155; 800-325-6433
FAX: 201-779-0759
Specialties: Imports Frost knives from Mora in Sweden, including the new Swedish soldier's knives. Knives are priced to sell.

EXECUTIVE EDGE (See B&D Trading Co.)

FALLKNIVEN AB
Box 46
S-960 30 Vuollerim
SWEDEN
Phone: Int. +46-976-10468
FAX: +46-976-10505
Specialties: Folders and hunting knives.

FORSCHNER GROUP, INC., THE
(See Swiss Army Brands Ltd.)

FREDIANI COLTELLI FINLANDESI
Via Lago Maggiore 41
I-21038 Leggiuno, ITALY
Phone: 0039 332 647 362
Specialties: Purveyors from Italy of fine Finnish knives, some with Italian decorative touches.

FROSTS KNIFE MANUFACTURING (Mora, SWEDEN)
(See Scandia International)

FURY (See Joy Enterprises)

GIESSER MESSERFABRIK GMBH, JOHANNES
P.O. Box 168
D-71349 Winnenden
GERMANY
Phone: +49-7195-1808-28
FAX: +49-7195-6 44 66
Specialties: Manufacturer of professional and kitchen cutlery.

GOODWIN ENTERPRISES
P.O. Box 4124
Chattanooga, TN 37405
Phone: 615-267-5071
Specialties: Imports German cutlery, including exclusive Red Stag pocketknives—jigged bone, etched blades in colors, and more.

GREEN HEAD GAME CALL CORP.
R.R. 1, Box 33
Lacon, IL 61540
Phone: 309-246-2155/800-247-8279
Specialties: Distributor of Canadian-made D.H. Russell belt knives; some two-bladed folders. Game calls also.

GUTMANN CUTLERY, INC.
120 S. Columbus Ave.
Mt. Vernon, NY 10553
Phone: 914-699-4044
FAX: 914-699-4217
Specialties: Edge Mark, Explorer, Hen & Rooster, Opinel and Russell Green River are the leading names in a selection of over 300 knives sold through retail stores and through the mail.

HENCKELS ZWILLINGSWORK, INC., J.A.
9 Skyline Dr., Box 253
Hawthorne, NY 10532
Phone: 914-592-7370
FAX: 914-592-7384
Specialties: U.S. office of world-famous Solingen cutlers—high-quality pocket and sportsman's knives with the "twin" logo.

HIMALAYAN IMPORTS
Box 327
Alpine, CA 91903
Phone: 619-561-3533
Specialties: Just one: Nepalese-made kukris, which they spell *khukuri*, hand-forged in that mountain kingdom.

HOFFRITZ/CUTLERY WORLD
515 W. 24th St.
New York, NY 10011
Phone: 212-924-7300
FAX: 212-627-5922
Specialties: Selected chef's kitchen and carving cutlery; elegant gentlemen's pocketknives; sports knives of all kinds, most with Hoffritz's own name; all sold in 80 Hoffritz stores and through catalog.

ILLINOIS CUTLERY
P.O. Box 607
Barrington, IL 60011-0607
Phone: 708-426-5002
FAX: 708-426-4942
Specialties: U.S. agent for Johannes Giesser Messerfabrik GmbH line of professional knives (butchers/cooks/household).

JOY ENTERPRISES
801 Broad Ave., P.O. Box 314
Ridgefield, NJ 07657
Phone: 201-943-5920
FAX: 201-943-1579
Specialties: Sporting and combat-style cutlery under the Fury label—full range. Folders and swords. Wholesale only.

KA-BAR KNIVES, Collector's Division
(See General Cutlers)

KELLAM KNIVES CO.
1770 Motor Pkwy. 2A
Hauppauge, NY 11788
Phone: 516-232-1747
Specialties: Handmade, all purpose knives for outdoorsmen.

KEN'S FINN KNIVES
Rt. 1, Box 338
Republic, MI 49879
Phone: 906-376-2132
Specialties: Puukkos and other Finnish knives. Broch. $2.

KNIFE COLLECTORS ASSN.-JAPAN
(See Murakami, Ichiro)

KNIFE IMPORTERS, INC.
P.O. Box 1000
Manchaca, TX 78652
Phone: 512-282-6860
FAX: 512-282-7504
Specialties: Eye Brand cutlery.

LEISURE PRODUCTS CORP.
P.O. Box 1171
Sialkot-1 PAKISTAN
Phone: 92-432-562009/86921
FAX: 92-432-558417; 92-432-561030
Specialties: Lockblade and slip-joint folders in old and new U.S.-style patterns; heavy-duty belt knives; low prices.

LIBERTY ORGANIZATION, INC.
P.O. Box 306
Montrose, CA 91020
Phone: 818-248-0618; 800-423-2666, Ext. 24
Specialties: Wholesale only. Distributor of Wenger, Estwing axes, backpack shovels, smith sharpening tools, etc.

MARKUSE CORP., THE
10 Wheeling Ave.
Woburn, MA 01801
Phone: 617-932-9444
FAX: 617-933-1930
Specialties: U.S. agent for Johannes Giesser Messerfabrik GmbH's "Creative Collection" range of knives.

MARTTIINI KNIVES
P.O. Box 44
96101 Rovaniemi 10, FINLAND
Phone: 358-60-21751
Specialties: Finnish knives straight from Finland's biggest cutler. Includes fancy Finn-type hunters.

MATTHEWS CUTLERY
4401 Sentry Dr., Suite K
Tucker, GA 30084
Phone: 404-939-6915
Specialties: Wholesalers only. Carries all major brands which include over 2,800 patterns. Has U.S. distribution for Linder-Solingen and others. Catalog $2.

MILITARY REPLICA ARMS, INC.
P.O. Box 360006, Dept. D
Tampa, FL 33673-0006
Phone: 813-968-1571
FAX: 813-935-0190
Specialties: Ron Hickox picks out dandies to copy—Ames naval cutlasses, Krag Bowie bayonets, a wide variety of U.S. sabers and such—and prices them pretty low. Catalog $3.

MUELA (See C.A.S. Iberia, Inc./Muela)

MURAKAMI, ICHIRO
Knife Collectors Assn.—Japan
Hashima-Gun
Gifu, Japan
Phone: (0582)74-1960-1
Specialties: Buys collector-grade and commercial U.S. knives for sale in Japan.

MUSEUM REPLICAS LIMITED
2143 Gees Mill Rd., Box 839 XZ
Conyers, GA 30207
Phone: 404-922-3703
Specialties: Battle-ready hand-forged edged weapons. Carry swords, daggers, halberds, dirks and axes. Catalog $2.

NICHOLS CO.
P.O. Box 473
Woodstock, VT 05091
Phone: 802-457-3970
FAX: 802-457-2051
Specialties: Importer/distributor of precision-engineered EKA pocketknives from Sweden; also fixed-blade knives from Norway and Finland.

knifemaking supplies

NORLANTIC INTERPRISE
200 High St.
Windsor, CT 06095
Phone: 203-688-0102
Specialties: Purveyors of advertising knives from penknives to lockback hunters—your logo, your message, gift-wrapped if you like. EKA brand.

NORMARK CORP.
1710 E. 78th St.
Minneapolis, MN 55423
Phone: 612-869-3291
Specialties: Scandinavian-made sturdy knives for fishermen; puuko-style belt knives for hunters; fillet knives. Good stainless steel.

PRECISE INTERNATIONAL
15 Corporate Dr.
Orangeburg, NY 10962
Phone: 800-431-2996
Specialties: Wenger Swiss Army knives.

PRO CUT
P.O. Box 2189
Downey, CA 90242
Phone: 800-356-8507
FAX: 310-803-4261
Specialties: Wholesale only. Imports historical medieval and samurai swords; armor and weapons, over 100 different models.

PUUKKO CUTLERY (See Suomi Shop)

PUMA CUTLERY (See Coast Cutlery)

RUSSELL CO., A.G.
1705 Highway 71 North
Springdale, AR 72764
Phone: 501-751-7341
Specialties: Morseth knives; Russell-marked special designs—"Woods Walker," Sting, CIA letter opener, Russell One-Hand knives.

SCANDIA INTERNATIONAL
118 English Neighborhood Rd., P.O. Box 218
East Woodstock, CT 06244
Phone: 203-928-9525
FAX: 203-928-1779
Specialties: U.S. importer of Frosts Knife Manufacturing AB of Mora, Sweden—over 800 models.

STAR SALES CO., INC.
1803 N. Central St., P.O. Box 1503
Knoxville, TN 37901
Phone: 615-524-0771
FAX: 615-524-4889
Specialties: New collector pocketknives; imports Star knives and Kissing Crane knives.

SUOMI SHOP
P.O. Box 303
Wolf Lake, MN 56593
Phone: 218-538-6633/winter: 512-968-9546
Specialties: A full and complete Finnish cutlery line, including the Puukko cutlery line, all custom/hand-forged. Offers Scandinavian or Nordic expertise on makers and knife values.

SWISS ARMY BRANDS LTD.
The Forschner Group, Inc.
One Research Drive
Shelton, CT 06484
Phone: 800-243-4032
FAX: 800-243-4006
Specialties: This is the Victorinox headquarters in the U.S.; all current production comes through here; manages service center also. Group also manages flow of excellent Forschner commercial and household cutlery.

TAYLOR CUTLERY MFG. CO.
320 Cherokee St.
Kingsport, TN 37662
Phone: 615-247-2406
Specialties: Taylor-Seto folders and straight knives, many other imports.

UNITED CUTLERY CORP.
1425 United Blvd.
Sevierville, TN 37862
Phone: 615-428-2532
FAX: 615-428-2267
Specialties: Wholesale only. Purchases for resale only; manufacture a number of items in the U.S. now.

VACAVILLE SURPLUS
501-C Main St.
Vacaville, CA 95688-3911
Phone: 707-448-1892
Specialties: Sports folders and straight knives in modern designs; utility belt buckles; knife kits and pouches.

VALOR CORP.
5555 N.W. 36th Ave.
Miami, FL 33142
Phone: 305-633-0127
Specialties: Emphasizes lockback folders from overseas in popular styles. Over 100 knife models imported.

ZEST INTERNATIONAL
1500 NE Jackson St.
Minneapolis, MN 55413
Phone: 800-453-8937/612-781-5036
FAX: 612-781-1452
Specialties: Full line of sports cutlery—dozens of models—with Zest trademark in 440A steel.

ZUM FLEISSIGEN BIBER
The Busy Beaver (H. Silk)
Postfach 1166
64343 Griesheim
GERMANY
Phone: 06155-2231
FAX: +49-6155-2433
Specialties: Wholesale/retail sales of American knives. Contact for details.

knifemaking supplies

The firms listed here specialize in furnishing knifemaking supplies in small amounts. Professional knifemakers have their own sources for much of what they use, but often patronize some of these firms. All the companies listed below have catalogs of their products, some available for a charge. For information about obtaining one, send a self-addressed and stamped envelope to the company. Firms are listed here by their request. New firms may be included by sending a catalog or the like to our editorial offices. We cannot guarantee the company's performance.

AFRICAN IMPORT CO.
Alan Zanotti
20 Braunecker Rd.
Plymouth, MA 02360
Phone: 508-746-8552
FAX: 508-746-0616
Specialties: Exotic African handle materials; exotic skins and leathers.

ARCTIC WILDERNESS ADVENTURES
(See Eklund's Arctic Wilderness Adventures, Neil)

ART JEWEL ENTERPRISES, LTD.
Eagle Business Center
460 Randy Rd.
Carol Stream, IL 60188
Phone: 708-260-0400; 800-260-0400 (orders only)
FAX: 708-260-0486
Specialties: Handles—stag, ivory, pearl, horn, rosewood, ebony.

ATLANTA CUTLERY CORP.
2143 Gees Mill Rd., Box 839XE
Conyers, GA 30207
Phone: 800-241-3595
Specialties: Many blades and fixings to choose from; occasional special buys in cutlery handles, pocketknife blades and the like; complete kits for buckskinner knives, small pocketknives. Catalog $2.

BILL'S CUSTOM CASES
4122 Branstetter St.
P.O. Box 2
Dunsmuir, CA 96025
Phone: 916-235-0177
Specialties: Knife cases made of 100 percent cotton duck-shell and synthetic shearling.

BLADEMASTER GRINDERS
P.O. Box 812
Crowley, TX 76036
Phone: 817-473-1081
Specialties: Manufactures knifemaking machine called "Blademaster." Wholesale and retail.

BLADES "N" STUFF
1019 E. Palmer Ave.
Glendale, CA 91205
Phone: 818-956-5110
Specialties: Full line of supplies and equipment, including excellent selection of tropical woods. Does big business in custom-ground heat-treated blades in dozens of shapes. Catalog $5.

BOONE TRADING CO., INC.
562 Coyote Rd.
Brinnon, WA 98320
Phone: 206-796-4330
Specialties: Exotic handle materials including elephant, fossil walrus, mastodon, warthog and hippopotamus ivory. Also sambar stag, oosic, impala and sheephorn.

BORGER, WOLF/IMPORT-EXPORT
Benzstrasse 8
76676 Graben-Neudorf
GERMANY
Phone: 07255-8314
FAX: 07255-6921
Specialties: Supplies European knifemakers, and others. German text catalog—write for details.

BOYE KNIVES, DAVID
P.O. Box 1238
Dolan Springs, AZ 86441
Phone: 602-767-4273
FAX: 602-767-3030
Specialties: Casts dendritic blades and bar stock for knifemaking. Information $1.

CHARLTON, LTD. (See Damascus-USA)

CHRISTOPHER FIREARMS CO., INC., E.
Rt. #128 & Ferry St., P.O. Box 303
Miamitown, OH 45041
Phone: 513-353-1321
FAX: 513-353-1322
Specialties: Blades and supplies, including modern guthook hunters; classic Bowies.

CRAZY CROW TRADING POST (See Mail-Order Sales)

CUSTOM KNIFEMAKER'S SUPPLY
Bob Schrimsher
P.O. Box 308
Emory, TX 75440
Phone: 903-473-3330
FAX: 903-743-2235
Specialties: Big catalog full of virtually everything for knifemaking. Their 21st year in business.

CUSTOM KRAFT
12922 127th Ave. N.
Largo, FL 34644
Phone: 813-972-5336
Specialties: Knifemakers Ron Miller and Reese Weiland make up Custom Craft; they specialize in hard-to-find knifemaking supplies like titanium naltex, safety gear, mills, taps, Fuller brand files, and Allen/spline drive screws, to name a few. Catalog $1.

DAMASCUS-USA
RR 1 Box 206-A
Tyner, NC 27980-9718
Phone: 919-221-2010
FAX: 919-221-2009
Specialties: Manufactures carbon and stainless Damascus bar stocks and blanks.

DAN'S WHETSTONE CO., INC.
130 Timbs Place
Hot Springs, AR 71913
Phone: 501-767-1616
FAX: 501-767-9598
Specialties: Traditional sharpening materials and abrasive products.

directory

DIAMOND MACHINING TECHNOLOGY, INC.
85 Hayes Memorial Dr.
Marlborough, MA 01752
Phone: 508-481-5944
FAX: 508-485-3924
Specialties: Quality diamond sharpening tools to hone all knife edges, including a unique serrated knife sharpener for all serration sizes.

DIXIE GUN WORKS, INC.
P.O. Box 130
Union City, TN 38261
Phone: 901-885-0700 info.; 800-238-6785 orders only
FAX: 901-885-0440
Specialties: Knife supplies for buckskinners; much early American hardware; blades; catalog $5 (outside U.S. $6). Also has knives made overseas, including Bowie replicas.

EKLUND'S ARCTIC WILDERNESS ADVENTURES, NEIL
P.O. Box 483
Nome, AK 99762-0483
Phone: NA
Specialties: Exotic handle materials like fossil walrus ivory, fossil whale and mammoth bone, mammoth ivory, oosic, horn and antler. Eskimo artifacts and trophy tusks; price sheet $1.

EZE-LAP DIAMOND PRODUCTS
15164 Weststate St., P.O. Box 2229
Westminster, CA 92683
Phone: 714-847-1555
Specialties: Diamond-coated sharpening instruments, various sizes.

FIELDS, RICK B.
330 N. Durango Ave.
Ocoee, FL 34761
Phone: 407-877-2339
Specialties: Fossil walrus and mammoth ivory.

FLITZ INTERNATIONAL, LTD.
821 Mohr Ave.
Waterford, WI 53185
Phone: 414-534-5898
Specialties: General line of polishers.

FORTUNE PRODUCTS, INC.
P.O. Box 1308
Friendswood, TX 77546
Phone: 713-996-0729
Specialties: "Accu-sharp" sharpeners.

GILMER WOOD CO.
2211 NW St. Helens Rd.
Portland, OR 97210
Phone: 503-274-1271
FAX: 503-274-9839
Specialties: They list 112 varieties of natural woods.

GOLDEN AGE ARMS CO.
115 E. High St.
P.O. Box 366
Ashley, OH 43003
Phone: 614-747-2488
Specialties: Many types of blades; stag for handles; cast items—much for the buckskinner. Catalog $4.

GRS CORP.
Don Glaser
P.O. Box 748
Emporia, KS 66801
Phone: 316-343-1084 (Kansas); 800-835-3519
FAX: 316-343-9640
Specialties: Engraving products such as the Gravermeister and the Gravermax.

HAWKINS CUSTOM KNIVES & SUPPLIES
P.O. Box 400
Red Oak, GA 30272
Phone: 404-964-1177
Specialties: Various size steel blanks, belts, buffing compounds and wheels; stag and drill bits.

HAYDU, THOMAS G.
2507 Bimini Lane
Ft. Lauderdale, FL 33312
Phone: 305-792-0185
Specialties: For knives that stay at home—deluxe boxes from Tomway Corp. have tambour covers.

HOUSE OF MUZZLE LOADING, THE (See Blades "N" Stuff)

HOUSE OF TOOLS LTD.
#136, 8228 MacLeod Tr. S.E.
Calgary, AB T2H 2B8
CANADA
Phone: 403-258-0005
FAX: 403-252-0149
Specialties: 440C and ATS34 handle and bolster material, sand belts, buff wheels and a large selection of tools.

INDIAN RIDGE TRADERS (See Koval Knives, Inc.)

JOHNSON WOOD PRODUCTS
RR 1
Strawberry Point, IA 52076
Phone: 319-933-4930 or 933-6504
Specialties: Fancy domestic and imported knife handle woods.

JONES, STANLEY A.
P.O. Box 30441
Mesa, AZ 85275-0441
Specialties: Ironwood and Karob Scales knifemaking supplies.

KNIFE & CUTLERY PRODUCTS, INC.
P.O. Box 12480
N. Kansas City, MO 64116
Phone: 816-454-9879
Specialties: Offers 14 pages of knifemaking supplies such as exotic woods, wheels, bar stock and blades in a variety of shapes. Catalog $2; list of pocketknives $1.

KNIFE AND GUN FINISHING SUPPLIES
P.O. Box 458
Lakeside, AZ 85929
Phone: 602-537-8877
FAX: 602-537-8066
Specialties: Complete line of machines and materials for knifemaking and metal finishing. Has wood, Micarta, ivory, horn.

KNIVES, ETC.
2522 North Meridian
Oklahoma City, OK 73107
Phone: 405-943-9221
Specialties: Exotic woods; variety of blade steels; stag.

KOVAL KNIVES, INC.
5819 Zarley St.
New Albany
Columbus, OH 43054
Phone: 614-855-0777
FAX: 614-855-0945
Specialties: Full range of Micarta and other materials for handles; brass, nickel silver, steels; machines and supplies for all knifemaking; some knife kits; catalog.

KWIK-SHARP
350 N. Wheeler St.
Ft. Gibson, OK 74434
Phone: 918-478-2443
Specialties: Ceramic rod knife sharpeners.

LINDER-SOLINGEN KNIFE PARTS
4401 Sentry Dr., Suite K
Tucker, GA 30084
Phone: 404-939-6915
Specialties: German-made knifemaking parts and blades. Wholesale catalog—send $2.

LOHMAN CO., FRED
3405 N.E. Broadway
Portland, OR 97232
Phone: 503-282-4567
FAX: 503—288-3533
Specialties: Sword polishing and handle wrapping service, quality replacement parts, for the restoration of Japanese-style swords, both new and old. Catalog $5.

MARKING METHODS, INC.
301 South Raymond Ave.
Alhambra, CA 91803-1531
Phone: 818-282-8823
FAX: 818-576-7564
Specialties: Manufacturer of electro-chemical etching equipment and supplies for the knifemaking trade—power units & kits, long life photo stencils, and accessories.

MASECRAFT SUPPLY CO.
170 Research Pkwy #3
P.O. Box 423
Meriden, CT 06450
Phone: 203-238-3049, 800-682-5489 (orders only)
FAX: 203-238-2373
Specialties: Handle materials.

MEIER STEEL
Daryl Meier
RR 4
Carbondale, IL 62901
Phone: 618-549-3234
Specialties: Supplier and creator of "Meier Steel." Contact for available sizes and prices of his Damascus.

MOTHER OF PEARL CO.
D.A. Culpepper
P.O. Box 445
401 Old GA Rd.
Franklin, NC 28734
Phone: 704-524-6842;
FAX: 704-369-7809
Specialties: Pearl, black pearl, abalone, pink pearl, sheephorn, bone, buffalo horn, stingray skin, exotic leathers, snake skin.

NORTHWEST KNIFE SUPPLY
621 Fawn Ridge Dr.
Oakland, OR 97462
Phone: 503-459-2216
FAX: 503-459-4460
Specialties: Coote grinders, Klingspor abrasives, exotic woods, Micarta, stag, other supplies. Catalog $2; foreign $4.

OREGON ABRASIVE & MFG. CO.
11303 NE 207th Ave.
Brush Prairie, WA 98606
Phone: 206-254-5400
FAX: 206-892-3025
Specialties: Sharpening stones made under their own roof, and sharpening systems based on those.

OZARK KNIFE
3165 S. Campbell, Suite A2
Springfield, MO 65807
Phone: 417-886-CUTT
Specialties: Shining Wave Damascus and mokume.

PARAGON INDUSTRIES, INC.
2011 South Town East Blvd.
Mesquite, TX 75149-1122
Phone: 800-876-4328; 214-288-7557
FAX: 214-222-0646
Specialties: Manufacturer of knifemaker's heat-treating furnaces in five available sizes.

POPLIN, JAMES/POP KNIVES & SUPPLIES
103 Oak St.
Washington, GA 30673
Phone: 404-678-2729
Specialties: Sanding belts, handle screws, buffing wheels and compound woods for knife handles, etc.

PUGH, JIM
917 Carpenter St., Azle, TX 76020
P.O. Box 711, Azle, TX 76098
Phone: 817-444-2679
FAX: 817-444-5455
Specialties: Kydex sheath material; limited.

RADOS, JERRY
Mlg: P.O. Box 531
Grant Park, IL 60940-0531
Shpg: 7523 E. 5000 N. Rd.
Grant Park, IL 60940
Phone: 815-472-3350
FAX: 815-472-3944
Specialties: Offers many distinct patterns of Damascus in forged-to-shape blades or customer designs.

REACTIVE METALS STUDIO, INC.
P.O. Box 890
Clarkdale, AZ 86324
Phone: 602-634-3434; 800-876-3434
FAX: 602-634-6734
Specialties: Phil Baldwin heads up another business and this is a source for titanium and like exotic metals plus the equipment for coloring or anodizing them.

REAL WOOD
36 Fourth St.
Dracut, MA 01826
Phone: 508-957-4899
Specialties: Exotic wood for knife handles; carry over 60 different species and are always adding more; catalog $1.

REPRODUCTION BLADES
Gary Kelley
17485 SW Pheasant Ln.
Beaverton, OR 97006
Phone: 503-649-7867 (evenings between 4:30 and 9:00 Pacific time)
Specialties: Custom cast blades.

RIVERSIDE MACHINE
Rt. 1, Box 488
DeQueen, AR 71832
Phone: 501-642-7643
Specialties: Grinders, belts, wood, steel, blade stamps, Riverside Stampmaster, trip hammer repair, parts and sales.

ROCKY MOUNTAIN KNIVES
George L. Conklin
P.O. Box 902, 615 Franklin
Ft. Benton, MT 59442
Phone: 406-622-3268
FAX: 406-622-5670
Specialties: Knife sharpening; supplies.

SANDPAPER, INC. OF ILLINOIS
P.O. Box 2579
Glen Ellyn, IL 60138
Phone: 708-629-3320
FAX: 708-629-3324
Specialties: Coated abrasives in belts, sheets, rolls, discs or any coated abrasive specialty.

mail-order sales

SCHELL, CLYDE M.
4735 N.E. Elliott Circle
Corvallis, OR 97330
Phone: 503-752-0235
Specialties: Knife and exotic wood material.

SCHEP'S FORGE
Box 83
Chapman, NE 68827
Phone: 308-986-2444
Specialties: Damascus steel made in Nebraska.

SHEFFIELD KNIFEMAKER'S SUPPLY
P.O. Box 141
Deland, FL 32721-0141
Phone: 904-775-6453
FAX: 904-774-5754
Specialties: Wood, stone, steel, brass, Micarta and more; catalog $5, foreign $8.

SHINING WAVE METALS
P.O. Box 563
Snohomish, WA 98290-0563
Phone: 206-334-5569
Specialties: Phil Baldwin makes and sells mokume, Damascus and a variety of Japanese alloys (for furniture, not blades) to order or from stock. Wholesale only.

SMITH WHETSTONE, INC.
1500 Sleepy Valley Rd.
Hot Springs, AR 71901
Phone: 501-321-2244; 800-221-4156 (orders only)
Specialties: Sharpeners of every kind, ceramic sharpeners, oils, kits and polishing creams.

SUEDMEIER, HARLAN "SID"
420 4th Corso
Nebraska City, NE 68410
Phone: 402-873-6603

Specialties: New headquarters for Little Giant/Mayer Bros. power hammer parts, information and advice.

TEXAS KNIFEMAKERS SUPPLY
10649 Haddington, Suite 180
Houston, TX 77043
Phone: 713-461-8632
FAX: 713-461-8221
Specialties: Bar stock, factory blades, much handle material; offers heat-treating; catalog $2.

THOMAS CUTLERY, CHARLES B.
902 Selma Blvd.,
Staunton, VA 24401
Phone: 703-885-1902
Specialties: Sharpening; repair, restoration; distributor for Stephen Bader grinders, Baldor buffers, Starrett precision tools, buffing wheels & compound, cabarundum abrasives, Foredom tools.

TRIPLE GRIT (See Oregon Abrasive & Mfg. Co.)

TRU-GRIT
11231 Thienes Ave., #A
So. El Monte, CA 91733
Phone: 818-444-5192
Specialties: Complete selection of 3M, Norton, Klingspor and Hermes belts for grinding and polishing, also Burr-King and square wheel grinders, Baldor buffers and an excellent line of machines for knifemakers; ATS-34 and 440C steel.

TUDOR II, HUGH SANFORD (SANDY)
Box 92
Vail, AZ 85641
Phone: NA
Specialties: Purveyor of desert ironwood.

WASHITA MOUNTAIN WHETSTONE CO.
P.O. Box 378
Lake Hamilton, AR 71951

Phone: 501-525-3914
Specialties: Knife sharpeners.

WILD WOODS
Jim Fray
P.O. Box 104
Monclova, OH 43542
Phone: 419-866-0435
FAX: 419-867-0656
Specialties: Stabilized woods in a variety of colors in four grades.

WILSON, R.W.
P.O. Box 2012
Weirton, WV 26062
Phone: 304-723-2771
Specialties: Full range of supplies, but sells nothing he doesn't use himself.

WOOD CARVERS SUPPLY, INC.
P.O. Box 7500
Englewood, FL 34295-7500
Phone: NA
Specialties: Carving tools, etc.

WYVERN INDUSTRIES
229 Flounce Rock Dr.
Prospect, OR 97536
Phone: 503-560-3355
Specialties: Purveyors of the hard-to-get for those who use anvils in their work.

ZOWADA, TIM
14141 P. Drive North
Marshall, MI 49068
Phone: 616-781-2458
Specialties: Damascus bars and billets, mokume and gas forge kits.

mail-order sales

The firms listed here have come to our attention over a period of years. All publish lists or catalogs. Their specialties are listed; send a self-addressed and stamped envelope for information. Firms are included here upon request. New firms wishing to be included should send a catalog or the like to our editorial offices. We cannot guarantee the company's performance.

A 'N J ENTERPRISES
P.O. Box 6071
Branson, MO 65616
Phone: 417-335-2171
FAX: 417-335-2011
Specialties: Buys, sells and trades collector-grade knives by mail and at major shows.

ADAMS INTERNATIONAL KNIFEWORKS
8710 Rosewood Hills
Edwardsville, IL 62025
Phone: NA
Specialties: Largest dealer of Linder-Solingen, Germany knives; offers Muela, Cold Steel, SOG, Kershaw, Ka-Bar-Boker and Henckels to name a few.

AMERICAN HISTORICAL FOUNDATION
1142 West Grace St.
Richmond, VA 23220
Phone: 804-353-1812
Specialties: Limited editions of replica military knives in collector and presentation grades; serves as headquarters for the Military Knife and Bayonet Collectors Club International.

AMERICAN TARGET KNIVES
1030 Brownwood NW
Grand Rapids, MI 49504
Phone: 616-453-1998
Specialties: Throwing knives

AMSPACHER, BRUCE
P.O. Box 9527
Newport Beach, CA 92658
Phone: 800-821-3985; 714-250-3187
FAX: 714-250-4412
Specialties: Sells, buys, trades custom-made, investment-grade knives; offers a free weekly price list.

ARIZONA CUSTOM KNIVES
Jay and Karen Sadow
10721 East Terra Dr.
Scottsdale, AZ 85258
Phone: 602-661-2142
Specialties: Collector quality handmade knives.

ARTHUR, GARY B.
215 Turkeyfoot Rd.
Forest, VA 24551
Phone: 804-525-8315
FAX: 804-525-8364
Specialties: Sells, buys and trades custom-made, invest-ment-grade knives.

ATLANTA CUTLERY CORP.
2143 Gees Mill Rd., Box 839XZ
Conyers, GA 30207
Phone: 404-922-3700
Specialties: Catalog on request; wide selection of knives; aims to provide working-quality knives and give good value; showroom. Catalog $2.

ATLANTIC BLADESMITHS
c/o Peter Stebbins
32 Bradford St.
Concord, MA 01742
Phone: 508-369-3608
Specialties: Factory and custom-made knives, over 100 in stock at all times, for immediate sale. List $3.

BALLARD CUTLERY
1495 Brummel Ave.
Elk Grove Village, IL 60007
Phone: 708-228-0070
FAX: 708-228-0077
Specialties: Special-purchase knives, all types. Tries for good buys.

BARRETT-SMYTHE, LTD.
127 East 69th St.
New York, NY 10021
Phone: 212-249-5500
Specialties: One-of-a-kind folding knives on sale in uptown Manhattan at prices suitable for their station.

BASCH ENTERPRISES, PAUL CHARLES
111 W. Del Amo Blvd., Suite I
Long Beach, CA 90805
Phone: 310-423-5362
FAX: 310-423-5792
Specialties: Buys, sells and trades handmade knives only; large stock; sets up 45 shows a year.

B&D TRADING CO., INC.
(See Importers & Foreign Cutlers)

BECK'S CUTLERY SPECIALTIES
Chatham Square Shopping Center
748F East Chatham St.
Cary, NC 27511
Phone: 919-460-0203
Specialties: South African Peter Bauchop's tactical designs; other U.S. big-ticket tactical names.

BLACK WHALE TRADING POST
3699 Quaker Lane
North Kingstown, RI 02852-3008
Phone: 401-885-0040

Specialties: Factory and custom-made knives and scrimshaw; inexpensive dive knives.

BLADES "N" STUFF (See Knifemaking Supplies)

BLAIR BLADES & ACCESSORIES
531 Main St. #651
El Segundo, CA 90245
Phone: 310-322-1063
FAX: 310-322-3112
Specialties: Sales reps for Anza File Knives.

BLUE RIDGE KNIVES
Rt. 6, Box 185
Marion, VA 24354
Phone: 703-783-6143
FAX: 703-783-9298
Specialties: Wholesale only; top brand knives.

BOONE TRADING CO., INC.
562 Coyote Rd.
Brinnon, WA 98320
Phone: 206-796-4330
Specialties: Ivory; catalog features scrimshawed and carved ivory-handled knives.

CARMEL CUTLERY
Dolores & 6th; P.O. Box 1346
Carmel, CA 93921
Phone: 408-624-6699
FAX: 408-624-6780
Specialties: Knife retailer; factory and custom knives.

CASANOVA'S
1601 W. Greenfield Ave.
Milwaukee, WI 53204
Phone: 414-672-3040 (info.); 800-627-4570 (orders)
Specialties: Factory and handmade collector knives. Has list.

CATOCTIN CUTLERY
P.O. Box 188, 17 Main St.
Smithsburg, MD 21783
Phone: 301-824-7416
FAX: 301-824-6138
Specialties: Wholesaler. Popular lines of domestic cutlery to dealers, as well as many import brands.

CLASSIC CUTLERY
39 Roosevelt Ave.
Hudson, NH 03051
Phone: 603-883-1199
FAX: 603-883-1199
Specialties: Factory knives and accessories, all discounted. Also custom, rare and discontinued knives. Huge catalog $5 (refundable).

directory

CRAZY CROW TRADING POST
P.O. Box 314
Denison, TX 75020
Phone: 214-463-1366
FAX: 903-463-7734
Specialties: Knife blades, books, knifemaking supplies; $3 for catalog.

CREATIVE SALES & MFG.
Box 550
Whitefish, MT 59937
Phone: 406-862-5533
Specialties: Patent knife sharpeners.

CUTLERY SHOPPE
5461 Kendall St.
Boise, ID 83706
Phone: 208-376-0430; 800-231-1272
Specialties: Discounts; custom and unusual balisongs; fighting and military-type knives; catalog $1.

DAMASCUS-USA (Charlton Ltd.)
RR 1 Box 206A
Tyner, NC 27980-9718
Phone: 919-221-2010
FAX: 919-221-2009
Specialties: Creating more handmade carbon and stainless Damascus blanks and knives than anyone.

DENTON, J.W.
102 N. Main St., P.O. Box 429
Hiawassee, GA 30546-0429
Phone: 706-896-2292
FAX: 706-896-1212
Specialties: Buys and sells Loveless knives—has lists.

EDGE CO. KNIVES
P.O. Box 826
Brattleboro, VT 05302
Phone: 800-732-9976, 802-257-3067
FAX: 802-257-1967
Specialties: A variety of opportunity knives.

EURO CHASSE
398 Greenwich Ave.
Greenwich, CT 06830
Phone: 203-625-9501

FROST CUTLERY CO.
P.O. Box 22636
Chattanooga, TN 37422
Phone: 800-251-7768, 615-894-6079
FAX: 615-894-9576
Specialties: Domestic and imported cutlery, especially folders and pocketknives; Hen & Rooster brand.

GENUINE ISSUE, INC.
P.O. Drawer S
Smithtown, NY 11787
Specialties: Representing the Digby line.

GODWIN, INC., G. GEDNEY
2139 Welsh Valley Rd.
Valley Forge, PA 19481
Phone: 610-783-0670
FAX: 610-783-6083
Specialties: Reenactment gear—18th and 19th century complete.

GOLDEN EAGLE CUTLERY
P.O. Box 1279; 16350 S. Golden Rd.
Golden, CO 80401
Phone: 800-828-1925
Specialties: Carry full line of Spyderco products, as well as many other quality knife companies.

HANDMADE CLASSICS
P.O. Box 578373
Chicago, IL 60614
Phone: 312-944-4307
Specialties: Scagel, Bowie, Early File Knife recreations, authentic and fully useable.

HOUSE OF TOOLS LTD.
#136, 8228 MacLeod Tr. SE
Calgary, Alberta
CANADA T2H 2B8
Phone: 403-258-0005
FAX: 403-252-0149
Specialties: 440C and ATS-34 handle and bolster material, sand belts, buff wheels and a large selection of tools.

JARVIS, PAUL M.
30 Chalk St.
Cambridge, MA 02139
Phone: 617-491-2900 (Days), 617-547-4355 (Evenings)
Specialties: Custom knives, Japanese sword fittings, metal carving.

JENCO SALES, INC.
P.O. Box 1000
Manchaca, TX 78652
Phone: 800-531-5301
FAX: 800-266-2373
Specialties: Sharpening gear.

KEN'S FINN KNIVES
Rt. 1, Box 338
Republic, MI 49879
Phone: 906-376-2132
Specialties: Puukko and Finnish-made knives. Brochure $2.

KENEFICK, DOUG
29 Leander St.
Danielson, CT 06239
Phone: 203-774-8929
Specialties: Excellent selection of Randall Made knives and custom knives at list prices; catalog on request.

KNIFE-AHOLICS UNANIMOUS, INC.
P.O. Box 831
Cockeysville, MD 21030
Phone: 410-628-6262
Specialties: David Cohen—purveyor of custom knives.

KNIFE & CUTLERY PRODUCTS, INC.
P.O. Box 12480
North Kansas City, MO 64116
Phone: 816-454-9879
Specialties: Sells brand-name commercial cutlery, some collectibles; 14-page list $2

KNIFE & GUN FINISHING SUPPLIES
P.O. Box 458
Lakeside, AZ 85929
Phone: 602-537-8877
Specialties: Complete line of machine and materials for knifemaking and metal finishing. Specializing in rare and exotic handle materials—oosic, ivory, rare hardwoods, horn, stag. Catalog $2.

KNIFE IMPORTERS, INC.
P.O. Box 1000
Manchaca, TX 78652
Phone: 512-282-6860
FAX: 512-282-7504
Specialties: Eye Brand cutlery.

KNIFEMASTERS/J&S FEDER
P.O. Box 2419
Westport, CT 06880
Phone: 203-226-5211
Specialties: Write for details.

KRIS CUTLERY
P.O. Box 133
Pinole, CA 94564
Phone: 510-758-9912
FAX: 510-223-8968
Specialties: Medieval swords and daggers, Indonesian and Moro krisses, Damascus balisongs.

LES COUTEAUX CHOISSIS DE ROBERTS
Ron Roberts
P.O. Box 273
Mifflin, PA 17058
Phone: 717-436-5010
FAX: 717-436-9691
Specialties: Handles all types and manufacturers knives and related items for collectors and users.

LONDON, RICK
P.O. Box 21303
Oakland, CA 94620
Phone: 510-482-2775
Specialties: Purveyor of collectible knives. A special eye for fine crafted folders.

MATTHEWS CUTLERY
4401 Sentry Dr., Suite K
Tucker, GA 30084
Phone: 404-939-6915
Specialties: Wholesale only. Carries major brands; monthly sale lists. Catalog (96 pages) $2.

MORTY THE KNIFE MAN
60 Otis St.
West Babylon, NY 11704
Phone: 516-491-5764; 800-247-2511
FAX: 516-491-6325
Specialties: The world's fish knives—all of them.

MUSEUM REPLICAS LTD.
2143 Gees Mill Rd.
Box 840XZ
Conyers, GA 30207
Phone: 404-922-3703
Specialties: Authentic edged weapons of the ages, battle-ready—over 50 models; subsidiary of Atlanta Cutlery; catalog $2.

NASHOBA VALLEY KNIFEWORKS
Box 35, 373 Langen Rd.
Lancaster, MA 01523
Phone: 508-365-6593
FAX: 508-368-4171
Specialties: Custom sales, emphasis on Guild members knives, plus Randall and Ruana. Large inventory; 6 lists a year. List $2.

NORDIC KNIVES
1634CZ Copenhagen Dr.
Solvang, CA 93463
Phone: 805-688-3612
Specialties: Custom and Randall knives; custom catalog $3; Randall catalog $2; both catalogs $4.

OZARK KNIFE
3165 S. Campbell, Suite A2
Springfield, MO 65807
Phone: 417-886-2888
FAX: 417-886-CUTT
Specialties: Offers list of custom knives for sale, plus general cutlery collectibles; Randall knives.

PEN AND THE SWORD LTD., THE
1833 E. 12th St., Suite 2D
Brooklyn, NY 11229
Phone: 718-382-4847
Specialties: Custom knives in a wide price range.

PLAZA CUTLERY, INC.
3333 Bristol, South Coast Plaza
Costa Mesa, CA 92626
Phone: 714-549-3932; or
Palm Desert Tower Center
Palm Desert, CA 92260
Phone: 619-341-3691
Specialties: List of custom knives for collectors, many top names every time; $1.

R&C KNIVES AND SUCH
P.O. Box 1047
Manteca, CA 95336
Phone: 209-239-3722
FAX: 209-825-6947
Specialties: Custom knives for collectors. Wide variety. Send stamps; can call anytime. Catalog $2.

RAMSHEAD ARMOURY
P.O. Box 653, Dept. K
Champaign, IL 61824-0653
Phone: 217-351-7232
Specialties: Stocks swords, daggers and such for the Renaissance dragon-slaying-tournament trade. Catalog $2.

ROBERTSON CUSTOM CUTLERY
P.O. Box 211961
Augusta, GA 30917
Phone: 706-650-0982
Specialties: Investment grade fighters, sub-hilt fighters, Bowies and Daggers.

RUSSELL CO., A.G.
1705 Highway 71 North
Springdale, AR 72764
Phone: 501-751-7341; 800-255-9034
Specialties: Regularly lists custom knives by all makers; sold on consignment; also commemoratives, Russell and Morseth knives.

SHAW, GARY
24 Central Ave.
Ridgefield Park, NJ 07660
Phone: 201-641-8801
Specialties: Investment-grade knives of all kinds.

SMOKY MOUNTAIN KNIFE WORKS
P.O. Box 4430; Hwy. 66
Sevierville, TN 37864
Phone: 615-453-5871
Specialties: Retail and wholesale sales of all kinds of knives and supplies.

STIDHAM'S KNIVES
Stidham, Rhett
P.O. Box 570
Roseland, FL 32957-0570
Phone: 407-589-0618
FAX: 407-489-3162
Specialties: Randalls, most of all; other high-end straight collectibles—keeps large inventory.

STODDARD'S, INC.
Copley Place
100 Huntington Ave.
Boston, MA 02116
Phone: 617-536-8688
FAX: 617-357-8263
Specialties: Oldest cutlery retailer in the country; handmade and Randall knives, other fine production knives—Spyderco and Al Mar knives, etc. Manager: Steven Weingrad. Two additional stores in MA area.

STONEWORKS
P.O. Box 211961
Augusta, GA 30917
Phone: 706-650-0982
Specialties: Investment grade fighters, sub-hilt fighters, Bowies and daggers with stone handles.

SWORD AND LANCE, THE
10051 Topanga Canyon Blvd. #11
Chatsworth, CA 91311-3673
Specialties: Provides swords, knives, axes, polearms in ancient, medieval and fantasy pieces. Catalog (60 pages) $2.

WASHITA MOUNTAIN WHETSTONE CO.
P.O. Box 378
Lake Hamilton, AR 71951
Phone: 501-525-3914
Specialties: Manufactures sharpening stones and wood products for custom wood boxes for many knife companies.

knife services

engravers

Alfano, Sam, 36180 Henry Gaines Rd., Pearl River, LA 70452/504-863-3364; FAX: 504-863-7715
Alpen, Ralph, 7 Bentley Rd., West Grove, PA 19390/215-869-9493
Allard, Gary, Creek Side Metal & Wood, Fishers Hill, VA 22626/703-465-3903
Allred, Scott, 2403 Lansing Blvd., Wichita Falls, TX 76309/817-691-9563
Bates, Billy, 2302 Winthrop Dr., Decatur, AL 35603/205-355-3690
Beaver, Judy, 48835 N. 25 Ave., Phoenix, AZ 85027/602-465-7831; FAX: 602-465-7077
Becker, Franz, Bruckbergstr. 23, 8261 Marktl/Inn, GERMANY
Bettenhausen, Merle L., 17358 Ottawa, Tinley Park, IL 60477/708-532-2179
Blair, Jim, P.O. Box 64, Glenrock, WY 82213
Blanchard, Gary, P.O. Box 1123, Burney, CA 96013/916-335-5445
Bleile, C. Roger, 5040 Ralph Ave., Cincinnati, OH 45238/513-251-0249
Bonshire, Benita, 1121 Burlington, Muncie, IN 47302/317-282-9073
Boster, A.D., 3744 Pleasant Hill Dr., Gainesville, GA 30504/404-535-8811
Bratcher, Dan, 311 Belle Aire Place, Carthage, MO 64836/417-356-1518
Brgoch, Frank, 1580 S. 1500 East, Bountiful, UT 84010/801-295-1885
Butler, Martin, 305 Robin Rd., London, Ont. N6J 1S5, CANADA/519-641-0652
Churchill, Winston, 20 Mile Stream Rd., RFD P.O. Box 29B, Proctorsville, VT 05153/802-226-7772
Coffey, Barbara, RR 3 Box 662, Monroe, VA 24574-9600
Cole, Larry R., P.O. Box 82, Broadbent, OR 97414-0082
Collins, David, Rt. 2 Box 425, Monroe, VA 24574/804-922-7465
Collins, Michael, Rt. 3075, Batesville Rd., Woodstock, GA 30188/404-475-7410
Creekside Metal & Wood (See Allard, Gary)
Cupp, Alan, Box 207, Annabella, UT 84711/801-896-4834
Dashwood, Jim, 255 Barkham Rd., Wokingham, Berkshire RG11 4BY, ENGLAND/0734-781761
Davidson, Jere, Rt. 1, Box 132, Rustburg, VA 24588/804-821-3637
Dean, Bruce, 13 Tressider Ave., Haberfield, N.S.W. 2045, AUSTRALIA/02-797-7608
DeLorge, Ed, 2231 Hwy. 308, Thibodaux, LA 70301/504-447-1633
Dibben, Melissa, Rt. 1, Box 80, Harrisville, MO 64701
Dolbare, Elizabeth, 39 Dahlia, Casper, WY 82604/307-266-5924
Drain, Mark, SE 3211 Kamilche Pt. Rd., Shelton, WA 98584/206-426-5452
Duarte, Carlos, 108 Church St., Rossville, CA 95678
Dubben, Michael, 414 S. Fares Ave., Evansville, IN 47714
Duguet, Thierry D., Rt. 250 W., Box 288, Ivy, VA 22945/804-977-4138
Eaton, Rick, 5560 Forbestown Rd., Forbestown, CA 95941/916-675-1632
Eldridge, Allan, 1424 Kansas Lane, Gallatin, TN 37066/615-452-6027
Engel, Terry (Flowers), P.O. Box 96, Midland, OR 97634/503-882-1323
Eyster, Ken, Heritage Gunsmiths, Inc., 6441 Bishop Rd., Centerburg, OH 43011/614-625-6131
Fisher, Jay, 104 S. Main St., P.O. Box 267, Magdela, NM 87825/505-854-2407
Flannery Engraving Co., Jeff, 11034 Riddles Run Rd., Union, KY 41091/606-384-3127
Foster Enterprises, Norvell, 619 Holmgreen Rd., P.O. Box 200343, San Antonio, TX 78220/210-333-1675
Fountain Products, 492 Prospect Ave., West Springfield, MA 01089/413-781-4651; FAX: 413-733-8217
French, J.R., 1712 Creek Ridge Ct., Irving, TX 75060/214-254-2645
George, Tim and Christy, Rt. 1, Box 45, Evington, VA 24550
Gilliam, Bill, 4078 Valley Fair, Simi Valley, CA 93063/805-527-7534
Glimm, Jerome C., 19 S. Maryland, Conrad, MT 59425/406-278-3574
Gournet, Geoffroy, 820 Paxinosa Ave., Easton, PA 18042/215-559-0710
Hand Engravers Emporium (See Maki, Robert E.)
Harrington, Fred A., Winter: 3725 Citrus, St. James City, FL 33956/813-283-0721; Summer: 2107 W. Frances Rd., Mt. Morris, MI 48458/810-686-3008
Henderson, Fred D., 569 Santa Barbara Dr., Forest Park, GA 30050/404-968-4866
Hendricks, Frank, HC03, Box 434, Dripping Springs, TX 78620/512-858-7828
Heritage Gunsmiths, Inc. (See Eyster, Ken) 649-0603
Heune, Benno, 934 Jack London Dr., Santa Rosa, CA 95405/707-539-1747
Holder, Pat, 4412 W. Diana, Glendale, AZ 85302/602-435-9589; FAX: 602-939-4408
Hudson, Tommy, P.O. Box 2046, Monroe, NC 28110/704-283-8556
Ingle, Ralph W., #4 Missing Link, Rossville, GA 30741/404-866-5589
Johns, Bill, 1412 Lisa Rae Dr., Round Rock, TX 78664/512-255-8246
Kelly, Lance, 1723 Willow Oak Dr., Edgewater, FL 32132/904-423-4933
Kelso, Jim, RD 1, Box 5300, Worcester, VT 05682/802-229-4254
Kostelnik, Joe and Patty, RD #4, Box 323, Greensburg, PA 15601/412-832-0365
Kraft, Brenda, Box 1143, Polson, MT 59860

Kudlas, John M., 622 14th St. SE, Rochester, MN 55904/507-288-5579
Lee, Ray, 209 Jefferson Dr., Lynchburg, VA 24502/804-237-2918
Letschnig, Franz, RR1, Martintown, Ont. KOC 1SO, CANADA/613-528-4843
Limings Jr., Harry, 5030 Patrick Rd., Sunbury, OH 43074/614-965-3272
Lindsay, Steve, RR2 Cedar Hills, Kearney, NE 68847/308-236-7885
Lister, Weldon, Rt. 1, Box 1517, Boerne, TX 78006/210-755-2210
Lyttle, Brian, Box 5697, High River, AB T1V 1M7, CANADA/403-558-3638
Lytton, Simon M., 19 Pinewood Gardens, Hemel Hempstead, Herts. HP1 1TN, ENGLAND/UK# 0443-55542
Maki, Robert E., Hand Engravers Emporium, P.O. Box 947, Northbrook, IL 60065/708-724-8238
Marek, George, 55 Arnold St., Westfield, MA 01085/413-562-5673
McCombs, Leo, 1862 White Cemetery Rd., Patriot, OH 45658/614-256-1714
McDonald, Dennis, 8359 Brady St., Peosta, IA 52068/319-556-7940
McKenzie, Lynton, 6940 N. Alvernon Way, Tucson, AZ 85718/602-299-5090
Mendenhall, Harry E., 1848 Everglades Dr., Milpitas, CA 95035/408-263-0677
Meyer, Chris, 712 Bergen Blvd., Apt. 4B, Ridgefield, NJ 07657
Morrow, Jimmy, 221 1/2 W. 28th St., Lorain, OH 44055/216-245-5230
Morton, David A., 1110 W. 21st St., Lorain, OH 44052/216-245-3419
Moschetti, Mitch, P.O. Box 27065, Denver, CO 80227/303-733-9593
Mountain States Engraving (See Warren, Kenneth)
Norton, Jeff, 2009 65th St., Lubbock, TX 79412/806-744-2436
Parsons, Michael R., 1600 S. 11th St., Terre Haute, IN 47802-1722/812-234-1679
Patterson, W.H., P.O. Drawer DK, College Station, TX 77841/409-846-9257
Perdue, David L., Rt. 1 Box 657, Gladys, VA 24554/804-283-5300
Pilkington Jr., Scott, P.O. Box 97, Monteagle, TN 37356/615-924-3475
Poag, James, RR1, Box 212A, Grayville, IL 62844/618-375-7106
Potts, Wayne, 912 Poplar St., Denver, CO 80220/303-355-5462
Poulakis, Jon, 160 French Rd., Rochester, NY 14618
Rabeno, Martin, 92 Spook Hole Rd., Ellenville, NY 12428/914-647-4567
Raftis, Andrew, 2743 N. Sheffield, Chicago, IL 60614/312-871-6699
Rece, Charles V., Wildwood Studios, 1949 E. Main St., Albemarle, NC 28001/704-982-1178
Reed, Chris, 4399 Bonny Mede Ct., Jackson, MI 49201/517-764-4387
Roberts, J.J., 7808 Lake Dr., Manassas, VA 22111/703-330-0448
Robidoux, Roland J., P.O. Box 4511, Deerfield Beach, FL 33442/305-426-9001; FAx: 305-426-9049
Robyn, Jon, 232 Meriweather Rd., Lynchburg, VA 24503/804-384-7240
Rosser, Bob, Hand Engraving, 1824 29th Ave. South, Suite 214, Birmingham, AL 35209/205-870-4422
Rundell, Joe, 6198 Frances Rd., Clio, MI 48420/810-687-0559
Shaw, Bruce, P.O. Box 545, Pacific Grove, CA 93950/408-646-1937
Sherwood, George, 46 North River Dr., Roseburg, OR 97470/503-672-3159
Shostle, Ben, 1121 Burlington, Muncie, IN 47302/317-282-9073
Silver Images, Silver Fox Studio, 21 E. Aspen Ave., Flagstaff, AZ 86001/602-774-6604
Sinclair, W.P., 3, The Pippins, Warminster, Wilts. BA12 8TH, ENGLAND/U.K. Code (44-985) 218544; FAX: (44-985) 214111
Skaggs, R.E., P.O. Box 34, 1217 S. Church, Princeton, IL 61356/815-875-8207
Smith, Jerry, 7029 East Holmes Rd., Memphis, TN 38125/901-755-2648
Smith, Ron, 5869 Straley, Ft. Worth, TX 76114/817-732-6768
Snell, Barry A., 172 Sexton Lane, Clinton, TN 37716/615-457-9138
Swartley, Robert D., 2800 Pine St., Napa, CA 94558/707-255-1394
Theis, Terry, P.O. Box 535, Fredericksburg, TX 78624/210-997-6778
Thierry, Ivan, 11 rue de la Vernade, 78630 Orgeval, FRANCE/39-75-61-76
Valade, Robert, 931 3rd Ave., Seaside, OR 97138/503-738-7672
Waldrop, Mark, 14562 SE 1st Ave. Rd., Summerfield, FL 34491/904-347-9034
Walker, Patricia, P.O. Box 2343, 555 Este Es Rd., Taos, NM 87571/505-758-0233; FAX: 505-758-4133
Wallace, Terry, 385 San Marino, Vallejo, CA 94589/707-642-7041
Warren, Kenneth, Mountain States Engraving, P.O. Box 2842, Wenatchee, WA 98807-2842/509-663-6123
Watson, Silvia, 350 Jennifer Lane, Driftwood, TX 78619/512-847-9679
Whitehead, James D., 204 Cappucino Way, Sacramento, CA 95838/916-641-7309; FAX: 916-641-1941
Wildwood Studios (See Rece, Charles V.)
Williams, Gary, 221 Autumn Way, Elizabeth, KY 42701
Willig, Claus, Siedlerweg 17, 8720 Schweinfurt, GERMANY/01149-09721-41446
Winn, Travis A., 585 E. 3065 S., Salt Lake City, UT 84106/801-467-5957
Wood, Mel, P.O. Box 1255, Sierra Vista, AZ 85636/602-455-5541
Young, Paul A., Rt. 1, Box 139-A, Vilas, NC 28692/704-297-4039

directory

heat treaters

Barbee, Jim, P.O. Box 1173, Fort Stockton, TX 79753/915-336-2882
Bay State Metal Treating Co., 6 Jefferson Ave., Woburn, MA 01801/617-935-4100
Bos, Paul, Shop: 1900 Weld Blvd., El Cajon, CA 92020/619-562-2370; Home: 2320 Yucca Hill Dr., Alpine, CA 91901/619-445-4740
El Monte Steel, 355 SE End Ave., Pomona, CA 91766
Hauni Richmond, Inc., 2800 Charles City Rd., Richmond, VA 23231/804-222-5262
Holt, B.R., 1238 Birchwood Dr., Sunnyvale, CA 94089/408-736-8500
Lamprey, Mike, 32 Pathfield, Great Torrington, Devon EX38 TBX, ENGLAND/0805-622651
Metal Treating, Inc., 710 Burns St., Cincinnati, OH 45204/513-921-2300 529-2439
O&W Heat Treat, Inc., One Bidwell Rd., South Windsor, CT 06074/203-528-9239; FAX: 203-291-9939
Pugh, Jim, P.O. Box 711, 917 Carpenter St., Azle, TX 76098/817-444-2679; FAX: 817-444-5455
Texas Heat Treating, Inc., 303 Texas Ave., Round Rock, TX 78664/512-255-5884
Texas Knifemakers Supply, 10649 Haddington, Suite 180, Houston, TX 77043/713-461-8632; FAX: 713-461-8221
The Tinker Shop, 1120 Helen, Deer Park, TX 77536/713-479-7286
Valley Metal Treating, Inc., 355 SE End Ave., Pomona, CA 91766/909-623-6316; FAX: 909-620-7304
Wilson, R.W., P.O. Box 2012, Weirton, WV 26062/304-723-2771

leatherworkers

Andre, John, Beadwork & Buckskin, 3955 NW 103 Dr., Coral Springs, FL 33065/305-345-0447
Anonymous Leather & Mfg., Vary Ltd., 519 Castro St., #M38, San Francisco, CA 94114/415-431-4555
The Astorian Ltd. (See Noone, George S.)
Baker, Don and Kay, 5950 Foxfire Dr., Zanesville, OH 43701/614-849-3044
Beadwork & Buckskin (See Andre, John)
Blade-Tech (See Wegner, Tim)
Cheramie, Grant, 4260 West Main, Rt. 3, Box 940, Cut Off, LA 70345/504-632-5770
Clements' Custom Leathercraft, Chas, 1741 Dallas St., Aurora, CO 80010/303-364-0403
Congdon Blade Leather, 1063 Whitchurch Ct., Wheaton, IL 60187/708-665-8825
Cooper, Jim, 2148 Cook Place, Ramona, CA 92065/619-789-1097
Cow Catcher Leatherworks (See Wilder, W. Barry)
Custom Leather Knife Sheaths (See Schrap, Robert G.)
Dawkins, Dudley, 221 N. Broadmoor, Topeka, KS 66606/913-235-0468
Dennehy Custom Leatherworks, John D., P.O. Box 431, 3926 Hayes, Wellington, CO 80549/303-568-9055
Fannin, David A., 2050 Idle Hour Center #191, Lexington, KY 40502
Foley, Barney, 8241 262nd St., Floral Park, NY 11004-1512/718-347-1646
Genske, Jay, 262½ Elm St., Fond du Lac, WI 54935/414-921-6505
Harris, Tom, 519 S. 1st St., Mount Vernon, WA 98273/206-336-2713
Hawk, Ken, Western Leather, Rt. 1, Box 770, Ceres, VA 24318-9630/703-624-3219
Homyk, David N., 8047 Carriage Ln., Wichita Falls, TX 76306/817-855-8425
John's Custom Leather (See Stumpf, John R.)
Kravitt, Chris, Tree Stump Leather, 18 State St., Ellsworth, ME 04605/207-667-8756
Lamprey, Mike, 32 Pathfield, Great Torrington, Devon EX38 7BX, ENGLAND/0805-622651
Layton, Jim, 2710 Gilbert Ave., Portsmouth, OH 45662/614-353-6179
Lee, Sonja, P.O. Box 1873, St. Johns, AZ 85936
Lefaucheux, Jean-Victor, Saint-Denis-Le-Ferment, 27140 Gisors, FRANCE/16.32.55-1410; FAX: 16.32.55-5087
Lively, Marian, P.O. Box 8847CRB, Tucson, AZ 85738/602-825-0679
Luck, Gregory, P.O. Box 2255, Greeley, CO 80632/303-686-7223
Mason, Arne, Mesa Case, 125 Wimer St., Ashland, OR 97520/503-482-2260; 800-326-9078
McGowan, Liz, 12629 Howard Lodge Drive, Sykesville, MD 21784/410-489-4323
McLuin, Tom, 36 Fourth St., Dracut, MA 01826/508-957-4899
Mesa Case (See Mason, Arne)
Metheny, H.A. "Whitey", 7750 Waterford Dr., Spotsylvania, VA 22553/703-582-3228
Miller, Michael K., M&M Kustom Krafts, 28510 Santiam Highway, Sweet Home, OR 97386/503-367-4927
M&M Kustom Krafts (See Miller, Michael K.)
Morrissey, Martin, 4578 Stephens Rd., Blairsville, GA 30512
Noone, George S., The Astorian Ltd., 8533 Gray Ct., Arvada, CO 80003-1337/303-429-4132
NQ Leatherworks (See Qvist, Niels)
Peele, Bryan, 215 Ferry St., P.O. Box 1363, Thompson Falls, MT 59873/406-827-4633
Poag, James H., RR #1 Box 212A, Grayville, IL 62844/618-375-7106
Pratt, Charles, 1953 Fillmans Bottom Rd., Port Washington, OH 43837/614-498-5404
Qvist, Niels, Leestrupvej #2, Hyllede, DK-4683 Roennede, DENMARK/(45)53 82 57 52
Ravon Industries, P.O. Box 670, Denton, TX 76202/817-382-1831
Red's Custom Leather, 9 Woodlawn Rd., Putnam Valley, NY 10579/914-528-3783
Riney, Norm, 6212 S. Marion Way, Littleton, CO 80121/303-794-1731
Rowe, Kenny, Rowe's Leather Goods, 1306 W. Ave. C, Hope, AR 71801/501-777-2974, 501-777-8216
Rowe's Leather Goods (See Rowe, Kenny)
Ruiz Industries, Inc., 1513 Gardena Ave., Glendale, CA 91204/818-242-4239
Schrap, Robert G., Custom Leather Knife Sheaths, 7024 W. Wells St., Wauwatosa, WI 53213/414-771-6472; FAX: 414-784-2996
Spragg, Wayne E., P.O. Box 508, Ashton, ID 83420/915-944-9630
Strahin, Robert, 401 Center Ave., Elkins, WV 26241/304-636-0128
Stuart, V. Pat, Rt. 1, Box 442-S, Greenville, VA 24440
Stumpf, John R., John's Custom Leather, 523 S. Liberty St., Blairsville, PA 15717/412-459-6802
Tierney, Mike, 447 Rivercrest Dr., Woodstock, ON N4S 5W5, CANADA/519-539-8859
Tree Stump Leather (See Kravitt, Chris)
Turner, Kevin, 17 Hunt Ave., Montrose, NY 10548/814-739-0535
Velasquez, Gil, 7120 Madera Dr., Goleta, CA 93117/805-968-7787
Watson, Bill, #1 Presidio, Wimberly, TX 78676/512-847-2531
Wegner, Tim, Blade-Tech, 8818 158th St. E., Puyallup, WA 98373/206-840-0447
Western Leather (See Hawk, Ken)
Whinnery, Walt, 1947 Meadow Creek Dr., Louisville, KY 40218/502-458-4361
Wilder, W. Barry, Cow Catcher Leatherworks, 3006 Industrial Dr., Raleigh, NC 27609/919-833-8262; FAX: 919-833-8262
Williams, Sherman A., 1709 Wallace St., Simi Valley, CA 93065/805-583-3821

photographers

A Bar V Studio (See Rhoades, Cynthia J.)
Allen, John, Studio One, 3823 Pleasant Valley Blvd., Rockford, IL 61114
Berchtold, Robert, Berchtold Studios, 820 Greenbriar Circle, Suite #26, Chesapeake, VA 23320/804-366-0653; FAX: 804-366-0122
Berchtold Studios (See Berchtold, Robert)
Berisford, Bob, 505 West Adams St., Jacksonville, FL 32202/904-356-4780
Bittner, Rodman, 3444 North Apache Circle, Chandler, AZ 85224/602-730-5088
Bloomer, Peter L., Horizons West, 427 S. San Francisco, Flagstaff, AZ 86001/602-779-1014
Box Photography, Doug, 1700 West Main, Brenham, TX 77833/409-836-1700
Bradley, Steven, Integrated Arts, P.O. Box 3252, Taos, NM 87571/505-758-1281
Brian Photography, Inc., 412 S. 5th St., Dade City, FL 33525/904-567-7569
Brown, Tom, 6048 Grants Ferry Rd., Brandon, MS 39042-8136
Buffaloe, Edwin, 104 W. Applegate, Austin, TX 78753/512-837-9746
Burdette, Roger W., Custom Images, 2421 Logan Ave., Des Moines, IA 50317/515-266-4743
Butman, Steve, P.O. Box 5106, Abilene, TX 79608/915-695-2341
Calidonna, Greg, 205 Helmwood Dr., Elizabethtown, KY 42701/502-769-2463
Carter, Art, 818 Buffin Bay Rd., Columbia, SC 28210/802-772-2148
Casey, Robert, 3590 Polk Ave., Ogden, UT 84403/801-394-9114
Catalano, John D., 56 Kingston Ave., Hicksville, NY 11801/516-938-1356
Chastain, Christopher, B&W Labs, 1462 E. Michigan St., Orlando, FL 32806/407-898-0266
Chiacchira, Don, P.O. Box 5788, Cary, NC 27512/919-469-3311
Clark, John, 304 15th St., #307, Des Moines, IA 50309/515-280-3954
Combs, Robert, 1386 Rambling Rd., Ypsilanti, MI 48197/313-482-6629

knife services

Cook, John, P.O. Box 642, Nambour 4560, AUSTRALIA
Cotton, William A., 749 S. Lemay Ave. A3-211, Fort Collins, CO 80524/303-221-5071
Country Visions Photography (See Wells, Carlene L.)
Courtice, Bill, P.O. Box 1776, Duarte, CA 91010-4776/818-358-5715
Criscooli, Walter, Via Aquilzia 14, 33100 Udine, ITALY/0432-26819
Crosby, Doug, RFD 1, Box 1111, Stockton Springs, ME 04981
Custom Images (See Burdette, Roger W.)
Davis, Marshall B., P.O. Box 3048, Austin, TX 78764/512-443-4030
Durant, Ross, 316 E. 1st Ave., Vancouver, B.C. V5t 1A9, CANADA/604-872-2717
Ehrlich, Linn M., 2643 N. Clybourn Ave., Chicago, IL 60614/312-472-2025
Ellison, Troy, 3709 19th, Box 436, Lubbock, TX 79410/806-793-7777
Elvens Foto AB (See Eriksson, Stig)
Eriksson, Stig, Elvens Foto AB, Box 103, S-828 00 Edsbyn, SWEDEN/0271-20197
Etzler, John, 11200 N. Island Rd., Grafton, OH 44044/216-748-3980
Everett, David, White Lotus Studio, 11 Custer St., West Hartford, CT 06110/203-953-5783
Fahrner, Dave, Photographics, 1623 Arnold St., Pittsburgh, PA 15205/412-921-6861
Faul, Jan W., 903 Girard St. NE, Rr. Washington, DC 20017/202-526-1122; FAX: 202-526-0905
Fedorak, Allan, 28 W. Nicola St., Amloops, B.C. V2C 1J6, CANADA/604-372-1255
Fisher, Jay, 104 S. Main St., Box 267, Magdalena, NM 87825/505-854-2507
Fitzgerald, Dan, P.O. Box 198, Beverly Hills, CA 90213/818-507-8418
Foster's, Star Rt., Box 259A, Topton, NC 28781/704-321-3561
Gardner, Chuck, 116 Quincy Ave., Oak Ridge, TN 37830/615-483-9411
Gawryla, Don, 1105 Greenlawn Dr., Pittsburgh, PA 15220/412-344-0787
Godby, Ronald E., 204 Seven Hollys Dr., Yorktown, VA 23692/804-898-4445
Goffe Photographic Associates, 3108 Monte Vista Blvd., N.E., Albuquerque, NM 87106/505-262-1421
Gray, Corey, 760 Warehouse Rd., Suite D, Toledo, OH 43615/419-382-3222
Griggs, Dennis, Tannery Hill Studios, Inc., 2 Middlesex Rd., Topsham, ME 04086/207-725-5689
Gustavsson, Hakan, Box 182, S-828 00 Edsbyn, SWEDEN/0271-236 00
Hansen, Claus Stahnke, Kastrupvej 75, 1 tv., 2300 Copenhagen KBH S, DENMARK/01 58 54 78
Hanusin, John, 3306 Commercial, Northbrook, IL 60062/708-564-2706
Hays, James A., 9515 W. 118th St. #10, Overland Park, KS 66210-3174/816-363-1344
Hodge, Tom, P.O. Box 4444, Highland Park, NJ 08904/201-247-8869
Holter, Wayne V., 125 Larking Ave., Boonsboro, ND 21713
Horizons West (See Bloomer, Peter L.)
Integrated Arts (See Bradley, Steven)
Jacobson, Stephen, 2336 Archwood Ln. #60, Simi Valley, CA 93065/805-581-2178
Jernigan, Craig, 290 Tunnel Rd., Milton, FL 32571/904-994-7262
Kelley, Gary, 17485 SW Pheasant Lane, Aloha, OR 97006/503-649-7867
Kerns, Bob, 18723 Birdseye Dr., Germantown, MD 20874/301-916-9092
Korsnes, Egil, Brakehaugen 2A, N-5050 Nesttun, NORWAY/55-135630
LaFleur, Gordon, 111 Hirst, Box 1209, Parksville, BC, CANADA V0R 270/604-248-8585
Lasting Images Photography (See Stittleburg, Jan)
Lautman, Andy, 4906 41st N.W., Washington, D.C. 20016
Lenz Photography, 939 S. 48th St., Suite 206, Tempe, AZ 85281/602-894-1229
Lester, Dean, 2801 Junipero Ave, Suite 212, Long Beach, CA 90806-2140/310-426-3960
Levinson, Lester, 13038 S. Brandon Ave., Chicago, IL 60633/312-646-1060
Lewis, K.J., 374 Cook Rd., Lugoff, SC 29078
Long, Gary W., 3556 Miller's Crossroad Rd., Hillsboro, TN 37342/615-596-2275
Long, Jerry, 402 E. Gladden Dr., Farmington, NM 87401
Lum, Billy, 16307 Evening Star Ct., Crosby, TX 77532/713-328-3521
Marshall Arts Photography (See Davis, Marshall B.)
McClintock, Robert, 111 Main St., Brattleboro, VT 05301/802-257-1100
McCollum, Tom, P.O. Box 933, Lilburn, GA 30226/404-972-8552
McCrackin, Kevin, 3720 Hess Rd., House Springs, MO 63051/314-677-6066

Moake, Jim, 18 Council Ave., Aurora, IL 60504/312-898-7184
Moya, Inc., 4212 S. Dixie Hwy., West Palm Beach, FL 33405/407-832-8457
Napier, Skip, 430 W. 15th Terrace, Anchorage, AK 99501/907-272-0019
Nevada Commercial Photography (See Parker, T.C.)
Newton, Thomas D., 136 1/2 W. 2nd St., Reno, NV 89501/702-232-0971
Norman's Studio, 322 S. 2nd St., Vivian, LA 71082/318-375-2932
Owens, William T., Box 99, Williamsburg, WV 24991/304-645-4114
Palmer Studio, 2008 Airport Blvd., Mobile, AL 36606/205-471-3523
Parker, T.C., Nevada Commercial Photography, 1720 Pacific, Las Vegas, NV 89104/702-457-0179
Parsons, 15 South Mission, Suite 3, Wenatchee, WA 98801/509-662-9576
Payne, Bob, 2385 Tyler Lane, Louisville, KY 40205/502-459-9602
Payne, Robert G., P.O. Box 141471, Austin, TX 78714/512-272-4554
Peders, Foto Atelier, Markevn 4A, 5012 Bergen, NORWAY/55-90-00-44
Photographic Multi-Services (See Smith, Earl W.)
Rasmussen, Eric L., 1121 Eliason, Brigham City, UT 84302/801-734-9710
Reinders, Rick, 1707 Spring Place, Racine, WI 53404/414-634-1246
Rhoades, Cynthia J., A Bar V Studio, Box 195, Hiway 14-16 3728, Clearmont, WY 82835/307-758-4460; FAX: 307-758-4331
Rice, Tim, 310 Wisconsin, Whitefish, MT 59937/406-862-5416
Richardson, Kerry, 2520 Mimosa St., Santa Rosa, CA 95405/707-575-1875
Ridolfi's Photographics, 830 Central Ave., Tracy, CA 95376/209-835-7551
Rogo, Penny L., Silhouettes Studio, 5720 W. Crenshaw, Suite F, Tampa, FL 33634/813-885-5334
Ross, Bill, P.O. Box 413, 405 Second Ave., Gallipolis, OH 45631/614-446-6700
Rubicam, Stephen, 14 Atlantic Ave., Boothbay Harbor, ME 04538-1202/207-633-4125
Ruby, Tom, Holiday Inn University, 11200 E. Goodman Rd., Olive Branch, MS 38654/601-895-2941
Rush, John D., 2313 Maysel, Bloomington, IL 61701/309-663-6766
Scadlock, David V., 406 Oak St., Mt. Horeb, WI 53572/608-437-4434
Schreiber, Roger, 429 Boren Ave. N., Seattle, WA 98109/206-622-3525
Semmer, Charles, 7885 Cyd Dr., Denver, CO 80221/303-429-6947
Silhouettes Studio (See Rogo, Penny L.)
Slobodian, Scott, 6519 Fountain Ave., Los Angeles, CA 90028/213-464-2341; FAX: 213-464-4060
Smith, Earl W., Photographic Multi-Services, 5121 Southminster Rd., Columbus, OH 43221/614-771-6487
Smith, Randall, 1720 Oneco Ave., Winter Park, FL 32789/407-628-5447
Stittleburg, Jan, Lasting Images Photography, P.O. Box 1115, Sturbridge, MA 01566
Storm Photo, 334 Wall St., Kingston, NY 12401
Strauss, Hans J., Bahnhofstr. 2, D-8262 Altotting, GERMANY/086 71-6979
Surles, Mark, P.O. Box 147, Falcon, NC 28342/919-483-8814
Tardiolo, Photo, 9381 Wagon Wheel, Yuma, AZ 85365/602-248-1302
Teger, Allan I., 248 Tremont St., Newton, MA 02158/617-527-0798
Third Eye Photos, 140 E. Sixth Ave., Helena, MT 59601/406-443-4688
Tocci, Tony, 41 Ellwood Rd., East Brunswick, NJ 08816/908-238-2289
Towell, Steven L., 1124 Wedgewood Dr., Franklin, TN 37064/615-794-9893
Troutman, Harry, 107 Oxford Dr., Lititz, PA 17543/717-626-0685
Tsutsumi, Naganori, World Photo Press, 3-39-2, Nakano, Nakano-ku, Tokyo 164, JAPAN/03-5358-1341; FAX: 03-5385-1347
Valley Photo, 2100 Arizona Ave., Yuma, AZ 85364/602-783-3522
Vallini, Massimo, Via Caduti della Via Fani 17, 40127 Bologna ITALY/0113951-516332
Vara, Lauren, P.O. Box 13511, Arlington, TX 76094/817-861-4299
Verhoeven, Jon, 106 San Jose Dr., Springdale, AR 72764-2538/501-751-5040
Wabnik, Jochen, Otto-Dix-Ring 66, 01219 Dresden, GERMANY/275-3035
Wanika, David, 881 E. 23rd St., Panama City, FL 32405/904-785-5687; FAX: 904-747-0992
Wells, Carlene L., Country Visions Photography, 1060 S. Main, Sp. 52, Colville, WA 99114/509-684-2954
Weyer International, 2740 Nebraska Ave., Toledo, OH 43607/419-534-2020; FAX: 419-534-2697
White Lotus Studio (See Everett, David)
Wildwood Studios, 1949 E. Main St., Albemarle, NC 28001/704-982-1178
Wise, Harriet, 242 Dill Ave., Frederick, MD 21701
Worley, Holly, 4186 W. Grand Ave., Littleton, CO 80123/303-794-5832

scrimshanders

Anderson, Terry Jack, 10076 Birnamwoods Way, Riverton, UT 84065-9073
Art of Scrimshaw (See Velasquez, Gil)
Bailey, Mary W., 3213 Jonesboro Dr., Nashville, TN 37214/615-889-3172
Baker, Duane, 2145 Alum Creek Dr., Cambridge Park Apt. #10, Columbus OH 43207/614-236-0915
Barrett, R.W., 3214 Montrose Dr., Huntsville, AL 35805/205-539-3439
Barrows, Miles, 524 Parsons Ave., Chillicothe, OH 45601/614-775-9627
Bellet, Connie, Fickle Finger Flats, P.O. Box 111, Ringling, MT 59642/406-547-2272

Bonshire, Benita, 1121 Burlington Dr., Muncie, IN 47302/317-282-9073 (Phone & FAX)
Boone Trading Co., Inc., 562 Coyote Rd., Brinnon, WA 98320/206-796-4330
Bouchard, Judy, 1808 W. Pleasant Ridge Rd., Hammond, LA 70403/504-345-2456
Bowles, Rick, 1416 Debbs Rd., Chesapeake, VA 23320
Brady, Sandra, P.O. Box 104, Monclova, OH 43542/419-866-0435; FAX: 419-867-0656
Burdette, Bob, 4908 Maplewood Dr., Greenville, SC 29615/803-288-0976

directory

Byrne, Mary Gregg, 1107 22nd St., Bellingham, WA 98225-6805/206-676-1413
Cable, Jerry, 332 Main St., Mt. Pleasant, PA 15666/412-547-8282
Capocci-Christman, Lynda, RR 4, Box 289A, Wabash, IN 46992/219-563-4634
Caudill, Lyle, 7626 Lyons Rd., Georgetown, OH 45121/513-876-2212
Collins, Michael, Rt. 3075, Batesville Rd., Woodstock, GA 30188/404-475-7410
Cosimini, Rene (See McDonald, Rene Cosimini-)
Courtnage, Elaine, Box 473, Big Sandy, MT 59520/406-378-2492
Cover Jr., Raymond A., Rt. 1, Box 194, Mineral Point, MO 63660/314-749-3783
Cox, J. Andy, 116 Robin Hood Lane, Gaffney, SC 29340/803-489-1892
Cricchio, Barbara, P.O. Box 91, Hackensack, NJ 07602-0091
Curtis, Jean E., 2809 Midwood, Lansing, MI 48910/517-393-9316
Dahl, Guy M., Box 308, Horsefly, BC VOL 1LO, CANADA/604-620-3349
DeYoung, Brain, 4140 Cripple Creek Way, Kennesaw, GA 30144/404-928-8051
DiMarzo, Richard, 2357 Center Place, Birmingham, AL 35205/205-252-3331
Dolbare, Elizabeth, 39 Dahlia, Casper, WY 82604/307-266-5924
Eldridge, Allan, 1424 Kansas Lane, Gallatin, TN 37066/615-452-6027
Engel, Terry (Flowers), P.O. Box 96, Midland, OR 97634/503-882-1323
Engnath, Bob, 1217 Crescent Dr., Apt. B, Glendale, CA 91205/818-241-3629
Eubank, Mary Ann, Rt. 1, Box 196, Pottsboro, TX 75076/903-786-3596; FAX: 903-786-3501
Evans, Rick M., 2717 Arrowhead Dr., Abilene, TX 79606/915-698-2620
Fields, Rick B., 330 Northern Durango Ave., Ocoee, FL 34761/407-877-2339
Fisk, Dale, Box 252, Council, ID 83612/208-253-4582
Fountain Products, 492 Prospect Ave., West Springfield, MA 01089/413-781-4651; FAX: 413-733-8217
Frazier, W.C., RR 3, Box 8720, Mansfield, LA 71052/318-872-1732
Garbe, Sandra, 900 Long Blvd. #278, Lansing, MI 48911/517-694-6736
Gigi, P.O. Box 624, Clovis, CA 93613/209-298-0685
Gill, Scott, 925 N. Armstrong St., Kokomo, IN 46901/317-452-3657
Gullette, Jim, Rt. 8, Box 265, Greer, SC 29651/803-877-7727
Halligan, Ed & Shawn, 14 Meadow Way, Sharpsburg, GA 30277/404-251-7720 (Phone & FAX)
Hargraves Sr., Charles, 10401 Snug Harbor Rd. #217, St. Petersburg, FL 33702/813-576-8271
Harless, Star, P.O. Box 845, Stoneville, NC 27048/919-573-9768
Harrington, Fred A., Winter: 3725 Citrus, St. James City, FL 33956/813-283-0721; Summer: 2107 W. Frances Rd., Mt. Morris, MI 48458/810-686-3008
Hawkins, Stan, 2230 El Capitan, Arcadia, CA 91006/818-445-3054
Hergert, Bob, 12120 SW 9th, Beaverton, OR 97005/503-641-6924
Hielscher, Vickie, HC34, P.O. Box 992, Alliance, NE 69301
High, Tom, Rocky Mountain Scrimshaw & Arts, 5474 S. 112.8 Rd., Alamosa, CO 81101/719-589-2108; FAX: 719-589-2826
Himmelheber, David R., 11289 40th St. N., Royal Palm Beach, FL 33411/407-795-1264
Holland, Dennis K., 4908-17th Place, Lubbock, TX 79416/806-799-8427
Hoover, Harvey, 14536 Asheville Dr., Magalia, CA 95954/916-873-3546
Images In Ivory (See Stahl, John)
Imboden II, Howard L., 620 Deerville Dr., Dayton, OH 45429/513-439-1536
Johnson, Corinne, W3565 Lockington, Mindora, WI 54644/608-857-3035
Johnston, Kathy, P.O. Box 9698, Spokane, WA 99209/509-326-5711
Journey Artistic Creations (See Nelson, Judith K.)
Karst, Linda K., 1020 San Jacinto #1318, Irving, TX 75063-8323/214-402-8022
Kelso, Jim, RD 1, Box 5300, Worcester, VT 05682/802-229-4254
Kirk, Susan B., 1340 Freeland Rd., Merrill, MI 48637/517-839-9131
Kondrla, Denise, P.O. Box 319, Bruceton Mills, WV 26525/304-379-9716
Kostelnik, Joe and Patty, RD #4, Box 323, Greensburg, PA 15601/412-832-0365
Land, John W., P.O. Box 917, Wadesboro, NC 28170/704-694-5141, 704-694-2001
Letschnig, Franz, RR1, Martintown, Ont. K0C 1S0, CANADA/613-528-4834
Little, Mary M., HC 34, Box 10301, P.O. Box 156, Broadbent, OR 97414/503-572-2656
Lovestrand, Erik, 703 Hillcrest Dr., Dublin, GA 31021/912-275-7932
Marek, George, 55 Arnold St., Westfield, MA 01085/413-562-5673
McCullough, Larry E., Box 556, Mocksville, NC 27028/704-634-5632
McDonald, Rene Cosimini-, 2300 N.W. 81 Avenue, Sunrise, FL 33322/305-748-5090
McFadden, Berni, 1402 E. Best Ave., Coeur d'Alene, ID 83814/208-664-2686
McGowan, Frank, 12629 Howard Lodge Dr., Sykesville, MD 21784/410-489-4323
McGrath, Gayle, 12641 Panasoffkee, N. Ft. Meyers, FL 33903/813-997-2215
McKissack II, Tommy, P.O. Box 991, Sonora, TX 76950/915-387-3253
McLaran, Lou, 603 Powers St., Waco, TX 76705/817-799-2234
McNamee, Nick T., 1005 W. Sumner Ave., Lake Elsinore, CA 92330
McWilliams, Carole, P.O. Box 693, Bayfield, CO 81122/303-884-0320
Mead, Faustina L., 2550 E. Mercury St., Inverness, FL 34453/904-344-4751
Miller, Anita, 450 S. 1st, Seward, NE 68434/402-643-4726
Miller, James K., 1012 Old Lee Hwy., Tuscumbia, AL 35674
Minds' Eye Metalmaster (See Smith, D. Noel)
Minnick, Joyce, 144 N. 7th St., Middletown, IN 47356/317-354-4108
Mitchell, James, 1026 7th Ave., Columbus, GA 31901/404-576-4014
Moore, James B., 1707 N. Gillis, Stockton, TX 79735/915-336-2113
Morris, Darrel, 29 Hawksmoor, Aliso Viejo, CA 92656
Nelson, Judith K., Journey Artistic Creations, 756 E. Date St., Cottonwood, AZ 86326/602-634-7011
Ochonicky, Michelle (Mike), Stone Hollow Scrimshaw Studio, 31 High Trail, Eureka, MO 63025/314-938-9570
Ochs, Belle, 124 Emerald Lane, Largo, FL 34641/813-530-3827
Parish, Vaughn, 103 Cross St., Monaca, PA 15061/412-495-3024
Peck, Larry H., 4021 Overhill Rd., Hannibal, MO 63401/314-221-5994
Peterson, Lou, 514 S. Jackson St., Gardner, IL 60424/815-237-8432
Petree, Linda A., Rt. 14, Box 2364A, Kennewick, WA 99337/509-586-9596
Pitt, Chris, P.O. Box 740, Bella Vista, CA 96008/916-275-1277
Poag, James H., RR #1 Box 212A, Grayville, IL 62844/618-375-7106
Polk, Trena, 4625 Webber Creek Rd., Van Buren, AR 72956/501-474-3828
Poulakis, Jon, 160 French Rd., Rochester, NY 14618
Purvis, Hilton, P.O. Box 371, Noordhoek, 7985, REP. OF SOUTH AFRICA/021-891114
Rece, Charles V., Wildwood Studios, 1949 E. Main St., Albemarle, NC 28001/704-982-1178
Roberts, J.J., 7808 Lake Dr., Manassas, VA 22111/703-330-0448
Rocky Mountain Scrimshaw & Arts (See High, Tom)
Rundell, Joe, 6198 Frances Rd., Clio, MI 48420/810-687-0559
Satre, Robert, 518 3rd Ave. NW, Weyburn, Sask. S4H 1R1, CANADA/306-842-3051
Schulenburg, E.W., 25 North Hill St., Carrollton, GA 30117
Schwallie, Patricia, 4614 Old Spartanburg Rd. Apt. 47, Taylors, SC 29687/803-292-8975
Selent, Chuck, P.O. Box 1207, Bonners Ferry, ID 83805/208-267-5807
Semich, Alice, 10037 Roanoke Dr., Murfreesboro, TN 37129/615-890-5146
Sherwood, George, 46 North River Dr., Roseburg, OR 97470/503-672-3159
Shostle, Ben, 1121 Burlington, Muncie, IN 47302/317-282-9073 (Phone & FAX)
Sinclair, W.P., 3, The Pippins, Warminster, Wilts. BA12 8TH, ENGLAND/U.K. Code, (0985) 218544; FAX: (0985)214111
Skaggs, R.E., P.O. Box 34, 1217 S. Church, Princeton, IL 61356/815-875-8207
Smith, D. Noel, Mind's Eye Metalmaster, P.O. Box 1363, Canon City, CO 81215-1363/719-275-2574
Smith, Jerry, 7029 East Holmes Rd., Memphis, TN 38125/901-755-2648
Smith, Peggy, 676 Glades Rd., Shop #3, Gatlinburg, TN 37738/615-436-3322; 615-436-3567
Smith, Ron, 5869 Straley, Ft. Worth, TX 76114/817-732-6768
Stearns, Glen, 209 N. Detroit St., Kenton, OH 43326
Stahl, John, Images in Ivory, 2049 Windsor Rd., Baldwin, NY 11510/516-223-5007
Stalter, Harry L., 2509 N. Trivoli Rd., Trivoli, IL 61569/309-362-2306
Stone Hollow Scrimshaw Studio (See Ochonicky, Michelle "Mike")
Talley, Mary Austin, 2499 Countrywood Parkway, Cordova, TN 38018/901-372-2263
Thompson, Larry D., 23040 Ave. 197, Strathmore, CA 93267/209-568-2048
Tisdale, Gerald, 10013 Album Ave., El Paso, TX 79925-5442/915-590-4188
Tong, Jill, P.O. Box 572, Tombstone, AZ 85638/602-457-9268
Toniutti, Nelida, Via G. Pascoli, 33085 Maniago-PN-, Italy/24-0594
Velasquez, Gil, Art of Scrimshaw, 7120 Madera Dr., Goleta, CA 93117/805-968-7787
Walker, Karen, Star Route, Alpine, WY 83128/307-883-2372
Walker, Patricia, P.O. Box 2343, 555 Este Es Rd., Taos, NM 87571/505-758-0233; FAX: 505-758-4133
Warren, Al, 1423 Santa Fe Circle, Roseville, CA 95678/916-784-3217
Wildwood Studios (See Rece, Charles V.)
Williams, Gary, (Garbo), 221 Autumn Way, Elizabethtown, KY 42701/502-765-6963

miscellaneous

custom grinders

Engnath, Bob, c/o Blades 'N' Stuff, 1019 E. Palmer Ave., Glendale, CA 91205/818-956-5110
Ferguson, Jim, Twisted Nickel Knives, P.O. Box 40247, Downey, CA 90239/310-862-7461 (evenings)
Forosisky, Nicholas, R32 Clover St., Johnstown, PA 15902/814-288-4543
High, Tom, 5474 S. 112.8 Rd., Alamosa, CO 81101/719-589-2826
Kwik-Sharp Optronics, Inc., 350 N. Wheeler St., Ft. Gibson, OK 74434/918-683-9514
Lamprey, Mike,, 32 Pathfield, Great Torrington, Devon EX38 7BX, ENGLAND/0805-622651
McGowan Manufacturing Company, 25 Michigan Ave., Hutchinson, MN 55350/612-587-2222; FAX: 612-587-7966
Twisted Nickel Knives (See Ferguson, Jim)
Wilson, R.W., P.O. Box 2012, Weirton, WV 26062/304-723-2771

knife services

custom handle artisans

Clements' Custom Leathercraft, Chas, 1741 Dallas St., Aurora, CO 80010/303-364-0403
Cooper, Jim, 2148 Cook Place, Ramona, CA 92065/619-789-1097
Cover Jr., Raymond A., Rt. 1, Box 194, Mineral Point, MO 63660/314-749-3783
DiMarzo, Richard, 2357 Center Pl. S., Birmingham, AL 35205/205-252-3331
Draghi, Juan Jose, Gral Alvear 345, CP 2760-San Antonio de Areco, Pcia. de Bs Aires, ARGENTINA
Eccentric Endeavors, J. Michel Santos, P.O. Box 13, Port Costa, CA 94569
Eldridge, Allan, 1424 Kansas Lane, Gallatin, TN 37066/615-452-6027
Eubank, Mary Ann, Rt. 1 Box 196, Pottsboro, TX 75076/903-786-3596
Ferguson, Jim, Twisted Nickel Knives, P.O. Box 40247, Downey, CA 90239/310-862-7461 (evenings)
Grussenmeyer, Paul, 101 S. White Horse Pike, Lindenwold, NJ 08021-2304/609-435-1859; FAX: 609-435-3786
Harrison, Ed, 10125 Palestine, Houston, TX 77029/713-673-6893
High, Tom, Rocky Mountain Scrimshaw & Arts, 5474 S. 112.8 Rd., Alamosa, CO 81101/719-589-2108; FAX: 719-589-2826
Hill, Russell S., 2384 Second Ave., Grand Island, NY 14072/716-773-0084
Holden, Larry, 1319 Gateway Blvd., Ridgecrest, CA 93555/619-375-5611 or 619-375-7955
Holder, Pat, 4412 W. Diana Ave., Glendale, AZ 85302/602-435-9589; FAX: 602-939-4408
Holland, Dennis K., 4908-17th Place, Lubbock, TX 79416/806-799-8427
Kelso, Jim, RD 1, Box 5300, Worcester, VT 05682/802-229-4254
Kemp, Mel, Scottsdale Casting, Inc., P.O. Box 130, Rimrock, AZ 86335-0130
Knack, Gary, 309 Wightman, Ashland, OR 97520/503-482-2108
Lee, Ray, 209 Jefferson Dr., Lynchburg, VA 24502/804-237-2918
Lefaucheux, Jean-Victor, Saint-Dennis-Le-Ferment, 27140 Gisors, FRANCE/32-55-1410; FAX: 32-55-5087
Letschnig, Franz, RR1, Martintown, Ont. K0C 1S0, CANADA/613-528-4843
Marlatt, David, 67622 Oldham Rd., Cambridge, OH 43725/614-432-7549
Miteaif, Oleg, Oboronnay 46/2, 300007 Tula, RUSSIA
Myers, Ron, 6202 Marglenn Ave., Baltimore, MD 21206/301-866-8435
Northwest Knife Supply (See Vallotton, A.)
Sayen, Murad, P.O. Box 127, Bryant Pond, ME 04219/207-665-2224
Smith, Glen, 1307 Custer Ave., Billings, MT 59102/406-252-4064
Snell, Barry A., 172 Sexton Ln., Clinton, TN 37716/615-457-9138
Twisted Nickel Knives (See Ferguson, Jim)
Vallotton, A., Northwest Knife Supply, 621 Fawn Ridge Dr., Oakland, OR 97462/503-459-2216
Vann Ausdle, Gary, 1812 E. Market St., Charlottesville, VA 22901
Watson, Silvia, 350 Jennifer Lane, Driftwood, TX 78619/512-847-9679
Williams, Gary, (GARBO), 221 Autumn Way, Elizabethtown, KY 42701/502-765-6963

display cases and boxes

American Display Company, 55 Cromwell St., Providence, RI 02907/401-331-2464; FAX: 401-421-1264
Bill's Custom Cases, Wm. C. Mittelman, P.O. Box 2, Dunsmuir, CA 96025/916-235-0177 (knife cases)
Clements', Chas, Custom Leathercraft, 1741 Dallas St., Aurora, CO 80010-2018/303-364-0403
Dennehy, John D., Custom Leatherworks, P.O. Box 431, 3926 Hayes, Wellington, CO 80549/303-568-9055
Gimbert, Nelson, P.O. Box 787, Clemmons, NC 27012/919-766-5216
Haydu, Thomas G., Tomway Corp., 2507 Bimini Lane, Ft. Lauderdale, FL 33312/305-792-0185; FAX: 305-792-0115
The Long Island Sutlers, 2169 Jones Ave., Wantagh, NY 11793/516-742-9495
M&M Kustom Krafts (See Miller, Michael K.)
Mason, Arne (See Mesa Case)
Mesa Case, Arne Mason, 125 Wimer St., Ashland, OR 97520/503-4872-2260
Miller, Michael K., M&M Kustom Krafts, 28510 Santiam Highway, Sweet Home, OR 97386/503-367-4927
Miller, Robert, P.O. Box 2722, Ormond Beach, FL 32176/904-676-1193
Mittleman, Wm. C. (See Bill's Custom Cases)
Retichek, Joseph L., W9377 Co. TK. D, Beaver Dam, WI 53916/414-887-8061
S&D Enterprises, 304 W. Second St., Manchester, OH 45144/513-549-2709, 513-549-2602
Tomway Corp. (See Haydu, Thomas G.)

etchers

Baron Technology, Inc., 62 Spring Hill Rd., Trumbull, CT 06611/203-452-0515; FAX: 203-452-0663
Eubank, Mary Ann, Rt. 1, Box 196, Pottsboro, TX 75076/903-786-3596; FAX: 903-786-3501
Fountain Products, 492 Prospect Ave., West Springfield, MA 01089/413-781-4651; FAX: 413-733-8217
Francis, Roger, 12215 Coit Rd., Dallas, RX 75251
Hayes, Dolores, P.O. Box 41405, Los Angeles, CA 90041/213-258-9923
Holland, Dennis, 4908 17th Place, Lubbock, TX 79416/806-799-8427
Kelso, Jim, RD1, Box 5300, Worcester, VT 05682/802-229-4254
Lefaucheux, Jean-Victor, Saint-Denis-Le-Ferment, 27140 Gisors, FRANCE/16-32-55-14-10; FAX: 16-32-55-50-87
Leibowitz, Leonard, 1025 Murrayhill Ave., Pittsburgh, PA 15217/412-361-5455
MacBain, Kenneth C., 30 Briarwood Ave., Norwood, NJ 07648/201-768-0652
Myers, Ron, 6202 Marglenn Ave., Baltimore, MD 21206/301-866-8435
Northwest Knife Supply (See Vallotton, A.)
Sayen, Murad, P.O. Box 127, Bryant Pond, ME 04219/207-665-2224
Smith, Glen, 1307 Custer Ave., Billings, MT 59102/406-252-4064
Vallotton, A., Northwest Knife Supply, 621 Fawn Ridge Dr., Oakland, OR 97462/503-459-2216
Watson, Silvia, 350 Jennifer Lane, Driftwood, TX 78619/512-847-9679

knife appraisers

Clements, Chas, 1741 Dallas St., Aurora, CO 80010-2018/303-364-0403
Levine, Bernard, P.O. Box 2404, Eugene, OR 97402/503-484-0294
Russell, A.G., 1705 Hwy. 71 North, Springdale, AR 72764/501-751-7341

organizations & publications

organizations

AMERICAN BLADESMITH SOCIETY
c/o E. Jay Hendrickson, President
4204 Ballenger Creek Pike
Frederick, MD 21701
Phone: 301-663-6923
If you're interested in the forged blade, you are welcome here. The Society has a teaching program, East and West, and awards stamps to Journeymen and Master Smiths after they pass tests—tough tests at a hot forge. You don't have to make knives to belong. A list of knifemaker members appears on page 281.

THE CANADIAN KNIFE COLLECTORS CLUB
c/o John Comber, President
2410 Lower Base Line, RR #1
Milton, Ont., L9T 2X5 Canada
Phone: 416-878-4955
One umbrella organization—the Canadian Knife Collectors Club—serves collectors and craftsmen alike. The CKCC holds its own shows and has a semi-annual newsletter.

KNIFEMAKERS GUILD
c/o Frank Centofante, President
P.O. Box 928
Madisonville, TN 37354-0928
Phone: 615-442-5767
This continues to be the big one. The Guild has prospered, as have its members. It screens prospects to ensure they are serious craftsmen; and it runs a big show in Orlando each July where over 250 Guild members show their best work, all in one room. Not all good knifemakers belong; some joined and later left for their own reasons; the Guild drops some for cause now and again. The Knifemakers Guild is an organization with a function. A list of Guild members appears on page 280.

KNIFEMAKERS GUILD OF CANADA
c/o George A. Roberts
149 Mill St.
Parkhill, Ont. N0M 2KO Canada
Phone: 519-294-0267
Newly formed group—1994.

MIDWEST KNIFEMAKERS ASSOCIATION
c/o Corbin Newcomb, President
628 Woodland Ave.
Moberly, MO 65270
Phone: 816-263-4639
The MKA currently has a membership of 49 makers from 10 states here in the Midwest; a list appears on page 282.

MINIATURE KNIFEMAKER'S SOCIETY
c/o Gary F. Bradburn
1714 Park Pl.
Wichita, KS 67203
Phone: 316-269-4273
The MKS is dedicated to improving the quality of custom miniature knives. The MKS welcomes miniature makers and collectors as members, publishes a bi-monthly newsletter, and awards miniature collectors who publicly show their collections. Send $1 for a list of members and an application. A list of knifemaker members appears on page 282.

PROFESSIONAL KNIFEMAKERS ASSOCIATION
1450 Prospect Ave., Suite 222
Helena, MT 88271
Phone: 406-449-8827

REGIONAL ASSOCIATIONS
There are a number of state and regional associations with goals possibly more directly related to promotion of their members' sales than the Guild and the ABS. Among those known to us are the Arizona Knifemakers Association; the Arkansas Knifemakers Association; the California Knifemakers Association; the South Carolina Association of Knifemakers; the Midwest Knifemakers Association; the New England Bladesmiths Guild; North Carolina Knifemaker's Guild; Ohio Knifemakers Association; and the Association of Southern Knifemakers. Lists of members of most of these may be found on page 282.

publications

THE BLADE MAGAZINE
Krause Publications
700 E. State St.
Iola, WI 54945
Phone: 800-272-5233
Editor: Steve Shackleford. Eight times yearly. Official magazine of the Knifemakers Guild. $3.25 on newsstand; $17.99 per year. Also publishes *Edges*, a quarterly ($12.95 for six issues); *Blade Trade*, a cutlery trade magazine; and knife books.

DBI BOOKS, INC.
4092 Commercial Ave.
Northbrook, IL 60062
Phone: 708-272-6310
FAX: 708-272-2051
In addition to this *Knives* annual, DBI publishes *Gun Digest Book of Knives*, by Jack Lewis and Roger Combs, *Knifemaking*, also by Lewis and Combs, and *Levine's Guide to Knives and Their Values*, by Bernard Levine.

FIGHTING KNIVES
P.O. Box 16598
N. Hollywood, CA 91615-9962
Phone: 818-760-8963
Publisher: Larry Flynt. Editor: Greg Walker. $3.95 newsstand; $14.95 subscription (6 issues). Covers knives from military/para-military point of view; wide-ranging commentary.

KNIFE WORLD
P.O. Box 3395
Knoxville, TN 37927
Phone: 800-828-7751
Editor/Publisher: Houston Price. Monthly. Tabloid size on newsprint. Covers custom knives, knifemakers, collecting, old factory knives, etc. General coverage for the knife enthusiast. Subscription $15 year.

KNIVES ILLUSTRATED
7745 S. Placentia Ave.
Placentia, CA 92670
Phone: 714-572-2255
Editor: Bud Lang. $3.50 on newsstands; $14.95 for six issues. Plenty of four-color, all on cutlery; concentrates on handmade knives.

NATIONAL KNIFE MAGAZINE
P.O. Box 21070
Chattanooga, TN 37424
Phone: 615-899-9456
Editor: Lisa Broyles. Monthly. Four-color cover. For membersof the National Knife Collectors Association. Lots of ads. Emphasis on pocketknife collecting, but has broadened coverage to include all phases of knife interest. Membership $29 year; $35 for new members.

TACTICAL KNIVES
Harris Publications
1115 Broadway
New York, NY 10010
Phone: 212-807-7100
FAX: 212-627-4678
Editor: Steve Dick. New publication aimed at emergency-service knife designs and users. On newsstands, October 1994.

WEYER INTERNATIONAL BOOK DIVISION
2740 Nebraska Ave.
Toledo, OH 43607
Phone: 419-534-2020
FAX: 419-534-2697
Publishers of the *Knives: Points of Interest* series. Sells knife-related books at attractive prices; has other knife-publishing projects in work.